Introduction to Computer Information Systems

Geoffrey Steinberg
Kent State University

Reviewed by Kamaljeet Sanghera
George Mason University

KENDALL/HUNT PUBLISHING COMPANY
4050 Westmark Drive Dubuque, Iowa 52002

Book Team

Chairman and Chief Executive Officer Mark C. Falb
President and Chief Operating Officer Chad M. Chandlee
Vice President, Higher Education David L. Tart
Director of National Book Program Paul B. Carty
Editorial Development Manager Georgia Botsford
Developmental Editor Lynnette M. Rogers
Vice President, Operations Timothy J. Beitzel
Assistant Vice President, Production Services Christine E. O'Brien
Senior Production Editor Mary Melloy
Permissions Editor Colleen Zelinsky
Cover Designer Suzanne Millius

Regional Managing Editor W. Ray Wood
Regional Acquisitions Editor Curtis Ross

Cover Image © Szymon Apanowicz, 2007/CORBIS

ISBN 978-0-7575-5191-8

Printed in the United States of America
10 9 8 7 6 5 4

Contents

PREFACE

Introduction to Computer Information Systems is for an introductory college level course in computing. It is suitable supporting an introductory survey course or as a first course in an Information Systems program. This book is current, including coverage of **Windows Vista** and **Office 2007.**

The subject of Information Systems is very broad as it involves understanding the needs that organizations have for computer automation. These needs are translated into information system designs and ultimately into hardware selections and computer programs. The chapters of this book address the major aspects of this broad discipline ranging from hardware, software, networks, and security to e-commerce, decision support, ethics, and the societal impact of computing.

This textbook is part of an integrated active learning environment designed to help the student gain mastery over a sequence of concepts that progresses from a foundation in data, data processing and information, through successively more sophisticated concepts and tools.

The chapters are divided between conceptual and hands-on active learning:

- **Conceptual** – These chapters present conceptual and factual topics that include hardware, software, the Internet, networks, and security and privacy. Other chapters present systems analysis, e-commerce and decision support. The impact of computing on society, an examination of computer use ethics, and a look at the future of computing are also discussed.
- **Hands-on** – These chapters present hands-on instruction and exercises that include **Windows Vista, Internet Explorer, Excel, Access** and other tools. File operations using Vista are presented. Internet Explorer is used to search for and acquire data. Excel is used to provide experience with decision support including forecasting and what-if analysis. Excel is also used to introduce macro programming and **VBA.** Access operations using **QBE** to perform simple queries and table joins are presented. Students learn how to design and implement an Access database and to ensure data integrity by defining primary and foreign keys.

  Hands-on exercises also use the **Data Lab, SQL Lab, HTML Lab, XML Lab,** and **Logic Lab.** Each lab provides an opportunity for the student to build and test solutions to exercises and receive immediate feedback about their work. Students first use the Data Lab to actively explore data, records, tables, and indexes. **HTML** and **XHTML** are introduced and students use the HTML Lab to build and test web pages and cascading style sheets. **XML** is presented and students actively explore its use in the XML Lab. Computer programming is presented with hands-on instruction in logic and coding of functions. Students build and test functions in the Logic Lab.

The student is exposed to a blend of material that includes mastering software programs as well as a conceptual framework provided by this book coupled with lecture oriented presentations. Lectures are presented with a selection of PowerPoint slides accompanied by demonstrations of software tools.

The student is exposed to many computing concepts which are woven together into a cohesive story.

For the Student: How to Use This Book

You will be assigned reading material from this book, which you should read before class to prepare for class discussion. This book contains many sections with specific instructions about how to use computers and software programs; you should use the step-by-step instructions in this book as a guide.

Bring this book to class. Many of the illustrations found in this book will be presented in class so you may want to write your notes directly on the pages where the illustrations are found. Follow along and take notes directly into the book. This will help make your studying more successful because your notes will more likely be complete.

Most importantly this entire course can and should be fun. You will be far more motivated to learn and stretch on your own if you are having a good time. This does not imply that the course should be easy, but the material can be presented in a compelling and exciting way.

For the Instructor

There are various tools provided to support the teacher as the course material is delivered. These features and the associated benefits they deliver are described here.

Features

Support is provided in several forms each of which is discussed.

PowerPoint presentations are provided for each chapter for classroom use. The material coordinates with but does not replace the textbook. It provides a framework for your lecture and discussion.

Lecture Notes are provided for each chapter. Use these notes as a suggestion for material that should be presented. The notes provide a suggested sequence for each chapter discussion.

Benefits

A significant benefit of this textbook's approach is that students learn as they are actively engaged. The objective of active experimentation is to help the students learn how to use software tools effectively and in support of the larger objective of becoming successful problem solvers. The use of Windows Vista and Microsoft Office amplify the conceptual content of the book.

About the Author

Dr. Geoffrey Steinberg is an associate professor of Information Systems at Kent State Universityís College of Business. He teaches at the undergraduate and graduate level and his courses cover end user computing, web development, programming and database design and development. His research interests include software interface design, automatic program and database schema generation and the development of tools that support the delivery of education in a distance environment.

Prior to earning his Ph D. at Temple University he had a long career in business which included both consulting and management. Among his clients were Citibank, The New York Daily News and Lockheed-Martin. Dr. Steinberg held significant information systems management positions at several national companies in the financial services industry. His focus, in business and as an academic, has largely been the development of tools that shield users from the technical details of computer system usage allowing users to be productive without knowing the underlying technical theory. Dr. Steinberg also earned an MBA at the Wharton School of the University of Pennsylvania.

INFORMATION SYSTEMS

CHAPTER 1

A computer-based information system, commonly referred to as CBIS or **IS,** is a set of components arranged to collect data, process it, and convert it into information. In effect, it is the integration of hardware, communication, and software technologies for the benefit of humans. While not all information systems need to be computer based, all support the objective of providing **timely, integrated, accurate,** and **useful** information for decision making purposes.

1.1 Input-Process-Output Model

Data are **facts** and can be thought of as raw material. Data alone is not particularly useful, but when data is associated with other facts information can be derived.

Data

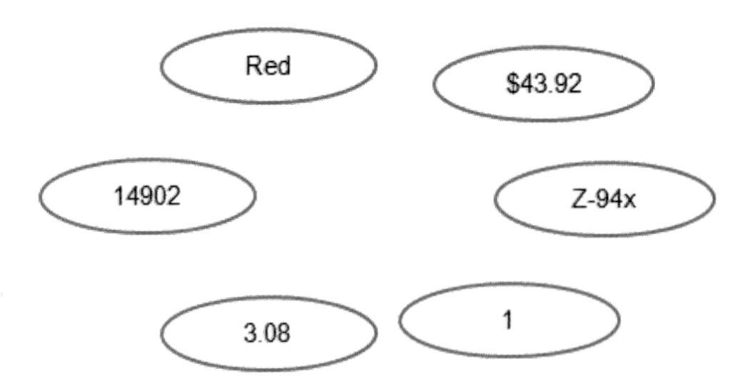

The process of providing a **context** for data is known as **data processing,** which is the fundamental activity of an information system. Facts alone may or may not be relevant to **decision making.** Facts (numbers, characters, words, images) alone mean nothing until they are combined with other data and thus provide a context for understanding—they then become the basis for information and decision making.

Data in a Context

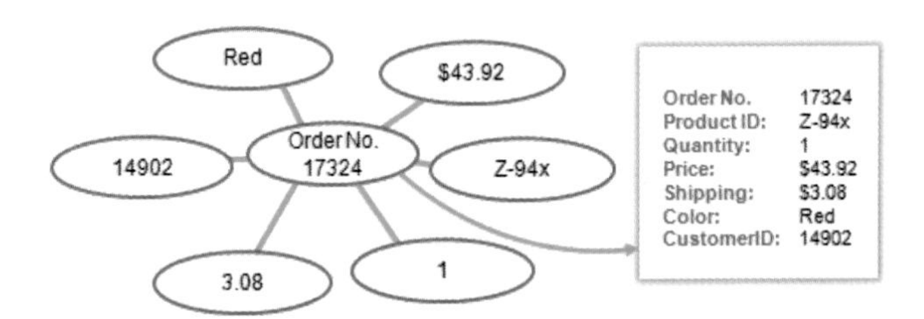

Consider data to be raw material. Raw material is generally of little use by itself but when processed, useful results may be produced. When data is processed, information (known as output) may result. In essence, an information system processes raw material into something that is useful to people. This relationship between data and information is summarized in the Input-Process-Output (IPO) model:

Input-Process-Output Model

Storage Processing data often requires including data that was stored earlier during collection or production. Storage is provided by hard disk, jump drive, CD and DVD, tape, and other storage devices. The IPO model is updated to reflect data storage this way:

Input-Process-Output Model with Data Storage

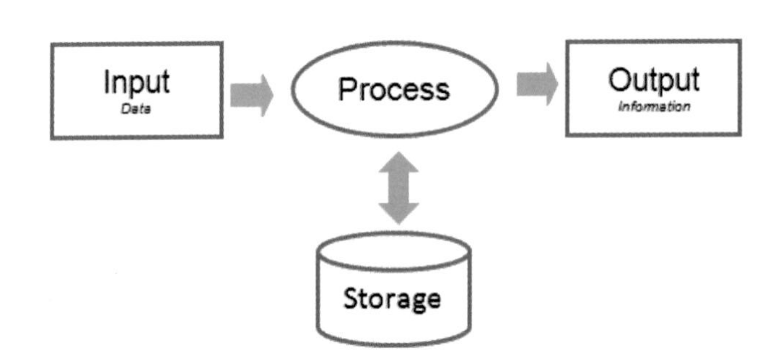

Feedback Often the information received is not completely sufficient for a decision we are making. The information we received is helpful but does not completely answer the question we are considering. So with our new knowledge we repeat the input-process-output sequence, this time asking a new question. The new question is refined by the knowledge we obtained in the first cycle of the model. This knowledge is known as **feedback** and is shown this way:

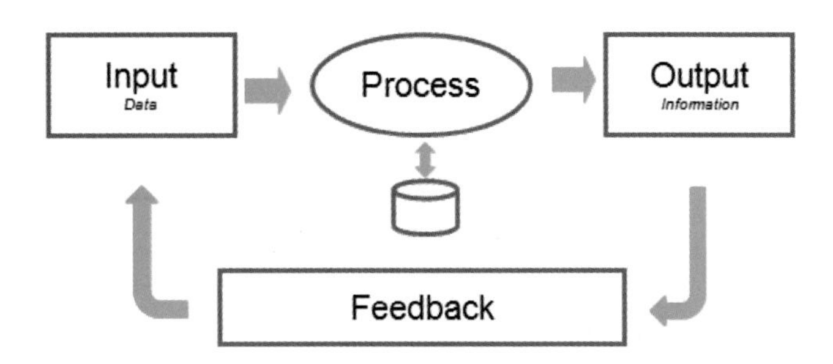

Input-Process-Output Model with Feedback

When information is used as input in a subsequent round of processing we describe the cyclical nature of data processing as **iterative.**

Here is an example of how feedback is used in decision making. When you want to withdraw money from your bank account at an ATM (automatic teller machine), you provide the computer with data (your account number) and instructions ("please report my balance") and the computer processes your request and gives you information (your balance). Then, based on your balance, you decide whether or not to make the withdrawal. This interchange illustrates the concept of feedback.

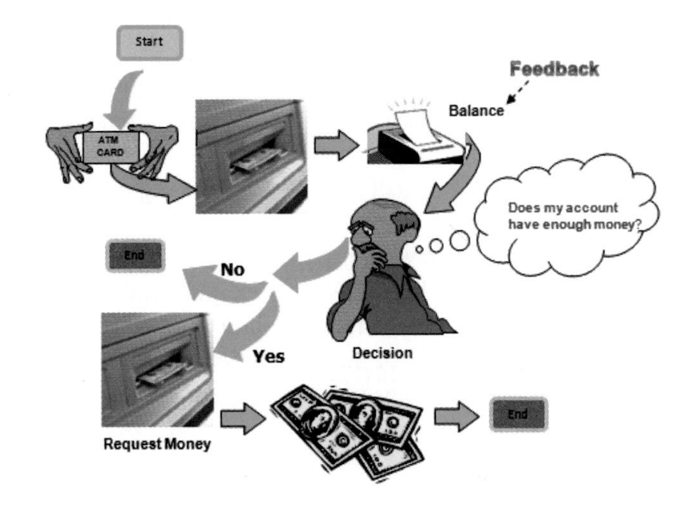

Feedback in Action

1.2 Information System Components

There are seven components of an information system:

1. Data
2. Database
3. Process

4. Information
5. System Life Cycle
6. Environment
7. Specifications

Each component is described individually in the remainder of this section. As an information system is developed, each of the IS components must be considered.

The Seven Components of an Information System

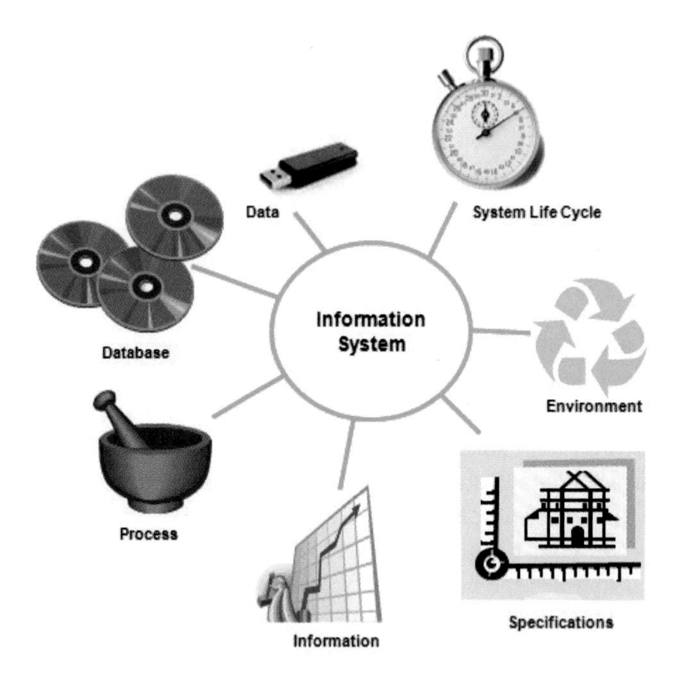

Data Data supports the objectives of an organization and is considered an organizational **asset.** Deciding what data is to be handled by the IS is perhaps the most significant aspect of system development. Since organizational goals change over time it is important that organizational data requirements be viewed as varying over time as well.

Database Data must be stored somewhere so that it is reliably available for future use. Databases which are commonly used for this purpose permit data storage to be transparent to the user and ensure **accuracy, integrity,** and no **data redundancy.** Data redundancy is a serious problem. As part of the IS development process, a database must be designed and specific database management software must be selected.

A Database Model

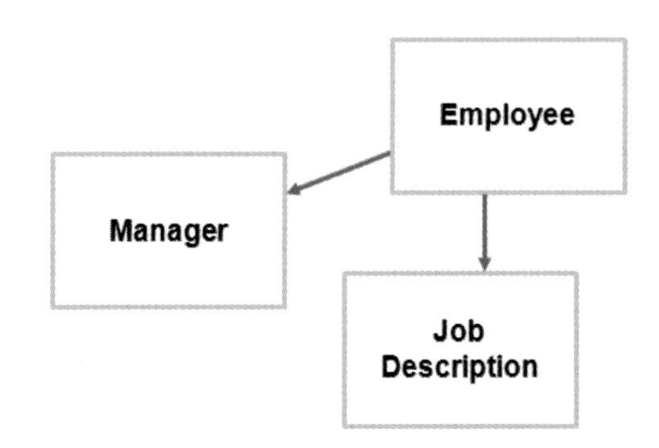

Process Consideration must be given to what is done with the organization's data to convert it into information. It is essential to be aware of the organization's objectives to ensure what processing rules are appropriate for the desired result. Data processing follows rules as implemented in computer programs.

```
Input Hourly Rate
Input Hours Worked
Multiply Hourly Rate X Hours Worked
    Giving Gross Pay
Multiply Tax Rate X  Gross  Pay Giving
    Net Pay
Print Paycheck
```

A Program Processes Data

Information The main objective for an information system is to provide a fundamental base for decision making. People making decisions require information that is timely, integrated, accurate, and useful. The IS must be designed and constructed so as to ensure that these requirements are fulfilled. Information may be presented in several ways.

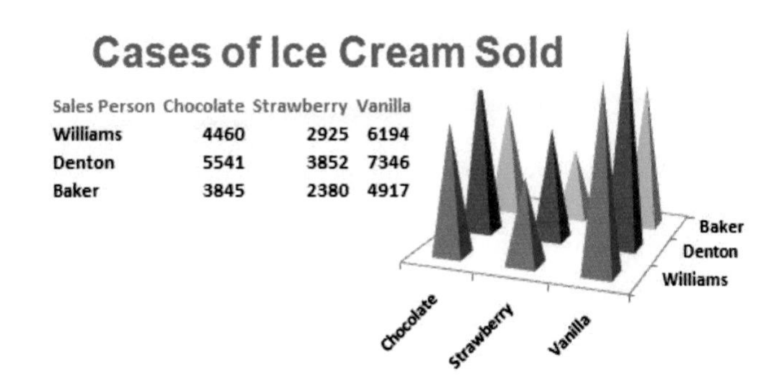
Cases of Ice Cream Sold

Sales Person	Chocolate	Strawberry	Vanilla
Williams	4460	2925	6194
Denton	5541	3852	7346
Baker	3845	2380	4917

Information

System Life Cycle Just like humans, each information system has a life cycle. An IS born as an initial concept is built and used until it is ultimately retired when no longer useful. The four phases of the Systems Life Cycle (SLC) are Conceptualization and Implementation, Growth, Maturity, and Decline.

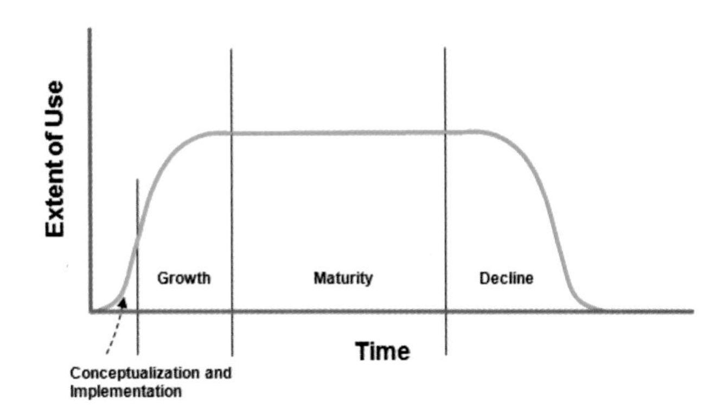

The System Life Cycle

- **Conceptualization and Implementation**—In this phase the information-related needs are identified. The requirement for a new (or upgraded) system is primarily due to environmental pressures (competition, regulation, needed functionality). The user requests the assistance of the systems analyst who studies the problem and offers a solution. During this phase the IS is designed, built, and installed.
- **Growth**—In this phase the IS has been installed and the users are gaining experience with it. They are exploring the system's potential and offering suggestions for upgrades that may be quite substantial. It is during this phase that a post-implementation audit is conducted as a quality assurance measure to ensure that the system addresses the needs of the users. During the growth phase usage spreads throughout the organization.
- **Maturity**—In this phase the IS is relatively stable. Major alterations have been primarily conducted in the previous stage. Although the IS may be modified during this phase, the changes are typically slight and the system is considered to be reliable.
- **Decline**—Here the system is becoming outdated and the need for change may become dramatic. Eventually the cost to modernize becomes excessive and a decision is made to replace it. Advances in technology that overtake a system often cause decline.

Environment No information system acts alone. The people who depend upon its information output for decision making are part of a larger network of **stakeholders.** These questions must be asked and answered: How will the IS be used? Who will resist changes in technology? How will the IS change how work is done? What is to be done to protect privacy?

All people concerned with the development of a new information system are considered its stakeholders. These groups of people represent the varying interests of those individuals who will interact with the new system in one capacity or another.

Stakeholders

© NorthGeorgiaMedia, 2007, Shutterstock.

Here are some groups of stakeholders. Specific categories of stakeholders will vary depending on the organization and the nature of the IS project.

- **Technical staff**—This group is responsible for the development of the new IS and is concerned with project schedules and resources available.

- **Clerical staff**—This group, usually the main users of the new IS, is often the most resistant to change. Typically a new system changes the way work is performed and change can cause anticipation and fear.
- **Managers**—These individuals receive the information typically generated by the system. Therefore, it is imperative to make sure that the reports are accurate and relevant.
- **Customers**—These stakeholders receive output from the IS and are quite concerned with its validity and efficiency. A bank customer, for example, receives a bank statement and expects that it is timely (once a month) and that all transactions are accurately reported.
- **Suppliers**—These stakeholders have many of the same concerns as customers. They conduct transactions with the organization and expect the transactions to be accurately recorded. A supplier expects to be paid correctly for products shipped to the business.
- **Investors**— This group has put up their money for the benefit of the business. They are entitled to be periodically appraised of the financial condition of the firm.
- **Regulators**—These stakeholders work in government agencies that have jurisdiction over business. Their need for accurate information should be obvious.

Specifications The IS's specifications form a **contract** between the system developers and other stakeholders. This contract stipulates what is going to be developed, in other words, what the stakeholders can expect to receive, for what cost, and when the development process will be complete. The design must accommodate the requirements of the stakeholders yet be flexible so that the IS can stay current as long as possible with minimal maintenance.

1.3 Information Systems and Decision Making

We studied the seven components of an IS to understand what an IS is built from. Before moving ahead, we must consider the classes of information systems and the types of people who will use them. We must also consider the different classes of decisions that a person may be called upon to make. In short order, we will learn that certain classes of information systems are of use to only certain types of stakeholders.

1.3.1 Classes of IS

There are four classes of information systems to be aware of. Each class can serve specific purposes and it is the job of the system designer (the system analyst) to understand each class and know what users may profit most from any particular IS class.

- **Electronic Data Processing**—The first ISs were EDP applications. Here computer hardware and software were employed to automate repetitive tasks such as bank balance computation and the preparation of insurance policies. Such systems were viewed as money saving, often putting groups of people out of work.
- **Management Information System**—MIS is a step above EDP in complexity and value to the organization. MISs prepare management control reports on a regularly scheduled basis. Managers use MIS reports to be aware of what is going on within

their part of the organization. MISs, for example, report employee attendance, production line productivity, and inventory levels.

- **Decision Support System**—A DSS is used to support higher level decision making. Often a DSS will integrate organizational data with models that are used to predict organizational outcomes. In effect, the DSS is used to preview the expected outcomes of decisions that might be made.
- **Executive Information System**—EIS is really an extension of a DSS. Here, external data (economic, industry specific, governmental) is integrated with organizational data. The software used frequently falls within the province of what is called artificial intelligence or AI. Decisions made with support of an EIS are often **one time only** decisions (for example whether or not to locate a new factory in a specific location).

1.3.2 Classes of Decisions

There are three classes of decisions that a person may be called upon to make:

- **Structured**—A structured decision is well defined and often involves repetitive tasks such as record keeping. There are limited possible actions based on the output of such decision making.
- **Semi-structured**—A semi-structured decision may involve trend spotting and forecasting. Mathematical, statistical and other models are frequently used. Although this kind of decision making is generally routine, it requires some human judgment for deciding actions.
- **Unstructured**—Unstructured decisions are more **what-if** oriented and deal mostly with the future. Much more human intuition is involved and these decisions are generally **one time only.**

One time decision: Where to locate a new factory?

These three classes of decision making are related to the three levels of management discussed in the next section.

1.4 Management Levels and Decision Making

As we examine any organization (commercial, educational, and governmental) we typically find managers at three levels: operational, tactical, and strategic. As we move up the **management pyramid,** fewer managers are found at each level.

Management Levels and Decisions

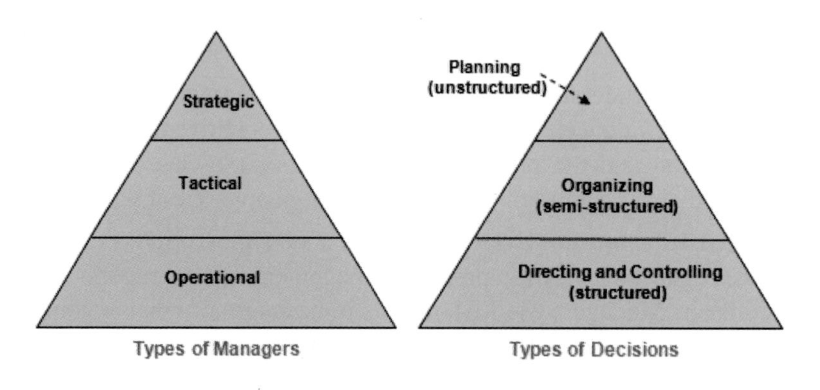

After putting it all together (IS classes, managers and) we arrive at the pyramid shown here:

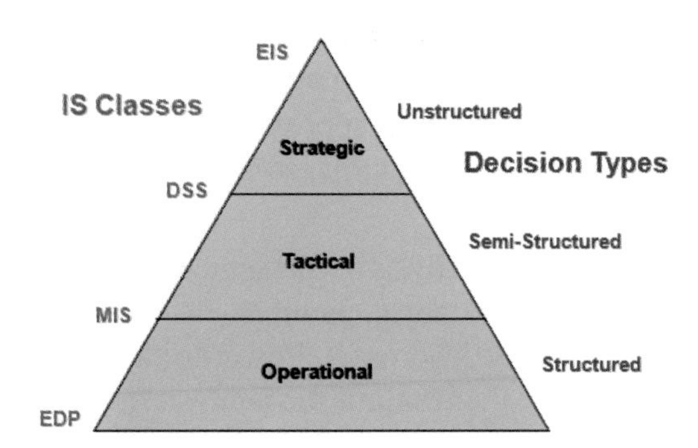

Management Levels and Information Systems

This pyramid serves as a guide that informs you of what class of information system is most useful for specific types of managers. For example, only an operational manager would use an EDP system and only a strategic manager would use an EIS. Tactical and strategic managers would use a DSS.

1.5 Computer Literacy

With the advent of the information age, computer literacy and information handling are two vital skills that will be needed for efficient job performance in most organizations. It will become superfluous to use the term "knowledge worker" because practically every worker will be handling computerized information of some sort for job-related decisions.

The personal computer is omnipresent. With the rapid growth in both computing and communicating technologies during the last decade, the domestic and global business environments have undergone vast transformations. Information technology (IT) is the root cause of major changes in business processes, products, services, and competitive strategies. Organizational processes are undergoing radical restructuring through IT. A direct result is the decline of middle management and the consequent empowerment of employees at all levels for greater organizational efficiency.

Earlier computers were mysterious machines, perceived as powerful yet difficult to use. Most people assumed that they should learn how to use a computer but were afraid to try. Assuming that they would fail, many people thought the best plan was to pretend that computers did not exist and would hopefully go away.

In fact, computers are much easier to use than most people expect. Graphics-based computer interfaces (such as Macintosh and Windows) are making it easier for people to use the computer effectively. The Internet is making data more easily available than ever before. With tools getting simpler and data more plentiful, there is really no excuse for not taking advantage of the opportunities computer use provides.

There are four facets to information handling:

- **Data Gathering**—Gathering data involves finding that which is of interest to you. Gathering may require searching through various sources, like the Internet or available databases, for what you want.
- **Manipulation**—Once the data is located you will need to obtain your own copy of it and may need to manipulate or alter its format for subsequent processing. You will

need to master various techniques for copying data, storing it, moving it between application programs, and even changing the data's format. You will use various tools for these purposes including: Windows, Web browsers, editors, and other programs.

- **Analysis**—Once data has been obtained and manipulated so it can be analyzed, analysis can determine the best deal for purchasing a particular automobile, the best mutual fund to invest in, the vacation spot with the most desirable climate, and so on. Analysis also requires the use of tools, some of which include Microsoft Excel and Access.
- **Presentation**—The result of analysis is presented to decision makers. It can be shown in various forms (charts, tables, pictures, etc.) depending on the content and the audience. Tools such as Microsoft PowerPoint, HTML editors, and Web browsers are used to present the result of the analysis.

Information Handling

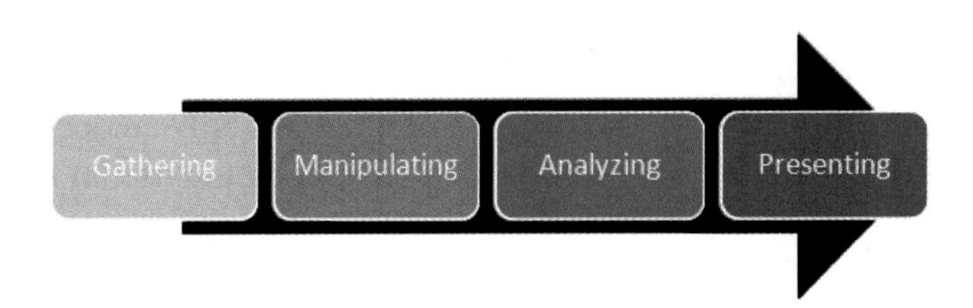

By **computer literacy,** we mean a broad understanding of the technology and its applications. Such an understanding is critically important for the individuals who will be using the technology every day. Computers are now an integral part of our lives (just like cars, cell phones, satellite radio, and microwave ovens). Computer literacy is a way to ensure that we are not overwhelmed by technology and are able to use it to our advantage. Computer literacy does not come without effort. You will find that it takes repeated **practice** to get it right and for you to feel confident about your abilities and skill.

1.6 Security and Privacy

Although we marvel at the power and convenience provided to us by technology we should also be thinking about **security** and **privacy.** With so much data in **digital form** it is not hard to imagine the opportunities for misuse.

If you consider the common use of credit cards for making purchases, it should not be hard to realize that a record of all that you purchased is stored in a **database** somewhere. The details of your transactions (cost, date, time, items, and merchants) are recorded and perhaps might be available for use in ways that you did not expect. Marketing companies may examine databases and look for new potential customers. Banks might look for loan customers who have overused credit cards.

While we have been accustomed to marketing solicitations directed to our mail and telephone systems, have you ever considered your e-mail and other "private" communication? Any words that you type are transmitted through the Internet, traveling among unknown **servers** until reaching their destination. How do you know that your message has remained unread and private while en route?

1.7 Information Systems Cover a Lot of Territory

The subject of Information Systems is very broad as it involves understanding the needs that organizations have for computer automation. These needs are translated into information system designs and ultimately into hardware selections and computer programs. The common use of networks makes access to data easy and opens the door to security concerns. The chapters of this book address the major aspects of this broad discipline.

Internet and World Wide Web The Internet is a worldwide inter-network of networks. Through its use we are able to communicate in ways never imagined before. The motivation to create a distributed packet-switching network came from the demands of the Cold War, but the benefits have spread throughout the world. The fundamental components of the Internet are packets, protocols, servers, and clients. Security has become perhaps the dominant concern of many Internet users and the issue of network neutrality is surfacing as important as well.

Hardware Hardware is the physical part of a computer system. It includes the electronic circuitry, input and output devices, data and program storage devices, memory for program execution, communication equipment, and, most importantly, the processor that performs calculations and controls all equipment. It is distinguished from software programs that execute within the hardware as data is processed. A computer system's hardware is infrequently changed in contrast to software as new programs are more frequently installed and older ones updated.

Software Hardware is only the physical part of a computer system, but it would be impossible to process data into information with a computer alone. The operating system gives a series of instructions that command the hardware to act in specific ways. The OS facilitates the operation of application programs and provides them access to resources like files, databases, and hardware. The operating system is the fulcrum that allows hardware and application software to balance.

Data Communications and Networking Data communications operates on the principles of the communication model which assigns the roles of sender and receiver to participants. Protocols govern how the roles are applied. Over time, networking evolved from highly centralized systems to the distributed systems that we know today. The Internet is a distributed system. Networks can be arranged locally as in a LAN or over a wide area in a WAN. A network's architecture takes into consideration various arrangements of components and follows established network topologies.

Systems Analysis Information Systems are designed and constructed to meet the needs of various stakeholders. System development is not a haphazard affair, but it is the result of planning, goal setting, management, and technical development activities. Strategic analysis may provide an opportunity for information system projects that have the potential to affect business performance. As the feasibility of projects is considered, the return on investment projection is often a critical determinant on whether or not a project is attempted.

Computer Programming Computer programming is about translating ideas into a reality that is experienced by a computer user. The reality can be visual (clicking a mouse button or viewing a Web page), informational (reviewing a stock portfolio or viewing a clothing catalog), entertaining (viewing a movie or playing a game), and transactional (reserving an airline ticket or taking a test). Programs provide e-mail, instant messaging, and Internet phone services. Everything that occurs when a computer is used involves software created by a computer programmer.

Data and Information, Database and SQL The relationship between data and information is described in the Input-Process-Output model. An understanding of the important difference between data and information is based on perception of the difference between facts and information that supports decision making. Records arranged in tables are the fundamental building block of an information system. The tables may be implemented as flat files or as part of a database. Designing a database correctly has a profound impact on the database's value. The purpose of a database is to store data, to ensure the data's integrity, and to provide the data in the form of information to users who require it. Query languages are used for this purpose. The standard language for interaction with a relational database is Structured Query Language or SQL.

HTML, XHTML, and XML HTML or Hypertext Markup Language is the set of markup codes inserted in a text file intended for display in a Web browser. The markup informs the browser how to display a Web page's words and images for the viewer. Each individual markup code is referred to as a tag. The current version of HTML is supported somewhat differently among different Web browsers so in the interest of standardization and adding advanced features Extensible Hypertext Markup Language or XHTML was developed. XML or Extensible Markup Language is a tool for structuring data in a document so that the data may be passed among and shared by programs. Its primary purpose is to facilitate the sharing of data across different systems, particularly systems connected by the Internet.

E-Commerce E-Commerce is commercial activity carried out using a technology infrastructure. It uses technology as a vehicle for performing business activities. As in all commerce, a supply chain carries raw materials eventually to consumers. Shortcuts through the supply chain are advantageous, perhaps lowering prices and transaction costs. Disintermediation of the supply chain (the creation of shortcuts) can be facilitated by electronic based commerce systems.

Security, Ethics, and Privacy Security and privacy is important to corporate and individual computer system owners. It is also important to consumers. Numerous recent events demonstrate how easy it is for personal data to be compromised. Security is the responsibility of a computer owner and network administrator. Software vendors provide tools to this end but unless the tools are installed, properly configured and maintained, privacy will be an accident and not an expected outcome. Some security measures that guard privacy are not software dependant and reply instead on the good judgment and actions of users when handling programs and data. The most important protection against unwanted intrusion and malicious data loss is you.

The Impact of Computers on Society Computing has influenced a very large impact on society. Whole new career paths have been created and the current job outlook for Information technology (IT) professionals is excellent. The widespread use of computing and networks opens doors to communication possibilities unheard of several decades ago, but security and privacy concerns go along with access and must be addressed and confronted. The work environment has changed as well with faster and more widespread communication channels flattening organizational structures. Jobs have been eliminated due to automation. A more recent development in personal communication and e-commerce, social networking, allows people to maintain communities of friends who share photos, journals, and interests.

Decision Support Information systems that support decision making activities are decision support systems. A DSS can take many different forms but a DSS is generally a computerized system for helping humans make decisions. A decision is a choice between alternatives based on estimates of the values of the outcomes. Supporting a decision means helping people who work alone or in a group to gather intelligence, generate alternatives, and make choices. Data integration tools which consolidate data from different sources into a consistent format provide a broader perspective to decision making. Tools such as digital dashboards and other business performance software allow faster decision making, identification of negative trends, and better allocation of business resources.

Future of Computing No one can foretell the roads that will open to advances in computing technology. It has been just more than a decade since the mouse and graphical user interface came into common use. The development of the Web is becoming old news as its use is routine in many people's lives. So what will come next? Certainly faster hardware and networks, greater data storage capacity and more intuitive user interfaces are not far around the corner. Advances in technology will certainly bring change to our lives. Hopefully it will be beneficial. Technology is rapidly altering medicine, law enforcement, banking, education, airline safety, commerce in general, personal communication, and much more. The only thing certain about the future is that it will be different from today.

1.8 Summary

Information Systems are designed and constructed to meet the communication and decision making needs of stakeholders. The IPO model can be used to understand the sequence of information handling activities in which data is gathered, standardized, and processed, and information is produced. The process depends on hardware and software operating within it. An information system blends people with hardware, communication, and software technologies.

Information systems are designed to accommodate the fundamental components of data, database, process, and information. Each system has a life cycle as it responds to the changing needs of stakeholders. An information system's success depends on its acceptance and use.

People make different types of decisions ranging from the well defined and repetitive to the one of a kind never to be thought about again variety. Information systems support all types of decision making and allow system use to match the task at hand.

With the Internet and the Web information is everywhere and those unable to capitalize on it are at a competitive disadvantage. Most people today are knowledge workers and are presumed to be computer literate that is, able to think about information and effectively use information handling tools. Collecting data and preparing it for processing are skills that we should all achieve. Understanding how to best present the resultant information is important, too.

Data flowing over massive networks and stored in large databases opens the possibility of our privacy being compromised. Securing servers and limiting exposure to unauthorized access will always likely be a major focus of information system management.

The study of Information Systems is quite broad. An information system combines hardware, software, and computer programs to enable a computer to perform the marvelous tasks we have grown accustomed to. Programs are designed to satisfy the requirements of stakeholders. Databases support e-commerce activities and are central to decision support environments. Markup languages provide data portability and information delivery independent of platform selection. This broad field covers quite a range and is the subject of this book.

EXERCISES

Exercise 1.1

Why are data considered to be raw material?

Exercise 1.2

What is the significance of adding storage to the IPO model?

Exercise 1.3

What is feedback? How can it assist in decision making?

Exercise 1.4

Data processing is said to be iterative. What does that mean?

Exercise 1.5

How do data and information differ?

Exercise 1.6

What is computer literacy and why is it important to a college student?

Exercise 1.7

What is a markup code? Why are they used?

Exercise 1.8

Who is responsible for protecting a computer system from attack?

Exercise 1.9

Consider a college's information system that you are aware of. Identify five categories of stakeholders and describe their interests in the information system.

Exercise 1.10

What does it mean that a specification is a contract between stakeholders and system developers?

Exercise 1.11

How do electronic data processing systems differ from management information systems? How might EDP systems provide input to a management information system?

Exercise 1.12

Why does it make sense that an executive information system would be used to support unstructured decision making?

Exercise 1.13

When considering information handling why might data manipulation be required before analysis? Give an example that supports your thinking.

Exercise 1.14

What is the System Life Cycle? Why do information systems enter a decline? What indicators might suggest that a system has outlived its usefulness?

Exercise 1.15

What is a decision and how might a decision support system assist decision makers?

Exercise 1.16

What are some of the workplace consequences of computer use?

Exercise 1.17

Why would a strategic manager have little use for an EDP system?

INTERNET AND WORLD WIDE WEB

CHAPTER 2

The Internet is a network of networks that consists of millions of smaller domestic and foreign, academic, business, and government networks. These networks together carry various information and services, such as electronic mail, online chat, file transfer, and search engines. The collection of interlinked Web pages and other documents, connected by hyperlinks that navigate to URLs, is known as the World Wide Web (or the Web).

The Internet provides the network architecture that enables the communication architecture we know of as the World Wide Web. In this chapter we discuss what the Internet is and where it comes from. Because the Internet is an enabling technology that makes the Web possible, significant Internet components, protocols, packets, DNS, and IP addresses are presented along with the Web's roles of clients, servers, and its services including search engines, chat rooms, and RSS. The chapter also discusses Web authoring and presents Internet Explorer 7 in depth.

The Internet is publicly accessible and it is international. As a network of interconnected local and wide area computer networks, it transmits data by switching packets among servers and routers. The data contained in the packets is the content of the Web. Computer networks are the infrastructure that makes the Internet possible, but the details of how networks are designed and operate are the topic of another chapter.

Many people use the terms Internet and Web interchangeably, but they are not the same. The Internet is a networking infrastructure that connects millions of computers together world-wide. Information that travels over the Internet uses a variety of languages known as protocols.

The Web is a way of accessing information over the medium of the Internet. It is an information-sharing environment that is built on top of the Internet. The Web uses the HTTP protocol, which is only one of the languages spoken over the Internet, to transmit data. The Web is just one of the ways that information can be shared over the Internet. The Internet, not the Web, is used for e-mail, which relies on the SMTP protocol. Instant messaging also uses the Internet and not the Web. The Web and the Internet are not synonymous and should not be confused.

In this chapter we discuss the Internet and Web. First we take a look at the Internet.

2.1 Internet

The Internet is a worldwide **packet-switching** network of computers connected by high-speed telephone and other communication links. These links allow data to be sent from one computer to another—usually very fast. Sponsors pay to support the computing and communicating equipment needed to maintain a site or **server.** These participating sponsors agree to follow certain **protocols** (rules) so that communication is ensured, but there is little control over who may use the Internet and what kind of data is carried on it.

The Internet Is a Client-Server Network Arrangement

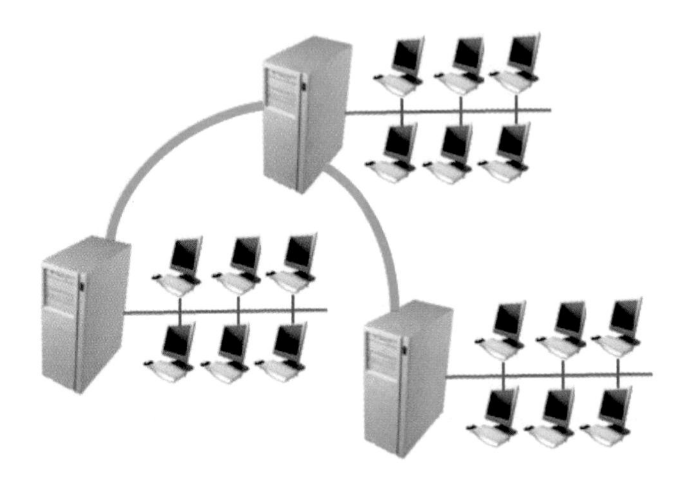

The Internet was once known as the Information Superhighway, a term popularized in the 1990s to describe ways of expanding the Internet beyond its then current state. Now that the Internet has developed into a major commercial, governmental, and social networking presence it is generally just known as the Internet.

2.2 History of Internet

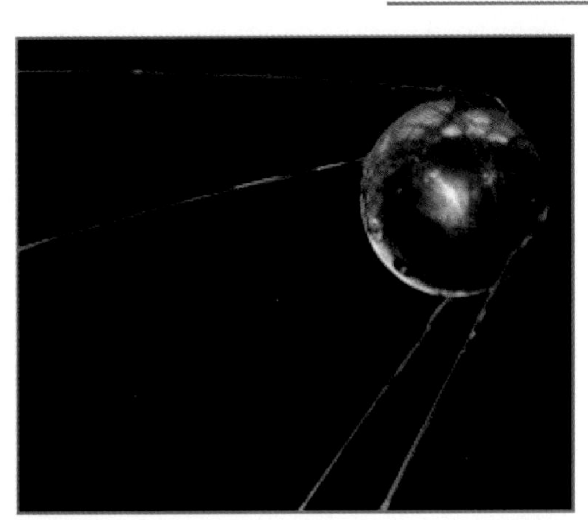

Sputnik Gave an Unexpected Boost to Internet Development

Much technology owes its birth to the pressures of wartime, with communication technology often playing an important role in war. The Internet was born of the Cold War with the need to communicate safely and quickly.

When Russia launched Sputnik in 1957, Americans panicked. In the scramble to keep up with the technologically advancing Russians, The Cold War brought a widespread fear of nuclear war as the power of weapons increased. The government in this period was partially concerned with how it could continue to function in the event of a nuclear strike.

The Union of Soviet Socialists Republics' launch of Sputnik spurred the United States to create the Advanced Research Projects Agency (**ARPA,** later known as the Defense Advanced Research Projects Agency, or DARPA) in February 1958 to attempt to regain a technological lead.

At the time, telephone communication was centralized, and destroying a central telephone switching location could leave portions of the country isolated. While computer networks of the time looked like a possibility, they also suffered in the same manner: one centralized computer controlled the others.

The Department of Defense commissioned the development of a decentralized computer information network in order to research the possibilities of networking. The plan included a network that lacked any type of central control, could easily add or remove any number of sites, and could still function even with major damage to other locations in the network. It was called a **packet-switching** network, and its first implementation was in 1961. The Advanced Research Projects Agency Network (**ARPANET**), developed by ARPA, was the world's first operational packet-switching network, and the predecessor of the Internet.

The technologies of networks and packet-switching are presented in another chapter where you learn about network architecture and network hardware. As you will find in that chapter, the Internet is a distributed network that follows the **client-server** model.

2.3 Protocol

Computers are able to communicate because they have an agreement about how to converse (send and receive messages). The agreement is known as a protocol. The Internet is a vast space in which many conversations occur simultaneously. To keep it all organized and working smoothly protocols coordinate the flow of communication. Several important protocols that govern the Internet include TCP/IP, HTTP, HTTPS, SMTP, POP, and FTP.

2.3.1 TCP/IP

The most fundamental protocol is Transmission Control Protocol/Internet Protocol (TCP/IP), which is the basic communication language or protocol of the Internet.

- **IP**—Responsible for moving packets of data from node to node.
- **TCP**—Responsible for verifying the correct delivery of packets from client to server.

But what are packets and nodes?

Packets The Internet transports data by dismantling it into packets which are addressed to a specific computer by using that computer's **IP address.** An IP address is a unique numeric address that each computer connected to the Internet is assigned.

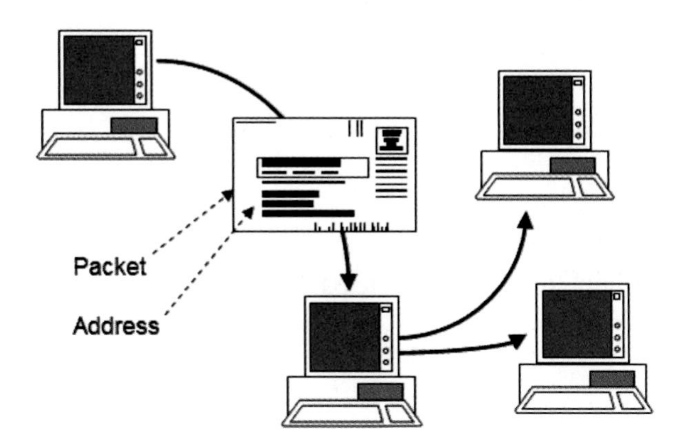

Internet Data Is Carried in Packets

The packets are passed from server to server over a **packet-switching** network in the general direction of the destination where they are reassembled into the original data. There is no fixed route on this network. This is how the network could still function even after many nodes had failed.

It turns out that everything you do on the Internet involves packets. For example, every Web page that you receive comes as a series of packets, and every e-mail you send leaves as a series of packets. Networks that ship data around in small packets are called packet-switching networks.

A Message Is Allocated into Several Packets

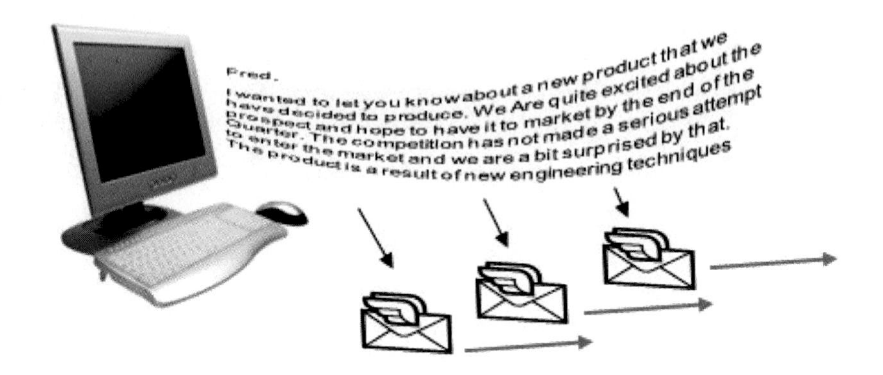

On the Internet, the network breaks an e-mail message into parts of equal size. These parts are known as packets. Each packet carries routing information that will help it get to its destination—the sender's IP address, the intended receiver's IP address, something that tells the network how many packets this e-mail message has been broken into, and the sequence number of this particular packet. A packet typically contains perhaps 1,000 or 1,500 bytes.

Think of a packet as an electronic envelope that contains data and is transported from server to server until it reaches its destination.

Each packet is then sent off to its destination by the best available route—a route that might be taken by all the other packets in the message or by none of the other packets in the message. This makes the network more efficient. First, the network can balance the load across various pieces of equipment on a millisecond-by-millisecond basis. Second, if there is a problem with one piece of equipment in the network while a message is being transferred, packets can be routed around the problem, ensuring the delivery of the entire message.

Packets Follow the Best Available Route

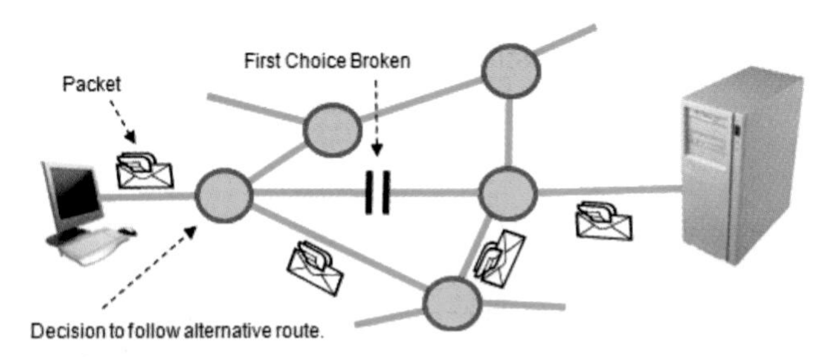

Generally, not all of a message's packets follow the same route. It is the job of the receiving computer, then, to reassemble the packets into the correct sequence. If a packet is dropped or lost then the receiver must request a retransmission from the sender.

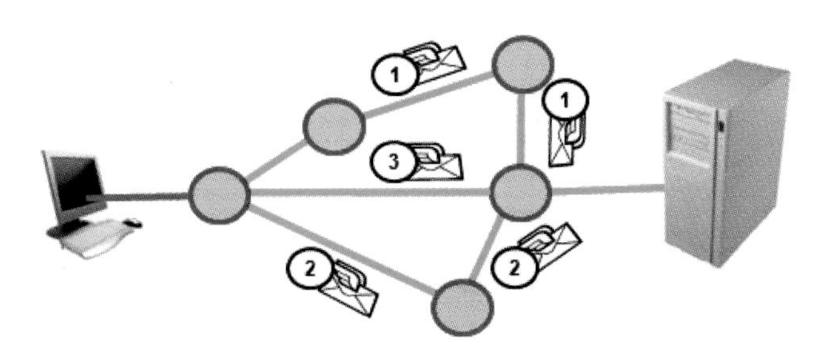

Packets Follow Different Routes

Packet switching, now the dominant basis for both data and voice communication worldwide, was a new and important concept in data communications. Previously, data communications was based on the idea of **circuit switching** as in the old typical telephone circuit, where a dedicated circuit is tied up for the duration of the call and communication is only possible with the single party on the other end of the circuit. With packet switching, a system could use one communication link to communicate with more than one machine by assembling data into packets and distributing them to various destinations.

Nodes A node is a term for a point in a network. Any computer connected to the Internet is considered a node. Machines like routers and gateways which direct traffic (packets) through the network are considered nodes, too. A node has an address and may be a point of origin, destination, or redirection.

2.3.2 E-mail Protocols

E-mail messages are generally sent to an e-mail server that stores received messages in the recipient's e-mail mailbox. The user later retrieves these messages with either a web browser or an e-mail client program that uses one of a number of e-mail retrieval protocols. Most clients and servers support the Internet standard protocols SMTP for sending e-mail and POP3 and IMAP4 for retrieving e-mail. Common use of these protocols allows **interoperability** with other servers and clients.

2.3.2.1 SMTP

Simple Mail Transfer Protocol (SMTP) is the de facto standard for e-mail transmissions across the Internet. Whenever you send an e-mail message, your e-mail client interacts with the SMTP server to handle the sending. The SMTP server on your host computer may have conversations with other SMTP servers to actually deliver the e-mail.

The SMTP server is a computer that runs special software allowing it to accept e-mail messages and redirect them to other servers. It understands that e-mail messages might spread over several packets. If the destination address is invalid, the SMTP server sends an informative response to the client that originated the message. Often a computer serving as an e-mail server performs no other tasks. This is to promote efficient transfer of messages and to assist with security.

2.3.2.2 POP

Post Office Protocol version 3 (POP3) is used to retrieve e-mail from a remote server over a TCP/IP connection. Nearly all Internet service providers grant e-mail accounts to

STMP Server Transmits E-Mail

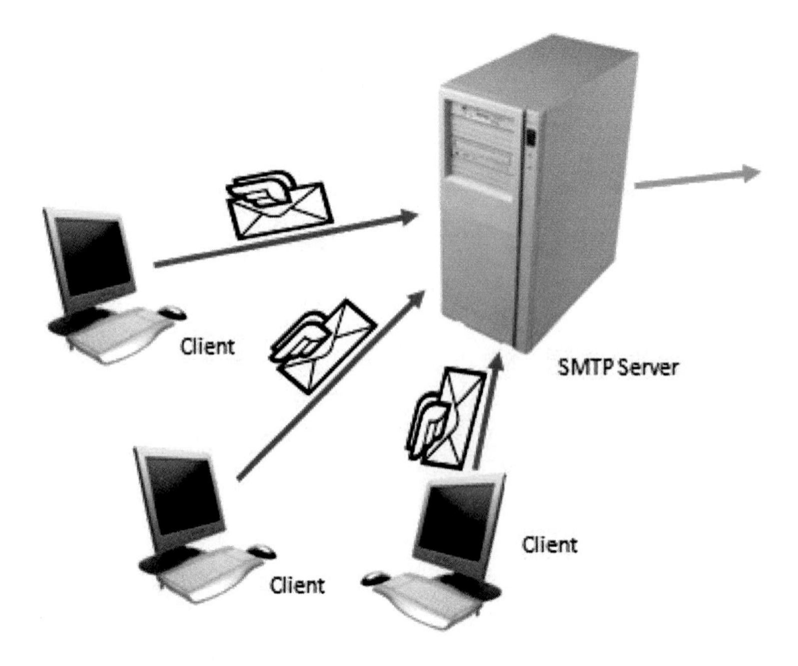

their subscribers who access their e-mail with client software that uses POP3. Some web-based services like **Gmail** also provide POP3 access for users who wish to download messages from the Gmail server. The POP3 server maintains e-mail boxes for storage of messages until they are downloaded.

Browser-based e-mail programs are a common alternative to the use of POP3 for delivery of e-mail. Stand alone client programs often provide greater functionality than web-based interfaces do. Client programs also house downloaded documents which can make the documents more accessible.

POP Server Stores and Forwards E-Mail

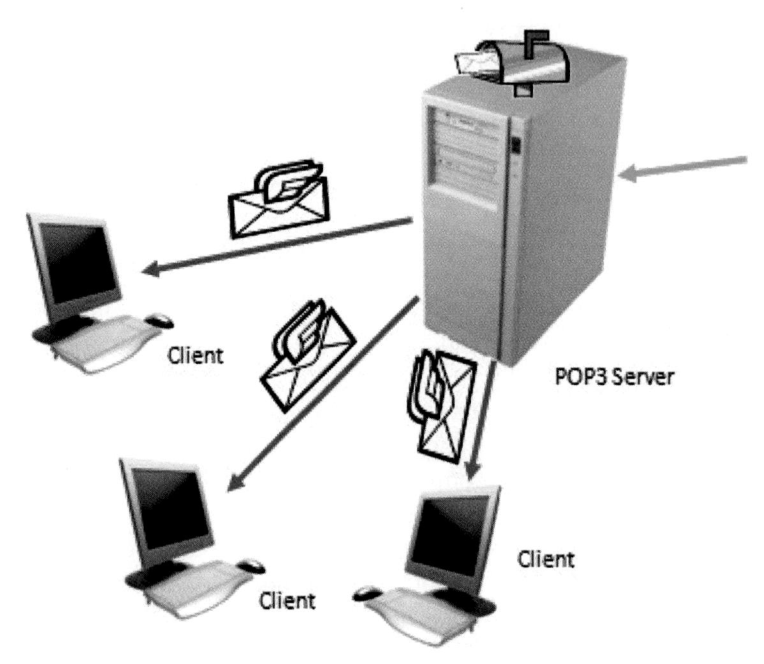

2.3.2.3 IMAP

IMAP (Internet Mail Access Protocol) is a more advanced e-mail protocol. With IMAP, your mail stays on the e-mail server. You can organize your mail into folders, and all the folders live on the server as well. This approach makes it extremely easy for you to access your e-mail from any machine, and regardless of which machine you use, you have access to all of your mail in all of your folders. IMAP is gaining in popularity. Several IMAP email service providers include **SAFe-mail, VFEmail,** and **FastMail.**

2.3.3 HTTP

Hypertext Transfer Protocol (HTTP) is a method used to transfer or convey information on the World Wide Web. Its original purpose was to provide a way to publish and retrieve HTML pages. HTTP is a **request-response protocol** between clients and servers. The originating client, such as a web browser, or other end-user tool, is referred to as the user agent. The destination server, which stores or creates resources such as HTML files and images, is called the origin server. In between the user agent and origin server may be several intermediaries, such as switches, routers, gateways, and other servers.

HTTP Is a Request-Response Protocol

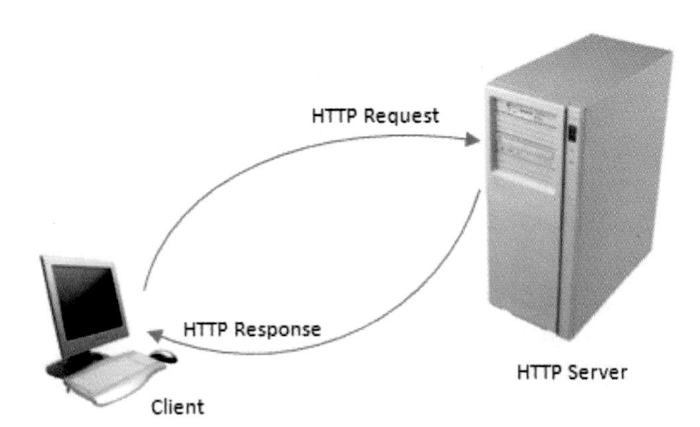

An HTTP client initiates a request by establishing a TCP connection to a particular port on a remote host. An HTTP server listening on that port waits for the client to send a request message. Ports are discussed in the chapter on networks.

2.3.4 HTTPS: Secure HTTP

HTTPS is a scheme almost identical to HTTP but which signals the browser to use an added **encryption** layer to protect the traffic. **SSL** (Secure Sockets Layer) is especially suited for HTTP.

Encryption to Disguise Data

Strictly speaking, HTTPS is not a separate protocol, but refers to the combination of a normal HTTP interaction over an encrypted Secure Sockets Layer. This ensures reasonable protection from eavesdroppers.

2.3.5 DNS

As you navigate among Web sites and pages, the browser must translate the English-like URLs you click on into the numeric addresses that the Internet requires for delivery of messages. These numeric addresses are known as **IP addresses.** The messages are known as **packets.** All Internet content is packaged and delivered in packets and each packet must carry the numeric address of the destination computer. The translation of URLs into IP addresses is performed automatically for you by Domain Name Service (**DNS**).

Domain Name Service

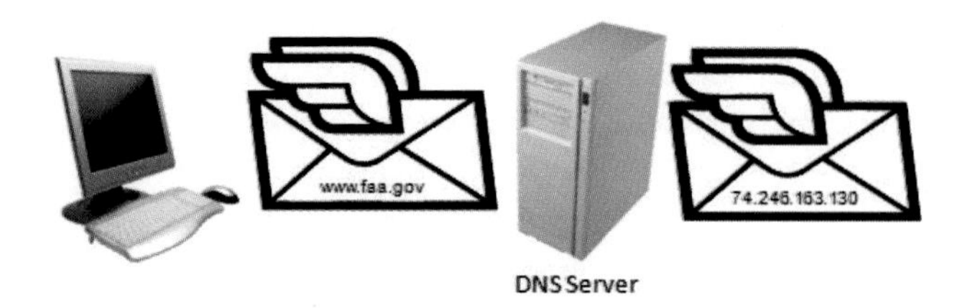

This service operates on specially designated servers scattered around the Internet. Your browser attempts to get URLs resolved into IP addresses from a local DNS server. If the server is down or unreachable due to a network blockage then you will not be able to send or receive emails, navigate to Web pages, download files, etc. If you suspect that this might be happening and are using Windows Vista, right-click the network icon in the lower right of the screen, and then select "Diagnose and repair." If DNS is the cause, this message will appear.

Vista Checking DNS

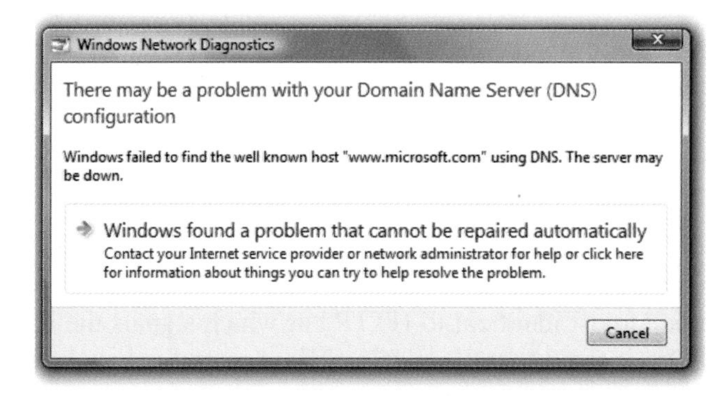

When this happens you have no alternatives other than to wait until the server returns to service.

URL, Universal Resource Locator A URL (i.e., sportsillustrated.com) is an Internet address. In this case, since the URL has no specific resource identified, a Web page is assumed by default. Since each web page must be fetched from a server before it can be displayed, it is important to understand what a **URL** is and how to use it.

All URLs combine a server name and the name of a resource on that server. The URL also identifies the type of resource. Sports Illustrated's home page is on a server with the name of sportsillustrated.com. Since we address it as http://sportsillustrated.com it is assumed to be a Web page which is normally named with a file extension of **.htm** or **.html.** In this case you do not see the name of the Web page. If no resource name is given, a default page (Web site home page) is assumed.

URLs are what make **hyperlinks** possible. Each is identified in a web page by underlined text. As you pass the mouse over any link the browser displays the URL of that hyperlink in the lower left corner of the screen. If you click on the underlined words (the hyperlink), the browser sends a message through the Internet to a server requesting that page which is then delivered to your computer where the browser displays it.

IP Addresses and Domain Names Every client and server on the Internet has a unique identifying number called an **IP Address.** IP stands for Internet Protocol, which is the language that computers use to communicate over the Internet. IP addresses are analogous to telephone numbers—when you want to call someone on the telephone, you must first know their telephone number. Similarly, when a computer on the Internet needs to send data to another computer, it must first know its IP address. IP addresses are typically shown as four numbers separated by three decimal points, or dots. For example, 10.24.210.3 and 67.144.63.11 are IP addresses.

If you need to make a telephone call but you only know the person's name, you look them up in the telephone directory (or call directory services) to get the telephone number. On the Internet, that directory is called the **Domain Name Service** (DNS). If you know the name of a server, say www.cnn.com, and you type this into your Web browser, your computer will then ask the **DNS server** (a special server somewhere on the Internet) what the numeric IP address is that is associated with that name. Generally you do not need to know IP addresses because DNS takes care of finding them for you.

The four numbers in an IP address can contain any value between zero and 255. Combine the four parts and you get a possible 256^4 or 4,294,967,296 unique values. Although this seems like a lot, it really is not when you consider the number of servers and clients connected to the Internet at any one time. It is not hard to imagine that we may be in for an IP address squeeze at some point. For this reason, projects like **Internet Protocol version 6 (IPv6) and Internet2** are oriented toward ensuring that Internet technology and protocols can keep up with expected future demand.

Internet Protocol Version 6 (IPv6) The main improvement proposed by IPv6 (Internet Protocol version 6) is the increase in the number of addresses available for networked devices, allowing, for example, each computer, mobile phone, and mobile electronic device to have its own address. IPv4 (the current standard) supports about 4.3 billion addresses, which is inadequate for giving even one address to every living person, let alone supporting other addressable electronic devices. IPv6, however, supports over 5,000 addresses for each of the roughly 6.5 billion people alive today. With such a large address space available the shortage of IP addresses mentioned earlier could be remedied.

Internet2 Internet2 or UCAID (University Corporation for Advanced Internet Development) is a non-profit consortium which develops and deploys advanced network applications and technologies for education and high-speed data transfer purposes. Students who belong to poor quality libraries now find themselves downloading not only text but sound recordings, animations, videos, and other resources. An important application is video conferencing. Using this technology over the Internet, neurosurgeons can video conference with other experts in the field during an operation in a high resolution format with no apparent time lag. The potential applications of this type of network are endless.

Dynamic and Static IP Addresses One approach to the absolute worldwide limit of IP addresses is to share addresses. While the IP addresses of servers must never change (so they can be found whenever a user wishes to visit that server) the IP addresses of clients can change without problem. For this reason two types of IP address assignments are used:

- **Static**—Addresses never change. Static IP addresses are used by servers.
- **Dynamic**—On many networks clients are assigned an IP address when connecting to the network. When a user logs off, the IP address may be assigned to another client.

Domain Name By allowing the use of unique alphabetical addresses instead of numeric ones, domain names allow Internet users to more easily find and communicate with Web sites and other server-based services.

Top Level Domain Names Every domain name ends in a top-level domain **(TLD)** name, which is always either one of a small list of generic names (three or more characters) or a two-characters territory code. The most commonly known top level domain name is **.com.** Other top level names are listed here:

Top Level Domain Names

ID	Description	ID	Description
.aero	Air-transport industry	.jobs	Companies
.biz	Business	.mil	United States Military
.cat	Catalan	.mobi	Mobile devices
.com	Commercial	.museum	Museums
.coop	Cooperatives	.name	Personal. Individuals, by name
.edu	Educational	.net	Network
.gov	Governmental	.org	Organization
.info	Information	.pro	Professions
.int	International organizations	.travel	Travel related sites

The Internet Assigned Numbers Authority (**IANA**) currently classifies top-level domains. In addition to the generic names, numerous two character country codes have been assigned as well. If a URL has no country extension, US for United States is assumed. The list of country codes is quite long. Here is an abbreviated list:

Two Character Country Extensions

ID	Country	ID	Country	ID	Country	ID	Country
.al	Albania	.bw	Botswana	.kg	Kyrgyzstan	.si	Slovenia
.aw	Aruba	.ck	Cook Islands	.mq	Martinique	.tg	Togo
.bo	Bolivia	.ee	Estonia	.ni	Nicaragua	.us	USA
.br	Brazil	.gd	Grenada	.nl	Netherlands	.uy	Uruguay
.bt	Bhutan	.ht	Haiti	.pn	Pitcairn Islands	.zw	Zimbabwe

2.3.6 FTP

Short for File Transfer Protocol, FTP is the protocol for exchanging files over the Internet. Specifically, FTP is a commonly used protocol for exchanging files over any network that supports the TCP/IP protocol (such as the Internet or an intranet).

FTP works in the same way as HTTP for transferring web pages from a server to a user's browser and SMTP for transferring electronic mail across the Internet, in that, like these technologies, FTP uses the Internet's TCP/IP controlling protocols to enable successful data transfer using packets. FTP is most commonly used to download a file from a server using the Internet or to upload a file to a server, for example, uploading a web page document to a server.

There are two computers involved in an FTP transfer: a server and a client. The FTP server, running FTP server software, listens on the network for connection requests from other computers. The client computer, running FTP client software, initiates a connection to the server usually supplying an ID and password. Once connected, the client can do a number of file operations such as uploading files to the server, downloading files from the server, renaming or deleting folders and files on the server, and so on.

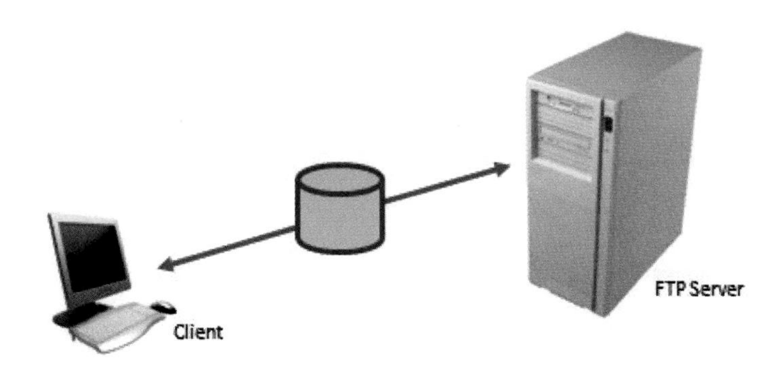

FTP Moves Data between Computers

2.3.7 Peer-to-Peer File Sharing

Peer-to-peer (**P2P**) file sharing is the activity of making files available for other users to download over the Internet and smaller networks. P2P file sharing follows the model where the files are stored on and served by the personal computers of the users. True P2P does not involve a server and permits direct communication between personal computers.

Napster, an example of a first generation P2P file sharing network had a centralized file list. After Napster's legal problems that caused bankruptcy, second generation networks like **Gnutella** and **FastTrack** emerged. These networks distributed the file list and true P2P file sharing was established.

2.4 Internet Access

Obtaining access to the Internet requires several components that are described in this section:

- **Service provider**—A business or organization that connects your message requests (http, ftp, smtp, pop3, etc.) to the Internet.
- **Communication hardware**—Computer and network interface hardware that translates electrical signals enabling different devices to send and receive them.
- **A line**—A physical connection that carries the packets that comprise your messages.

2.4.1 Service Providers

A service provider (SP) is a business or organization that provides consumer's access to the Internet and related services. There are two types of service providers:

- **Internet service provider (ISP)**—Provides connectivity.
- **Application service provider** (**ASP**)—Provides an application platform for Web services like on-line shopping, e-mail, chat rooms, and others.

2.4.1.1 Internet Service Provider (ISP)

ISPs provide basic end-user access to the Internet. Local businesses, AOL, the phone and cable companies, and so on are ISPs. Governments and universities are ISPs, too. Each ISP that provides end-user Internet access consolidates the **traffic** (messages) of all customers onto larger capacity lines that connect to the greater Internet.

Just as their customers pay them for Internet access, ISPs themselves pay upstream ISPs for Internet access. Ultimately there are a few significant SPs that form the **backbone** of the Internet.

Internet Backbone

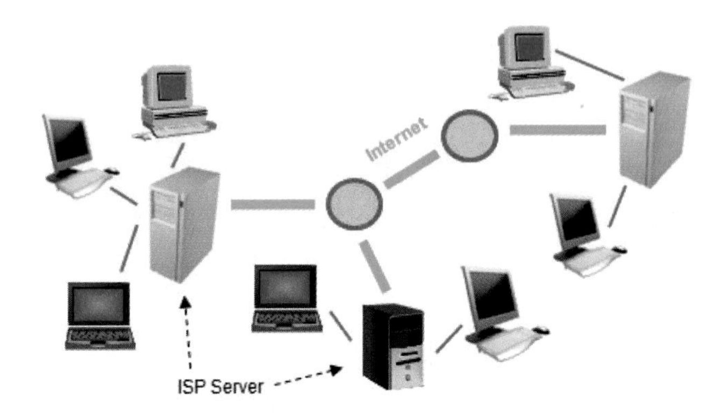

2.4.1.2 Application Service Provider

An Application service provider (ASP) is a business that provides computer-based services to customers over a network. Software offered using an ASP model is also sometimes called On-demand software. The most limited sense of this business is that of providing access to a particular application program (such as medical billing) using a standard protocol such as HTTP.

The need for ASPs has evolved from the increasing costs of specialized software that have far exceeded the price range of small- to medium-sized businesses. Likewise, the growing complexities of software have led to huge costs in distributing the software to end-users. Through ASPs, the complexities and costs of such software can be cut down. In addition, the issues of upgrading have been eliminated from the end-user firm by placing the responsibility on the ASP to maintain up-to-date services, physical and electronic security, and round-the-clock technical support.

2.5 E-mail

Electronic mail, one of the oldest and most commonly used services on the Internet, permits the exchange of letters. Your letter travels through the Internet, from server to server (computer to computer), until it reaches the addressee. E-mail is generally reliable, but not very secure. As your letter hops through the net, its contents could easily be read as it passes through a server.

E-mail is a way to electronically share (send and receive) typed messages between people. Both you and the other person must have e-mail accounts. A message that you type is stored in a shared computer (server) until the other person accesses the computer and is then shown the mail message waiting from you. When the other person reads the message a reply may be typed and electronically sent back to you. If the server with your account is connected to the Internet then you may communicate with people throughout the world.

Your E-mail Account Your account is really a globally (worldwide) unique mailing address. Since each message must be delivered to the specified person it is essential that each address (e-mail account) be unique. Your address is comprised of two sections (local and global) separated by the @ sign. The sections are divided among three parts this way:

- **Local address**—Your local address is simply your USERID on the computer that your account is registered on. If you are communicating with a person who has an account on the same server then you only need use the USERID of the other person. If you wish to e-mail to another server then the global address is used.
- **Global address**—Global addresses are a little different. If you want to send a message to someone with a mailbox on a different computer you must include the domain name and server name as part of the address. For example, if you want to send a message to Betty Rubble (user id brubble) at Crop Circle University you would use her global address: brubble@salamander.cropc.edu

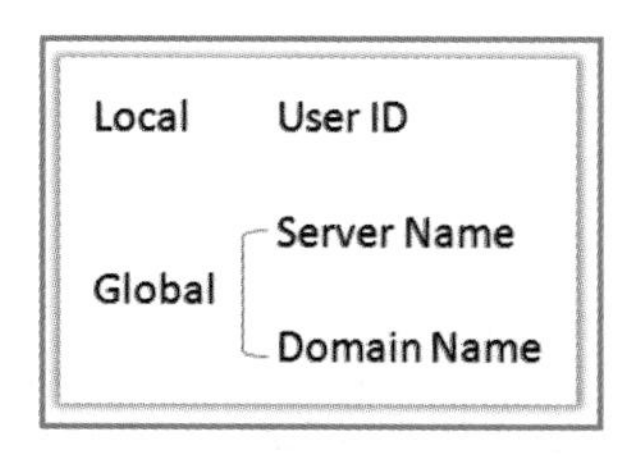

Two Sections of an E-mail Address Are Divided into Three Parts

Here, salamander is the name of the school's server which houses Betty's account and cropc.edu is the school's domain. The **server** name together with the **domain** uniquely identifies a computer connected to the Internet. So, the global address gets the message to a particular computer and the local address takes over from there. All domain-server names are registered world-wide with the Domain Name Service (DNS). This global registration permits users anywhere to send e-mail messages to servers anywhere.

How to Send E-mail Your e-mail account is registered on a local server. That server holds the local post office including your personal mailbox. You enter your mailbox (to send and read mail) from any client workstation on the server's local network. If you are sending mail to someone with an account on a different server you use his or her global address. Your server recognizes the address as global and it ships the message out to the Internet. There, a worldwide collection of connected servers has the intelligence to read e-mail addresses and forward the message to the proper server. How it happens is not important, but the beauty of e-mail and the Internet is that all you need know is a friend's e-mail address and let the servers and Internet do the rest.

2.6 Browser

When surfing the Web, you need to use two fundamental resources: browsers and search engines. You need a **browser** to view Web pages and you need a **search engine** to help you figure out where to go. You will also need to understand **domain names, URLs** and **IP addresses.**

A Web browser is a software application that enables a user to display and interact with text, images, and other information typically located on a Web page at a Web site on the World Wide Web or on a local area network. Text and images on a Web page can contain hyperlinks to other Web pages at the same or different Web site. Web browsers allow a user to access quickly and easily information provided on many Web pages at many Web sites by traversing these links. Web browsers format HTML information for display, so the appearance of a Web page may differ between browsers. The browser is the primary tool for visiting Web sites and displaying Web pages. Internet Explorer is more widely used than any other browser.

Internet Explorer 7 provides a safer, more personalized, and more productive browsing experience for users than earlier versions of Internet Explorer. A redesigned interface maximizes the area of the screen that displays a Web page. Quick and easy access to favorites, browsing history, and RSS Feed subscriptions is available, too. Multiple sites are viewed in a single browser window and you may easily switch from one site to another through tabs at the top of the browser frame. You can easily select and navigate through open tabs by displaying thumbnails of them all in a single window.

Internet Explorer uses a **zone-based security** framework, which means that sites are grouped based upon certain conditions. It allows the restriction of broad areas of functionality, and also allows specific functions to be restricted. ActiveX control allows Web pages to extend their functionality by providing access to native operating system calls. This has been the source of security concerns, as this access was originally unrestricted and unchecked. Internet Explorer 7 has significantly tightened up security about ActiveX controls and other similar technologies.

Internet Explorer 7 (IE7) is the current version of Microsoft's browser. When Microsoft redesigned version 6 of Internet Explorer three design objectives were paramount.

- **Make everyday tasks easier** with improved navigation through tabbed browsing, Web search right from the toolbar, advanced printing, easy discovery of RSS feeds, reading and subscription to RSS feeds, and much more.
- Provide **dynamic security protection** through a new architecture, security features that help defend against malicious software (also known as malware), and new ways to better protect against the theft of personal data from fraudulent Web sites, a practice known as phishing.
- Develop an **improved platform for Web development and manageability,** including improved support for cascading style sheets (CSS), a RSS feeds platform, and tools for deploying and managing Internet Explorer 7 in large enterprise environments.

2.6.1 Internet Explorer Is a Client Program

All of the computers connected to the Internet can be categorized as two types: servers and clients. Those machines that provide services to other machines are **servers.** And the machines that are used to connect to those services are **clients.** The most common activity of Internet users is to navigate to Web sites and view Web pages. Servers provide Web pages and a client browser is used to request and display Web pages. Internet Explorer is a client program.

Internet Explorer

2.6.2 Features

Internet Explorer provides several tools and features that enhance your use of the browser.

2.6.2.1 Menus

The standard menus that are familiar from earlier IE versions are not displayed unless you want them. The right side of the tool bar provides a Tools button. When you click on it a mini menu appears. From there, select Menu bar and the Menu bar appears.

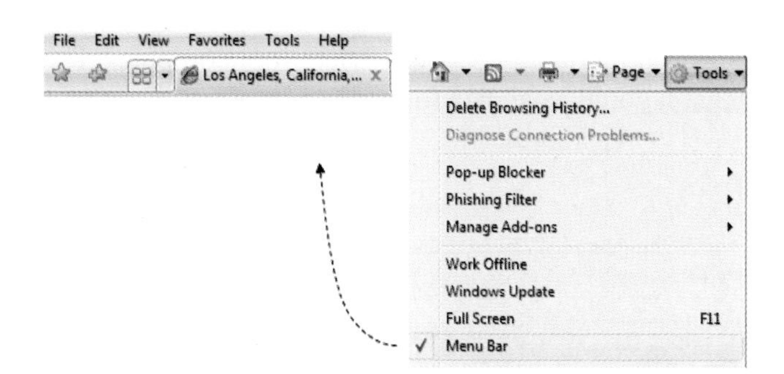

Un-hiding the Menu Bar

2.6.2.2 Address Bar

When you type an address (URL) into the Address bar and press Enter the browser navigates to that Web site which then appears in the browser window. Since typing URLs is such a common activity the Address bar was designed to help you complete URLs as you type. The History list (explained elsewhere) is the source of prospective URLs that IE considers and contains visited URLs of the last three weeks.

2.6.2.3 Status Bar

The status bar at the left bottom of the browser tells you what is happening (Opening a page, Page Loaded, etc.). When you hover over a link to another page, the Status bar displays the URL of that page. When you click a link, the Status bar displays a bar graph showing the progress of downloading the page and its associated content (images, sound, etc.) that comprises the page.

2.6.2.4 Control Buttons

- **Back and Forward buttons**—The standard button for prior and next page look a little different from earlier browser versions.
- **Go, Refresh, and Stop**—With IE 7 the traditional Stop, Go, and Refresh buttons are merged into two buttons that change state. The Go and Refresh buttons have been combined into one control, and have been moved up next to the right hand edge of the Address bar. While a page is loading, the Go button displays. Once a page finishes loading, the Refresh button displays. When you type in the Address bar, Go displays.

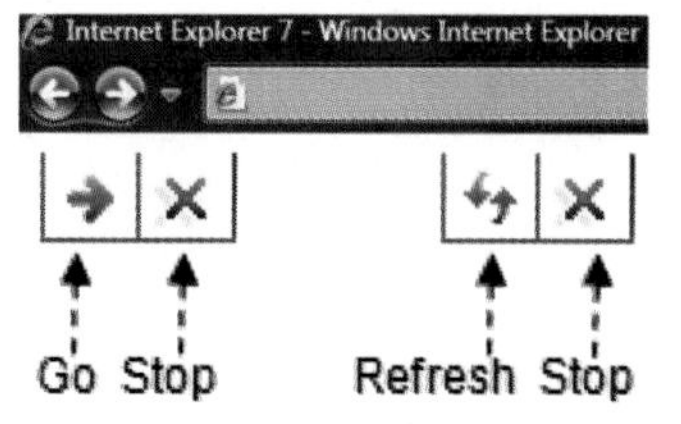

- **Home Button**—You will probably want to designate a Web site that you frequently like to visit as your home page. Each time you open IE the browser will initially navigate to your selected home page. Designating a home page can be accomplished several ways but the easiest is to click the arrow next to the home page button on the toolbar. From the menu that appears select Add or Change Home Page.

  Any time you click the Home Page icon the browser returns to your home page.

2.6.2.5 Auto Complete

Internet Explorer can remember user IDs and passwords as well as other data that you frequently type into Web page forms. This is convenient for sure but can also present a security risk if someone other than you were to use your computer. The first time IE detects a form field that it could save data for it asks you if you want to use this feature.

Adding a Search Provider

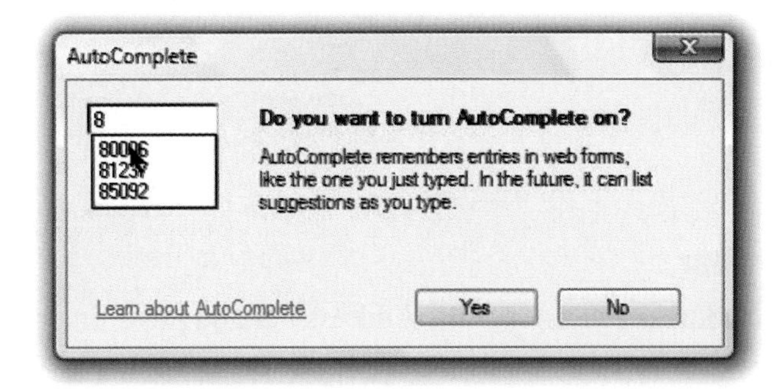

If you later change your mind or wish to exercise more control over automatic form completion, click Internet Options on the Tools menu and then click AutoComplete Settings.

Opening AutoComplete Settings

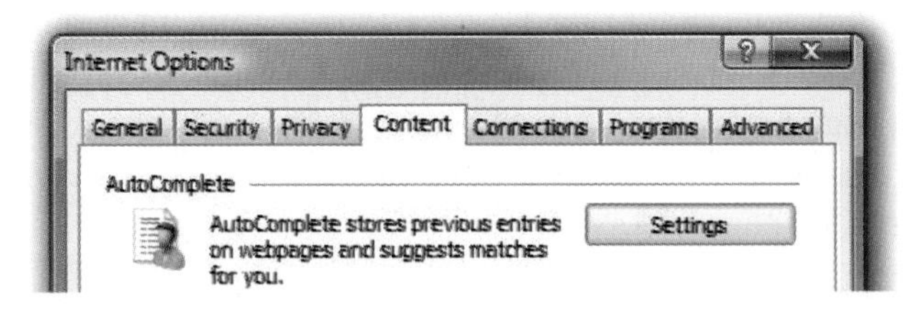

The AutoComplete dialog box allows you to control what to auto-fill and provides directions for deleting all stored form data including user IDs and passwords.

AutoComplete Settings

2.6.2.6 Tabbed Browsing

Tabbed browsing is the most-requested browser navigation feature among users seeking to visit multiple Web sites within one browser window. To create or open tabs in Internet Explorer 7, users can click on the empty tab on the Toolbar or right-click on any hyperlink in a Web page and choose Open in New Tab. They also can right-click on a tab to refresh each page as an individual tab or refresh all of them as a group, close individual tabs or the entire group, and reorder tabs on the tab bar by simply dragging and dropping.

Opening a New Tab When a new tab is opened this message appears:

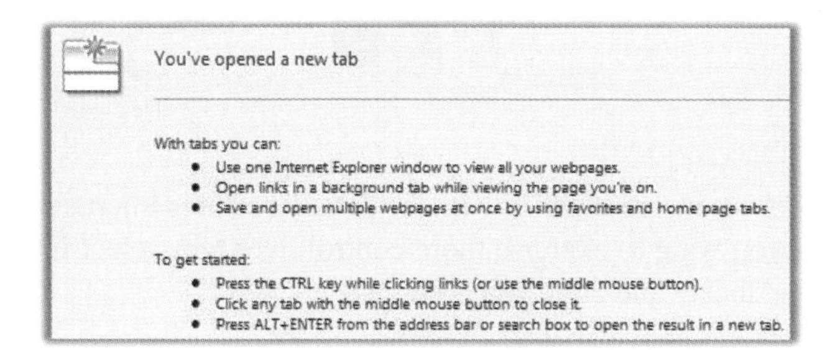

Open a New Tab

Dragging Tabs As you open tabs you may decide to rearrange their order. This is easily accomplished by dragging any tab to a new location in the tab sequence. This is illustrated here.

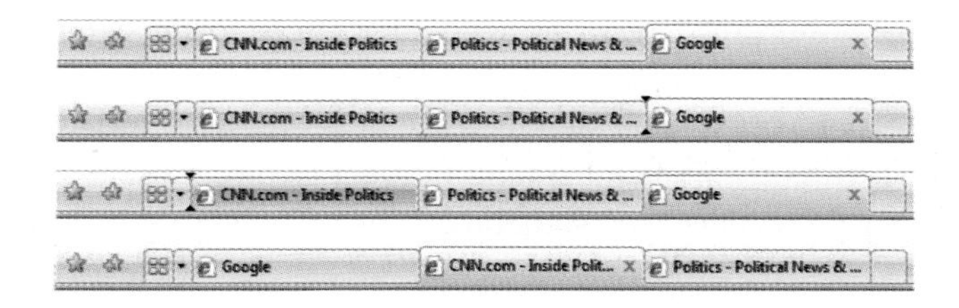

Dragging Tabs

Close All Tabs If you close the browser when one tab is displayed the browser closes. If more than one tab is displayed when you try to close the browser it asks you if you want to close all tabs.

Close All Tabs?

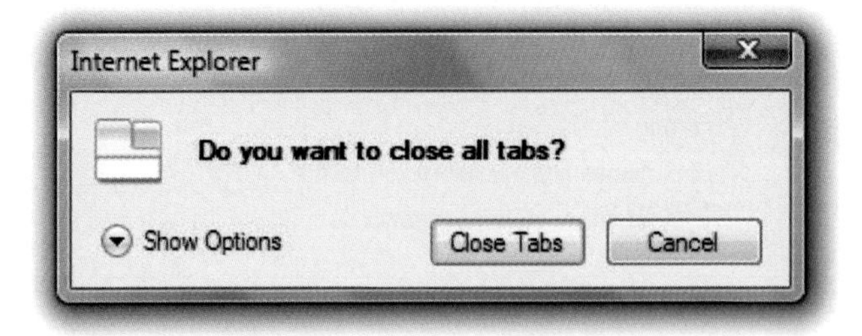

Quick Tabs Internet Explorer 7 helps manage multiple tabs with a feature called Quick Tabs. Quick Tabs enable the user to view thumbnail images of all open tabs in one view. By clicking the Quick Tab icon just to the right of the Favorites icon, users can view all open tabs. From the Quick Tabs view, the user can open any tab by simply clicking anywhere on the tab image and can close any tab by clicking the "X" in the far right corner of the image.

The Quick Tabs page will scale to the number of tabs the user has open. If a user has nine tabs open, Quick Tabs will preview thumbnail images of all nine tabs; if a user has more than 20 tabs open, they will see smaller thumbnail images of each tab but will still be able to see all tabs in single view. The Quick Tabs icon appears next to the Favorites Center and Subscribe buttons as soon as two or more tabs are open.

Selecting Quick Tabs

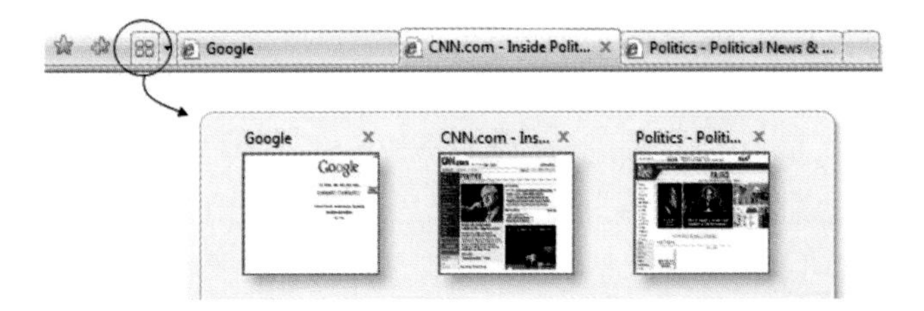

Tab Settings Most users are satisfied with the default features Internet Explorer provides to control tabs. If you want to exercise more control over tabs select Internet Options on the Tools menu and locate and click Tab Settings.

2.6.2.7 Printing

To help simplify common tasks like printing, Internet Explorer includes enhanced functionality that makes it easier to print a Web page without content at the left or right margin being cut off, which has been common in the past.

By default, the Internet Explorer 7 shrinks a Web page's text just enough to ensure that the entire page prints properly, so users no longer need to cut and paste the page into a text-editing program. Users are also able to adjust Web page margins, change the page layout, remove headers and footers, and increase or decrease the print space.

It has been a common complaint among Internet Explorer users that the right hand edge of a Web page's content was sometimes cut off when the page is printed. The workaround has always been to set Internet Explorer to print in Landscape mode, which of course uses more paper than Portrait.

Internet Explorer 7 introduces a new setting, Shrink to Fit, which is now the default setting when a Web page is printed. Shrink to Fit, as the name implies, automatically shrinks a Web page so that it fits perfectly on to your paper, no matter what its size may be.

Print Preview (on the File menu) provides a wide array of control over how printing is accomplished.

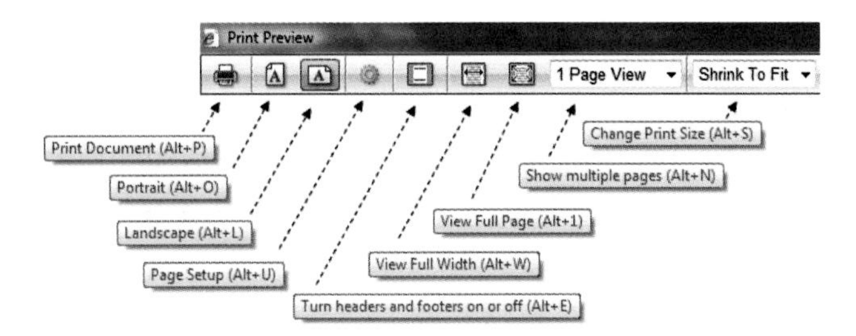

Print Preview Menu

2.6.2.8 Import/Export

Internet Explorer can import feeds and export your favorites, cookies, and RSS feeds. On the File menu, click on Import and Export. To export, select the type of content you wish to export then navigate to the location where the export will be saved. To import, all you need to know is where the file for your existing content is saved.

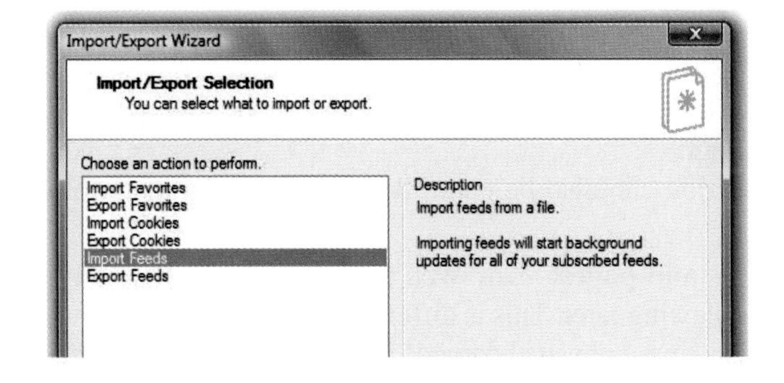

Import RSS Feeds

Exported content is stored in different file types:

- **Favorites**—stored in an HTML document (extension htm).
- **Cookies**—stored in a text file (extension txt).
- **RSS libraries**—stored as XML documents (extension xml) in a format known as OPML (Outline Processor Markup Language).

2.6.2.9 Instant Searching

The Instant Search box makes it quick and easy for users to search the Internet directly from the browser frame using their favorite search provider. Users can choose a search provider from the drop-down list and easily add more providers to the list.

Adding a Search Provider

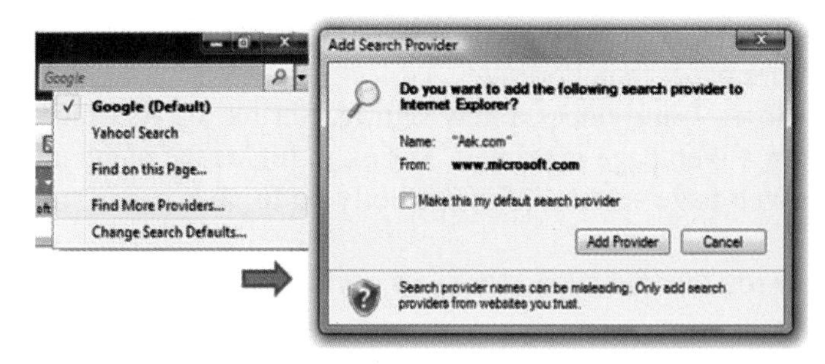

2.6.2.10 Other Control

There are several other ways to control your browsing experience:

- **Full screen browsing**—The menus, toolbars and controls in IE 7 and Vista take up less screen space than in earlier browsers and operating system versions but they still occupy space. If you want to view the page and only the page press **F11** to enter full screen mode. Press F11 again to return to regular mode.
- **Text size**—Depending on your eyes, different levels of text magnification will be desirable. This is manipulated selecting Text Size from the **View menu.** Keep in mind that this setting affects only text size. The Zoom control affects text and images.
- **Zoom**—To improve the user experience, Internet Explorer 7 has added a page zoom feature, which enables users to increase or decrease the page size for easier viewing. Not only can the user change the text size, but any graphics or embedded text in graphics can also be modified. Hard-to-read text or small thumbnail images on Web sites can now be enlarged. The keyboard shortcuts to manipulate Zoom settings are:
  - **Ctrl +**—zoom in
  - **Ctrl -**—zoom out
  - **Ctrl 0**—set to 100%

  If you have a wheel mouse, hold down the Ctrl key then spin up to zoom in, spin down to zoom out.

  Zoom selection can also be controlled by the Zoom menu on the status bar as shown here.

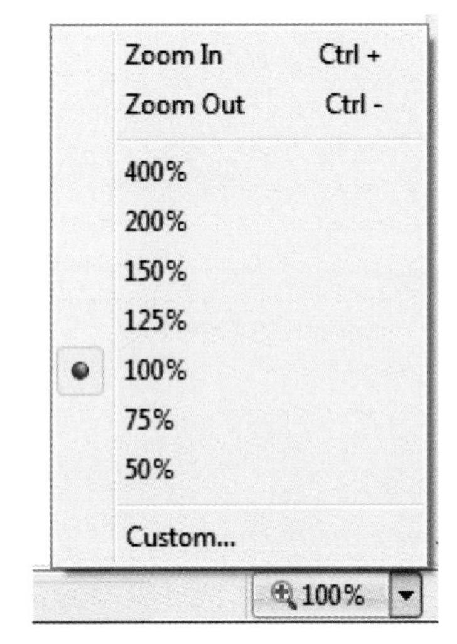

- **Saving images and pages**—Any Web page you are visiting may be saved to your computer for viewing later. This is different from saving a favorite (discussed later). Here you are saving a physical copy of the page and perhaps images and other content as well. Since saving pages consumes storage space it should be used wisely.

  To save a page select Save As on the file menu and then the Save Web page dialog box (partially shown) appears. The name of the page is taken from the Web site you visited. Select the Save as type. The four choices are explained here:

Saving a Web page

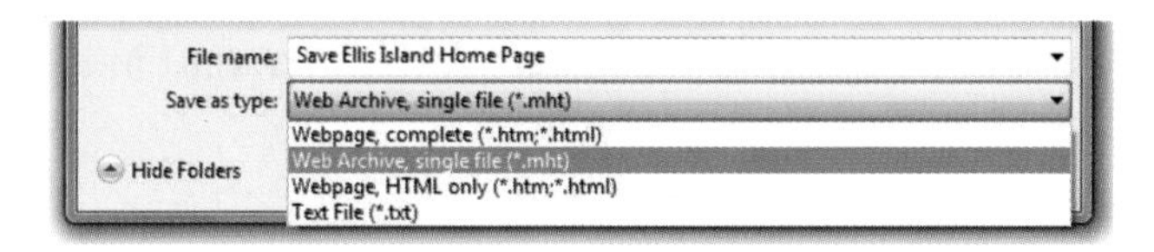

- **Web page, complete**—The Web page's HTML (the Web page text and formatting instructions) and all images and all other page content is saved in an HTML document and an associated folder. If you use this option keep in mind that images can be sizeable and a page with numerous images may consume more storage space than you want to use. If you save the page this way and ever move the page to a different folder you must be sure to move the page together with the folder this option creates.

- **Web archive, single file**—When you select this type the Web document gets saved in a Multipurpose Internet Mail Extension HTML (MHTML) format file with a **.MHT** file extension. All relative links in the Web page are remapped and the embedded content (images, sound files, etc.) is included in the .MHT file, rather than being saved in a separate folder as the case is with Web Page, complete option.

  MHTML enables you to send and receive Web pages and other HTML documents using e-mail programs. MHTML embeds images directly into the body of your document rather than attaching them separately as in a conventional Web page.
- **Webpage, HTML only**—If you only want to save a Web page as a raw HTML you would select Web Page, HTML only (*.htm, *.html). It will simply save the current page's source HTML to your drive intact. This action will NOT save the graphics from the page or any other files used within the page, which means that if you loaded the file back from the local disk, you would see broken image links.
- **Text file**—Here the page text is stored. No HTML formatting is included and no images or other content is stored. The resulting file is a text file with an extension of **txt** that can be opened in Notepad (open Accessories menu or type Notepad in the Start Search window of the Start menu).

2.6.3 Selecting a Home Page

The advantage of selecting a home page was described earlier in the discussion of control buttons. The home page button allows you to select the page currently displayed in the browser as your home page. If you want a bit more control, select Internet Options from the Tools menu.

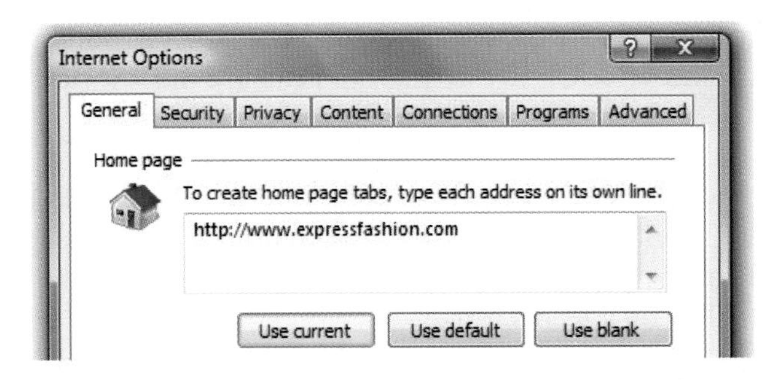

Selecting a Home Page

2.6.4 Favorite Center

Internet Explorer 7 no longer has separate History, Search, and Favorite panes. Instead, the History and Favorites panes have been combined with a Web Feed (RSS) pane in a new feature called the Favorites Center:

Favorites Center

The Center has three displays shown in a left side panel of the browser window.

- **Favorites**—Web pages that you have added to your favorites list.
- **RSS Feeds**—News feeds that you subscribe to.
- **History**—Pages that you have recently visited.

2.6.4.1 Favorites

As you surf and visit Web sites you may want to save the addresses (URL) of some sites so you can easily return for another visit. Adding a site to the list of your favorites can be accomplished either of two ways:

- **Press Ctrl-D**—The Web site displayed in the browser when you press Ctrl-D is added to the favorites list.
- **Click Add to Favorites**—Click the Add to Favorites option in the Favorites menu. This method allows you to rename the URL if you wish.

You may access your favorites directly on the Favorites menu or in the Favorites Center as shown above.

2.6.4.2 RSS

RSS (Really Simple Syndication) is a way of sharing information over the Internet. Basically, a Web site designer creates a specially coded page that can be registered with special Web services (called **aggregators**). Internet users can then use such aggregators to subscribe to the RSS feed, and be automatically notified when its content changes. Or, if the user visits a site with an RSS service, he or she can subscribe to a feed without using an aggregator if they happen to have an RSS feed reader or aggregator available on their computer. IE 7 provides an aggregator.

RSS content is typically indicated on a Web page by one of two icons shown here. There are a couple of ways to access this content. First, you can simply click on the orange button to view the page. Or, if you wish, you can use the RSS icon on Internet Explorer's toolbar.

XML RSS

Subscribing to an RSS Feed Users can subscribe to a feed with a single click, a process that is very similar to adding a Web site favorite. First you need to know what feeds are available on the page you are viewing. Click the arrow to the right of the RSS toolbar icon. Next click on a feed's name:

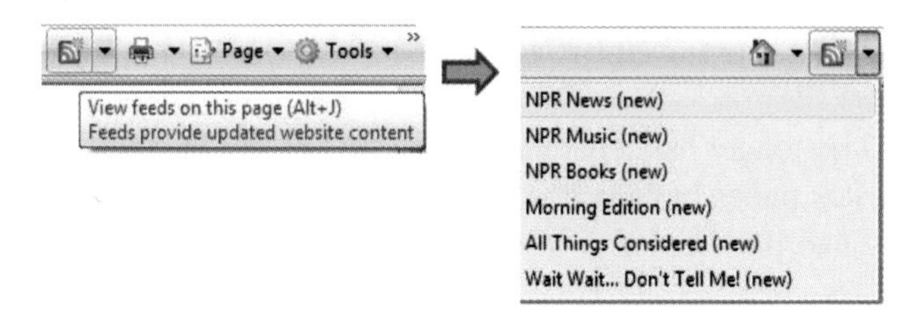

Listing Available RSS Feeds

Now you can subscribe by clicking the link shown.

Viewing RSS Feeds before Subscribing

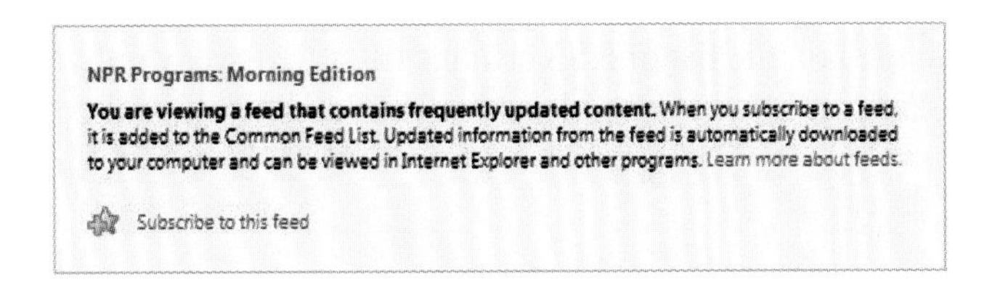

After viewing the current feed and clicking the subscribe link this confirmation dialog box appears:

Confirming Subscription to a RSS Feeds

Reading Feeds In previous versions of Internet Explorer, RSS feeds were rendered in the browser in raw Extensible Markup Language (XML), which is unreadable by anyone but the most technical users. In Internet Explorer 7, users can read the feed directly in the browser, scan for important stories, and get a description of the content. Once you have subscribed to RSS feeds, reading them is a simple procedure:

View Feed List

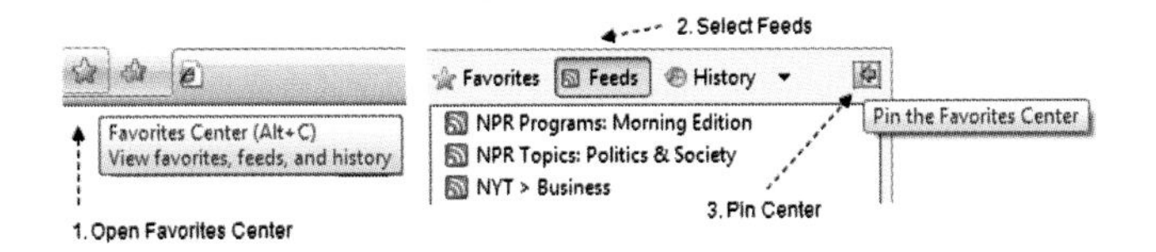

Any feed name listed in bold indicates a feed has new content. This visual indicator always informs you of which feeds have fresh news so that you do not have to examine each feed yourself. Most aggregators provide some equivalent indicator.

Fresh News Indicator

Click on a feed name to view the feed in a browser tab.

Searching for Content Internet Explorer 7 allows display of feed content sorted by Date, Title, or Author (the Author option only appears if there is more than one contributor to a feed). There is a text box in the top right hand corner of a subscribed feed page. As you type text in the box the list of RSS articles filter to display only those articles that contain the text. Click on Show All to clear the filter and display all content.

Filtering News

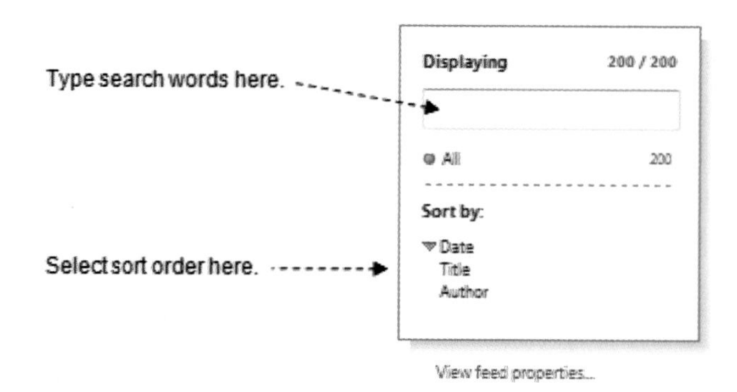

Feed Settings Once you have subscribed to any news feeds, click on View Feeds in the Favorites Center to adjust feed subscription settings. Right click on any feed entry, and then select Properties to access various options. The Feed Properties dialog box that appears allows you to:

- Rename the feed entry.
- Specify how often IE checks for new content.
- Indicate whether you wish to download attached content (not recommended).
- Define how many old news items to archive.

You can also change the default for when Internet Explorer searches for feed updates. The installation default settings are sufficient for most users but if you are interested in controlling the settings select:

1. Tools menu
2. Internet Options
3. Click Content tab
4. Click Feeds Settings

The settings are mostly understandable but turning off the feed reading can have several interesting consequences—none of which are desirable.

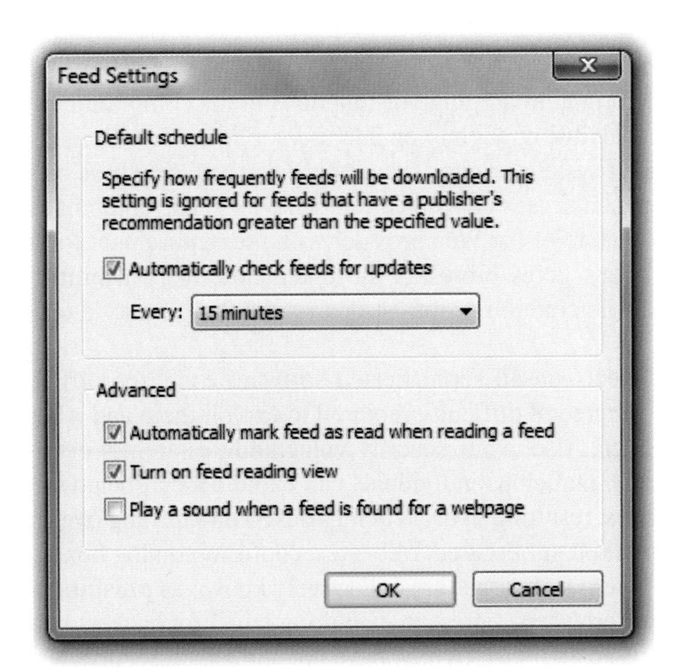

Feed Settings

2.6.4.3 History List

This is the history of all Web sites you visited. As you can see there are several ways that the history list may be sorted and presented. Most of the time, the sites that you wish to revisit are stored in your Favorites list. There may be sites that you recall and wish to revisit but did not record the URLs—that is where the History List comes in. The tools available may help you locate the lost Web site.

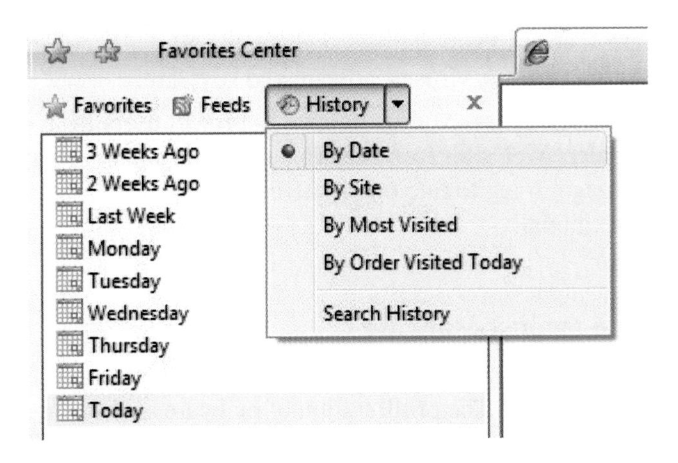

History List

The History list also presents a security risk. Apart from Web site URLs personal identification data including IDs and passwords may be stored, too. Give proper consideration to the history that you maintain.

2.6.5 Security

Web browsers perform a broad range of functions in the computing environment. They must be open and flexible enough to enable users to interact with multiple data sources housed on a range of systems around the globe and at the same time be secure enough to prevent unwanted data access or application behaviors. The combination of the ubiquitous and essential nature of the Web browser with the requirement for bidirectional network communications gives browsers the unenviable responsibility of being both a critical element of the computing infrastructure and the primary attack point for malicious software.

Vulnerabilities exist in all sophisticated software code; the differences essentially come down to the degree of difficulty required to exploit them and what a hacker can do upon exploiting them. Also, some security vulnerabilities are not even technological in nature. For example, malicious individuals can exploit social behaviors and use misinformation techniques, resulting in users being tricked into turning over personally identifiable information through obscured Web sites, confusing dialog boxes, and unexpected add-on behavior. These techniques are collectively known as **phishing** and have become a big problem. Web browsers represent an alluring target for hackers because many users can be easily confused and, historically, have not applied all security updates in a timely manner.

When combined with Microsoft Windows Defender, Internet Explorer 7 helps users achieve an unprecedented level of security protection.

2.6.5.1 Objectives

Two primary security objectives of Microsoft with Internet Explorer 7:

- **Protection against malware**—Microsoft is committed to giving users more confidence in their security while browsing and helping to prevent the installation of malicious software. The company defines malware as all malicious code or unwanted software, including worms, viruses, adware and spyware.
- **Personal data safeguards—**Microsoft aims to protect users from phishing attacks, to prevent fraudulent Web sites from stealing user data, and to help users more safely and securely engage in legitimate e-commerce without divulging their personal information unintentionally.

2.6.5.2 Protection against Malware

Malware, short for malicious software, refers to software applications designed to damage or disrupt a user's system. The proliferation of malware and its impact on security is a driving force behind the design of Internet Explorer 7. The new version has been improved to reduce the potential for hackers to compromise a user's browser or system. In addition, Internet Explorer 7 includes several technical features designed to thwart hacker efforts to lead users into giving away personal data when they should not. Core parts of the browser's architecture also have been fortified to better defend against exploitation and improve the way the browser handles data.

2.6.5.3 Pop-up Blocker

Ads and other windows that pop up are bothersome enough, but some are dangerous. It is not uncommon to receive pop-up windows that seem to display an information or error message that requires you to click a confirmation that you have received the message. Your click might be a trigger to install spyware or other malicious malware.

When Internet Explorer detects a pop-up in a Web page, it displays a message in the Information Bar at the top of the browser window and reminds you with this message:

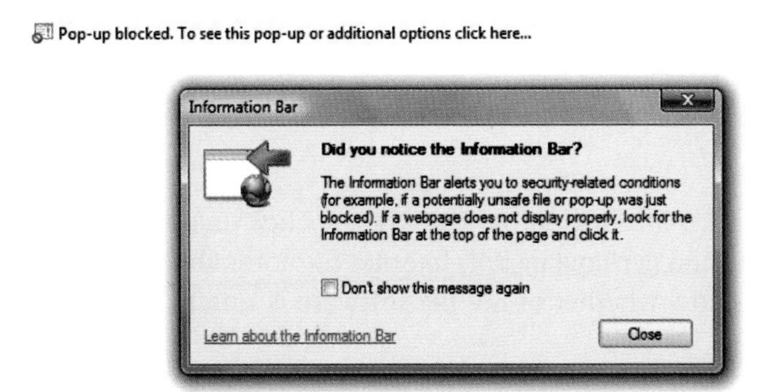

Information Bar

Clicking the Information Bar displays a menu, where you can elect to temporarily or always allow the pop-ups from that Web site.

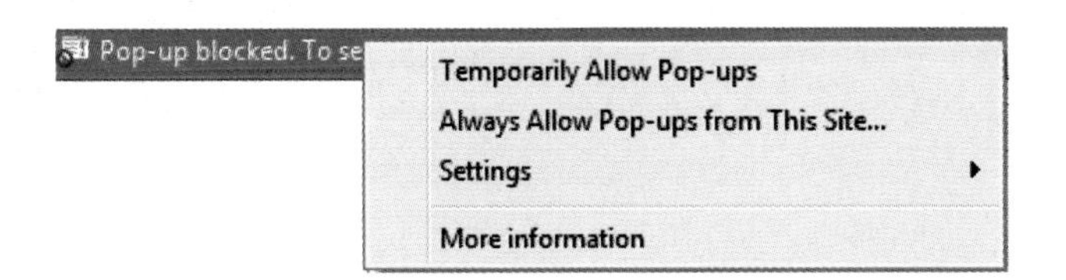

Information Bar Menu

A better choice is to open Settings and take full control over the list of sites that pop-ups are permitted for.

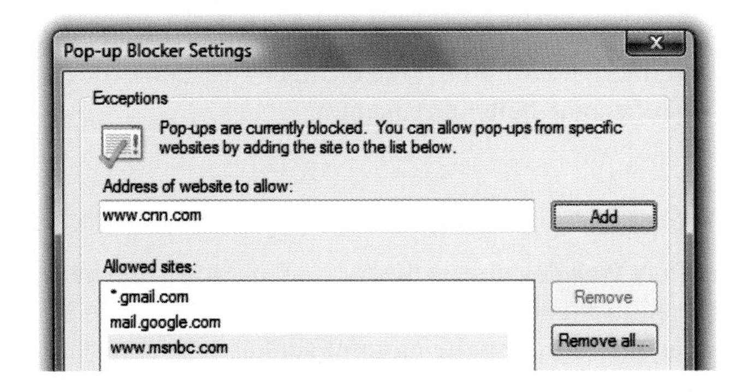

Controlling Pop-ups

Active Content Active content is identified by Internet Explorer using the Information bar, too. You respond in a similar fashion. Active content is material that is part of a Web page that is controlled by active programs like Active-X, Flash, or Shockwave. If you know of and trust the source then it is okay to allow the active content to run. If you are unsure, do not. Active content mostly is harmless but since it can access your computer's file system, harmful content can compromise your documents and other vital data. Active-X content is discussed later in this section.

Install Active Content?

Downloading and Installing Software If you click on a link that would cause a program to download and perhaps install, Internet Explorer checks with you first. It is your responsibility to know whether or not the software is safe to install.

Do You Want to Install?

2.6.5.4 URL Handling and Display Protections

Historically, attackers have taken advantage of internal code weaknesses within the Web browser to attack a system. A hacker would rely on a user clicking on a hypertext link referencing some type of malformed URL that contains odd or excessive characters. In the process of parsing the URL, the system's buffer would overflow and execute some code the hacker wanted to install. Updates to Internet Explorer 6 attempted to patch these vulnerabilities. With Internet Explorer 7, the browser's baseline code was rewritten and this type of attack has become quite infrequent.

2.6.5.5 ActiveX Opt-In

Internet Explorer offers Web developers the ActiveX platform as a mechanism to greatly extend browser capabilities and enhance online experiences. Some malicious developers have co-opted the platform to write harmful applications that steal information and damage user systems.

Internet Explorer 7 offers users a new security mechanism for the ActiveX platform known as the ActiveX Opt-In. ActiveX Opt-In automatically disables this category of active content. Users are now prompted by the Information Bar before any ActiveX content can be accessed. This notification mechanism enables users to permit or deny access when viewing unfamiliar Web sites.

2.6.5.6 Protection against Cross-Domain Scripting Attacks

Cross-domain scripting attacks involve a script from one Internet domain manipulating content from another domain. This allows an attacker to embed malicious JavaScript code in a webpage and execute the script on the machine of any user that views that website. An attacker who uses this type of attack might compromise confidential information, steal cookies, and execute malicious code on the end-user system.

Internet Explorer 7 has been improved to help deter this malicious behavior by appending the domain name from which each script originates and limiting that script's ability to interact only with windows and content from that same domain. These cross-domain script barriers will help ensure that user information remains in the hands of only those the user intentionally provides it to. This new control, which operates invisible to the user, will further protect against malware by limiting the potential for a malicious Web site to misuse flaws in other Web sites.

2.6.5.7 Protected Mode

Available only to users running Internet Explorer 7 in Windows Vista, Internet Explorer's Protected Mode provides new levels of security and data protection. Designed to defend against elevation of privilege attacks, Protected Mode provides safety by helping prevent hackers from taking over the browser and executing code through the use of administrator rights.

In Protected Mode, Internet Explorer 7 in Windows Vista does not allow modifications to user or system files and settings. All communications occur via a negotiation process that mediates between the Internet Explorer browser and Vista. The highly restrictive process prohibits work-arounds from bypassing Protected Mode.

Internet Explorer Protected Mode helps protect users from malicious downloads by restricting the ability to store anything on your computer other than temporary Internet files. Attempting to write to the Windows Registry or other locations will require the negotiation process to provide the necessary elevated permissions. Internet Explorer's Protected Mode also offers tabbed browsing security protection by opening new windows—rather than new tabs—for content contained outside the active security zone.

2.6.5.8 Security Zones

The security model of the browser divides the world of the Internet into four zones. Each is controlled on the Security tab of the Internet Option dialog box.

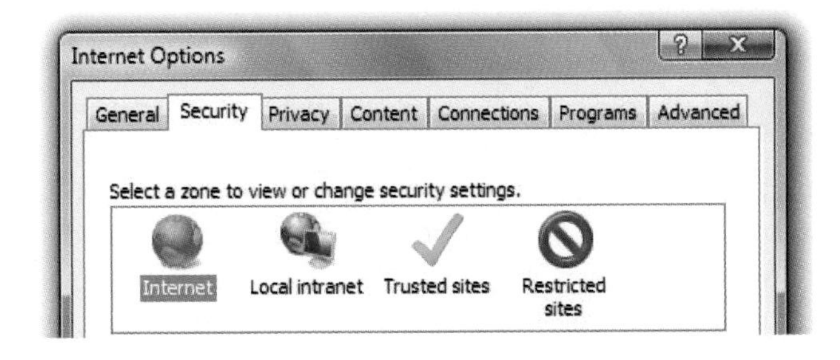

Security Zones

In this dialog box you select a zone and then set the security level for that zone. By default all Web sites are grouped into the Internet Zone and security is usually set higher in this zone than in the others. Web sites associated with your work (Local Intranet) and

Web sites that you visit regularly for personal use and trust may be added to those other zones where security may be more relaxed. The restricted zone is where you list Web sites that you consider dangerous and want controlled by high security.

Opening a Page from a Different Zone

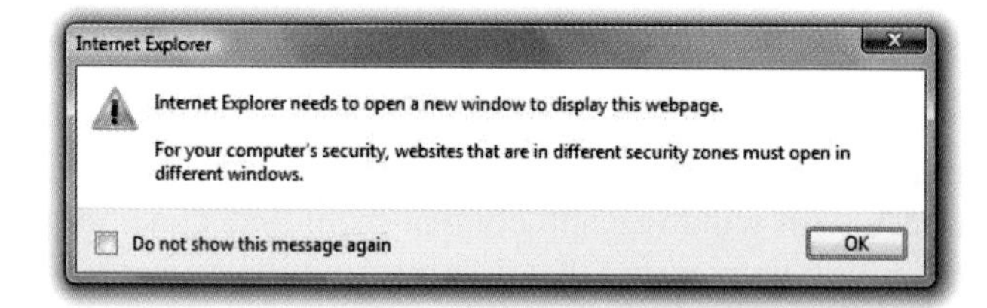

2.6.5.9 Fix My Settings

Knowing that most users are likely to install and operate applications using the default configuration, Internet Explorer 7 ships with security settings designed to provide the maximum level of usability while maintaining controlled security. There are legitimate reasons why a custom application may require a user to lower security settings from the defaults, but it is critical the user reverse those changes when they are no longer needed.

Internet Explorer 7 adds the Fix My Settings feature to keep users protected from browsing with unsafe settings. This feature in Internet Explorer 7 warns users with an Information Bar message when current security settings may put them at risk. When a user makes changes in the security settings the Information Bar provides an option to return to default security settings. Users can instantly reset the security settings to the Medium-High default level by clicking the Fix My Settings option in the Information Bar.

2.6.5.10 Windows Defender

Microsoft Windows Defender enhances security and privacy protections when used with Internet Explorer 7. Extending the protections against malware at the browser level, Windows Defender helps prevent malware entering the machine via piggy-back download, a common mechanism by which spyware is distributed and installed silently along with other applications.

Although the improvements in Internet Explorer 7 cannot stop non-browser-based spyware from infecting the machine, using it with Windows Defender will provide a solid defense. Windows Defender is available for download with Windows XP and is also installed with Windows Vista.

2.6.5.11 Cookies and Privacy

Most users are unaware of how much personal, traceable data is transmitted with every click of the mouse while they are browsing the Web. Much data is stored on the user's client computer in small text files known as cookies. Local storage is convenient because users need not retype IDs and passwords when re-visiting Web sites. Data typed into Web page forms may also be preserved for future visits. Commercial Web sites may store the customer's shopping preferences, making it easier for a person to shop in a subsequent visit.

Cookies get a lot of press but they may be an over-rated security concern. Compared with spyware, viruses, and Trojan horses that is certainly the case. Cookies are like little posted notes that Web sites leave on your computer to remind the Web site about you the next time you visit the site. They are often used to remember your name or address and perhaps user ID and password for Web sites that require them. They might be used to remember your shopping preferences, too.

Most cookies are innocent but some are not. If you wish to control use of cookies, click Internet Explorer's Tool menu and select Internet Options. Click the Privacy tab and move the slider as desired.

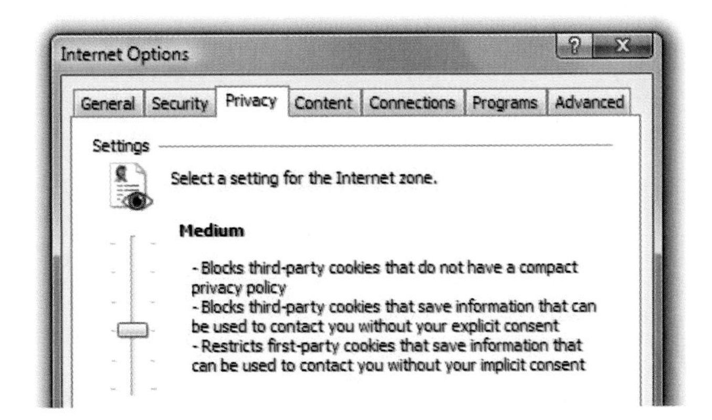

Controlling Cookies

2.6.5.12 Microsoft Phishing Filter

A technique used by some malicious Web site operators to gather personal information is known as phishing. This activity occurs while a Web site masquerades as a legitimate business but its real purpose is acquiring sensitive information. Such fake Web sites are designed to look like the legitimate sites and lure the user to divulge private or sensitive information.

Developers of phishing and other malicious activities thrive on lack of communication and limited sharing of information. Using an online service that is updated several times an hour, the new Phishing Filter in Internet Explorer 7 consolidates the latest industry information about fraudulent Web sites and shares it with Internet Explorer 7 installations to warn and help protect them.

The Phishing Filter combines client-side scans for suspicious Web site characteristics with an opt-in online service. It helps protect users from phishing scams in three ways:

1. It compares the addresses of Web sites a user attempts to visit with a list of reported legitimate sites that is stored on the user's computer.
2. It analyzes sites that users want to visit by checking those sites for characteristics common to phishing sites.
3. It sends the Web site address that a user attempts to visit to an online service run by Microsoft to be checked immediately against a frequently updated list of reported phishing sites.

Internet Explorer 7 uses the Security Status Bar to signal users (in yellow) if a Web site is suspicious.

How Does the Phishing Filter Work? The Phishing Filter is off by default; meaning that it does not transmit any suspect data to Microsoft and will only check visited Web sites against locally stored data until the user decides to turn the Filter on. The locally stored data is a list of Safe Sites that is downloaded and installed with Internet Explorer 7 when it is installed.

When you visit a Web site, IE7 first checks the local Safe Sites list. If the URL is there or it appears in the local cache (because you visited it already), things will go no further. If, on the other hand, the site is not in those lists then the users must opt in to use the Phishing Filter. If it is enabled IE7 will then transmit details of the URL being visited for checking.

Internet Explorer 7 uses a notification area called the Security Status Bar. If a Web site is suspected as a phishing site the Address Bar turns yellow and the Security Status Bar warning will appear.

Suspected Phishing Site

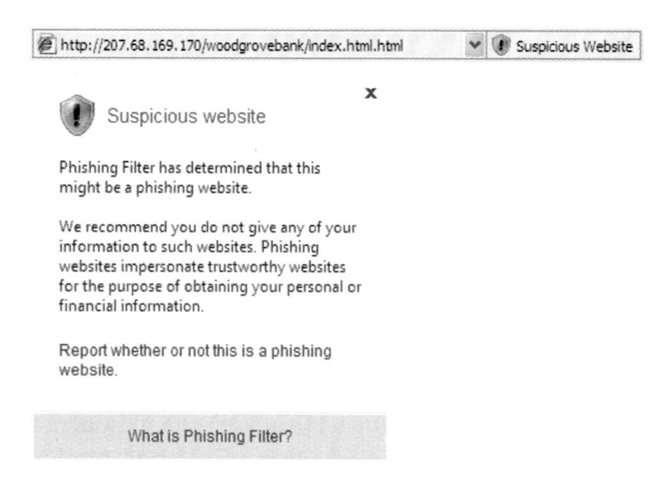

If the Web destination has been confirmed as a known phishing site, Internet Explorer 7 signifies the threat level in red and automatically navigates the user away from that site.

Known Phishing Site

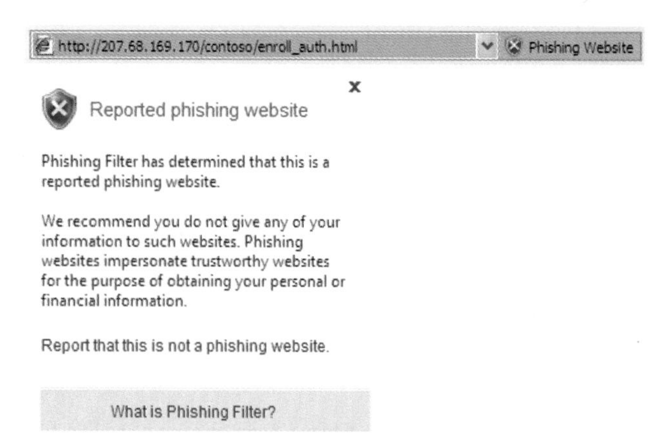

Internet Explorer permits you to report a suspected or confirmed phishing site. Microsoft maintains a list of confirmed phishing sites that you will be alerted to as you surf in the future.

Report Phishing Site

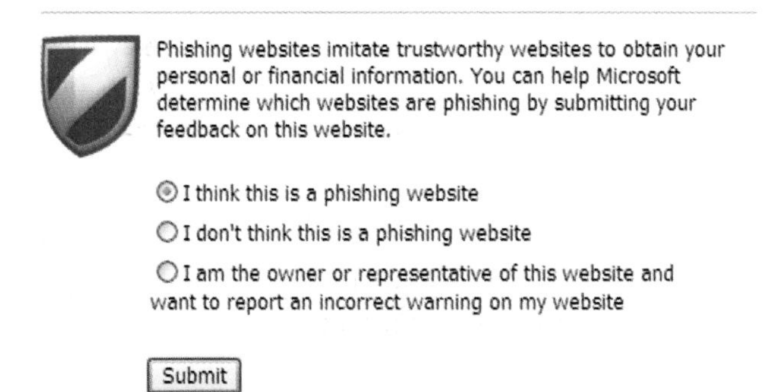

If you do not wish to be warned about phishing sites the Phishing Filter can be turned off at any time via Internet Explorer's Advanced settings tab.

Phishing Control

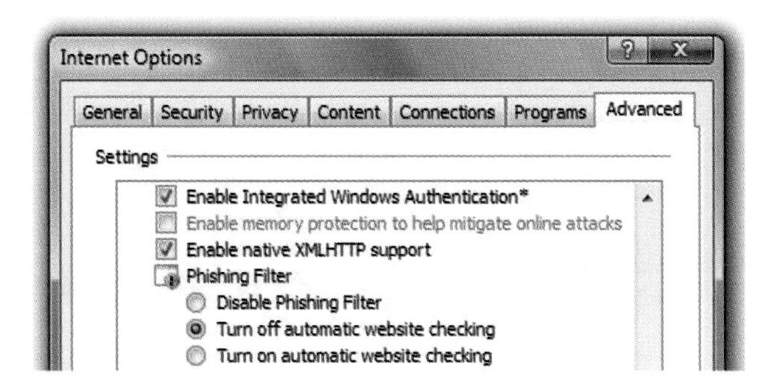

2.6.5.13 Delete Browsing History for Better Protection of Privacy and Passwords

All Web browsers provide mechanisms to delete history information, clean the **cache,** and erase automatically completed form history. Internet Explorer 7 provides a Delete Browsing History option that provides users with one-click cleanup to easily and instantly erase personal data. Delete Browsing History is especially valuable in shared-resource environments. Accessing online resources using a friend's computer seems harmless enough, but the user then becomes reliant on the security of the friend's system to protect his or her data. Also, in public environments such as libraries, schools, and senior citizen centers, computers may be used by hundreds of people and potentially expose personal data and history information to every one of those users. Delete Browsing History provides a simple mechanism to instantly erase your personal information and eliminate any concern for data privacy on other systems.

Browsing History

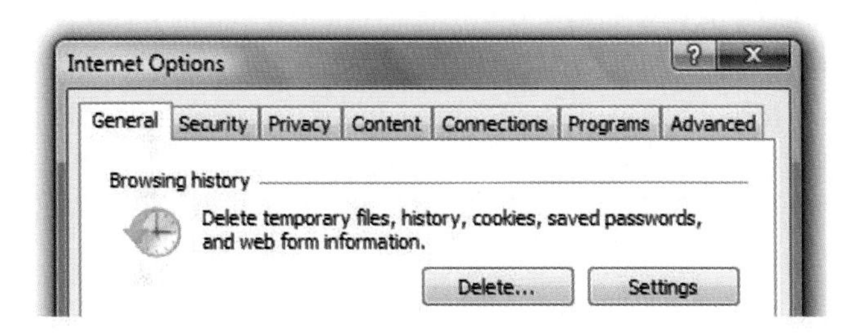

Click the Delete button and the Delete Browsing History dialog box appears. As you can see from the illustration below, we can choose to delete specific information types or all types at the same time. The various categories of stored data are described elsewhere in this and other chapters. Of most particular interest from the standpoint of security is the storage of your identification and passwords in cookies.

Delete Browsing History

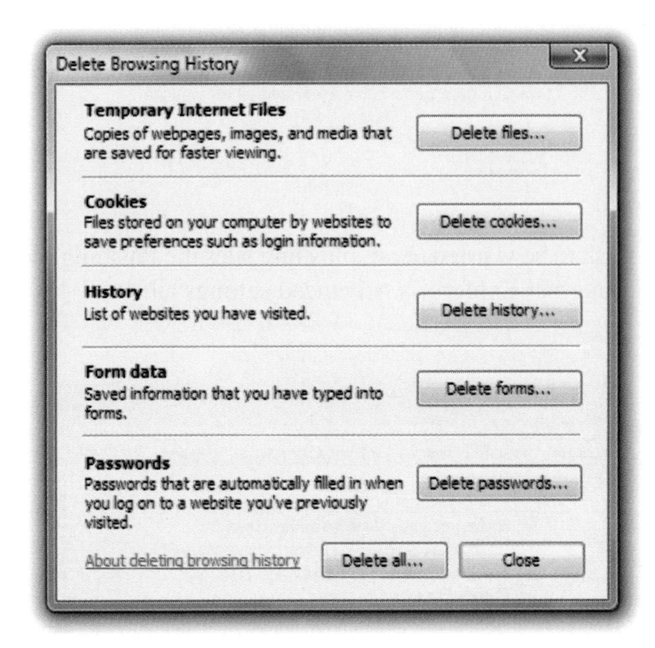

2.6.6 Other Browsers

Several other browsers are popular, too. Since most Web browsers communicate primarily using HTTP (hypertext transfer protocol) to fetch Web pages and HTML as a formatting language, it is reasonable to assume that other browsers can handle the same content as Internet Explorer.

2.6.6.1 Firefox

Mozilla Firefox is a graphical Web browser developed by the Mozilla Corporation and has a large community of external contributors. Mozilla Firefox is a cross-platform (multiple-operating system) browser, providing support for various versions of Microsoft Windows, Mac OS X, and Linux. Firefox's source code is freely available under the terms of the Mozilla license as free and open source software.

The significant features of Firefox are:

- **Tabbed Browsing**—Firefox supports tabbed browsing in which all links that would normally open in a new window are instead opened in a new tab. This feature allows users to open multiple pages in the same window.
- **Pop-up Blocking**—Firefox also includes integrated customizable pop-up blocking. This blocks pop-ups from all Web sites by default, but can be configured to allow individual sites to show pop-ups. It can also be turned off entirely to allow pop-ups from all sites.

- **Download Manager**—Downloads can be opened automatically depending on the file type, or saved directly to disk. By default, Firefox downloads all files to a user's desktop on Mac and Windows or to the user's home directory on Linux, but it can be configured to prompt for a specific download location.
- **Live Bookmarks**—RSS feeds are used by Live Bookmarks, another Firefox feature, to allow users to dynamically monitor their favorite news sources.

2.6.6.2 Safari

Safari is a Web browser developed by Apple Inc., and is available as part of Mac OS X. It is the only browser bundled with Mac OS.

Safari uses Apple's brushed metal user interface, and has a bookmark management scheme that functions like the iTunes jukebox software. The browser integrates Apple's QuickTime multimedia technology, and features a tabbed-browsing interface similar to that of Explorer, Opera, and Firefox. A Google search box is a standard component of the Safari interface. Safari also automatically fills out Web forms, manages passwords, and spellchecks entries in Web page text fields. The browser also includes an integrated pop-up ad blocker.

2.6.6.3 Opera

Opera is a cross-platform Web browser and Internet suite which handles common internet-related tasks including visiting Web sites, sending and receiving e-mail messages, managing contacts, and chatting online. Opera's mobile Web browser, Opera Mini, and most current versions of its desktop browser application are offered free of charge.

Opera was designed to run on low-end and small computers, with an emphasis on a commitment to computer accessibility for users who may have visual or mobility impairments. Page zooming, for example, allows text, images, and other content such as Flash, Java, and Scalable Vector Graphics (**SVG**) to be increased or decreased in size to help those with impaired vision.

Opera is proprietary software developed by Opera Software based in Oslo, Norway. It runs on a variety of operating systems including Microsoft Windows, Mac OS X, Linux, FreeBSD, and Solaris.

2.6.6.4 Netscape

Netscape is the general name for a series of Web browsers originally produced by Netscape Communications Corporation, but now developed by AOL. The original browser was once the dominant browser in terms of usage share, but as a result of the first browser war (1990s), which they lost, many of their customers migrated to Internet Explorer. As of September 2006, the usage share of Netscape browsers is under 1% and falling. This number, however, could be misleading as Netscape users have largely moved to other browsers in the same family (Mozilla and Firefox), while Internet Explorer has lost market share, giving the Netscape/Mozilla/Firefox family approximately 1/6 of the browser use.

2.6.6.5 3-D Browser and Virtual Reality

Since the Web first became public, various attempts have been made at providing a three-dimensional Web surfing interface. Early on, browser support for **VRML** or Virtual Reality MarkUp Language became common. VRML is a standard file format for representing three-dimensional interactive vector graphics for display in browsers and similar objects. VRML files are commonly called worlds and have the WRL extension.

The term "browser wars" is given to the competition for dominance in the Web browser marketplace. It most commonly refers to two time periods: the struggle between Internet Explorer and Netscape Navigator during the late 1990s, and the threat which Firefox poses to Internet Explorer now.

A variation on VRML is the use of **QuickTime** for display of **VR Panorama** images. The user navigates through and around 360 degree images. The mouse is used to change direction or scan speed. Numerous examples are found on the Web. The Apple QuickTime viewer is required. A fine collection of VR panoramas can be found at: http://geoimages.berkeley.edu/.

Blender is a well known open source animation program that can export VRML. It can be used for modeling, texturing, animating, and rendering interactive 3D applications.

Virtual Reality Virtual Reality (VR) is a technology which allows a user to interact with a computer-simulated environment. Most current virtual reality environments are primarily visual experiences, displayed either on a computer screen or through special stereoscopic eye-piece displays, but some simulations include additional sensory information, such as sound through speakers or headphones.

Virtual Worlds Web browser software that combines the concepts of virtual reality with 3D display mechanisms like VRML provides the opportunity to create artificial interactive worlds. A currently popular example is **3B Browser.** In these various virtual environments participants are represented by **avatars** engaging in behavior representative of the humans controlling the software.

Avatar An avatar is an electronic image that represents something or someone and is manipulated by a computer user. Often avatars are animated and respond to commands through a graphical user interface. It is not uncommon for the interface to include **speech recognition** and **synthesis.**

2.7 Intranet vs. Extranet

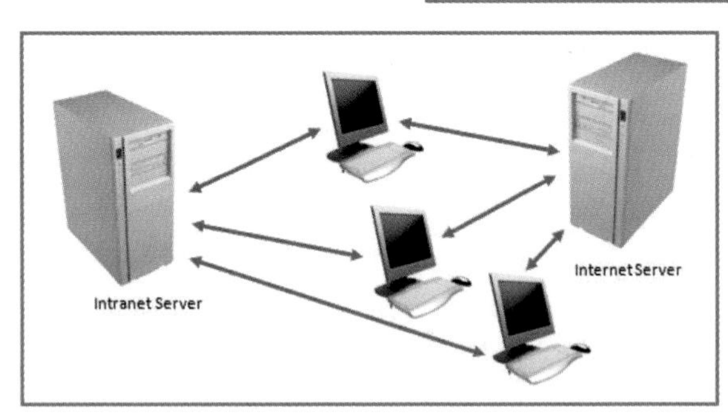

Intranet

Two networking arrangements that make use of Internet protocols and equipment are intranets and extranets. An intranet can be understood as a private version of the Internet, or as a version of the internet confined to an organization. Intranets are used by organizations to facilitate internal communication but present barriers to external access (inbound and outbound).

An extranet is used by a group of organizations to provide communication among their members. An industry group might wish to share data between members and an extranet is perfect for this. Since the network is external to a single organization specific safeguards must be in place to ensure that unauthorized users do not gain access.

2.8 World Wide Web

The Web, or World Wide Web, is an information service of the Internet. It is based on a technology called **hypertext** (see the HTML chapter), which allows documents to be connected, or linked, to each other. When you jump from a **hyperlink** to another page, you have no concern for where that other page is physically located; your browser figures out how to fetch the page for you and how to display it. Since the page could contain a variety of types of data (text, numbers, sound, images, video, etc.) we call Web pages **hypermedia.** Pages are formatted using a special language called Hypertext Markup Language, or **HTML** for short. As you can follow hyperlinks, you use HTTP (Hypertext Transfer Protocol) and a browser.

2.8.1 Clients and Servers

Let's say that you are sitting at your computer, surfing the Web, and you get a call from a friend who says, "I just read a great article! Type in this address and check it out. It's at http://msnbc.com." So you type that URL into your browser and press return. And magically, no matter where in the world that URL lives, the page appears on your screen:

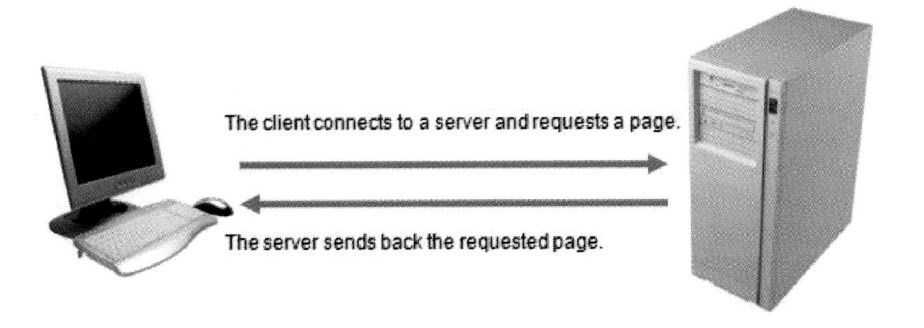
The client connects to a server and requests a page.
The server sends back the requested page.

Client and Server

Search engines run on a server and provide the client's browser program with a list of page links in response to the search request.

In general, all of the machines on the Internet can be categorized as two types: servers and clients. Those machines that provide services (like Web servers or FTP servers) to other machines are **servers.** And the machines that are used to connect to those services are **clients.** When you connect to Yahoo! at http://yahoo.com to read a page, Yahoo! is providing a machine to service your request. Yahoo! is providing a Web server. Your machine, on the other hand, is probably providing no services to anyone else on the Internet. Therefore, it is a user machine, also known as a client.

A server machine may provide one or more services on the Internet. For example, a server machine might have software running on it that allows it to act as a Web server, an e-mail server, and an FTP server. Clients that come to a server machine do so with a specific intent, so clients direct their requests to a specific software server running on the overall server machine.

The Internet is a distributed network that follows the client-server model. Networks and the communication hardware that make it possible are discussed in another chapter.

2.8.1.1 Server

A server is a computer system that provides services to other computer systems—called clients—over a computer network. The term server can refer to hardware (such as a Sun computer system) or software (such as a database server).

2.8.1.2 Client

A client is a computer system that accesses a (remote) service on another computer by some kind of network. The term was first applied to devices that were not capable of running their own stand-alone programs, but could interact with remote computers via a network. These dumb terminals were clients of the time-sharing mainframe computer.

The client-server model is used today on the Internet, where a user may connect to a service operating on a remote system through Internet protocols. Web browsers are clients that connect to Web servers and retrieve Web pages for display. Many people use e-mail clients to retrieve their e-mail from their internet service provider's mail storage servers. Online chat uses a variety of clients, which vary depending on the chat protocol being used. Game clients allow players to communicate in real time with other players via a server.

Clients and Server

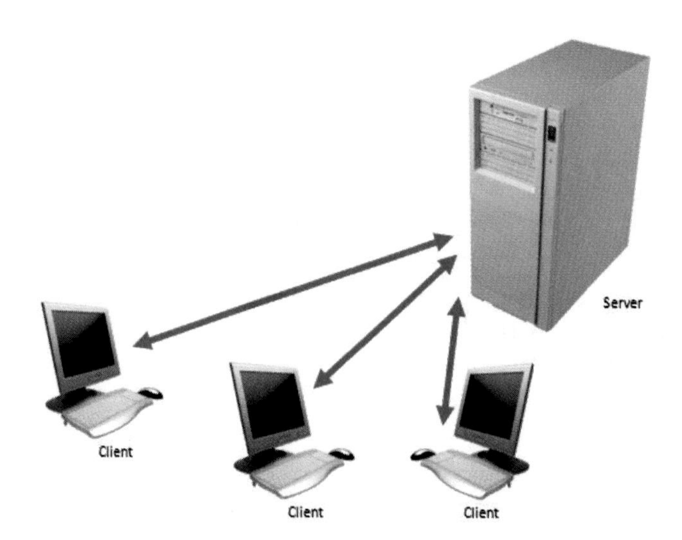

2.8.2 Web Sites

A Web site is a collection of Web pages, images, videos, and other digital content and hosted on a particular domain on the Web. A Web page is a document, typically written in HTML and almost always accessed via HTTP, that transfers information from the Web site's server for display in the user's Web browser. All publicly accessible Web sites are seen collectively as constituting the World Wide Web.

The pages of Web sites can usually be accessed from a common root URL called the **homepage,** and all of a site's pages usually reside on the same physical server.

Web Pages: Hypermedia Web pages are said to be **hypermedia** pages meaning that a Web page could contain more than one type of data (text, images, sound, etc.). A corporate logo is an image that is included with Web page's text. HTML weaves them together into a cohesive unit.

Hypermedia is a logical extension of the term **hypertext,** in which Web pages using hyperlinks intertwine to create a generally non-linear medium of information.

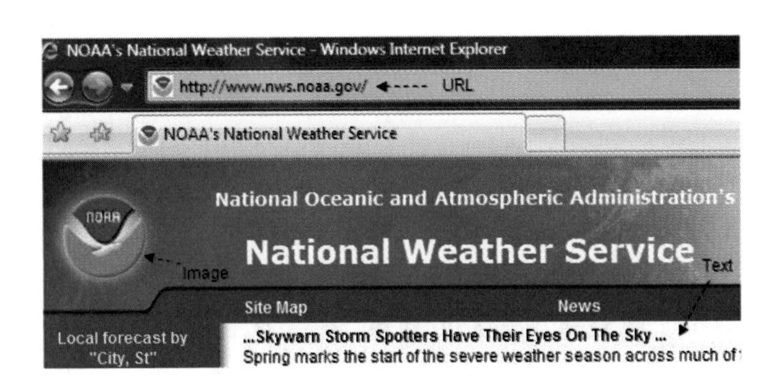

A Hypermedia Page Contains Text, Images and Other Objects

2.8.3 Hyperlinks

A hyperlink (often referred to as simply a link), is a reference or navigation element in a document to another section of the same document, another document, or a specified section of another document, that automatically brings the referred information to the user's browser when the navigation element is selected (clicked). The familiar mouse click on a Web page is the action that causes the Web browser to navigate to the Web address of the element that was clicked.

Hyperlinks are part of the foundation of the World Wide Web, but are not limited to HTML or to the Web. Hyperlinks may be used in almost any electronic media.

2.8.4 Search Engines

A search engine is an information retrieval system designed to help find information stored on a computer system, such as on the World Wide Web. The search engine allows one to ask for content meeting specific criteria (typically those containing a given word or phrase) and retrieves a list of items that match those criteria. Hyperlinks provide navigational access to the selected links. This list is often sorted according to some measure of relevance of the results. Search engines use frequently updated indexes to operate quickly and efficiently.

Without further qualification, search engine usually refers to a Web search engine, which searches for information on the publicly accessible sites on the Web. An alternative is enterprise search engines which search on private intranets.

Popular Search Engines Numerous search engines are found on the Internet. Many are special purpose or impose limited access. Several public engines that are heavily used and well known include:

- **Google**—Google is a search engine owned by Google, Inc. whose mission is to ". . . organize the world's information and make it universally accessible and useful." It is the most used search engine on the Web.
- **Yahoo**—Yahoo! Search is the second largest search engine on the Internet; Yahoo! also provides many services including e-mail, radio, news, Yahoo messenger, and more.

- **MSN**—MSN is not only a content provider and search engine, it is additionally an Internet Service Provider.
- **Ask**—The original idea behind Ask.com was the ability to answer questions posed in natural language. Ask.com was the first commercial question-answering search engine for the Web. It supports user queries in plain English (natural language), as well as traditional keyword searching.

Special Purpose Search Engines The popular search engines are not limited by subject matter or personal access. Many search engines are tuned to efficiently handle a specific type of information request. Here are some examples:

- **Switchboard.com**—Find people, businesses, phone numbers, e-mail addresses, etc.
- **Download.com**—Internet download directory Web site; part of CNET. Downloads are often rated and reviewed by editors and users.
- **MapQuest.com**—MapQuest is a map publisher and a free online Web mapping service.
- **Monster.com**—One of the largest job search Web sites on the Internet.

Meta-Search Engine A meta-search engine is a search engine that sends user requests to several other search engines, and perhaps databases, and returns the results from each engine in one consolidated Web page. Meta search enables users to enter search criteria once and access several search engines simultaneously. Since it is hard to catalogue the entire Web, the idea is that by searching multiple search engines you are able to search more of the Web in less time and do it with only one click. Meta-search engines create what is known as a **virtual database.**

An emerging type of search engine, **tag search engines,** rely on meta tags to index pages of interest. Meta tags use several properties including name and content. Name might equal "keywords", "author", or "description." The content property would contain a list of key words, the page author's name, or a description of a document. Tags are found in most Web content.

2.8.5 Chat Rooms

A chat room is a term used primarily by mass media to describe any form of synchronous conferencing. The term usually means real-time online chat over instant messaging and online forums. Online chat is a way of communicating by sending text messages to people in the same chat room in real-time. The oldest form of chat rooms is the text-based variety. The most popular of this kind is Internet Relay Chat (IRC).

Topics in chat rooms are as varied as the people in them. The primary use of a chat room is to share information via text with a group of other users. New technology has enabled the use of file sharing and Webcams to be included in some programs. Chat rooms usually have stringent rules that they require users to follow in order to maintain integrity and safety for their users. Particularly in rooms for children, rules usually discourage users from using offensive language, or promoting hate, violence, and other negative issues.

Netiquette Netiquette is commonly taken to mean Internet etiquette. It is a term for the common standards of politeness and respect that people expect in normal life and assume are carried over to Internet chat room use. Examples of these guidelines are:

- No posting in all uppercase characters—it is considered shouting.
- No typing of repetitive text to fill the screen. This is known as **flooding.**
- Refrain from commercial advertising.
- Not being offensive to the group or other individuals.

Internet Relay Chat (IRC) Internet Relay Chat (IRC) is a form of real-time Internet chat or synchronous conferencing. It is mainly designed for group (many-to-many) communication in discussion forums called channels, but also allows one-to-one communication and data transfers via file and private message.

IRC was created in 1988 and gained prominence when it was used to report on the Soviet coup attempt of 1991 throughout a media blackout.

Instant Messaging Instant messaging or IM is a form of real-time communication between two or more people based on typed text. Instant messaging requires the use of a client program that connects to an instant messaging service. IM differs from e-mail in that conversations happen in real-time.

Most services offer a feature which indicates whether people on one's list of contacts are currently online and available to chat. It is possible to save a conversation's transcript, so as to refer to it later. Popular instant messaging services are provided by **MSN, AOL, Google,** and **Yahoo.**

2.8.6 VoIP: Internet Telephony

Internet telephony, commonly known as Voice over Internet Protocol (VoIP), is the routing of voice conversations over the Internet or through any other IP-based network. VoIP offers several advantages including:

- Incoming phone calls can be automatically routed to your VoIP phone, regardless of where in the world as long as you are connected to the network. Take your VoIP phone with you on a trip, and wherever you connect to the Internet, you can receive incoming calls.
- Call center or customer service agents using VoIP phones can work from anywhere with a sufficiently fast and stable Internet connection.
- VoIP phones can integrate with other services available over the Internet, including video conferencing, data file exchanging, and managing address books.
- VoIP can save expense over traditional telephone network use.

Computer to Computer VoIP

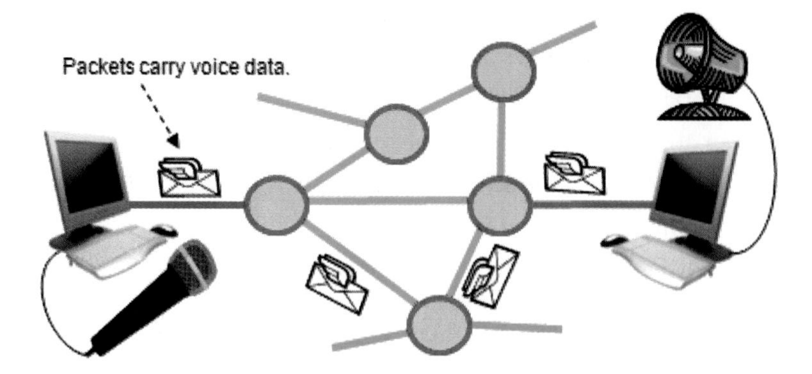

VoIP service is reliant upon another separate service—an Internet connection. Users can choose different service types:

- **Computer to computer**—Users with a microphone, speakers, a sound card, and an Internet connection can connect to and speak with other users similarly equipped. There are no usage charges and even long-distance calls are free. Several companies offer free or low-cost software that can be used for this type of VoIP.
- **Computer to public telephone network**—Users make calls from their computer but are able to reach others who are connected to the public telephone network. This service must be paid for and allows the user to operate a physical or software telephone.
- **Analog Telephone Adaptor**—An ATA (analog telephone adaptor) is a device that allows a standard phone to be connected to a computer. The ATA is an analog-to-digital converter which takes the analog signal (described in the network chapter) from the phone set and converts it into digital data for transmission over the Internet.
- **IP Phones**—These specialized phones look like normal phones with a handset, cradle, and buttons. IP phones have an Ethernet connector and connect directly to a router and have the hardware and software necessary to handle IP calls. Wi-Fi IP phones will be available, allowing subscribing callers to make VoIP calls from any Wi-Fi hot spot.
- **Softphone**—A softphone is software that looks like a traditional telephone on the computer screen. Computer-to-computer service uses a softphone, but it may be used by computer to public telephone network users also.

Computer-to-Public Telephone Network

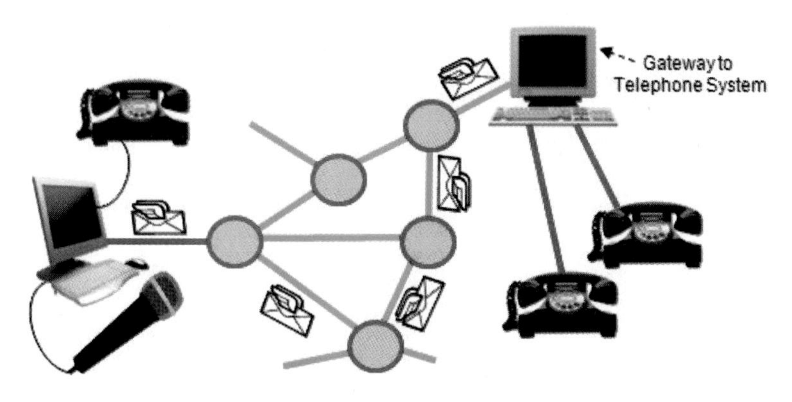

Well known providers include: **Qwest, Skype, Time Warner, Verizon,** and **Vonage.** The quality and overall reliability of the phone connection is entirely reliant upon the quality, reliability, and speed of the Internet connection it is using. Additionally, there are several other challenges that VoIP providers will be called on to address:

- Conventional phones are connected directly to telephone company phone lines, which in the event of a power failure are kept functioning by back-up generators or batteries located at the telephone exchange. However, household VoIP hardware uses broadband modems and other equipment powered by household electricity, which may be subject to outages dictating the use of an uninterruptible power supply or generator to ensure availability during power outages.
- Some broadband connections may have less than desirable quality. Where IP packets are lost or delayed at any point in the network between VoIP users, there will be a momentary drop-out of voice. This is more noticeable in highly congested networks or where there are long distances or interworking between end points.
- The majority of consumer VoIP solutions do not support encryption yet. As a result, it is relatively easy to eavesdrop on VoIP calls and even change their content. There are several open source solutions that facilitate sniffing of VoIP conversations.

VoIP technology has improved the reliability and quality of voice transmission over time and will likely continue to improve as the flexibility and low cost it offers is appealing.

2.8.7 Newsgroups

A newsgroup is a repository for messages posted from many users at different locations. The term is somewhat confusing because it is usually a discussion group. Each newsgroup pertains to a specific topic that is of interest to members. In that respect it is similar to a chat room. The primary difference between the two is that chat room messaging occurs in real time and newsgroup participation is asynchronous and involves reading the messages posted by members and responding to the postings.

2.8.8 RSS—Aggregators

An aggregator or **news aggregator** or **feed reader** is software that uses a Web feed to retrieve syndicated Web content such as blogs, podcasts, and RSS feeds. Aggregators reduce the time and effort needed to regularly check web sites for updates, and essentially allow creating a unique information space or personal newspaper.

Once a feed is subscribed to, an aggregator is able to check for new content automatically at user-determined intervals and retrieve updates. The aggregator blends together content from multiple providers and consolidates the result in one place for the user's access. The content is sometimes described as being pulled to the subscriber.

The syndicated content an aggregator will retrieve and interpret is usually supplied in the form of RSS or other XML formatted data. An earlier section of this chapter discussed the use of RSS feeds in Internet Explorer.

2.8.9 Mailing List—ListServ

ListServ is an electronic mailing list software application. When e-mail is addressed to a ListServ mailing list, it is automatically broadcast to everyone on the list. The result is similar to a newsgroup or forum except that the messages are transmitted as e-mails and are therefore available only to individuals on the list.

LISTSERV is currently a commercial product marketed by **L-Soft** International.

2.8.10 Web Auction

The best known online auction is e-Bay. There are many others as well more special purpose than e-Bay which serves all markets.

The online auction business model is one in which participants bid for products and services over the Internet. The functionality of buying and selling in an auction format is made possible through auction software which regulates the various processes involved.

2.8.11 BLOG

A blog (short for Web log) is a user-generated Web site where entries are made in journal style and displayed in a reverse chronological order.

Blogs provide commentary or news on a particular subject, such as food, politics, or local news; some function as more personal online diaries. A typical blog combines text, images, and links to other blogs, Web pages, and other media related to its topic. The ability for readers to leave comments in an interactive format is important. Most blogs are primarily textual although some focus on photographs (photoblog), videos (vlog), or audio (podcasting), and are part of a wider network of social media. The search engine **Technorati** is specifically oriented to searching blogs.

BLOG Software Many Weblog applications are available for users to download and install on their own systems. Other Weblog applications are offered only through their developers' hosts, either free of charge or for a fee.

2.8.12 Wikipedia

Wikipedia is an online encyclopedia where anyone can edit and post an article on any subject. Once an article is submitted it then can be edited and added to by other users. Wikipedia has rapidly grown into the largest reference Web site on the Internet with over 1.7 million topics and growing rapidly. The content of Wikipedia is free, and is written **collaboratively** by people from all around the world. This makes it a very current tool for research and information on most subjects.

Wikipedia has been criticized for their editing policies where anyone can edit the site, hide behind fake names, and make fraudulent claims about his/her credentials.

2.8.13 Podcasting

A podcast is a digital media file, or a series of such files, that is distributed over the Internet using syndication feeds for playback on personal computers and portable media players. A podcast is a specific type of Webcast and the host or author of a podcast is often called a podcaster.

Though podcasters' Web sites may also offer direct download or streaming of their content, a podcast is distinguished from other digital media formats by its ability to be downloaded automatically, using software capable of reading feed formats such as RSS.

2.9 Multimedia

Multimedia is media that uses multiple forms of information content (text, audio, graphics, animation, and video, interactivity) to inform or entertain the (user) audience.

Multimedia means that computer information can be represented through audio, graphics, image, video, and animation in addition to traditional media (text and graphics).

2.9.1 Image Formats

Image file formats provide a standardized method of compressing, organizing, and storing image data. Several formats common in Web pages are:

- **GIF**—Suitable for sharp-edged line art (such as logos). This takes advantage of the format's lossless compression which preserves very sharp edges (in contrast to JPEG). GIFs are used for small animations and low resolution film clips.
- **JPEG**—The format most used for storing and transmitting photographs on the Web. It is preferred to formats such as GIF, which has a limit of 256 distinct colors that is considered insufficient for color photographs.
- **PNG**—Created to improve and replace the GIF format. It generally can achieve greater **compression** than GIF, and give a wider range of transparency options and wider range of color depths than GIF. It does not support animation. PNG images are widely supported, but not as widely supported as GIF images.
- **SVC**—Scalable Vector Graphics is an XML markup language for describing two-dimensional vector graphics that can be animated and interactive.

Numerous image editing programs may be found on the Web. Many are shareware or freeware. These programs can copy images from one format to another. Additionally, most provide common and complex graphic editing capability.

2.9.2 Audio and Video

Audio and video content is commonly delivered through the Web. Sound and moving images are embedded in Web pages and delivered whole for later viewing. Since both data types are dense (video especially) consideration must be given to the delivery mode selected.

There are two delivery modes in common use:

- **Streaming**—Streaming media is multimedia that is continuously received by the client while it is being delivered by the provider. Since files are not stored on the client computer's hard drive it is not possible to make illegal copies. Radio and television content is delivered this way.
- **Download**—Downloading involves accepting a media file for later play and replay. It is copied to a local hard drive or other storage device. Since media file size can be quite large downloading can take considerable time.

Codec Storing sound or video requires encoding it into a sequence of binary 1s and 0s. A codec performs this task. It is a device or program capable of performing encoding and decoding on a digital data stream or signal. The word codec is derived from the two functions it performs: **coding** and **decoding.**

Several common audio and video formats include:

Audio

- **WAV**—Standard digital audio file format for storing sound data; allows audio recordings to be captured and stored; often used to save CD-quality audio.
- **WMV**—Video or audio file, based on the Microsoft Advanced Systems Format (ASF), formatted and compressed with Windows Media compression. It requires a Windows media codec.

- **MP3**—An encoding format that uses a compression algorithm designed to greatly reduce the amount of data required to represent audio recording, yet still sound like a faithful reproduction of the original uncompressed audio.
- **MIDI**—Standard MIDI (Musical Instrument Digital Interface) file which contains music data such as what notes are played, when they are played, how long each note is held, and the loudness of each note.

Video

- **AVI**—Audio Video Interleave, known by its acronym AVI, is a multimedia video format with minimal compression and excellent quality.
- **MPEG**—A family of digital video compression standards. MPEG-4 is the global multimedia standard, delivering professional-quality audio and video streams over a wide range of bandwidths, from cell phone to broadband and beyond.
- **MOV**—Video and animation system built into the Macintosh operating system. PCs can also run QuickTime files, but they require a special QuickTime driver.
- **RM**—Media file format used by RealPlayer; contains audio or video data or both; may be a downloaded file or may be a streaming media file, which is played back as it is downloaded.

2.10 Web Authoring

Creating web pages and Web sites requires knowledge of various tools. At a minimum a document preparation (markup) language is needed, but programming and database storage or sophisticated animation might be called for as well. Most Web applications are categorized as **thin client.** This is because the application depends primarily on a central server for processing activities, and mainly focuses on conveying input and output between the user and the remote server.

Thin Client Architecture

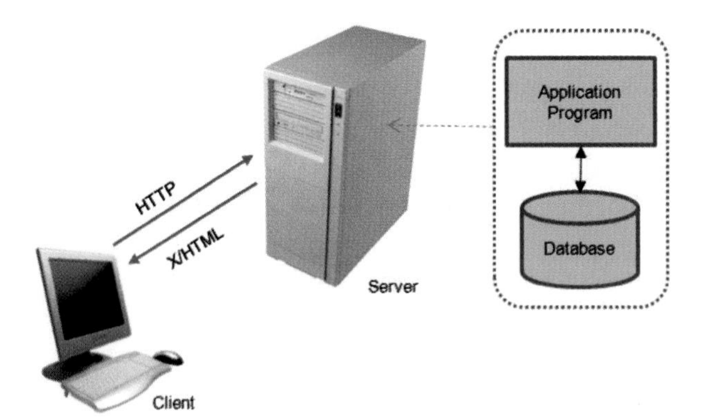

2.10.1 Languages

All Web pages are written in a markup language and stored in a text file. The most commonly used markup languages listed here are developed fully in another chapter:

- **HTML**—Hypertext Markup Language is a particular form of **hypertext** that is used to create Web pages.

- **XHTML**—Extensible Hypertext Markup Language, or XHTML, is a language that is at least as expressive as HTML, but has a stricter syntax. XHTML addresses the need for greater standardization of HTML as Web content is now delivered to many devices like mobile equipment in addition to traditional computers.
- **XML**—Extensible Markup Language was designed to describe data and to focus on what the data is about. Use of XML allows **data portability** as it is transported among computers and devices running different operating systems.
- **CSS**—Cascading Style Sheets is a style sheet language used to describe the presentation of a document written in a markup language.

2.10.2 Programming Languages

A programming language is used to add interactive potential to a Web site. Programs can control options given to users and react to their actions. On a server, a program can retrieve data from a database and present results to the user. Programs can run on either a Web server or in the client's Web browser. Several popular languages are:

- **PHP**—PHP programs run on a server and dynamically generate (X)HTML; the (X)HTML, which contains the Web page content, is then sent to the user's Web browser. PHP programs often interact with a server based **MySQL** database manager. MySQL and PHP are **open-source** programs and are developed openly and distributed for free to all who wish to use them.
- **JavaScript**—JavaScript code is contained in a Web page and run on the client computer. Use of this language permits interactive control within a Web browser. JavaScript is a key element in the **AJAX** (Asynchronous JavaScript and XML) development technique which makes Web pages feel more responsive by exchanging small amounts of data with the server behind the scenes.
- **.NET**—.NET is a collection of products and technologies from Microsoft. Most have in common a dependence on the .NET Framework which is a component of the Windows operating system. Commonly used programming languages within the Framework are **C#** and **Visual Basic.**
- **Java Server Pages**—JSP technology provides a simplified, fast way to create dynamic web content. JSP technology enables rapid development of web-based applications that are server- and platform-independent.

The programming chapter presents an introduction to Web development programming with connection to databases. Generation of (X)HTML output for the browser is also discussed.

2.10.3 Web Development Tools

As Web site complexity increases so does the value of using automated development tools. Numerous tools exist to edit HTML, XHTML, and XML. Tools are also found to add animation and other special features to a Web site. A few tools are mentioned here:

- **Dreamweaver**—A WYSIWYG (What You See is What You Get) HTML editor that incorporates support for other Web technologies including CSS, JavaScript, and various server-side scripting frameworks.
- **Flash**—A popular method for adding animation and interactivity to Web pages.
- **Other Tools**—Other popular web development tools are: **Homesite** and **Adobe Golive.**

2.11 Accessories

Browser functionality can be extended to accommodate content produced by certain authoring platforms. Small accessory programs, known as **plug-ins,** are attached to the browsers. Here are some popular examples:

ActiveX is a common means of distributing malware such as adware and spyware to unsuspecting users of Internet Explorer; as such, Internet Explorer users should configure their browsers to not install ActiveX controls from untrusted sites.

- **Flash Player**—The Adobe Flash Player is an application player that runs SWF (Shockwave) files created by the Adobe Flash authoring tool.
- **QuickTime**—QuickTime is a multimedia framework developed by **Apple** capable of handling various formats of digital video, media clips, sound, text, animation, music, and interactive panoramic images.
- **Adobe Reader**—Formerly known as **Acrobat Reader,** uses Adobe's Portable Document Format (PDF) as the native file format.
- **Applets**—An applet is a small application program that performs a narrow function and has no independent use. It is a software component that runs in the context of another program like a Web browser.
- **ActiveX Control**—ActiveX control is a Microsoft term that is used to denote reusable software components that are based on Microsoft's Component Object Model (COM). ActiveX controls, like applets, provide encapsulated functionality to programs.

2.12 What Is Information Security, and Why Is it Important?

Computer security is the process of preventing and detecting unauthorized use of your computer. Prevention measures help you to stop unauthorized users (also known as **intruders**) from accessing any part of your computer system. Detection helps you to determine whether or not someone attempted to break into your system, if they were successful, and what they may have done.

We use computers for everything from banking and investing to shopping and communicating with others through e-mail or chat programs. Although you may not consider your communications top secret, you probably do not want strangers reading your e-mail, using your computer to attack other systems, sending forged e-mail from your computer, or examining personal information stored on your computer (such as financial statements).

Information security is concerned with three main areas:

- **Confidentiality**—information should be available only to those who rightfully have access to it.
- **Integrity**—information should be modified only by those who are authorized to do so.
- **Availability**—information should be accessible to those who need it when they need it.

These concerns apply to all Internet users. You probably would not let a stranger look through your important personal documents. In the same way, you may want to keep the tasks you perform on your computer confidential, whether it's tracking your investments, reading work-related correspondence, or sending e-mail messages to family and friends. Also, you should have some assurance that the information you enter into your computer remains intact and is available when you need it.

A Computer Virus is: A parasitic program written intentionally to enter a computer without the users's permission or knowledge. The word parasite is used because a virus attaches to files or boot sectors and replicates itself, thus continuing to spread. Though some viruses do little but replicate, others can cause serious damage or effect program and system performance. A virus should never be assumed harmless and left on a system. —Symantec

Intruders Intruders (sometimes also known as **hackers**) may be able to watch all your actions on your computer, or cause damage to your computer by reformatting your hard drive or changing your data.

Unfortunately, intruders are often discovering new vulnerabilities (informally called holes) to exploit in computer software. The complexity of software makes it increasingly difficult to thoroughly test the security of computer systems. When holes are discovered, computer vendors will usually develop patches to address problems. However, it is up to you to obtain and install the patches, or correctly configure the software to operate more securely.

The most common methods used by intruders to gain control of home computers are briefly described below and fully examined in the chapter that covers security and privacy:

- **Virus**—A virus is a small piece of software that piggybacks on real programs. For example, a virus might attach itself to a program such as a spreadsheet program. Each time the spreadsheet program runs, the virus runs, too, and it has the chance to reproduce (by attaching to other programs) or wreak havoc. An e-mail virus moves around in e-mail messages, and usually replicates itself by automatically mailing itself to dozens of people in the victim's e-mail address book.
- **Trojan horse program**—Trojan horse programs are a common way for intruders to trick you into installing "back door" programs. These can allow intruders easy access to your computer without your knowledge. The program claims to be what it is not (it may claim to be a game) but instead does damage when you run it (it may erase your hard disk). Trojan horses have no way to replicate automatically.
- **Denial of service**—Another form of attack is called a denial-of-service (**DoS**) attack. This type of attack causes your computer to crash or to become so busy processing data that you are unable to use it. In most cases, the latest patches will prevent the attack.
- **Being an intermediary for another attack**—Intruders often use compromised computers as launching pads for attacking other systems. You are unlikely to know if this is happening.
- **Spyware**—When a PC is infected with spyware every keystroke and every Web site visited can be recorded or monitored by the people or companies that may have secretly installed software on the PC. In general, spyware is any technology that aids in gathering information about a person or organization without their knowledge.

How to Protect Your Computer Here are several suggestions that are highly recommended:

- **Firewall**—Any Internet user should want to protect their computer from intrusion. One of the best forms of protection is called a firewall. Intruders are constantly scanning systems for known vulnerabilities. A firewall is a program or hardware that examines packet addresses as they arrive at the computer (client or server) and only allows those with safe addresses to pass through.
- **Anti-Virus Software**—Use anti-virus software on all Internet-connected computers. Be sure to keep your anti-virus software up-to-date. Many anti-virus packages support automatic updates of virus definitions.

- **Anti-Spyware Software**—Install and run anti-spyware software. These protective programs scan the hard disk and the system registry for malicious spy programs and delete them. Anti-spyware software uses a list of known spy programs. Typically the list is frequently updated by the vendor of the anti-spyware program. Two free and excellent anti-spyware programs are:
  - Spybot http://www.safer-networking.org
  - Ad-Aware http://www.lavasoftusa.com
- **Do not open unknown e-mail attachments**—Before opening any e-mail attachments be sure you know the source of the attachment. It is not enough that the mail originated from an address you recognize. If you must open an attachment before you can verify the source, do the following:
  - Be sure your virus definitions are up-to-date.
  - Scan the file using your antivirus software.
- **Backup all data**—Make frequent and complete copies of all significant data (spreadsheets, term papers, photographs, etc.). Put copies on storage media (jump drives, CDs, etc.) that can be stored physically away from your computer. In the worst case, if a virus, or other intruder, overtakes your computer you can use your backup copies to restore your data to a clean machine.
- **Maintain your computer's performance**—Make regular use of programs like Disk Defragmenter and Check Disk, etc. to ensure that your computer is always running as efficiently as possible.
- **Keep all applications, including your operating system, patched**—Vendors will usually release patches for their software when vulnerability has been discovered. Some applications will automatically check for available updates, and many vendors offer automatic notification of updates via a mailing list. Look on your vendor's Web site for information about automatic notification. Microsoft makes it easy to keep Windows and other Microsoft programs current. Run Windows Update from the browser's tool menu.

Keeping Windows Current

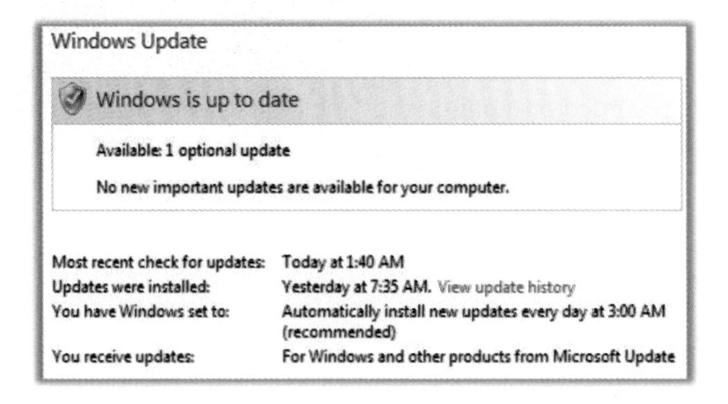

2.13 Net Neutrality

Network neutrality or net neutrality refers to a principle applied to broadband networks. Precise definitions vary, but a broadband network free of restrictions on the kinds of equipment attached and the modes of communication allowed would be considered neutral by most people. Net neutrality is a political issue that is being considered by Congress and the FCC.

Activists fear that telecommunication companies may use their power to discriminate between traffic types, charging tolls on content from some providers such as specific Web sites or services. They are concerned that failure to pay the tolls would result in poor service or no service for certain Web sites or certain types of applications. The ultimate concern is maintenance of an open-market and support for free-speech.

Proponents counter that Quality of Service (**QoS**) standards should depend on the price specific users pay for access. They say that large on-line retailers would likely pay a premium for faster delivery of their Web pages to viewers. Non-commercial users, they claim, have little need for faster delivery of e-mail messages and other similar services, so end-users would not be harmed.

2.14 Summary

The Internet is a world-wide inter-network of networks. Through its use we are able to communicate in ways never imagined before. The motivation to create a distributed packet-switching network came from the demands of the Cold War, but the benefits have spread throughout the world. The fundamental components of the Internet are packets, protocols, servers, and clients. Security has become perhaps the dominant concern of many Internet users and the issue of network neutrality is surfacing as important, too.

The World Wide Web is a communication architecture that is enabled by the Internet. The Web depends on protocols for governing communication sessions between clients and servers. DNS provides for the translation of URLs into numeric server addresses to enable delivery of messages where intended. Hyperlinks in hypermedia documents allow the user to navigate through the Web. The Web provides services that include electronic mail, online chat, file transfer, VoIP, and search engines. The client's browser is the most commonly used program for navigating the Web. Use of Internet Explorer was presented in depth and other browsers were discussed as well.

The network architecture that forms the Internet is well defined and the participants agree to follow certain protocols so that communication is ensured. There is little control, however, over who may use the Internet and what kind of data is carried on it.

EXERCISES

Exercise 2.1

Why is a browser a client program?

Exercise 2.2

What is hypertext?

Exercise 2.3

How does a local e-mail address differ from a global address?

Exercise 2.4

Why is it that a single e-mail message might travel in several packets? Why is it that the packets might not all follow the same route to the destination?

Exercise 2.5

What is information security? What does it involve and who is responsible for it?

Exercise 2.6

What is the significance of DNS and how would our use of the Internet be different if DNS did not exist?

Exercise 2.7

There are three markup languages that support much web activity. Identify them, describe them and provide an example of each.

Exercise 2.8

The Web uses the client-server architecture for delivering requested Web pages to web site visitors. How does this architecture differ from peer-to-peer?

Exercise 2.9

What are blogs and why have they become popular?

Exercise 2.10

What is the significance of packet-switching? Do you think the Internet as we know it could have been developed had packet-switching not been invented? Why?

Exercise 2.11

Describe what phishing is. What would your strategy be to protect yourself against a phishing attack?

Exercise 2.12

What is an RSS feed? What is a news aggregator?

Exercise 2.13

What are some reasons why VoIP is becoming popular?

Exercise 2.14

What is a cookie? Discuss how cookies are useful. Are there dangers in using cookies? If so what are they?

Exercise 2.15

Assume that you use a public access computer for browsing and visiting websites. What should you do to protect your privacy?

Exercise 2.16

Describe the difference between the POP and IMAP protocols.

Exercise 2.17

Explain the difference between the Web and the Internet.

Exercise 2.18

Discuss three protections that you should use to protect your computer from attack.

Exercise 2.19

What is a protocol and why are they essential to the smooth operation of the Internet and the Web? Identify three protocols and describe their importance.

Exercise 2.20

What is the difference between intranets, extranets and the Internet?

Exercise 2.21

What is an IP address and what limitation is inherently built into the current method of assigning IP addresses?

Exercise 2.22

If you were a member of Congress you might be expected to take a stand on net neutrality. How would you evaluate the tug between the constitutional guarantee of free speech with the commercial demand for profit?

HARDWARE

CHAPTER 3

Hardware is one of the three building blocks of an information system; software and the community of stakeholders are the other two. Each is important in its own right, and software and systems analysis are the subjects of other chapters. Here the topic is hardware, which is defined as:

> *Hardware is the physical part of a computer system. It is tangible—It can be seen, touched and held. It is the physical components of the system and is comprised of electronic, magnetic and mechanical devices. Computer equipment includes processors, memory and storage devices, input and display devices, and communication equipment. The hardware of a computer system is infrequently changed. Hardware functions to accept and store data and execute operations on the data.*

It is the operating system software that provides the instructions and manages the Input/Output devices, memory RAM and hard drives, files and processors. Software is comprised of data and sets of instructions that the computer can interpret and execute. It is not physical and cannot be directly seen without the aid of hardware to display it or process it. Programs are written to satisfy the needs of those who will use it. These people are known as stakeholders. The job of the system analyst is to design programs that meet stakeholder needs.

The central hardware component in a system is the computer itself. We will discuss that first.

3.1 Computer

A computer is a machine that can be programmed (it follows the commands in computer programs) to accept data (software - input) and process it into useful information (software - output). The computer may store data for future retrieval on storage devices and share data and messages over a network with other computers. Modern computers have a two hundred year legacy. Long before electronic computers there were mechanical devices.

The Computer and Input-Process-Output

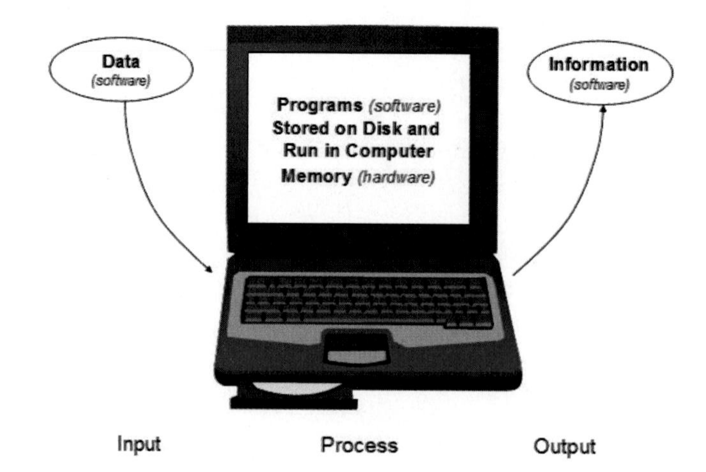

The computer plays a major role in the processing depicted in the **Input-Process-Output** model (**IPO**). This model is fundamental to data processing and to an information system. It is the basis for our discussion about data, information and databases in another chapter, however, a brief introduction is beneficial here.

Data are facts that may or may not be relevant to decision making. Alone, facts mean nothing until they are combined with other data which provides a context for understanding—they then become the basis for information. The process of providing a **context** for data is known as **data processing** and that is the fundamental activity of an information system. The relationship between data, processing and information is presented in the IPO model:

Input-Process-Output Model

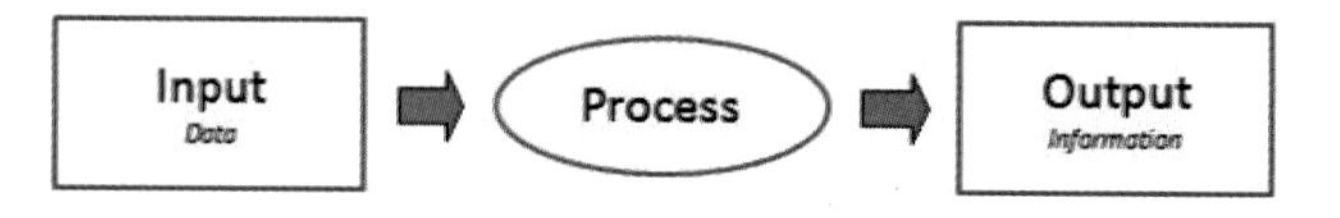

The computer plays a pivotal role as it accepts input, runs programs that process the data, and generates output. In addition to data entered from a keyboard or received in an e-mail or spreadsheet, data processing often involves including data preserved in a storage device (disk, jump drive, CD, etc.) and the IPO model can be updated to reflect data storage this way:

IPO Model with Data Storage

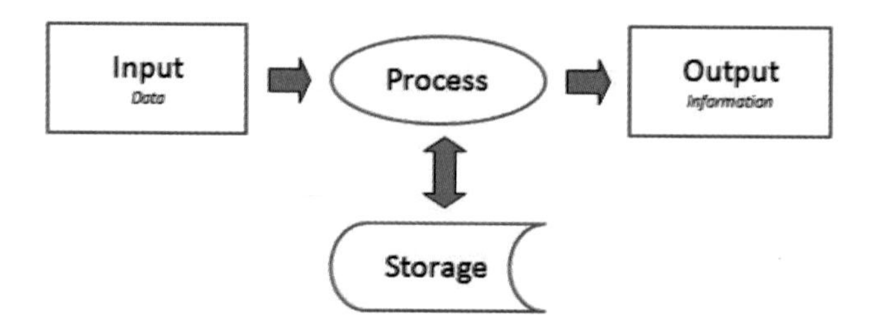

Before we delve into the particulars about what comprises a computer and how it works we consider the perspective of how and when computers came about.

3.2 Computer History

The electronic digital computer, that we use today, has its roots in machines invented in the 1800s. One of the most significant was the non-electrical machine, the **Analytical Engine,** designed by an English inventor, **Charles Babbage.** The Analytical Engine was too complex to be built with the technology of the early 1880s. However, in the 1980s, a model was produced from Babbage's original blueprints, and it worked! So Babbage is considered to be the father of the computer. But what is a computer if it cannot be programmed? The answer should be obvious: it does nothing. So who invented programming?

Babbage's Analytical Engine
Science Museum/Science & Society Picture Library.

A friend of Babbage's, mathematician **Ada Lovelace,** wrote **procedures** that gave the Analytical Engine a set of instructions for processing data. Of course, Ada Lovelace's programs could not be tested until the Engine was built about 150 years later, but her programs worked! Ada Lovelace is often considered the first computer programmer. In 1979, the programming language, Ada, was named in her honor.

While many other inventors and inventions are historically important because they helped pave the way for computing as we know it today, several people and milestones are worth mentioning.

Jacquard Loom The Jacquard Loom, invented by **Joseph Jacquard** in 1801, used the holes punched in wooden cards to control the weaving of patterns in textiles. The loom enabled even unskilled weavers to produce complex designs. Each punched card corresponded to one row of the design and the cards were strung together in order of the pattern.

This loom was the first machine to use data stored as holes in punch cards to control a sequence of operations. While it performed no computations on the data, it is considered an important step in the history of computing hardware because it was the first example of a machine that used stored data to guide operations. This was important to the development of computer programming. Charles Babbage planned to use punch cards to store programs in his Analytical Engine. Although he did not live to see his ideas fulfilled, punch card data storage did prove to work reliably, as you will learn next.

Jacquard Loom
Science Museum/Science & Society Picture Library.

Hollerith's Punch Card Data Storage After graduating from college, **Herman Hollerith** took a job with the **U.S. Census Bureau** collecting and analyzing statistical information on the use of water and steam to power in the iron and steel industries. This assignment motivated his inspiration to devise a machine to automatically collect and store data for later analysis. He successfully found an outlet for his creativity when he developed equipment for recording census statistics.

The Census Bureau offered a substantial reward to the developer of devices that would streamline the collecting and counting of census data for the 1890 census. The rapid influx of immigrants to the United States in the 1880s caused the Census Bureau to believe that continued use of manual data collection practices would not permit a timely tabulation of the census.

Hollerith knew, from a relative who was involved in the textile industry, of the Jacquard Loom's use of punch card for data storage. He was also inspired by the use of punch cards by railroad conductors when issuing railroad tickets. Holes punched in the tickets represented not only destinations and seat assignments but also provided an area in which passenger details (such as height and hair color) were recorded. He concluded that census takers could do the same, with the resulting cards being sorted and processed by machines. His device sensed holes electrically rather than mechanically and, unlike the loom, was sophisticated enough to accumulate data and calculate summaries.

Hollerith's Punch Card Data Storage System

With some of the award he received from the Census Bureau Hollerith founded the Tabulating Machine Company. In 1911 his firm merged with two others to form the Computing Tabulating Recording (CTR) Corporation and it was renamed International Business Machines (**IBM**) in 1924.

Early Digital Computers Modern computing began with accelerated development before and during World War II. During this period developments in electronics produced important inventions including electronic circuits, relays, vacuum tubes, and other devices replacing mechanical equivalents. The computers designed and constructed from these new devices have often been referred to as **first generation computers.** Computers such as the Atanasoff-Berry Computer, the Colossus and ENIAC, were built individually in research laboratories and typically used punched cards for input and as the primary data storage medium.

The **Atanasoff-Berry Computer** (ABC) was the first electronic digital computing device. The machine was developed in the late 1930s for the special purpose of solving simultaneous linear equations. The ABC lifted the curtain on modern computing, including binary arithmetic and electronic switching, but its special-purpose and lack of an alterable, stored program delineate it from modern general purpose computers. This machine was largely forgotten until the 1970s when a U.S. District Court invalidated the ENIAC patent and concluded that the ABC was the first "computer."

The ABC was the first computer to use binary arithmetic. Earlier machines, including The Analytical Engine, based calculations on decimal numbers using "base 10" arithmetic. The advantage of binary is simplicity: there are two possible values, 1 and 0. Handling two values requires less complicated circuits or machinery than what is needed to process the 10 decimal digits: 0, 1, 2, 3, 4, 5, 6, 7, 8, and 9.

ABC: First Binary Computer
Courtesy of the Computer History Museum.

The **Colossus,** an early electronic digital computer, was used by British code breakers to read encrypted German messages during World War II. The encrypted message was read at high speed. The Colossus, a semi-special purpose computer, reduced the time to break German messages from weeks to hours. It was developed just in time for deciphering messages which gave significant information to the Allies prior to D-Day. The deciphered messages showed that Hitler had fallen for the deception campaigns designed to avert German opposition during the D-Day invasion.

Colossus: World War II Code Breaker
Courtesy of the Computer History Museum.

ENIAC, the abbreviation for Electronic Numerical Integrator and Computer, is usually considered to be the first modern, general purpose computer. It was large (weighed thirty tons) power hungry (consumed two hundred kilowatts of power), all electronic, digital, and capable of being reprogrammed to solve general computing problems. ENIAC was designed and built originally to calculate artillery firing tables for the U.S.

Army's Ballistics Research Laboratory. Due to war-time needs the first problems run on the ENIAC were related to the design of the atomic bomb.

A drawback on the machine was a side effect of its reliance on vacuum tubes, which tended to burn out often. This caused the machine to go through up and down periods.

ENIAC: First Large Scale Programmable Computer
Courtesy of the Computer History Museum.

All of the early electronic computers incorporated vacuum tubes for controlling the circuits that computers use while processing data. These tubes look and behave very much like light bulbs; they generate a lot of heat and have a tendency to burn out. The development of computing depended on a new breakthrough.

The Impact of the Transistor The next major step in the history of computing was the invention of the transistor in 1947. This device rapidly replaced the fragile and power hungry vacuum tube as an electronic switch. Transistorized computers are normally referred to as **second generation computers** and became available in the late 1950s and early 1960s. The use of transistors allowed a significant reduction in size and power requirements accompanied by an increase in reliability. Second generation computers were expensive and were primarily used by universities, governments, and large corporations.

Transistors

Through the 1950s all computers manufactured were large scale and often referred to as **mainframe** computers. Several companies (most notably Digital Equipment Corporation) used the new second generation technology to design and market smaller computers known as mini computers but the technology was mostly no different from that of mainframes. The introduction of integrated circuits allowed the design and then rapid development of the next generation of computers.

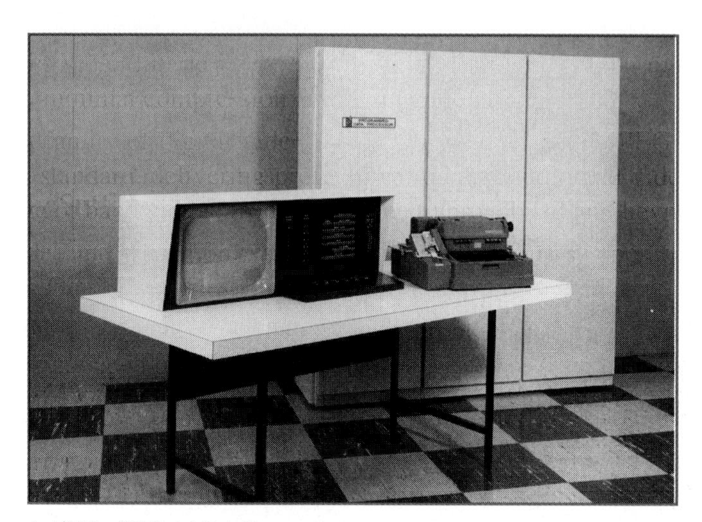

A 1960s PDP-1 Mini Computer
Courtesy of the Computer History Museum.

Integrated Circuits Promote Powerful Computing Expansion When building a circuit, it is very important that all connections remain solid. If conections are loose the electrical current may be interrupted and the circuit fails. Before the integrated circuit, first and second generation computer circuits were assembled by hand, soldering each component in place and connecting them manually with wires. Engineers understood that manually assembling the substantial number of tiny components required in more powerful computers would be impossible without generating some faulty connections.

Another challenge was the complexity of the circuits and the distance between components. A complex computer circuit is dependent on speed for efficient operation. If the circuit's components were large, or the connections too distant, the electric signals could not travel rapidly enough, and the computer would not operate well, or at all. A new breakthrough was needed to advance beyond the second generation.

The **integrated circuit** combines numerous transistors and other electronic components and their connections in a single package thus eliminating the problems of distance between components. The circuits are machine manufactured therefore eliminating the tedious effort of hand soldering transistor based circuits and at the same time increasing the reliability of the circuits. Mass production coupled with enhanced reliability fueled the remarkable explosion in the use of computers known as the **third generation.**

An Integrated Circuit
© Andrew Brookes/Corbis.

The **microprocessor** (an integrated circuit that serves as a **central processing unit** or **CPU** in a computer system) made possible the development of the **microcomputer,** small, low-cost computers that could be owned by individuals and small businesses. Microcomputers which first appeared in the 1970s, became commonplace in the next two decades. Today such computers are known as **personal computers. Apple Computer** introduced the first mass-market personal computer.

By integrating the processor onto one integrated circuit (containing the equivalent of millions of transistors and other components), production and assembly cost was greatly reduced. Since the emergence of the integrated circuit the microprocessor has become the most common implementation of the central processing unit.

Data Representation Before we discuss modern hardware, we first consider data representation and why it is important. Computers only understand a very limited vocabulary comprised of 1 and 0. Certainly computers process business transactions, allow e-mail communication, stream video and audio from servers, and allow us to print pictures from our digital cameras. Yet ultimately all content that is processed or handled by a computer system is just 1s and 0s. Each 1 or 0 is known as a **bit.** This is called the **binary** system and is integral to what makes computers and data processing using computers plausible.

Binary means counting by twos. It is a numbering system that has two possible values: 0 and 1. As humans we count in the decimal system which has 10 values: 0, 1, 2, 3, 4, 5, 6, 7, 8, and 9. A decimal machine must have 10 possible states, one for each value that can be represented.

Binary works perfectly with the electrical nature of a digital computer system. Electrical currents can carry different voltages to represent a 1 or a 0. Early attempts at building computers were mechanical and so no inherent orientation toward binary existed. As a result the mechanics required to handle more complicated systems were too complicated to build. Babbage's Analytical Engine suffered from this problem.

A Binary Digit

So far so good, but we have a problem. What use would a computer be if it only could store and process 0s and 1s? We are interested in processing much more complex forms of data. What about the 26 letters of the alphabet? If a bit can have only two values how can we store and process all 26 letters?

If all data is represented as 1s or 0s (sometimes referred to as on or off) then the familiar letters of the alphabet, punctuation, numerals, and so on must be translated from key strokes with familiar symbols (A, B, . . ., Z, 0,1, . . .,9) to numbers with just two values. Since a bit can only have two values (1 or 0) it would be impossible to represent every key on the keyboard as a single bit. The solution is to group bits together and assign the group to represent particular keys. Today a group of eight bits is known as a **byte.**

To permit data transfer and sharing between computers and software of different manufactures it is necessary for vendors of participating equipment and programs to agree on the specific bit pattern (bytes) for each keystroke. An industry agreement in 1963 did just that by becoming the basis for data interchange. The American Standard Code for Information Interchange, **ASCII** for short, established standard bit pattern representations.

ASCII A document typed into a word processor would be of little interest if it were all 0s and 1s. While it is true that everything stored in a computer is stored as binary, when we use a keyboard we type letters of the alphabet, punctuation, numbers and so on. The computer must be able to accept what we type and yet still store it in binary.

The trick used is to group bits together so that more than two states (0 and 1) can be represented. Normally, eight bits are combined to form a byte, and a byte can represent one character from the keyboard. The sequence of bits 01000001 represents the capital letter "A".

Eight Bits (One Byte) Makes the Letter "A"

01001000	=	H
01010100	=	E
01011100	=	L
01011100	=	L
01011111	=	O

Bytes Are Grouped to Make Words

How in the world could the sequence of bits 01000001 represent the letter "A"? The answer is that most of the computer hardware and software manufacturers agreed on the ASCII convention that specifies what each sequence of bits is to represent. The figure shown here illustrates how the word "HELLO" is built from a sequence of five eight bit bytes.

The chart that follows displays selected ASCII codes and the characters they represent. Notice that upper and lower case require separate codes. The decimal equivalent of each binary code is also presented in this portion of the ASCII table:

ASCII Code

Binary	Dec.	Character	Binary	Dec.	Character	Binary	Dec.	Character
010 0000	32	Space	011 0000	48	0	100 0001	65	A
010 0001	33	!	011 0001	49	1	100 0010	66	B
010 0010	34	"	011 0010	50	2	100 0011	67	C
010 0011	35	#	011 0011	51	3	100 0100	68	D
010 0100	36	$	011 0100	52	4	100 0101	69	E
010 0101	37	%	011 0101	53	5	100 0110	70	F
010 0110	38	&	011 0110	54	6	110 0001	97	a
010 0111	39	'	011 0111	55	7	110 0010	98	b
010 1000	40	(	011 1000	56	8	110 0011	99	c
010 1001	41	)	011 1001	57	9	110 0100	100	d
010 1010	42	*				110 0101	101	e
010 1011	43	+				110 0110	102	f

How Many Different Characters Can Be Represented? The ASCII coding scheme actually uses seven bits to represents characters (letters, numbers, and punctuation). Since each bit can be a 1 or 0 then the seven bits can have 2^7 or 128 possible arrangements. Bytes are formed of eight bits and the eighth bit is used to form **Extended ASCII.** This is not part of the formal ASCII specification but rather a collection of an additional 128 combinations that are used by manufacturers for proprietary function. It is the first 128 characters that are defined as ASCII.

So how many different characters can eight bits together represent? One bit can represent two things: 0 or 1. What about a byte with two bits? Since each bit can be a 0 or 1 then there are four possible sequences that two bits can represent. This can be determined algebraically as

$$2^{\text{number of bits}}$$

and is summarized here. The table on the left shows how many characters can be generated from bytes of different sizes and the chart on the right shows the four two-bit sequences possible if the code set uses two bits per character. Most computers use eight bit bytes. From the table you can see that 256 characters are possible.

The Relationship between Bits per Byte and Character Set Size

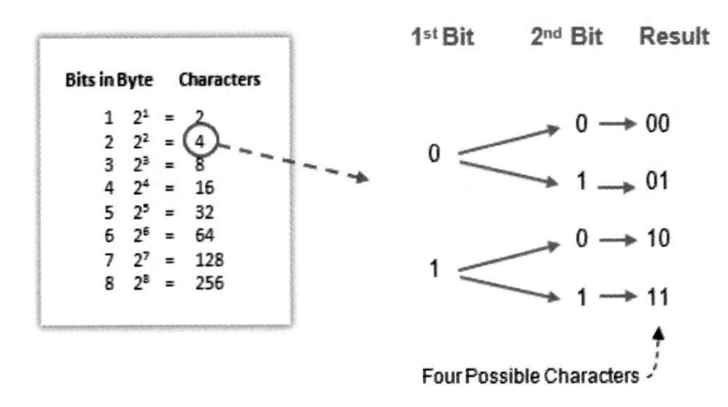

Unicode Unicode is an industry standard designed to allow text and symbols from all of the major writing systems of the world to be consistently represented and manipulated by computers. A **writing system** limited to 128 distinct representations is not sufficient for more than one alphabet, numbering system, and punctuation. The world has many such systems. Unicode handles multiple writing systems by using two bytes (16 bits) for each character's representation. This scheme provides about 65,536 distinct combinations of 16 bits and that is sufficient for human writing systems currently known. A few examples are shown here:

Unicode

Decimal	Unicode name	Display
65	Latin capital letter A	A
223	Latin small letter Sharp S	ß
254	Latin small letter Thorn	þ
916	Greek capital letter Delta	Δ
1049	Cyrillic capital letter Short I	Й
1511	Hebrew letter Qof	ק
1605	Arabic letter Meem	م
3671	Thai digit 7	๗
4688	Ge'ez syllable Qha	ቐ
12354	Hiragana letter A (Japanese)	あ
21494	CJK Unified Ideograph-53F6 (Simplified Chinese "Leaf")	叶
33865	CJK Unified Ideograph-8449 (Traditional Chinese "Leaf")	葉
46507	Hangul syllable Tteolp (Korean "Ssangtikeut Eo Rieulpieup")	떫

Other Data Encoding Numerous other data encoding arrangements have been and are important. Here are a few that handle various types of data:

- **EBCDIC**—Extended Binary Coded Decimal Interchange Code is an 8-bit character encoding used on IBM mainframe operating systems. It originated in the 1950s.
- **BCD**—Binary-coded decimal is an encoding for decimal numbers in which each digit is represented by its own binary sequence. It allows easy conversion to decimal digits for printing or display and faster decimal calculations.

Data Compression Compression techniques are used to reduce the number of bytes required to store certain kinds of data. Compression is also used to permit faster transmission of data between computers.

- **MPEG**—A family of digital video compression standards. Storing sound or video requires encoding it into a sequence of binary 1s and 0s. A codec performs this task. It is a device or program capable of performing encoding and decoding on a digital data stream or signal. The word **codec** is derived from the two functions it performs: **coding** and **decoding.**
- **GIF**—The Graphics Interchange Format is an 8-bit-per-pixel bitmap image format that was introduced by CompuServe and is widely used on the Web.
- **WAV**—Standard digital audio file format for storing sound data; allows audio recordings to be captured and stored; often used to save CD-quality audio.

3.3 Modern Hardware

When we speak of hardware we are considering a collection of devices that allow us to enter, store, and process data, and display output. You are surely familiar with some of these devices. Today most computers are physically small (desktop and laptop) but mainframe computers are still quite important as they are used to process large volumes of data for governments, businesses, schools, the military, and research laboratories for example. Although physically large, mainframe computers share the same basic components of small computers. In this section the most common and important computer components are listed here and described afterward:

- **Motherboard**
  - Processor (CPU)
  - Bus (internal and external)
  - BIOS
- **Power Supply**
- **Input**
  - Keyboard
  - Mouse
  - Microphone
  - Camera
- Output
  - Monitor

  - Printer
  - Speaker
- **Storage**
  - Primary Memory: RAM
  - Secondary Memory
    - Hard and Floppy Disks
    - Flash Drives
    - CD/DVD
    - Zip Disk
    - Magnetic Tape
- **Communication devices**
  - Modem
  - Network Interface Hardware

Important Terms Your understanding of computer hardware and software depends on understanding the following:

- **Bit**—A logical data value may be 0 or 1. Sometimes a bit is said to take on the values True or False.
- **Byte**—A unit of data storage consisting of 8 bits. It represents a single character, digit, or punctuation.
- **Kilobyte (KB)**—A unit of data storage consisting of about one thousand bytes.
- **Megabyte (MB)**—A unit of data storage consisting of about one million bytes.
- **Gigabyte (GB)**—A unit of data storage consisting of about 1000 megabytes or a billion bytes.
- **Terabyte (TB)**—A unit of data storage consisting of about 1000 gigabytes.
- **Hertz**—A unit of frequency describing the number of electrical cycles that occur in a second. The speed of a computer's processor is measured in hertz. The larger the number, generally the faster the microprocessor.
- **Kilohertz (Khz)**—One thousand hertz.
- **Megahertz (Mhz)**—One million hertz.
- **Gigahertz (Ghz)**—One billion hertz.
- **RAM**—Random Access Memory. This memory holds programs as they execute and temporarily holds data as it is processed.
- **ROM**—Read-Only Memory. It cannot easily be written to and its main uses are the distribution of firmware (software that is very closely related to hardware).
- **bps**—Bits Per Second. The number of bits transmitted per second.
- **Kilobits per Second (Kbps)**—One thousand bits per second.
- **Megabits per Second (Mbps)**—One million bits per second.
- **Gigabits per Second (Gbps)**—One billion bits per second.

3.3.1 Motherboard

This is the one component of a computer system that ties all other components together. This is where the core components of a computer reside. A computer is typically constructed with the processor (**CPU**), main memory (**RAM**), and other basic components on the motherboard.

The **system unit** is the main body of a computer. It provides an enclosure containing the motherboard, power supply, cooling fans, internal disk drives, and the memory modules and expansion cards that are plugged into the motherboard.

Components such as external storage, control circuits for video display and sound, and peripheral devices (printers, communication devices, etc.) are typically attached to the motherboard via cables plugged into connectors on the motherboard. The motherboard also supports expansion of the computer's functionality by providing a place for additional components to be added. Clearly the ability to expand is an important aspect of the computer.

A Computer's Motherboard

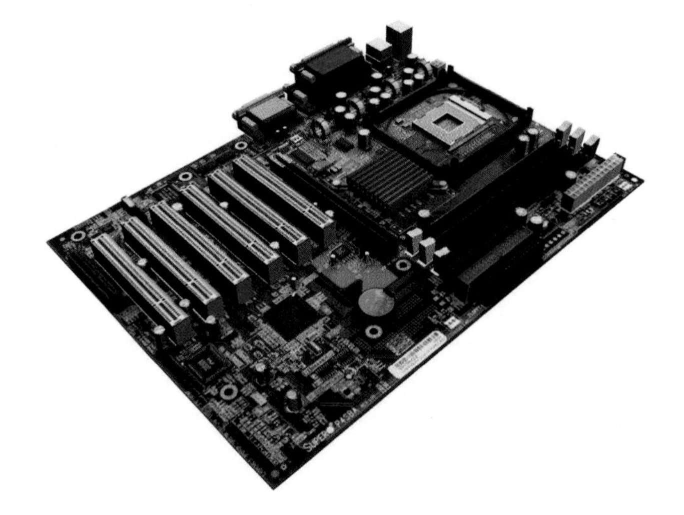

Several of the important components found on the motherboard are described next.

Processor The **central processing unit** (**CPU**), also called the processor, is the critical component in a digital computer that processes data by interpreting and executing instructions that are contained in computer programs. Generally a CPU that is manufactured using integrated circuits is known as a microprocessor.

This device responds to a program's commands and has a **clock** to keep all activities in the computer synchronized. Inside the CPU we find the **control unit** and the **arithmetic logic unit,** ALU. The control unit is like a **manager** who keeps things organized and synchronized and the ALU is where mathematical and logical operations are performed. The control unit fetches data and copies it into registers. The ALU performs operations on data in registers such as addition and subtraction. The ALU also perfoms logical tests on data which permits branching within programs.

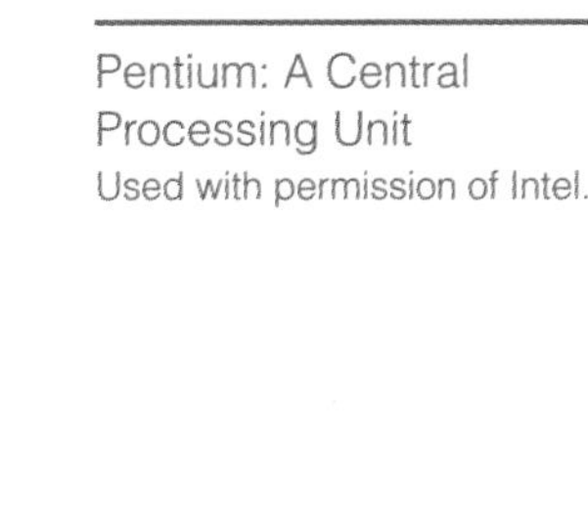

Pentium: A Central Processing Unit
Used with permission of Intel.

Several important terms that relate to the CPU or processor are:

- **System clock**—Time keeper that provides a synchronizing signal that the CPU follows.
- **Clock speed**—The rate in cycles per second (measured in hertz) at which a computer performs its most basic operations such as adding two numbers or transferring a value from one register to another.
- **Machine cycle**—The machine cycle is a four phase cycle that includes reading and interpreting the machine language, executing the code, and then storing that code. The execution of program code (machine code) follows this cycle.
- **Machine instruction**—A small segment of code that contains steps that need to be executed by the computer processor. Normally an instruction performs one action like adding two numbers. Machine instruction speed is measured in the number of cycles an instruction requires for operation.
- **Machine language**—Sometimes referred to as machine code or object code, machine language is a collection of binary digits or bits that the computer reads and interprets. Machine language is the only language a computer is capable of understanding.
- **Instruction set**—This is the set of instructions that the processor knows how to perform. Instruction sets are built into the processor's circuitry, so different processors are not likely to be able to run the same version of the same program.
- **RISC**—A reduced instruction set computer is a processor designed for speed. It is a special purpose computer that requires only a subset of all operations to perform the processing it is assigned.
- **CISC**—Complex Instruction Set Computers preceeded RISC. The primary goal of CISC architecture is to complete a task in as few lines of program code as possible.
- **Cache**—High speed memory that allows the processor to fetch data faster than from memory located elsewhere on the motherboard or on secondary storage like disk.
- **Serial processing**—The processor must execute all phases of the machine cycle before the next instruction is begun.
- **Pipelining**—A method for boosting performance in which the processor begins execution of the next instruction before the current instruction is complete.
- **Parallel processing**—Multiple instructions are processed simultaneously. This and pipelining improve system performance.

- **Multiprocessing**—The combination of several processors working together in a computer system. A multiprocessing system will allocate tasks among the several processors. This is not the same as parallel processing in which multiple instructions are simultaneously executed on the same processor.
- **Benchmarks**—Standard measures of performance used to allow comparison between processors.
- **Register**—A location within a processor used to store and process data. Registers are 16, 32, or 64 bits wide.
- **Word size**—The number of bits that can be manipulated by a single instruction. Registers hold one or more words but never parts of a word.
- **Data bus**—Part of the motherboard that allows transfer of data among the computer's components. A bus operates in parallel fashion so that all bits of each single byte travel together in unison. The data bus size (number of bits) will be the same as the word size.

A key feature of the processor is the amount of data that it can operate on simultaneously. Originally four or eight bit architectures were available. Although it was possible to build a working computer with such chips it would not be particularly powerful. Advances have increased processor capability to 64 bit architectures allowing today's computers to process data quite efficiently.

Another measure of the processor's power is its speed. There are two measures that are relevant:

- The clock speed of the processor (measured in cycles per second or Hz)
- The number of instructions executed per clock cycle (IPC).

The clock speed is advertised when a computer is purchased, and numbers in the 3 Ghz+ range are common for desktop computers while laptop computers tend to run somewhat slower. The IPC is not advertised but the true horsepower of the processor is calculated by multiplying the IPC by the clock speed.

Another factor contributing to the computer's power is the amount of installed real memory (RAM).

Popular processors today include Intel's **Pentium** and **Core Duo** and Advanced Micro Devices (AMD) **Athalon** and **Opteron.**

Dual Core Processor A dual- or multi-core microprocessor is one that combines two or more independent processors into a single package, usually in a single integrated circuit. A multi-core device contains two or more independent microprocessors and permits multiprocessing without including multiple microprocessors in separate physical packages. This form of processing is often known as chip-level multiprocessing.

Processor Speed As processor and computer architecture have advanced, it has become more and more difficult to compare the performance of various computer systems simply by looking at their specifications. Here are some measures of performance:

- **Ghz**—One billion hertz—one billion cycles per second. Generally the faster that the processor cycles per second the faster the processor. As you will see in a moment, though, this is not always true. This is because no two processors are equally efficient per cycle.

- **MIPS**—Instructions per second (IPS) is a measure of a computer's processor speed and one MIP is one million instructions per second. MIPS is used to benchmark processors against others.
- **FLOPS**—Floating Point Operations per Second is the measure of a computer's performance. FLOPS is an especially useful measure in systems that perform scientific calculations and make heavy use of floating point (non-integer) operations.

As an example, an Intel Pentium 4 processor generally operates at a higher clock frequency than AMD Athlon XP processors, but this does not necessarily mean the Pentium has more computational power. In other words an AMD processor with slower clock frequency can perform as well on benchmark tests as an Intel processor operating at a higher frequency.

Intel and AMD Announcements Recent announcements by the premier processor manufacturers (Intel and American Micro Devices) indicate their intent to produce ultralow-power chips. In March 2007 Intel announced that it was on track in developing a new generation of chips that would achieve a significant increase in performance without consuming more power. The new processor families, named **Penryn** and **Nehalem,** may in some cases help Intel catch up technically with its archrival, AMD.

AMD announced plans to introduce an improved processor code named **Barcelona** based on technology that uses four processing cores rather than the two currently used in AMD processors. The company believes that Intel would not be able to catch up with AMD's existing designs until it introduces the Nehalem microprocessor in 2008.

Bus In a computer, a bus is a subsystem of the motherboard that transfers data or power between computer components inside a computer or between a computer and external components which are typically controlled by device driver software.

A device driver is computer software developed to allow computer interaction with hardware devices. Each external device requires a unique driver. Vendors of hardware supply drivers for the hardware they manufacture. Without the correct driver, hardware would not operate properly or at all.

Computers usually have **internal** and **external** busses. The internal bus (or local bus) connects the internal components of a computer to the motherboard (and therefore to the CPU and primary memory—RAM). The internal bus connects to devices that are local to the computer and not to those in other machines or to those external to the computer. An external bus connects external devices (peripherals) to the motherboard.

The internal bus is really three busses that work in a coordinated fashion:

- The **control bus** is used by CPUs for sending commands to other devices within the computer.
- The **address bus** carries the information about which device the CPU is communicating with.
- The **data bus** carries the actual data being processed.

The external bus provides card slots which are used to hold device controller cards for devices such as video cards, sound cards, external storage units, or network cards. This is a mechanism by which external devices are connected to the computer. To gain access to the external bus the computer's case is opened and cards are plugged in to open slots in the bus. Some motherboards today include video and sound or even communication devices thus eliminating the need for the addition of extra cards.

USB Today the use of the **Universal Serial Bus** (**USB**) allows peripheral devices to be connected without the need to plug expansion cards into the computer's external bus. In effect the USB **port** is an extension of the external bus. Devices with a USB plug are connected to the computer by inserting the plug into the USB port. A major advantage of this arrangement (aside from eliminating the need to open the computer's case when attaching a new device) is that devices may be **hot-swapped** (connected or disconnected without powering down or rebooting the computer). When a device is connected the computer identifies it and loads the appropriate device driver.

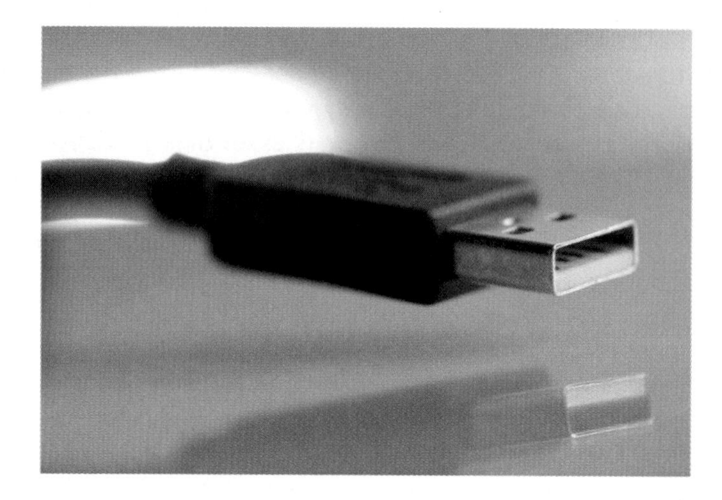

A USB Plug
Corbis.

USB 2.0 (the current standard) has a raw theoretical data rate at 480Mbps, and it is rated about 40 times faster than the earlier USB 1.1, with top speed at 12Mbps.

Plug and Play Plug and play is not a component of the motherboard but describes the process for attaching a new device to the computer system. It is a feature that allows the addition of a new device, normally a peripheral, without requiring reconfiguration or manual installation of device drivers. It allows the device to be added without requiring rebooting of the computer. Normally the device is added by connecting with a USB plug. The processor senses this connection and assigns an internal bus address to the device. Plug and play is a significant advancement over the manual and arduous process that was required in earlier days when adding peripherals.

The operating system provides a set of services for the programs running on a computer, and it also provides the fundamental user interface for use of the computer.

BIOS The **Basic Input/Output System** (BIOS) is a small program run by a computer when first powered on. Its primary function is to stabilize the machine and devices on the motherboard so that the **operating system** can be loaded and take control of the computer. This process is known as **booting up.**

The **BIOS** is software code (known as **firmware**) embedded in a chip that recognizes and controls various devices that make up the computer. It resides in read only memory (**ROM**) and therefore cannot be altered unless the chip is removed and replaced. Without the BIOS the computer cannot start.

At times it may be desirable to interrupt the boot process to reconfigure certain aspects of the computer's environment. How to enter setup mode differs on various computer systems but generally a specific key is pressed (Esc, Del, F1, F2, Ctrl-Esc, etc.) during the start sequence. Once in setup mode, numerous options are available, including these:

- **System Time/Date**—Set the system time and date.
- **Drive Configuration**—Configure hard drives, CD-ROM, and floppy drives.

- **Boot Sequence**—The order that storage devices will be searched for the operating system.
- **Mouse/Keyboard**—Enable Num Lock; Enable the Keyboard; Auto-Detect Mouse.
- **Security**—Set a password for accessing the computer's hardware.
- **Power Management**—Set various power management parameters.
- **Exit**—Save changes, discard changes, or restore default settings.

Expansion Slots Some peripherals require more than a USB port for installation. Certain devices, especially devices with substantial electronics (sound and graphics cards especially) that must be close to the motherboard's bus, are usually connected to the computer with a card placed into an extension slot. Cards that fit into expansion slots are known as **expansion cards** and they provide additional functionality for the computer.

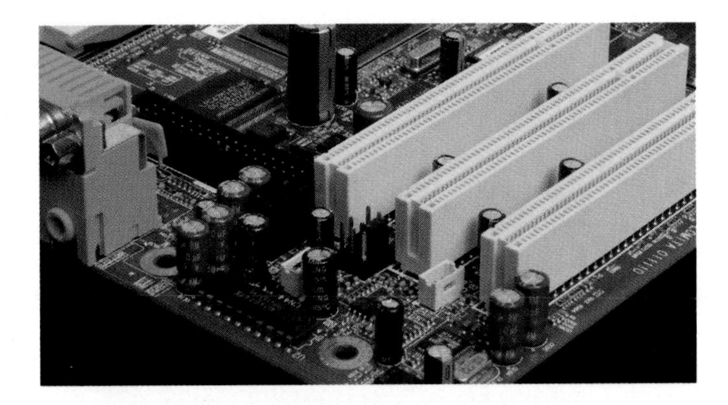

Expansion Slots on Motherboard
© Wayne Johnson, 2007, Shutterstock.

Once the board is inserted into the expansion slot, data is transferred between the expansion board and the computer's devices including RAM, disk, and other peripheral devices. The data bus is the vehicle that transports the data. Expansion cards are engineered to be compatible with one of several types of expansion slots. The slots vary in size depending on the number of data bits (data bus size) that the card requires. The slot provides data, address, and control bus lines.

Today, the Peripheral Component Interconnect bus (**PCI**) is commonly used. This high speed slot provides a 32 or 64 bit data bus (the number of bits that are simultaneously transferred per operation). It has largely replaced the older **ISA** (Industry Standard Architecture) technology.

Another common expansion card conforms to the **AGP** (Accelerated Graphics Port) standard. It is a high-speed port for attaching a graphics card to a computer's motherboard and is used primarily to assist in the acceleration of computer graphics.

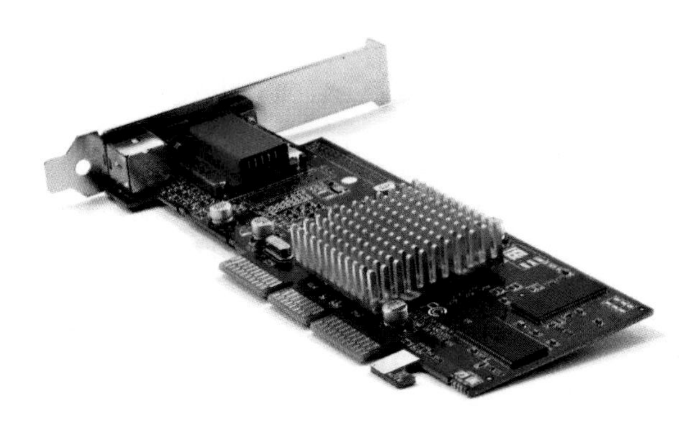

Accelerated Graphics Card
© Dion van Huysseteen, 2007, Shutterstock.

Network Adapter Card A network card, network adapter or **NIC** (network interface controller) is a piece of computer hardware designed to allow computers to communicate over a computer network. It allows users to connect to each other either by using cables or wirelessly and provides an addressing scheme through the use of **MAC** addresses. The networking chapter provides additional information about NICs.

Disk Controller Card The disk controller is the electronic circuit which allows the processor to communicate with a hard disk, floppy disk or other kind of disk drive. A computer will usually have disk controller hardware built onto the motherboard. If additional disks are added to the computer it may be necessary to add additional controllers by installing expansion cards.

Sound Card A sound card is an expansion card that can output and input sound under control of computer programs. Typically sound cards provide the audio for multimedia applications such as music composition, editing video or audio, and games. Many computers have sound capabilities built in, while others require these expansion cards if higher quality audio is desired.

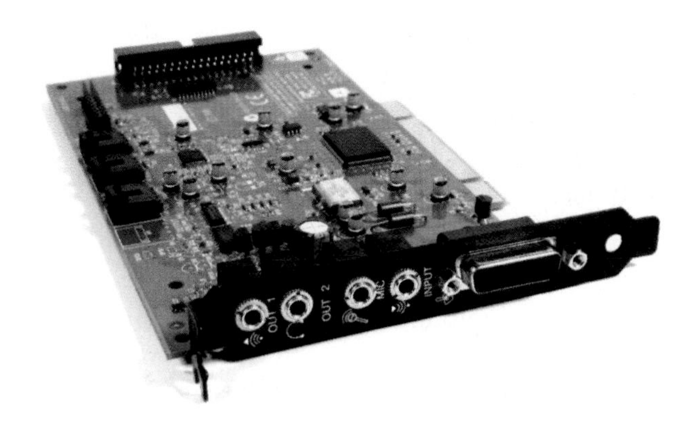

A Sound Card Connects Speakers and Microphones
© David Brimm, 2007, Shutterstock.

Video Card A video card, also referred to as a **graphics accelerator card, display adapter,** and **graphics card,** is responsible for generating output images to a display. The term usually refers to a separate expansion card plugged into a slot on the computer's motherboard and not a graphics controller integrated into the motherboard chipset.

Some video cards offer added functionalities, such as **video capture** and **TV tuning.**

Port A communication port is a doorway between an external device and a computer system. The port may carry data, voice, video, or other types of transmission. A port is used to send computer signals to a printer and to receive data from a scanner. Ports are vital to a computer's functionality. Ports are defined by the function they perform and the physical number of connections they provide. Specific connectors (plugs) fit into ports and must be physically matched.

Today the **USB** port is the most common. Specialty port types (for printers and other devices) have largely been replaced by USB ports. A **FireWire** port is of a different size and allows a FireWire to be connected for fast data transfer. Similarly a **Bluetooth** port allows connection of short distance wireless devices. The most common ports allow connection of a **mouse** or **keyboard.**

FireWire FireWire is used for fast data transfer with peripheral devices. It is Apple Computer's brand name for the IEEE 1394 interface used for high-speed data transfer. It is often used for connecting video sources to a computer. It is also used for connection of external hard-drive storage devices. Most digital camcorders include this connection and many computers intended for home or professional audio/video use have built-in FireWire ports. FireWire connectors have a similar appearance to USB and other plugs.

FireWire Plugs

Bays A bay is a standard-sized area for adding hardware to a computer. Bays are most commonly used to store disk drives, although they can also be used for front-end USB ports, I/O bays, card readers, fans, and other uses. Most bays are fixed to the inside of a case, but some newer ones can be removed. Two types are commonly in use today:

- **Half height bay**—Approximately 5.75" wide by 1.75" high, they are the standard housing for CD and DVD drives.
- **3.5′ bay**—Approximately 4" wide by 1" high, those with an opening in the front of the case are generally used for floppy or Zip drives. Hard drives in modern computers are typically mounted internally.

Cooling Computers generate heat while running. Processors especially get hottest because they consume the most electricity. Several techniques are used to dissipate the heat because otherwise the electronic components would cease to function.

- **Fan**—A fan moves air and is used in a computer to move cooler air over a hot area (like a processor) and to vent hot air to outside the computer's cabinet.
- **Heat sink**—A heat sink is an object that absorbs heat from a hot object and dissipates it—usually into the air.
- **Heat pipe**—A heat pipe is a mechanism that transports heat with a very small difference in temperature between the hot and cold interfaces. It is used to move heat from where it is generated to somewhere that is not sensitive to heat. Heat pipes are generally quite efficient.

Heat Sink for Cooling
© Pekka Jaakkola, 2007, Shutterstock.

3.3.2 Power Supply

A computer power supply is designed to convert 110 volts AC (alternating current) power to the low power DC (direct current) used by the internal components of a computer. The power supply is a metal box usually found inside the computer's case. It is next to the wall of the case allowing the installation of a cooling fan that is vented to the outside air. The power-cord receptacle is usually found outside the case next to the cooling fan. The power supply in laptop computers is usually external to the case.

Computer Power Supply
© akva, 2007, Shutterstock.

Power supplies are rated for certain wattages based on their maximum power requirements of the computer. Wattages in the range of 200 W to 500 W are typical, although computers used as servers or by gamers (video and processor intensive) often require more power.

3.3.3 Input

Data and commands are given the computer through input devices. The most common input devices are the keyboard and the mouse. Microphones and cameras are increasingly important as input devices too.

3.3.3.1 Keyboard

A **keyboard's** primary function is to act as an input device. With a keyboard, you can type a document, use keystroke shortcuts, access menus, and perform a variety of other tasks. Keyboards can have different special purpose keys depending on the manufacturer, the operating system they're designed for, and whether they are attached to a desktop computer or part of a laptop. Most keyboards have between 80 and 110 keys, including:

- **Typing keys**—These keys (letters, numbers, and punctuation) most often follow the **QWERTY** arrangement that was devised in the 1870s when typewriters were introduced. The name QWERTY comes from the first six letters in the top alphabet row. Although the pattern of keys seems to make no sense, it was designed so that consecutive keystrokes were unlikely to cause a typewriter jam as it pressed letter and number patterns into the paper. While this is no longer a concern with paperless systems (computers and monitors) the QWERTY arrangement remains the most common in use today.
- **Function and Control keys**—These keys were introduced by IBM. Function keys, and control keys when pressed simultaneously with typing keys, allow specific commands to be issued by the typist. In effect, function and control keys act as additional shift keys.
- **Windows Key**—Pressing this key brings up the Windows Start Menu. It also causes the icons on the task bar to appear. The Windows key or Windows logo key was originally introduced for the Windows 95 operating system. The key is usually near the space bar and is identified by the Windows logo on it.

Modifications to the QWERTY design are an attempt to make them safer or easier to use. For example some people have associated keyboard use with **carpal tunnel syndrome. Ergonomic** keyboard designs are intended to prevent injuries while keeping a person's hands in a more natural position while typing.

3.3.3.2 Mouse

A pointing device is a computer hardware component (specifically a **human interface device**) that allows a user to input spatial movements to the computer. The mouse is the most common pointing device in use.

The **mouse** is a **point and click** interface for entering commands which works well in graphical environments. Apple Computer did not invent the mouse but was the first to introduce it commercially in 1984 with the Apple Macintosh. The main goal of any mouse is to translate the movements of your hand into signals that the computer can use. The hand motion is displayed and tracked on the monitor as a pointer known as the **cursor.** When the mouse is over an active word processing document or text file it becomes known as the **insertion point.**

A Basic Two-Button Mouse
© Pchemyan Georgiy, 2007, Shutterstock.

Today mice are available as mechanical (least expensive—a ball senses movement) or optical (a light signal senses movement). Mice may be connected to a computer with a wire or wireless transmitter. A mouse has one or more buttons that are pressed ("clicked") to indicate the initiation of an action. The two-button mouse has become the most commonly available design. The left button generally is used to select an object (**single click**) or act on the object (**double click**). The right button displays a menu of options relevant to an object—the menu is said to be **context sensitive.** Operating systems, like Windows, allow the use of the mouse buttons to be reversed for left-handed people. Window's Control Panel provides access to selecting left/right mouse preferences.

- **Mechanical mouse**—The original mouse was mechanical. A ball on the bottom of the mouse rolled over a surface and the ball's movement was converted into electrical signals that reflected the mouse's movement.
- **Optical mouse**—An optical mouse replaced the ball as a sensor of movement with light—most commonly, infra red light. The lack of movable parts makes the optical mouse more durable and allows it to be more accurate. The optical mouse comprises of a camera that takes pictures of the surface that it rests upon and compares the pictures to deduce its direction of travel.
- **Touchpad**—An input device commonly used in laptop computers. They are used to move the cursor by following motions of the user's finger. They are a substitute for a computer mouse.
- **Trackball**—A pointing device consisting of a ball housed in a socket containing sensors to detect rotation of the ball. It is like an upside-down mouse. The user rolls the ball with the thumb, fingers, or the palm of the hand to move a cursor.

3.3.3.3 Tablet

The touch screen of a tablet PC allows the user to operate the computer with a stylus or digital pen, or a fingertip, instead of a keyboard or mouse. Since the tablet accepts movements of the **electronic pen** for input it is possible for the tablet PC to recognize human handwriting.

3.3.3.4 Microphone

A microphone can be used for input when a computer is recording voice or live music. It is also needed when a computer is used for making Internet phone calls (known as **VoIP**). More sophisticated use of this input device involves speaking commands to the computer known as **speech recognition.**

3.3.3.5 Camera

Digital cameras are easily connected to a computer, and since the images are in digital form a computer is an excellent device for storing and editing these images. When a computer is used for live communication a web-camera (or webcam) may be used. Chat services like Yahoo messenger permit users to speak and view each other in real time.

- **Digital camera**—A digital camera is an electronic device used to capture and store images electronically in a digital format, instead of using photographic film. It can be used as an input device for a computer. Images are stored in **flash memory** and transferred to the computer using a cable or by inserting the memory card into a special slot inside the computer's case. Digital cameras normally store images using the **JPG** image format.

Digital cameras record an image as a sequence of dots or **pixels.** The number of pixels per image is an indicator of the **resolution** or clarity of the image. Images with a larger number of pixels can be blown up to larger size without distortion.

- **Video camera**—Video cameras are digital photographic devices whose main purpose is to record moving images. Video recordings are mostly stored in **AVI** or **MPG** format. Once captured, video may be converted to other formats for streaming to clients or for compatibility with different systems. Codecs are devices or programs capable of performing encoding on a digital data stream or signal. More information about video formats and codecs is found in the World Wide Web chapter.
- **Web camera**—A web camera records a continuing sequence of digital images and transmits the images to the computer. Web cameras can also take single pictures, but most are for motion purposes. Generally, web cameras offer lower resolution than digital or video cameras but at a much lower price. Popular uses for webcams include instant messaging and video conferencing.

A Basic Web Camera for a Laptop Computer
© Eric Ferguson, 2007, Shutterstock.

3.3.3.6 Touch Screen

A touch screen is an overlay that covers the computer's monitor and can receive movements of a user's finger in a fashion similar to the touchpad. The difference is that a user interacting with a touch screen views the monitor's image and moves or clicks a finger as if using a mouse over the same surface.

Touch screens are particularly useful in museums and retail settings where user input is required but a mouse and keyboard are undesirable because they require additional space and could easily be taken.

3.3.3.7 Scanner

A scanner is a device that analyzes an image (most commonly a photograph) or document (printed text or handwriting) and converts it to a digital image. The most common are flatbed scanners.

- **Flatbed Scanner**—This type of scanner has a flat surface on which to place the item to be scanned and a top that closes holding the item securely during scanning.
- **Handheld Scanner**—Hand-held scanners are more portable but more difficult to use because of hand movements.

Scanner resolution is important because, just as with digital cameras, the resolution dictates the clarity and potential for enlargement of the scanned digital image.

Flatbed Scanner

3.3.3.8 Barcode Readers

A barcode reader is a peripheral for reading printed barcodes. It is similar to a scanner because it consists of a light source, a lens, and a photo conductor translating optical impulses into electrical ones.

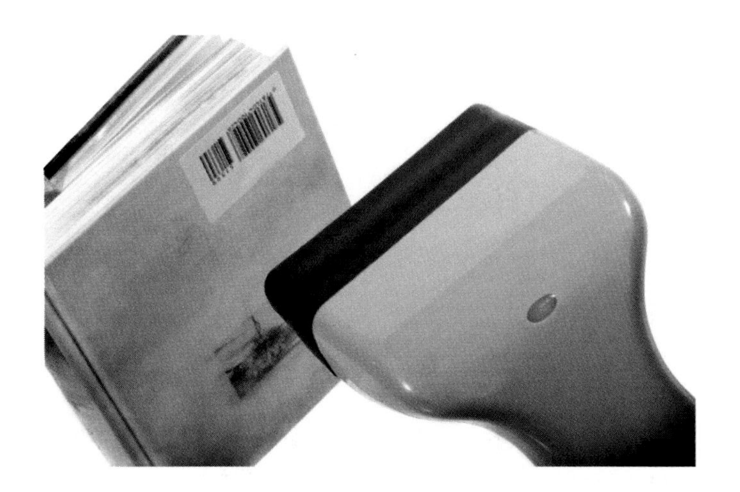

Barcode Reader

3.3.3.9 Speech Recognition

Speech recognition is an input procedure that uses a microphone and other hardware to capture a speech signal and convert it into a sequence of words. The conversion is performed by an algorithm implemented as a computer program. The performance of a speech recognition system is often specified in terms of **accuracy** (word error rate—percent of words not understood) and **speed** (the lag behind spoken word that the conversion consumes).

Microsoft has included speech recognition capabilities in Windows for several versions. The implementation in **Windows Vista** is considerably better than earlier versions. It is, however, limited to being an alternative to giving commands from the mouse or keyboard. Other systems like **Dragon Naturally Speaking** have excellent algorithms and transcribe dictation rapidly with good accuracy. Systems of this type are commonly used for medical record keeping and court reporting.

3.3.4 Output

The three most common computer output devices are monitors, printers, and speakers.

3.3.4.1 Monitor

A monitor is the device that displays data on its screen—it displays signals generated by a computer as images on a screen. An image is made up of numerous dots, called **pixels,** so you want a monitor that can pack as many pixels onto the screen as possible! This device, which operates like a TV set, lets the user see how the computer is responding to their commands.

Older monitors (also known as **CRTs**) were based on cathode ray technology but most monitors today use **LCD** (Liquid Crystal Display) technology and are known as flat panel displays.

An Image Is Composed of Pixels

Monitors are used to view your data on a computer. The characteristics of a monitor are important for a system's performance since the quality of the video display will significantly affect the user's computing experience. Some of the more important specifications on the monitor are:

- **Screen size**—Expressed in inches, it is the size of the image measured diagonally from the lower left to the upper right corners.
- **Pixel spacing**—Expressed in **dot pitch** or known as **dots per inch.** This describes how close the pixels are spaced apart in the screen. Smaller is better.
- **Resolution**—It is the number of individual pixels contained on a display and it is expressed as the ratio of pixels on the horizontal axis to the number on the vertical axis. Currently, 1280 by 800 is the ratio supported by new monitors. If the past is a guide, that ratio will improve over the next years.
- **Refresh rate**—The frequency with which the monitor's display is refreshed or completely redrawn.
- **Color depth**—The array of colors that a monitor can display. A **24 bit** color monitor can display over 16 million distinct colors.

Graphics Card A graphics card takes data from the CPU and turns it into images displayed on the monitor. The CPU generates a binary stream of bits that are converted by the graphics card into a video signal that can be viewed on a monitor. The card accepts the CPU's bits and decides how to use the pixels on the screen to create the image. It then sends that information to the monitor through a cable.

The graphics card adapts the computer's signal for display in conjunction with the particular display hardware that is connected to the computer. The card must be compatible with the display type.

- **VGA**—Video Graphics Array is an analog computer display standard. It has been technologically outdated for some time due to its relatively low resolution (640 × 480 pixels).
- **SVGA**—Super Video Graphics Array was an extension to VGA. Originally it mandated 800 × 600 4-bit pixels allowing each pixel to be any of 16 different colors. It has been extended to 1024 × 768 8-bit pixels (256 colors) and beyond.

- **Widescreen**—Widescreen adapters allow a wider **aspect ratio** (width to height) than the standard monitor (4:3). Widescreen aspect ratios are in the range of about 16:9 allowing a wider display surface. Almost all new laptops sold today have widescreen displays. Apart from the aspect ratio, the technology for producing images remains the same. Note: The concept of aspect ratio applies to images as well. As an image is resized the aspect ratio must be retained to ensure no distortion of the image.

3.3.4.2 Printer

This is the device that puts data or information on paper. Printers are much less expensive than ever before. And that includes color printers, too. There are two fundamental styles of printers: **impact** and **non-impact.** An impact printer pushes pins into a ribbon and then the paper to create an image. Each pin displays a "dot" of ink on the paper. The arrangement of the dots (similar to pixels) creates the image that you see. These printers are louder than non-impact printers, but are required when you want to print on multipart forms. A non-impact printer, like a **laser or ink-jet,** can produce a much finer image. Color lasers are more expensive, but color ink-jets can be purchased for less than $100.

Laser printers use technology virtually the same as that of copier machines. As ink is sprayed onto the page it is guided by an electro-magnetic force. Ink-jet printers use a series of nozzles to spray small droplets of ink onto the page.

Two measures of the printer's performance are important:

- **DPI**—Printed pages are produced in a way similar to images displayed on a monitor. The page is comprised of thousands of dots, and more is better. When you review printer advertising look for the number of dots per inch (DPI) the printer places on the paper,.
- **PPM** (pages per minute)—this indicates how many pages a printer is able to produce each minute. Since not all pages are equally dense this is an average estimate.

Several types of printers are in common use. Other older types may still be found in use. Here several printer types are described:

- **Laser printer**—Laser printers are more common now than in the past since prices have dropped over the last several years. Originally black and white only, color laser printers are becoming more available. They produce high quality text and graphics on plain paper. Like photocopiers, laser printers employ a xerographic printing process in which the image is produced by the direct scanning of a laser beam across the printer's drum. The drum charge attracts ink that is directed to specific locations by the electrostatic charge of the latent image on the drum surface. Laser printers are fast and quiet.

  Color laser printers add colored toner (usually cyan, yellow, and magenta).

Laser Printer
© Wojcik Jaroslaw, 2007, Shutterstock.

- **Ink-jet printer**—Ink-jet printers operate by propelling tiny droplets of liquid ink onto paper. They are the most common type of computer printer for the general consumer due to their low cost, high quality of output, capability of printing in vivid color, and ease of use.

  When compared to earlier consumer-oriented printers, ink-jets have a number of advantages. They are quieter in operation than impact printers: dot matrix or daisy-wheel. They can print finer, smoother details through higher print head resolution, and many ink-jets with photorealistic-quality color printing are widely available. Ink-jet printers require two or more ink sources. One container always holds black ink, and the color ink is stored in one or several other containers.

  The most common criticisms of ink-jet printers are:

  - **Clogging of the print head**—This happens as a result of the printer not being used for a period.
  - **High cost of the ink**—This is especially true when all color inks are contained in the same dispenser, so if blue is dry the other colors must be replaced anyway at additional expense.

Ink-Jet Printer
© Wayne James, 2007, Shutterstock.

- **Dot-Matrix printer**—A dot matrix printer or impact matrix printer refers to a type of printer with a print head that runs back and forth on the page and prints by impact. It operates much like a typewriter by striking an ink-soaked cloth ribbon against the paper. Letters are drawn out of a dot matrix, and thus, varied fonts and some graphics can be produced. Since printing involves mechanical pressure, dot-matrix printers can create carbon copies.

These machines are relatively noisy because of the mechanical movement and used mostly where multiple copies are required.

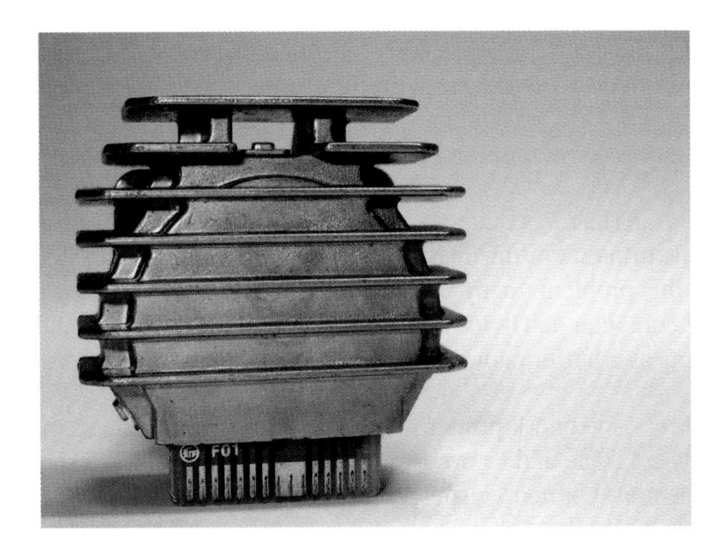

Dot-Matrix Printhead
© Egidijus Mika, 2007, Shutterstock.

- **Photo printer**—A photo printer is a printer (usually an ink-jet printer) that is specifically designed to print high quality digital photos on special photographic quality paper. These printers usually have a very high number of nozzles and are capable of printing very small droplets. Good quality photo printers may have more than the standard three-color ink sources.

Photo Printer
© rixxo, 2007, Shutterstock.

- **Thermal printer**—A thermal printer produces a printed image by selectively heating coated heat-sensitive paper or thermal paper as the paper passes over the thermal print head. The coating turns black in the areas where it is heated, producing an image or characters. Two-color direct thermal printers are capable of printing both black and an additional color (most often red), by applying heat at two different temperatures.

Thermal printers are in use where customer receipts are required for transactions based on automated machines like ATM and gasoline dispensers. Some FAX machines print using a thermal process.

Printer Duty Cycle The maximum usage level per month for a printer is considered to be the duty cycle. This rating takes into account printer specifics such as the paper-handling capacity and cartridge replacement. Running a printer at the top end of its duty cycle will require users to intervene with the printer to replace supplies more often. Choose a printer with a duty cycle that exceeds your production needs by a substantial margin to minimize interventions and maximize printer life expectancy.

Printer Memory Printers operate slower than a computer does as it sends documents and images to the printer. For this reason the actions of a printer can slow down a computer. To avoid this problem, many printers may have built-in memory that accepts the stream from the computer and holds it temporarily until the print mechanism catches up. This memory acts as a buffer between the computer and the printing process.

Network Printer A network printer is not a special type of printer but it is a printer attached to a network. One of the purposes of networking is to share resources, and printers are one of the most common resources shared.

3.3.4.3 Plotter

Plotters print their output by moving a pen across the surface of a piece of paper. Because of using a pen, plotters are restricted to line art. They can draw complex line art, including text, but do it very slowly because of the mechanical movement of the pens. Plotters cannot create a solid region of color, but can draw close regular hatch lines to define an area.

Plotters may use paper supplied on long roles which allow very long images (measured in feet or yards) to be produced.

3.3.4.4 Speaker

Originally an after-thought, the computer's speaker (or speaker system) has become an important output component. The first speakers made simple noises like squeaks, beeps, and squeals. Today computers come with stereo speaker systems that in some cases rival stand alone music boxes. Computers usually also have an output jack allowing users to attach headphones to the computer.

3.3.4.5 All-in-One

An MFP (Multi-Function Peripheral) is an office machine which incorporates the functionality of several devices in one, allowing a smaller footprint in a home or office. The most common MFP combination includes these devices:

- Printer
- Scanner
- Photocopier

No multi-functional machine can be optimized for all functions that it performs. If high-quality printing or scanning is desired a dedicated machine should be considered.

3.3.5 Storage

Computer storage, or computer memory, refers to computer components, devices, and recording media that retain data or programs for some interval of time (short or long term). Data and program retention is one of the key functions of the modern computer.

Computer memory refers to temporary (but fast) storage known as **primary memory** and permanent storage known as **secondary storage.** The former uses chip technology (integrated circuits) and is known as random access memory (RAM). Secondary storage is based on mechanical or electronic devices and is known as disk, flash memory, CDs, or DVDs, and other devices. Primary memory is faster than secondary memory.

3.3.5.1 Primary Memory

A computer's RAM is considered main memory (or primary storage): the working area used for loading, displaying, and manipulating programs and data. This memory is usually in the form of integrated circuits. These are commonly called memory sticks because they are manufactured as small circuit boards with plastic. Most computers have slots for adding and replacing memory chips.

RAM This type of storage is within the computer, closely connected to the processor. This is where programs are held while running. Data that is being processed may be held here, too. The name for primary storage is **RAM.** RAM is **volatile,** which means that when the computer's power is shut off any program or data within it is lost. When you develop a spreadsheet, or other document, make sure to save your work periodically, because if the computer accidentally loses power you will lose your work. For that reason it is important for the user to save work in progress on a secondary storage device. Note: It is typical of some operating systems to periodically save files automatically so that in case a failure occurs, the file may be presented to the user as a recovered file.

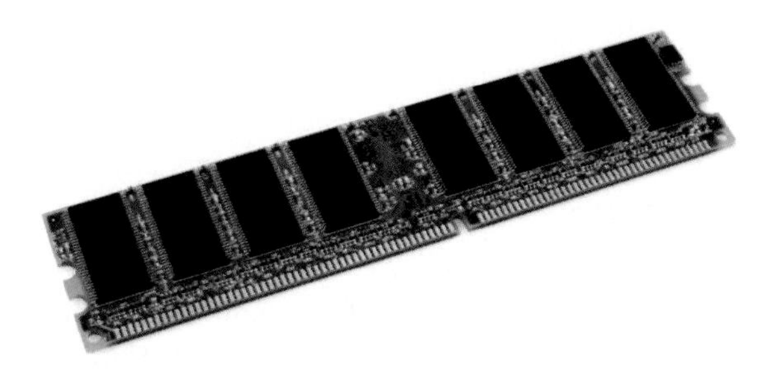

Random Access Memory (RAM)
© Wojcik Jaroslaw, 2007, Shutterstock.

Primary storage in new computers is usually measured in **gigabytes.** This is especially true of computers running Windows Vista operating system.

Computers use RAM to hold programs and associated data during computation. An important characteristic of RAM is that all memory locations can be accessed at almost the same speed (hence "random access"). Most other secondary storage technologies have inherent delays for reading data because they have moving parts or because they are physically farther from the processor.

Computer capacity is a measure of how many programs can be run at once, and how big the programs can be. The computer's capacity will also impact how fast programs can run. The capacity, or amount of memory, is commonly measured in **bytes.** The computer's storage capacity relates to two types of storage: primary and secondary. This table presents the common measures of computer memory. Recall that one byte is the equivalent of one character, letter, or digit:

Storage Capacity in Bytes

Name	Amount of Bytes
Kilobyte (KB)	1,000
Megabyte (MB)	1,000,000
Gigabyte (GB)	1,000,000,000
Terabyte (TB)	1,000,000,000,000

The numbers above are approximations. 1KB is actually 1024 bytes.

Memory Access Time Memory **latency** is the time between the processor initiating a request for a byte (eight bits) or word (usually 16 bits) in memory until it is retrieved. Latency is a fundamental measure of the speed of memory: less latency defines faster reading operations.

If the requested data is in the processor's **cache** (special high-speed memory) it is not necessary for the processor to communicate with RAM.

Memory Configuration Several configurations of RAM are commonly available:

- **DRAM**—Random access memory that stores each bit of data in a separate capacitor within an integrated circuit. Since real capacitors leak charge, the information eventually fades unless the capacitor charge is refreshed periodically. Because of this refresh requirement, it is a **dynamic** memory as opposed to SRAM and other static memory. Its advantage over SRAM is its architectural simplicity.
- **SDRAM**—Synchronous dynamic random access memory has an asynchronous interface which means that it reacts as quickly as possible to changes in control bus inputs. SDRAM waits for a clock signal before responding to its control inputs. It is synchronized with the computer's system bus and with the processor. Because of the asynchronous nature, SDRAM can be used in pipelining architectures.
- **DDR SDRAM**—Effectively it nearly doubles the transfer rate of SDRAM by transferring data on the leading and trailing edges of the clock signal in a process known as double pumping. Basically DDR SDRAM transfers twice the data per machine cycle and it does it more frequently. It takes advantage of the chips electronic cycles to move data two times in the same period while SDRAM moves it only once.
- **SRAM**—Static random access memory retains its contents as long as power remains applied, unlike DRAM that needs to be periodically refreshed. SRAM should not be confused with read-only memory and flash memory since it is **volatile** memory and preserves data only while power is continuously applied.

Memory Packaging RAM is packaged in many configurations with names like: **DIP** (dual inline packages), **SIMM** (single inline memory module), and **DIMM** (dual inline memory module). These names relate to the physical configuration of the chip and its packaging.

The main difference between SIMMs and DIMMs is that DIMMs have double the **data path** (the **bus**) meaning that a DIMM can transfer twice the amount of data in a single operation. DIMMs come in two configurations: **SDRAM** (dynamic random access memory) and **DDR SDRAM** (double-data-rate synchronous dynamic random access memory).

- **SIMM**—A single in-line memory module is a type of memory module that differs from a DIMM (the most predominant form of memory module today) in that the contacts on a SIMM are redundant on both sides of the module.
- **DIMM**—The main difference between SIMMs and DIMMs is that SIMMs have a 32-bit data path, while DIMMs have a 64-bit data path. Since Intel's Pentium has (as do several other processors) a 64-bit bus width, it requires SIMMs.

Memory cards are added to the computer by inserting the card into a slot on the motherboard as shown here:

Adding RAM to the Motherboard

Cache Memory Cache memory is special memory that operates much faster than RAM memory. It is impractical to use this memory for the entire system because it is relatively expensive. Cache memory is often between the microprocessor and RAM. There are some levels of cache memory that also reside within the microprocessor. Cache is used as a buffer to reduce the time of data transfer between the processor and devices like the monitor and storage devices.

Cache is used to store a copy of frequently required data. The original copy is in RAM, but if the processor requests data that happens to be also found in cache it will retrieve it faster.

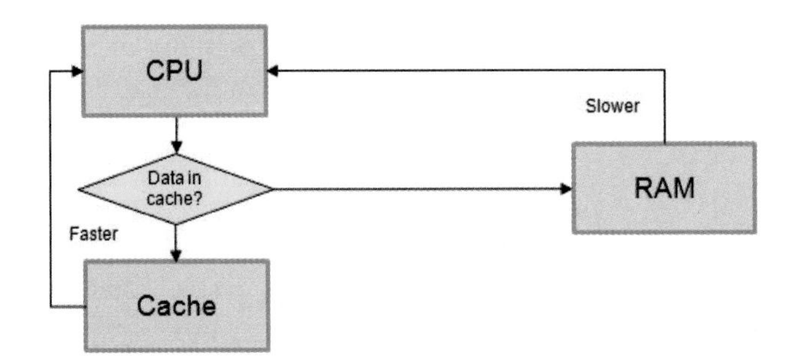

Cache Provides Data Faster than RAM

ROM Read-only memory cannot (easily) be written to, so its main uses lie in the distribution of **firmware** (software that is very closely related to hardware and not likely to need upgrading). Several variations of ROM are often found in computer systems.

- **PROM**—Programmable ROMs are used to store programs permanently. The key difference from a ROM is that the programming is applied after the device is constructed unlike a ROM in which programs are burned in during the manufacture process.
- **EEPROM**—Electrically Erasable Programmable ROM is a non-volatile storage used to store small amounts of data. Usually EEPROM is used to store system configuration data. When larger amounts of data are to be stored other memory types, like flash memory, are more economical.
- **BIOS**—The Basic Input/Output System is firmware code run by a computer when it is first powered on. The primary function of the BIOS is to prepare the machine so that the operating system can take over control of the hardware. This process is known as **booting** up.

CMOS Complementary metal–oxide–semiconductor is the technological base for many integrated circuits. It is used in RAM and processors. It has replaced earlier technologies including Transistor-Transistor Logic (TTL) because of these benefits:

- High immunity to circuit noise, thus high reliability.
- Low power consumption, thus easier on power supply.
- Less generation of heat.
- High density of logic functions per chip.

Virtual Memory Virtual memory is a memory management technique, used by **multitasking** computer operating systems like Windows. It is important because when several programs are running simultaneously (multitasking) they often require more RAM than is physically available in the computer. This technique allows the computer to pretend it has more real primary memory than it actually does. The computer's hard disk is used to swap running programs and their data in and out of RAM so fast the illusion of multitasking is maintained. Operating systems allow the user to control the amount of disk space allocated as virtual memory to support program swapping.

In this illustration when program 1 pauses the operating system moves it to disk and allows another program (in this case program 4) to have an opportunity to run for a little while. Later program 4 may be swapped with a program that is in virtual memory. Program 2 will eventually be swapped as well. This happens so frequently and so fast that computer users never know that it is occurring. A computer's processor can actually only run one program at any specific time so this technique really does create the illusion of multitasking.

Virtual Memory

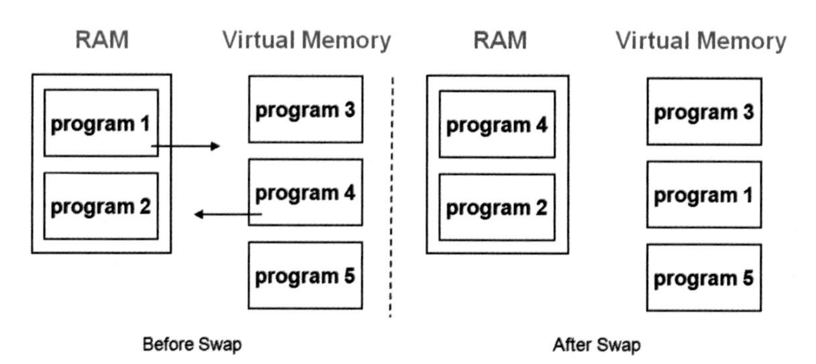

Memory at the Speed of Light Intel has experimented with the use of laser light to move data between devices inside the computer. Their experimentation has proven successful so far. Removing wires from inside chips would allow more components to be packaged in the same space. If their technology can be commercialized then extremely fast memory (and processors) could be expected in the future.

Future Memory Architecture The electronic switches that hold and manipulate the binary 1s and 0s are very small. Nevertheless they each contain billions of atoms. Scientists are experimenting with **quantum computing** which uses individual atoms to hold a value of one or zero. The obvious implication of such an achievement is the potential for extremely small computer processors or extremely powerful processors of current size. The binary value 1 or 0 is based on the atom's spin. A related variation on this concept is known as **nanotechnology.**

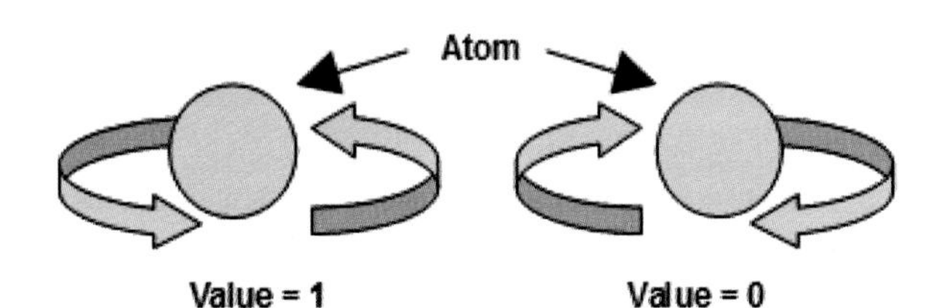

Quantum Computing

- **Nanotechnology**—Engineering of functional systems at the molecular scale. This applies to memory and processors. Nanotechnology involves the manufacture of components at the nanometer scale, i.e. one billionth of a meter.
- **Quantum computing**—The basic principle is that the quantum properties (such as atomic spin) of particles can be used to represent and structure data.
- **Optical computing**—An optical computer uses light instead of electricity to manipulate, store and transmit data.

3.3.5.2 Secondary Storage

Secondary storage is **non-volatile.** This means that it holds data and programs even when there is no power in the computer. The most common kind of secondary storage is a hard disk. Other examples of **persistent** storage include floppy disks, CD-ROMs, DVDs, and flash memory (often known as jump drives).

Hard Disk Hard disks are built into the computer's cabinet or in external units, usually have a very large capacity, and are fast. These days, the storage capacity on hard disks is measured in **gigabytes** (one GB is 1,000 megabytes or one billion bytes). That's a lot of storage, but in a few years it will seem like next to nothing. In fact, the next size up, 1,000 gigabytes, is called a **terabyte.** Today a new desktop computer may have a hard disk of several hundred GB and a laptop computer would have somewhat less.

Hard drives consist of a series of round rotating metal plates called platters. They are coated with an electromagnetic material which can be electrically altered allowing the binary digits 1 and 0 to be recorded on the surface. Different areas of the surface move under the **read/write head** allowing data to be stored over all portions of the surface as the platter rotates. Data is written to the disk at high speed (a hard disk may spin at 7,200 rpm). The read/write head flies very close over the magnetic surface, often as close as the diameter of a single strand of cigarette smoke.

Hard Disk Rotating under Read/Write Head

Each platter has data stored on it in a specific pattern for read and write access. The data is organized into concentric rings around the platter known as **tracks.** The distance the head moves into the platter will determine which track is read. A **sector** is a pie-shaped section of the platter. The intersection of a track and sector is a **block.**

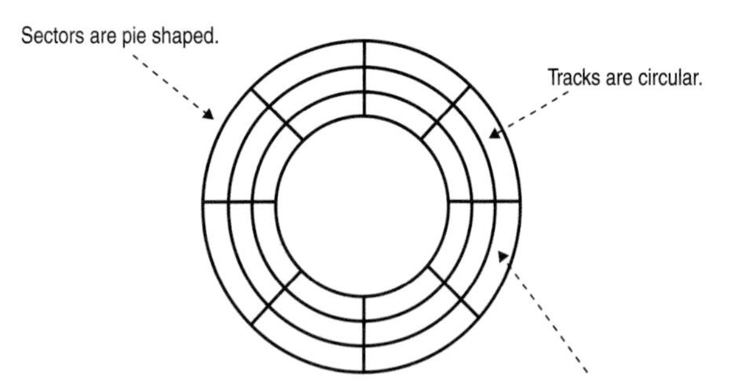
Sectors are pie shaped.
Tracks are circular.
The intersection of a track and sector is a block.

A Disk Surface

Hard disks provide **random access** to data. This means that any data (file, document, image, video) stored anywhere on the disk may be retrieved when requested by the processor. There are three ways to measure the performance of a hard disk:

- **Data transfer rate**—The number of bytes per second that the drive can deliver to the CPU.
- **Seek time**—The time is the amount of time between when the CPU requests a file and when the first byte of the file is sent to the CPU.
- **Latency time**—The average delay until a desired sector rotates to under the read/write head.

Disk Organization Content stored on a disk is arranged in a **hierarchical** collection of **folders.** The first folder encountered when a disk is examined is the **root** folder. Each folder may hold additional folders or files as shown here.

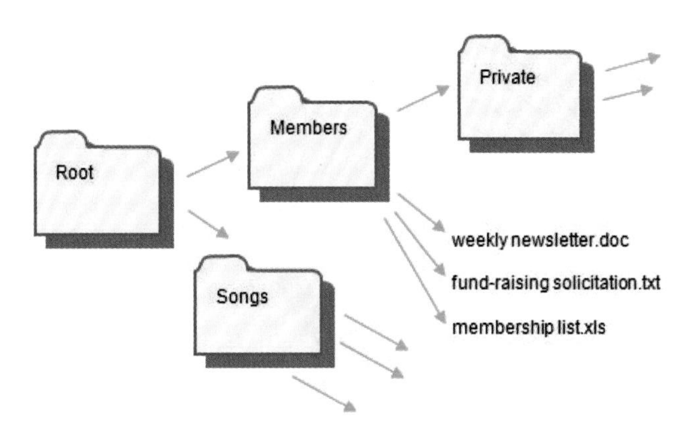

Disk Content Is Arranged Hierarchically in Folders

Navigation through a disk begins with the root folder and progresses until the desired content is located. Navigation is **logical** and not **physical.** This is because the actual (physical) location of a file on a disk is really of no concern to the user. The operating system stores files where it finds available space and not in a specific sequential order. To allow the user to navigate the operating system's file system maintains a directory that links logical content (folders) to the physical locations of files on the disk. This linkage is known as **mapping.**

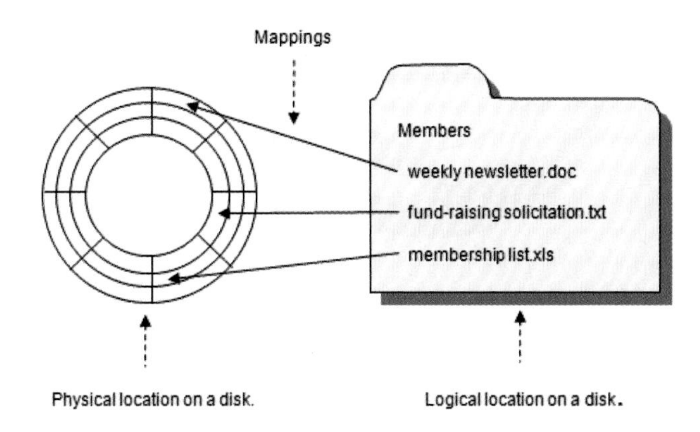

Disk Mapping

Disk Fragmentation As the disk fills with data, performance may suffer. When a file is saved to the hard drive, the operating system tries to keep everything in the same area (or cluster). Over time files will be deleted, leaving blank areas between files. When new programs are installed or large files saved, the hard drive tries to fill the holes thus breaking up the program or file into blocks. This situation is known as **disk fragmentation** and can cause serious performance degradation.

To understand how a disk gets fragmented and understand why it can harm your computer's performance you must understand how a disk is structured. Hard disks, CDs, and floppy disks are round and rotate. All rotating secondary storage defines sectors and tracks which intersect in blocks.

When a file (or document) is placed in secondary storage it fits in one block or, if it is too large for one block, it spreads over several blocks. No block ever contains parts of more than one file. It is desirable for files to be stored in **contiguous blocks** because the entire file can be accessed fastest that way. Suppose the first file stored on an otherwise empty disk requires four blocks of space. After that file is stored the disk would look as shown here:

A File Is Stored on the Disk

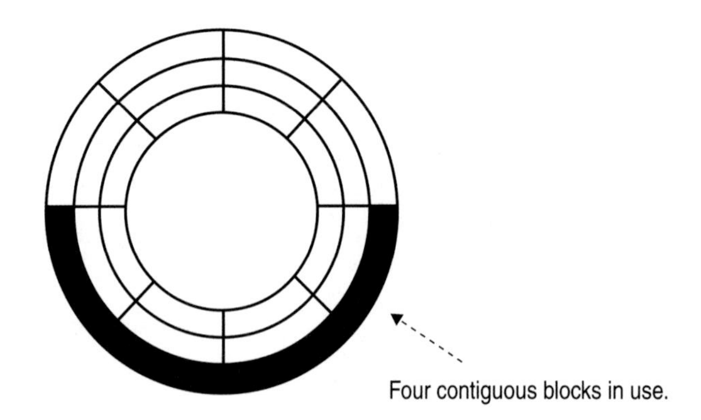

As the disk fills up, fewer contiguous blocks of free disk space remain. As the disk fragments it becomes increasingly hard for the operating system to find open space for file storage.

A Fragmented Disk

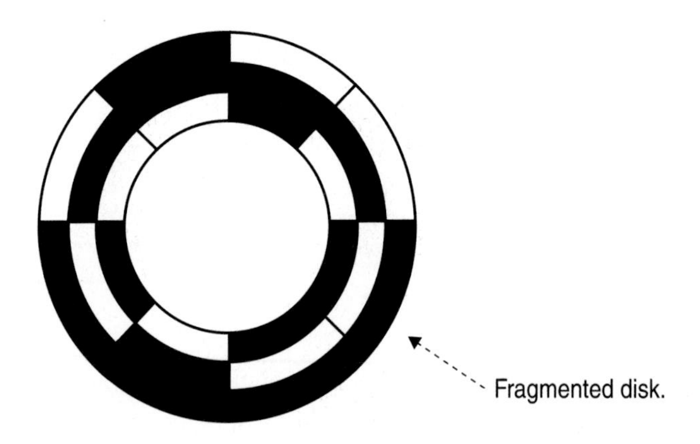

The solution to this problem is to **defragment** the disk. Windows includes a program called **Disk Defragmenter** which scans the entire disk drive and looks for segments of unused disk area. The segments are consolidated resulting in larger areas of contiguous space for the storage of larger files. Regular use of this program will help keep a computer running more efficiently and may prevent unexpected loss of data. It will also help the computer find files and documents faster.

Another disk performance factor that is worth considering is reliability. This is expressed as mean time between failures (MTBF). The higher the number, the better.

Deleting All Files from a Hard Disk Sometimes it is desirable to delete all files from a disk. Often this is done when a previously used computer is sold or given away so that the new owner will not have access to the original user's data. Unfortunately most people believe that simply using Windows Explorer or Vista's Computer (or an equivalent program) to delete files and/or folders will do the job. This is not the case. This problem is relevant to people who sell, donate, or even throw away computers.

Explorer and Computer allow the user to manipulate entries in the disk's **directory** but do not actually allow the user to manipulate files directly. The directory is a logical list of folders and files on the disk with mapping references to the specific physical location of each file. Deleting a file does not remove the file's data from the storage device. Only the directory entry is removed.

For example, when a file is deleted it is moved to the Recycling Bin. What actually happens is that the directory entry for the file is altered to indicate that the file is now in the Recycling Bin folder. The actual physical location of the file is not changed. If the user empties the Recycling Bin the directory entries of all affected files are deleted but the files actually remain on the disk right where they were. The disk space used by the deleted file may now be re-used, but until it is re-used, a sophisticated user running a special program would be able to recover and view the "erased" data!

The solution to this problem is to use a **scrubber.** This special program overwrites each bit of data with a zero. For most users this is sufficient. For the United States Defense Department a more thorough cleansing is demanded. The DOD requires three separate overwrites, first zeros, next ones, finally a random zero or one. After scrubbing, the data truly is gone.

Floppy Disk A floppy disk is similar to a hard disk in that it stores data on a surface that rotates. Unlike the hard disk the platter is a flexible circular piece of metal-coated plastic. Floppy disks are considerably slower than hard disks and have limited storage capacity (1.44MB).

The main appeal of floppy disks was their portability. They were typically used to copy data or programs from one computer to another. Floppy disks were commonly used for file backup. Today floppy disks have largely been replaced by flash memory which offers portability with considerably greater storage capacity.

Flash Memory Flash, or solid state, memory is attractive because it is non-volatile, offers fast read access times (though not as fast as volatile RAM memory used for primary memory), has large data storage capacity (several GB is common), and has better shock resistance than hard disks. Flash memory is packaged in small portable units known as flash or jump drives which connect to the computer's USB port.

Although flash memory is **solid state** (an integrated circuit) and not rotational like a disk, the operating system and the flash hardware work together as if the memory were divided into track, sectors, and blocks. The flash drive is accessed by the user as if it were any **mass storage** device. Unlike a hard drive, which requires a hardware controller to operate, flash memory requires a device driver, software that allows the operating system to access the memory without consideration to its physical construction.

Flash Memory Packaged as a USB Drive
© u-nat, 2007, Shutterstock.

A flash drive consists of a circuit board encased in a plastic or metal casing, making the drive robust enough to be carried about in a pocket or on a lanyard. Only the USB connector extends from this protection, and is usually covered by a removable cap.

Flash Memory for a Digital Camera
© emin kuliyev, 2007, Shutterstock.

RAID Redundant Array of Independent Disks (RAID) is a technique that divides or replicates data among multiple hard drives. Its benefits are increased data reliability (redundant storage) and throughput (allocation of data to separate devices). RAID is often found in **fault tolerant** computer systems where redundant data storage reduces the likelihood of data loss.

Disk Mirroring Disk mirroring is a technique that involves the replication of logical disk volumes (folder structures) onto separate hard disks in real time to ensure continuous availability of data. A mirrored volume is a complete copy of a logical disk volume. In the event of a disaster, disk mirroring can assist with recovery since the backup is a current and exact replication of the original that was lost. Mirroring is a function of the operating system and requires no manual intervention.

In a disaster recovery plan, disk mirroring can be arranged so that the mirror copy is in a different location, often at a substantial distance. Since the likelihood of disaster striking simultaneously at two distant locations is low this method provides a good level of data security.

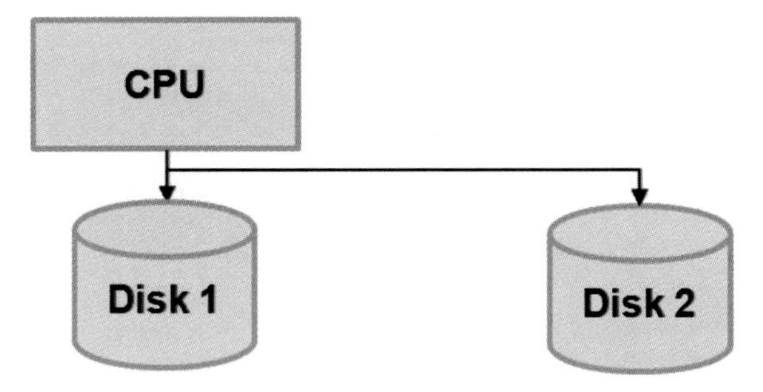

Disk Mirroring

CD-ROM and DVD The CD-ROM is an **optical** storage device that contains data accessible by a computer using a CD-Rom Drive. The compact disc format was originally designed for music storage and playback but the format was later adapted to hold any form of binary data. CD-ROMs are often used to distribute computer software, though any data can be stored on it. Unlike the hard disk which is magnetic, data is stored on the CD-ROM as a series of microscopic indentations called **pits** and the gaps between them called **lands.** A laser shines on the reflective surface of the disc to read the pattern of pits and lands. The pattern of the changing light intensity of the reflected beam is converted into binary data.

The storage capacity of most CD-ROMs is about 650MB of data. Originally CD-ROMs were read only devices (that is why they were called ROMs), but read/write technology has developed. The primary performance concern of CD-ROM drives is their speed. Speeds are expressed in terms of 1X, 2X, 4X, which is the number of times the drive is faster than the original CD-ROM reader.

CD-Recordable drives are usually sold with three different speed ratings, one for write-once operations, one for re-write operations, and one for read-only operations. The speeds are typically listed in that order.

DVD (Digital Versatile Disc) is also an optical rotational storage media format that can be used for storage of any type of data. DVDs appear similar to CDs because their physical dimensions are the same but they are encoded differently and at a much higher data storage density. DVDs offer considerably more storage capacity than CDs (4-5GB is common) but access speed is an issue as it is with CDs. Like CDs, DVDs can be used as rewriteable memory.

Several types of optical storage formats include:

- **CD-R**—Compact Disc-Recordable is a Write Once, Read Many (**WORM**) optical media which refers to a kind of computer storage media that can be written to once, but read from multiple times.
- **DVD-R**—Similar to CD-R but uses DVD technology and has higher capacity.
- **DVD+R**—Also DVD technology and similar to CD-R but not compatible with DVD-R.
- **CD-RW**—Compact Disc ReWritable is a rewritable optical disc CD format that is also known as CD-Erasable (CD-E).
- **DVD-RW**—A rewritable optical disc using DVD technology with equal storage capacity as a DVD-R.
- **DVD+RW**—Similar to, but not compatible with, DVD-RW.

Zip Disk Zip disks are a removable cartridge storage device that may be generally used to store compressed data. A zip drive has at least 100MB of storage capacity although its physical size is close to that of a floppy disk. A zip drive has considerable more tracks than a floppy (thousands compared to about 270) which results in greater storage capacity and faster access.

Magnetic Tape A tape drive is a data storage device that reads and writes data stored on a magnetic tape. Tape is generally used for archival storage of data stored on hard drives, and tape media generally has a lower cost per byte stored and offers longer archival stability.

Tape drives only allow for **sequential-access** of data and not random-access to data as hard disk drives do. A hard-disk drive can move its read/write head to any random part of the disk platters in a short amount of time while a tape drive spends considerable time rolling tape back and forth between reels to locate particular data. Tape drives, therefore, have slow average seek times. Despite this disadvantage, tape drives can **stream** data to tape very quickly.

Magnetic Tape

3.3.6 Communication Devices

Early computers were said to be stand-alone units because they were not connected to other computers and usually had no need for sharing data. The opposite is true today as almost all computers are connected to the Internet. Connectivity requires that a computer's digital signals be translated into signals that are carried by a communication network. This is usually the task of a modem. Several communication components are described here. A thorough discussion of communication and networking equipment is found in another chapter.

Modem A modem is a device that **modulates** a carrier's signal to encode a computer's digital data, and later **demodulates** the signal to decode the data at the receiving end. The purpose is to produce a signal that can be transmitted easily and decoded to reproduce the original digital data. Modems are rated by the amount of data they can send in a given time, measured in **bits per second,** or **bps.**

Historically the most common example of a modem turns the computer's digital 1s and 0s into sounds that can be transmitted over **analog** telephone lines. The process is reversed at the receiving end as **digital** signals are detected in the sounds as they are received. Modems of this type generally run up to 56Kbps (56,000 bits per second). In reality, this is a theoretical limit and a 56 kbps modem will not be able to transmit at this rate.

Modem with Phone In/Out Ports

Today newer modems are commonplace because the local communication backbone for computer transmission has shifted from **dial-up** to **cable** and **DSL** carriers.

Cable modems are designed to deliver **broadband** Internet access by modulating a data signal over the cable television system's infrastructure. Like DSL modems, cable modems are capable of transmitting 256Kbps or more—in fact much more.

Broadband is a high data-transmission rate, Internet connection.

Digital Subscriber Line (DSL) a technology that provides high-speed digital data transmission over the wires of the local telephone network which is known as the **local loop.** Computer signals are modulated and transmitted over the local network where they are delivered to high-speed Internet carriers. Use of this technology permits simultaneous use of a telephone line for phone calls and data transmission. Generally DSL service is not as fast as cable-based communication which relies on the television system for transmission.

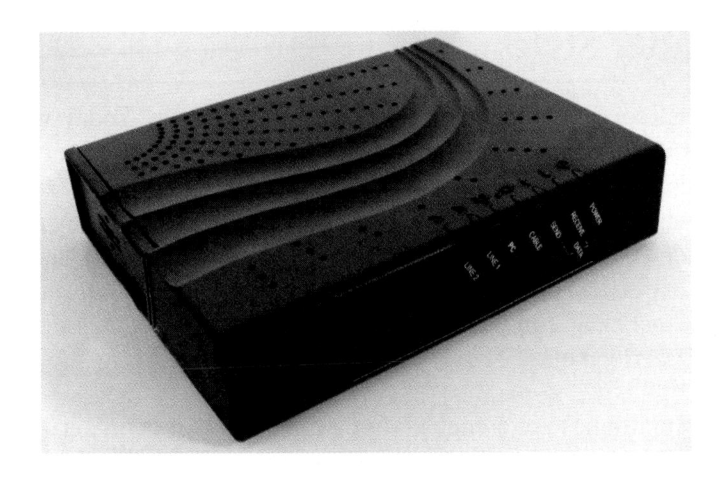

A Cable Modem
© Cristi Matei, 2007, Shutterstock.

The signal delivered to the computer from the cable or DSL modem enters the computer through a network adaptor. Today virtually all new computers have the adaptor built in. In fact, the same adaptor can accept a signal from either type of modem.

Wireless A variation on the delivery mechanism between the modem and the computer is to use a wireless system to transmit the modem's signal to the computer which has a receiver. The modem is connected to a device known as a **wireless router** which attaches the data signal to a radio-based carrier signal for transmission to computers in the local vicinity. The router is known as an **access point** (AP). This arrangement, also known as **Wi-Fi,** provides a signal to any computer within range to receive it.

Such open signals can present a security risk for these reasons:

- **Intercepted data**—Data transmitted "over the air" can be intercepted.
- **Security breach**—Intrusions into the computer system are possible.
- **Unauthorized use**—Illegitimate use of the wireless router can slow down the transmission rates of legitimate users.

For these reasons it is best to **encrypt** wireless signals. Encryption involves disguising the bytes being transmitted so that an intruder is unable to read the bytes and to understand their content.

Wireless Router

3.4 Computer Styles

There are several configurations that computers are found in. Today we are most familiar with personal computers, but there are **mainframes** and **super computers** as well. Personal computers, generally used by one person at a time, are available in **desktop** and **laptop** models. Mainframe computers, used typically by many people simultaneously, provide the processing power required by large organizations. Super computers are extremely powerful and expensive machines and are used for special proposes. Since personal computers are generally understood, mainframe and super computers are described here.

Mainframe Mainframes are computers used mainly by large organizations like government agencies, large companies, universities, the military, and research laboratories for **mission critical** requirements. Typically these machines are used for bulk data processing activities like census tabulation, preparation of customer statements, and maintenance of student information systems, human resource record keeping and inventory management.

The term mainframe originated during the 1960s to contrast with the newly introduced smaller computers which became known as minicomputers. As previously noted, mainframes and minicomputers generally shared the same technology but were packaged differently.

Mainframes have proven powerful and robust over the years. In fact, most mainframes operate continuously and maintenance is performed while the machines remain in operation. Dependability is a hallmark of these computers—since they are used for support of critical applications, downtime could be catastrophic. Reports of intrusive attacks against mainframes are rare even though they often support thousands of simultaneous users.

Mainframe Computer

Super Computer A super computer is a machine that processes data exceptionally fast. Super computers are used for calculation-intensive tasks such as economic and weather **forecasting,** climate research, molecular modeling, **simulations** of physical events (like nuclear fusion experimentation and airplane wind tunnel tests), and computer-based cryptography. Major universities, military agencies, and scientific research laboratories are heavy users and may share super computers due to the high expense. Super computers are typically one-of-a-kind custom designs and often become outdated as newer and faster technology is developed.

Super Computer

3.5 Moore's Law

Moore's Law is based on the empirical observation made in 1965 by Gordon E. Moore, a co-founder of Intel, that the number of transistors on an integrated circuit for a given cost doubles every 24 months. Moore's Law relates to the rapidly continuing advance in computing power per unit cost, because increase in transistor count is also a surrogate measure of computer processing power.

The implication of Moore's Law for computer component suppliers is significant. A typical major design project (such as a new CPU) takes between two and five years to reach production. Consequently, component manufacturers face timescale pressures to complete projects and get new products into production quickly and achieve sales.

The law also has an impact on information system developers. System development projects take a long time (usually years) and the price of computer processing power will fall between the beginning and end of a project. This is because the **price/performance ratio** of a product, which refers to a product's ability to deliver performance for its price, changes over time. This means that one dollar spent 24 months from now will buy twice the processing power than if spent today. Knowing this, a project director should attempt to defer purchase of hardware until it is absolutely needed and not early in a project.

3.6 Source Data Automation

Did you ever use an ATM (automatic teller machine), vote at the ballpark for the major league all-star team, register for college courses by telephone, pay at the store with a bank card, or have items you wish to purchase scanned at the checkout line? If you did, then you have experienced source data automation. Simply put, it is the use of special equipment to collect data at the source and send it directly to the computer for processing.

Why is this important? Well, think about it. If your data is directly collected and sent to the computer then:

- It will get there **faster.**
- May have **fewer errors** because it does not have to be entered by an intermediary (like a bank teller).
- Will be **less expensive** (because there are no intermediaries to hire).

There are many uses for source data automation. Look around, you will surely think of others!

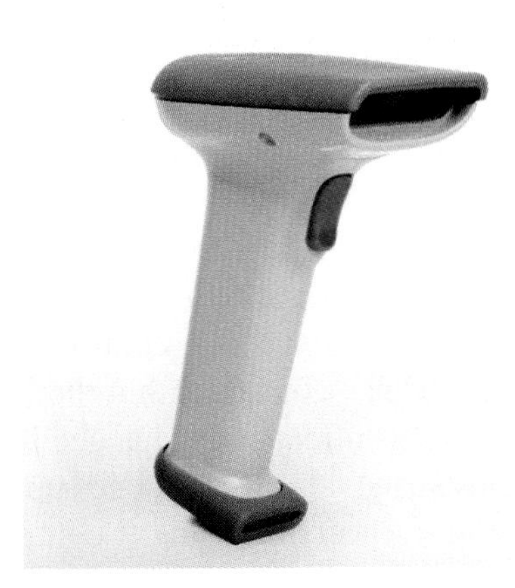

Source Data Automation
© Dino Ablakovic, 2007, Shutterstock.
© Slawomir Fajer, 2007, Shutterstock.

3.7 Recycling Hardware

When hardware ceases to operate properly or when it ceases to meet your requirements, it may be disposed of in several ways.

Donating a Computer Organizations exist that reuse old hardware and distribute the resulting systems to those who would benefit even from an older computer. Since discarding old electronic equipment in landfills or incineration not only wastes valuable resources, but also releases potentially hazardous materials into the environment, donation should be considered. Prior to donating a computer, be sure that any personal or private data on the hard drive is permanently erased. A scrubber program should be used for that purpose.

If donation is not possible or if the equipment is beyond continued use, some companies also recycle hardware, such as discarded printers. However, unlike toner cartridge recycling, these can involve a cost to the consumer for shipping and handling.

Toner Cartridges Toner cartridges have a life span limited by the volume of toner they contain, and toner cartridge manufacturers design the components of their products to be able to function throughout this life span. When the toner supply is exhausted recycling is an option. All the major manufacturers of toner cartridges offer some way to recycle their cartridges, usually in the form of a prepaid mailer that comes with the cartridge.

3.8 Summary

Hardware is the physical part of a computer system. It includes the electronic circuitry, input and output devices, data and program storage devices, memory for program execution, communication equipment, and, most important of all, the processor that performs calculations and controls all equipment. It is distinguished from software programs that execute within the hardware as data is processed. A computer system's hardware is infrequently changed in contrast to software as new programs are more frequently installed and older ones updated.

Data processing using a computer follows the Input-Process-Output model. The computer's input (keyboard, mouse, etc.) and output hardware (monitor, printer, etc.) support the activities of the model. As data is processed it may be necessary to store (for later use) or retrieve additional data. Data storage is provided by persistent memory devices (hard disks, CD/DVD-ROMS, and jump drives). During the data processing activity programs are loaded into RAM (volatile memory) for execution. To assist with speeding up processing, a computer system employs special high-speed cache memory.

While electronic computers are a relatively new invention, a long history of research and development preceded their introduction around the time of World War II. Early mechanical attempts were remarkable in their time but hampered by reliance on a decimal scheme for coding data and program instructions. Electronic computers are binary machines, and data representation, using schemes like ASCII, greatly simplified and promoted interoperability among products of different vendors.

EXERCISES

Exercise 3.1

Write a description for these concepts and components:

- IPO Model
- CPU
- Transistor
- Integrated Circuit
- ASCII
- Motherboard
- BIOS
- Port
- Primary Memory
- Secondary Memory
- Virtual Memory
- Mainframe
- Super Computer

Exercise 3.2

Your instructor will provide you with illustrations of computer hardware. Identify the components indicated.

Exercise 3.3

Identify and describe three each of:

- Input Devices
- Output Devices
- Storage Devices
- Bus

Exercise 3.4

Using the information provided in this chapter, what is the ASCII bit pattern and decimal equivalent for these characters? Assume the first bit for each character is a zero. The remaining seven bits are to be determined by you.

- &
-)
- 6
- b
- G
- g
- F

Exercise 3.5

What is the sequence of bits that represents **Good Morning!**? Assume that the first bit for each character is a zero. The remaining seven bits per byte should be determined by you. Provide a total of eight bits per character. You will need to consult a complete ASCII table to answer this question.

Exercise 3.6

Describe what disk fragmentation is and what to do about it.

Exercise 3.7

Some people prefer to use on-line storage services. Discuss why using on-line storage might be desirable and identify three such services.

Exercise 3.8

Considering the history of pre-electronic inventions that preceded the electronic computer, which do you believe contributed most significantly to the development of electronic data processing? Why?

Exercise 3.9

Not all computer users require the same CPU power or amount of RAM or secondary storage. How would you assess the hardware needs of a user?

Exercise 3.10

Considering secondary storage options available for data backup, what are the trade-offs between using different storage media?

Exercise 3.11

Considering the needs of the visually impaired, investigate hardware solutions available to assist such persons with computer usage.

Exercise 3.12

What are the advantages of using speech recognition software? Investigate speech recognition software and discuss challenges to be overcome if it is to be widely used.

Exercise 3.13

When purchasing new equipment at a retail store, a customer is usually offered an extended service contract for an additional charge. Determine the details of service contracts offered by two large retail vendors and compare the coverage provided as well as the cost.

SOFTWARE

CHAPTER 4

Software is one of three building blocks of an information system; hardware and the community of stakeholders are the other two. Each is important in its own right, and hardware and systems analysis are the subjects of other chapters. Here the topic is software which is defined as:

> ***Software*** *– Software is data and computer programs. It is not physical and cannot be directly seen. Computer programs execute within the hardware and enable a computer to perform specific tasks. Programs include* ***system software*** *such as an operating system, which enables other software to run properly and* ***application software*** *such as a word processor or database manager, which enables a user to perform a task.*

The differences between software and hardware seem straight forward, but can be confusing. Hardware is easier to understand than software. You see hardware and you see data on a computer screen, too, yet data is software. Hardware makes it possible to view data. In fact, without hardware you could not store data or computer programs.

This may help: you take notes in class and your notes are data. You use hardware (paper and pencil) to record and store your notes (data). To view your data (notes) you must take out your notebook (hardware). The same is true of computer-based data. Data (and programs) are stored on disks or on other storage devices. Disks are hardware not software.

4.1 Software

Software is **data** and it is also **programs** that enable a computer to perform specific tasks. It is not hardware which is the physical component of the computer system. Programs include **application software** such as a word processor, which enables a user to perform a task, and such as the **operating system** (known as system software), which enables other programs to run properly by interfacing the hardware, other software, and the computer user.

Charles Babbage proposed the idea of reading instructions into a machine's memory for the purpose of controlling computations. His plan for the Analytical Engine was to use punch cards as the source of program and data. While Babbage's ideas of the early 1800s could not be tested until the last century, they did prove valid and modern computing environments that process data are based on his conceptualization.

Before discussing what computer programs are and what they do, how they are written, and what programming languages are available, we will investigate the relationship between programs and three important partners: hardware, data, and users. The following illustration partitions the world of software to programs and data. The focus of this chapter is computer programs; data is the subject of another chapter. For the balance of this chapter the term software will refer to computer programs.

Software: Programs and Data

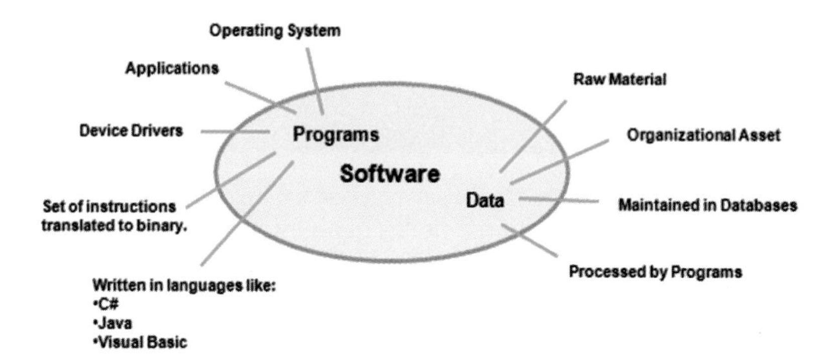

Software's Relationship to Hardware Computer software directs the actions of computer hardware. Software is loaded into memory (**RAM**) and executed in the central processing unit (**CPU**). The operating system determines when specific application programs are loaded for execution. Programs that require access to files on the disk drive communicate with the **file system** (system software) which retrieves or updates data. The file system communicates to storage device (hardware) through special system programs known as **device drivers.** When an application program wishes to print or perform other external functions, device drivers are activated by the operating system after the application program makes a request.

Software and Hardware

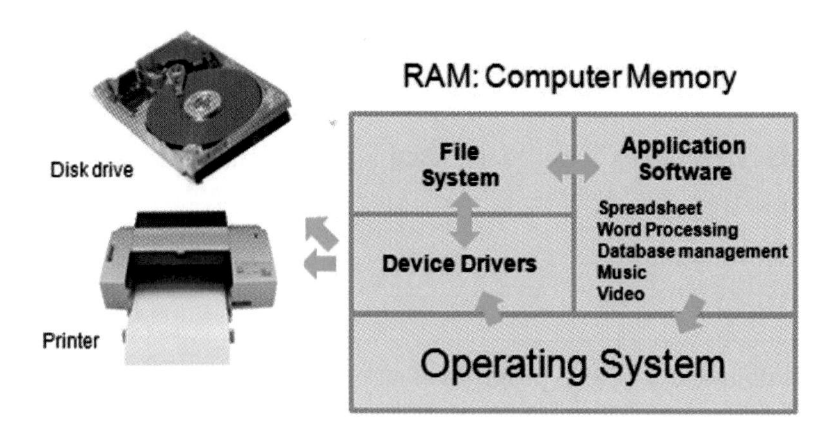

Software's Relationship to Data Software is the intermediary between electronic hardware and data, which hardware processes according to the sequence of instructions given in computer programs. Data is generally considered the input or output of executed software. Data is visually presented by hardware (monitor, printer, speaker, etc); it cannot be seen by itself.

Software's Relationship to Computer Programming Application software is usually written in **high-level** programming languages that are easier and more efficient for humans to use than the machine's native language. These high-level languages are translated into machine language. Software at its most basic level is a collection of binary digits (1 and 0) that are defined by the **machine language** specific to the individual processor. Machine language is defined groups of binary digits signifying processor instructions (**object code**), Software is an ordered sequence of instructions that change the state of the hardware.

Computer Programs

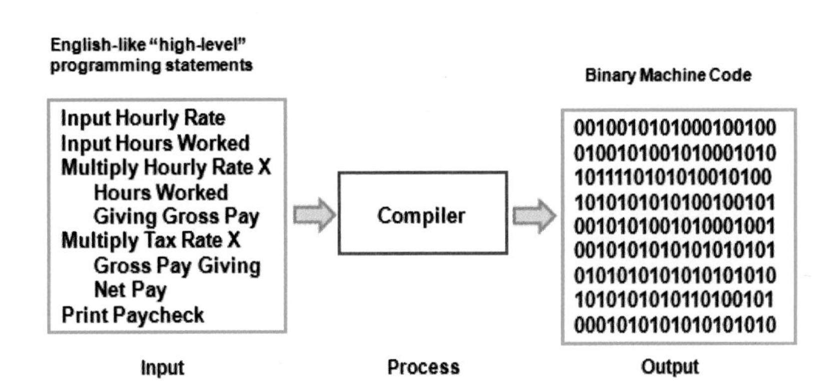

Software's Relationship to People Programs execute because users want them to. The operating system (**OS**), a program which allows the execution of programs, runs because a person has booted a computer. When the user, interacting with the operating system's interface, requests that a program be started, the OS responds by directing the hardware to fetch the program from storage (usually a disk) and load it into RAM. It is the user who initiates these activities.

Software's Relationships These relationships between software and its partners can be summarized as follows:

No computer could be useful without programs to give it commands. A computer cannot even run without a specific type of program called an operating system, or OS. This program is like the government in that it is in charge. Once the computer starts up, the OS tells each piece of hardware when it is allowed to act. The OS is also responsible for loading programs from disk into RAM for execution. The OS authorizes generation of the images seen on a monitor or printed on paper. Nothing happens without the approval of the OS.

The relationship between hardware, user, OS and other programs (**application programs**) is depicted in the figure below. As you can see neither the user nor the application software directly commands the hardware. Any command given by the user, such as requesting the display of a folder's content, printing a document, or updating a database, is intercepted by the OS which then constructs a formal command for the hardware to perform.

In a spreadsheet program like Excel, each time the mouse is moved making a new cell active the spreadsheet program asks the OS to command the hardware to allow the screen to be re-drawn showing the new active cell.

It all sounds pretty complicated, and it is, but it does work. There are a variety of very excellent technical reasons for this arrangement. The primary reason is that by allowing the OS to know how to command each hardware device the same knowledge is not needed redundantly in each application program. And besides, what user would want to memorize the binary commands required to get a disk folder listing?

Software's Relationships

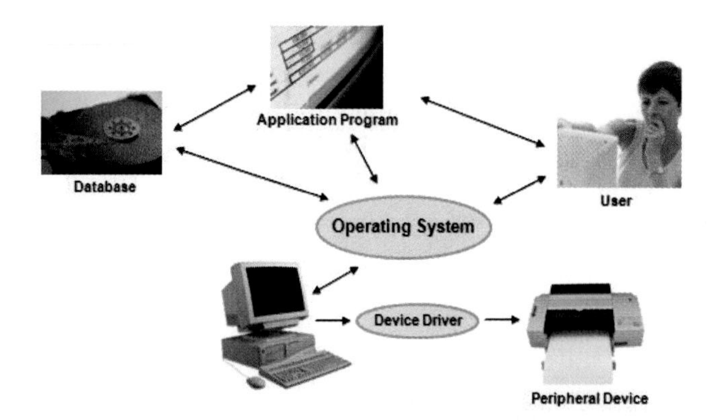

From our earlier discussion, recall that software is data and programs. Software is stored in files as a collection of bytes. Each file could be either a program or data. You probably know about data (images sound, etc.) which is why the focus of this chapter is on the other kind of software, computer programs. This chapter discusses operating systems and application programs followed by consideration of system architecture and design.

4.2 Software Milestones

Numerous events in the history of software are notable. The chronology below presents some of the highlights that are significant. Some events are about hardware, but in those cases the accomplishment presented allowed further advances in software development. Some dates are approximate.

1801	Jacquard used the holes punched in wooden cards to control the weaving of patterns in textiles.
1838	Samuel Morse invents a code (later called Morse code) that used different numbers to represent the letters of the English alphabet and numeric digits.
1890	Hollerith's punch card data storage system used by the U.S. Census Bureau.
1937	ABC computer uses binary system for program control and data storage.
1945	The term "bug" as computer bug was termed by Grace Hopper while programming the MARK II.
1954	The first version of FORTRAN (formula translator) is published by IBM.
1960	The Common Business-Oriented Language (COBOL) programming language is invented.
1963	BASIC language developed at Dartmouth College.
1970	Codd proposes the Relational Database Model.
1970	C language developed.
1970	Pascal language developed.
1975	Structured programming paradigm proposed.
1975	Paul Allen and Bill Gates write the first computer language program for personal computers—a form of BASIC.
1975	Steve Wozniak and Steve Jobs co-found Apple Computers.
1980	IBM hires Allen and Gates to create an operating system for a new PC.
1981	IBM introduces IBM PC, which runs the new MS-DOS operating system.
1982	Lotus Development Corporation is founded and Lotus 1-2-3, a spreadsheet program, is introduced.

1983	C++ developed.
1984	Apple introduces the Macintosh, a computer with graphical user interface instead of needing to type in commands.
1985	Microsoft releases Excel for the Macintosh and follows two years later for the PC.
1990	Tim Berners-Lee proposes a 'hypertext' system, which is the first start of the Web as we know it today.
1990	Microsoft releases Windows 3.0 considered to be the first viable version of Windows.
1991	Linux is introduced by Linus Torvald.
1992	Java language developed.
1993	Intel releases the Pentium, a 60 MHz processor. Software development accelerates.
1993	Mosaic (an early and important Web browser) is released.
1994	Netscape is founded by Marc Andreesen and James H. Clark.
1994	Vice President Al Gore makes a speech where he coins the term "Information Superhighway."
1995	Amazon.com, one of the largest and well known e-commerce sites, opens its Web site.
1996	Google is first developed by Sergey Brin and Larry Page.
1996	IBM computer Deep Blue beats chess master Garry Kasparov in two chess matches.
1996	Active server pages (ASP) first released by Microsoft expanding the potential of the Web.
1999	Microsoft acquires Access.
2002	Microsoft releases .NET Framework.
2007	Windows Vista and Office 2007 released.

4.3 The Operating System

General-purpose computers, including mainframes and personal computers, have an operating system to control hardware, present a user interface, manage files, and run other programs. Examples of operating systems for personal computers include Microsoft Windows, Linux, and Mac OS X. Original electronic computers did not have operating systems. However, software tools for managing those systems appeared soon afterward, and gradually expanded in scope becoming the basis for operating systems of today. Several operating systems are presented here.

An **operating system** (OS) is the master program controlling all resources within a computer. Control of the operating system is up to the user. A significant advantage gained by using Windows is the **GUI,** making the use of the computer and associated programs visually intuitive thus eliminating the obtuse command languages of the past which required memorizing command **syntax** (*the words and grammar of a language*).

Once the computer starts up, the OS tells each piece of hardware when it is allowed to act. The OS is also responsible for loading programs from disk into **RAM** (computer memory) for execution. The OS generates the images seen on a monitor or printed on paper. Nothing happens without the approval of the OS. This process of starting the computer is known as **booting up.** When power is applied to the computer, a small program in firmware known as the **Basic Input/Output System** (BIOS), is run. Its primary function is to stabilize the machine and devices on the motherboard so that the **operating system** can be loaded and can take control of the computer.

The relationship between hardware, user, OS and other programs (**application programs**) is depicted here. As you can see neither the user nor the application software directly commands the hardware. Any command you give is intercepted by the OS which then constructs a formal command for the hardware to perform.

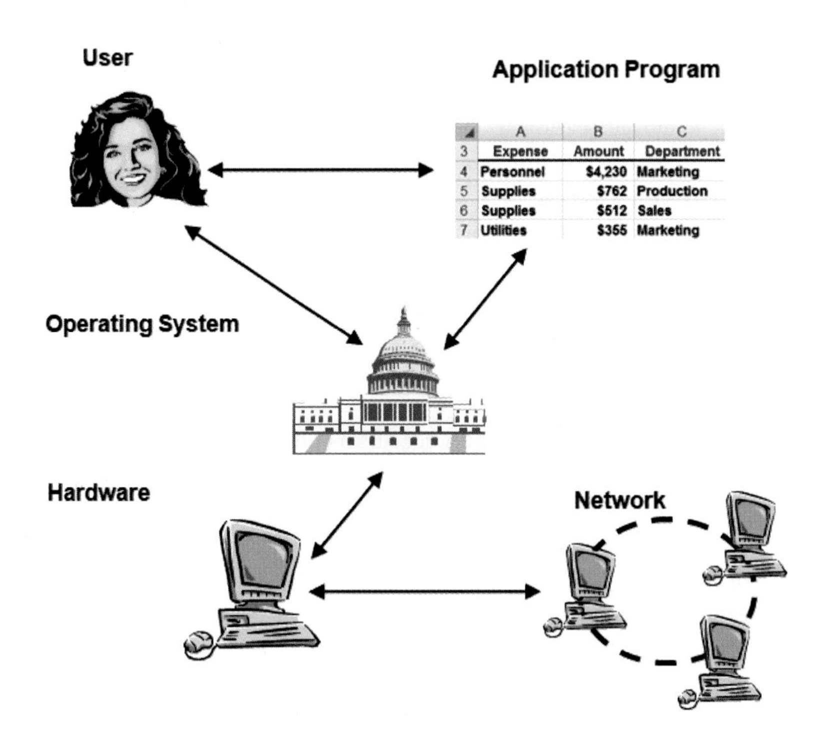

The Role of the Operating System

It may sound pretty complicated but there are a variety of very excellent technical reasons for this arrangement. The primary reason is that by allowing the OS to know how to command each hardware device the same knowledge is not needed redundantly in each program that you use. This feature is known as **device independence.**

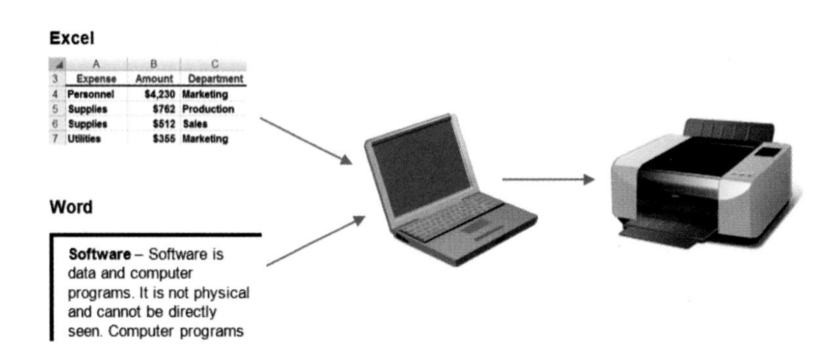

Windows Permits Device Independence

4.3.1 What an Operating System Does

All operating systems perform the same collection of basic tasks. In this section those tasks are enumerated and described.

- **Process management**—The operating system runs programs and allocates memory. Every action on a computer is run as a **process.** Only one process per CPU can actually be run at a time. Modern operating systems are able to simulate the execution of many simultaneous processes by doing what is known as **multitasking.** Process management is the operating system's way of dealing with running multiple processes. Multitasking is accomplished by simply switching from one process or another quickly and is known as **context switching.** As more processes run, the time available for each diminishes and may result in the system **thrashing.** It is the responsibility of the OS to recognize this situation before it becomes a problem by prioritizing time allocations.

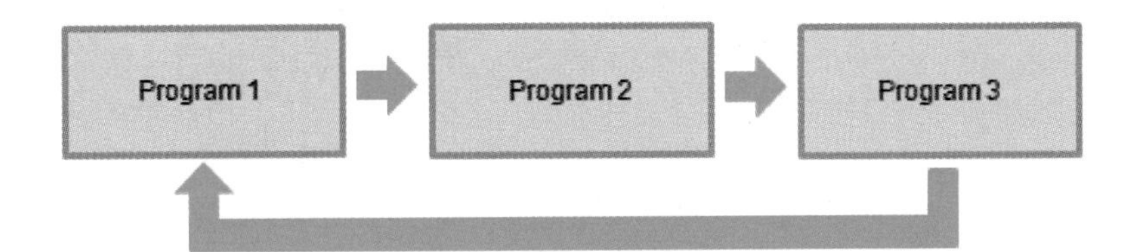

The Operating System Controls Multitasking

- **Memory management**—There are many demands for the computer's memory and the OS must allocate memory sensibly. Although there are several types of memory to manage (cache, RAM, disk), as the OS tracks what is needed and what is available it allocates and deallocates memory accordingly. One of the most important tools available to the OS is swapping between main memory and secondary memories. This is known as **virtual memory** management and greatly increases the amount of memory available for a process.
- **File System**—Any operating system has thousands and possibly hundreds of thousands of files stored in directories and subdirectories that must be managed. Files are persistently stored on disk (or other storage device) and must be located, read, and copied into RAM for processing as needed. This happens frequently (even continuously) as programs execute. Keeping track of the physical location of files is an important task. Large files (especially databases) may not occupy contiguous portions of the disk (consecutive **blocks**) thus making the task more difficult to manage. As the disk fills and files are added, updated, and deleted the disk may become **fragmented** and performance suffers. The file system should provide tools like disk defragmenters for managing the disk's hygiene.
- **Mapping**—Navigation through a disk begins with the route folder and progresses until the desired content is located. **Navigation** is **logical** and not **physical.** This is because the actual (physical) location of a file on a disk is really of no concern to the user. The operating system stores files where it finds available space and not in a specific sequential order. To allow the user to navigate, the operating system's file system maintains a directory that links logical content (folders) to the physical locations of files on the on the disk. This linkage is known as **mapping.**

- **File Associations**—All files (documents) of the same type will have the same file extension. For example: all files with the extension DOCX are Microsoft Word documents. This means that they were created using Word and that Word must be used to edit or print those documents. For instance, the name of a file containing a term paper might be "English Term Paper.docx". "English Term Paper" is descriptive of the contents of the file and "docx" indicates that this is a Microsoft Word document.

The linkage between a file and a program is important. Windows handles this **association** automatically since it knows that DOCX means a Word Document, XLSX means an Excel Workbook and so on. The significance is that if you double-click an icon for an XLSX file it opens in Excel automatically. If you right click an icon for a PPTX file it displays a menu of options for a PowerPoint presentation automatically!

Right Click on an Icon to Display a Menu Based on Associated File Type

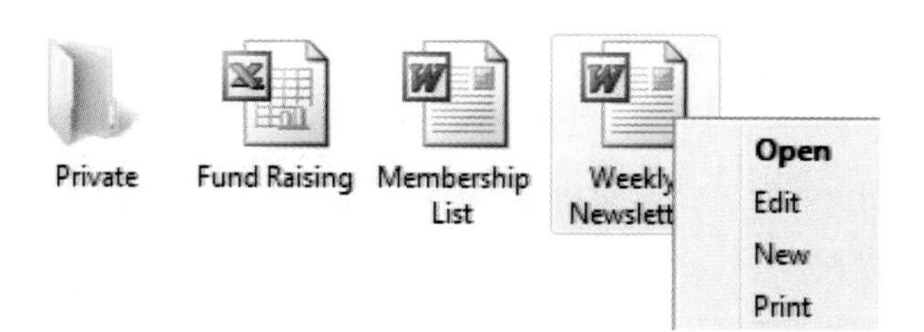

The complete list of all file extensions is too extensive to display here—no one knows for sure how many different extensions exist because many are proprietary. Several commonly used file types and their associated extensions are listed here:

Common File Extensions

Extension	Purpose
BMP	Image File
DOCX	Word Document
EXE	Computer Program
GIF	Image File
JPG	Image File
ACCDB	Access Database
MP3	Music File
PPTX	PowerPoint Presentation
TXT	Text File
WAV	Sound File
XLSX	Excel Workbook

- **Networking**—Most operating systems are capable of using networking **protocols** like **TCP/IP.** This means that systems can appear on a network and share resources such as storage devices, printers, and scanners with other computers. It also means that computers can connect to the Internet and operate as **clients** or **servers** (special server software required). Some operating systems (especially mainframe systems) support older vendor specific protocols like IBM's SNA.
- **Security**—Security involves **authenticating** users (people and other computers) prior to allowing access and limiting user access to functions that are permitted. Since computers are now attached to networks, a critical aspect of security is preventing unauthorized **intrusion** into a computer system. Common violations include: virus attachment, Trojan horse penetration, denial of service attack, being an intermediary for another attack, and spyware installation.
- **Graphical User Interfaces**—Today, most operating systems provide Graphical User Interfaces (**GUIs**, pronounced "gooey") enabling users and computer operators

to command the computer using a mouse or other **pointing device.** Pictures representing objects (**icons**) make it easier to provide access to system components. Some operating systems are more graphical than others and some are more flexible in that commands may also be entered on the **command line.** The interface is more a matter of style and not an indication of the operating system's power.

- **Device drivers**—A device driver is computer software that allows interaction with hardware devices. This constitutes an **interface** for communicating with the device through the computer bus or communications system the hardware is connected to. Each device driver is specific to a particular hardware device coupled with a specific operating system.

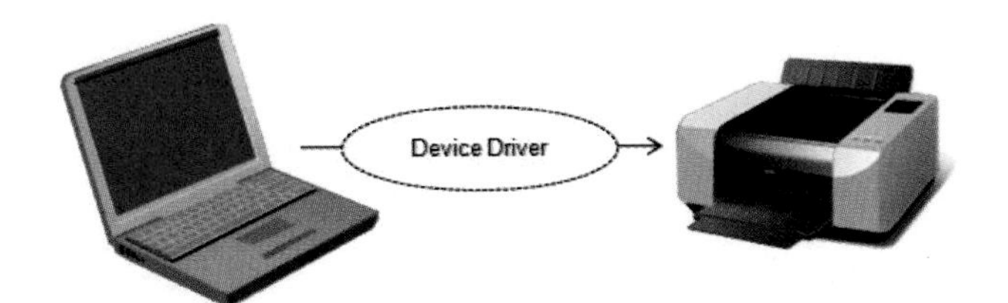

Device Driver Directs Hardware

The objective of this arrangement is **abstraction.** Every model of peripheral hardware is different (for example all printers). As newer models are released operating systems cannot be expected to know how to control every new device. To solve this problem the OS relies on the device driver to translate application requirements (print this page, store this image, etc.) to device specific actions.

4.3.2 Windows

Microsoft's Windows operating system originated as a **graphical** layer on top of MS-DOS for the IBM PC. In essence the original versions of Windows were not operating systems but a shell that surrounded the challenging **syntax** of the operating system DOS. Later versions of Windows became operating systems in their own right and the DOS interface faded into obscurity. The most recent addition to the member of the Windows family is **Windows Vista** which was released in 2007. Windows is a 64-bit operating system that runs on 32-bit and 64-bit Intel and AMD processors. Microsoft remains the dominant vendor of desktop operating system software.

Windows offers a **graphical user interface** (GUI) but did not present the first graphically oriented **point and click** environment. Apple was the first company to commercialize that concept but itself borrowed it from research of the 1960s at Xerox Palo Alto Research Center (PARC). The concept of the **mouse** interacting with **icons** was first developed there.

While Windows provides many excellent features (including **multitasking**—the ability to run several programs simultaneously), perhaps its most significant contribution was that it opened the computing door to many people afraid of or unable to use the command syntax and structure of DOS.

Specific operations using Windows Vista are presented later in this chapter.

Windows Registry

An important component that assists Windows in remaining organized and running efficiently is the **Registry.** It is a database which stores settings and options for the operation of the computer including information about the hardware, software, and users. Changes made, for example, to **Control Panel** settings, file associations, or by software installations are reflected and stored in the registry. The Windows Registry was introduced to clean up the disorganized distribution of configuration files (INI files) that had previously been used to store configuration settings for individual programs. These files tended to be scattered all over the system, which made them difficult to keep track of.

Windows Registry

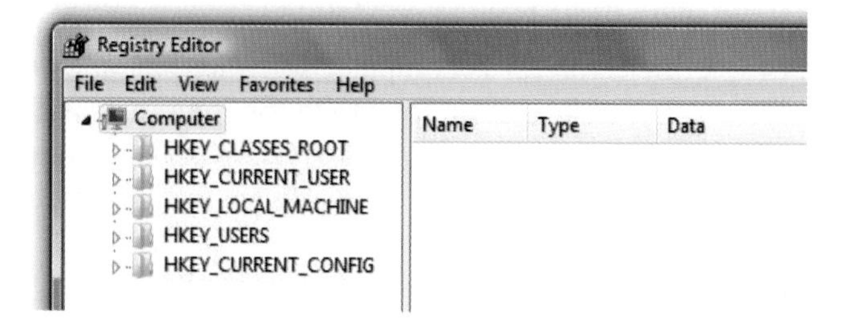

4.3.3 Linux

Linux is a **Unix-like** computer operating system and is one of the most significant examples of **open source development** and **free software.** Unlike proprietary operating systems such as Windows or Macintosh OS X, all of its program code is available for anyone to use, alter, and redistribute freely.

Linux was initially developed and used by hobbyists on personal computers. Since then, however, Linux has gained the support of major corporations such as Sun Microsystems, IBM, and Novell for use in servers. It is used in numerous systems ranging from appliances like digital cameras, Sony PlayStation 3, and cell phones to mainframes and super computers.

The Linux **kernel** (the core of the operating system) was first developed by Linus Torvalds in 1991. It was originally designed only for Intel 80386 (pre-Pentium) microprocessors, but now supports a wide variety of computer architectures. Linux is one of the most widely **ported** operating systems. Linux has historically been used mainly as a server operating system as the platform for server based web development applications like **Apache** (web server), **MySQL** (database server), **PHP** and **Python** (both programming languages).

The main concern of personal computer users wishing to base their operations on Linux is the lack of application software. Most end-user software is developed for Windows and has not been ported to other operating systems. Unlike Windows, Linux is not prone to be the target of hacking and other intrusive activities.

4.3.4 Unix

Unix or UNIX was originally developed in the 1960s and 1970s by a group of engineers at AT&T's **Bell Labs.** Although it did not initially catch on commercially, Unix gained attention in academic environments. The most notable Unix offspring, **BSD-Unix,** was created at the University of California, Berkeley and later deployed by Sun Microsystems which offers a version of Unix as it's **Solaris** operating system. Today, Unix is used in both servers and workstations. The Unix environment and the client-server model that defined it were important constructs in the development of the Internet as computing became centered in networks rather than in individual computers.

The programming language **C,** also developed at AT&T and used in the development of Unix, was distributed with Unix for free to academic institutions and government agencies. The wide deployment of both caused them to be ported to a greater variety of platforms than any other operating system or programming language. Unix became synonymous with **open systems** or **free software.**

As an operating system perhaps ahead of its time, Unix was designed as portable, multi-tasking, and multi-user. Architecturally, Unix was assembled from a large number of small programs that were strung together as **pipes** to complete larger functions. This arrangement efficiently delivered software components as required rather then relying on larger programs that provided more functionality than was necessary. It also permitted customization of the OS installation giving more flexibility.

Unix is based on a master control program, the **kernel** which provides services to start and stop programs, handles the file system, schedules access to hardware to avoid conflicts, and provides common "high level" tasks that many programs require.

4.3.5 Macintosh OS

Mac OS, which stands for Macintosh Operating System, is Apple Computer's graphical user interface-based operating system. It is usually given credit for popularizing the graphical user interface. It was first introduced in 1984, long before the first stable version of Windows was available. Apple actually avoided the term operating system in the Macintosh's early years because of the public perception of operating systems (like DOS) as unintuitive and difficult to use. Apple stressed the computer and not the software. Early versions of Mac OS ran on the Motorola 68000 processor but recent versions are compatible with Intel's architecture.

Mac **OS X** was introduced in 2001 and incorporated Unix-style management and multitasking to the Mac. It is derived from the BSD implementation of UNIX, and had been used as the basis for NeXTSTEP, the **object-oriented** operating system developed by Steve Jobs's NeXT company. The new OS allowed more programs to run simultaneously and virtually eliminated the possibility of one program crashing another.

4.3.6 DOS

DOS or **Disk Operating System** is a generic term for a class of operating systems that were disk based. These operating systems were without graphical interface relying instead on the **command line** where the user's instructions were typed in a somewhat arcane grammar. These systems were an advance over older systems that relied on available system memory (RAM) and could not take advantage of the additional storage provided by a disk. The most commonly known disk operating systems were **PC-DOS** (created by Microsoft for the original IBM-PC in 1981) and **MS-DOS** which Microsoft licensed to users of other systems. Neither DOS version was designed to be a multi-user or multitasking operating system.

PC/MS-DOS has effectively disappeared. It dominated the desktop computer industry from 1981 until 1995 when Windows '95 was released. Since the first several versions of Windows (95, 98, and Me) were actually shells surrounding DOS, the older operating system really powered computers until 2000 with the release of Windows 2000.

4.3.7 Mainframe and Other Operating Systems

Operating systems in mainframes usually must support thousands of simultaneous users running hundreds of programs. Large databases are rapidly accessed and updated as well. Normally mainframes are too costly to be brought down for maintenance so their operating systems must handle operations while hardware components are removed, serviced, and replaced. The fundamental chores of mainframe operating systems are no different from the systems previously discussed and described in more detail below. Several important mainframe operating systems were: MVS, VM, OS/390, TOPS-10 and TOPS-20. As noted, Unix (and Linux) are used for mainframe operations as well.

4.3.8 Virtual Machine

A virtual machine essentially mimics a computer so that several copies of an operating system, for example Windows and Linux, can run on one physical machine at the same time. It allows computing chores to be done on fewer computers, using less electricity and taking up less space, offering a potential way to control costs. A virtual machine is implemented in software and allows multiple operating systems to be run at the same time on the same physical computer. This technology allows hardware to be shared by applications running on different operating systems.

Microsoft's **Virtual PC** permits creating separate virtual machines on the Windows desktop. Each machine (remember, the virtual machine is really just software) virtualizes the hardware of a complete physical computer. This feature allows the user to run multiple operating systems at once on a single physical computer and switch between them with a mouse click.

Virtual Machine

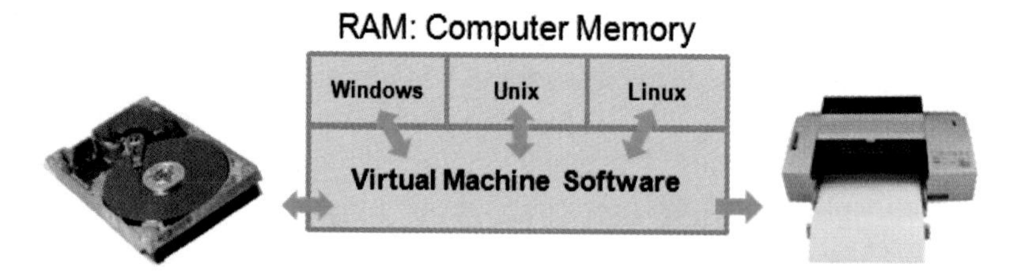

4.4 Operations with Windows Vista

Vista is the newest version of Windows. While many of the time-tested features of earlier versions of Windows are maintained, this version represents a complete overhaul of the operating system in look and functionality. Here are some of the key changes included in Vista:

- **Security**—The predominant driving factor as Microsoft created Vista was making Windows more secure. Windows XP had become a frequent, and some say, easy target for hackers. Indeed Vista is much tighter than XP in numerous areas, including:
  - **User Account Control** (UAC)—Any time a program is installed a dialog box pops up and asks your permission to proceed. This is especially important because viruses will no longer be able to install without your explicit permission.
  - **Windows Defender**—This is a new program that protects your computer from spyware.
  - **Phishing filter**—This feature alerts you when you are visiting a fake Web site (representing a bank, eBay, etc.) and possibly are being scammed.
  - **Service hardening**—This safeguard prevents invisible background programs from altering system files, the network, and registry settings.
- **Cosmetics**—Vista looks different. The common reaction is that it looks more Mac-like. This is accomplished with the new design scheme called Aero combined with menus and windows that fade away when closed. The taskbar shows actual thumbnail images of open documents. You will also find the Start menu better organized.

- **Programs and features**—Many new or upgraded programs come with Vista. Several are highlighted here:
  - **Windows Mail**—This is the native e-mail program included with Vista. It is an upgraded version of Outlook Express. A notable improvement is the addition of a spam filter that works well.
  - **Speech Recognition**—If you have a microphone you can speak to your computer and control its operation by talking instead of typing. You can also dictate e-mail and other documents.
  - **SuperFetch and ReadyBoost**—These features enhance your computer's performance. SuperFetch analyzes when you tend to use certain programs and preloads them for you in anticipation of your next use. ReadyBoost lets you use RAM (active memory) on a flash drive as extra memory.
  - **Sidebar**—This feature is a floating panel that hosts single purpose programs, called gadgets, that provide useful functionality including: weather reporter, stock ticker, calendar, etc.
- **Computer**—This is a major upgrade to the familiar My Computer from earlier Windows versions. This program is where you navigate through all icons, folders, and documents that are stored on your computer's storage devices (hard disk, jump drive, etc.). Several new features are:
  - **Stacking, filtering and grouping**—Vista offers three new methods for arranging, sorting, and displaying documents in folders.
  - **Document preview**—Now you can see what is in a document before opening it. The icon for a document is the document's first page content. This feature displays an image's thumbnail version as you hover the mouse over the image's name in a folder's document list.
  - **Address bar**—This displays a document's path. It also allows you to select other branches from the path if you want to explore related documents.
- **Versions**—Windows Vista comes in five different versions: Home Basic, Home Premium, Business, Enterprise, and Ultimate. Each has different hardware requirements, features, and pricing. Consult the Microsoft Web site for more information.

While Windows is a complex and powerful program there are several aspects of it that you must understand if you are to use its capabilities effectively.

4.4.1 Windows Security

Microsoft's number one objective in developing Vista was making Windows more secure. When Windows/XP was developed the Internet was less dangerous and hacking attacks were less common than today. Microsoft left open "back doors" to Windows that were designed for convenience, for example allowing system administrators to communicate with your computer through a network. Since these openings were known they became obvious targets for hackers. No doubt Vista will be targeted but it will be much harder for outsiders to compromise your computer than before.

This section describes features that are available for you to use. Before we discuss them, several features invisible to you but built into Vista are mentioned:

- **Application isolation**—No program is allowed to take over tasks performed by Windows itself.

- **Service hardening**—Invisible background programs are prevented from altering system files, the network, and registry settings.
- **Protected mode**—This isolates Internet Explorer and prevents actions taken by Explorer in response to Internet hacks from affecting Windows.
- **Code integrity**—Before a program runs, Vista checks to ensure that the program has not been altered somehow.

Security Center The security center gives you consolidated information about the current state of your computer's Internet security. To open the Center, follow these steps:

1. On the Start menu open the Control panel.
2. Click Security.
3. Click Security Center.

The page provides color coded status information about the firewall, automatic Vista updating, malware (virus, spyware, etc.) protection, and other security settings. The color status for each item is:

- Green—fully protected.
- Yellow—partially protected.
- **Red**—open to attack.

Vista's Security Center

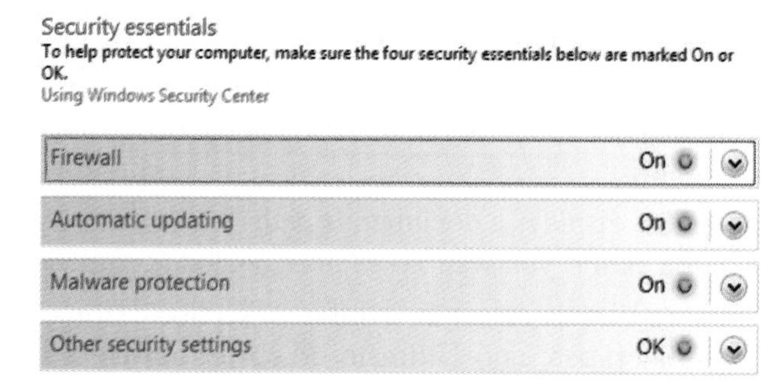

Windows Firewall A firewall acts as a gatekeeper allowing only communication that it knows is safe. The firewall operates on a set of predefined rules that open or close specific ports which are openings between your computer and the Internet. The firewall guards against dangerous inbound and outbound traffic. Most of the time Windows Firewall sets up the correct rules automatically, but there may be occasions when you would like to fine tune the settings. Do it this way:

- Open the Control Panel.
- Click Security and then select Windows Firewall.
- Click Change Settings.

Once you confirm that you wish to change settings the Windows Firewall dialog box appears. The middle tab, Exceptions, is most useful. You will find a list of all programs installed on your computer. Check the programs that you wish to allow access to the Internet. All other programs will be blocked. You also may add or remove ports from protection. Ports are numbered and you will need information about specific programs to know what ports are relevant.

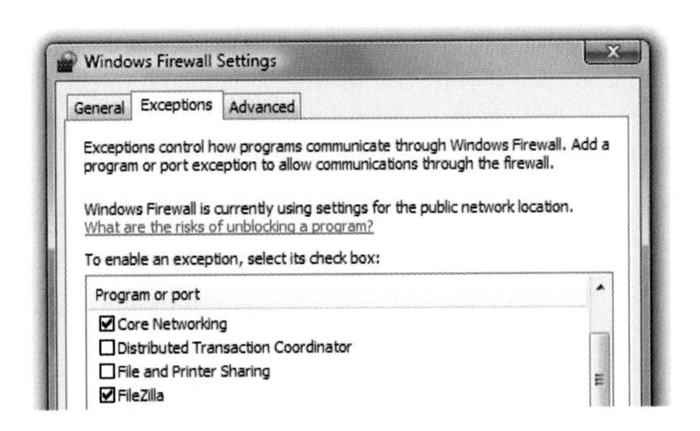

Changing Firewall Settings

Windows Defender Defender is an anti-spyware program. It should be used together with an anti-virus program (not supplied with Vista). Spyware arrives and is installed without you being aware of it. You might accidentally download it from a Web site or find it included in a compromised program that you installed. Spyware is described more fully in another chapter, but it can track what you do with your computer, harvest data about you, record and report your keystrokes, and perform other damage.

Defender works in the background protecting your system without your intervention. It monitors your computer and if it detects spyware attempting to install itself the spyware is deleted. Defender also scans your hard disk daily (usually about 2am) and removes any infections that it finds.

If you want to see what Defender has accomplished open it this way:

- Open the Control Panel.
- Click Security and then select Windows Defender.

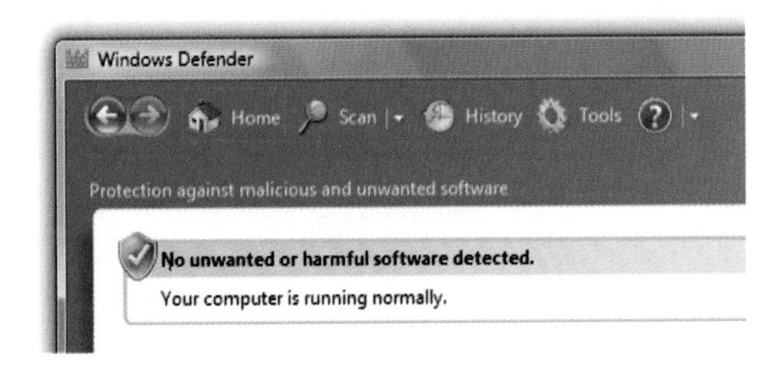

Defender Settings

The tabs in Defender's page are used this way:

- **Scan**—Perform an immediate system scan. Scans may be quick or complete.
- **History**—View a log of actions Defender has taken.
- **Tools**—Here is where advanced options are found. These tools include resetting the daily scan time, examining quarantined software, and obtaining a detailed look at all programs running.

Phishing Filter Phishing is an increasingly common attack where you are asked to provide personal data (often account numbers and passwords) for what appears to be a legitimate request but is not. If you respond to these requests you arrive at what looks like a proper Web site but, in fact, is a fake.

There is not much for you to control with the Phishing Filter but several tools are available in Internet Explorer. If you click the tools menu and select Phishing Filter you will find options that include checking Web sites you visit against lists of known bogus Web sites and warns you if you attempt to access such a site.

Phishing Actions

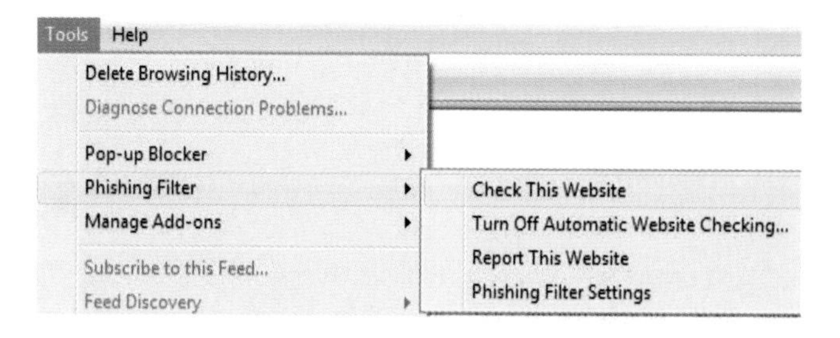

Cookies and Privacy Cookies get a lot of press but they may be an over-rated security concern. Compared with spyware, viruses, and Trojan horses that is certainly the case. Cookies are like little posted notes that Web sites leave on your computer to remind the Web site about you the next time you visit the site. They are often used to remember your name or address. They might be used to remember your shopping preferences, too.

Most cookies are innocent but some are not. If you wish to control use of cookies click Internet Explorer's Tool menu and select Internet Options. Click the Privacy tab and move the slider as desired.

Controlling Cookies

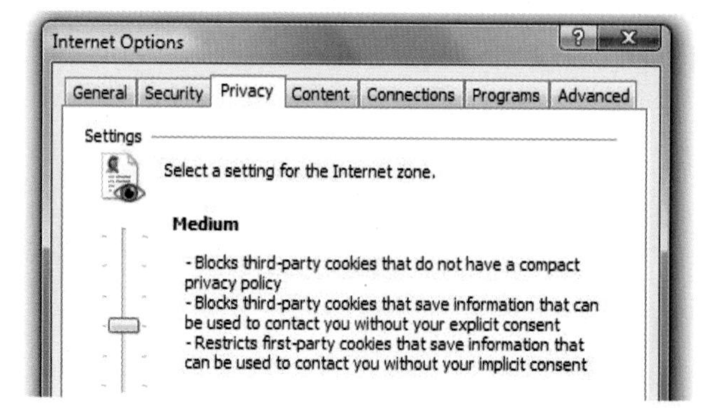

Pop-up Blocker Pop-up windows have been annoying Web surfers for a long while. These bothersome windows pop up when you visit a Web site. Some are simply in your way and some are actually dangerous. It is not uncommon to receive pop-up windows that seem to display an information or error message that requires you to click a confirmation that you have received the message. Your click might be a trigger to install spyware or other malicious malware.

When Internet Explorer detects a pop-up in a Web page it displays a message at the top of the browser window and reminds you with this message:

Pop-up Detected

You may then elect to view the pop-up if you wish. By default all pop-ups are prevented. If you wish to relax the prohibition or allow certain Web sites to always present pop-ups here is how to do it:

1. In Internet Explorer's Tool menu select Pop-up Blocker.
2. Click Pop-up Blocker Settings

A dialog box appears in which you may add a Web site that is permitted to display pop-ups.

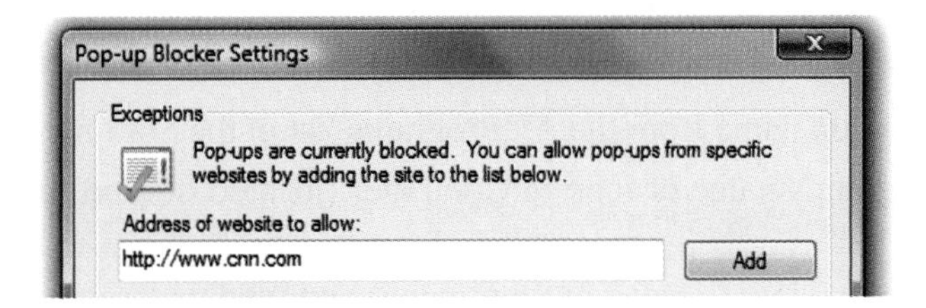

Pop-up Blocker Settings

Home Wireless Considerations Wireless, or **WiFi** as it is known, transmits your computer's messages to an Internet **access point** through the air where it could potentially be intercepted by an unknown intruder. Another breech might involve an outsider detecting your network and piggybacking on it and using it to download and distribute pornography or other offensive or inappropriate material that you do not wish to be associated with. A less offensive, but unacceptable action is freeloading where a neighbor uses your WiFi for Internet access and in doing so places additional load on your service thus possibly slowing down your access.

WiFi intrusion is easily prevented but many users do not realize this. The solution is to turn on **encryption.** The wireless router (access point) can be directed to require that each connecting computer provide a correct password before access is granted. Since only authorized users would know the password, security is maintained. Encryption is more than passwords. It involves scrambling messages so that outsiders cannot read them without properly unscrambling them. Encryption is built into most routers which may offer either of two methods: WEP and WPA. Select the more secure WPA if it is available.

User Accounts Vista was designed to be a multi-user operating system. Each person who uses the computer must log on by typing a name and potentially entering a password. Vista remembers the particulars for each user including:

- **Desktop**—The Desktop is maintained exactly as each user left it.

- **Start menu**—Each user's organization of the Start menu is preserved.
- **Favorites**—The Web favorites of each user are maintained separately and are not viewed by the other users.
- **Control Panel**—The settings established for each user are maintained. This includes wallpaper, screen saver and mouse, sound and keyboard settings.
- **Cookies**—Data in cookies are about individual users. Two users visiting the same Web site each have data in separate cookies.

Accounts are established and edited by opening the Control Panel and clicking User Accounts. These are known as **standard** accounts. Only users with administrator rights may perform those actions. Normally the primary user of the computer, the computer owner, or the person who installed Vista is the **administrator.**

All users should operate standard accounts. Even the administrator should create a personal standard account and use that except when administrative actions are required. This is suggested because a standard user who accidentally downloads or installs infected software will not infect the work of other users. An administrative user who downloads the same will infect all users.

4.4.2 Programs, Documents, and Files

Vista allows you to run programs several different ways. Use what is most convenient for you:

- Click the program name from the All Programs list in the Start menu.
- Locate a program's name or icon in Computer (located in Start menu) and double click it.
- Open the Run window (located in Start menu) and type the program's name.
- Open a document that is specific to a particular program. Locate the document name or icon and double click it. The document opens and so does the program that hosts it. This is due to what is known as **file association** and is described elsewhere in this chapter.

Windows keeps track of the programs that you use most frequently and attempts to maintain your favorites in RAM memory to allow faster loading when you select the program. See the section of this chapter about performance considerations for more information about this topic.

When a Program Locks Up On occasion a program will fail while it is running. This is known as a program **crash** or lock up. The typical symptoms are the mouse moves but menus and the toolbar do not respond. If this happens you need to remove the program from memory and start it again. Here is how:

1. Press Ctrl-Alt-Del simultaneously.
2. The Windows Security screen appears – click Start Task Manager.
3. A list of all programs currently in memory appears. Select the program to be stopped and click the End Task button.

Be aware that when a program crashes you will lose any data or work completed since you last saved the document you are working with. For this reason it is essential that you frequently save your work.

Moving between Open Programs and Documents The beauty of multi-tasking is that several programs may run simultaneously. While you can personally interact with only a single program at the same time you will want to move between open documents or programs as you use your computer. Vista provides several ways to move between programs and documents. The following methods are familiar from earlier versions of Windows:

- **Click the window**—If any part of the window holding the program or document you want to work with is visible, click it and that window will come to the front of your monitor.
- **Alt+Tab**—If you press Tab while holding down the Alt key a window appears with icons presenting all open windows. As you keep Alt pressed down, each time you press Tab the next window icon is highlighted. Release both keys when you reach the desired window.
- **Taskbar**—The Taskbar (at the bottom center of the desktop) displays an icon for each open window. Click the icon that represents the window you wish to work with.

4.4.3 File Operations

Now that you understand the importance of file names and file types we will focus on storing, locating, updating, and deleting files. We will look at a tool that Windows provides for organizing files in folders, it is called **Computer.**

The program allows you to navigate through the storage devices and folders on your computer. It provides you many options for viewing folders and their contents. You also use Computer to run programs, open files and documents, and create new folders. To run it, click the start menu and find and click the Computer icon. When the program runs it will initially display something like this:

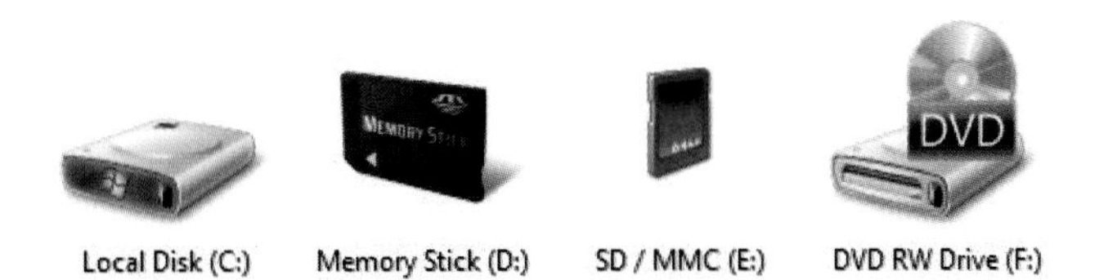

Computer Provides Access to All Storage Devices

If you prefer a different display click on the **toolbar**'s view icon and select your preference. You should also explore the View menu for other options.

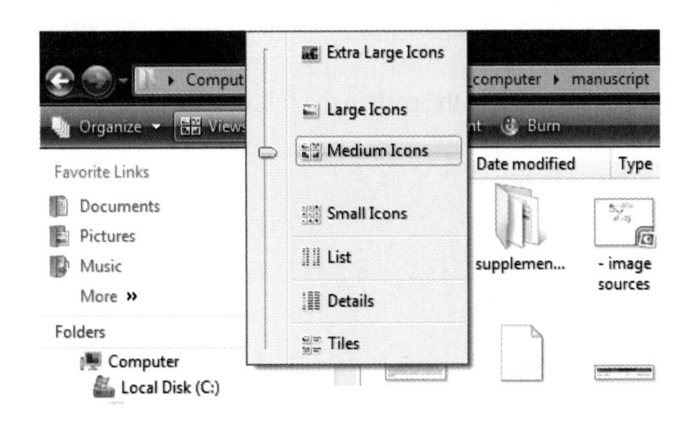

Click Views on the Toolbar to Select Computer's Display Mode

With Computer running it is now possible to **navigate** a storage device. Start by double-clicking the icon or name of what you wish to explore. Here the D:\ Drive (a memory stick) is opened and the content of the D:\ drive's **root folder** is displayed in this expanded view of Computer:

The Root Folder of a Storage Device Is Displayed

The first folder to be explored when a storage device is opened in Computer is the **root folder** for that device

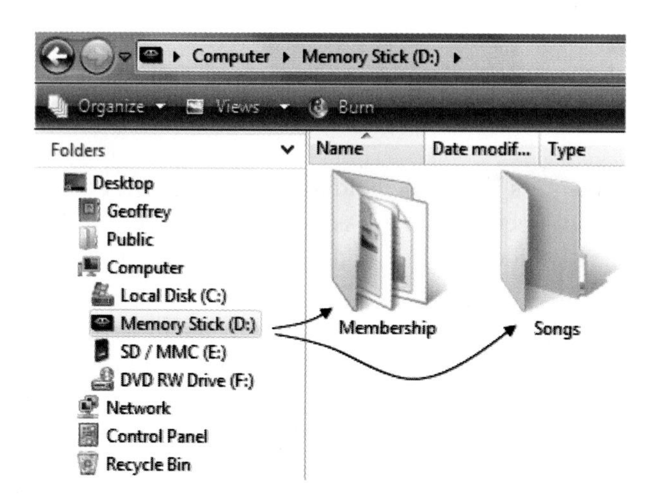

If the Membership folder (above) is double-clicked it opens and the display changes to this:

The Membership Folder Is Opened

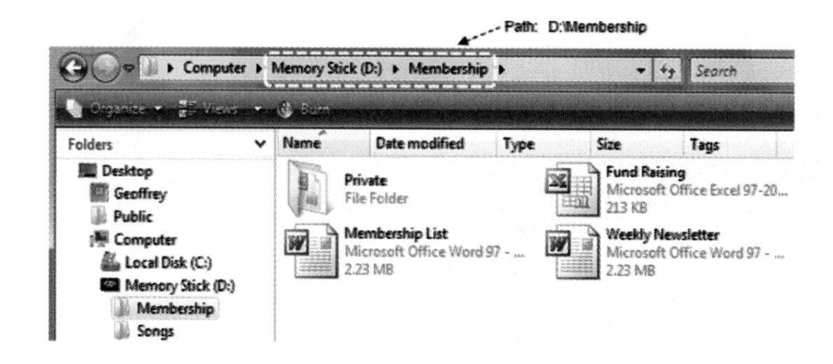

Paths File **paths** are important because that is how the location of a file is described. Examine the previous illustration and be certain that you understand the relationship between a file's path (examine the Address bar) and the folder display by Computer. The membership folder (D:\memberhsip) contains a folder ("private") and three files (documents). The path to the Excel workbook "Fund Raising," for example, is: "D:\membership\fund raising.xlsx".

Make sure that you understand the path in the following illustration is D:\Membership\Fund raising.XLSX:

File Paths Describe the Location of a File

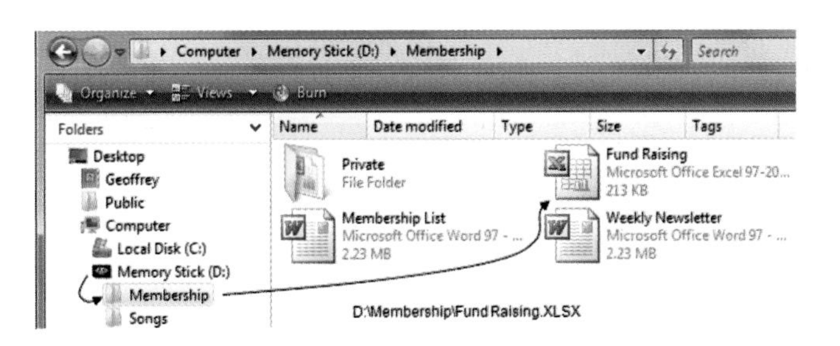

Searching for Files Sometimes you do not know the path to a file. Windows can find the file for you. Click the Start button then click Search and then the Search form appears. Type the file name in the search box and, as you type each letter, Vista narrows down the search as it attempts to locate what you are looking for.

Beginning a Search

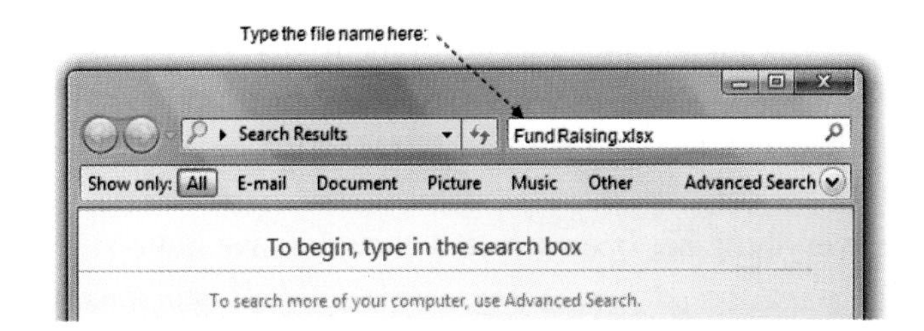

Once the file or document is located double-click on the file's name in the Search Results window to open the file:

Document Located

If you only know the file name and are unsure of the file extension then use a **wildcard** to locate the file. If you replace the file extension with an asterisk (*) then all files with the same name but with any extension are located. The search my books.* would return "my books.xlsx," "my books.accdb," and "my books.txt" assuming that those three files were found on the disk.

Searching with a Wildcard

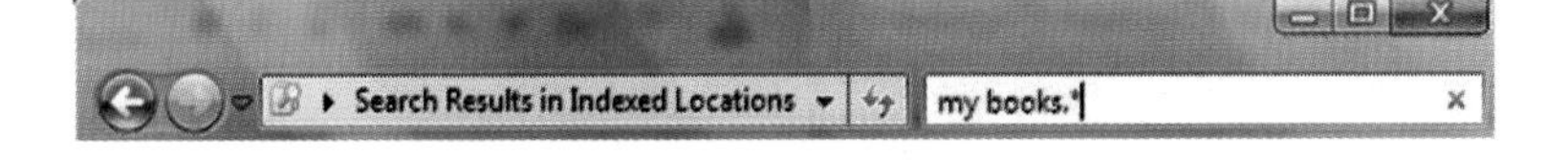

It is also possible to use the same wildcard to locate all files of a specific type. If you wanted to search for all Excel books (file extension XLSX) then the search would be *.xlsx. This search would return my "mybooks.xlsx" and "expenses.xlsx" assuming that those two files were found on the disk.

Wildcards can even help you if you do not know the full name of a file. Suppose that you want to search for an Access database but you only know that it ends with the word "book," type "*book.accdb." This search would return "expense book.accdb" and "gradebook.accdb" assuming these files were found on the storage device.

Actions on Files Now that you understand how to navigate among storage devices and how to locate files there are several operations that are important to understand. Each is described below.

Save When you save a file (document) Windows provides a **dialog box.** To view the Save As dialog box select the Save As option from the File Menu, then there are five things you must do:

1. Give the document a name. The name should be descriptive of your document.
2. Select the type of file that you want to save. Most of the time the proper file type already is selected.
3. Decide what storage device to save your work on. If you want to select a particular device then click the arrow to the right of Computer. A list of the computer's storage devices appears.
4. Select the folder on the storage device in which to store the file. Click the name of the folder that you want and the contents of the folder will be displayed. Continue until you find the folder that you want. If you go too far and want to return to a parent folder then click the icon with the left pointing arrow (*found at the top of the dialog box*).
5. Finally, after everything has been selected click the save button.

Steps to Follow when Saving a File

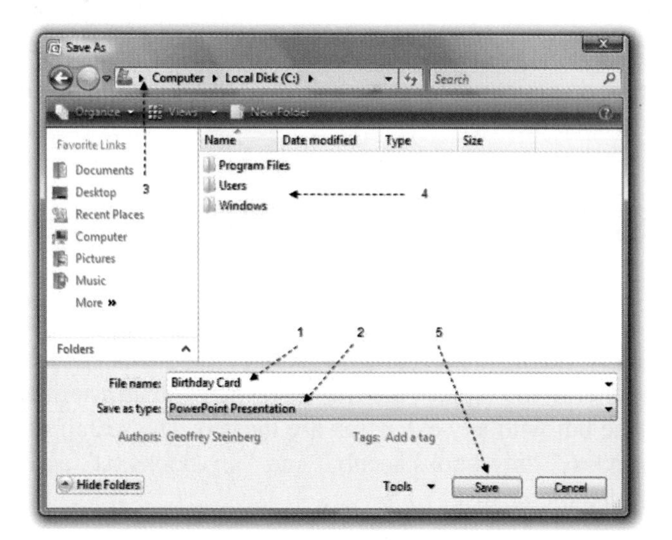

Rename Find the file (in Computer) to be renamed and right-click on its name and click the Rename option. The file name to be edited appears surrounded with a thin line. Type a new name in the box or edit the existing name. When you are finished, left click anywhere outside of the box or press the <enter> key.

Copy Start by using Computer to locate the file that you wish to copy. Right click on the file name and select the "Copy" option on the menu that pops up. Now navigate to the folder that you wish to place the copy in and click the right mouse button again. This time select the Paste option. A copy of your file is pasted into the target folder. After a copy operation two copies of the file exist.

Copy a File to Another Folder

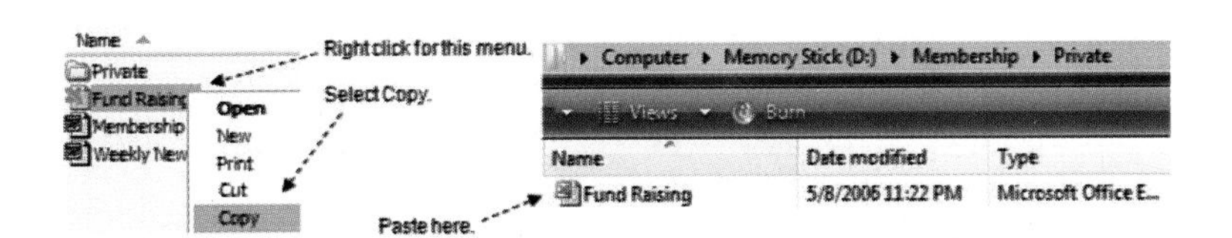

As you create and edit documents, put copies on floppy disks or jump disks for safe keeping. Hard disks fail at times--**backup** your work!

Note: If you copy a file and paste the copy in the same folder the name of the copy begins "Copy of" followed by the original name.

Move Moving a file involves relocating a file from a source folder to a destination folder. The folders may be on the same or different disk drives. A move often is done as a cut and paste operation.

Move a File with Cut and Paste

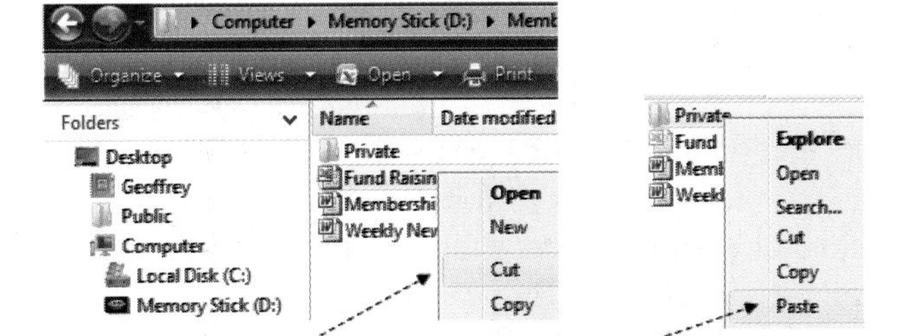

Move a File by Dragging The move operation is also made possible as a drag and drop operation. Either way, after a move is complete the file is no longer found in the source folder.

Move a File by Dragging It

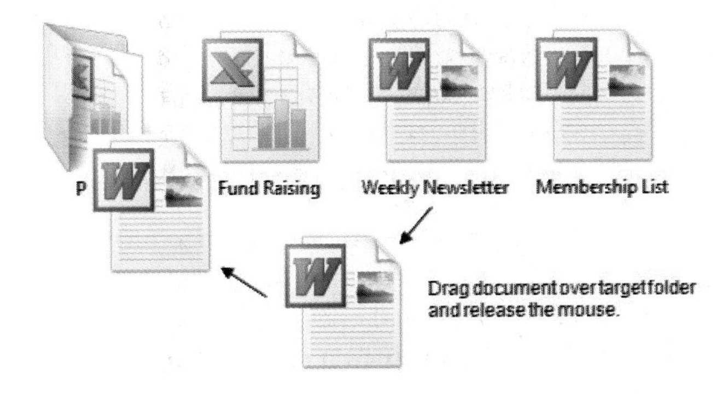

Be aware: If you drag a document or file to a different storage device the original is retained and in effect you have a copy not a move.

Creating a Folder Creating a folder to hold a group of files or folders is also done with a right mouse click. Use Computer to locate the folder that you wish the new folder to be created within. Click the right mouse button and select New and then the Folder option. A folder is added within the current folder and it is given the name New Folder. You should change the folder's name to something meaningful. See next page:

Creating a New Folder

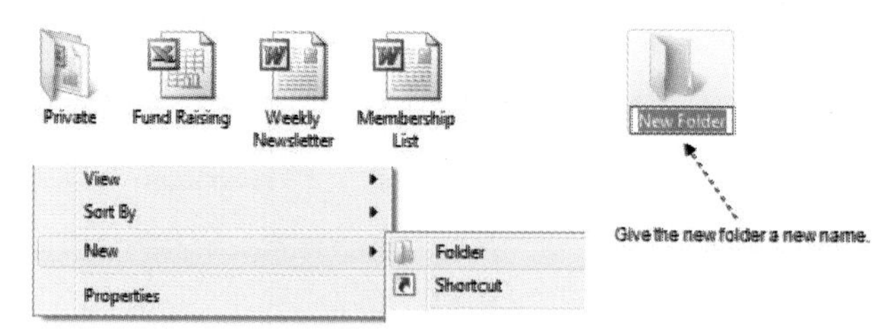

The **Recycle Bin** temporarily holds deleted files until they are permanently erased from the computer's disk. Only files from the hard disk are saved here.

Delete Deleting a file from the hard drive moves it to the **Recycle Bin** where it may be recovered if accidentally deleted. Deleting a file from other storage devices immediately removes the file with no possibility of recovery.

To delete a file first locate it with Computer and then click the right mouse button. Select the Delete option from the menu that pops up. A follow up dialog box verifies that you really wish to delete the file. Once deleted, the file is moved to the Recycle Bin.

To restore a file open the Recycle Bin (click the icon on the Desktop), locate the file you wish to restore and then right click on the file's name. From the menu that pops up select the Restore option. The file is restored to its original folder. To permanently remove all files in the Recycle Bin select Empty Recycle Bin from the Bin's file menu or right-click the Bin's icon and click Empty. Once this option is selected no possibility exists to restore any deleted files. Only empty the Recycle Bin to recover the disk space occupied by files no longer needed. Recovering disk space allows space for new files and may enhance performance.

Formatting Formatting a disk is useful only if you want to completely erase everything that is stored on it. Do this to a floppy disk or jump drive only—never format a hard disk unless you are an expert! Once a disk is reformatted there is no possibility of restoring files. They are not moved to the Recycle Bin, they are lost forever. Be careful!

To format a storage device right click on the drive name in Computer's left panel. Select the Format option from the pop menu. Next, the Format dialog box appears. Normally select the default option Quick Format and then click the Start button.

4.4.4 Performance Considerations and System Hygiene

As your computer is used your hard drive becomes increasingly cluttered. Three useful programs can help remove clutter, fix file errors, and generally improve performance. You should run these programs reasonably frequently. These programs are:

- Error Checking
- Disk Defragmenter
- Disk Cleanup

Other tools for enhancing system performance include:

- SuperFetch
- ReadyBoost

Error Checking This program scans the file folders and searches for errors within files. Those errors that can be corrected are fixed and those disk areas that cannot be fixed are avoided by Windows in the future. To check a disk, follow these steps:

1. Start Computer.
2. Right-click on the icon for the disk you want to check.
3. From the menu that pops up select Properties.
4. Click the Tools tab and locate and select Error-checking and click Check Now.

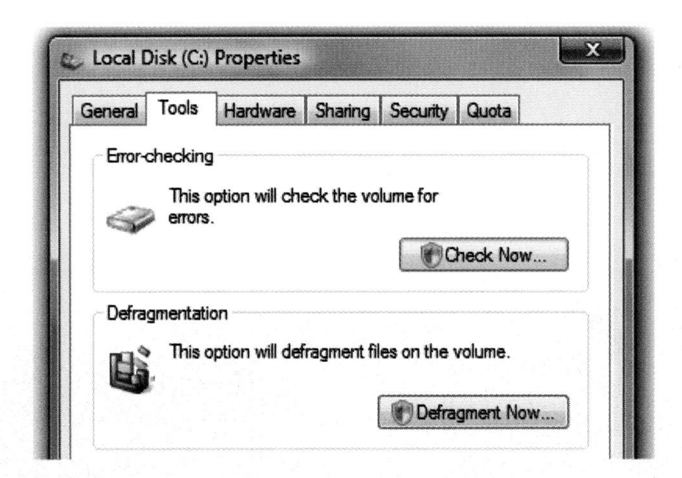

Error Checking

Next you are asked what you want to check. It is recommended that you select both options.

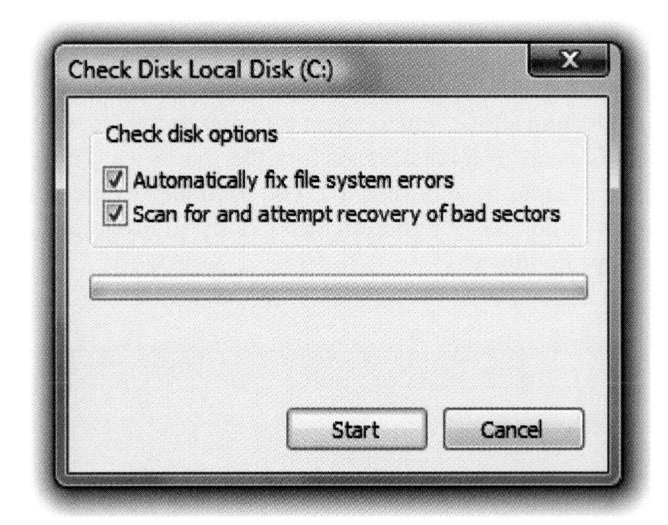

Options to Check

Windows will perform the check the next time the computer is restarted.

Permission Required to Check Disk

Disk Defragmenter As files are created, edited, and deleted the hard disk may become fragmented. Disk defragmenter scans the entire disk drive and looks for segments of unused disk area. The segments are consolidated resulting in larger areas of **contiguous space** for the storage of larger files. Regular use of this program will help keep your computer running more efficiently and may prevent unexpected loss of data. It will also help your computer find files and documents faster.

Disk Defragmenter runs immediately when you request it and you may continue to use your computer as the program runs. Locate this program one of these two ways:

1. From the Tools tab, or
2. Click the Start menu then click All Programs/Accessories/System Tools

Disk Defragmenter May Run Immediately or Scheduled for Later

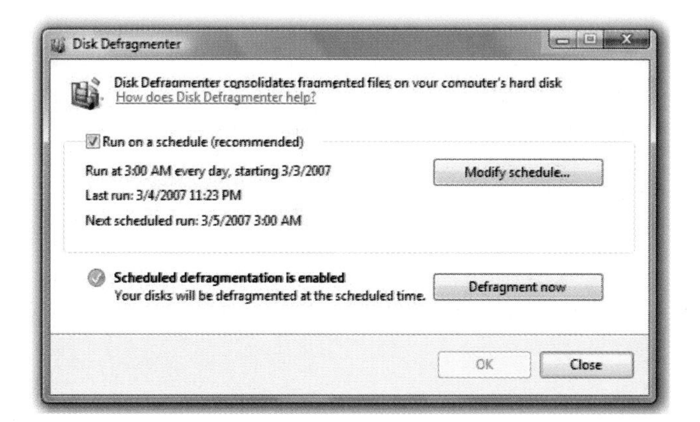

Disk Cleanup Use of your computer results in a buildup of files that may never be needed again. Disk cleanup allows you to select for deletion of unused or little used files. Removal of unused files opens up disk space for other purposes. This program finds infrequently used files in areas of your disk that you normally would not consider. When you start this program (click the Start button then Click: All Programs/ Accessories/System Tools) it first appears this way:

Disk Cleanup

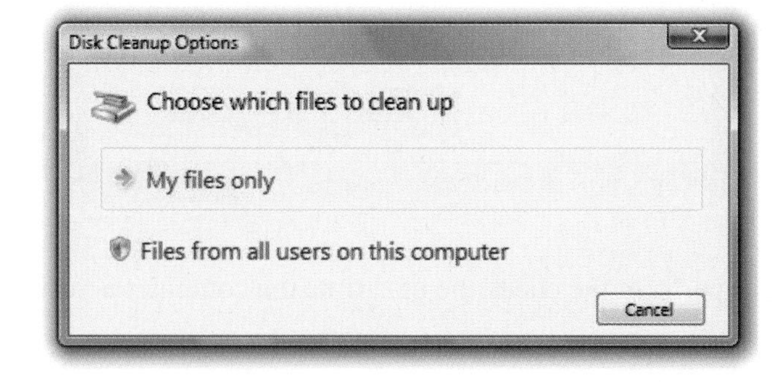

Disk Cleanup takes a while to run and it keeps you aware of its progress.

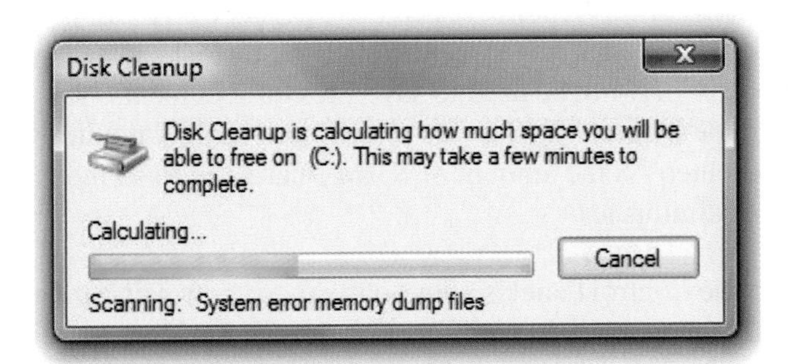

Disk Cleanup in Progress

When it is ready it asks you to confirm the deletion of files that it has determined are little used. Normally the files it locates are truly not needed so there is very little risk using this feature of Windows. Here is how Disk Cleanup presents what it found. Notice especially that the majority of unused (or little used) files were downloaded while surfing the Internet (Temporary Internet Files) and are stored in **cache.**

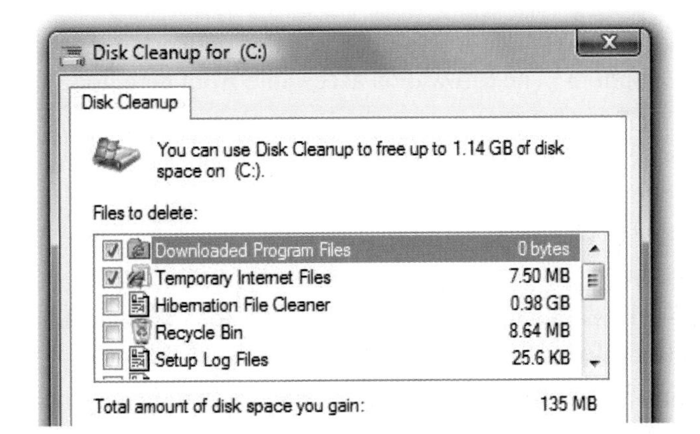

Disk Cleanup and Findings

SuperFetch A computer can access RAM (primary memory) much faster than it can access disk storage. For this reason Vista tracks what you do as you use your computer and it maintains copies of frequently used programs in RAM. This way frequently used programs start much faster. RAM memory used this way is known as **cache.**

When you leave your computer for a while (for lunch or overnight) various background programs like spyware scanners, anti-virus programs, and backup programs take over when the idle nature of the computer is realized. So after you return from the break the computer might seem sluggish because your frequently used programs have been washed from RAM and replaced with the background utilities.

SuperFetch tries to overcome this sluggishness. Vista remembers your use cycle and attempts to restore to RAM your favorite programs just before it anticipates your return. There is nothing for you to configure or turn off. SuperFetch is on all the time.

ReadyBoost This feature extends the amount of RAM available and thus increases the performance of SuperFetch. ReadyBoost allows you to use external memory in flash drives or camera memory cards as additional cache memory. This has the same effect as installing additional real memory in your computer. The external memory must be at least 256MB and not more than 4GB. Additionally some flash memory is excluded because it does not operate fast enough.

To take advantage of this feature, attach the external device. In the AutoPlay dialog box that appears click Speed up my system. Once you have dedicated the external memory for ReadyBoost it may not be used to save files or documents. The best speed boost is achieved when the external device has exactly the same amount of memory as the RAM in your computer. As the amount of RAM relative to flash memory increases the performance boost diminishes.

Control Panel The Control Panel is your doorway to control of hundreds of your computer's individual components. In an effort to help you navigate as quickly as possible to the controls you wish to manipulate the panel divides these components into broad categories:

- **System and Maintenance**—Here you will find administrative tasks that include backing up data and documents, managing Windows Update, changing power settings, indexing content for Search, and controlling hardware drivers.
- **Security**—Here is the entry to the Windows Security Center as well as specific protections including Windows Firewall and Defender. Windows Update is also available here.
- **Network and Internet**—Here you manage your network connections and control some browser options. The Firewall is accessible from here, too.
- **Hardware and Sound**—Here you control just about any hardware you can imagine from printers, to mouse, keyboard, speakers, and tablet PC accessories. All device drivers are controlled from here, too.
- **Programs**—Here you remove undesired programs. Windows Defender may be reached here, too.
- **Mobile PC**—This is for laptop or tablet PCs. Use it for controlling battery power settings and use it for touch screen and pen input device control.
- **User Accounts and Family**—This option allows you to manage all accounts on the computer. Administrative authority is required to add or edit accounts.
- **Appearance and Personalization**—Anything cosmetic is controlled from here. This includes the Desktop, the Start menu, the Taskbar, and the Ease of Use Center including Speech recognition.
- **Clock, Language, and Region**—Set the date, time, and time zone. Language options are available, too.
- **Ease of Access**—Here you find the hardware (mouse, keyboard, etc.) for ease of use. A magnifier is available if you require visual magnification. The Speech Recognition system is here, too.

Windows Update Maintain current versions of operating software by downloading and installing **service packs** provided by Microsoft. These updates are typically created to provide additional security protection, close security loopholes, and add additional functionality to the software. Use the **automatic update** feature of Vista to keep current.

Vista updates are delivered to your computer directly and automatically. You have the option of reviewing the updates before installation if you wish. Vista offers a wider range of updates than earlier versions of Windows as it delivers driver updates for hardware and patches for programs like Microsoft Office 2007.

If you purchased a new computer with Vista installed, then Windows Update is turned on. If you installed Vista you were asked questions about your update preferences. If you want to make adjustments, follow these steps to open Windows Update:

1. Open the Start menu and then open the Control Panel
2. Click System Maintenance and then click Windows Update
3. On the left side of Windows Update (not shown) click Change settings

Windows Update

Windows is up to date

Available: 1 optional update

No new important updates are available for your computer.

Most recent check for updates:	Yesterday at 10:13 PM
Updates were installed:	2/28/2007 at 7:22 AM. View update history
You have Windows set to:	Automatically install new updates every day at 3:00 AM
You receive updates:	For Windows

Windows Update

4.5 Application Programs

Application programs are software that is dedicated to performing specific tasks for users. These programs are differentiated from system software which is used to control the computer system and allow applications to execute and use system resources. Hundreds of application categories exist; several important ones are described here.

Memory Use Once your work is complete (for example, your Word document or Excel workbook) make sure to save it for future use. Until now your work in progress is stored in the computer's active memory (**RAM**) but will be lost if the computer is turned off before the work is saved permanently. Permanent storage is said to be **persistent** while RAM is said to be **volatile.** Active memory is also known as **primary memory.**

RAM Memory Is Volatile

4.5.1 Word Processor

The word processor is, perhaps, the most commonly used computer application (e-mail is a likely alternative candidate). It is used for the creating, editing, formatting, and publishing or printing of any sort of written material. The most commonly used word processor is Microsoft **Word.** Other word processor applications include the commercial product **Word Perfect** and open-source applications such as **OpenOffice.**

Word processors evolved from text editing programs. Their value as a tool for letter and document preparation was quickly evident and the application developed rapidly. In addition to the uses already noted, common features of modern word processor include:

- Spell checking
- Grammar checking
- Thesaurus
- Tables of contents
- Tables of figures
- Indices of keywords
- Footnote numbering
- Batch mailings (mail merge) using a form letter and address database
- Web enabled (HTML) output

Word processors use a graphical interface that allows the author to view and directly edit an accurate representation of the end result as the document is being created. This style is known as "what you see is what you get" and referred to as **WYSIWYG** (pronounced "wizziwig").

The Word screen is shown below with each highlighted item explained afterward.

The Word Workspace

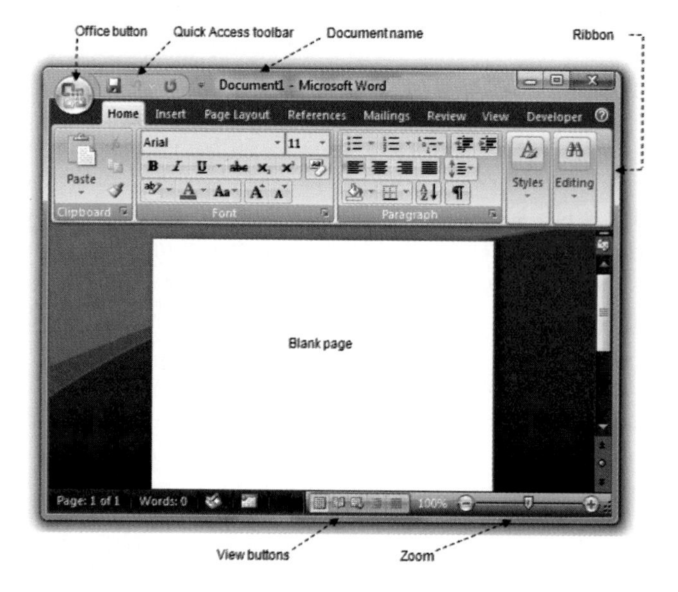

- **Office Icon Button**—This button provides a menu of options for creating new documents and saving, sharing, and printing documents. It also provides a list of recently opened Word workbooks.
- **Quick Access Toolbar**—This is one of the few toolbars found in Word 2007. It remains visible regardless of which Ribbon tab is displayed. It is a place to store most frequently used commands and have them visible at all times. Any command anywhere on the Ribbon may be added to the toolbar.
- **Document Name**—Word stores your document in a single file (a "document") with the extension of **DOCX.** New documents are given default names. When you save your work you should change the name in a meaningful way.
- **The Ribbon**—All features of Word are available through the Ribbon tabs. Since there are no longer menus in Word 2007 the Ribbon can be thought of as providing that function. The content and organization of tabs cannot be customized as menus were in earlier versions of Word.

- **View Buttons**—These provide different views of the work in progress including print layout, full screen, Web layout, outline, and draft.
- **Zoom Slider**—This slider allows you to zoom in and out by dragging it left and right. As you zoom out, more of a document is increasingly displayed.

4.5.2 Spreadsheet

Spreadsheet programs permit the manipulation of data arranged in a grid of rows and columns which define cells. A spreadsheet is a rectangular table (a grid) of information and a spreadsheet program is designed to perform computations on data stored within the cells of the grid. Each **cell,** the intersection of a row and a column, may contain a **data value** or a **function** or **formula** used to compute the value of the cell. Functions and formulas may use the contents of other cells as input to calculations. Spreadsheet programs update data in cells when data in the cells on which they depend have been changed.

The most common spreadsheet program in use is Microsoft's **Excel.** The Excel screen is shown below with each highlighted item explained afterward.

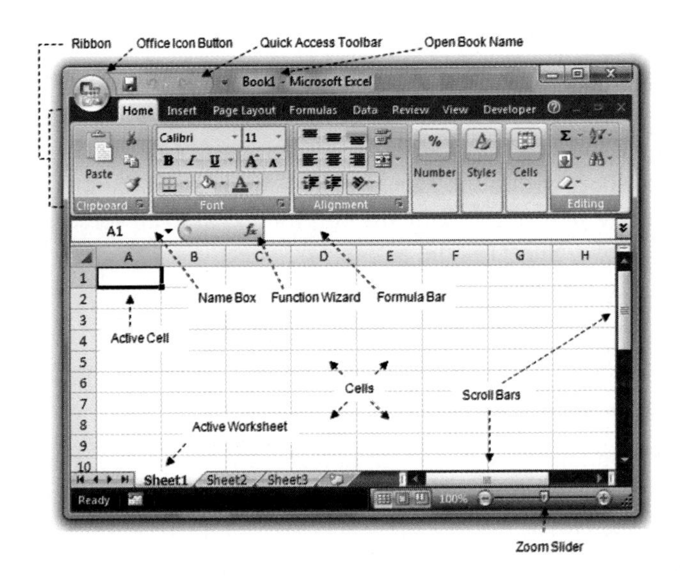

The Excel Workspace

- **Office Icon Button**—This button provides a menu of options for creating new documents and saving, sharing, and printing documents. It also provides a list of recently opened Excel workbooks.
- **Quick Access Toolbar**—This is one of the few toolbars found in Excel 2007. It remains visible regardless of which tab is displayed. It is a place to store most frequently used commands and have them visible at all times. Any command on any Ribbon tab may be added to the toolbar.
- **Open Book Name**—Excel automatically allows you to group several spreadsheets together in what is called a book. The book is a single file (a "document") with the extension of **XLSX.**
- **Ribbon Tabs**—All features of Excel are available through the Ribbon tabs. Since there are no longer menus in Excel 2007, the tabs can be thought of as providing that function. The content and organization of tabs are not customizable as menus were in earlier versions of Excel.

- **Cells**—The intersection of a **row** and **column** is a cell. A spreadsheet is made up of many cells. Cells are referenced by column then row. Valid cell names are: A1, B92, Z47, D3094, etc.
- **Active Cell**—Only one cell on the spreadsheet at a time can be the target of your typing; that cell is called the active cell. In the figure above A1 (column A row 1) is the active cell.
- **Name Box**—Every cell has a name which is the column name (a letter or group of letters) followed by the cell's row number. The active cell name is always clearly shown by Excel. The active cell is also highlighted with a dark border. You should easily see that cell A1 is active.
- **Function Wizard**—The Function Wizard is a search utility that provides access to all of the functions Excel provides. Functions are categorized (financial, statistical, logical, etc.) and the wizard guides you through selection and completion of your selection.
- **Formula Bar**—The content of the active cell is displayed here and may be edited. Place the cursor here and edit as desired. If the content of the active cell is a formula or function then that appears here and the result of the calculation is displayed in the active cell. Remember: The Formula Bar always displays the content of the Active Cell.
- **Active Worksheet**—Since a workbook contains several spreadsheets only one can be active at a time. In other words, the screen displays just one spreadsheet at a time. The tabs on the lower left of the Excel screen allow you to click to get access to a different worksheet within the same book. Use the scroll bars at the bottom left of the Excel window to scroll through the tabs for access to all spreadsheets in the book. In the figure above, Sheet1 is the active worksheet.
- **Scroll Bars**—A vertical and horizontal scroll bar allows you to see more of the spreadsheet than can be displayed on the screen at one time.
- **Zoom Slider**—This slider allows you to zoom in and out by dragging it left and right. As you zoom out more cells are increasingly displayed.

Spreadsheet programs have been said to foster the commercial success of early personal computers. They have been referred to as the killer applications that motivated sales. **VisiCalc** helped drive Apple's early success and the IBM PC's growth was fueled by **Lotus 1-2-3.** Microsoft released **Excel** for the Mac in 1985 and followed for the PC two years later. Today Excel is the dominant spreadsheet program due to its large base as part of Microsoft Office.

The real usefulness of spreadsheets lies in its ability to calculate formulas—and recalculate them automatically when values change. Spreadsheets are great for budgets, financial statements, and other tasks that require calculations. Spreadsheets permit what-if analysis on data and the preparation of charts for the presentation of results. Data may be stored in multiple spreadsheets that are linked when needed to support data analysis.

Macros Microsoft Office allows you to repeat tasks more efficiently and accurately by recording a task's steps for later use. The recording is known as a **macro** and is easily accomplished using the **Macro Recorder** provided by Excel and some other Office programs. More sophisticated Office automation goes beyond macro recording and permits the implementation of a dynamic user interface using **Visual Basic for Applications** (VBA). VBA is a complex and powerful topic. Macros and VBA are discussed in depth in the computer programming chapter.

The keystrokes and mouse actions that are recorded as a macro are written in a **scripting language.** VBA is such a language. VBA has access to most Microsoft Windows system calls and executes (if allowed) when an Office document is opened. It is relatively easy to write computer viruses in VBA—they are commonly known as macro viruses—and distribute them by e-mail in an Office document. To assist in prevention of macro virus infestation the current version of Office provides much stricter control over macro execution than earlier versions did. Refer to the chapter on security for more information.

4.5.3 Presentation and Multimedia Software

A commonly used example of a **presentation graphics** package is **PowerPoint.** It gives you everything you need to produce professional-looking presentations. Your presentations are enlivened with color, text, images, and other objects. It is very easy to insert images that were developed or edited with other software. As you build your presentation you have the convenience of viewing your work as a slide show (one image at a time in full screen display) or as if using a slide sorter (all images laid out in rows and columns on your desktop). PowerPoint allows the recording for notes for assisting a presenter to remember the narrative that accompanies each slide during a public presentation. The program also allows recoding of voice narration for accompaniment when the presentation is displayed in slide show mode.

Other categories of presentation and multimedia software include:

- **Image editing software**—Numerous programs are easily found for editing digital images. Among the most commonly used are the Windows program **Paint** and Adobe's **Photoshop.** Common image formats include **GIF, JPG, PNG,** and **BMP.**
- **Audio and video editing software**—There are also many programs for editing audio or video. Features typically included are the ability to import audio and video source, cut and paste sections, and save completed compilations to disk. Some programs also enable the creation of **streaming** output that can be sent via the Web to clients. Adobe **Premiere** is a high quality, feature rich video editor used by television studios and artists.
- **Animation software**—Software that is used when creating moving images via the use of computers. Computer animation is essentially a digital successor to the art of stop motion film animation of 3D models and frame-by-frame animation of 2D illustrations. For 3D animations, objects are built on the computer monitor and 3D figures are rigged with a virtual skeleton. The open source animation package **Blender** is complex but popular.
- **Scalable Vector Graphics**—SVG is an XML markup language for describing two-dimensional static and animated vector graphics. SVG images are defined by the series of points, lines, and shapes they are comprised of. Since they are XML based SVG images are easily included as Web content. Because they are vector graphics (essentially line drawings) they are not used for photographic content. **Inkscape** is an open source vector graphics editor with a substantial array of features.

4.5.4 Personal Organization

An example of a personal information manager is Microsoft's **Outlook.** Although often used mainly as an e-mail application, it also provides a calendar, note taking, task and contact management, and a journal. It can be used stand-alone or in conjunction with

Microsoft Exchange Server to provide enhanced functions for multiple collaborators in an organization, such as shared mailboxes and calendars, public folders and meeting time negotiation.

Numerous other personal data organizers may be found quickly with a Web search.

4.5.5 Database

A database is a collection of data that is of interest to people in support of decision making and record management activities. The concepts of database are rooted in our understanding of tables where data is arranged in records defined by rows and columns. Tables are related using logical values known as keys. Databases of this type are known as **relational databases** and most commercially installed databases are relational. A **database management system (DBMS)** is a computer application designed to manage a database.

Tables of Records Logically Connected

Customer Records

Primary key — Foreign keys reference primary keys — Foreign key

First_Name	Last_Name	Suffix	Phone	Prefix
Buster	Jones	Dr.	401-1902	
Wilma	Sanders		401-2510	
Zoe	Green		401-1507	Ms.

Customer Purchase Records

Last_Name	Product	Price
Green	Coat	$ 109.53
Jones	Sweater	$ 43.77
Sanders	Pants	$ 31.45
Green	Sweater	$ 43.77
Jones	Shoes	$ 62.83
Green	Scarf	$ 17.50

The functions of a DBMS are:

- **Data management**—recording of data as records in tables
- **Data integrity**—accuracy in data recording and update
- **Rule enforcement**—accurate enforcement of user defined rules governing data
- **Response to queries**—use of languages like SQL to request records and summaries
- **Security**—authentication of users
- **Backup and recovery**—replication of data and restoration if errors occur
- **Concurrency**—multiple simultaneous users

Popular database managers include **Oracle,** Microsoft's **SQL Server,** and **MySQL** which is free software. IBM's mainframe database manager is **DB2,** more recently renamed as Information Management software. Microsoft's popular **Access** is part of the Office Suite.

The relational concept was invented by Edgar F. Codd of IBM during the late 1960s. Popular database managers of the time stored data in complicated architectures known as **hierarchical** and **network** structures. The appealing simplicity and inherent power of Codd's model languished until the 1970s when Oracle began development of the product of that name. The relational algebra that Codd proposed was implemented as the **Structured Query Language** or **SQL.** Today SQL is the language used in most commercial **database management systems** (**DBMS**).

Security is a major concern to **database administrators** (DBA). Apart from the use of passwords and other authorization techniques, few users are given access to an entire database and are limited to portions of a database defined in a **subschema.** As an example, a university database can contain extensive data about an individual student, but staff in the registrar's office would only have access to academic data and staff in the bursar's office only to financial data. A student would presumably have access to view all personal data but would not be permitted to update it.

A **transaction processing system** (TPS) is a type of information system that typically relies on a DBMS to collect, store, modify, and retrieve the transactions of an organization. A transaction is an event that generates or modifies data that is eventually stored in a database. There are two styles of transaction processing:

- **Batch updating**—Transactions are collected and updated as a batch when it's convenient or economical to process them. The cost per transaction processed is assumed to be lower with batch processing but response time to the client is slower. Monthly statements from a financial institution are an example of batch processing.
- **Real-Time updating**—This involves the immediate processing of data and instant confirmation of a transaction. The cost for real-time processing is higher because resources must always be available to handle peak demand. Because of advances in technology, consumers have grown to expect real-time processing. ATMs and online reservation systems are examples.

The history of commercial relational database management systems (**RDBMS**) is long and involved with many dead ends. Today the marketplace is dominated by these offerings:

- **DB2**—Now known as IBM's Information Management software, is considered to be the one of the first database products to use SQL. Today DB2 is available on other platforms including UNIX, Windows servers, and Linux.
- **MySQL**—This is a freely available **open source** product and runs on a variety of platforms including Linux and Windows. It is especially popular supporting Web-based applications.
- **SQL Server**—This relational database management system is offered by Microsoft and is commonly used by businesses for small to medium-sized databases.
- **Oracle**—Oracle is one of the most popular RDBMSs today. It runs on many platforms including UNIX, Apple Mac OS X, IBM, Linux, Windows, and Sun Solaris.

Data Mining Data mining is the process of searching large volumes of data for patterns that reveal information embedded in the data. Statistical tools that are employed include classification, pattern recognition, association rule mining, and clustering. As an example of association rule mining, consider a retail store that records data about all customer purchases in a database. Data mining might reveal that consumers of silk dresses also tend to purchase patent leather purses. Realizing the association, the store would have the opportunity to cross-sell purses to silk dress customers.

4.5.6 Enterprise Resource Planning

Enterprise Resource Planning systems (**ERP**s) integrate the data and data processing activities of a government, business, or other organization into a single system. The key to most ERP installations is the use of a single **database** which is accessed and updated by applications from all areas of the organization. This arrangement allows the complete integration of data that the organization depends on for management and planning.

ERP Architecture

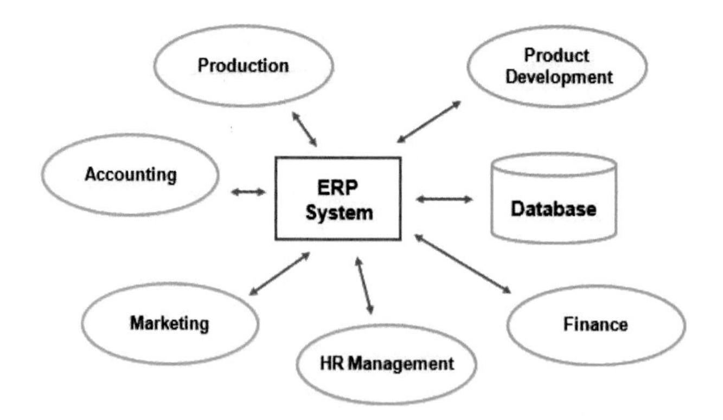

There is no specific formal definition of an ERP. The needs of organizations differ depending on many factors including orientation (business, non-profit, military, governmental, and academic), competition, financial and legal requirements, etc. While no "one size fits all" solution is possible, various vendors, the most notable being **SAP** and **PeopleSoft,** provide software that can be customized to conform to an organization's needs, purpose, and structure.

4.5.7 Groupware

Groupware is a generic term that defines software that supports **collaborative work** among people engaged in a common task. This software can support small or large groups and, being dependent on a electronic communication component, the physical proximity of the collaborators is not relevant. A significant advantage to organizations is bringing collaborators together with less time and expense spent than in travelling were necessary. Meeting attendees can assemble electronically from a great distance without leaving their offices. Common applications in this category include **email, calendaring, chat, wiki,** and **video conferencing.**

More generally this category may include social and business networking software like **Facebook, MySpace,** and **Craigslist.** Dating services are included here, too. These applications, strictly speaking, do not support a group of people applied to the same task, but the underlying software has components virtually identical to those mentioned earlier.

Project Management Software Project management software is a form of groupware that automates many functions including scheduling, budget management, resource allocation, collaboration software, communication, quality management, and documentation or administration systems, which are used to deal with the complexity of large projects. Pert and Gantt charts are used to display project schedules and the critical path method is used to evaluate project status. Project management software is explained fully in the systems analysis chapter.

4.5.8 Browser

A Web browser is an application that enables the user to retrieve, display, and interact with **Web pages** provided by a **server.** Text, images, and other objects on a Web page may contain **hyperlinks** to other pages at the same or different Web sites. Browsers interpret a document's **HTML** (Hypertext Markup Language) code and display the page's content as defined by the formatting and program instructions (most often **JavaScript**) in the code. Hypertext Transfer Protocol (**HTTP**) is a method used to govern the navigation and transport of pages from servers to **clients.**

Numerous browsers are available including Microsoft **Internet Explorer,** Mozilla **Firefox,** Apple **Safari, Netscape,** and **Opera.** Although browsers are mostly used to access the Web, they are also used to access information provided by servers in private networks known as **intranets** and extranets.

4.5.9 Search Engine

An Internet search engine is a program that runs on a **server** and helps users find Web pages of interest. It provides hyperlinks allowing navigation to the selected pages. The application allows one to ask for content meeting specific criteria and retrieves a list of references that match those criteria. Search engines depend on massive indexes which are engineered to operate quickly and are updated frequently. The most commonly used search engines are **Google, Yahoo Search,** and **MSN.** In pre-Web days, Internet searches used the **Archie** and **Veronica** search engines operating under the **Gopher** protocol.

4.5.10 Speech Recognition Software

Speech recognition is the prospect of a computer understanding spoken words and translating them into commands directed to the computer. It also translates words spoken into a document or e-mail message. This technology is not new but was not particularly well developed in earlier versions of Windows. With Vista, Microsoft has improved the quality and simplicity of the technology.

Speech recognition allows you to control your computer by voice (a microphone is required) and to dictate text into documents. Instruction in the use of speech recognition is beyond the scope of this book but **Vista** provides an excellent tutorial and training tool that will get you started. Open speech recognition this way:

1. Attach a microphone if one is not connected.
2. On the Start menu click Accessories.
3. Click Ease of Use.
4. Click Windows Speech Recognition.
5. The tutorial is visible the first time you open Speech recognition.

Professional quality speech recognition software, **Dragon Naturally Speaking,** is used in many applications for dictation and is manufactured by **Nuance Corporation.**

4.5.11 Other Application Software

The categories of applications are as endless as the imagination of designers and programmers. In this section, several other examples of application software are presented.

Instant Messaging Instant messaging or IM is a form of **real-time** communication between two or more people most commonly based on typed text. The text is transmitted between computers connected over a network such as the Internet. Instant messaging speeds communication and supports collaboration. In recent years IM has extended to include voice and video with voice communication. Popular IM applications include AOL's **Instant Messenger** and Yahoo's **Messenger.**

Instant messaging can be used for **one to many** group discussion, as in a chat room, or for one to one discussion. Group discussion requires a server but one to one does not because a faster **peer-to-peer** connection can be used.

Web Development and Editing Tools Web development tools are programs that assist developers of Web sites. Websites are formed from combinations of Web pages, server programs, and databases. Numerous tools are available to help in all aspects of Web development and several are identified and explained here:

- **Dreamweaver**—A what you see is what you get (WYSIWYG) editor of HTML (Web) pages. Dreamweaver provides tools for accessing server databases and returning data to visitors of a Web site.
- **Expression Web**—Microsoft's WYSIWYG HTML editor and general Web design program that replaced Microsoft **FrontPage.**
- **Visual Studio**—This is Microsoft's premier development platform for programmers. While it can be used to create stand alone programs (EXEs) it is also used to build Web interfaces with connection to server databases.
- **WAMP**—This is a Web developer server suite that is an open-source, free, and non-proprietary. It runs on a Windows-based server and includes several important components:
    - **Apache**—Web server software that enables a computer to receive HTTP client requests and respond by sending HTML pages to the client. The Internet and Web chapter explains the client-server role in depth.
    - **MySQL**—MySQL is a relational database manager (RDBMS).
    - **PHP**—A programming language designed for producing dynamic Web pages (pages that are created on the spot in response to client requests).
- **LAMP**—Identical to WAMP except that it runs on a Linux server.

Desktop Publishing Desktop publishing is commonly used to describe page layout procedures. This activity combines a personal computer and page layout software (**QuarkXPress, InDesign, Publisher**) to create publication documents for large-scale publishing at a commercial printer or small scale in-house publishing. The skills employed apply to pamphlets, books, CD labels, posters, signs, and advertising.

Statistical Software A statistical package is a collection of programs that is designed to perform statistical analysis. It enables people to obtain the results of standard statistical significance tests without knowledge of the underlying statistical procedures or mathematics. Most statistical packages also provide facilities for data management.

4.5.12 Installing Application Software

Software is normally installed by running a procedure which performs the act of putting the program into a computer system so that it can be executed. Most programs are supplied in a compressed form to enable less costly distribution. For installation they must be unpacked and the relevant components (files) placed correctly in specific locations on the computer's hard disk folders.

During the installation process the user may be asked to make choices regarding which of the program's options to install. This is known as a **custom installation.** Not all software allows custom installation because in some cases all of the software must be installed for it to operate properly. A common example of where a custom installation is permitted is **Microsoft Office.** Office includes Word, PowerPoint, Excel, and several other programs each with its own selection of options. The user chooses which programs and which features of each to install.

Application software is installed in one of two ways:

- **Package Management System**—This is a function of the operating system and installs all packages from all vendors. Mac OS uses this technique.
- **Installer**—This is a separate program, often called SETUP.EXE, which is responsible for the installation of the program it is bundled with. Installers are common with Windows-based software.

4.6 Software Ownership

Questions of software ownership are frequently raised. Depending on the type of license offered by the software's author programs may or may not be copied and given to friends or colleagues. Various types of software license and the overall consideration of copyright are discussed in this section.

Copyright Software authors may copyright their work and most software is covered with that protection. Some advocates of free software use software copyrights to ensure that the software they write will remain free. Ownership of software usually remains with the author and users license software for their use on machines they own or operate.

License A software license grants permission to a user to do things with computer software. For example, a software license might grant permission to make copies of the software, or distribute it to a specified number of co-workers. The license may be permanent or may terminate in a specified amount of time or after a limited amount of use. It is rare that the user of software owns the software even when having possession of the physical media the software was distributed on.

Site License A site license is a type of software license that is commonly used to license software to an organization (business, educational, governmental). A site license grants permission to make a large or unrestricted number of installations throughout the organization. The vendor supplies one copy of the software and the organization assumes responsibility for the multiple installations.

End User License Agreement An end user license agreements or **EULA** accompanies most licensed software and is presented to a user during the installation process. The user has the choice of accepting or rejecting the agreement. The installation of the software is conditional to the user accepting the agreement and thereby agreeing to abide by its terms. Typically a EULA grants the right to make a certain number of copies of the licensed software.

When software is installed it is copied to the user's hard drive. Without the consent of the licensor the action of copying violates copyright law. The EULA is used to grant permission to make such a copy. If the user chooses not to accept the license agreement, the software may not be used. The license is the only mechanism provided by the licensor for granting permission for use. The EULA may also specify that a user may install a second copy on a backup computer and some EULAs allow a user to install a copy on a business and home computer.

Beta License A beta version of software is the first version released outside the organization that develops the software. It is distributed for the purpose of evaluation and real-world testing. The users of a **beta version** are said beta testers. They are usually customers or prospective customers of the company that develops the software. They receive the software for free or for a reduced price and act as testers. The agreement governing their use of the software is known as a beta license. Normally permission is granted for a period of time that ends when the software reaches the commercial production stage.

Shareware Shareware is a method for marketing commercial software in which a trial version is distributed in advance and without payment. Frequently shareware is downloaded from a Web site providing a convenient **try before you buy** environment. Typically the trial period is limited by time or usage or both. At the end of the period the user must decide to purchase a usage license or allow the software to deactivate. This distribution method is thought to result in a reduced end-user price compared to the brick and mortar retail channel. It also contributes to higher user satisfaction because of the opportunity to try before purchase. Vendors often encourage users of shareware to copy and distribute unregistered versions of the programs in the hope that other users will find it useful and decide to purchase their own license.

Freeware Free software is software which is specifically licensed to grant the recipient freedom to modify and redistribute the software. Normally that would be prohibited by copyright law, so the copyright holder of free software must give recipients explicit permission by license to modify and redistribute. A variation in freeware is open source software.

Open Source This is software whose program **source code** is available under a copyright license that permits users to review, alter, and enhance the software, and redistribute it as modified. The best known open source program is the operating system **Linux.** The open-source "movement" blossomed during the dot-com boom of the late 1990s and contributed to Sun Microsystems **StarOffice,** and IBM's endorsement and support for Linux. A notable example of open source software is the database manager **MySQL.** Various programming languages including **PHP, Perl,** and **Python** are open source projects. The animation package **Blender** and the scalable vector graphics program **Inkscape** are open source. The Apache Web server is also open source as is the **Linux** operating system.

Software Piracy Copyright infringement of software refers to a collection of actions performed without the permission of the copyright holder. Of course, whether or not each activity is an infringement depends on the license as granted by the software owner. Actions include:

- Creating a copy and selling or giving it to someone.
- Creating a copy to serve as a backup. Some see this as a fundamental right of the software-buyer but legally it can be an infringement, depending on the laws and license.
- Renting the original software to others.
- Posting copies on the Internet for users to download.

4.7 Software Architecture

Software architecture is the structure and arrangements of the components of an application. It also includes the interface requirements of a program, and relationship of the program to database managers and to communication utilities. This topic is differentiated from programming paradigms like structured and object oriented programming and the important topic of data storage structures, which are discussed in another chapter.

Operating System – Application Program Relationship The relationship between the operating system and the application program is that of a client (the program) requesting services from the host (the operating system). As a program runs, files are requested, communication to other programs established, and results displayed on output devices. The role of the OS is to load programs into RAM, begin program execution, and provide these services and access to other hardware in a timely fashion without unduly denying other applications needed resources.

Application Program – Database Management System Relationship Modern application development follows the general design orientation that programs are more flexible and more quickly written and tested when the management of a program's data (it's primary resource) is left to a DBMS that specializes in that task. This **two-tier** arrangement separates the application into parts that can be maintained separately thus minimizing risk and affording opportunities for more efficient operation.

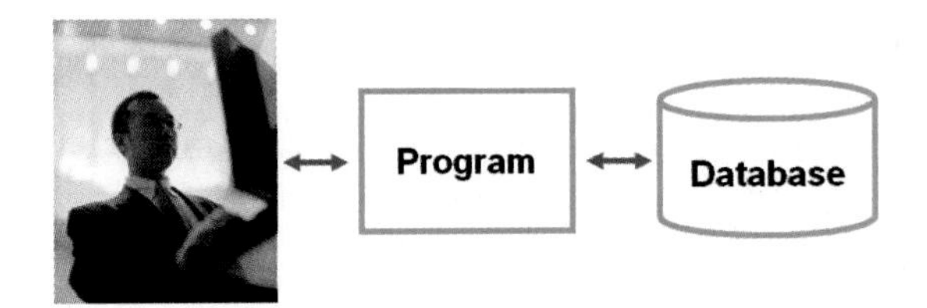

Two-Tier Architecture

Application Program – User Interface Relationship Some software developers separate the application into three tiers by removing responsibility for the user interface from the program. This arrangement permits the interface to be altered without affecting the underlying logic embedded within the application code.

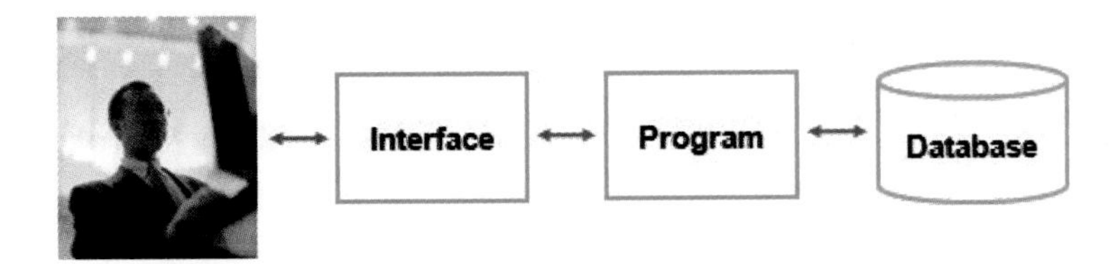

Three-Tier Architecture

Client-Server Client-server is an architecture which typically revolves around a network (although a network is not required) and separates the client (the consumer of data and other resources) from the server (which distributes those resources). Numerous clients are typically connected to the server at the same time. Common server applications include file, data, image, and e-mail serving. The server may also provide access to a shared hardware resource such as a printer or communication gateway. In the illustration here the interface is distributed to the client making what is depicted a **three-tier** deployment.

Client-Server Architecture

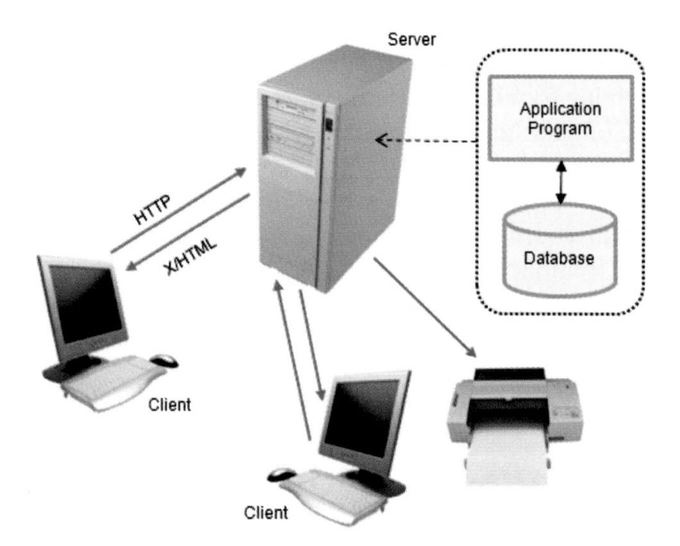

.NET Tying together the components can be difficult when they are made of different designs or use incompatible interfaces for the transport of data between the tiers. Microsoft has attempted to provide a **run-time** environment that manages a program's requirements while standardizing the definitions of data storage structures in memory and providing a standard interface between software components. This environment is called the **.NET Framework.** It is intended for use in new applications created for the Windows platform.

Web Services A Web service is a software system designed to support **interoperable** between machines over a network. Interoperability is important when machines run different operating systems and different Web servers. The essence of Web services is that **program functionality** and the data that it accesses may be distributed over a network of incompatible computers.

Web services are frequently revealed to programmers as application program interfaces (**API**—discussed in the computer programming chapter) that can be accessed over a network, such as the Internet, and executed on a remote system hosting the requested services. The standard definitions of Web services apply to many different computer systems, but the common thread is the use of XML to communicate content following the **SOAP** (Simple Object Access Protocol) architecture.

SOAP Transports Requests and Responses

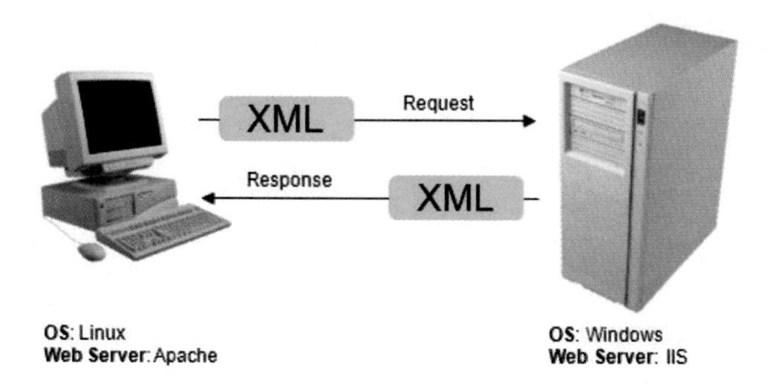

SOAP is a **protocol** that defines the format of messages exchanged in XML envelopes. HTTP is a foundation for SOAP. The most common format is the Remote Procedure Call (**RPC**) in which one network node (the client) sends a request message to another node (the server), and the server sends a response message to the client.

Since Web services are distributed among servers it is useful for software developers to have access to a directory of the technical specifications of available services. **WSDL** (Web Services Description Language) is one such directory. It is an XML-based service providing descriptions on how to communicate using Web services. The directory provides information about what services are available on which servers. It also identifies the data requirements for using each service. Programs on the client computer format requests using SOAP to actually call the functions listed in the WSDL.

If a business wishes to use Web services on the server of different firms, Web developers must learn what firms provide what services. To assist developers in finding businesses that offer Web services the **UDDI** (Universal Description, Discovery and Integration) exists. It can be thought of as a protocol for publishing a telephone like directory of Web service sources. Businesses wishing to permit access to their servers' Web services are listed in the UDDI. Essentially, the UDDI serves as a broker between businesses. The integration of SOAP, WSDL, and UDDI is summarized here:

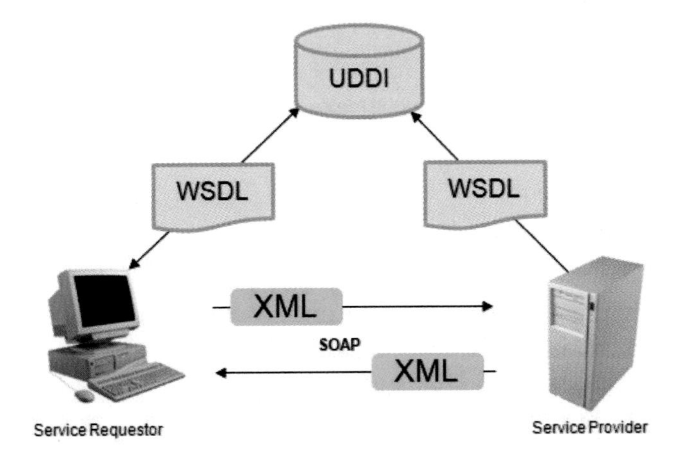

Web Services Architecture

4.8 Software Engineering and Software Design Tools

Software Engineering is the application of a systematic, disciplined, and quantifiable approach to the development of software. The discipline of software engineering includes the use of tools and methods for defining software requirements, performing software design and software construction, testing software, and performing software maintenance. Software Engineering arose in response to the perceived failure of earlier software development procedures that were considered by some to be haphazard at best.

Software is often found where very high reliability is expected (FAA aircraft traffic control, medical imaging, nuclear power plant control, etc.). These applications contain millions of lines of code, making them as complex as many modern machines. It should be no surprise that the possibility of error is great and the allowance for error is minimal.

There are many manual and computer assisted tools available to provide aide during the system analysis and design activity. Several important and frequently used tools are described briefly here and more completely in the systems analysis chapter.

4.8.1 Data Flow Diagram

A data flow diagram (**DFD**) is a graphical representation of the movement of data through an information system. A DFD can also be used for the visualization of structured design because this tool facilitates breaking down processes into increasingly smaller units—in effect decomposing the process until individual program blocks are defined.

This is a **top-down** approach

- The designer makes a **context level** (top level) DFD, which shows the data flows between the system and the external environment (**stakeholders**).
- The system is **decomposed** into increasingly more detailed DFDs that represent portions of the system.
- This approach continues until a sufficiently **granular level** of design is accomplished (program blocks).

Context Level Data Flow Diagram

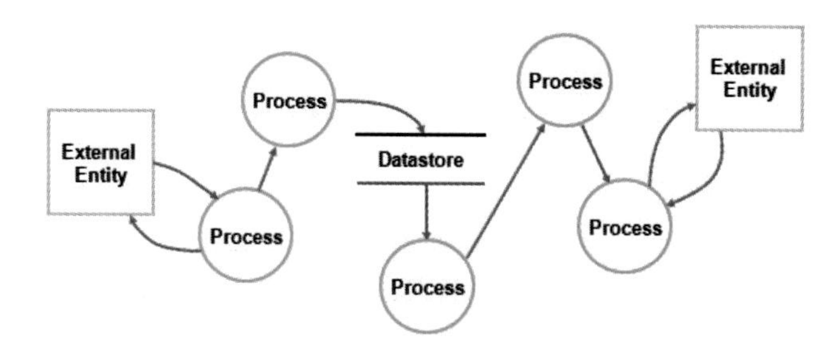

4.8.2 Flowcharts

A flowchart is graphical representation used to illustrate the logical steps to be performed by a process. The starting and ending points of a process are identified and the sequence of actions in the process, and the decision points (branches) are shown, too. Flowcharts use semi-standard shapes to represent different types of actions in a process:

- **Start/End**—The terminator symbol usually contains the word "Start" or "End."
- **Input/Output**—Represents data entering or leaving the system.
- **Action or Process**—A box can represent a single step ("add two numbers"), or an entire sub-process ("get average of two numbers").
- **Decision**—A decision or branching point depicted as a diamond. Lines representing different decisions emerge from different points of the diamond.
- **Flow Line**—Connects other symbols and indicates the direction of flow.
- **Data Storage**—Indicates a source of data storage.

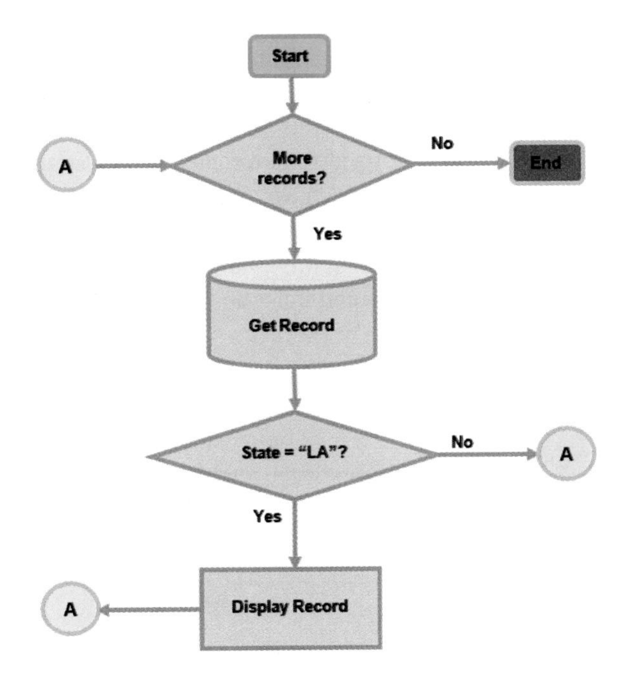

Flow Chart

4.8.3 Data Modeling

Data modeling is the process of designing structures for organizing data. The data structures are created in a database which is controlled by a DBMS. The model may define constraints or limitations on the data placed within the structure. A **conceptual data model** is developed early in a software development project. This model evolves into a **logical data model** and eventually into **physical data model.**

The conceptual model for a relational database is often prepared in graphical form as an **entity-relationship diagram** (ERD). An ERD represents the objects of a database and the relationships that connect them. The objects are **entities** which can be thought of as nouns and **relationships** among the entities can be thought of as verbs. The following illustration depicts the ERD for a system that manages products, customers, and their purchases.

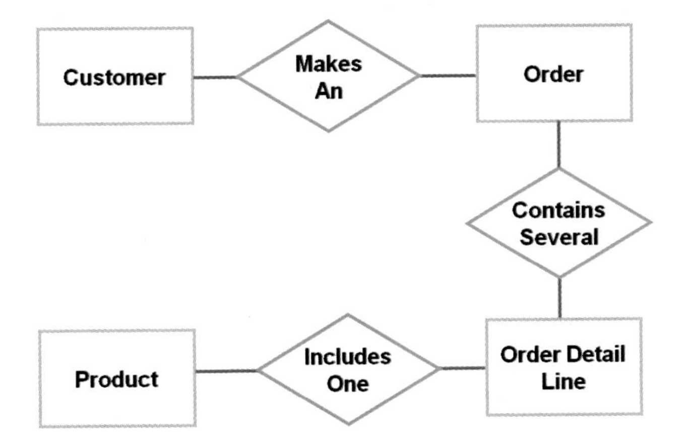

Entity-Relationship Diagram

4.8.4 Computer Aided Software Engineering

Computer Aided Software Engineering, usually abbreviated **CASE,** is the use of programs to assist in the analysis of requirements and the design, development, and maintenance of software. CASE tools are used to automate the preparation and distribution of the analysis and design diagrams (known as "upper CASE") and can also operate as **code generators** (known as "lower CASE") producing program code based on the designs contained within the diagrams. Generally, automatically generated program code is somewhat generic (and not efficient) and must be refined by human programmers before installation is attempted.

CASE Code Generator

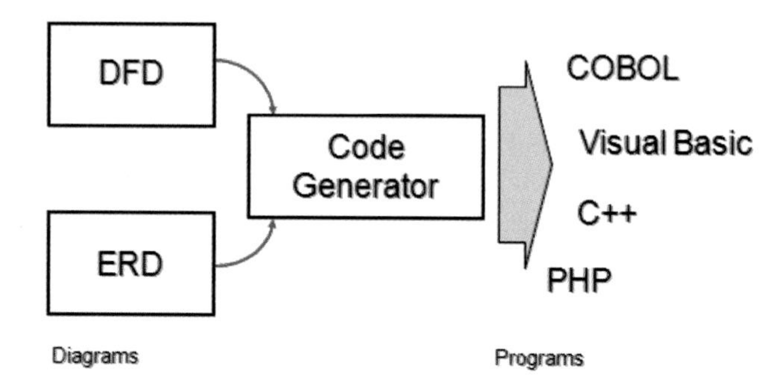

4.9 Summary

Hardware is the physical part of a computer system but it would be impossible to process data into information with a computer alone. The operating system gives a series of instructions that command the hardware to act in specific ways. The OS facilitates the operation of application programs and provides them access to resources like files and databases and hardware.

In a sense, the operating system is the fulcrum that allows hardware and application software to balance. The OS brings order to the mass of electronic signals running through hardware and the binary 1s and 0s of computer programs. Many operating systems exist but the most common are Windows, Linux, and Mac OS. The primary functions of the OS are management of resources: memory, disk, and processing time. The file management subsystem of the OS is used to place files on disk for later retrieval. The file system allows users to navigate among the folders, the logical grouping of files, without regard to the files' physical placement. The logical to physical mapping of files is automatic and not a burden to the user.

The types of application programs seem endless but several categories are most common. Most users are familiar with e-mail and word processing and many are knowledgeable about spreadsheets and their usefulness. Database management is a more sophisticated topic and plays an important role in business processing and Web applications. Enterprise resource planning ties together different aspects of an organization and is centered on a common database. Personal organization and project management software assists people and project teams to work effectively.

Ownership of software is often misunderstood and users should be aware of the legal aspects of software licensing. Site licenses are frequently used when multiple persons within an organization or multiple labs in a university require use of the same software. Shareware, freeware, and open source projects, all formerly non-traditional software licensing arrangements, are common now.

Software engineering involves the application of a structured framework on the software development process. Consideration is given to different software architectures and development techniques. Tools used during the analysis and design stages of system development include various diagramming techniques. The diagrams can be input to code generators as a way of lowering software development cost.

EXERCISES

Exercise 4.1

Open the Notebook program (usually found on the Accessories menu). This is a simple yet very effective and handy program. It is used primarily for creating and editing text files—files that contain no images or special formatting. There is no spell checking feature.

Run Notepad by clicking the Start button and then click Programs and then Accessories. The cursor, or **insertion point,** indicates where Notepad will display characters as they are typed. Do these things:

1. At the insertion point type your first name followed by your last name. Separate them with a space.
2. Save your work with the name SOFTWARE_01.TXT (type SOFTWARE_01 only since .TXT is automatically added for you). *SOFTWARE_01 is the file name and TXT is the file extension.*
3. Save it in the root folder of any storage device.
4. Submit your work to the instructor.

Exercise 4.2

Using the program Paint, create a corporate logo of your design. Use Search if you do not know where Paint is. Follow these requirements:

1. Set image size to 1" × 1". If you ignore this requirement your work can not be graded! Hint: Look in the IMAGE drop down menu at the top of your screen and find the ATTRIBUTES option.
2. Include your name or initials in the logo.
3. Include a minimum of 2 shapes and 2 colors.
4. Save the logo on your homework disk as LOGO.BMP. It is best to save using the 256 color bitmap option. If you ignore this requirement your work can not be graded!
5. Hint: Make sure you save your work in the root folder of a floppy disk or jump drive.
6. Submit your file.

Exercise 4.3

Search the Internet for The Northwest Ordinance. Copy it to the Clipboard and paste it into a new file in Notepad. Save the file as SOFTWARE_03.TXT and submit to your instructor.

The Northwest Ordinance begins: "Be it ordained by the authority aforesaid . . ."

Exercise 4.4

Perform these operations using Vista's Computer and Notepad programs:

1. Download SOFTWARE_04.TXT from your course Web site.
2. On your storage device create a folder named doorway.
3. Inside the doorway folder make a folder named flower.
4. Move the downloaded file to the flower folder. Move means move and not copy.
5. Use NOTEPAD to create a text file. Type your first name and last name and save the file in the doorway folder giving it the filename HELLO.TXT. Separate your first and last names with a space.
6. Create a folder named goldfish in the flower folder and copy HELLO.TXT to that new folder.

Exercise 4.5

Visit the Federal Aviation Administration's (FAA) Web site (http://www.faa.gov). Click Data and Statistics then select Airline On Time Statistics. Select all carriers and the Baltimore, MD airport. View the On Time Arrival Performance for February 2007. View the Tabular Version of the Data and then copy the table that you see to the Clipboard. Paste the table into Notepad and save the file as SOFTWARE_05.TXT. Submit the TXT file to your instructor.

The first two rows of the table are exactly this:

On Time	5,890	73.55%	N/A	N/A
Air Carrier Delay	495	6.18%	24,059	28.14%

Exercise 4.6

Provide short answers to these questions:

A. What is system software compared to application software?
B. Why is data considered software?
C. What is machine language and why is it needed?
D. What is the role of the compiler and how does it differ from that of an interpreter?

Exercise 4.7

Provide short answers to these questions:

A. What are the basic functions of an operating system?
B. What is file mapping and why is it important?
C. File associations performs an important role—describe it.
D. What is a graphical user interface? Discuss how the introduction of GUI based software broadened the community of computer users.
E. What is a device driver? What advantage is derived from their use?
F. When using Vista's Computer utility, what is the difference between moving a file and copying one?
G. How is the Recycle Bin able to hold on to deleted files?

Exercise 4.8

Provide short answers to these questions:

A. Identify and describe two activities that promote system hygiene. Describe their use.
B. Identify and describe the importance of three specific application programs.
C. Who owns software? What is the EULA?
D. Why is open source software development important? What advantages does it offer to commercial and private computer users?
E. Is the client-server architecture compatible with SOAP? If so, how and what advantages does SOAP offer?
F. What is shareware? Why has it become popular?
G. Is it illegal to make copies of commercial software and distribute them among your friends?

Exercise 4.9

While using Vista make sure that you can perform these operations:

A. Clean up using the Disk Cleanup Wizard.
B. Install and uninstall a program.
C. Create a shortcut for a program.
D. View and sort files and folders using Computer.
E. Retrieve a deleted file from the Recycle Bin.
F. Unzip compressed files and folders.
G. Use Task Manager Utility to stop a program. This is an important Vista program, if you are not sure where it is use Vista to help you locate it.
H. Defragment your computer's hard drive.
I. Install a hardware device and its associated driver.

Exercise 4.10

What are the strengths and weaknesses of the Windows, Mac, and Linux operating systems?

DATA COMMUNICATIONS AND NETWORKING

CHAPTER 5

Communication is about the exchange of data. Whether the exchange is between humans or machines there are certain technologies that may be employed and certain rules that must be followed. Although communication is as old as humanity electronic communication has been possible for less than 200 years. The first **electronic** medium for telecommunication, the telegraph invented in the 1840s, was slow, awkward to use and carried little information content. However, it is interesting to note that this was the first form of digital transmission where voltage "ON" can be conceived as a "1" and voltage "OFF" would be a "0". By today's standards it could be considered primitive. Where a skilled telegraph operator could perhaps transmit 50 words per minute a computer network today can carry in excess of 500,000,000 words per minute. With such an incredible increase in speed comes a dramatic rise in the potential for the use of information. The risks to **security** and **privacy** associated with the ability to deliver large quantities of data anywhere in the world in almost no time must also be considered.

Today most people that we know depend on computers and communication equipment to stay in touch. We e-mail friends, perform banking transactions, purchase tickets, take college exams, and chat with family all by using a computer connected to the Internet. Several of the most commonly used communication services of the Internet are shown here:

Service	Description
Chat Rooms	Typed, real-time conversation. Audio, video and other media may be exchanged.
E-Mail	Transmission of typed messages by a computer network.
FAX	Sending and receiving FAX messages using a computer.
FTP	A standard that permits up and downloading files to and from a server.
Instant Messaging	Real time typed messaging that notifies you when your contacts are on-line.
Newsgroups	Written discussion about a topic posted to an interested group..
Phone	Known as VoIP, using a computer as a replacement for traditional phone service.
Video Conferencing	Real time conference using video and audio equipment.
WWW	Use of browser to navigate to various documents and perform transactions.

Internet Communication Services

Although computer and voice communication technologies grew rapidly during the period after World War II, it was not until the 1960s that serious attempts were made to link the technologies together. Until that time computers operated independently of other computers and corporations that required information to be shared among various locations and that relied on the postal service to deliver it. Now, in the age of the Internet, it is almost unheard of for a business organization to be without some form of electronic data communication.

The earliest forms of communication involved speaking or drawing symbols that represented concepts. Surely, these forms of communication seem simple and commonplace to people today, but, in fact, they represented significant advances in human development. Inherent in both modes of communication is the notion that the **speaker** (the transmitter) and the **listener** (the receiver) must have a common understanding of the meaning of words or symbols. Both must have an agreement that when one speaks the other listens. They further agree that after a period or a pause the listener may become the speaker and the other the listener. Thus both people are sharing the air time or, in effect, sharing the **communication channel.** This concept of a set of rules that govern communication (known as a **protocol**) applies to people and machines alike.

Communication Roles: Transmitter and Receiver

A discussion of communication architecture and technology would not be complete without consideration given to security and privacy. With the wide distribution of computers, databases, and computer users the possibility of illicit entry into a network for the purpose of data theft or sabotage is not remote. Discussion of security and privacy is presented in another chapter.

5.1 History and Background

Prior to electronic communication humans employed various means of exchanging information. Romans used light (torches) to communicate between mountaintops. When used during wartime the light signals were **encrypted** (the data content was disguised) so an enemy observer could not intercept valuable information. Information encoding for security and privacy remains in practice today. Smoke signals and drumbeats were used by many peoples as communication carriers. Drumbeats were effective in places where line of sight communication was not possible (like in jungles) and smoke signals were used in open spaces. Today consideration is given to whether line of sight (direct visibility between transmitter and receiver) communication is possible when selecting a communication channel. In a city where buildings get in the way, telephone or wireless radio channels can be more effective than line of sight channels. Each of these means of communication, light, smoke, and sound involved packing as much meaning into as little symbolic representation as possible.

Clearly, the simple communication systems described above were limited in the information content that they could carry. Since there was little variety among light patterns that torches could form, the number of different messages was limited. To overcome that limit, semaphore (flag-based) systems were developed. Individual flags, each with a pattern representing a different letter of the alphabet, were strung together to form words. The words were combined together into sentences. Essentially this method could be considered an optical telegraph system because Morse's telegraph system replaced each flag pattern with a pattern of electronic dots and dashes. The concept of stringing together a series of letters into words remains the same to this day.

Drumbeats Provide a Communication Channel

Electronic communication advanced quickly in the later part of the 1800s. In 1861 the first transcontinental telegraph was complete, rapidly putting the Pony Express out of business. In 1866 an international telegraph line linking Europe with the United States became operational.

The Telegraph Replaced the Pony Express

In 1874 Emile Baudot developed the means for sending several different information signals through the same wire simultaneously. This process called **multiplexing** opened the way for cost reduction in communication. In 1876 Alexander Graham Bell introduced the telephone, which, unlike the telegraph, carried sound and opened the way for even richer communication content. The next important advance was called voice multiplexing in which several conversations can be carried over the same telephone wire simultaneously. This advance gave the impetus to rapid proliferation of telephony and paved the way later for wide spread use of the telephone network for computer-based communication.

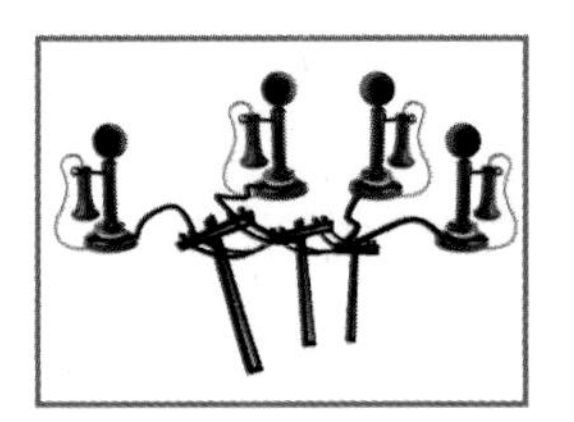

Voice Multiplexing

There were other notable advances in electronic communication. The radio was first effectively used to guide the Titanic's rescue effort in 1912; today it forms the backbone of wireless communication that has become commonplace. Radio wave communication (radio based) permitted long distance communication between cities without the need for underground wires which are expensive to place and maintain. Satellite-based communication allows huge volumes of data to be moved almost instantly almost anywhere around the earth. Finally, cable television networks are used to bypass the traditional broadcast systems to bring extremely large selections of programming directly to people's homes. Such **broadband** systems also permit two way communications between the broadcaster and the home viewer.

Radio Helped Locate the Titanic

Computing technology, described in depth in the hardware chapter, did not advance quite as fast. Charles Babbage invented the first computer, the Difference Engine, in the 1830s. The required technology was too advanced for the time so his computer was not practical. Since the computer was not constructed it could not be programmed, but his friend, a mathematician Ada Lovelace, wrote computer programs that were later proven as logically correct. Ada Lovelace is considered to be the world's first programmer. William Burroughs invented the first commercial mechanical adding machine in 1855 and the first stored data electronic tabulating machine was developed by Herman Hollerith for use in counting the 1890 census.

While electronic communication technology was rapidly advancing, computing technology had a long way to go. Computer development activity picked up. The first practical electronic computer, the ABC computer, was developed in the late 1930s. The first general purpose, electronic computer, the ENIAC, was developed by Eckert and Mauchly in the 1940s at the University of Pennsylvania, and used by the military to calculate artillery shell trajectories. During the 1950s computers were first deployed in business, and in the next decade the marriage of computer and communication technology began.

5.2 Why Link Computers?

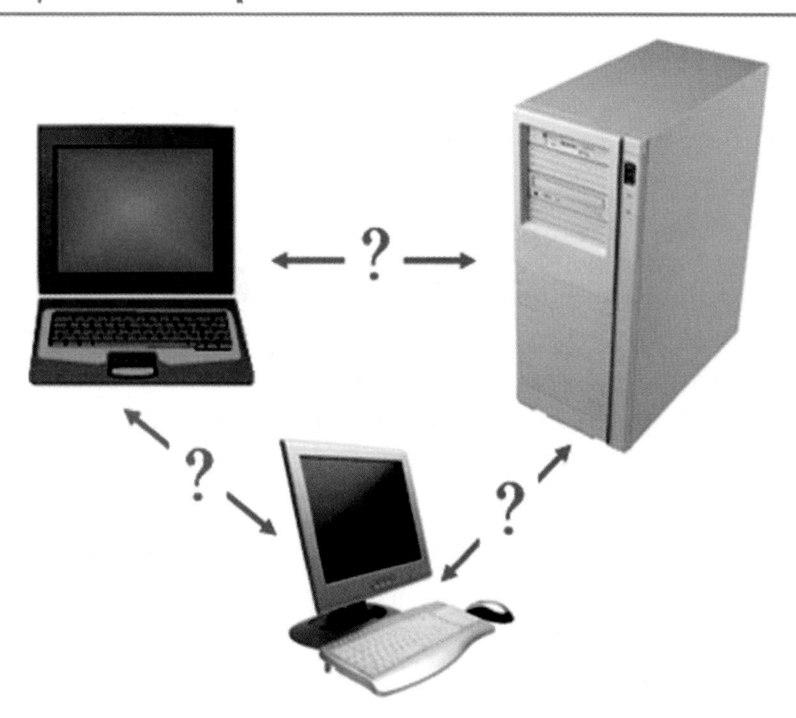

For many years, most computers were stand-alone and on the rare occasion when it was required that data be shared by two computers the data was copied to magnetic tape or punch cards and physically carried to the second machine. This primitive kind of network, where data was manually transported, was jokingly referred to as sneaker-net.

Today things are different. The majority of computers communicate regularly with other computers. In business few computers are stand alone; in a college laboratory most computers are linked on a local area network; and most home computers are used to connect with others using the Internet.

Electronically connecting computers permits sharing of resources among a pool of users. Students in a school laboratory share **site licensed** copies of software thus reducing the cost of providing programs to a large group of users without requiring that a large number of individual copies be purchased. The laboratory network can also be used to distribute homework to students who download their assignments from the network server. In a business, workers share hardware resources (printers, fax machines, external communication gateways, etc.). Since hardware devices are expensive, a network can provide the benefits of laser printing to all connected users without requiring that each user purchase an expensive printer.

Data is another resource that can be shared through a network. Multiple users can gain access to a corporate database through a network. Bank tellers at any branch can access any account of any customer of that bank. Imagine if a teller could only get your account information if you were at the branch where you opened the account. Users can send and receive electronic mail messages and other documents through the network. An organization's procedure manual can be maintained online so that all employees can get access to current updates of the manual rather than wait for the next printing. New software can be distributed to, and installed on all employees' computers through a network thus avoiding the time and expense of manually performing the task many times.

When we consider linking computers for the purpose of communication it is important to differentiate between the following:

- **Telecommunication**—The transmission of signals over a distance for the purpose of communication. Today telecommunication almost exclusively involves the sending of electromagnetic waves (radio, light) and electrical currents by electronic transmitters via wireless or cable transmission systems. In earlier years it may have involved the use of smoke signals, drums, lights, or semaphores.
- **Data Communications**—The engineering devices and circuits that permit signals to be communicated between computer systems. Such communicating computer systems form a computer network and these networks involve at least two devices capable of being networked with at least one usually being a computer.

Telecommunication is about the coding of data and data communication is about the transmission and delivery of data in a network. Neither would be useful alone. Together they form the basis of electronic communication that we have grown to depend on.

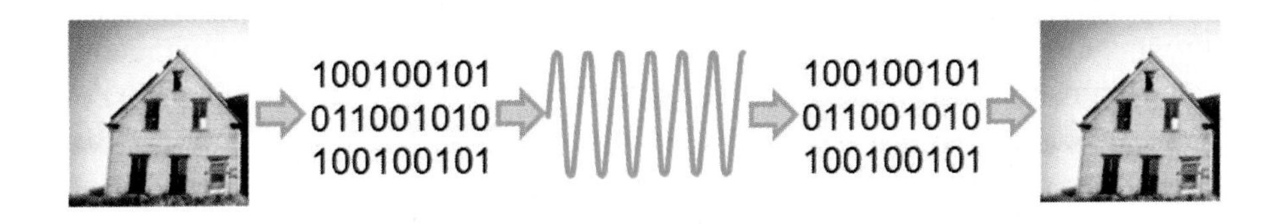

Communication: Encoding, Transmission, and Delivery of Data

5.3 Types of Network Processing

There are three categories of data processing architectures that apply to our discussion of communication networks. Each type has advantages and disadvantages, which are summarized next.

5.3.1 Centralized Processing

In a centralized system one computer system handles all of the data processing responsibilities for the organization. User terminals are wired to the central computer and all programs and data reside at the central site. In the early days of computing, organizations had no choice but to use a centralized approach. This was due to several factors: electronic computer-to-computer communication was not reliable or cost effective; skilled technical employees were rare and it would be difficult for an organization to afford deployment of technicians at multiple sites. The advantage of a centralized architecture, therefore, had been primarily one of economies of scale. One large central computer and one centralized staff cost less than many smaller computers operated by several staffs.

Centralized Processing

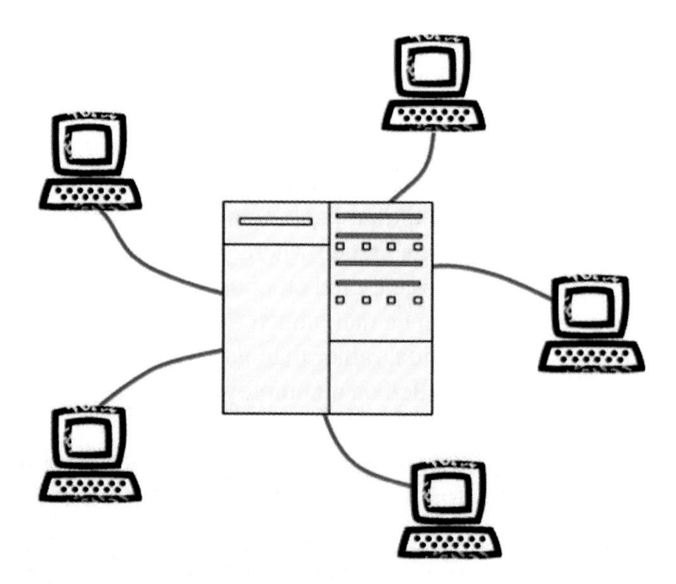

Changes in the way businesses operate caused reconsideration of whether the centralized approach was the way to go. Reliance on a central staff can leave some departments feeling that they do not get the attention they deserve. Since employees were increasingly computer literate the knowledge needed to purchase and operate computers has become more distributed through organizations. For that reason, too, many corporations are allowing the various departments to take responsibility for their own data processing.

5.3.2 Decentralized Processing

The decentralized approach is totally the opposite of centralized processing. Each part of an organization does its own data processing. Each unit is totally independent of the others. Programs and data are not shared (unless manually transported between computers) and hardware resources (printers, communication gateways) are replicated as needed for each site.

Decentralized Processing

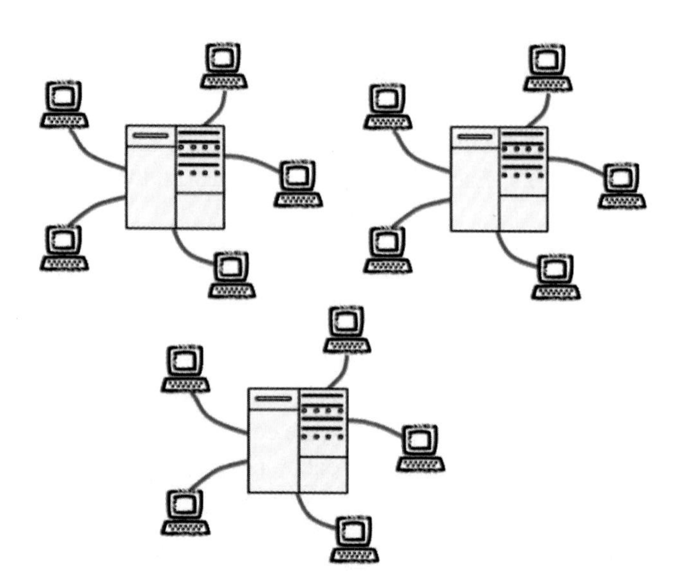

While it may be a more expensive option for an organization (more hardware, software, and staff) with less opportunities for data sharing and data integration there are advantages to this architecture. Data processing activities will be more responsive to local staff needs because there is no competition among departments for a slice of a centralized technical staff's time. Data processing is not dependent on one single computer, which, if it goes down, would cause all data processing for an organization to stop. A disadvantage of this approach is the replication of efforts and data at various locations.

5.3.3 Distributed Processing

The distributed architecture tends to solve the problems inherent in the other approaches. It affords the opportunity for shared resources without reliance on a single computer. Local staff can be responsive to local needs but data can be shared throughout the organization without redundancy of effort. How is this accomplished?

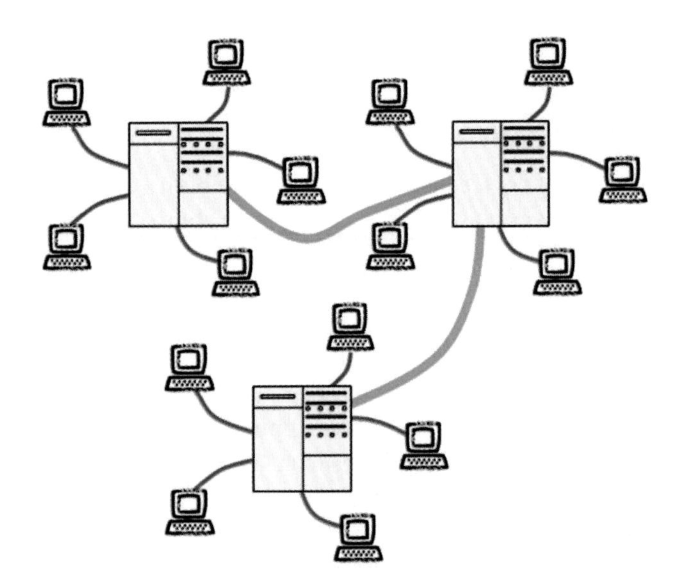

Distributed Processing

Computers are linked together in a network. Data processing responsibilities for the organization are handled by local parts of the organization where data originates and is most frequently accessed. When data is needed in other parts of the organization it is electronically shipped between computers. Programs and other software can be distributed to all sites through the network, and e-mail and other messages make communication among remote workers easy. System reliability is generally higher because one malfunctioning computer will not cause all processing activities to cease. In fact, some organizations can move processing tasks from one computer to another if the first computer is down. In that case the workers at the down computer's site can still communicate with the backup computer via the network.

5.3.4 The Internet

The Internet is a very large distributed network. Numerous **host** computers (servers) are interconnected and even more numerous client computers connect to servers. While not all clients share the same host all clients could find an electronic pathway to all other clients.

The Internet Is a Distributed Network

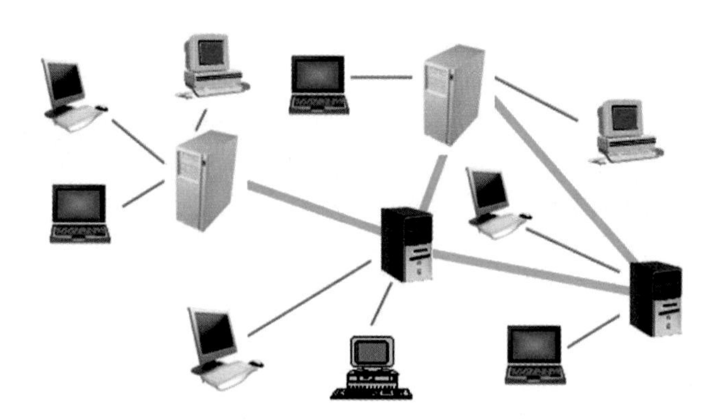

5.4 How Computers Are Connected

Linking computers requires certain accessory hardware devices, special software programs, and the use of electronic connecting channels.

5.4.1 Roles: Sender/Receiver

Normally, each computing device has the capacity to be both a sender (a transmitter) and a receiver (listener). Rarely is it useful for a device to be able to only perform one of those roles. There are several examples of sender/receiver devices: A **dumb terminal** has no computing ability but are attractive because of low cost. It has no processor, disk drive, or main memory. Its use is fully dependent on a host computer to which it is connected. It must, however, be able to send and receive data. Some airline reservation systems use a dumb terminal. The agent types in a request for a seat reservation, which is transmitted by the terminal to the host computer. The computer then checks the reservation database and determines whether the seat request can be fulfilled. A confirmation or denial message is sent back to the dumb terminal where it is displayed for the clerk. A **workstation** is a computer which can perform stand alone processing or serve as a data entry and display device. This type of machine will clearly take on the sender and receiver roles when in data entry mode and when participating in network activities like e-mail.

5.4.2 Communication Channel

A Communication Channel: An electronic or optical highway that carries a communication signal between computers or other electronic devices.

Some means must be provided for carrying the sender's signals to the receiver. This connection is a communication channel and is frequently referred to as a carrier.

The key word in the definition is highway. The carrier is just that, a right of way that transports an electronic signal between a pair of communicating devices. There are seven important types of carriers (media) that will be described shortly. Each type of carrier can be considered from the perspectives of cost, reliability, capacity, distance signal that can be carried, and security.

Communication Channel

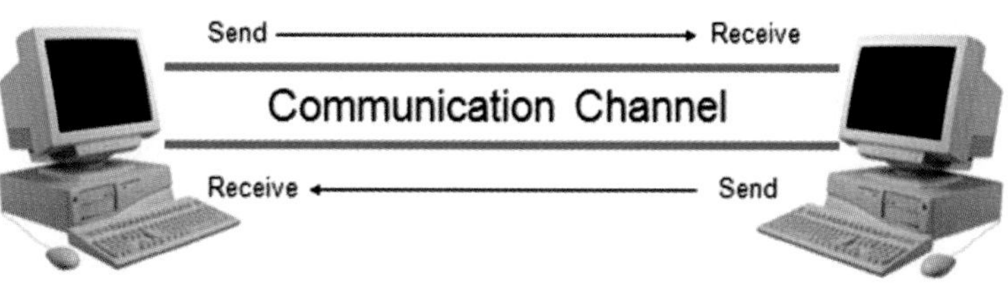

5.4.3 Bandwidth

The communication channel's transmission speed dictates the amount of data than can be moved over the channel per unit of time. Think of a channel as a highway. Bandwidth, the measure of a channel's capacity, is higher for a three-lane highway than for a smaller road with two lanes. Obviously, higher transmission rates are more desirable, but less obviously, higher speed typically costs more.

To determine the number of characters per second that can be transmitted, divide bps by ten.

The most common measurement of transmission speed is **bps** or bits per second. Often, measures are in multiples like **kbps** (1000 bits per second), **Mbps** (million bits per second) or **Gbps** (billion bits per second).

Different types of data require different data rates to transmit properly. Voice communication uses a lower bandwidth channel than video does. The bps capacity of a communication channel is referred to as its bandwidth. The amount of data that can be passed along a communications channel in a given period of time is the bandwidth. The higher the bandwidth the greater the amount of data that can be sent through a channel at once. This is no different than the water supply system in a community. Wider diameter pipes can carry more water. Pipes leaving the water treatment plant (the host) get progressively smaller until they reach individual houses.

Bandwidth

A **data transfer rate** (sometimes just data rate) is the quantity of digital data that is moved from one machine to another in a given time. Data transfer rates are usually measured in bits per second as mentioned before. The data transfer rate can be viewed as the amount of data that travels from one place to another per second. In general, the greater the bandwidth of a given path, the higher the data transfer rate.

5.4.4 Channel Media

Channel media carries communication signals between computers and other network devices. There are seven common types of electronic "water pipes," and each is described in this section:

Channel Media

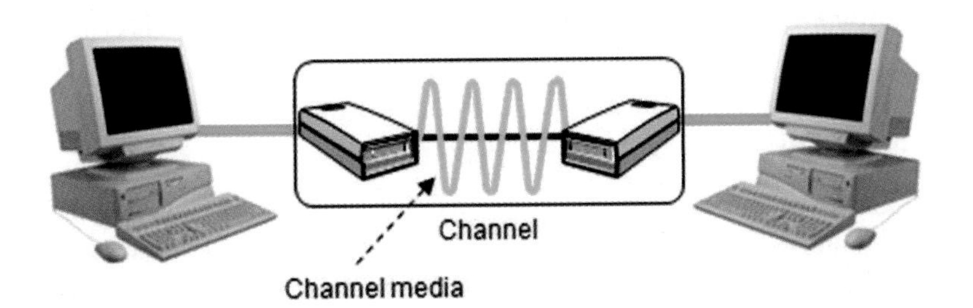

The seven common channel media types can be divided into two groups, **guide media** and **wireless,** depending on whether or not a physical connection is used:

Guide Media Some media are physical and wire-like. From the original telephone and telegraph wires of more than 130 years ago to glass wires of today, these examples are known as guide media.

- **Wire Pair**—The oldest and most common form of medium is ordinary telephone wire known as wire pair or **twisted pair.** Wire pair has been around for more than one hundred years so there is plenty available for use. Nearly every home and business in the United States is wired and therefore has the potential to participate in electronic communication. The telephone system is setup to carry voice (analog) transmission so when used for computer- based communication the computer's digital signal must be converted to one that can be accepted by the phone network. You will learn about this conversion process and the device that performs it later when we discuss modems.

Wire pair channels are perhaps, because of their wide spread availability, the least expensive of all but there are some drawbacks. Data moves more slowly on wire pair than on any other medium. Signals that are carried through the phone system may be subject to security breach because they pass through so many pieces of equipment between sender and receiver (normally wire pair is not used to directly connect two communicating devices but rather the signals are switched through the telephone network).

Wire Pair
© Anthony Bolan, 2007, Shutterstock.

This simple type of medium is not shielded well from external static or other disturbances so data may be lost or otherwise polluted when transmitted. The telephone system was built to carry voice communication. If you are listening to a friend speak and a word or two are garbled up because of momentary noise on the line you will probably still be able to get the message because you can try to fill in the words based on the context of what is being said. A computer is not able to do that. If a single bit (one eighth of a byte) is lost then the character represented by the byte is wrong and the computer has no way of understanding the rest of the message based on context. Consequently, systems must rely on error detection and error correction software to trap and correct such errors. This software is good but not perfect, so when communication is critical, wire pair might not be the best choice. **DSL** communication is carried by wire pair and simultaneously shares the line with analog voice communication using a technique called **multiplexing** which is discussed later in this chapter.

- **Coaxial Cable**—This type of medium consists of a thick copper wire surrounded by insulating material which itself is surrounded by an electrical conductor formed as a braided mesh. A protective plastic coating covers the whole package.

Coaxial Cable
© Igor Smichkov, 2007, Shutterstock.

This type of cable delivers high-speed transmission, which is relatively free from outside noise. Coaxial cable, or **coax** for short, is classified as baseband and broadband. The former is easily used for computer communication: it is easy to attach to devices and is relatively inexpensive but it can carry only one transmission channel. Broadband coax provides higher transmission speeds and can be subdivided into several channels. Speeds of and above 600 Mbps are possible making this media desirable for cable television systems which must carry many television pictures simultaneously. Broadband is more expensive and more difficult to install. It is used for computer communications in cable modem services. Since coaxial cable networks are private, security is of less worry than with other types of media.

- **Fiber Optics**—Here the transmission medium is the glass or plastic cable itself that is transparent and carries **light waves.** Since the signal is being carried by light, data travels at the speed of light which is extremely fast. So fiber optics provides a very fast channel. The light signal travels through a glass strand which is generally impervious to environmental interference. A small diameter strand can carry up to 30 billion bits per second (30 giga bits or 30 Gbps); recent experimentation demonstrated that a single fiber optic cable could carry close to 26 Terabits per second of data.

© Stephen Coburn, 2007, Shutterstock.

There are other advantages that fiber optics provide. The signal is about as clean as can be because the light signal is guided by an internal mirror like reflection so it is not possible for a signal to escape and interfere with other signals in other glass strands that it is usually bundled with. Since the signal is light and not electric or radio, it is not subject to the common types of interference that plague wire pairs and the other kinds of media. It is also secure. It is not possible to tap into an optic strand and extract the data moving through it. If an attempt to physically tap into the glass is made, most likely the glass will break and the signal will be lost. The downside of fiber optics is that it is still relatively expensive compared to other land-based media (wire pair and coaxial cable) and like other guide media the owner must obtain right of way permission to lay cable between points. However, it is interesting to note that while fiber is expensive to deploy it is less expensive in terms of cost per bps.

Wireless Media Channels with media not tied to wires and cables have some advantages: easier installation and lower cost. There are some downsides too as discussed here.

- **Microwave**—Microwave is based on the use of radio to carry a communication signal. Since radio signals are sent over the air security should be a concern, but since the signal follows close to a straight line it may be difficult for unauthorized people to intercept it. As microwaves travel they undergo effects such as scattering and reflection just as other radio waves do. This makes it possible for microwaves to be intercepted by third parties even though they are highly directional forms of electromagnetic energy. Speed of transmission, about 50 Mbps, is generally acceptable for voice or low level data communication demands. A significant advantage is that microwave use avoids the cost of laying and maintaining coax cables underground.

Because the signal is out in the air it can be subject to environmental static. Also, the line of sight nature of microwave is the main drawback when using this media type. The sender and receiver must be able to clearly see each other—line of sight. There may be no physical obstructions between them. If a company uses microwave to communicate between buildings in the same city (not an uncommon practice) then the carrier will be lost if a new building is built between them and it obstructs the clear line of sight.

A further problem involves distance. If the sender and receiver are too far apart the curvature of the earth gets in the way. Every 30 miles or so, the line of sight between two microwave antennas is broken by the Earth's curvature. To overcome this problem relay stations are built about that distance apart so that the signal can continue on its way.

Microwave—Line of Sight Limitation

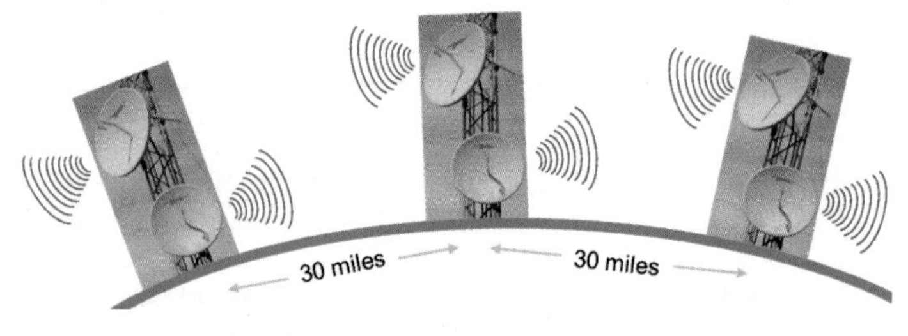

- **Infrared**—This is a medium that is similar to microwave. Light rather than radio waves carries the signal but it has the same line of sight restriction. Infrared light is not visible to humans and it is well suited to data transmission. This type of medium is mostly used for communication in the same room—like remote control devices. It is a very short range medium because it is blocked by almost anything.
- **Satellite**—Satellites are used to overcome the distance limitations imposed by the line of sight restriction of microwave and infrared. An earth station sends a signal up to an orbiting satellite where the signal bounces back to another earth station. The earth stations may be very far apart. In fact, it is possible for a signal to travel all the way across the United States on one **uplink** and **downlink.** The area on the surface of the Earth where the signal from the satellite is received is known as the **footprint.** It is not possible, however, for a single satellite to carry a signal all the way from one side of the earth to the other. To send a signal from New York to Beijing several bounces must occur. In that sense there really is a line of sight restriction on satellite transmission, but since the distance covered in one bounce is so great the restriction is not generally a problem.

For this method to work the satellite must appear to be motionless in the sky. We realize that for a satellite to remain in orbit it must rotate around the Earth. So how are these conflicting requirements resolved? The trick is to put the satellite in a special orbit called a **geostationary** earth orbit which is 22,241 miles directly above the equator. It turns out that anything orbiting the Earth at that altitude above the equator takes exactly 24 hours for each orbit. Since the Earth itself rotates once each 24 hours the satellite and the associated **ground stations** appear to move together, and from the Earth's perspective the satellite appears not to move therefore providing a seemingly stationary electronic mirror on which to reflect signals. This solves one problem but creates another.

Satellite in Geostationary Earth Orbit

Satellites must not be too close together or else the signals bouncing off each satellite will pollute the signals bouncing off other satellites. Until recently, technology permitted no satellites to be closer than 4 degrees apart in Earth orbit. Since there are 360 degrees in a circle only 90 satellites could occupy the ring 22,241 miles above the equator. Ninety is not a large number when used by all countries is considered. Recent advances in technology now permit satellites to be closer so more can be placed in use and with the use of higher frequencies the effective bandwidth is increased; but no matter how far technology advances there is some physical limit that eventually will be reached.

Security is a concern with satellite transmission because anyone can install a satellite receiver (a round dish antenna) and intercept the signal as it returns to Earth. This is because the signal spreads out as it leaves the satellite and when it reaches Earth it covers a fairly large area. Encoding the signal and only allowing the designated receivers access to the decoding scheme provides protection against unauthorized reception.

- **Radio Frequency**—Radio Frequency or RF is also known as wireless technology. It is gaining popularity as more and more families and small businesses are wiring homes and offices. The technology enabling wireless connections is known as 803.11b/g and is more fully explained later in this chapter.

Radio Frequency (RF)—Wireless Technology

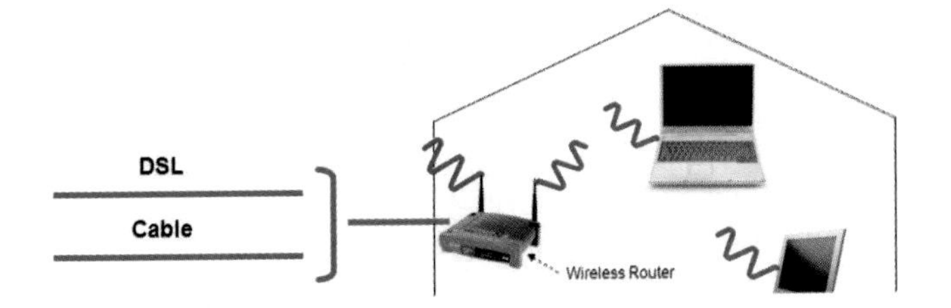

When installed in a home or business a single DSL or cable modem connection can be shared by multiple clients without running wire through the building. The data transfer rate between the base station and the remote units can reach 54 Mbps. The advantages are obvious. The only restriction is that the distance between base and remote units is normally not more than 300 feet. This restriction does not limit use in most homes or small businesses.

There is one caution, however. Since this is wireless the signal can travel outside of buildings thus enabling outsiders to tap into the wireless network and steal Internet access or even possibly hack into home or business computers.

Bluetooth is a specific radio frequency wireless connection limited to very short distances. It is used for connection between computers and peripheral devices.

5.4.5 How a Channel Works

Now that you know what media types are available it is important to understand how a pair of computers uses a channel to communicate. It is not possible to simply connect a computer to each end of a channel. Usually other hardware devices and software are involved.

5.4.5.1 Protocol

Protocol is a word used to refer to an established procedure of conduct. When a head of state visits another country the rules followed for greeting a person of the other country are used. In the United States we greet one another with a handshake. In other countries a hug or a kiss may be traditional. At the start of a **communication session** a handshake occurs. After the initial **handshake,** protocols take over as the rules governing communicating computers connected to other electronic devices.

Devices Connect with a Handshake

If two computers did not follow the same rules it would be impossible for them to communicate. Numerous protocols exist in data communications, but two classes are most common and worthy of notice.

- **Asynchronous**—Data transmission that is asynchronous is the slower of the two but it is also the less expensive. Here special signal bits are added to each transmission to indicate the beginning and end of each block of data that is sent. This protocol is easier to install and is commonly used by personal computers communicating with the various online services. While this protocol requires synchronization (as does the synchronous protocol) it is less complex.
- **Synchronous**—Synchronous protocols also require that the sender and receiver be synchronized in time. This means that the receiver knows when to expect a transmission from the sender. This protocol can be thought of as polite because each device knows when it is time to be the sender or receiver. There is less potential for confusion.

5.4.5.2 Line Configuration

Each channel can be arranged for a particular style of communication. The costs and benefits associated with each style differ.

- **Simplex**—Here the line permits communication in one direction only. This is the least expensive configuration. An example of where simplex could be used is the daily transmission of data from a remote sales office to a central office. Another example is the one-way transmission of telemetry data from a space probe to an Earth station.

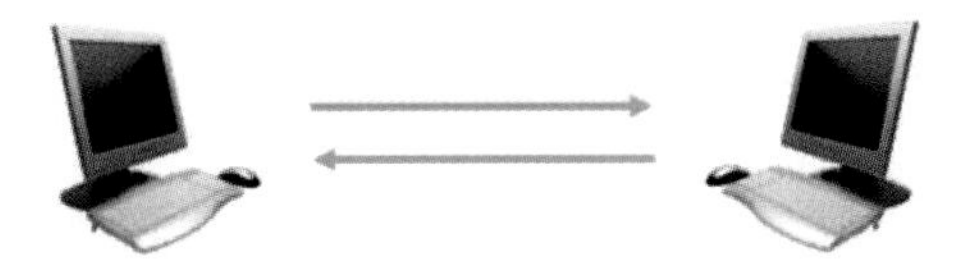

- **Half Duplex**—Data flows in both directions on a line but not at the same time. The same sales office should use a half duplex line if the only communication activity of the day included transmitting daily sales data to the main office followed by receiving a summary report sent back to the sales office.

  Imagine that you and a friend are talking and as you listen to your friend talk you may not respond until your friend tells you that it is your turn. You then speak and, when finished, tell your friend that you are done and now your friend speaks. What an awkward way to have a conversation. That is an example of half duplex communication which is one direction at a time and the receiver must wait until it is time to become a sender.

- **Full Duplex**—A full duplex line permits data to flow in both directions at the same time. Here the receiving device can transmit messages to the sending device before the incoming data transmission is complete. This is particularly useful in systems that send and receive e-mail.

Humans operate in full duplex mode all the time. We may be listening to a friend speak and while still listening begin to respond. The sender (the friend—the original speaker) begins to hear our response (and is becoming a receiver, too) while still speaking. The human brain is able to deal with sending and receiving simultaneously and computers do also.

- **Multiplex**—A multiplex configuration involves several computers sharing the same channel. The line (usually full duplex) can carry several signals simultaneously in both directions between several computers.
- Multiplexing is used to mix two or more signals together onto one line and it is employed to permit a resource to be shared. There are two basic methods used for multiplexing:
    - **Time Division**—Two or more signals are transmitted along the same circuit but only one signal occupies the circuit at any moment. The circuit is shared with each signal getting a small amount of time for access. The time slices are interrupted by the transmissions of the other signals. Each signal takes a turn, but all signals are transmitted.

Time Division Multiplexing

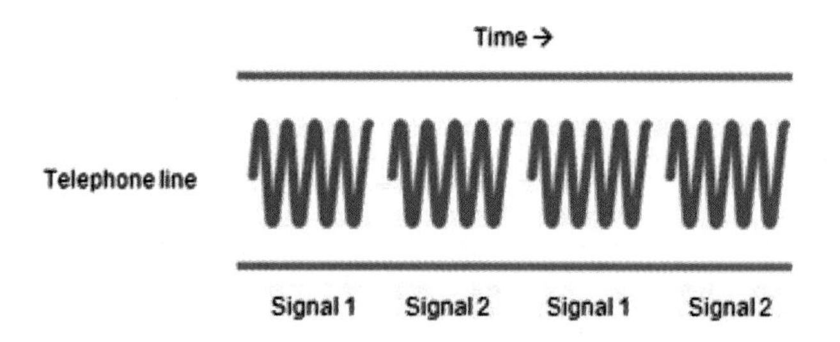

- **Frequency Division**—All signals sharing the circuit are transmitted at once and allocated a portion of the circuit's frequency range. Each signal occupies the circuit at all times. Signals are modulated to different frequency ranges thus allowing each signal a simultaneous portion of the bandwidth.

Frequency Division Multiplexing

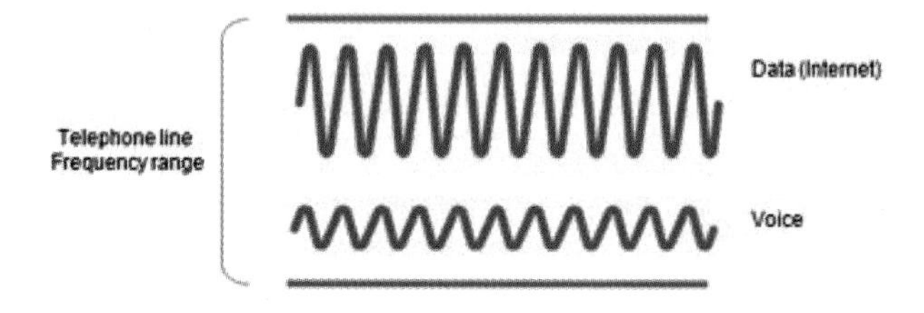

DSL modems modulate digital signals to high frequencies from 25 KHz (kilohertz; one thousand cycles per second) to above 1MHz, in order not to interfere with voice service on the same line in the 0-4 KHz range. Note: a non-DSL modem using the telephone line would not allow simultaneous use of the line because that type of modem modulates the digital signal into the voice signal range.

Multiplexing is what permits **broadband** communication. Broadband is a telecommunications term which refers to a signal processing method which handles multiple simultaneous signals. A **baseband** transmission uses the channel to carry one signal only. The full channel is used to carry one signal at a time. Dial-up network access works this way as does 10base-T Ethernet.

5.4.5.3 Modem

A modem (modulator demodulator) permits a computer's **digital** signals to be carried over an **analog** channel. The modem is a device that modulates an analog carrier signal to encode digital information, and also demodulates such a **carrier signal** to decode the transmitted information. A carrier signal is a specific frequency in a communication channel that is modulated with an information-carrying signal. The most familiar example is a voice-band modem that turns the digital 1s and 0s of a computer into sounds that can be transmitted over the telephone lines of the telephone system, and once received on the other side, converts those sounds back into 1s and 0s. Modems are generally classified by the amount of data they can send in a given time, normally measured in bits per second, or **bps.**

- **Digital signals**—The computer's signals are digital, also known as discrete or square waves. Remember that a computer's signal is a series of bits (1s and 0s) that in sequence make up characters or bytes. It is called discrete because each bit is represented as up (1) or down (0). In a **binary system** that is a very convenient and efficient way to represent data.

Digital Square Wave

- **Analog signals**—A telephone system that was designed to carry voice was built to carry analog signals. These types of signals are called continuous because there is no discrete pattern as with digital signals. Your voice is not comprised of a series of 1s and 0s but rather a continuous sequence of sounds blended together. Since the telephone network was designed for human voice it was designed to carry analog signals. So if the telephone network is to be used to provide a communication channel between computers, the computers' digital signals must be converted from digital to analog and back at the receiving end.

Analog Continuous Form

A modem accepts the digital signal of the sender and converts (modulates) it to an analog signal. This means that the output of the modem can be heard but not understood by humans. The sound that it produces is meaningless to a human but it is a sound that can be carried over a telephone wire or other analog carrier. At the receiver's end another modem is used. Here the second modem receives the analog signal and converts it back (demodulates) to a digital signal that can be accepted by the receiver. The point where the signal enters the computer or network device is known as a **port.**

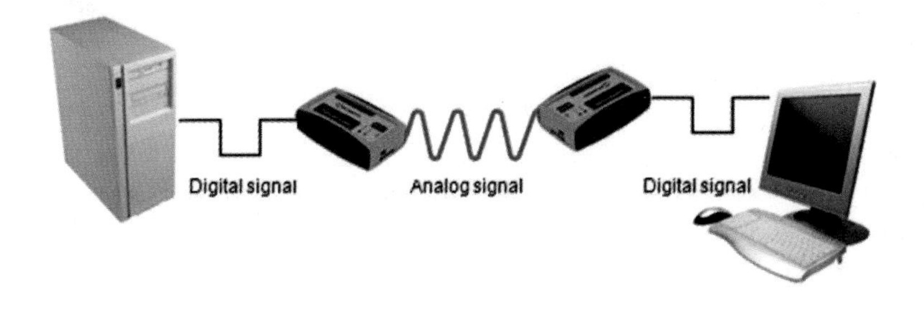

A Modem Converts between Digital Square Waves and Analog Continuous Form Waves

Modems can process data at varying transmission rates. Original computer modems operated at about 300 bps but today home computers often use 56 Kbps modems. At that speed a modem can process about 5600 characters per second (CPS). As an astute reader you are probably wondering why a 56,000 bps modem processes 5600 bytes (characters) per second and not 7000 (56,000/8). This is because each byte that is transmitted has extra two bits added to it to permit synchronization and error detection and correction. So it is easy to compute bytes per second from bps bydividing by ten.

Faster modems, notably cable modems and **ADSL** (Asymmetric Digital Subscriber Line but generally referred to as DSL) modems are becoming common place as Internet users turn to **broadband** Internet access.

5.4.5.4 DSL (Digital Subscriber Line)

Until fairly recently the only option for connecting to the Internet was with a standard analog modem and a phone line. Often busy signals got in the way because the connection point (the ISP—Internet service provider) could handle only a certain number of inbound calls at a time. Also, while connected to the Internet it was impossible to use your phone line for conventional phone calls. DSL is offered as a service that solves these problems and increases connection speed at the same time.

DSL Shares the Telephone Line with Internet Access

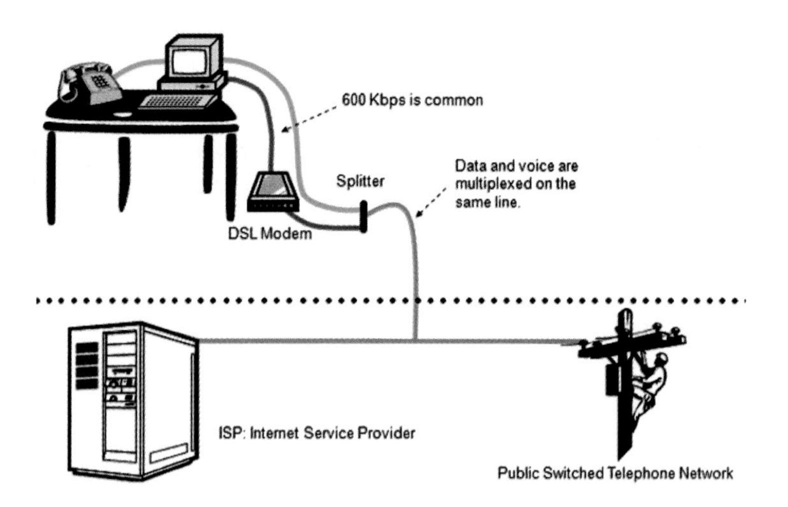

DSL transmits Internet data at relatively high speeds over standard telephone lines and it does this while sharing the telephone line (wire pair) with voice communication. It is able to do this because it squeezes data onto the regular phone line using frequency division multiplexing to blend the two types of signals (data and voice) together.

5.4.5.5 Cable Modems

Cable technology offers speeds generally higher than DSL. Since the heart of the television network provides cable connections at very high bandwidth and speed it is possible to use some of the capacity for other services such as data transmission.

The Cable TV Line Also Carries Internet Access

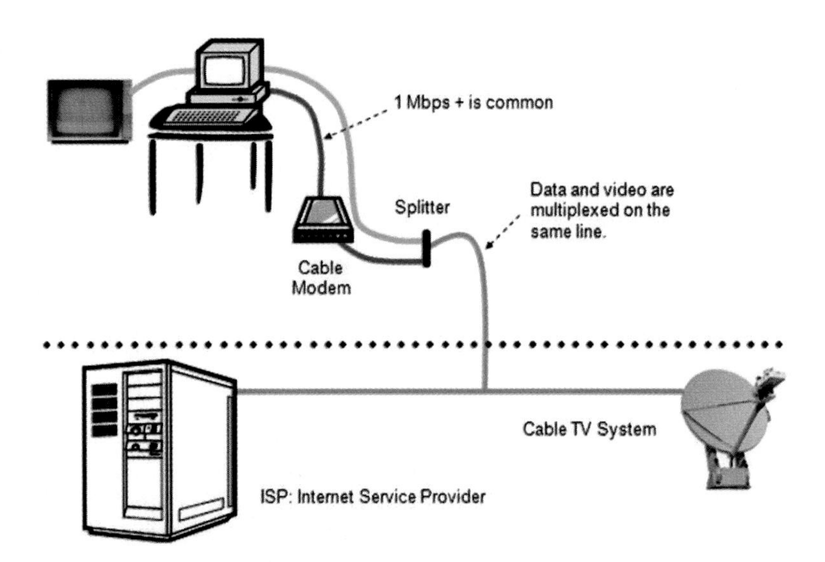

Similar to DSL the data signal is multiplexed with other signals (in this case video) for transmission on the cable. Generally each cable video channel occupies 6 MHz (megahertz) of the bandwidth allowing potentially more than 100 video channels on the cable. The cable provider selects one 6MHz slice and allocates that for data transmission.

Cable is different from DSL in that the line is shared. Essentially the bandwidth for carrying data is shared by all customers in the neighborhood. Cable architecture is **one-to-many** (unlike DSL which is one-to-one). The cable office (head end) supplies bandwidth to the local area and it is divided among all users. If the head end is delivering 30 Mbps to 300 users who are each simultaneously downloading data then each will have 100Kbps available. If there are only 50 simultaneous users then each obtains 600Kbps.

5.5 Networks

A network is a collection of computers and other devices connected by channels. Several important uses of a network are:

- **Enable Communication**—The basic function of a network is to provide an infrastructure that enables communication content to be carried from a sender to the receiver. The hardware, software, other equipment, channel media, and other components must be running consistently and reliably to ensure a smooth communication flow.
- **Share Data**—In most organizations many people have a need to access and use data that relates to business activities. Data is often stored in databases that are maintained on servers in secure locations. The network must be arranged to provide a path to the data for all personnel with appropriate authorization to access the data.
- **Share Hardware Resources**—Certain hardware devices are too expensive to purchase for all users. A color laser printer, a communication gateway, and a database server are examples of commonly shared hardware resources.
- **Share Software Resources**—Organizations with many employees find it less expensive to provide shared access to commonly used software than to purchase a license for each person individually. Since licensing copies for all employees is costly, often a **site license** is used. A license of that type permits multiple installations but at a lower cost since the installations are to be used only by employees and no outsiders.

- **Perform Transactions**—Business **EDI** (electronic data interchange), airline ticket reservations, purchase of clothing, register of college courses, and payment of taxes are all examples of network facilitated transactions.
- **Transfer Funds**—Movement of funds between financial institutions, called Electronic Funds Transfer (**EFT**), is a very common use of networks. Examples of fund transfers are payments made to accompany EDI transactions and payroll checks automatically deposited in employee bank accounts.

Networks are often described based on the geography they cover: wide, metropolitan, and local. The definitions are not specific and are subject to discussion.

5.5.1 WAN: Wide Area Network

A WAN is a wide area network that covers a large geography and includes connections to many MANs (metropolitan area network) or LANs (local area network). A WAN will include many different communication channels linked together in a coordinated fashion. The largest WAN in the world is the Internet.

A Wide Area Network (WAN)

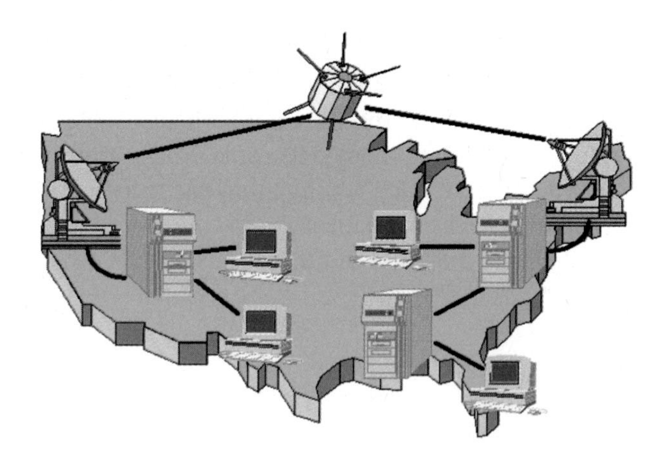

Wide area networks provide connections for computing devices that are geographically diverse. A corporation, for example, with numerous manufacturing plants, sales offices, and warehouses would most likely employ a WAN to provide data and voice transmission between its facilities. The company would lease communication carrier channels from a common carrier (**Verizon, Sprint, AT&T,** etc.) but provide its own equipment for connection to the carrier's channel. The interconnections between portions of the carrier's network (satellite earth stations, microwave relay stations, or other equipment) are the responsibility of the common carrier. Networks designed this way produce an economy of scale that allows many corporations to use the same communication facilities that would be prohibitively expensive for most to build or operate on their own.

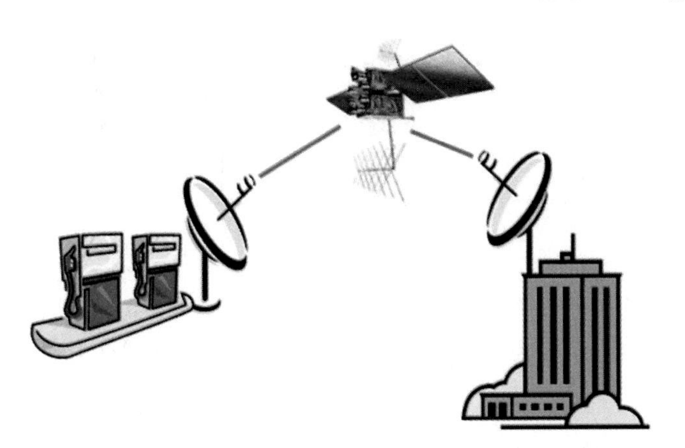

Business Use of a Wide Area Network

Some companies have plunged rapidly into the data communications world. Kmart, for instance, installed satellite ground stations on most of its stores. These communications links allow rapid credit checks for credit card purchases and fast inventory order requests, as stores require replenishment of stock. British Petroleum, an international giant, makes extensive use of a WAN. Various computer centers throughout the world are connected so that oil fields, refineries, wholesale distributors, and shippers are able to rapidly balance oil extraction, refining and stocking as world economic conditions and currency exchange rates change. BP also uses the WAN to provide teleconferencing between international locations. Managers can meet via television instead of traveling to foreign locations. The cost and time savings to the corporation are substantial. The biggest WAN user in the United States, and probably the world, is the US Defense department. Most of the computers at military bases, supply centers, and even major defense contractors are linked to the same network. Here issues of security are a real concern.

5.5.2 MAN: Metropolitan Area Network

A Metropolitan Area Network (MAN) is one of a number of types of networks (see also LAN and WAN). It usually networks together LANs in a region such as a city or college or corporate office campus. Local and state governments made use of MAN architectures to link state agencies. A MAN is a relatively new class of network.

While a MAN is not as large as a WAN there are three important features which discriminate MANs from LANs:

- **Geographic Scope**—Many MANs cover an area the size of a city, although in some cases MANs may be as small as a group of buildings or as large as a state.
- **Shared Access**—Unlike a LAN, a MAN is not generally owned by a single organization. The MAN, its communications links, and equipment are generally owned by either a consortium of users or by a single network provider who sells the service to the users. This level of service provided to each user is negotiated with the MAN operator, and performance guarantees are normally specified.
- **Resource Sharing**—A MAN often acts as a high speed network to allow sharing of regional resources (similar to a large LAN). MANs connecting research universities might, for example, provide access to a shared super computer.

Metropolitan area networks connect businesses to businesses, and businesses to WANs and the Internet. MANs consolidate the interconnection of networks in a city into a single larger network which then offers more efficient connection to a wide area network and the Internet. It is also used to mean the interconnection of several local area networks by bridging them with **backbone** lines as in a campus network.

5.5.3 LAN: Local Area Network

Local area networks, LANs for short, are generally in a single geographical area. It is not uncommon for a LAN to provide connectivity within a single building or even within a single department of a business. LANs today even carry voice communication (telephone or intercom) bypassing the telephone companies—this use is known as Voice over Internet Protocol or **VoIP.** There are principally three topologies that are in common use.

LANs are used to provide local connectivity and to permit sharing of resources among users. Printers, scanners, secondary storage, and tape backup units are a few of the types of hardware that may be shared. Databases and other data may be shared, too. Multiple users may access software that is installed on the server if the organization is properly licensed. Software maintenance is easier when software is distributed through and maintained on a LAN. The **topologies** (map of a network) of three common LAN configurations are presented next.

LAN Topologies: BUS, RING, STAR Networking electronically links data processing and data communication devices. A network may spread over a large area (a Wide Area Network or WAN) or be localized (a Local Area Network or LAN) to one department in an organization. Regardless of the geographic scope covered by the network the prior discussion of media, modems, signals, and line types applies. Each network has a structure or topology that depicts how the various devices are connected.

Star Topology The star topology involves a collection of nodes (terminals or workstations) connected to a single central computer. This is the simplest and easiest form of LAN. The central computer is called a server because it provides disk storage for all users and may provide processing power for some. Dumb terminals (terminals without local processing power) may be used because each is directly connected to the host. This presents the possibility of low cost hardware because dumb terminals are less expensive than computers. The advantage of lower cost equipment may be mitigated by the relatively higher expense for wiring the network—the direct connection between the central computer and each of the users' machines is more expensive. There is one major drawback to the star topology—if the central computer goes down (crashes) then everyone is out of work. This problem is solved with the other topologies.

Star LAN Topology

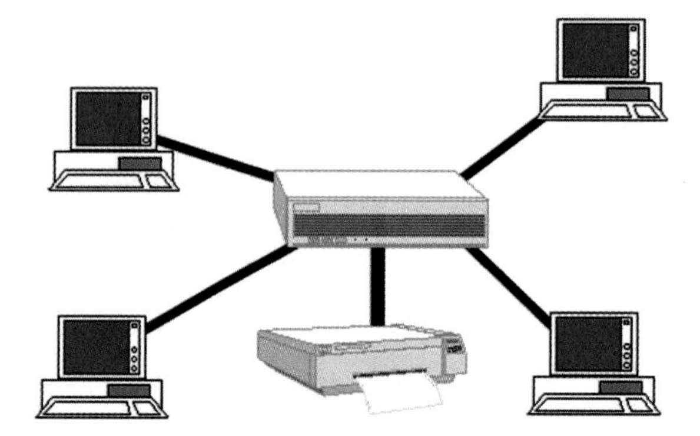

Ring Topology The ring topology involves a single cable that connects each workstation in a circle. Dumb terminals cannot be used with this topology because there is no central computer (server) to provide processing power for them. There may be other devices (printers, FAX, communication gateways, etc.) connected to the ring, too. Communication does not depend on a single host computer (or server) so network communication will not stop if one computer stops functioning. Wiring is usually less expensive than with the star topology because the wire runs from computer to the next closest computer.

The ring topology is like a telephone party line since there is no central authority controlling communication. When a computer has a message to send to another computer it puts the address of the destination computer on the front of the message and then sends the message out on the ring. Messages travel on the ring only in one direction. As the message passes each computer, the computer reads the destination address and determines whether the message is addressed to it. If so it reads the rest of the message, otherwise it lets the message pass without reading. When the message travels all the way back to the sending computer that computer may assume that the message has been received, however the sender may wait until an acknowledgement is actually received. Ring networks can be used where reliable high-speed communication is required.

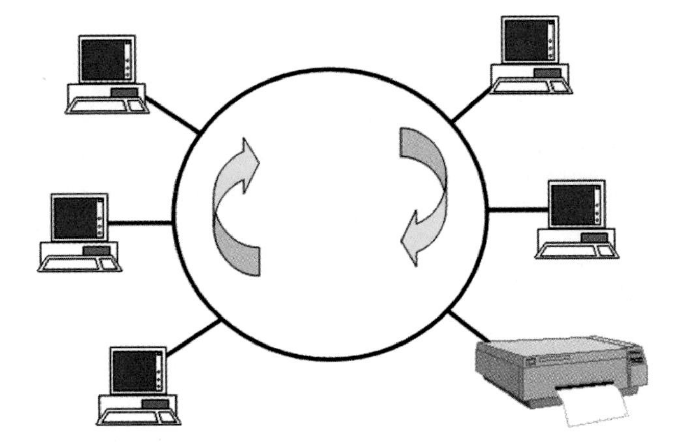

Ring LAN Topology

Bus Topology The bus topology involves a single cable (bus) that all computers and other devices are connected to, but it is not connected in a loop as in the ring topology. This topology is the least expensive to wire. If the wire breaks then the computers on either side of the break will still be able to communicate but computers on opposite sides of the break will not. The ring topology does not provide this protection.

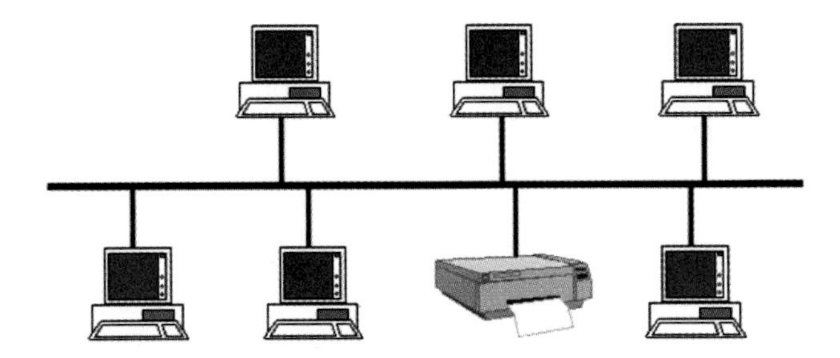

Bus LAN Topology

The bus topology is less orderly than the ring topology. Here a computer sends a message with a destination address on to the bus and hopes that it gets to the designated receiver. Hope is important because in a bus network the messages travel in both directions on the wire and collisions are possible if two or more computers transmit simultaneously. When the computer signal reaches the bus it goes both left and right because the bus has no guiding intelligence telling it which way is the route to the receiving computer. There is a strong possibility that another signal from another sender may hit. When a collision happens both messages involved are destroyed and must be resent. Complex algorithms are employed to govern when the senders should attempt transmission again—if they try to re-send simultaneously then a collision would happen again so the senders back off for different time periods.

5.5.4 Intranets and Extranets

An intranet is a **private** computer network that uses Internet protocols and software (servers and browsers), network equipment and connectivity, and possibly external telecommunication services to securely share part of an organization's information or operations with its employees. The public has no access to an intranet. Corporate communication including e-mail, access to the Benefits Department database, and access to job postings might be available to employees only through an intranet.

An Intranet Is a Private Network

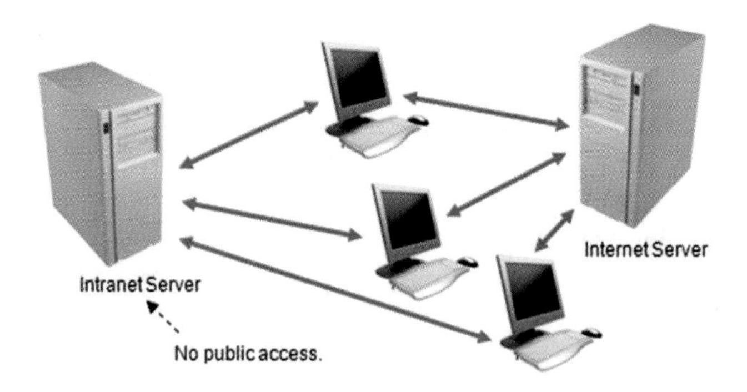

Extranets use the same hardware, software, and communication components as intranets but participation is limited to members of an organization instead of to one specific business. Examples include trade organizations that include representatives from several businesses in the same industry group. As with intranets, access by the public is prohibited.

5.6 Network Architecture

Computers are not randomly wired together. The specific arrangement of computers connected with various media and following specific protocols is not random, it is a thought out design that is known as a network's architecture. Just as a contractor would not build a house without an architect's blueprint, a network is not constructed without architecture to define it.

Packet Switching Networks deliver data transmitted from sender to receiver. On most networks, data (words, voice, numbers, video, e-mail, etc.) is broken into small segments and placed into **packets.** The packets are carried from node (computer or other network device) to node until the destination is reached. This arrangement is known as **packet switching** and is commonly used today. Although other types of networks exist, packet switched networks are most common and form the basis for most discussion in this chapter. More detail about packet switching is found in the Internet and World Wide Web chapter.

Network Operating System The Network Operating System (**NOS**) is software that provides special functions necessary for connecting computers and devices into a local-area network (LAN) or for inter-networking between networks (a gateway). The NOS controls a network and its packet traffic controls access by multiple users to network resources, and provides for administrative functions including security. The NOS must be consistent with the selected network architecture.

5.6.1 Client-Server

Client-server is both a hardware- and software-based network architecture. In hardware computers are servers and clients. Servers provide connection to the larger network and also provide access to shared resources.

- **Server**—Generally a powerful computer system that has been designated for running a specific application or applications. The functionality provided is shared by multiple clients. Servers are also known as **hosts.** Servers provide access to shared data and hardware resources including databases and centralized storage.
- **Client**—Generally a single user computer that depends on a server for connection to the Internet and the delivery of resources.

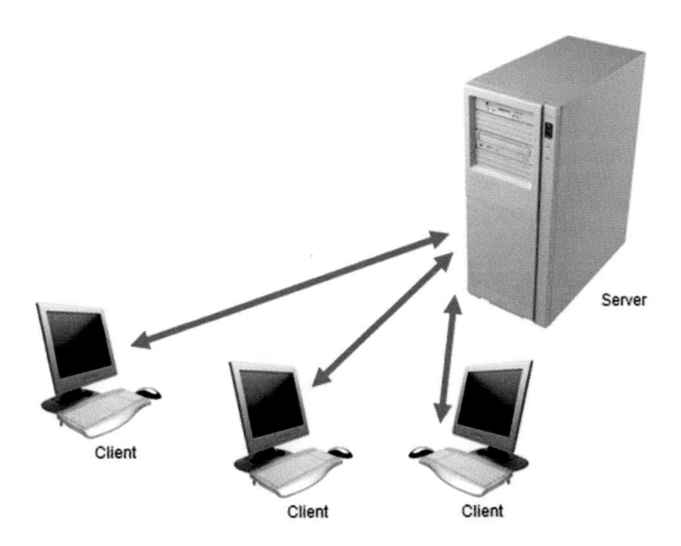

Clients and a Server

Some servers are dedicated to specific tasks and become known by the name of the task as: file servers, print servers, database servers, security servers, Web servers, e-mail servers, FTP servers, and network servers.

In software, a client program interacts with applications on a server (perhaps a search engine). Each client instance of the software can send requests to a software server. Specific types of software servers include Web servers, application servers, data servers, terminal servers, and e-mail servers. While their purposes vary somewhat, the basic architecture of software servers remains the same: they respond to client requests delivered through a network.

Although this idea is applied in a variety of ways, on many different kinds of applications, an easy example to visualize is an Internet website. For instance, if you are browsing an online store, your computer and Web browser would be considered a client, and the computers, databases, and applications that make up the online store would be considered the server. When your Web browser requests a particular page from the online store, the server finds all of the information required to display the article in the database, assembles it into a Web page, and sends it back to your Web browser for you to look at.

5.6.2 Peer-to-Peer

A peer-to-peer system is a distributed system whose computers (**nodes**) participate in similar roles, and are therefore peers to each other. Peer-to-peer can be viewed as decentralized network architecture in which there is no server.

Even though the computers have similar roles, not all computers have the same peripheral devices (printers, scanner, mass-storage devices, etc.). One aspect of a peer-to-peer network is that participants (peers) may share the peripherals attached to other computers. Because each computer has a similar role each must have its own copy of the operating system, network software, and all application software. There is no server to provide access to shared software or data resources. A network of this type is primarily for sharing hardware resources and sending messages among participants.

Peer-to-Peer Architecture

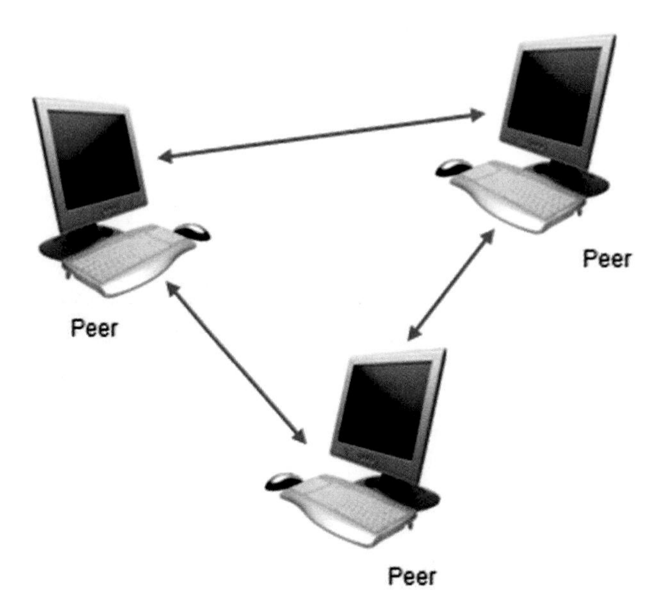

Because there is no server the peer-to-peer system possesses some degree of self-organization where each node finds its peers and helps maintain the system structure. This makes a peer-to-peer network node more complex than a client in client-server architecture. The main benefits of peer-to-peer system are scalability, fault-tolerance (each node is self-sufficient), and the lack of resource bottlenecks in servers.

5.7 Communication Standards

Different specifications exist to implement the various network architectures. Networking could not exist without standards because participating equipment would not be able to coordinate communication. Standards are agreed upon by international committees like **IEEE** (Institute of Electrical and Electronics Engineers, Inc.) who represent business, manufacturers, government, academia, and the military. The Internet Engineering Task Force (**IETF**) is involved too and develops and promotes Internet standards, cooperating closely with the World Wide Web Consortium (**W3C**).

Since equipment and software is produced by many developers and manufacturers, the absence of standards would make communication impossible. Software and hardware is designed to comply with standards so that devices and programs can communicate. Network standards define how equipment accesses the physical medium of the network. Other standards dictate how data and message **packets** (an electronic envelope) are formed and delivered on a network. Standards that define how two devices will communicate is known as a **protocol.** In networking, the term protocol refers to a set of rules that govern communications. For two devices on a network to successfully communicate, they must both understand the same protocols.

When any two devices need to talk to each other, they have to agree on a number of points before the conversation can begin. The first point of agreement is physical: Will they talk over wires, or through some form of wireless signals? If they use wires, how many are required—one, two, four, eight, 16? Once the physical attributes are decided, other questions like how much data will be sent at a time arise.

This section presents some of the more commonly used standards that govern local area networks.

5.7.1 Open System Interconnect Model

The Open System Interconnect Model (**OSI**) was a pre-TCP/IP effort by the International Organization for Standardization (ISO) to standardize networking. Prior to OSI, networking was largely vendor-developed and proprietary. OSI was an industry attempt to get everyone to agree to common network standards enabling multi-vendor interoperability. It was common for large networks to support multiple network protocol suites, with many devices unable to talk to other devices because of a lack of common protocols between them. However, while OSI standards were being developed TCP/IP (packet switching) came into widespread use with both Ethernet and token ring providing data transport.

5.7.2 Ethernet

The Ethernet standard defines a network with no centralized server. Individual nodes control what is transmitted without external governance. The original Ethernet described communication over a single cable shared by all devices on the network. Once a device is attached to this cable, it had the ability to communicate with any other attached device. This allows the network to expand to accommodate new devices without requiring any modification to those devices already on the network.

Each node takes responsibility for data transmission. If two nodes send messages at the same time a collision will occur and both messages are lost. All the computers back off a random amount of time and resend the messages. The backbone of the network is a **bus** that all devices are attached to. The bus is not a loop and devices may be attached at any point.

The IEEE designated 802.3 as the standard that defines Ethernet. Ethernet is formally known by the acronym **CSMA/CD** which signifies carrier-sense multiple access with collision detection. Ethernet is a local area technology, with networks usually operating within a single building, connecting devices in close proximity. At most, Ethernet devices typically have only a few hundred yards of cable between them, making it impractical to connect geographically remote locations. The original Ethernet standard called for a 10 Mbps transmission rate but considerably faster Ethernet networks (802.3ae) can achieve data rates in the Gbps range today.

5.7.3 Token Ring

The most common local area network alternative to Ethernet is a network technology developed by IBM, called token ring. Where Ethernet relies on the random gaps between transmission attempts to regulate access to the bus, token ring implements a strict, orderly access method. A token-ring network arranges nodes in a closed physical ring following the ring topology. The nodes send messages in one direction around the ring, removing each message when it has circled the ring once. Each message carries a unique identifier enabling nodes to detect a message that returns to the point of origin.

This network has no server, but unlike Ethernet it is organized. When the network is booted this process is followed:

1. The ring initializes by creating one message known as a token. It is a special type of message that gives a node permission to transmit. The token is represented by a specific pattern of bits understood by all nodes as a token.
2. The token circles the ring like any message until it encounters a node that wishes to transmit data.
3. This node then captures the token by replacing the message with a data-carrying message which encircles the network.
4. Once that data message returns to the transmitting node it removes the data message, creates a new token, and forwards that token on to the next node in the ring.

Token-ring nodes do not have collisions among packets; the presence of the token gives the node permission to transmit a message without any concern of another node interrupting. Because a node transmits only a single message before passing the token along, each station on the ring gets a turn to communicate in a fair manner. The IEEE designated 802.5 as the standard that defines token ring. Token ring speeds of 4 Mbps, 16 Mbps, 100 Mbps and 1 Gbps have been standardized by the IEEE.

Fiber-distributed data interface (FDDI) is another token-passing technology that operates over a pair of fiber optic rings, with each ring passing a token in opposite directions. FDDI networks offered faster transmission speeds of up to 100 Mbps. While initially quite popular for high-speed networking, the advent of 100-Mbps Ethernet, which is cheaper and easier to administer, has caused interest in FDDI to decline.

5.7.4 Asynchronous Transfer Mode (ATM)

The big difference between an ATM network and packet-switched networks is that the latter use variable sized packets and ATM does not. An ATM network encodes data traffic into small fixed-size **cells** (53 bytes; 48 bytes of data and 5 bytes of header information). In theory, small, fixed-size cells should operate more efficiently than flexible size packets because less overhead is needed to operate the network. While complex protocol overhead is reduced, each new packet introduces more data bits into the transmission and more bandwidth is required. This is not an issue with ATM because the bandwidths of ATM Optical transmission systems usually connected to an ATM switching machine are immense.

ATM technology has proved very successful in WAN implementations. Many ADSL networks use ATM. ATM has failed to gain wide use as a general LAN technology, however.

5.7.5 TCP/IP

The first Transmission Control Protocol/Internet Protocol (TCP/IP) wide area network was operational by January 1, 1983, when the National Science Foundation (NSF) constructed a university network backbone that would later become the NSFNet. The ability of TCP/IP to work over pre-existing communication networks allowed for a great ease of growth.

TCP/IP is a suite of communications protocols that define how messages are created and routed to destinations through the Internet. The protocols include rules for dividing messages into smaller pieces called **packets.** Destination addresses are encoded with each packet and specifications dictate rules for regulating the flow of packets through the network. Procedures for handling undelivered or corrupted packets are included, too.

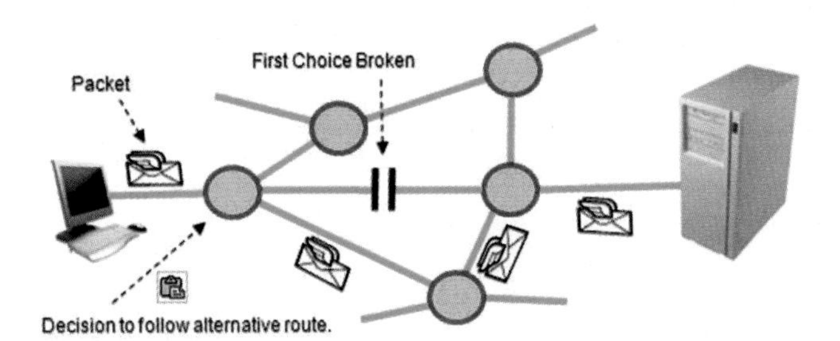

Packet Switching

As packets travel through the Internet the best route between servers and routers is determined dynamically as conditions on the network are monitored. Excessive traffic or a down link will motivate routing decisions. Although all of a transmission's packets may not take the same route or arrive at the same time these protocols ensure that the packets are reassembled into the full message in the correct sequence. The method of sending individual packets on the best route is known as **packet switching.** Each packet is labeled with the **IP address** of the destination computer. This numeric, four byte address is unique to each computer on a TCP/IP network thus enabling reliable delivery to any network destination.

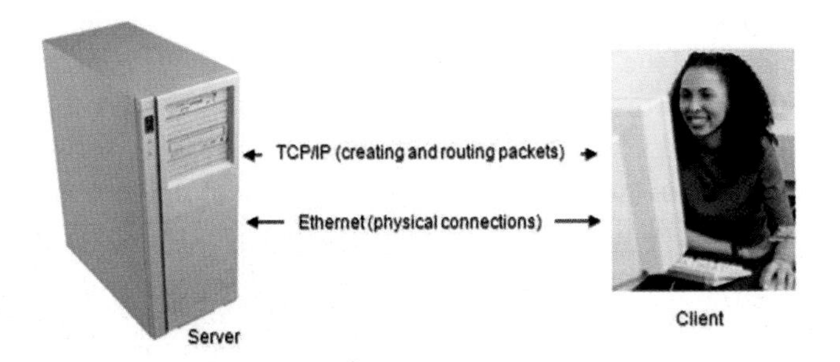

Communication Standards

Additional information about packets, IP addresses, and packet switching is found in the Internet and WWW chapter.

Circuit Switching A circuit switching network is in contrast to a packet switching network. In circuit switching a dedicated circuit (or channel) is established between nodes before the users may communicate. Each circuit that is dedicated cannot be used for any other transmission of data until the circuit is released and a new connection is set up. Even if no actual communication is taking place in a dedicated circuit, then, that channel still remains unavailable to other users.

The demand for rapid, unscheduled data links makes circuit switching impractical for the Internet. The original telephone system was based on a circuit switching network architecture.

Circuit Switching

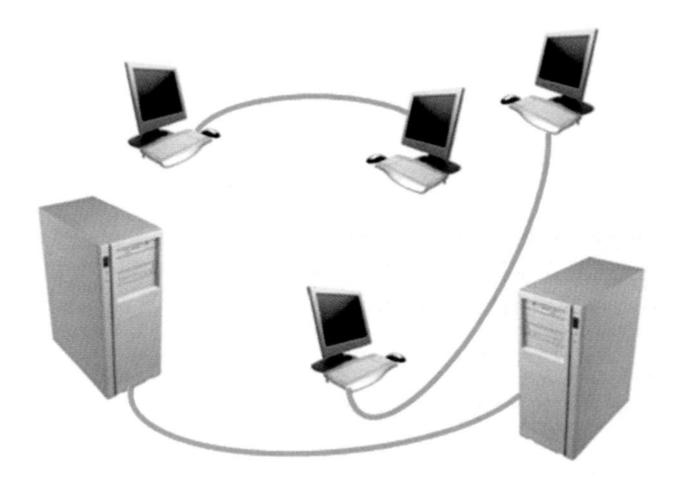

5.7.6 Wi-Fi

The 803.11 standard, known as Wi-Fi, developed by IEEE specifies how devices will connect with each other over the air. Radio is used as the transmission media. 803.11 is similar to the Ethernet bus in how devices are to connect. The standard is really a family of wireless standards that use several frequency range portions of the broadcast spectrum and provide different data transmission rates. When first popularized the **803.11b** standard offered speeds up to 11 Mbps. Today **803.11g** provides rates up to about 54 Mbps. A new standard, **803.11n** promises faster rates but it is still in the development stage.

A typical Wi-Fi setup contains one or more **access points** (APs) and one or more clients. An AP broadcasts its **SSID** (Service Set Identifier or network name) via packets that are called **beacons.** Since Wi-Fi transmits in the air, it has the similar properties to an Ethernet network, and therefore collisions can occur.

802.11b is usually used in a point-to-multipoint configuration, where an access point communicates via an omni-directional antenna with one or more clients that are located in a coverage area around the access point. Typical indoor range is up to 300 feet. Transmission speed falls off as distance between access point and remote device increases. 802.11b uses the 2.40 GHz (gigahertz) radio band and because of this can incur interference from microwave ovens, cordless telephones, Bluetooth devices, and other appliances using this same band. The 802.11g standard also uses this frequency range and is subject to the same interference.

5.7.7 WiMax

This IEEE standard, 802.16, known as WiMax, is the specification for the deployment of broadband Wireless Metropolitan Area Networks (**WMAN**). WiMax provides wireless communication over long distances, in a variety of different ways, from point-to-point links to distributed systems like those that provide cellular access. WiMax is an alternative to broadband access by cable and DSL. In areas without pre-existing physical cable or telephone networks WiMAX can be a viable alternative for broadband access that is economically unavailable. Prior to WiMAX many used proprietary fixed wireless technologies for broadband services.

WiMax and Wi-Fi sound similar but are deployed for the following different reasons:

- **WiMax**—A long range (many miles) system to deliver a point-to-point connection to the Internet from an ISP to an end user. Different 802.16 standards provide different types of access, from mobile (analogous to access via a cell phone) to fixed (an alternative to wired access, where the end user's wireless termination point is fixed in location).
- **Wi-Fi**—A shorter range (typically measured in hundreds of feet) system that typically covers only the network operator's own property. Wi-Fi is often used by end users to access their own home or business network.

5.7.8 Bluetooth

Bluetooth is a standard that defines how two Bluetooth enabled devices will communicate. These devices use radio waves to carry short distance transmissions. A Bluetooth connection is wireless and automatic, and is limited to about 33 feet. Bluetooth is primarily used for short-distance connection between computers and peripheral devices like microphones, headsets, mice, keyboards, cameras, phones, and printers.

Bluetooth and Wi-Fi are both wireless and use the same Industrial, Scientific and Medical (**ISM**) radio band. Bluetooth connects special purpose devices over a short distance while Wi-Fi provides faster data transfer rates and is used for general purpose connections between computers and networks.

5.7.9 RFID

Radio-Frequency Identification (RFID) is an automatic identification method, relying on storing and remotely retrieving data using devices called **RFID tags** or transponders. An RFID tag is an object that can be attached to or incorporated into a product, animal, or person for the purpose of identification using radio waves. Chip-based RFID tags contain silicon chips and antennas. A receiver, called a transceiver, accepts the signals and delivers them to a waiting computer.

RFID can be passive or active. Active tags contain a battery and are always transmitting. Passive tags have no internal power and must be triggered from an external source that sends out radio waves. Passive tags can be manufactured small enough to be placed in a person's skin.

Common uses of this technology include tagging items in a warehouse which permits automated inventory management. Cars equipped with tags can speed through a tollbooth and the driver billed later for the tools. Potentially, tags could be embedded in people and provide identification when paying with a credit card or withdrawing cash at a bank. Certainly it is not too farfetched to imagine this technology used to identify travelers boarding airplanes.

5.7.10 IrDA

The Infrared Data Association (IrDA) defines physical communication protocol standards for the short range exchange of data over **infrared light.** Typically IrDA is used for connecting peripheral devices in a personal area network. Infrared requires line of sight transmission meaning that the sender and receiver must have a direct view of each other. Devices communicating with infrared must generally be close to each other. Since Bluetooth does not have the line of sight restriction it is assumed that it will replace IrDA for control and communication with local devices.

5.8 Connecting to a Network

Access to a network requires a connection between your computer and a server. The server is the pathway to the Internet. Accessing the Internet depends on having a reliable, rapid, consistent path to a server. Your computer's connection is carried by a communication channel which includes among its components the line or media that carries the signal.

5.8.1 Serial and Parallel Transmission

When bits are transmitted from sender to receiver they may be sent one bit at a time (serial transmission) or all bits of one byte may be sent together at once (parallel transmission). The difference between a parallel and a serial communication channel is the number of distinct wires at the physical layer used for simultaneous transmission. Parallel communications implies more than one such wire (a standard eight bit byte requires eight wires working in unison).

Generally, parallel channels are preferred because of:

- **Speed**—It is faster to transmit several bits at once if each is following a separate wire than it is to transmit several bits one after the other on the same wire.

Parallel and Serial Transmission

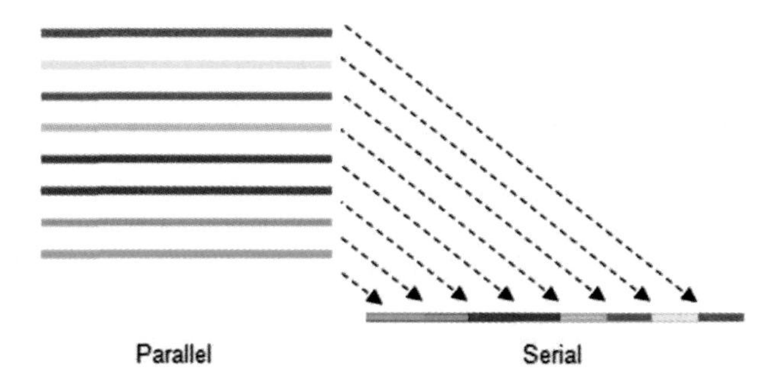

- **Hardware**—It is easier to implement parallel channels in hardware. Serial transmissions originate with the parallel signals of the computer's data bus being serialized and transmitted one by one. The serial flow is reconstituted to parallel signals at the receiving end by a **UART** (Universal Asynchronous Receiver Transmitter).

While parallel transmission may be preferred it must be noted that overall data throughput will be limited by the speed of the slowest parallel wire. Further, the possibility exists that the several parallel lines may interfere with each other due to **crosstalk.** Parallel channels are mostly used for short-distance communication such as inside a computer

Parallel Printer Connector

(the data address and control buses) and between computers and printers. The decreasing cost of integrated circuits and the greater cost of parallel channels, combined with greater demand for speed and cable length, has led to growth in importance of serial channels.

5.8.2 Dial-up Lines

Dial-up access is a form of Internet access through which the client uses a modem connected to a computer and a telephone line to dial into an Internet service provider's (ISP) node to establish a modem-to-modem link, which is then routed to the Internet. Dial-up requires time to establish a telephone connection and perform handshaking before data transfers can take place.

Dial-up requires no additional infrastructure on top of the telephone network. As telephone points are available throughout the world, dial-up remains useful to travelers. Dial-up is usually the only choice available for most rural or remote areas where getting a broadband connection is impossible due to low population and demand. Under some circumstances dial-up access may be an alternative to people who have limited budgets.

Dial-up access is a transient connection, because either the user or the ISP terminates the connection. Internet service providers will often set a limit on connection durations to prevent hogging of access, and will disconnect the user—requiring reconnection.

Performance Modern dial-up modems typically have a maximum theoretical speed of 56 Kbps, although in most cases only up to 53 Kbps is possible due to overhead. These speeds are currently considered the maximum possible; in many cases transfer speeds will be lower, averaging anywhere between 33 to43 kbps. Factors affecting connection speeds include phone line noise and conditions, as well as the quality of the modem itself.

In recent years broadband Internet access (cable and DSL) has been replacing dial-up access in many places. The reason for this is mostly due to broadband connections featuring speeds which far exceed the capacity of dial-up, many of which provide speeds greater than 1 Mbps. As an increasing amount of Internet content such as streaming media and Flash animation require large amounts of bandwidth, dial-up can no longer keep up with the needs of many users.

5.8.3 Dedicated Lines

A dedicated line is a communications cable dedicated to a specific connection. It is said to be **always-on.** Dedicated lines are faster than dial-up lines and can be less susceptible to external noise (static or other factors) that might interfere with dial-up transmissions.

As more general-purpose systems have improved, dedicated lines have been steadily replaced by intranets and the public Internet, but they are still useful for time-critical, high-bandwidth applications such as video transmission. Access to the Internet, however, can be facilitated by use of dedicated lines as DSL and cable have become the primary vehicle for home users.

Businesses used dedicated lines because public access to server has become standard business practice. Businesses also use dedicated lines to connect sales office and manufacturing plants in other locations. By leasing these lines and associated equipment it becomes cost effective for a business to support WANs that they could not afford if required to alone.

5.8.3.1 DSL (Digital Subscriber Line)

DSL is a family of technologies that provides digital data transmission over the wires of a local telephone network—that is, the link between the central phone switch and the end-point: a residence or business. DSL originally stood for digital subscriber loop, although in recent years the acronym has become **digital subscriber line.** The DSL technologies enable faster data transmission over copper telephone lines than a conventional voice modem can provide. It does this by utilizing frequencies that are normally not used by a voice telephone call, in particular, frequencies higher than normal human hearing.

Communication providers usually offer ADSL (Asymmetric Digital Subscriber Line)—an **asymmetric** version of DSL in which the volume of data flow is greater in one direction than the other. Providers usually market ADSL as a service for consumers who mostly download or receive data, e-mail, and Web pages. In other words, most of their traffic is inbound. In ADSL more of the bandwidth is dedicated to download than to upload.

ADSL uses **frequency division multiplexing** (explained earlier) to blend the data and voice signals together on the customer's telephone line. ADSL uses two separate frequency bands—the **upstream** and **downstream** bands. The upstream band is used for communication from the end user to the telephone central office. The downstream band is used for communicating from the central office to the end user.

ADSL Uses Frequency Division Multiplexing

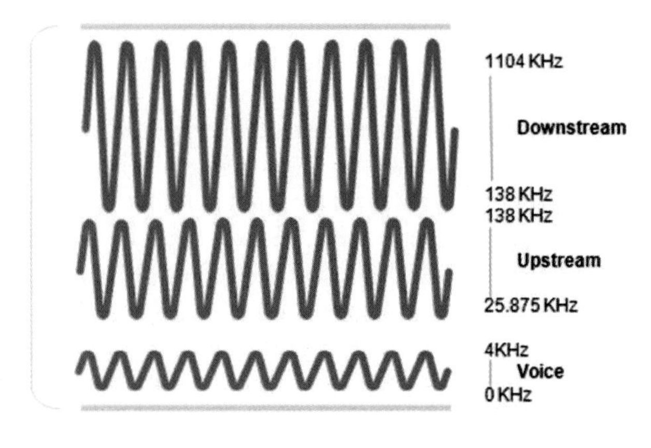

Note: KHz is a measure of signal frequency. The number of times that a signal modulates (swings up and down) per unit of time is the frequency of the signal. One Hz (Hertz) is one cycle per second. The top of the voice range is 4,000 cycles per second.

5.8.3.2 Cable Access

Cable modems deliver **broadband** Internet access by taking advantage of unused bandwidth on a cable television network. The term broadband refers to advanced communications systems capable of providing high-speed transmission of services such as data, voice, and video over the Internet and other networks.

Access via a cable company network is much faster than dial-up because these companies set up cabling to provide television signals which require considerably more bandwidth (data transfer) than the voice communication carried by the dial-up phone system. Cable networks use coaxial or fiber-optic cabling directly into the home or business which is capable of delivering vast amounts of data at high speed. Most telephone subscribers have old copper wire (twisted pair) connecting them to their telephone company's network. Note: coaxial cabling does not provide the same throughput as fiber-optic.

Cable modem access is about 30 times that of a 56 Kbps modem, and about 15 times that of an ISDN connection and about as fast as a T1 line (both described shortly). The most common method for cable modems to be attached to your computer is by using an Ethernet connection utilizing 10base T cables. This uses a cable that is similar to a telephone cable with a small plastic connector at either end. One end connects to the cable modem and the other connects to a computer's Ethernet card.

5.8.3.3 ISDN

Integrated Services Digital Network (ISDN) is a **circuit-switched** telephone network system, designed to allow digital transmission of voice and data over ordinary telephone copper wires, resulting in better quality and higher speeds than that available with the phone system. ISDN is a set of protocols for establishing and breaking circuit switched connections.

A special ISDN modem is required and the distance between the computer and the telephone company's ISDN modem is limited to a few miles. This distance restriction and the generally lower speeds than those provided by cable and DSL are limiting interest in ISDN.

5.8.3.4 T1

Digital signal 1 (also known as T1 or DS-1) is a long distance telephone-carrier line that carries multiple signals at the same time. These fast lines use **multiplexing** to carry multiple signals. T-lines are expensive and usually afforded only by large institutions or businesses.

A T1 line can carry about 1.544 Mbps which is considerably more data than a normal residential modem carries. It is also extremely reliable. Depending on what they are doing, a T1 line can generally handle quite a few people. For general browsing, hundreds of users are easily able to share a T1 line comfortably. If they are all downloading streaming video simultaneously it would be a problem, but that still isn't extremely common.

A T3 line is the equivalent of 28 T1 lines bundled together and it is very expensive. T3 lines are used by the phone system itself, very large companies and also Internet service providers. A T1 line might cost between $1,000 and $1,500 per month. You can imagine the cost of a T3 line.

TIP: Position the wireless access point above the devices it connects to for best results.

5.8.3.5 Wireless Access Points

A wireless access point (WAP or AP) is a device that connects wireless communication devices together to form a wireless network. The wireless network allows devices to communicate among themselves or to transfer data to a larger network. The WAP usually connects to a wired network, and can relay data between wireless devices and wired devices. Several WAPs can link together to form a larger network that allows roaming. Roaming networks are common in large businesses, in hotels, or in institutions like universities.

Wireless networking lags behind wired networking in terms of increasing bandwidth and throughput. Typical wireless devices for the consumer market can reach speeds of 11 Mbps (802.11b) or 54 Mbps (802.11g) while wired hardware of similar cost reaches 1000 Mbps. Once the new standard 802.11n is complete speeds of up to 540 Mbps are expected and older wired network use is expected to decline as the common 100Mbps speed is surpassed.

Interference can commonly cause problems with wireless networking reception, as many devices operate using the 2.4 GHz frequency. A nearby wireless phone, garage door opener, microwave, or other device can markedly reduce the perceived signal strength of a wireless access point.

Public Internet Access Data Points Increasingly computer users are expecting to access the Internet via a wireless connection just about anywhere. Many people carry laptops to a coffee shop, the airport, a meeting, etc. and expect a connection. As public wireless access points are becoming more common, various Web sites list known public access points and encourage viewers to report newly discovered sites.

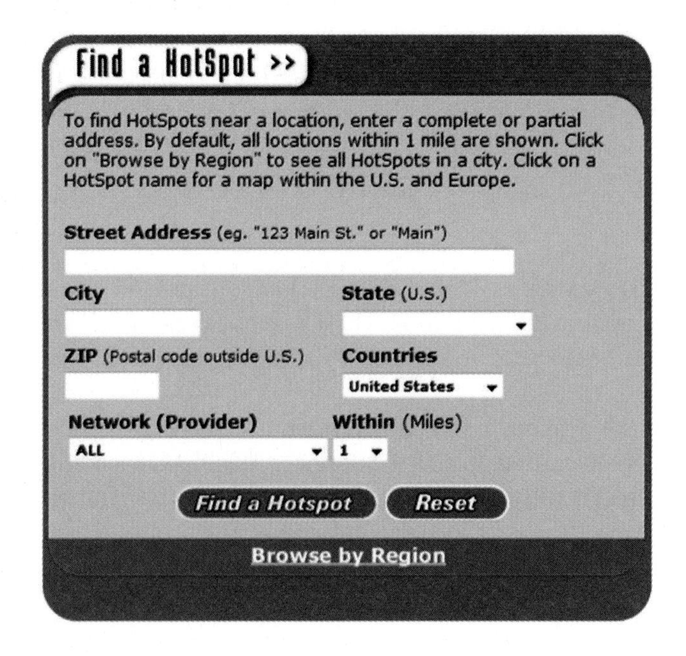

Reporting a Wireless Public Access Point

Known as **hot spots,** public Internet access points are becoming more common. Some are free and some require that a fee be paid. In some cities the municipal government is providing Wi-Fi access to all citizens. Philadelphia is a notable example. Shopping malls, quick car lube stops, transportation centers, bookstores, and restaurants often provide hot spots.

Fixed-Wireless For customers out of cable or phone system range, broadband Internet access is possible. These systems offer broadband service that is based on fixed-wireless technology. Fixed wireless refers to wireless devices or systems that are situated in fixed locations, such as an office or home. **Sprint** and other communication companies are offering this service.

The **point-to-point** signal transmissions occur through the air over **microwaves** rather than through copper or fiber cables; therefore, fixed wireless does not require cable or local phone service. Fixed wireless technology uses a device called a transceiver that is mounted on the outside of a home or office, usually on the roof. The transceiver is pointed toward a radio transmission tower that sends and receives microwave signals. Once the signal is received by the transceiver, it is sent to the modem and computer in your house.

The advantages of fixed wireless include the ability to connect with users in remote areas without the need for laying new cables and the capacity for broad bandwidth that is not impeded by fiber or cable capacities.

Broadband Wireless Internet Access Some people want network access to travel with them rather than search for public access points (hot spots) as they travel. Now, wireless broadband technologies include new services from companies such as **Sprint, Cingular,** and **Verizon** which allow a more mobile version of broadband access. Consumers can purchase a PC-card or USB equipment to connect their PC or laptop to the Internet through cell-phone towers.

Wireless Internet Access Card
© Alex Melnick, 2007, Shutterstock.

Wireless Encryption One issue with wireless networks in general involves the need for security. Many early access points could not discern whether or not a particular user had authorization to access the network. The fact that radio signals bleed outside of buildings and across property lines makes physical security largely irrelevant to intruders. Anyone within the geographical network range of an open, unencrypted wireless network can sniff on all the network traffic, and can gain unauthorized access to internal network resources as well as to the Internet.

Wired Equivalent Privacy or Wireless Encryption Protocol (**WEP**) is a scheme to secure IEEE 802.11 wireless networks. It is part of the IEEE 802.11 wireless networking standard. Several serious weaknesses were identified and WEP was superseded by Wi-Fi Protected Access (**WPA**) in 2003. In 2004 it was followed by the full IEEE 802.11i standard **WPA2.**

The content of communication between your computer and a wireless router should be hidden by using encryption. This technique encodes data so that the information content remains intact but outsiders are prevented from interpreting intercepted data. The prevalent use of **Wi-Fi** for home and small business use provides a wide open door as many users do not encrypt their network. The major concerns that encryption addresses are:

- **External access**—Anyone with a wireless equipped computer in proximity to an unencrypted network can potentially use that network for personal access to the Internet. This is common in urban areas where users at times piggy-back on their neighbors' networks thus avoiding Internet connection fees and potentially implicating them in criminal behavior.

- **Data loss**—Once access is obtained to an unencrypted network that is not password protected it is not much of a stretch to examine data communicated by the network.

What Encryption Is Encryption is the process of obscuring information to make it unreadable without special knowledge. It is sometimes referred to as scrambling. An algorithm is used for performing encryption and decryption (returning the information to its original state). A key is used for encoding and decoding the information.

Early encryption algorithms had been symmetric in that the same cryptographic key is used with the underlying algorithm by both the sender and the recipient, who must both keep it secret. **Public key** encryption (developed in 1976) changed the way cryptographic protection works. The process is mathematical and quite complicated but in essence it works this way: Data set to be encoded is run through a complicated mathematical computation to generate a single large number, called a **hash.** The original data and the hash are linked. If either changes, the hash won't match and the message cannot be decoded. Two keys are used to code and decode data—each participant (sender and receiver) has a public key and a private key. Public keys are used by a sender to encode messages designated for a specific recipient who then must use a personal private key for decoding.

5.9 Networking Hardware

Connecting to a service provider requires an electronic pathway which starts with hardware devices that enable a computer's signals to be translated onto a network.

5.9.1 Network Adapter Card

A network card, network adapter, or NIC (network interface controller) is a piece of computer hardware designed to allow computers to communicate over a computer network.

It allows users to connect to each other either by using cables or wirelessly and provides an addressing scheme through the use of **MAC** addresses.

Every network card has a unique 48-bit serial number called a MAC address, which is stored in ROM (read only memory) carried on the card. Every computer on a network must have a card with a unique MAC address. No two cards ever manufactured share the same address. This is accomplished by the IEEE, which is responsible for assigning unique MAC addresses to the vendors of network interface controllers.

Whereas network cards used to be expansion cards that plug into a computer bus, the low cost and common presence of the Ethernet standard means that most new computers have a network interface built in to the motherboard. A separate network card is not required unless multiple interfaces are needed or some other type of network is used. The network interface card or motherboard chip implements the electronic circuitry required to communicate using a specific standard.

Network Adaptor Card
© Marc Dietrich, 2007, Shutterstock.

5.9.2 Dial-up and Broadband Modems

A computer's digital signals must be converted so that they may be carried over a communication channel. The device that performs this translation is a modem. Depending on the type of channel, modems will differ. In this section several popular modem types are described. The word modem is an abbreviated combination of **modulate** (convert to an analog signal) and **demodulate** (convert to a digital signal). Although only a dial-up modem performs that task of providing compatibility with an analog network (most other networks are digital) the name modem is used for many devices that enable a computer to connect to a network.

Dial-up Modem The telephone system is an analog network. This means that a computer's digital signals must be converted to analog before the phone system can be used to carry data or other messages.

Both ends of the channel must be connected to modems because the translation at the receiving end is the exact opposite of the translation performed at the sending end. Most computers have built-in modems that are able to transmit at the maximum theoretical speed of 56 Kbps or the practical speed of 53 Kbps. Older computers might require a modem card if one was not installed as part of the computer.

A Modem Modulates and Demodulates Signals
© OlgaLis, 2007, Shutterstock.

Before modems there were **acoustic couplers.** These devices provided the link between a computer and the telephone system through acoustic (sound) signals rather than through direct electrical connection. Usually, a standard telephone handset was placed into a cradle that fit closely around the microphone and earpiece of the telephone handset. A modem would modulate a loudspeaker in the cup attached to the handset's microphone, and sound from the loudspeaker in the telephone handset's earpiece would be picked up by a microphone in the cup attached to the earpiece. In this way signals could be passed in both directions. Speeds were typically 300 bps. This awkward arrangement was required because legal restrictions prohibited direct electrical connections to the telephone system. When those restrictions were removed acoustic couples were no longer needed.

Before Modems Acoustic Couplers Were Used
Courtesy of Computer History Museum.

DSL and ISDN Modems DSL and ISDN are protocols that involve coordinating with the regular telephone system. This is an analog system (as already mentioned) but the type of modulation used here is different. Unlike a dial-up modem which converts the digital signal to analog which then occupies the entire line, a DSL or ISDN modem takes advantage of portions of the line's frequency range that is not used for voice communication (and is otherwise unused). The modem converts the digital signal to operate in the range of the unused frequencies. The technique (explained earlier) is known as **frequency division multiplexing** and allows a line to be used more efficiently.

Most DSL and ISDN modems are external to the computer with an attachment to both the computer and the telephone line as shown here:

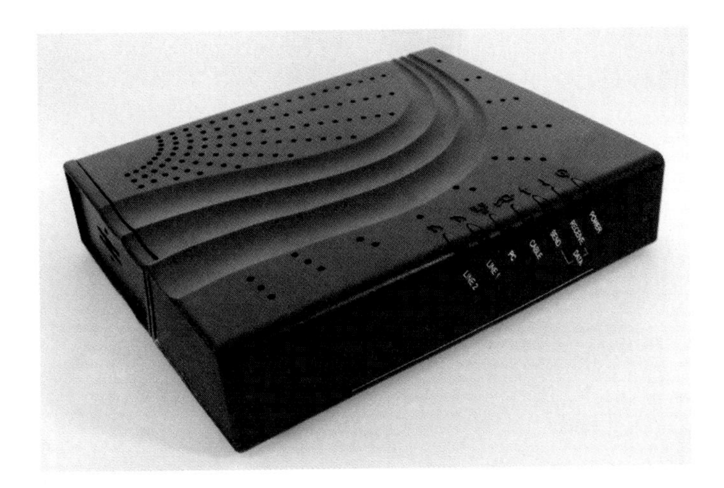

DSL Modem

Cable Modem A cable modem is at times known as a **broadband** modem because it takes advantage of the high capacity of the cable television system's lines. In theory a cable system based Internet connection will be faster than DSL and certainly faster than dial-up, but it can slow down because it is a shared line and sensitive to the use of others.

The cable television system delivers a connection to a residence in a single line which is usually coaxial cable or perhaps fiber optics. Since television does not consume all of the frequency range available in the channel the unused portions are available for other use such as data communications. Similar to a DSL modem, the cable modem multiplexes the data signals (in digital form) onto the unused portions of the channel—a similar modem at the receiving end removes the digital signal from the line using a **splitter** and delivers it to a server.

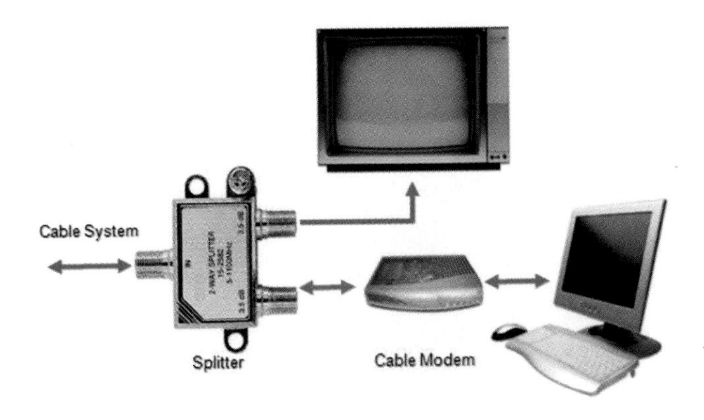

A Cable Modem Makes Use of Available Portions of Cable System Lines

Note: Since the cable line is shared by several households in a community, as more computers connect during peak usage periods (afternoons and evenings) access speeds might slow down. This does not happen with DSL because the telephone line into a house is dedicated to that house and is not shared by neighbors.

Wireless Modem These types of modems operate in the radio frequency range of cell phones and allow a computer to connect to a wireless network. This technology, although similar to Wi-Fi, does not connect to a local access point in a home network. This broadband allows a more mobile version of broadband access. Users purchase a PC-card, laptop-card, or USB equipment from a provider like Sprint to connect their PC or laptop to the Internet via cell-phone towers.

Wireless Modem

5.9.3 10base T Cables

This is a twisted-pair cable used for **Ethernet** connections that is similar to a telephone wire with a small plastic connector (8P8C) at either end. The network jack found in most new computers is designed for a 10base T connection—this is used for connection to DSL and cable modems and to local area Ethernet networks. 10baseT, specified in the IEEE 802.3 standard for Ethernet local area networks (LANs), is twisted pair wire. There are actually three standards for Ethernet over twisted pair cable. The most widely used are 10base T, 100base T, and 1000base T (IEEE 802.3ab), running at 10 Mbps, 100 Mbps, and 1000 Mbps respectively.

The names of these standards are derived from several aspects of the physical media. The number refers to the transmission speed in megabits per second (Mbps); Base is short for baseband, meaning that there is no frequency division multiplexing in use; and T designates twisted pair, the type of cable that is used.

Ethernet 10base T Cable

5.9.4 Switch

A switch is a networking device that directs packets to a specific hardware device attached to a network. Since this level of traffic direction is based on the **MAC address** stored in ROM no address decoding or translation is required enabling switches to direct packets at the speed of hardware. No software intervention is required.

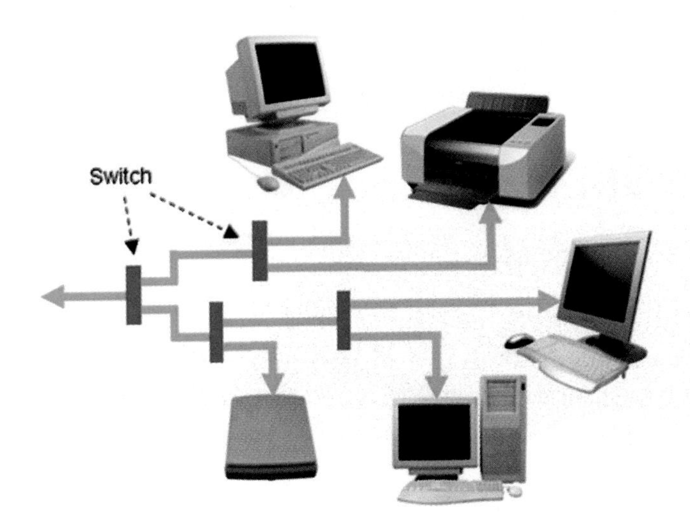

Switches Direct Local Traffic in a LAN

5.9.5 Hub

At first glance a hub is similar to a switch. An Ethernet hub or **concentrator** is a device for connecting multiple lines together, making them act as a single segment. Hubs essentially repeat a line's signal without regard for destination address. Hubs work at the physical layer (layer 1) of the OSI model. The device is thus a form of **multipart repeater.**

An Ethernet hub, or repeater, is a fairly unsophisticated broadcast device. Hubs do not manage any of the traffic that comes through them, and any packet entering any port is broadcast out on every other port (every port other than the port of entry). Since every packet is being sent out through every other port, packet collisions result—which greatly impedes the smooth flow of traffic.

Historically, the main reason for purchasing hubs rather than switches was price. This has largely been eliminated by reductions in the price of switch.

Ethernet Hub

5.9.6 Router

A router is a computer networking device that buffers and forwards data packets across networks toward their destinations through a process known as routing. A router also acts as a junction between two or more networks to buffer and transfer data packets among them. The router uses a packet's destination **IP address** to determine the route the packet will follow. The path from one router to the next is called a **hop.**

Routers Direct Packets

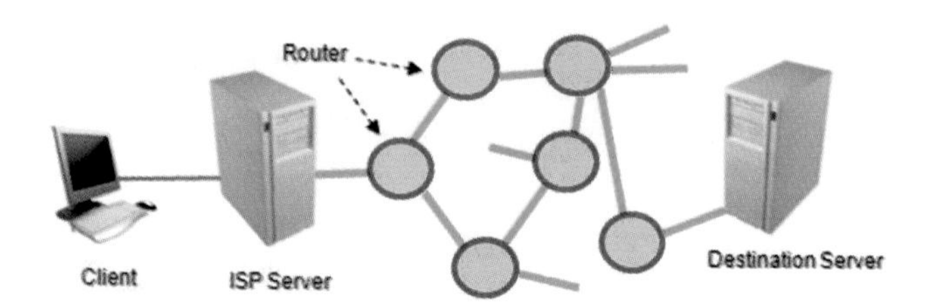

Packets are routed from network to network until the destination network is reached. Routers direct packet traffic among LANs and MANs that follow the same protocols. The illustration is redrawn showing the role of routers in a broader WAN.

Routers Connect Networks

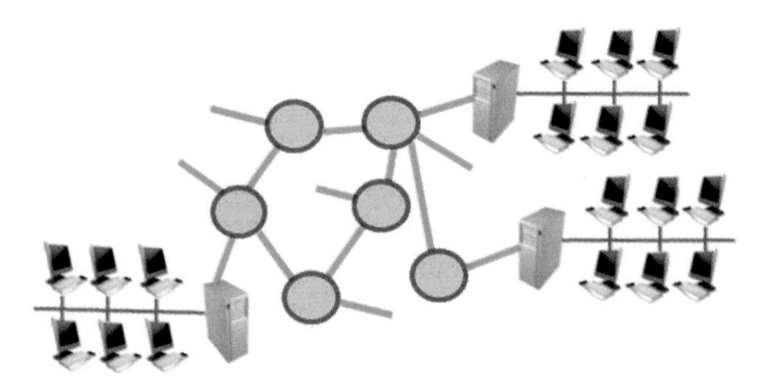

5.9.7 Multiplexer

A multiplexer or **mux** is a device that selects one of many data-sources and outputs that source into a single channel. In digital signal processing (DSP), the multiplexer takes several separate digital data streams and combines them together into one data stream usually of a higher data rate. This allows multiple data streams to be carried from one place to another over one physical link, which saves cost.

The two most commonly used forms of multiplexing are:

- **Time Division Multiplexing**
- **Frequency Division Multiplexing**

A de-multiplexer (or **demux**) is a device taking a single input and translates (demodulates) it into the several signals that originated.

Multiplexer

5.9.8 Repeater

A repeater is an electronic device that receives a weak or low-level signal and retransmits it at a higher level or higher power so that the signal can cover longer distances without reduction in signal quality. Because repeaters work with the actual physical signal, and do not attempt to interpret the data being transmitted, they operate on the physical layer, the first layer of the OSI model.

Repeater

5.9.9 Gateway

A gateway is an entrance from one network to another to another network. In particular, gateways are required when networks use different protocols. While routers direct packets among servers in a distributed network, gateways are used:

- To transfer data between private networks and the Internet.
- Connect networks that use different protocols. These gateways are known as **protocol converters.**

A gateway task is more complex than that of a router or switch. Gateways are computers.

A Gateway Bridges Networks

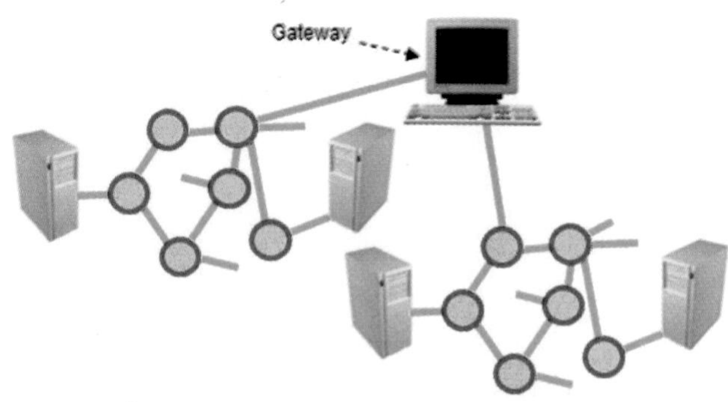

5.9.10 Home Networks

A home network is simply a method of allowing computers to communicate with one another. If you have two or more computers in your home, a network can let them share:

- Files and documents
- Printers, scanners, and other devices
- An Internet connection

The two most popular home network types are wireless and Ethernet networks. In both of these types, the router or switch does most of the work by directing the traffic between the connected devices. By connecting a router to your dial-up, DSL, or cable modem, you can also allow multiple computers to share one connection to the Internet.

The easiest, least expensive way to connect the computers in your home is to use a wireless network, which uses radio waves instead of wires. The absence of physical wires makes this kind of network very flexible. You can, for example, move a computer between rooms without handling network cables and without losing your connection. The downside is that wireless connections are generally slower than Ethernet connections.

If you want to build a wireless network, you'll need a **wireless router.** Signals from a wireless router extend to several hundred feet in all directions, but walls can interrupt the signal. Depending on the size and shape of your home and the range of the router, it may be necessary to purchase a **range extender** or **repeater** to get thorough coverage.

You'll also need a **wireless adapter** in each computer you plan to connect to the network. You can add printers and other devices to the network as well.

If you decide to build a wireless network, you'll need to take steps to protect it—you don't want your neighbors taking a free ride on your wireless signal. Be sure to **encrypt** the signals and use a password for access. Encrypted networks cannot be intruded into easily. Use of password prevents unauthorized use.

Some people feel more secure when using a wired network, and others want to move lots of data very quickly. In either case, a wired Ethernet network is the better choice. Ethernet networks are faster than wireless networks, and they can be very affordable. However, as the number of computers on your network and the distance between them increases the more expensive your network will be. In addition, unless you're building a new house and installing Ethernet cables in the walls, you'll be able to see the cables running from room to room and floor to floor around your home.

Web Cams A web camera (or webcam) is a real-time camera whose images can be accessed using the World Wide Web, instant messaging, or a PC video calling application. It has many uses:

- **Video-conferencing**—Group discussion including video
- **Instant messaging**—Video and audio chat instead of text-based chat

- **Location monitoring**—The camera uploads images to a Web server, either continuously or at regular intervals. Web site visitors refresh the page to view subsequent images.

A Web Cam
© Olivier Le Queninec, 2007, Shutterstock.

5.10 Network Applications

People in business are finding that communication networks provide excellent opportunity for collaboration. Programs like Microsoft's **Live Meeting** enable individuals to collaborate online with colleagues, customers, and partners in real time. Meetings may occur between individuals or large groups. Only a computer and Internet access are required. During meetings, participants share documents, view changes made to the shared document by others, type messages to each other, and keep notes. Some collaborative systems provide a common **whiteboard** that displays the comments, drawings, and notes made by any participant.

If participants can not all meet at the same time e-mail can be used to route comments and updated documents to all teams members. Although not as fast as a live meeting, e-mail can be an effective way to get things done. The use of **digital signatures** can help to ensure that all participants view the same version of a document without subsequent changes as it is distributed.

Collaborative software, sometimes known as **groupware,** is designed to help people involved in a common task achieve their goals. Collaborative software is the basis for computer supported cooperative work. The software is typically designed to support a specific task but sometimes it is generic. Such software systems as e-mail, calendaring, text chat, and wiki belong in this category. Another example of groupware is **Google Documents** which is a publically available free service that permits collaborators to jointly develop and edit documents. Several users simultaneously view and edit changes to the same document while on-line.

5.10.1 Voice Mail

Similar to e-mail combined with a voice answering machine; this system allows a person to leave messages for one or more people. The speaker's voice is converted from a telephone analog signal to a digital signal than can be stored in a **voice mail box** on a computer hard drive. Since the voice is in digital form it can be re-played for recipients as often as desired.

5.10.2 Web Services

Web services is a description of standardized software components that programmers use to communicate with programs on remote computers. Programs written to these standards encapsulate program code and data in a **platform neutral** form using languages like **XML.** This technique allows software systems to incorporate functionality provided by software written in different programming languages running on remove machines. Web services is described fully in the software chapter.

5.10.3 Calendar

Many large businesses use a common corporate calendar to assist those scheduling meetings. Determining the dates and times of all meeting participants is considerably easier with a networked calendar. Individuals mark off time slots when they are not available and the system does the rest. Once a meeting is scheduled and participants notified the calendar system is used to distribute the agenda, discussion material, and later on the minutes.

5.10.4 Wiki

A wiki is a Web site that allows visitors to add, remove, edit, and change content, typically without the need for registration. This ease of interaction and operation makes a wiki an effective tool for mass collaborative authoring. Generally, there is no review before modifications are accepted. Many wikis are open to the general public without the need to register any user account. A single page in a wiki is referred to as a wiki page, while the entire body of pages, which are usually highly interconnected via hyperlinks, is the wiki. A wiki runs on a server and numerous Internet hosts provide platforms for wikis.

5.10.5 EDI

Electronic Data Interchange (EDI) is a set of standards for structuring information to be electronically exchanged between and within businesses, government agencies, and other groups. Since EDI standards were designed to be independent of communication and software technologies EDI transactions can be transmitted using any communication protocols agreed to by the sender and recipient.

EDI standards mostly define the content and form of data required in specific transactions. For example, an electronic purchase transaction between two companies would include price, quantity, and packaging data about products ordered. EDI defines the specific data values and data types that comprise a purchase transaction. If both parties agree to the definition of a transaction it can be automated.

5.10.6 Blackberry

A Blackberry can do everything that a cell phone can do, including sending text messages. It's also an organizer, a calendar, an e-mail client, a Web browser, a two-way pager, and a palm-top computer. Although it can do some of the same things a computer can, it doesn't have to be in a Wi-Fi hot spot to work because it uses the cell phone network as well as 802.11b LANs.

Blackberry: A Wireless Communication Device

5.11 Summary

Data communications operates on the principles of the communication model which assigns the roles of sender and receiver to participants. Protocols govern how the roles are applied. Over time, networking evolved from highly centralized systems to the distributed systems that we know today. The Internet is a distributed system.

Messages that are transmitted between sender and receiver are carried by a communication channel that is provided by several different types of media. Bandwidth is a measure of the channel's capacity and the configuration of the channel determines what directions communication may flow in. For the Internet to work, an arrangement of physical components is required to provide electronic pathways for packets to move to and from servers and clients. Equipment including routers, gateways, and switches helps ensure the proper delivery of messages.

Networks can be arranged locally as in a LAN or over a wide area in a WAN or MAN. A network's architecture takes into consideration various arrangements of components and follows established network topologies.

EXERCISES

Exercise 5.1

Why must the sender and receiver have an agreement about the rules of conversation?

Exercise 5.2

What is a communication channel? What are its components?

Exercise 5.3

What is multiplexing and why is it important?

Exercise 5.4

How does a switch differ from a router?

Exercise 5.5

What is the point of linking computers? Why were early computers rarely networked?

Exercise 5.6

Explain the difference between data communication and telecommunications. Which enables the other?

Exercise 5.7

What is modulation and demodulation?

Exercise 5.8

What is a protocol converter? Where might they be used?

Exercise 5.9

What is encryption? What protection does encryption offer? What wireless encryption standards does IEEE support?

Exercise 5.10

What is a MAC address? What communication devices use the MAC address for routing packets?

Exercise 5.11

What type of network processing is like the Internet? Explain why.

Exercise 5.12

Why does the selection of channel media impact on the cost and usefulness of a channel?

Exercise 5.13

What is EDI? What role might it have in e-commerce?

Exercise 5.14

What are the advantages and disadvantages of the three types of network processing?

Exercise 5.15

What is the value of a fiber optic channel? Contrast it with the advantages offered by satellite.

Exercise 5.16

Discuss three network applications from the perspective of how business might benefit from their use.

Exercise 5.17

What is a protocol?

Exercise 5.18

What are the differences between line configurations and what is significant about the differences?

Exercise 5.19

Discuss the differences between time division and frequency division multiplexing.

Exercise 5.20

What is the difference between a WAN and LAN? How do they work together?

Exercise 5.21

What does a modem do?

Exercise 5.22

What is a topology? Discuss the differences between LAN topologies.

Exercise 5.23

What are communication standards and why are they important?

Exercise 5.24

Discuss four important uses of networks. Give examples to support your ideas.

Exercise 5.25

How do intranets and extranets differ? How do they relate to the Internet?

Exercise 5.26

Discuss Ethernet from the perspective of collisions.

Exercise 5.27

How does client-server architecture differ from peer-to-peer architecture?

Exercise 5.28

How do DSL and cable model lines differ?

Exercise 5.29

How are token ring and Ethernet similar and how are they different?

Exercise 5.30

What is Wi-Fi? Is Bluetooth an example of Wi-Fi? What is Bluetooth used for? Identify two specific commercial products that are Bluetooth ready.

Exercise 5.31

What is TCP/IP? Could the Internet exist without it? Why?

Exercise 5.32

Serial and parallel are two ways to transmit data. Discuss the advantages and disadvantages of each.

Exercise 5.33

If given a choice between using dial-up and dedicated lines what would you select? Why?

Exercise 5.34

What is a T1 line? If DSL and cable were not available would it be used in residential connections?

Exercise 5.35

If you were designing a network for a business what would you consider?

SYSTEMS ANALYSIS

CHAPTER 6

Systems analysis is the process of understanding the needs that organizations have for computer automation. These needs are then translated into information system designs and ultimately into hardware selections and computer programs. The person who performs some of these duties is the **system analyst.** This person is the intermediary between business users of computers and computer programmers and operators. The pressure of cost reduction, government regulation, and increased competition contribute to the demand for upgraded information systems. The system analyst can be a very busy person.

Definitions When computers first became available the task of systems analysis was mostly left undone or was performed poorly. This was because highly technical people who typically had little understanding or appreciation of business issues programmed the computers. In the 1950s and 1960s computer programming was a far more complicated task than it is today so programmers really had little time to be concerned with other than technical issues. Computer hardware was somewhat unreliable thus demanding the constant attention of the technical staff to those concerns rather than to the concerns of business. To bridge this gap the role of system analyst emerged.

Today there remains opportunities for business automation that have gone unfulfilled. This is partly because business people do not fully understand the potential of computer technology, or because business users are not completely aware of how their competitors are using computer technology to improve their business. So the system analyst is a communication bridge between technical and non-technical staff. The analyst helps the business user understand the capability of technology and teaches the technician about business.

Sometimes the results of business computing activities are disappointing. Frequently such situations can be traced to lack of communication. Computer programmers often are concerned only with hardware and software and the businessperson is concerned only with business. Sometimes the information system is built without real regard for the people who will use it. Just because a system analyst is placed between the computer and business professional is no guarantee that the job will be done right. The system analyst does, however, have an arsenal of tools that, when used properly, can help increase the likelihood of a successful result.

6.1 System Development

Significant and successful information systems (IS) are the product of careful thought, planning, implementation, and management. Often IS projects involve many people, are costly, and have a long time-line from conception to conclusion. Up-front attention to open-minded analysis and receptivity to those with an interest, the stakeholders, are important ingredients that help promote success. Unplanned projects have little likelihood of a satisfactory ending.

SWOT SWOT analysis (Strengths, Weaknesses, Opportunities, and Threats) is a **strategic planning** tool used to evaluate a business and the environment it operates within. By taking a close-up and honest look at itself and its competitors; a business can craft a strategy that distinguishes itself from its competitors. As a strategic planning tool SWOT is not a tool for designing an information system, but a SWOT analysis may identify opportunity where automation can support and enhance business performance. Strengths and weaknesses are often internal to an organization. Opportunities and threats often relate to external factors. For this reason the SWOT Analysis is sometimes called **Internal-External Analysis.** The SWOT analysis asks these questions:

- **Strengths:**
    - What advantages does the business have?
    - What does it do better than others?
    - What unique or lowest-cost resources are available?
- **Weaknesses:**
    - What could be improved?
    - What should be avoided?
    - What do competitors in your market see as weaknesses?
- **Opportunities:**
    - Where are good opportunities identified?
    - What are the business trends of interest?
    - What useful opportunities can come from changes in technology, markets, government policy, and social patterns?
- **Threats:**
    - What obstacles are present?
    - What is the competition doing?
    - Is changing technology threatening business?
    - Could any weaknesses seriously threaten business potential?

The analysis may reveal opportunities to enhance existing information systems or acquire or build new ones.

Buy or Build Companies pursue the buy option because it can be easier and faster than building custom software. Nevertheless, buying the right software is a project in itself. When buying software, it is often difficult to determine which product packages are worth looking at seriously. Marketing literature can be vague and unhelpful. Even referrals from other users with the software already installed may not be sufficient because no two businesses are alike or operate in the same way.

Buying off-the-shelf software usually gives most of the desired functionality at lower cost than if custom built. Sometimes simple changes such as redesigning the layout of a data entry screen could make the software much more suitable but off-the-shelf software can not usually be customized. Measured over the lifetime of the software, such changes might save the users a lot of time (and therefore money), but the changes often cannot be made to off-the-shelf software.

Software that exactly matches business requirements is customized by internal staff, consultants, and off-shore outsourcers. The risk associated with developed applications is significant because these projects involve many people and consume considerable resources. Skilled project management is essential to successful conclusion of these projects. The business and system analyst is called on to assess organizations opportunities and requirements and offer judgment on the buy vs. build decision.

Stakeholders Stakeholders are individuals or organizations who stand to gain or lose from the success or failure of an information system project. This can include managers, designers, developers, and users of a system. Since, by definition, stakeholders are impacted by or have an impact on the project, consideration of their perspectives is important for a project to be successful. Stakeholders often do not agree with one another, making it a challenge to reconcile their objectives and viewpoints.

Return on Investment In finance the **ROI** is the ratio of money gained or lost on an investment relative to the amount of money invested. With an information system project ROI is not as clear, yet the system developer must establish that there is expected value in completing the system project. With the exception of transactional information systems (**EDP**—electronic data procession systems) it is hard to estimate with precision the expected return derived from system development.

Managers must make the most of scarce resources and at the same time respond to ever-increasing demands for improved performance and new technology. Competing demands compel close scrutiny of proposals for new information technology investments. High profile **IT** system failures raise concerns about why these investments often fail to live up to expectations. As a result, many IT investment planning processes now require deep analysis of the costs and returns expected from proposed investments.

System Development Issues The traditional Systems Development Life Cycle (SDLC) model has been used successfully for many years. It is worth noting, however, some of the challenges that the SDLC can cause:

- **Long delivery time**—System development time can be extensive. This is especially true of large and complex projects. Not only may the stakeholders become impatient but also the needs of the organization may change during the development period and the finished result may not match initial needs.
- **High expense**—Systems are expensive to build. Staff (programmers, analysts, users, etc.) must be paid and provided workspace. Time spent by other stakeholders during system development is usually considered not productive because they are taken away from their regular job responsibilities. A consequence of long development can be opportunity cost to the organization. As resources (people, hardware, etc.) are tied up in the development effort those resources are not available for other organizational needs.
- **Missed targets**—The SDLC (and especially the Waterfall Model-see the next section) has been labeled **monolithic.** That is because, as the development project

moves through its various stages, it can be difficult to back up to earlier stages to correct problems. As unbelievable as it may seem, sometimes problems that are identified during development are not fixed until after the system is installed and are then corrected as maintenance activities.

- **High maintenance costs**—Maintenance for most information systems is estimated at about 70 percent of the system's total expenses during its full life cycle. That means that about 30 percent of cost goes toward analysis, design, implementation, training stakeholders, and testing the system. How could it be that maintenance costs so much? The answer is that long delivery time coupled with missed targets contributes to systems delivered that may not really meet all user requirements. Fixes to missed requirements can be expensive and during the life of the IS they typically add up to about 70 percent of total expense.

Open Source Development Issues Despite the growing success of the Open Source movement, much of the general public continues to feel that Open Source software is inaccessible to them despite the low cost. Several issues are holding the movement back:

- **Interface Design**—The lack of focus on intuitive user interface.
- **Documentation**—Lacks the complete documentation that users expect.
- **Features First**—Focus on software features rather than program stability.
- **Prejudice**—Desire to be different from what the public knows and likes—commercial software.

If Open Source software is to become widely used and embraced by the general public, these issues will have to be overcome.

System Development Lifecycle When software is developed, a standard process is followed that imposes a formalized structure on the project. Information system projects are big and complex and teams of software developers (architects, analysts, programmers, testers, and users) must work together to create the systems that enterprises depend on.

Here, several stages of the process are identified. As you see, once a project is complete, maintenance is required because **stakeholder** needs and requirements change over time thus necessitating updates to the software.

- **Problem Definition and Analysis**—The first activity is to clearly define the problem to be solved and to develop a solution that meets the needs of clients and stakeholders. This may involve **negotiation** between **stakeholders** that is facilitated by a system analyst.
- **Program Design**—Once the solution is accepted by all parties a technical design or **blueprint** is prepared. This document defines all technical aspects of the program or programs including: selection of programming language, design of program logic and of the database structure, interface design, and design of output (reports and screen display). During this phase acceptance criteria should be established so that success can be measured.
- **Coding**—This phase is for the programmers. Apart from maintenance, it is usually the most time-consuming and costly phase of the development cycle.
- **Testing**—Here work is tested and certified to meet the already established acceptance criteria. Errors that are identified must be corrected before moving to implementation.

- **Implementation**—Once the system is satisfactorily tested it is time to create user documentation, train users, and convert data for use by the software.
- **Maintenance**—It is rare that completed systems are static. Changes in business requirements, governmental regulation, and stakeholder needs demand software modification and upgrade. In the lifetime of a system considerable time and money is spent on maintenance so a good design and thorough testing is important because they could affect the cost and extent of maintenance expenditures.

The software engineer or system analyst uses various tools to better understand system requirements and specify the design for programmers. The system designer uses various diagramming and prototyping tools to create charts that depict the structure and flow of data and events in a system. The designer may also use tools to document the system's processing logic and even create **pseudocode** that is the basis for program code.

6.2 Waterfall Model

To manage the SDLC, several models have been created. The oldest of these, and the best known, is the Waterfall Model: a sequence of stages in which the output of each stage becomes the input for the next. These stages can be characterized and divided up in different ways. The Waterfall Model contains both a sequence of stages that are conceptual and implementation phases of the SDLC. Work completed in each stage is passed on and becomes the input for work at the next stage—at each point of transfer between stages it is possible that miscommunication may occur and therefore assumptions used for the work in a particular stage may be based on an incorrect understanding. There is little opportunity to back up and correct problems that are **propagated** this way.

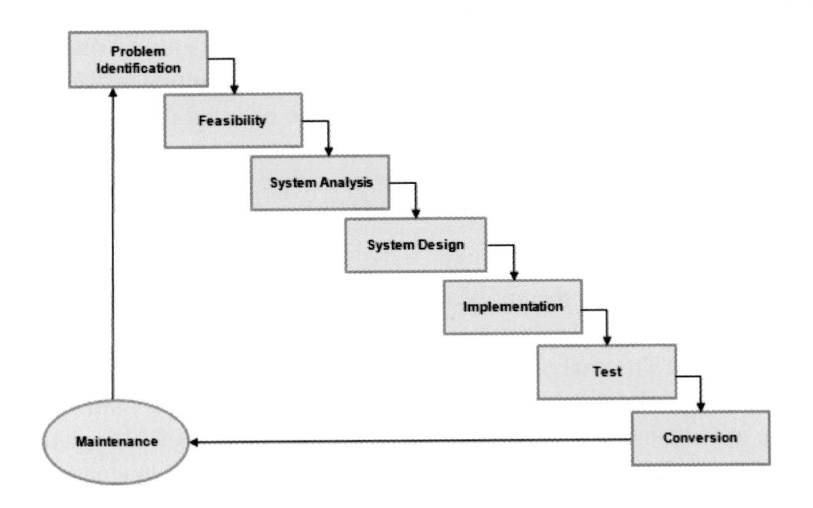

The Waterfall Model of System Development

6.2.1 Problem Identification

In this stage the client and analyst work together to identify the specific problem to be considered. The client most likely was motivated to ask the system analyst for help because of experiencing symptoms of a problem. Symptoms might be, for example, customer invoices printing incorrectly or inventory restocking requests not being transmitted to vendors on a timely basis. Here a high-level view of the intended project is established and the project **goals** are determined.

6.2.2 Feasibility Study

Once the problem is identified a feasibility study is conducted to assess whether or not it is possible and practical to solve the problem. The analyst evaluates various concerns including considerations of technology (can it be applied to the problem area), finance (does the organization have the resources to attempt to solve the problem), and human resources (will the staff accept a solution to the problem and, if not, then what will it take to gain the staff's acceptance). The feasibility study is concluded with a report to management.

6.2.3 Systems Analysis

Assuming the feasibility of creating a solution to the problem the analyst develops a set of alternative solutions. After much analysis and consideration of data, the analyst recommends a solution for management's approval. End-user information needs are analyzed and the project goals are refined into the defined functional aspects of the intended application. The analyst collects organizational and environmental data for evaluation. Data collection and analysis methods are discussed later in this chapter. The outcome of the analysis phase is a **functional specification** of an information system and is sometimes called the **logical design.**

Ultimately the fundamental question of build, buy, or outsource must be addressed:

- **Buy**—Easier and faster and perhaps more reliable than building a customized solution. The purchased software may not exactly fit needs and stakeholder frustrations may surface after installation.
- **Build**—System will be designed to exactly match stakeholder requirements. Risks associated with project development should be considered and weighed against the benefit of a matched solution.
- **Outsource**—Building a system can be an in-house or outsourced project. In-house development can be more effective because of the proximity between developers and clients. Outsourcing can save money because external developers may be in a location where labor rates are lower.

6.2.4 System Design

The system design describes the application's desired features and operations in detail, including screen layouts, business rules, process and schema diagrams, pseudocode, and other documentation. The analyst's proposed solution is developed into a technical specification used as a **blueprint** by programmers and other technical staff. The design is very specific and includes detailed instruction for the creation of files, databases, processing algorithms, data entry screens, and reports. Programming languages and a database management system (DBMS) may be selected. Hardware and software are selected and computer program logic is completely spelled out often in **pseudocode.**

The system design is also known as the system's physical design and includes several important considerations:

- **System Architecture**—Standalone systems are becoming rarer as systems are increasingly expected to enable data sharing among users. Today, the client-server architecture of the Internet has become virtually standard. Local, LAN based architectures are used especially for corporate Intranets. Extranets, that straddle organizational boundaries, are important, too, but add security risks and other management concerns.

- **Programming Language Selection**—Numerous programming languages are available to choose from among. To be considered are: scalability, integration, platform independence, code distribution, speed of development, and availability of programmers. These concerns are discussed in the computer programming chapter. Specific consideration should be given to the possible need to interface with existing or **legacy** systems.
- **Database**—Virtually all information systems require data storage and retrieval. Most often a Database Management System (DBMS) is called for. Today most DBMSs are relational and several prominent options are available including **MySQL, Access, Oracle, DB2,** and **SQL Server.** While they all support SQL each has different features that aid in design and management including backup and recovery.
- **Web Applications**—A request-response protocol is followed and several technology options are available for consideration. Matching programming language and database manager with Web server is an important choice as various combinations work harmoniously. The computer programming chapter discussed request-response options in more detail.
- **E-Commerce**—Depending on Web applications for infrastructure, e-commerce also demands consideration be given to marketing, interface design, ease of use, and security.
- **Data**—Information systems are about processing data into information to support decision making. Data is input and information is output, but invalid or corrupted data produces little output of any use. The system design must give thorough attention to **data validation** and the maintenance of data integrity. Individual data values should be checked for correct data type and completeness, and also checked for inclusion in a list or range of values considered valid.
- **Security**—All systems require security checks to authenticate all user access attempts. Security should be designed in up front and not as an afterthought. Security also includes provisions for data backup and the preparation and testing of disaster recovery plans.

6.2.5 Implementation

Here the system design is made a reality. Hardware and other software is purchased and installed. Programs are written and databases are created. Interfaces between the emerging and existing systems are prepared. Implementation follows the technical design blueprint created in the prior phase. This phase is typically the most clearly understood and apart from maintenance it is the most time consuming of all.

6.2.6 Testing

In the testing phase all the pieces of the application are brought together into a special testing environment, then checks for errors, bugs, and interoperability are conducted. First individual programs are tested in what is called **unit testing** then all programs are tested together in what is called a **system test.** Finally if the programs integrate properly the system is **stress tested.** Large volumes of real data are processed by the system and an evaluation is made about whether or not the system can handle the load.

Quality Assurance Quality assurance (**QA**) is the activity of providing evidence to stakeholders establishing that the entire project has been completed successfully and is ready to be operational.

Testing software is one of the most important and often overlooked phases in system development. It is the process used to help identify the completeness, correctness, security, and quality of developed computer software. There are many approaches to software testing, but effective testing of complex software is essentially a process of investigation, it is not a process that follows a set road map. The testing is somewhat subjective as it is particular to each specific software development project.

Testing is used to certify that the individual programs and complete system are free of **syntax, logical,** and **run-time** errors, each of which is explained in the computer programming chapter. Testing is a broad topic, but there are two complimentary methods commonly in use:

- **Unit Testing**—Individual units of source code are evaluated and determined to be working as expected. Errors that are found are corrected and recertified. A unit is the smallest testable part of an application. For this reason unit testing is often known as **bottom up** testing. All three types of errors are addressed while unit testing is conducted. The unit test eliminates uncertainty about the systems components. Testing the individual parts first makes testing the full system easier.
- **System Testing**—The complete integration of all units is subjected to a comprehensive test. The purpose of integration testing is to determine that the system components works together and to identify incompatibilities between units where they exist. At this level of testing, run-time and logical errors are detected but syntax errors are addressed only in unit testing.
- **User Acceptance Testing**—User Acceptance Testing (UAT) is the determination of stakeholders that the system development meets original requirements. Stakeholders assess system perform against standards derived from system specifications. Only upon user acceptance should the system be activated.

Software Testing

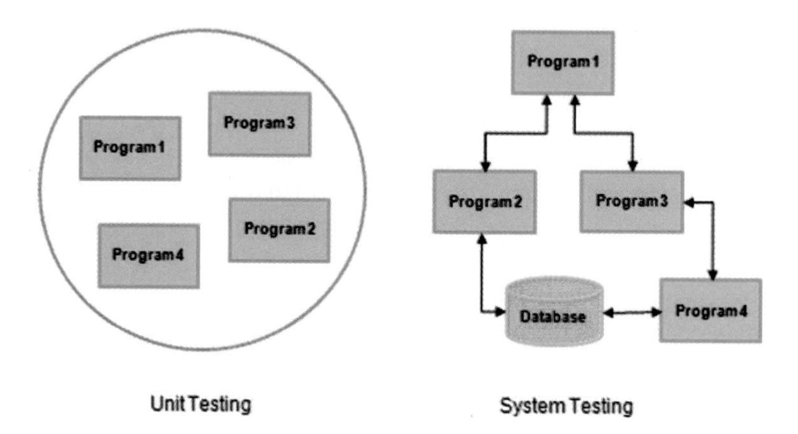

6.2.7 Conversion

The final stage of development, where the software goes into production and runs actual business is the conversion phase. Here the staff is **trained** to use the information system. User manuals and **documentation** are prepared before training begins. For training to be effective it should be provided away from the normal work site so that the staff's attention is not diluted with concerns about other work responsibilities. Next, it is time to go live with the new system. There are three common approaches to putting the new system into production as depicted shortly.

Information System Conversion Options

- **Direct Conversion**—The old IS is abruptly turned off and the new IS turned on. This can be risky because, if the new IS fails, the organization may have little to fall back on. This approach is often the least costly.
- **Phased Conversion**—The old IS is gradually turned off and the equivalent parts of the new system gradually turned on. This approach requires the continued use of resources to support both systems but provides a fall back if problems occur with the new system.
- **Parallel Conversion**—The old and new ISs are run at the same time with no concern about new system failure because the old system is completely up and running as a fallback. After a period of time (usually one to three months) the old IS is shut down as long as the new IS has operated properly during this period. This approach is the most costly since resources are provided to operate both systems and the staff must enter all transactions into both systems in parallel.

Each method of conversion has its associated risks and costs. The system analyst would consider these factors when planning this part of a project.

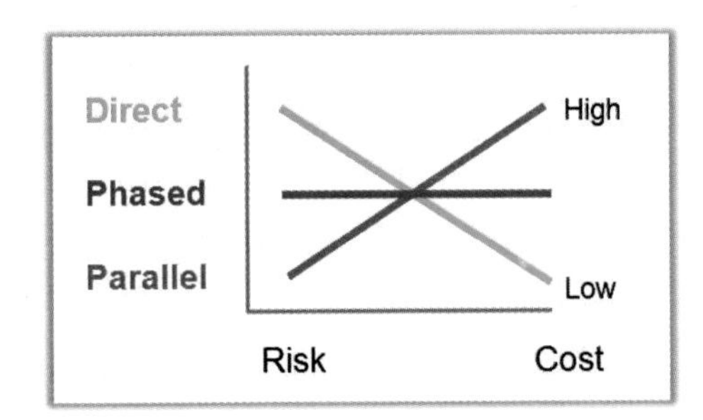

System Conversion Risk and Cost

6.2.8 Maintenance

What happens during the rest of the software's life: business and regulatory changes, changes in competition other companies and from replacement products, and technology changes. Maintenance, unexciting yet perhaps the most important phase in a system's life cycle, goes on seemingly forever. Most system resources are expended in maintenance. Systems are not always delivered as the specifications originally defined. Changes in technology, in competition, and in business practice place demands on a system that may require upgrading over time. Typically 70 percent of a system's lifetime budget is expended in this stage.

Backup and Recovery Backup refers to copying data onto portable or remote media in order to facilitate data restoration in the event of a system failure or corruption of databases. Backups are useful primarily for two purposes: to restore a computer system to operational following a **disaster** (called disaster recovery) and to restore data files after they have been accidentally deleted or corrupted. Backups differ from **archives** in the sense that archives are a copy of the data as of a specific date. Archives provide a permanent record of a system's data. Backups reflect the current status of a database at the time of failure. Backups are use do restore system databases enabling recovery from a system failure. Backup systems differ from **fault-tolerant** systems in the sense that backup systems assume that a recovery due to a data loss event and fault-tolerant systems assume a loss will not occur.

Since a backup system contains at least one copy of all data that might require recovery, the data storage requirements are considerable. Organizing this storage space and managing the backup process can be a complicated and expensive undertaking.

Disaster Recovery Plan Disaster recovery is the process of regaining access to data, computer systems, and software to resume operations after a disaster. An Information Disaster Recovery Plan (DRP) should be part of a larger process known as **Business Continuity Planning.** Replacement of key personnel and obtaining access to financial markets are essential for business recovery.

6.3 Other SDLC Models

The waterfall model is well understood and works well when systems are built to automate transactional activities. It does not work as well if building non-transactional systems for knowledge workers—customer service representatives, marketing analysts, investors, or executives. The Waterfall Model can be perceived as monolithic. It assumes that best role for a user is in specifying requirements, and that all requirements can be completely specified in advance. Experience shows that requirements are not static. Requirements grow and change throughout the project and beyond. This reality calls for feedback and iterative adaptation. Because of this other SDLC models have been developed.

- **Spiral Model**—This model is iterative and repetitive. Prototyping emerges as important tool for this model. The Spiral Model emphasizes the need to go back and reiterate earlier stages a number of times as the project progresses. It's a sequence of mini Waterfall cycles, each producing an early prototype representing a part of the entire project. This approach helps demonstrate a proof of concept early in the cycle, and it more accurately reflects the disorderly, even chaotic, evolution of technology.
- **Rapid Application Development**—In RAD the initial emphasis is on creating a **prototype** that looks and acts like the desired system in order to test its usefulness. The prototype is an essential part of the requirements determination phase, and may be created using software development tools that are different from those used for the final product. Once the prototype is approved, it is discarded and properly architected and tested software is written.
- **Incremental Model**—The project is divided into separate smaller projects where each is created and tested separately. This approach will likely find errors in user requirements quickly, since user feedback is solicited for each stage and because code is tested sooner after it's written. Each smaller project can be organized using any system development model.

- **Build and Fix**—This is not really a model but a crude approach that involves writing code then modifying it until the stakeholders are happy. With little or no planning, this is very open-ended and can be risky.

6.4 Prototyping

In the past, system design has usually been a pencil and paper exercise following the stages of the Waterfall Model. The analyst drew illustrations that depicted the data entry screen and reports from the new system. These pictures were presented to the users for their approval. As the users requested changes the analyst repeated the time-consuming process of redrawing them and presenting the illustrations again (and again) until the users were satisfied. Frequently, even if the users accepted the system design based on the pictures, the design might prove inadequate when the system development phase began because underlying technical and human usage concerns were not gauged accurately simply by looking at pictures. To address this problem prototyping is used.

A prototype is a **model** of what is being built. Before the Wright brothers built their first airplane they made sure that an exact model of it flew in a wind tunnel first. They figured that it was better to destroy a model before risking their necks anymore than was necessary. This same rule can profitably be applied to information system development. These days system development is costly (in time, money, and human resources) and the risk of failure can be quite high (unneeded computer hardware, lost business opportunity, rebelling employees, etc.). To reduce risk, analysts are increasingly turning to the use of prototypes.

The real advantage of prototyping lies in the process of **iteration.** The analyst builds a prototype based on an understanding of the users' requirements. The prototype is shown to the users who operate it and make recommendations for change. The prototype is updated to reflect the suggestions and the users operate it again. This process continues until the users are satisfied. When this iterative process ends the users and analyst have essentially agreed on a **design** that will be used during system development. A further, but subtle, advantage of this method is that it draws users rapidly into the design process and demands that users become "owners" of the developing design. It will surely be harder for a user to complain about a system that is developed based on a design that they partly were responsible for. Another advantage is speed. Placing a working model of a system before a group of users usually gives the analyst **feedback** more rapidly than if the users were expected to review and react to pictures and reports that described the new system.

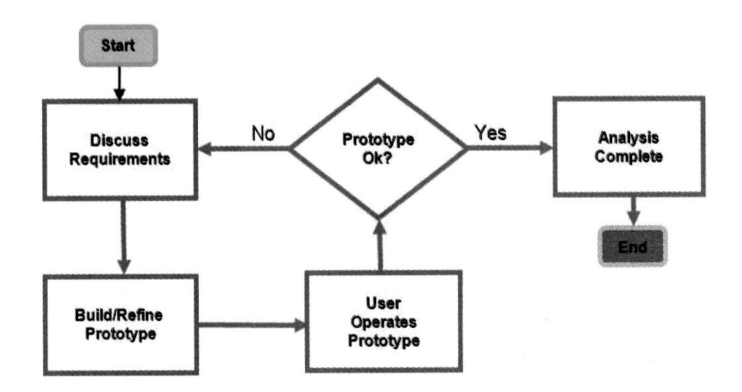

Prototyping Features
Iterative Development

Prototyping, however, has its disadvantages. The most common may be called "seduction by first impression." This means that users may be so overwhelmed by the excitement of using the first prototype version that a common reaction is "That's it! Build that system!" The danger, of course, is that the user will fail to explore all possibilities that the new system could offer and limit the design to what is apparent in the first prototype. Another danger is that the analyst may want to use the prototype as a substitute for formal system specifications. The prototype is merely used to help define the system characteristics but does not reflect the detailed aspects of the system design including selection of programming language, database management system, hardware, training materials, etc. A final trap to watch for may be called "expanding user expectations." As the user views prototypes and is impressed with the speed with which they are constructed the user may begin to assume that anything is possible and may continue to enlarge a wish list of what is to be included in the system. The analyst must be fully aware of these dangers and manage the expectations of the user so that the system development project is not jeopardized.

6.5 The System Analyst

System analysts are responsible for designing computer information systems, modifying systems to improve production or work flow, or expanding systems to serve new purposes. The system analyst studies the information related needs of an organization to determine how people, business processes, and computer technology can be best arranged to help accomplish the objectives of the business. Because the result of analysis may be the recommendation for change within the organization the system analyst is known as a **change agent.** A job description for the system analyst might include these items:

Purpose Gather and analyze data for developing information systems. Study existing business procedures and computer programs to determine how both can be better organized. Study technology and business trends to be able to recommend changes to take advantage of advances in both.

Duties

- Analyze existing business operations and existing information systems (computerized or not).
- Study trends in technology.
- Study trends in business and be aware of competitors' exploitation of technology.
- Propose alternative solutions to business problems and select and justify the preferred solution.
- Recommend technology products (hardware and software) for purchase.
- Design new systems including process flow, user interface, reports, and security procedures.
- Prepare training material for users of new systems.
- Supervise implementation of new systems.

Skills and Qualities

- Excellent communication abilities (oral and written).
- Problem solving abilities and drive.
- Understanding of the potential of computer technology.
- Appreciation for the business's objectives.
- Ability to guide people through periods of change.

- Patience.
- Creativity.

6.5.1 Preparing for a Career as System Analyst

The system analyst is the bridge between computer programmers and business computer users. Many organizations assume that computer-programming experience is a vital prerequisite to system analysis and design responsibility. This assumption is based on the incorrect expectation that the job of system analyst is mostly technical in nature. While a decent understanding of technology is quite important, the most important characteristic of a system analyst is excellent communication skills!

The Analyst Is a Communicator

A Communicator The system analyst must be able to communicate in writing and orally. Poor use of language will immediately reduce the credibility of the analyst in the view of the business user. Practice in business and technical writing is very good preparation for work as a system analyst. It is a good idea for an analyst to become familiar with software like **PowerPoint,** or other programs that are used to prepare graphics for presentation.

The analyst must easily get along with people. The analyst must also be a good **listener** and able to react to what people say, and be persuasive in helping others overcome anxiety caused by fear of the unknown (change after all presents an unknown future to most people). There is also a political perspective: people are often more interested in their own welfare than in the success of the organization. Because people are looking out for themselves, the system analyst can feel pulled by several competing sets of needs from the people involved in a project. If the analyst appears to play favorites then project participants may feel slighted and lose trust in the analyst. It is up to the analyst to be fair, honest, and open but at the same time be aware of hidden agendas and be sensitive to the needs of all individuals involved.

When an analyst is designing a new information system for use by data entry clerks the analyst should be mindful of their concerns. Often ISs are developed to make business more efficient. Data entry clerks may believe that a more efficient system will require them to work faster, in effect requiring them to do more work. Or they may believe that the purpose of the new system is to weed out the poorly performing clerks. Such concerns have resulted in stakeholders banding together and refusing to use a new system. Make sure that such fears are adequately addressed!

6.5.2 Technology Aware

It should not be surprising that knowledge of technology is quite important. The analyst is not expected to know the intricacies of programming logic but a decent general knowledge of concepts and terms is essential. Awareness of the different development tools (programming languages, databases, operating systems, types of hardware, and communication devices, etc.) helps the analyst properly represent the capabilities of technology for solving business problems.

The Analyst Considers Technology

How does the analyst gain this knowledge? Certainly course work while in college is helpful. Many analysts either major in IS (Information Systems) or at least minor in that subject. Often additional non-credit courses or workshops are helpful. Regularly reading trade publications and attending industry trade shows are helpful, too. The analyst's ears should always perk up when a television story about technology is broadcast because in all likelihood some of the analyst's clients (business users) may have seen the same show and may want to discuss it with the analyst. Joining professional organizations often provides another rich source of information.

Computer programming experience is a good prerequisite, too; many organizations require this skill anyway. It is not uncommon to start a career as a programmer and be promoted to system analyst. This means that, even if you have the communication and interpersonal skills already discussed, you may still be required to demonstrate some programming ability to be considered for a system analyst position. It is highly recommended that a student learn at least one programming language while in college. The key point is that businesses believe that experience programming will help give the analyst an awareness of the issues faced by the technical staff.

6.5.3 Business Is Important, Too

Just as knowledge of technology is important so is business knowledge. Clearly it would be quite difficult for a system analyst to contribute to the organization without understanding the organization's mission, products, and competition. The analyst need not be an expert in business but should have a decent understanding of it. A system analyst designing an IS for the accounting department should understand debits and credits. An analyst designing an IS for a rental company should understand the significance of security deposits and late payment fees.

The Analyst Considers Business

Recall from earlier the discussion on the traditional IPO Model. In effect the system analyst is responsible for all three stages of the model when analyzing and designing an information system. Gathering the input (data about business needs, corporate objectives, technological capabilities, etc.) is important, but analyzing (processing) that data is the most crucial aspect of the analyst's work. The analyst must be able to evaluate the data and creatively suggest alternative solutions to the business problems being addressed. The analyst must be able to "see" beyond solutions that worked in the past and be able to "paint a new horizon." Being able to see beyond the barriers that hold others back is often what drives the success of the system analyst.

6.6 Data Gathering Techniques

During analysis, the system analyst evaluates many different kinds of data from many sources. This section discusses data gathering and analysis tools employed by the system analyst.

6.6.1 Interviews

Interviews are the first tool used by the system analyst. The interview is first conducted with the primary user of the information system under analysis. The purpose of this first interview is to learn the owner's objectives in having a new system built.

Subsequent interviews should be held with representatives of as many classes of stakeholder as possible. The purpose of these further interviews is to get "the other side of the story." Each person probably has a different point of view, and each will interact with the system differently when it is built. For example, in a manufacturing company, work supervisors will want daily reports that show how productive the assembly workers are. Upper management will be more interested in reports that periodically report on the overall quality of the assembly work. Thus the data collected and reported by the system must address the needs of varying audiences.

6.6.2 Surveys

Surveys may be used because it is not always possible for the system analyst to interview all stakeholders. If the IS to be built automates the job of order takers in a large mail order company it would probably not be possible to interview all employees, but a survey could help. The use of a survey may allow the analyst to get input from many or all employees without taking the time to personally interview each one. Sometimes a survey is used when it is impossible to interview a stakeholder at all. Rarely can a system analyst get access to customers, suppliers, or other outside stakeholders. To obtain information from these people surveys are frequently used.

6.6.3 Focus Group

When it is desirable but impossible to interview a group of stakeholders a focus group may be used. This concept is borrowed from marketing. A meeting is arranged where several stakeholders are gathered and discuss the IS. The analyst who leads participants through a relevant discussion facilitates the meeting. The benefit of this method is that firsthand knowledge of the concerns and desires of stakeholders is obtained without requiring significant amounts of time.

6.6.4 Observation

Observation and review of relevant data is useful because all facts relevant to the analysis of the new information system do not become evident in an interview or survey. Sometimes it may be useful for the system analyst to observe workers interacting with the existing system. This method can provide a rich source of information to the analyst because people often perform their job duties differently from the way they describe their work activities.

The analyst may find it especially helpful to evaluate the business forms that are used by the organization to record data. This review can help uncover the names and types of data that the new system must accommodate. Further, the rules of the business are often described on the business forms. For example, a bank credit card application form (a business form) usually lists the minimum income that a credit card applicant must have (a rule). These rules become the basis for the logic of computer programs that are written as part of the new information system.

6.7 Modeling and Analysis Tools

As the analyst collects and records data about the information system being designed there are various tools available to assist with the analysis. Most of the tools are visual in nature because experience has shown that there is something to the expression "A picture is worth a thousand words." While printed reports may be used to present the details that have been collected, pictures often can help someone get the big picture quickly. Several of the tools described in this section are employed as part of what is called structured methodologies because the process of using the tool follows a series of predetermined steps.

Software Engineering is the application of a systematic, disciplined, and quantifiable approach to the development of software. The discipline of software engineering includes the use of tools and methods for defining software requirements, performing software design and software construction, testing software, and performing software maintenance. Software Engineering arose in response to the perceived failure of earlier software development procedures that were considered by some to be haphazard at best.

Software is often found where very high reliability is expected (FAA aircraft traffic control, medical imaging, nuclear power plant control, etc.). These applications contain millions of lines of code, making them as complex as many modern machines. It should be no surprise that the possibility of error is great and the allowance for error is minimal.

There are many manual and computer assisted tools available to provide aide during the system analysis and design activity. Several important and frequently used tools are described briefly here and more completely in the systems analysis chapter.

6.7.1 Data Flow Diagrams

Data Flow Diagrams or **DFDs** depict the flow of data through a system. Unlike a flow chart that presumes a linear flow of operations, a DFD does not relate to the sequence of events but rather to the flow of data between events and stakeholders. The DFD provides a **context** for the existence and operation of an information system. It provides the **big picture.**

It is understood that events may happen in parallel. For example, you could be withdrawing money at an ATM machine from your checking account at the same time that your spouse is withdrawing from the same account at a teller window. The DFD shows where the data about your account goes from the ATM and the teller window but does not show the processing logic that deals with the data itself. For example, what happens if the checking account does not have an adequate balance to cover both withdrawals (remember they are happening at the same time). The DFD will not resolve this problem.

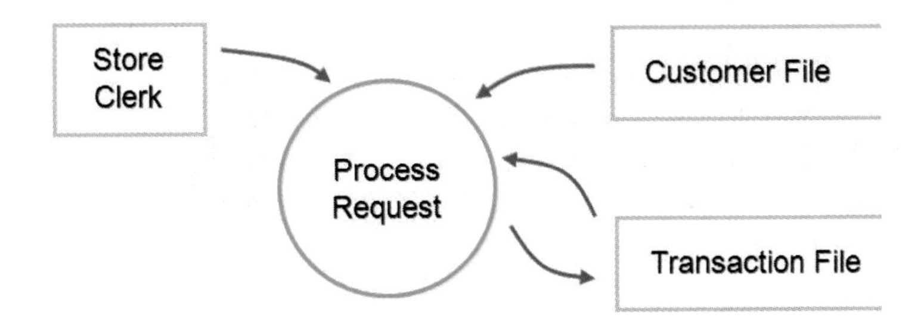

Context Level Data Flow Diagram

DFDs are considered to be a **structured methodology tool** because they facilitate breaking down processes to their smallest components. The symbols used in a DFD depict the different components of the problem area. Most notably each data processing activity (shown as a circle) can be subdivided into smaller processes that comprise the parent process. This process of decomposition ultimately results in a sub process that cannot be further divided—that process becomes a computer program.

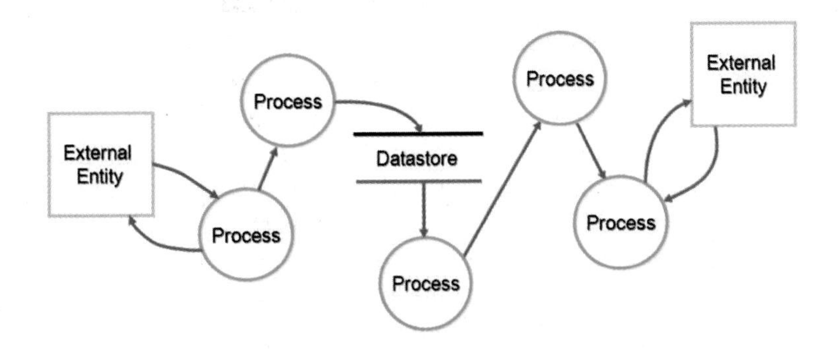

Context Level Exploded

A data flow diagram is a **graphical representation** of the **movement of data** through an information system. A DFD can also be used for the visualization of structured design because this tool facilitates breaking down processes into increasingly smaller units—in effect decomposing the process until individual program blocks are defined.

This is a **top-down** approach

- The designer makes a **context level** (top level) DFD, which shows data flows between the system and the external environment (**stakeholders**).

- The system is decomposed into increasingly more detailed DFDs that represent portions of the system.
- This approach continues until a sufficiently granular level of design is accomplished (program blocks).

One drawback of the DFD and other graphical approaches is their labor intensity. Computer automated drawing tools ease the burden. As DFDs are exploded to the ultimate detailed level the analyst must draw a fresh diagram for each level.

Top Down Design

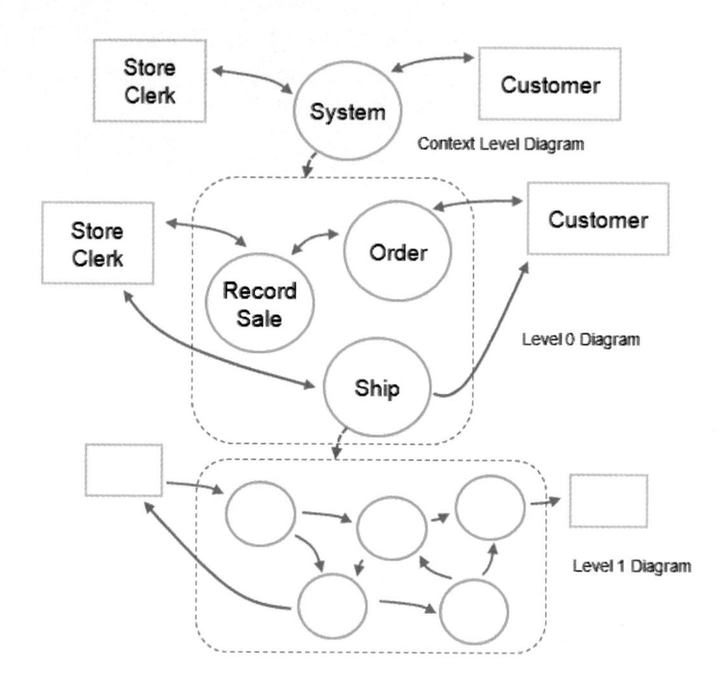

6.7.2 Entity Relationship Diagrams

Entity Relationship Diagrams (ERD) describe the system's data. The DFD depicts the flow of events and data within a system but omits consideration of the other important part of the system: the **structure** of data. Data cannot magically move from process to process or from process to data storage without computer programs that understand the structure of the data. Data is stored in a database as records that are defined as a collection of fields. This data structure is called the database **schema** or **data model.** No system design is complete without a data model.

The Entity-Relationship Diagram (ERD) can be used to present the information contained within the data model. Each file in the database (each entity) is shown as a rectangle with the name of the entity inside the rectangle. Since all files in a database are related the diagram shows lines that depict the relationship between pairs of entities.

Entity Relationship Diagram—Database Design

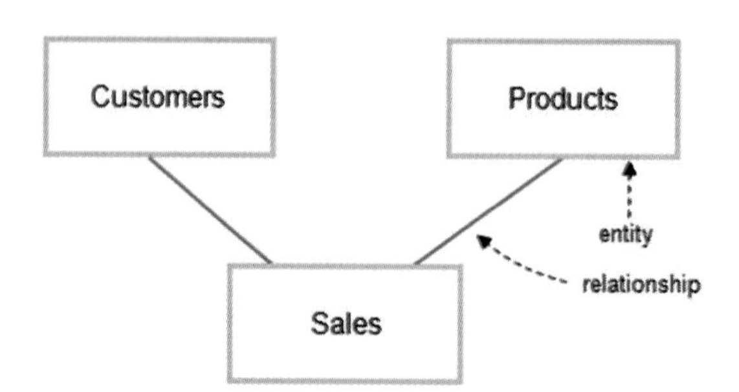

Data Modeling Data modeling is the process of designing structures for organizing data. The data structures are created in a database which is controlled by a DBMS. The model may define constraints or limitations on the data placed within the structure. A **conceptual data model** is developed early in a software development project. This model evolves into a **logical data model** and eventually into **physical data model.**

The **conceptual model** for a relational database is often prepared in graphical form as an ERD. The ERD represents the objects of a database and the relationships that connect them. The objects are **entities** which can be thought of as **nouns,** and **relationships** among the entities can be thought of as **verbs.** The following illustration depicts the ERD for a system that manages products, customers, and their purchases. Various aspects of data modeling including defining relationship cardinality and primary and foreign keys is discussed in the database chapter.

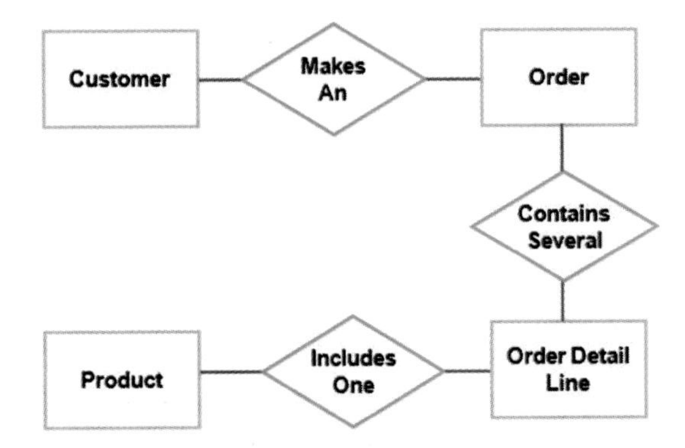

Entity Relationship Diagram—Database Design

During implementation, the creation of the database will involve using the SQL language to **create tables** and define their relationships and specify other constraints.

```
CREATE TABLE ORDERS (
    Order_ID integer,
    Order_Date date,
    Customer_ID integer,
    Amount double,
    Primary Key (Order_ID),
    Foreign Key (Customer_ID) references CUSTOMER(ID)
);
```

Creating Tables Using SQL

6.7.3 Decision Table

Decision tables are used to **model** complicated **logic** precisely. Decision tables associate conditions with resulting actions. Decision tables can tie together independent conditions with several actions in a simple and clear way.

Conditions:			
Valid Customer	Y	Y	N
Charge + Balance Within Limit	Y	N	N
Action:			
Authorize Transaction	X		
Reject Transaction		X	X

Decision Table

6.7.4 Flow Chart

These charts are used to depict the sequence of activities that a system must perform. The assumption in a flow chart is that activities occur in a linear sequence; an event occurs first always followed by a specific second event, then a third, and so on. The sequence is constant and always predictable. Programmers use flow charts as the basis from which the logic of a computer program is derived.

The activity represented by a circle in the middle of a DFD can be depicted in a flow chart.

Logic Flow Chart

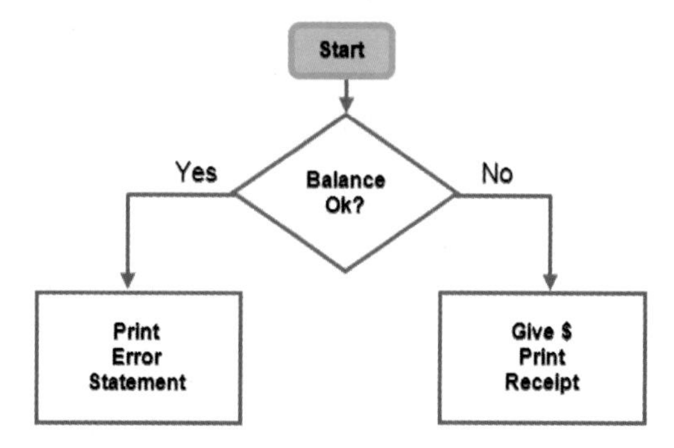

A flow chart is graphical representation used to illustrate the logical steps to be performed by a process. The starting and ending points of a process are identified and the sequence of actions in the process, and the decision points (branches) are shown, too. Flow charts use semi-standard shapes to represent different types of actions in a process:

- **Start/End**—The terminator symbol usually contains the word Start or End.
- **Input/Output**—Represents data entering or leaving the system.
- **Action or Process**—A box can represent a single step (add two numbers), or an entire process (get average of two numbers).
- **Decision**—A decision or branching point depicted as a diamond. Two lines representing different decisions emerge from different points of the diamond.
- **Flow Line**—Connect other symbols and indicate the direction of flow.
- **Data Storage**—Indicates a source of data storage.

Flow Chart

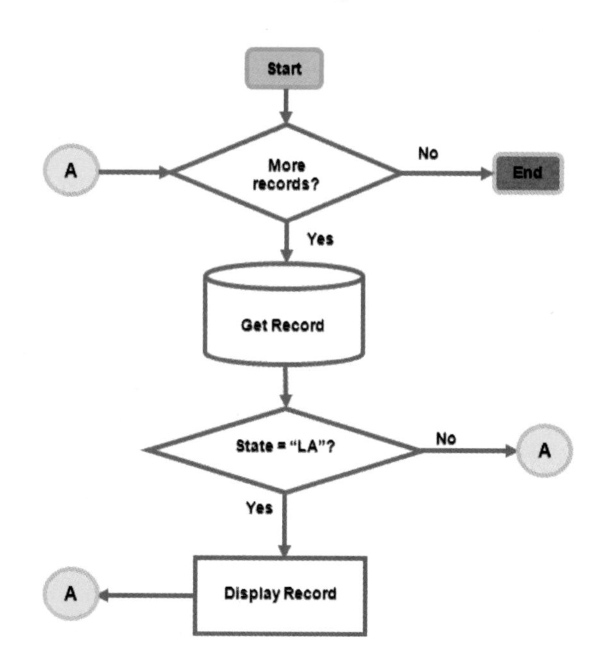

Additional information and illustrations about flow charts is available in the computer programming chapter.

6.7.5 Structure Charts

Structure charts are used to specify the high-level design, or architecture, of a computer application or individual program. As a design tool, they aid the programmer in dividing a large software problem, by **recursively** breaking a problem down into parts that are small enough to be self-standing or **atomic** routines. The process is called **top-down design,** or **functional decomposition.**

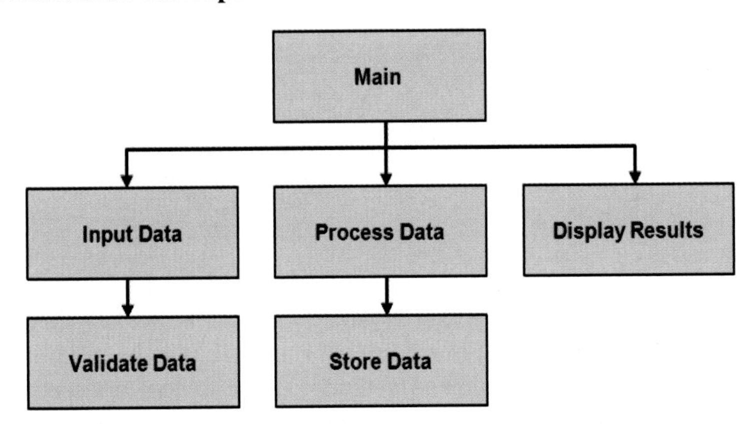

Structure Chart

6.7.6 Pseudocode

Pseudocode is a compact natural language-like description of a computer programming algorithm that uses the structural conventions of programming languages, but omits implementation details, variable storage declarations, or language-specific syntax. Pseudocode follows no specific form, that is, it does not conform to the syntax rules of any particular programming language.

```
If account balance is the same or more than withdrawal request
   update balance and dispense cash
else
   show a failure message
end if
```

Pseudocode

6.7.7 UML

Unified Modeling Language (UML) is a standardized specification language for **object modeling** with **graphical** notation. Used to create an abstract model of a system, UML is an **Object Modeling Language** which provides a set of symbols and ways of arranging them to model an object-oriented software design or system design.

The **Object Management Group** (OMG) is an industry consortium that created the standard definition for UML. Their purpose is to set standards for distributed object-oriented system design with portable model's that work in varied development environments and on different development platforms. Their work promotes system integration.

OMG defines UML this way:

> *The Unified Modeling Language (UML) is a graphical language for visualizing, specifying, constructing, and documenting the artifacts of a software-intensive system. The UML offers a standard way to write a system's blueprints, including conceptual things such as business processes and system functions as well as concrete things such as programming language statements, database schemas, and reusable software components.*

UML Model

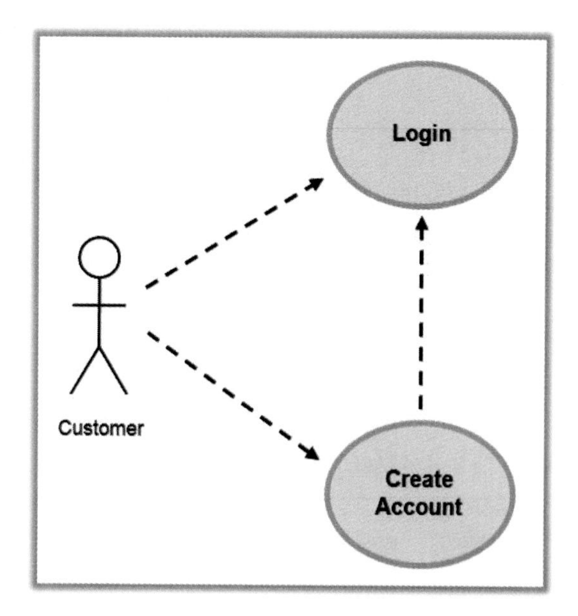

The UML is used to define a software system; to detail the artifacts in the system—it is the language that the blueprint is written in. The UML may be used in a variety of ways to support a software development methodology but it does not specify a particular methodology or process.

Features of a UML model include:

- **Actors**—Human or machine entities that interact with the system to perform meaningful work that helps them to achieve a goal. *The customer in the diagram above is an actor.*
- **Sequence Diagrams**—Sequence diagrams provide a graphical representation of object interactions over time. These typically show a user or actor, and the objects and components they interact with.
- **Implementation Diagram**—A formal description of functionality that the system will have when constructed.

6.7.8 Computer-Aided Software Engineering

Computer-Aided Software Engineering, usually abbreviated **CASE,** is the use of programs to assist in the analysis of requirements and the design, development, and maintenance of software. CASE tools are divided among **upper case** tools used to automate the preparation and distribution of the analysis and design diagrams and **lower case** tools used as **code generators** producing program code based on the designs contained within the diagrams. Generally, automatically generated program code is somewhat generic (and not efficient) and must be refined by human programmers before installation is attempted.

CASE Code Generator

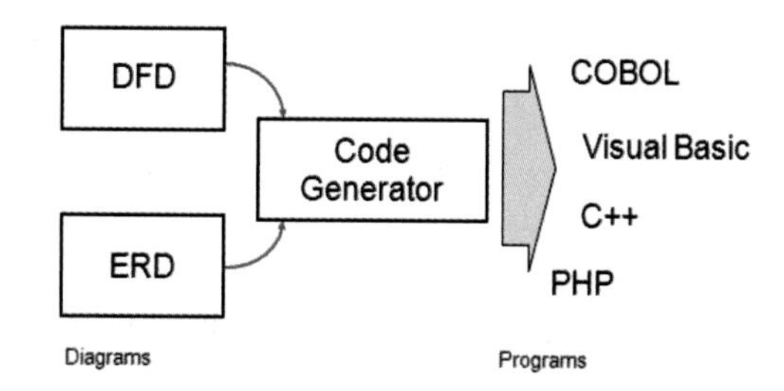

The idea behind computer-aided software engineering is that the tool should aid the development of software. The tools should save labor by simplifying parts of the development process. Some CASE tools are simply tools that help to create and manage documentation. Using these tools is not actually part of the creative design process, but rather recording the design decision afterwards. Creating design tools that are used during the actual creative design process is a lofty goal. However, if a CASE tool is to be used in the design process, it should support the design methodologies that the designer feels comfortable with.

CASE Tools and UML UML is a **semantic** modeling language and many CASE tools were not originally designed to process models of that type. Because of that, early support for UML in CASE tools was somewhat ad-hoc and mostly involved retrofitting old applications with a notation that more or less corresponded to UML symbols. Newer CASE tools routinely use UML models.

6.8 Project Management

Project management is the activity of organizing and managing resources in such a way that these resources deliver all the work required to complete a project within defined scope, quality, time, and cost constraints. The challenge of project management is to ensure that a project is delivered within defined constraints with the consumption of resources optimized to reduce expense and time till delivery. A project is a carefully defined set of activities that use resources (money, people, materials, energy, space, provisions, communication, quality, risk, etc.) to meet the pre-defined objectives.

The project manager considers and manipulates three constraints: time, cost, and project scope.

- **Time**—The time required to produce each deliverable (a project component) is estimated. The estimates are rolled up into the final deliverable estimate. Tasks are prioritized and dependencies between tasks are identified. This information is documented in a project schedule. The dependencies between the tasks can affect the length of the overall project. Allocation of additional resource may shorten the time to deliver a component. The manger must always consider the trade-off between time and cost.
- **Cost**—The cost to develop an information system project depends on several variables including: labor rates and software and hardware material cost. Developer training expense might also be considered. Additional cost can purchase the use of additional resources that may shorten development time. Note, however, that as a project team grows so does the management effort required keeping it on track.
- **Scope**—Requirements are specified for the end result to be delivered at a certain time. The scope defines what the project is supposed to accomplish, and a specific description of what the end result should be or accomplish. A major component of scope is the quality of the final product. The project time frame and specified level of quality affect project cost.

Together, time, cost, and scope are considered by the project manager who has many responsibilities including:

- Identifying Objectives
- Assessing and Controlling Risk
- Planning the Work of Others
- Acquisition and Allocation of Resources
- Organizing and Monitoring Work

- Tracking and Reporting Progress and Expenses
- Quality Management
- Communicating to Stakeholders

Project control is activity within a project that keeps it on-track, on-time, and within budget. Project control begins early in the project with planning and ends late in the project with post-implementation review, having a thorough involvement of each step in the process. Numerous tools are available to the manager control projects. The tools are automated and integrated giving the manger multiple perspectives on project activities. As the manager monitors progress, slippage should be corrected by reallocation of resources. Stakeholders should always be apprised of progress and informed when discrepancies from the plan occur.

6.8.1 Gantt Chart

Gantt chart is a popular type of bar chart that illustrates a project schedule. Gantt charts illustrate the start and finish dates of all project tasks. Some Gantt charts also show the dependency relationships between activities. Gantt charts can be used to show current schedule status using percent-complete shadings for each task symbol.

Although a Gantt chart is easily comprehended for small projects that fit on a single screen, they can become quite unwieldy for projects with many activities. Larger Gantt charts may not be suitable for most computer displays. Gantt charts are criticized for communicating relatively little information and that projects are often considerably more complex than can be communicated effectively with a Gantt chart.

Gantt Chart

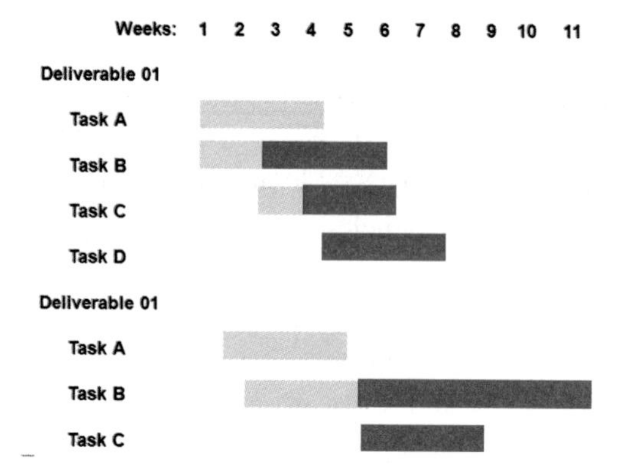

6.8.2 Critical Path Analysis

The Critical Path Method or **CPM** is based on a mathematical algorithm for scheduling a set of project activities. Projects with interdependent activities can apply this method of scheduling.

The essential technique for using CPM is to construct a model of the project that includes the following:

- A list of all activities required to complete the project.
- The duration that each activity will take to completion.
- The dependencies between the activities.

Using these values, CPM calculates the starting and ending times for each activity, determines which activities are on the path critical to the completion of a project and reveals those activities with float time that are less critical. The duration of each task is shown and the longest route is identified as the critical path.

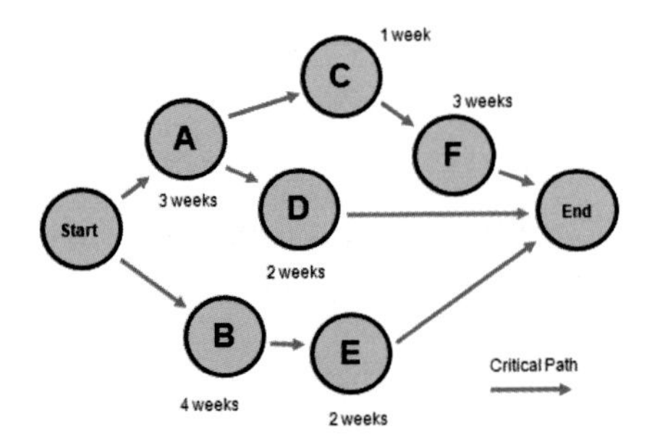

Critical Path Analysis

6.8.3 PERT Chart

The Program Evaluation and Review Technique (PERT) method is used to analyze the tasks involved in completing a project. Particular emphasis is placed on the time needed to complete each task, and therefore, identifying the minimum time needed to complete the total project. A PERT chart is similar to a critical path display as it identifies the tasks with no **slack time.** The PERT chart determines the fastest route to project completion.

PERT analysis follows these steps:

- Determine the tasks that the project requires.
- Identify task inter-dependencies.
- Sort the tasks in the order which they must be completed.

In a PERT chart the **circles** (also called **nodes**) mark the beginnings and ends of project tasks. The **arrows** are the tasks, identified by letters, and with numbers after the task names showing the duration of the task.

When a node has two or more tasks branching from it, it means those tasks can be done concurrently. When a node has incoming arrows, it means all incoming tasks must be completed before progress may continue to any arrows heading away from the node.

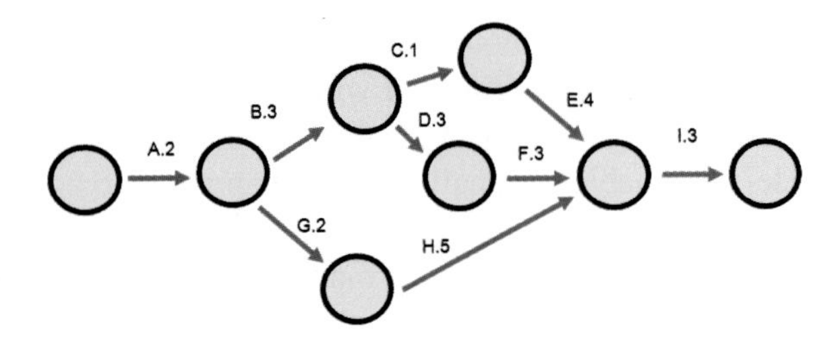

PERT Analysis

6.8.4 Project Budget

A project budget is a list of all planned expenses. One of the project manager's responsibilities noted earlier involves monitoring and reporting expenses. During the course of a project the manager must always know how the project's planned expenses compare to what is actually spent. Spending less is acceptable, but spending more will require explanations to management and perhaps jeopardize project success.

Many programs provide budget vs. actual reporting. Excel spreadsheets can be used as well.

Budget Analysis

	Budget	Actual	Variance
Deliverable 01			
Task A	$2,430.00	$2,430.00	$0.00
Task B	$1,701.00	$1,600.00	$101.00
Task C	$3,500.00	$4,000.00	($500.00)
Task A	$1,450.00	$1,500.00	($50.00)
Total			($449.00)
Deliverable 01			
Task A	$600.00	$650.00	($50.00)
Task B	$1,550.00	$1,300.00	$250.00
Task C	$2,500.00	$2,400.00	$100.00
Total			$300.00
Project			($149.00)

Microsoft Project MSP is Microsoft's project management software program which is designed to assist project managers in plan development, task assignment, progress tracking, budget review, and workload analysis and reallocation. The application creates critical path evaluations, schedules can be resource balance, and critical path chains are displayed in a Gantt chart. Microsoft project is a popular tool and is part of Office 2007. Numerous other commercial and Open Source project management software may be found on the Web.

6.9 Summary

Information Systems are designed and constructed to meet the needs of various stakeholders. System development is not a haphazard affair but it is the result of planning, goal setting, management and technical development activities. Strategic analysis may surface the opportunity for information system projects that have the potential to affect business performance. As the feasibility of projects is considered, the return on investment projection is often a critical determinant on whether or not a project is attempted.

System development is a long and expensive process. Many resources, including people, are applied to a project and should be organized and deployed effectively. Various development models have been proposed with the Waterfall Model of System Development being in use the longest. Prototyping is a technique that can soften the rigidity of the Waterfall model and enable the analyst and stakeholders to agree on system specifications faster and with lower likelihood of error.

The system analyst is at the center of information system development. This person must straddle both worlds of business and technology. Most importantly the analyst must be a communicator, able to hear and balance the sometimes conflicting desires of stakeholders. The analyst gathers information about the environment, stakeholders, competition and business objectives using various data collection techniques. Modeling and analysis tools, many of them visual, assist the analyst in consolidating information and presenting findings to clients.

Projects must be managed well to enhance the likelihood of successful completion. Various automated tools assist the manager in scheduling project resources and tasks and monitoring progress against plans.

As organizations face constant change their information processing needs change, too. Systems age, technology advances, businesses introduce new products and face new competition, and government regulation changes and creates new demands. These, and a host of other factors, keep the information systems staff, and in particular the system analyst, very busy.

EXERCISES

Exercise 6.1

A new system is to be built to automate grading for instructors. Who are the stakeholders?

Exercise 6.2

List the phases important in building an online student registration system. What should the outcome of each phase be?

Exercise 6.3

Assume you are called on to design a system to automate student course registration for a college. How would you justify the ROI for that project? Quantify your answer (make assumptions) and compile your result in a spreadsheet. Clearly identify your assumptions.

Exercise 6.4

Perform a brief, but not insignificant, SWOT analysis of a fast-food chain that you select. What opportunities for automation did you identify?

Exercise 6.5

Describe how prototyping differs from the Waterfall model. How might an analyst use prototyping to clarify system requirements?

Exercise 6.6

Draw a PERT Chart that reflects these task dependencies. Also determine the least time until project completion.

Task	Duration	Before	After
A	3	Start	A
B	4	A	C,D
C	2	B	End
D	1	B	F
E	2	C	End
F	1	D	End
G	4	A	H
H	1	G	End

Exercise 6.7

Create an expense budget for yourself for the coming week in a spreadsheet. Track your actual expenses against the amount you budgeted for each expense category. Display the variance.

Exercise 6.8

Consider your college education as a large project with interdependent components (courses). Draw a Gantt chart that displays your academic progress to date along with your curriculum plans through graduation. Keep in mind course pre-requisites and major course and distribution requirements.

Exercise 6.9

Prepare a decision table that describes this set of rules:
A student may enroll in more than 18 credits only with a GPA of at least 3.25 or with permission of an advisor. Under no circumstances may more than 18 credits be taken in the student's final semester of school.

Exercise 6.10

Prepare a flow chart that depicts the logic of Exercise 6.9.

Exercise 6.11

Write pseudocode that describes the logic of Exercise 6.9.

Exercise 6.12

Explode this context level diagram one more level. Your answer should show processes for checking customer credit, car availability, and registration completion. Depict the flow between processes and connect processes correctly to appropriate stakeholders or data stores.

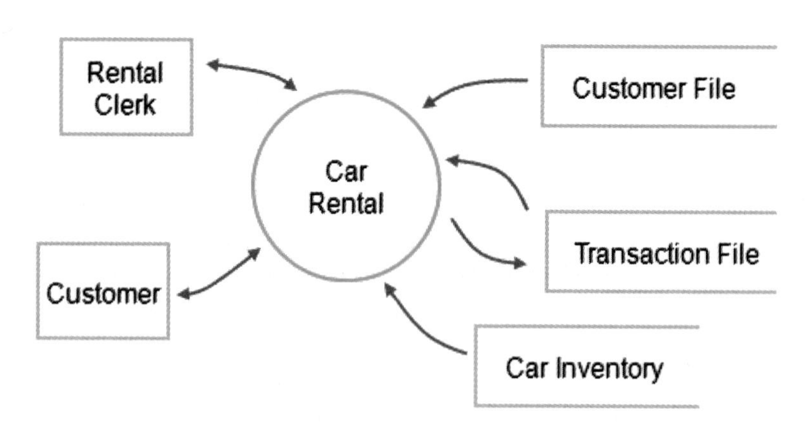

Computer Programming

Chapter 7

Computer programming (sometimes known as coding) is the process of writing, testing, and maintaining the code of computer programs. The code is written in programming languages like Java, Visual Basic, C, C#, or scripting languages like PHP, Perl, or VBScript. The process of writing program code requires expertise in many different subjects, including knowledge of the application domain and algorithms to implement the hardware's desired behavior.

Computer programs execute within the hardware and enable a computer to perform specific tasks. Programs include **system software** such as an operating system, which enables other software to run properly and **application software** such as a word processor or database manager, which enables a user to perform a task. System software is commercially available and necessary for the operation of a computer. Application software is commercially available, too, but it is also custom created by programmers for clients. Regardless of the type of software, computer programming follows certain techniques and principles, which is the subject of this chapter.

It would be impossible to process data into information with a computer alone. The operating system (OS) gives a series of instructions that command the hardware to act in specific ways. The OS facilitates the operation of application programs and provides them access to resources like files and databases and hardware. The computer's horsepower impacts greatly on the amount of data that can be processed in a given portion of time.

Computer programming involves writing instructions for a computer to follow as it processes data. The instructions are usually written in a **high-level language** and later translated into the computer's native language: **machine language.** There are different **programming paradigms** with object-oriented programming having become quite popular in the last decade. Numerous programming languages exist and each has its own **syntax** and form.

Who are these people who create computer programs and what do they do? Sometimes a programmer works alone but more often the programmer is part of a larger development team. Coordination among team members is, of course, essential.

- **Programmer** — A person who writes, tests, and maintains the source code of computer programs. A programmer normally follows specifications provided by an analyst.
- **Software Engineer** — A person who follows a systematic, disciplined, quantifiable approach to the development of software. This person has a broader project perspective than a programmer and must consider systems analysis, system design, and project management.

This chapter discusses what programming is as well as the issues faced by programmers. Different design and development paradigms are considered. The fundamentals of programming including data structures, logic, and the binary system are here as well. Programming languages and development tools are presented with code examples. The chapter also teaches programming with a hands-on section. Macro programming using Microsoft Excel as a prelude to VBA and procedural programming using VBScript are included. Numerous automatically graded programming exercises at the end of the chapter give ample opportunity to practice the concepts and skills presented in this chapter.

In this chapter's discussion of logic and coding, no distinction is made between compiled computer programs and interpreted scripts. While the former is generally considered computer programming, applications are built with both technologies.

7.1 Computer Programming

A **computer program** is a series of commands that instructs the computer **how to process data.** It is, in effect, a sequence of rules. Ada Lovelace's algorithms were the first example of a set of rules for processing data. Today's programs are exactly the same. Without a program running within it, a computer is nothing more than an expensive paperweight because it could not operate. The main thing to understand about computer programs is that they must be given to the computer in a language that the computer understands: **machine language** (code with only 1s and 0s). Machine language is comprised of an arrangement of 0s and 1s; it is called **binary.**

Since humans (computer programmers) do not speak binary they write computer programs in languages such as PHP, C, Java, and Visual Basic. Programs written in these **high level languages** must be translated into machine language before the computer can use them. The programmer creates **source code** which is translated into **binary code.** A special program, called a **compiler** performs this translation. The good news is that, as end-users, we do not need to know how to operate a compiler because the programs that we run have already been compiled for us and stored in the native machine language of the computer. Since each processor has a unique set of instructions designed into the chip, programmers must provide separate compilations for each processor they expect to distribute their software for. The compiling process is depicted here. Compiled programs are known as **executables** and usually have a file extension of **EXE, COM, DLL, or JAR.**

The Compiler Translates Source Code to Binary Machine Code

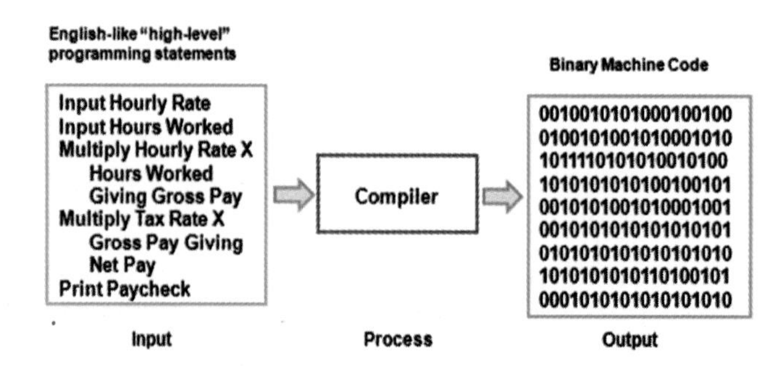

The process is actually a bit more complex because the compiled code (known as **object code**) is combined with other code already compiled that is stored on disk in libraries. Libraries contain code for many purposes including: sorting data, displaying graphics, spell checking content, etc.

A special program, the **linkage editor** (linker), assembles object and library code and produces an executable known as a **load module.** The load module is so named because it can be loaded into memory and executed.

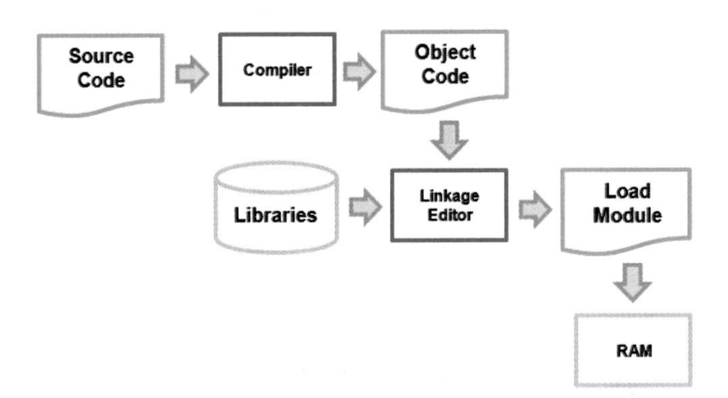

The Role of the Linkage Editor

Interpreter versus Compiler An alternative approach to program execution involves interpretation of program code as the program is running. The translation is not done once and distributed to users as the product of a compiler: machine code. Here the **source code,** known as a **script,** is translated to the required binary line by line during execution. This is not a particularly efficient approach for program execution but since compiling can be a long process, using an interpreter can be quite useful during program development and debugging as software is prototyped because programmers can quickly and repeatedly test their work. Interpreted code is also valuable as a teaching tool. For example, interpreted Pascal is used this way. Some languages are always interpreted as noted below.

The interpreter is part of the operating system (OS) and some interpreters have been ported (distributed) to various operating systems. **Perl** and **PHP** are two interpreted languages that are hosted on a variety of platforms. A commonly used scripting protocol is **Active Server Pages** (ASP) which is hosted by Windows servers. The file extension of the script varies depending on the programming language used.

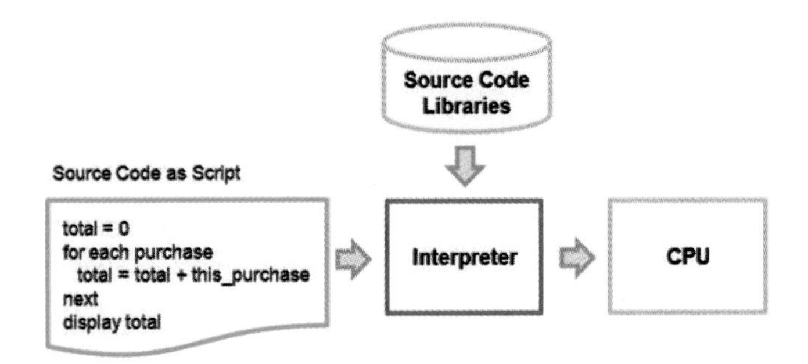

How a Script Executes

Bytecode Interpreter A compromise between compiling and interpretation is a **partial translation** that yields what is known as bytecode. The translation is not into machine code that is native to any particular processor, but instead an efficient **platform independent** representation of the program is produced and distributed that undergoes a final (and quick) translation to machine code when it runs. This process is known as **just-in-time compilation** (JIT) because the bytecode is compiled to native machine code at runtime. Since the code is ultimately rendered in machine language, the high execution speed of running native machine code is achieved. Programs written in **Java** are distributed using this approach.

Byte Code Is Pre-Compiled

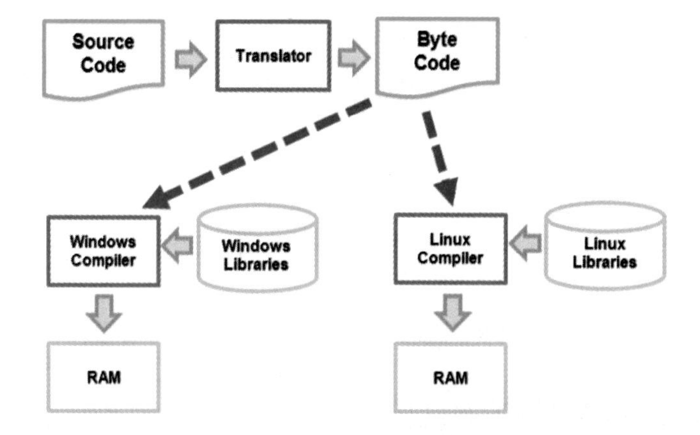

7.2 Programming Design, Paradigms, and Architecture

Good programs are well thought out in advance. They are designed before coding begins and tested before being turned over to stakeholders for use. The design process follows the **System Development Lifecycle** or **SDLC** and the architecture of programs broadly follows established **paradigms** or style of programming.

7.2.1 System Development Lifecycle

When software is developed a standard process is followed that imposes a formalized structure on the project. Here, several stages of the process are identified. The systems analysis chapter has more information. As you see, once a project is complete maintenance is required because **stakeholder** needs and requirements change over time thus necessitating updates to the software.

- **Problem Definition and Analysis** — The first activity is to clearly define the problem to be solved and develop a solution that meets the needs of clients and stakeholders. This may involve negotiation between stakeholders that is facilitated by a systems analyst.
- **Program Design** — Once the solution is accepted by all parties a technical design is prepared. This document defines all technical aspects of the program or programs including: selection of programming language, design of program logic and of the database structure, interface design and design of output (reports and screen display). During this phase acceptance criteria should be established so that success can be measured.
- **Coding** — This phase is for the programmers. It is usually the most time-consuming and costly phase of the development cycle.
- **Testing** — Here work is tested and certified to meet the already established acceptance criteria. Errors that are identified must be corrected before moving to implementation.
- **Implementation** — Once the system is satisfactorily tested it is time to create user documentation, train users, and convert data for use by the software.
- **Maintenance** — It is rare that completed systems are static. Changes in business requirements, governmental regulation and stakeholder needs demand software modification and upgrade. Program errors not detected during testing may surface as the system ages and require fixing. In the lifetime of a system considerable time and money is spent on maintenance so a good design and thorough testing is important because they could affect the cost and extent of maintenance expenditures.

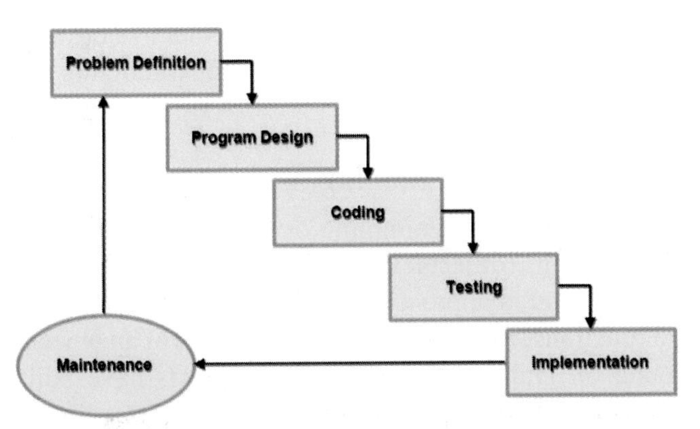

Program Development Lifecycle

The software engineer or systems analyst uses various tools to better understand system requirements and to specify the design for programmers. The system designer uses various diagramming and prototyping tools to create charts that depict the structure and flow of a system. The designer may also use tools to document the system's processing logic and even create **pseudocode** that is the basis for program code.

7.2.2 Program Design Paradigms

A programming paradigm is style of programming. The relationship between programming paradigms and programming languages can be complex since a programming language can support multiple paradigms. Two of the best known paradigms are discussed here.

7.2.2.1 Structured Programming

(Structured programming is a task-oriented design technique. There are two approaches: Top-Down Design and Bottom-Up Design.) Programmers working with this approach break larger pieces of program functionality into smaller sections called subroutines, functions, procedures, and methods. These **code blocks** are generally small, self-contained and reasonably easy to understand. Code blocks are combined to build larger functional structures, thus the paradigm's name. The idea is to build large numbers of small program units that can be individually tested and placed into **libraries** of code **modules** affording code **reuse** as larger programs are assembled. In the structured approach data is maintained in a common area generally shared among all code blocks.

Structured programming is frequently considered a **top-down** approach to design. Programmers map out the full structure of a program in terms of smaller operations, which are implemented and tested individually and then tied together in a whole program. Each unit of code is called a **subroutine** or **function.** Each unit can be called by any number of other units. Ultimately the top level unit, the main program, orchestrates the sequence of calls and operations.

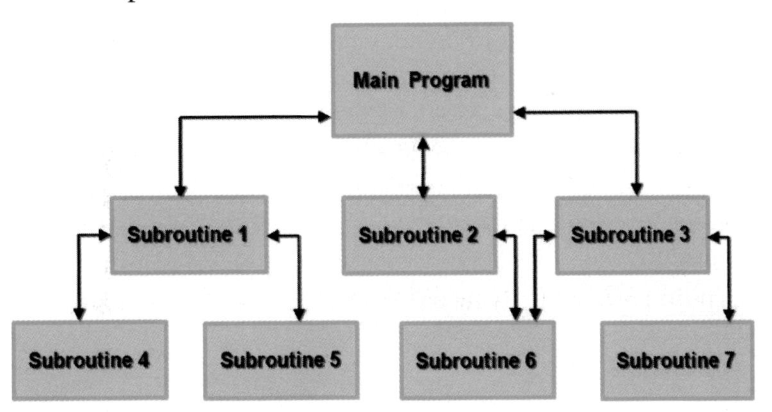

Structured Programming

Bottom-up design is a structured approach to a problem where the programmer uses smaller pieces, already created, in developing the larger solution to the problem.

7.2.2.2 Object-Oriented Programming

The concept of object-oriented programming or **OOP** is that a computer program is a collection of individual units (**objects**) that maintain their own data and behaviors. This is different from the structured approach in which a program is considered a collection of subroutines and functions with shared data. An example of an object is a clickable button frequently found on graphical interfaces. All objects have built in functionality (known as methods) that defines certain behaviors for all **instances** of that object. Each instance of a button has common properties (screen location, size, color, etc.) and common methods (depress when clicked, take action when clicked).

By instances we mean examples of the object active in a single program. We may find several buttons on an interface. While each may be at a different screen location and have a different label each will behave the same predictable way because each is an instance of the same **template** (the object). Objects provide an alternative approach to code **reuse** that is claimed to promote greater flexibility and maintainability in programming. The details of process implementation are shielded from the programmer as the principle of **information hiding** (hiding design code logic and structure) is employed. This ensures the programmer need not worry about implementation and only use an object's properties and methods as revealed in the **interface.** Information hiding is sometimes known as **encapsulation.**

Some fundamental concepts of object oriented programming are:

Object — A template for all instances that have identical behaviors and properties which are known as methods and properties.

Class — A class is a blueprint, base, or prototype from which objects are created. For example, a student class would be used as the basis for defining undergraduate and graduate student objects. Programmers create classes that model the abstract characteristics of a thing (object), including the thing's characteristics (attributes, fields or properties) and the things it can do (behaviors or methods).

Instance — A specific example of an object. For example, the object "person" with properties like name, birth date, and hobby may be used to create the instances "Joe," "Sally," and "Wilma."

Method — An object's behavior. Objects know how to do things. For example, an object representing a bank account knows how to compute the account's balance.

Property — The characteristics of an object. For example, a bank account has an account holder, a balance, and an interest rate.

Inheritance — The process of defining new objects as descendents of existing objects. For example, an object inheriting the properties of the parent class. For example, a car object inherits characteristics from vehicle, the parent object.

Encapsulation — The process of shielding an object's implementation details from the programmer. This allows the programmer to focus on assembling object instances into a whole program without requiring knowledge of the objects inner workings and architecture.

Polymorphism — The ability for an object to take multiple forms (properties and methods).

These concepts are summarized here:

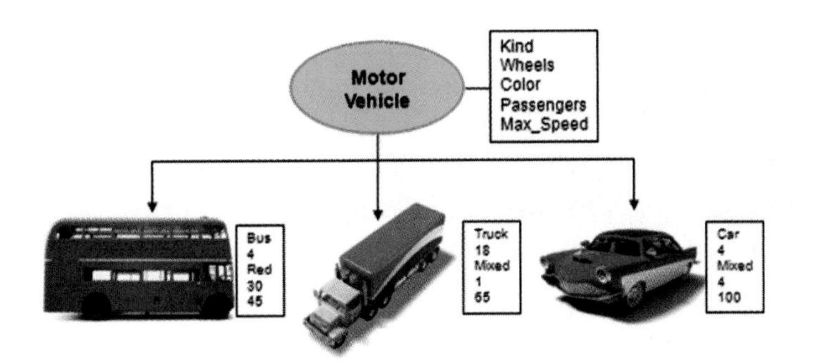

Object-Oriented Programming

7.2.3 API — Application Program Interface

An application programming interface (API) is a description of classes and their properties and methods written by another developer that can be used by a programmer. It is a language that enables communication between computer programs. The API is provided to programmers so that they can write applications consistent with the system's operating environment. An API is a set of routines, protocols, and tools for building software applications. A good API makes it easier to develop a program by providing all the building blocks. A programmer puts the blocks together. The blocks are pre-existing code modules provided by a host environment like an operating system.

An application program interface is a specific class definition prescribed by a computer operating system or by an application program by which a programmer writing a program can make requests of the operating system or another application to perform tasks that are already programmed.

Although the API is an abstraction of a process implemented in code it is not the code itself. The software that provides the functionality described by an API is said to be an implementation of the API. The API informs the programmer how to link a program to the process defined by the API. The actual implementation of the code defined by the API is of no concern to the programmer; only the description of how each method works, what information the method needs to succeed in the task, and the result of the method are important. If the code were to change, as long as the API does not change, the programmer need not be aware of the alteration.

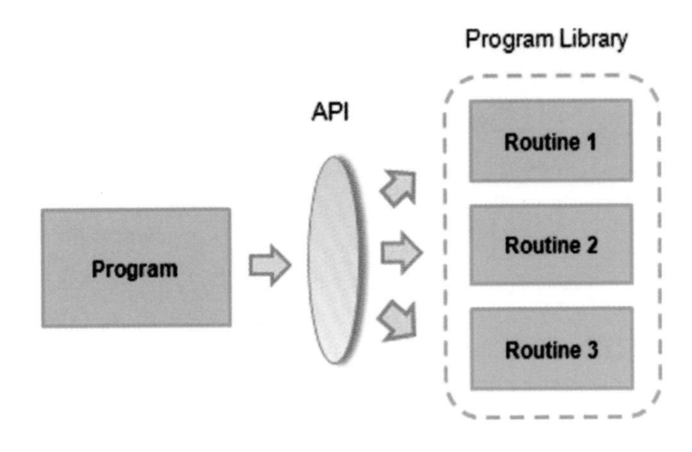

Application Program Interface

7.2.4 Software Testing

Testing software is one of the most important and often overlooked phases in system development. It is the process used to help identify the completeness, correctness, security, and quality of developed computer software. There are many approaches to software testing, but effective testing of complex software is essentially a process.

Testing is used to certify that the individual programs and complete system are free of **syntax,** and **logical** and **run-time** errors, each of which is explained later in the chapter. Testing is a broad topic, but there are two complimentary methods commonly in use:

- **Unit Testing** — This is a procedure used to validate that individual units of source code are working as expected. A unit is the smallest testable part of an application. For this reason unit testing is often known as **bottom up** testing. All three types of errors (syntax, logical, run-time) are addressed while unit testing is conducted.

  A unit may be an individual program, function, or subroutine. In object-oriented programming, the smallest unit is a Class. The goal of unit testing is to isolate each portion of the code and show that the individual parts are correct. A unit test is quantifiable and when the expectations are satisfied the code may be certified to use within the full system. Unit testing helps to eliminate uncertainty in the units themselves. By testing the parts of a program first and then testing the sum of its parts, integration testing becomes easier.

- **System Testing** — A full test is conducted on a complete, integrated system to evaluate the system's compliance with its specified requirements. The purpose of integration testing is to detect any inconsistencies between the software units as they are integrated together. At this level of testing, run-time and logical errors are detected but syntax errors are addressed only in unit testing. Often, for large development projects, there are two distinct groups of software professionals: developers and testers. During system testing, identified errors are shared with the developers who resolve them and return to the testers. This can be a very long process.

Software Testing

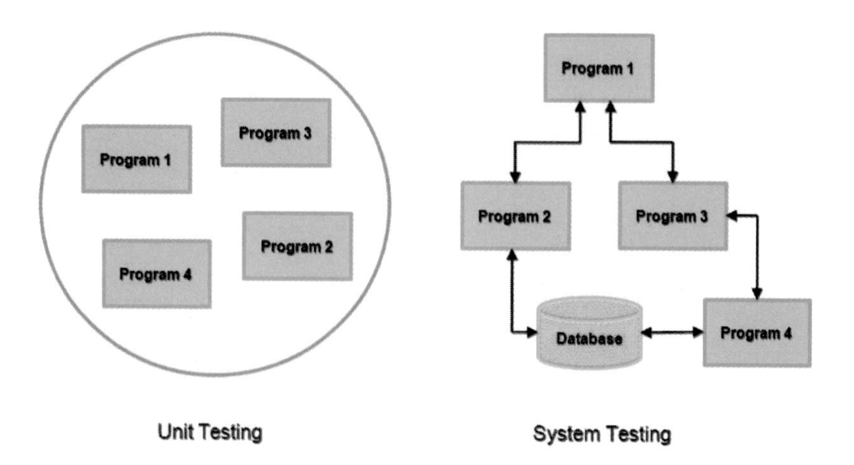

7.3 Data Structure

A data structure is an arrangement of storing data in a computer's memory (primary and secondary) so that it can be used reliably and efficiently. The choice of the data structure usually models the purpose of the application. Different data structures are suited to different types of applications.

Several important data structures include:

- **Arrays** — a list of data elements (or objects) that are of the same data type (number, string, date, etc.) and occupy a predetermined quantity of **contiguous memory.** For example, a list of customer balances could be stored in an array. A second array could hold customer account numbers.

RAM: Computer Memory

Balance	AcctNum
235.00	74-AJ-947
100.00	89-BX-617
53.95	91-GQ-392

Two Arrays

- **Queue** — a list (that might be implemented as an array or linked list) in which data added to the list first is processed first. This is like a line of customers waiting to purchase tickets at the movie box office. A queue is said to be **FIFO** (first in, first out).

  Here is how a queue operates. In the following illustration the images from left to right show the contents of a queue as data values arrive and depart. Notice that each new data value is added to the end of the queue. Each departure from the queue is from the front of the line.

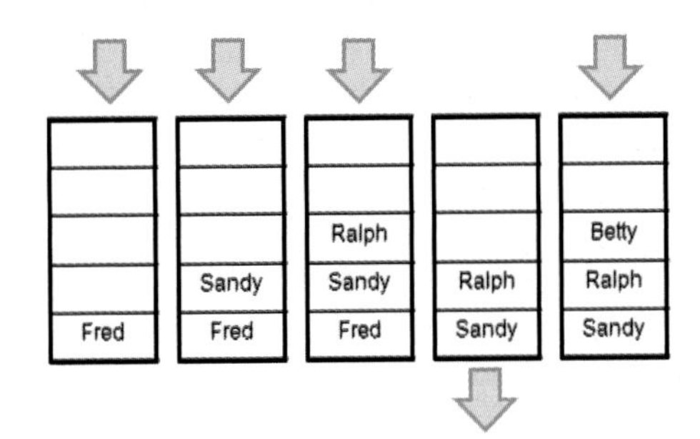

Data Structure: Queue

- **Stack** — a list (that might be implemented as an array or linked list) in which data added to the list last is processed first. This is like a group of airline passengers where those at the back of the plane board first and those who board last depart first. A stack is said to be **LIFO** (last in, first out).

  In the following illustration the images from left to right show the contents of a stack as data values are added ("pushed onto the stack") and removed ("popped off the stack"). Initially the stack is empty. This stack is implemented as an array with a fixed capacity for five data values.

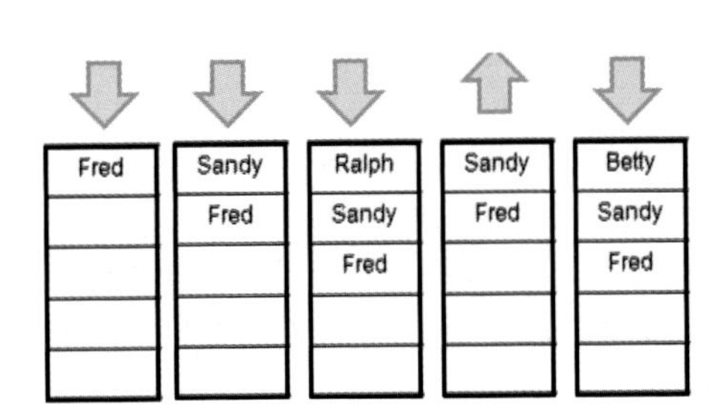

Data Structure: Stack

- **B-trees** — well-suited for implementation of binary database indexes,

  An index search always starts with a root node. Branches from the root go off to collections of index records (child nodes). For every node the branch to the left leads to lower index values and the node to the right offers higher index values. The process of following the nodes until an index record is found is known as **traversing** the tree. An index that supports a binary search involves successively splitting the unexamined nodes between those that might contain the desired value and those that can not contain it.

  Suppose we are searching for the index value 15. We start by examining the root node (the one at the top) and find 10. Since it is not what we are looking for we look to the right because 15 is higher than 10. The notes to the left (values: 2, 5, 6, 8) are now ignored and we examine the first node to the right: 17. We are not searching for 17 so we may go left (lower) or right (higher). We go left (lower) and immediately find our target, 15.

Data Structure: B-Tree

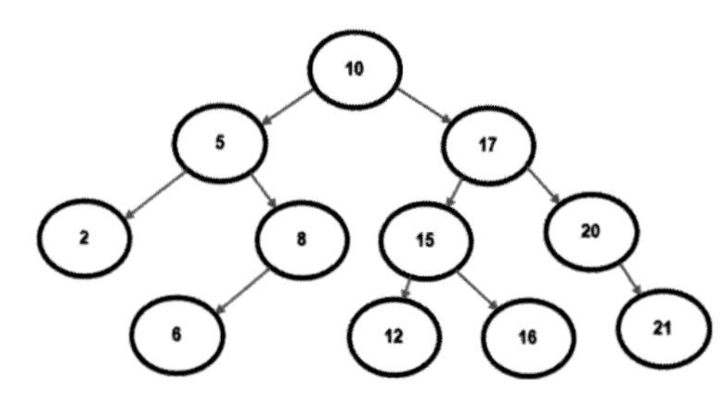

- **Linked List** — a linear list of data elements (or objects) that is dynamically sized as a program is running depending on the immediate storage requirements of the program. The B-Tree illustrated above is often implemented as a non-linear linked structure. This allows the structure to grow as needed and not consume more memory than required.

String values are always surrounded by double quotes and numeric values are never surrounded by quotes.

Data can be expressed in two ways: **constant values** and **variables** that hold values. Examples of constant data are: 3, -7.2, and "William." The first two examples are **numbers** and the last example is a **string.** The important thing is that the value of a constant is always the same — it is constant!

Variables are names for storage locations that hold data values. The value in a storage location may change but the name of the location (the variable name) never changes.

Data Values

RAM: Computer Memory

Last_Name	First_Name	Phone_Number
"Boyes"	"William"	"391-217-4817"
Age	Balance	Tax_Rate
26	235	10%

Never use a space in a variable or constant name. Many programmers use _ instead of a space, or separate parts using capital letters as: firstName

Each specific location in memory is accessed by use of that location's address. Addresses are usually defined as the number of bytes relative to the beginning of memory, address zero. This is known as the **offset** or **relative** addressing. Fortunately, for most programmers it is only necessary to use the name of a variable when referring to it in memory. When a program is compiled to prepare it for execution memory names are translated automatically to relative addresses. The list of memory names and offset values is maintained in what is known as a **symbol table.**

Symbol Table Translates Memory Names

Variable Name	Byte Offset
Last_Name	0
First_Name	20
Phone_Number	50
Age	64
Balance	66
Tax_Rate	70

The data structures discussed so far reside in RAM which is volatile memory. If the data is to be preserved for future use then persistent storage (disk, CD-ROM, DVD, Flash memory) must be used. Secondary storage is random, meaning everything stored is accessible without processing all of the data prior to it (such as using a cassette tape) but not at the level of individual data values as RAM is. When data is stored persistently values are stored collectively in a file which is then placed on a storage device. When data is accessed from persistent storage the file is read and individual data values are retrieved from it.

Persistent Storage Uses Files

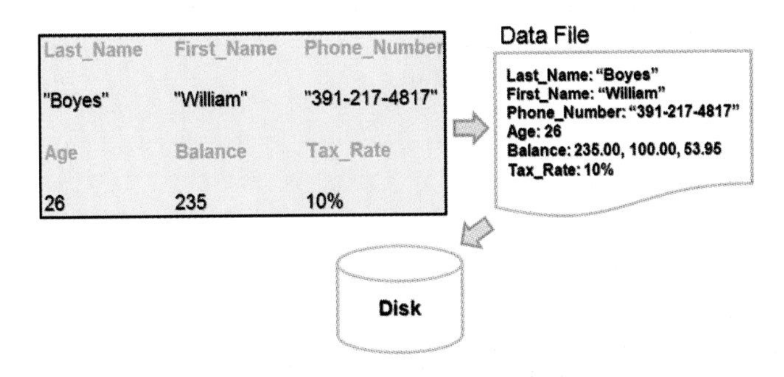

Data stored persistently is often much like a database table, that is arranged in records with a common set of data fields (columns). The type of data up and down any column must be the same. This arrangement makes it possible to process the data in each record using the same program code for each record. Repetitive processing is known as **iteration.** The data and information chapter has more information about records and tables.

There is a big difference between **text files** that can be shared by multiple types of applications and **binary files** that tend to be proprietary to specific applications. In OOP, binary files can be used to store object-based data.

A Table of Records

Origin	Destination	Ticket_Cost
San Diego	Boston	$ 59.00
Denver	Philadelphia	$ 198.00
San Diego	Tampa	$ 215.00
Portland	Boston	$ 112.00
San Diego	Tampa	$ 205.00
Denver	Chicago	$ 157.00
Tampa	San Diego	$ 200.00

7.4 Logic

A computer program follows the step-by-step **sequence** of instructions that informs the computer how to complete a task. The process is known as an **algorithm** and follows a specific pattern which depends on the nature of the processing to be accomplished. The sequence of instructions is often linear but the flow can be interrupted and redirected by two common **control structures: branching** and **iteration.**

Before a programmer begins coding the logic, or sequence of operations, is presented graphically and sometimes in other forms. A flow chart is a commonly used graphic depiction of logic. The flowchart presented here depicts the algorithm for determining the net pay for an employee earning $10.00 per hour who worked 40 hours in the pay period. A tax rate of 15% is assumed.

A Flowchart Depicts an Algorithm

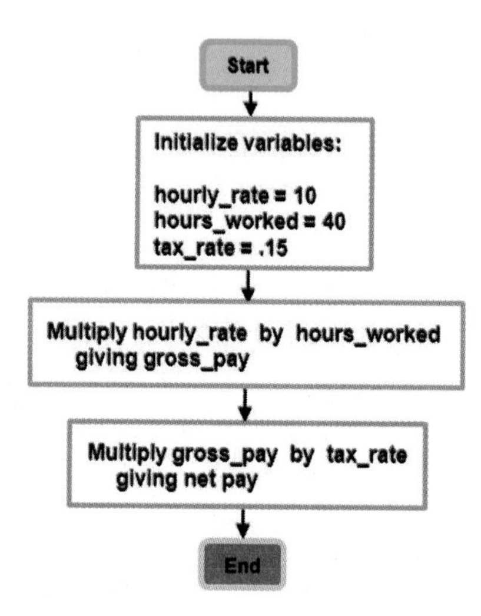

All flowcharts have a beginning and an end. In between is where the processing steps are defined. The basic flowchart is used for structured programming and UML (discussed in the systems analysis chapter) is the choice for OO development.

Branching Linear algorithms provide little opportunity for complexity in processing. In the flowchart above the process is linear: each step flows directly into the next with no possibility of deviation. While that simplicity is attractive, it is not commonly found. An algorithm that involves **choices** incorporates branching into the design.

Branching allows choices. The choice to go one way or the other in an algorithm is based on evaluating a condition and taking action based on the evaluation. Conditions are **binary**; only two possible outcomes ever exist. Conditions are displayed in flowcharts in a **diamond.**

If the net pay algorithm were to incorporate the possibility of different tax rates depending on an employee's income then branching would be employed. If we assume that the 15% tax rate applies to gross pay of no more than $400 and otherwise a 17% tax rate applies the flow chart would be redrawn this way:

Branching: Decision Making

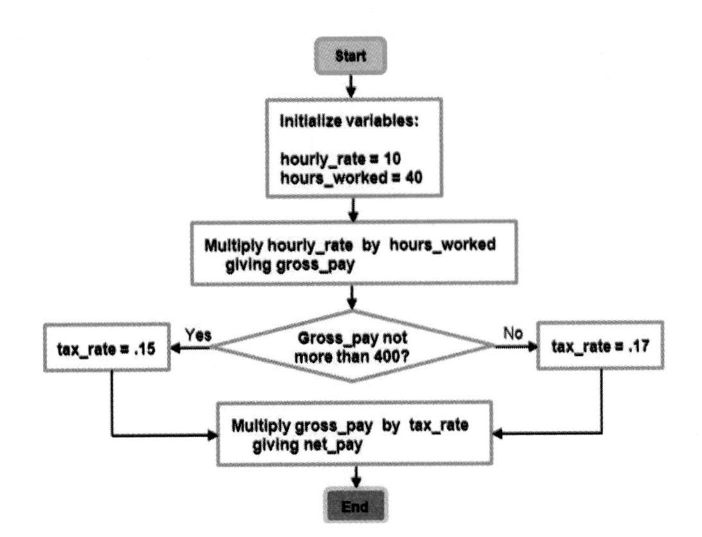

Each condition is a binary logic question in which there are two and only two possible answers. This is known as binary logic because only two outcomes exist. The condition involves comparing two values and determining the relationship between them. The determination of the relationship is based on the logical operator that associates the two values.

In binary logic there are only two possible outcomes: the condition is either **True** or **False.** Deciding whether the result is True or False depends on the values (in this case, gross pay and the constant 400) and the operator (not more than).

The example we are working with could be stated in English this way:

"If it is true that gross pay is not more than $400 the tax rate will be 15% otherwise it will be 17%."

When the algorithm is implemented in code the <= operator will be used because it means "not more than."

Conditions require an operator and evaluate to True or False. "Maybe" is never an option. There are no other possibilities.

Operators A condition is evaluated by comparing two values connected with a **logical operator.** The operators are easy to understand and should be familiar:

Logical Operators

Logical Operator	Meaning
=	Equal
<>	Not Equal
>	Greater Than
<	Less Than
>=	Greater or Equal
<=	Less or Equal

Truth table A truth table can be used to summarize the possible outcomes as a logical condition is evaluated. A simple condition tests one value and has two possible outcomes. Assume we want to apply a 10% discount to senior citizens at least 70 years old. The program code written in BASIC and the associated truth table are as follows:

Truth Table

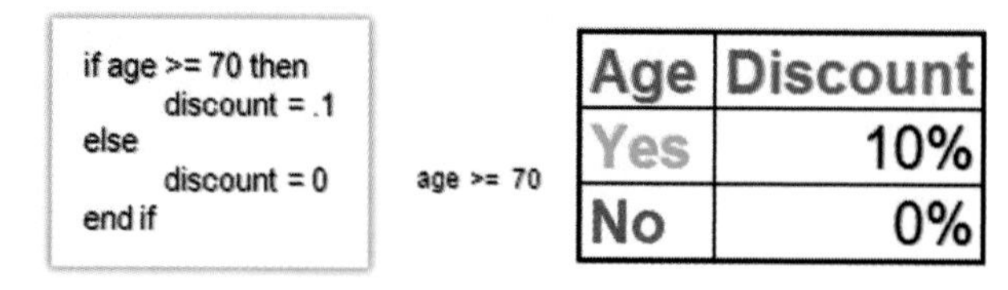

A complex condition tests two or more values. If the discount were based on a customer 70 years and more making more than $10.00 in purchases the BASIC code and truth table would become this:

ComplexTruth Table with And Logic

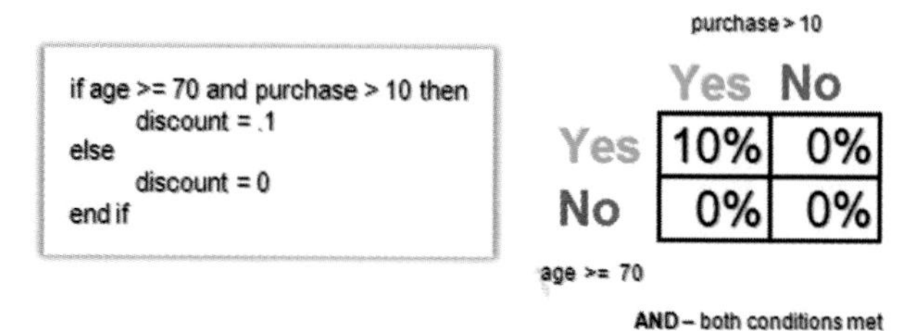

As you see the customer must be at least 70 years old **and** purchase more than $10.00. If the condition were changed a little and required that either the customer be at least 70 **or** that the purchase must be more than $10.00 the code and truth table change this way:

ComplexTruth Table with Or Logic

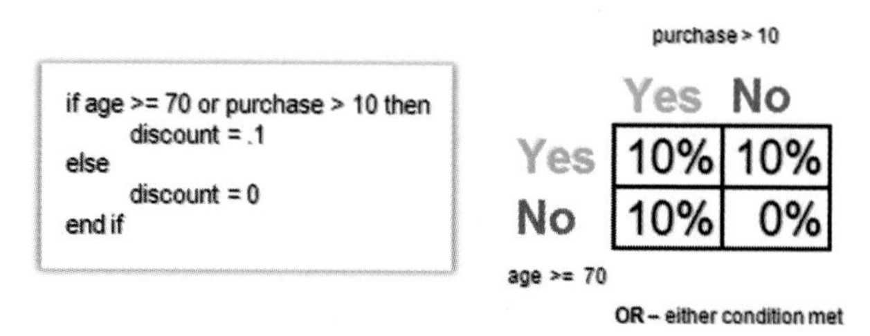

Iteration With data arranged in records and stored in tables, data processing can be repetitive. The recurring nature, known as iteration, allows programs to be more compact and less complex because no code is customized to specific records. The logic that processes one record applies to all. Iteration is a foundation of programming.

The code that iterates is known as a **loop.** To illustrate the concept of a loop, an example that calculates the average ticket price for all flights recorded in a table is shown here:

Iteration: Loops

Origin	Destination	Ticket Cost
Washington	Boston	$290.45
Denver	San Francisco	$198.00
Portland	Grants Pass	$168.23
Washington	Nashville	$112.00
Phoenix	Selma	$208.32
Denver	Los Angeles	$157.00
Selma	Washington	$198.00

```
total_ticket_cost = 0

flights = 0

for each flight
    total_ticket_cost = total + ticket cost
    flights = flights + 1
next

average = total_ticket_cost / flights
```

7.5 Programming Languages

Computer languages are considered to have been developed in several **generations.** The first level, or generation, is the binary language understood by the machine itself: **machine code.** In fact, programmers of the original computers were required to perform all of their work in binary. This was a tedious process using only abstract symbols: 0s and 1s. A second-generation language, **assembly,** became popular in the 1950s as a short hand version of machine language. The development of this language removed some of the abstraction of machine language, but was more or less just as tedious. The third generation of languages, **high level** languages, saw the eventual introduction of most of the popular computer languages in use today: Java, Visual Basic, and C#. The first three generations are grouped together as **procedural languages,** so named because these languages are used to tell a computer ***how to behave.***

Fourth and fifth generation languages are considered to be **non-procedural** because the user tells the computer ***what to produce,*** not how to do it. These languages are used mostly by users other than programmers. When performing a database query in Microsoft Access a fourth generation **query language** is used telling Access what data is wanted but not directing the steps needed to retrieve that data. Examples of query languages are **SQL** (Structured Query Language) and **QBE** (Query by Example). A fifth generation language is very much like English and is known as **natural language.** The idea is to allow the user to converse with the computer in a comfortable (preferably spoken), non-technical form. The sequence of language introduction with examples of each is summarized here:

Generation	Language	Example	Introduced
1	Machine	01100011100010	1940s
2	Assembler	LDXACC	1950s
3	High Level	pay=gross-tax	1956
4	Query Language	List customers in 'Spain'	1970s
5	Natural Language	spoken English	1980s

Programming Language Generations

Choosing What Language to Use Most procedural third generation languages provide the same fundamentals: **data structures, branching,** and **iteration.** The question, therefore, of which language to select for a project depends on several other factors:

- **Integration** — The potential for integration with existing data processing systems.
- **Platform Independence** — The ability to run the application on systems governed by different operating systems.
- **Scalability** — The extent to which the language can properly handle increasingly large processing loads defined as quantity of data and number of concurrent users.
- **Distribution** — The method by which the programs can be distributed to clients in an important factor. For example, programs written in some languages are more easily embedded in a Web page and others work best on a server or as stand alone executables.
- **Programmers** — Some languages are known by more programmers and some by less. Finding sufficient seasoned staff to develop a project is an essential ingredient to successful project completion.

- **Speed** — Certain languages lend themselves more to prototype development and others to a more traditional development approach. Project deadlines can be a significant determining factor.

Programming Issues Programming is an activity in which precision is exceptionally important. There are three broad categories of errors a programmer may encounter while developing an application. They are summarized here:

- **Syntax errors** — These are errors in use of the programming language. These must be fixed before the program will compile or before the statement will execute, if an interpreted language is being used. The syntax of a language is the grammar of the language. Grammar dictates the use of certain words and punctuation used in proper sequence. A syntax error involves violations of grammar, or rules of the programming language.
- **Logic errors** — Here the program executes but produces incorrect results. This is likely due to incorrect steps within the program and is often the case of faulty design. Logic errors often manifest as performing incorrect calculations, permitting unauthorized user access to an information system, and sending communication (e-mails usually) to an incomplete or incorrect list of customers.
- **Run time errors** — The program runs but fails due to situations that the programmer did not anticipate. The consequence is a program crash after the program begins running. A common example is attempting to perform an operation that is not possible, like division by zero. Another frequent run time error is attempting to process records in a table after the last record has been dispatched with. Errors can occur in handling data entered by users. For example, if a data field expects numeric data but the user types "two," a program without **error trapping code** will terminate.

Languages In the history of computer programming hundreds and possibly thousands of languages were developed. A smaller number stands out as historically significant or currently important and several of those are briefly described next. Each description is followed by a small example of the language. The examples are not intended to teach programming in any specific language but do provide a glimpse at the wide variation found in language **syntax.**

All programs ultimately must be represented in the computer's memory (RAM) as a sequence of binary digits (1 and 0). Digital computers are binary machines, so only two states are possible: on and off. Only machine language is exclusively binary. Programs written in all other languages are a higher level abstraction and must be translated into binary. A complete discussion of binary code, ASCII codes and Unicode are found in the hardware chapter.

7.5.1 Machine Language

This is the native language of a specific processor. The language is fully expressed in 0s and 1s making use of the language tedious at best. The 0s and 1s are exact representations of the state of computer memory (digital computers are binary and a bit in memory may have only two values: 1 or 0) so programs written in machine language execute rapidly because no translation is required.

```
1001010100100001000100100
1000100011010010000010001
0011010001000110110001 01
```

7.5.2 Assembly Language

This is shorthand for machine language. Each assembly instruction is actually a name for an arrangement of a group of machine language bits. Since each group identifies a specific processor instruction the programmer is not far removed from the details of machine language. The difference here is use of words (known as a **mnemonic**) rather than memorization of a sequence of bits.

```
mov   cx, size
repe  cmpsw
jnz   not_equal
mov   al, 'y'
int   10h
jmp   exit_here
```

7.5.3 Fortran

FORTRAN, originally called Formula Translator, was the first third generation programming language. It is well suited to numeric computation and scientific computing. Developed in the 1950s it has withstood the test of time and remains in use in computationally intensive applications.

```
DO
    PRINT*,'Enter a number or 0 to exit:'
    READ*,NUMBR
    IF(NUMBR.EQ.0) EXIT
    SUM = SUM + NUMBR
ENDDO

WRITE(2,*) NUMBR
```

7.5.4 Cobol

Its name is an acronym, for **CO**mmon **B**usiness **O**riented **L**anguage, and is primarily of use in business and administrative applications. It was initially released in 1959 and designed to be English-like which was expected to open the programming door for many people. Today COBOL is still in use, primarily in **legacy systems** that were developed in the past and have been maintained since. COBOL is almost exclusively used on mainframe systems.

```
COMPUTE LW-PMT-AMT ROUNDED =
        (LW-LOAN-AMT * LW-INT-PMT) /
        (1 - 1.00000000 / ( (1 + LW-INT-PMT) ** LW-NBR-PMTS) )
MOVE 1 TO LW-LOAN-ERROR-FLAG
GO TO 004000-EXIT.
```

7.5.5 Pascal

Pascal is a language that is particularly suited to structured programming. It was developed in 1970 to be used as a teaching tool in undergraduate programming courses. Few commercial projects were implemented in Pascal and it has largely disappeared after considerable use during the 1970s through the mid-1990s.

```
for I := 1 to max do
  for J := (I=1) to max do  { set J to start one ahead of I }
   if test_array[J] < test_array[I] then
     begin
       temp := test_array[J];
       test_array[J] := test_array[I];
       test_array[I] := temp;
     end;
  end;
end.
```

7.5.6 C

Originally developed in the early 1970s at Bell Labs and was the language used for the development of Unix. It allows the programmer excellent communication with the operating system and with hardware devices. It has been influential in the development of numerous other languages and is commonly used in Computer Science programs as a teaching vehicle. It is also largely used in legacy systems involved in scientific solutions.

```
unsigned char ser_data;

static unsigned int crc;
crc = (unsigned char)(crc >> 8) | (crc << 8);
crc ^= ser_data;
crc ^= (unsigned char)(crc & 0xff) >> 4;
```

7.5.7 C++

C++ is an object oriented derivative of C. It was developed at Bell labs in 1993 and remains popular although less so than before. The formal definition of the language was published in 1998 and it continues to evolve. Large libraries of C++ code are freely available enhancing its popularity.

```
void MoveLVSelectedItemsUp(HWND hListView)
{
        int iCount = ListView_GetItemCount(hListView);

        for (int iIndex = 1; iIndex < iCount; iIndex++)
           if (GetLVItemState(hListView, iIndex, LVIS_SELECTED) != 0)
                  SwapLVItems(hListView, iIndex, iIndex - 1);
}
```

7.5.8 C#

C# (pronounced C Sharp), is an object-oriented programming language developed by Microsoft as part of their **.NET** initiative. C# has a procedural and object-oriented syntax based on C++ that also includes aspects of several other programming languages including Java. C# can be considered to be a simpler version of C++ with enhanced features. The language was developed in part to compete with Java and to enhance productive development of Web applications. C# is included within Microsoft's development environment, **Visual Studio.**

The language was designed to take advantage of the **Common Language Infrastructure** (CLI), developed by Microsoft, that defines the data structure and run-time environment that form the core of the .NET Framework. The environment allows multiple high-level languages to be used on different computer platforms without being rewritten for specific architectures.

7.5.9 Ada

Originally targeted at embedded and real-time systems, the language is strongly typed and is used in **mission-critical** applications, such as avionics software. It is used almost exclusively by the United States Defense Department. Although the syntax is different, it provides many of the features and constructs of C and languages derived from C. Ada was named after Ada Lovelace, who is often credited with being the first computer programmer.

```
with Ada.Text_IO;

procedure Welcome is
begin
  Ada.Text_IO.Put_Line("Welcome to Ada!");
end Hello;
```

7.5.10 LISP

Lisp derives from List Processing and linked lists are the Lisp language's major data structure. Lisp source code is itself made up of lists and as a result, Lisp programs can manipulate source code as a data structure. This unusual arrangement allows programmers to create new syntax or even new languages embedded in Lisp. Lisp became a preferred programming language for artificial intelligence research because AI operations often involved processing large lists of data and looking for patterns of data value and structure within the lists. Lisp is not a general purpose programming language like C#, Visual Basic and PHP, for example.

```
(append '(1 2) '(3 4))
;Output: (1 2 3 4)

(defun factorial (n)
 (if (<= n 1)
  1
  (* n (factorial (- n 1)))))
```

7.5.11 Java

Java is an object-oriented programming language developed in the early 1990s. Different from other languages, Java is compiled to **bytecode** for distribution (although it can be compiled to native code if desired). When it runs it is compiled to native code using JIT (Just in Time) compilation implemented by the **Java Virtual Machine.** The implication of this approach is platform independence and Java is used in a wide variety of applications ranging from graphical interfaces to programs that are embedded in products like digital cameras, microwaves, and automobile control devices.

```
private static int getRandom(int mod) {
    Random rand = new Random();
    return Math.abs(rand.nextInt()) % mod + 1;
}
```

Java applets Java applets are small programs written in Java and delivered in the form of Java bytecode. Java applets can run in a Web browser using a Java Virtual Machine. Applets are used to provide interactive features to Web applications that cannot be provided by HTML. Running an applet requires that the Java plug-in be installed.

Applets offer several advantages including:

- **Cross Platform** — Since it is delivered in bytecode it is simple to make it work on Linux, Windows, and Mac OS platforms.
- **Safe** — It runs in a **sandbox,** so the user does not need to trust the code, so it can work without security approval. Programs in a sandbox cannot access the local machine's file system.
- **Available** — Java is supported by most Web browsers.
- **Fast** — Applets will cache in most Web browsers, so will be quick to load when returning to a Web page.

There are a few disadvantages, but none so severe as to suggest that Java not be used:

- **Support Environment** — It requires the Java plug-in, which is not available by default on all Web browsers.
- **Startup Time** — It cannot start up until the Java Virtual Machine is running which might have significant startup time the first time it is used.
- **Interface** — It is considered more difficult to build and design a good user interface with applets than with HTML-based technologies.

7.5.12 BASIC

BASIC is an acronym for Beginner's All-purpose Symbolic Instruction Code. It was originally designed in 1963 at Dartmouth College to enable shared access to the school's limited computer resource, it has remained a popular language since and is available today in a variety of dialects.

```
10 INPUT "How many stars do you want: "; N
20 S$ = " "
30 FOR I = 1 TO N
40 S$ = S$ + "*"
50 NEXT I
```

7.5.13 Visual Basic

Visual Basic is one of the most used languages today, especially in business. Visual Basic is available in several forms and is heavily supported by Microsoft. It is used in Windows server based applications in the older Active Server Page (**ASP** — interpreted script) format or compiled in **.NET** as VB.NET. It is also contained in all Microsoft Office products (Word, Excel, PowerPoint, and Access) as **VBA** (Visual Basic for Applications).

```
Screen.MousePointer = vbHourglass
sSysDir = Space$(256)
GetSystemDirectory sSysDir, Len(sSysDir)
sSysDir = Left(sSysDir, InStr(sSysDir, Chr(0)) - 1)
If Right(sSysDir, 1) <> "\" Then
        sSysDir = sSysDir & "\"
End If
```

7.5.14 PHP

PHP is a scripting language, introduced in the mid-1990s, that generally runs on a Web server host. Like programs written using Microsoft's active server page environment, PHP programs generally produce Web page output in response to client requests of a server. PHP can be used with a variety of relational database management systems (most commonly **MySQL**), and runs on several popular operating system-web server combinations including **Linux-Apache** and **Windows-IIS** (Internet Information Service).

```
<?
include "config.php";
$query_invoice = "SELECT *,DATE_FORMAT(inv_date,'%D %M %Y') as
idate,DATE_ADD(inv_date,INTERVAL 30 DAY) as duedate  FROM
invoices ORDER BY invno DESC";
$result_invoice = mysql_query($query_invoice);
$num_invoice = mysql_num_rows($result_invoice);
?>
```

7.5.15 JavaScript

JavaScript is a language primarily used in HTML pages providing program control while a page is displayed in a browser and as the user interacts with the page. Although similar in name to Java, the languages are not closely related. The major use of JavaScript is to perform actions not possible in HTML alone. JavaScript makes use of the **Document Object Model** (DOM) as it performs tasks such as:

- Changing browser images as the mouse moves over objects.
- Opening or popping up a new window.
- Validating Web form input values before they are submitted to the server.

```
<SCRIPT language=JavaScript>
function open1() {
    var windowHandle
    window.open('http://yahoo.com','','scrollbars=yes,height=600,
    width=800,resizable=yes');
}
</SCRIPT>
```

7.5.16 Ajax

Ajax, which is short for **Asynchronous JavaScript** and **XML,** is not so much a programming language but a Web development technique designed to make Web pages appear to operate more like programs found on the user's computer. Specific objectives are increases in Web page speed and interactivity resulting in greater usability. **Google Earth** is a well known application that uses this technology.

7.5.17 Structured Query Language

SQL or Structured Query Language is an **English-like,** non-procedural language designed to make possible the easy manipulation of data managed in a **relational database.** SQL is not a programming language in that program instructions are not given when using it. It is presented here to illustrate the power available to non programmers who might have a need to perform data retrieval and analysis.

SQL is commonly used by Web-based programs to retrieve database managed data required by the application. Once a **connection** is established between the application and the database manager, SQL is used to convey data requests to the server. The connection is also used by the server to return selected data to the application.

```
SELECT department, SUM(sales) as "Total sales"
    FROM order_details
        GROUP BY department
            HAVING SUM(sales) > 1000;
```

The section on web development later in this chapter explores the use of a DBMS (database management system) as part of a web application. The SQL chapter presents the SQL language and its use.

7.5.18 XML

The Extensible Markup Language (XML) is a general-purpose **markup language** used to describe almost any kind of data structure. XML uses **tags** to define data structure and the individual data values contained within the structure. It is not a programming language but is used primarily to allow data sharing across different systems, especially systems connected via the Internet. This is particularly important when the computer systems run with different operating systems and use different programming languages.

```
<?xml version="1.0" standalone="yes" ?>
<DOCUMENT>
        <STATE>
                <NAME>Louisiana</NAME>
                <TREE>Bald Cypress</TREE>
                <FLOWER>Magnolia</FLOWER>
                <CAPITOL>Baton Rouge</CAPITOL>
        </STATE>
        <STATE>
                <NAME>Mississippi</NAME>
                <TREE>Magnolia</TREE>
                <CAPITOL>Jackson</CAPITOL>
        </STATE>
</DOCUMENT>
```

XML specifies neither tags nor their meaning. In fact XML is really a **meta language** for describing languages because it provides a facility to define tags and the structural relationships between them. Since there is no predefined tag set, there cannot be any preconceived semantics. All of the meaning of an XML document's data will be defined by the programs that process them. The XML chapter has additional information about this language.

7.6 Program Development Tools

Building an information system is always a complexity that often involves the efforts of many people. Managers are always under budgetary and time pressure. Business users want results immediately and may be hard to pin down with regard to the specifics of their requirements. Tools and techniques that assist with rapid development are valuable if used wisely. Some tools automate the activities of designers and programmers.

A binary machine need have only two states, one for 0 and the other for 1.

7.6.1 Code Generators

Code generators perform tasks that normally programmers do. Generators allow programmers to work on a higher level and not spend time getting their hands dirty in the low-level details. Experience has shown, however, that code generated by off-the-shelf software may not deliver code with the quality or operational efficiency that code crafted by programmers themselves does. Tools that fall into the category of code generators are part of the larger category known as **Computer Aided Software Engineering** or **CASE.**

CASE tools not only provide code generation but also include design tools that assist with drawing Data Flow Diagrams (DFD), Entity-Relationship Diagrams (ERD), flow charts, and with designing pseudocode. The diagrams are input to the generator and finished code and database models are produced. CASE tools also incorporate software that assists with project management (schedules, PERT charts, and critical path analysis).

Generators have successfully produced good quality interface design and database schemas from static design diagrams for a long time. That success, however, changes when it comes to modeling and generating code logic that implements algorithms. This is because algorithms are dynamic, and the resulting code would be more complex and more likely to inaccurately follow user requirements.

7.6.2 Report and Form Generators

Report generators are found in programs like Excel and Access enabling the user to quickly define a report layout and the data that the report presents. In those programs the generators are known as wizards.

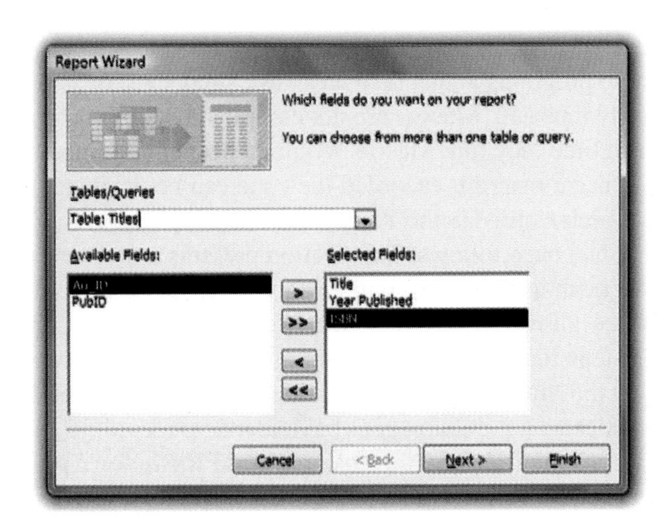

Report Wizard

Form generators are similar. The outcome, however, is a template used to view or enter data one record at a time. Forms make data entry easier and enable the developer to ensure that data values are of the correct type and fall within acceptable ranges (for example, any person's age must be a non-negative integer).

7.6.3 Data Dictionary

The data dictionary is a database that holds information about all data that an organization's information processing activities might encounter. The names, meaning, data types, rules of use and access permissions for all data elements are stored in the dictionary.

As programmers write and test code the dictionary is queried to ensure that the data elements referenced in programs are valid and that the particular program has authorization to access the data specified. A dictionary that provides this linkage to the development environment is considered to be an **active dictionary.**

7.6.4 RAD: Rapid Application Development and Prototyping

Rapid Application Development is a set of techniques fostered by automated support that enables developers to implement systems when time and budgets are tight. RAD involves **iterative** development, construction of **prototypes,** and the use of CASE tools, screen and report designers, database schema validators, and various wizards. The downside of this technique is that RAD may compromise system usability, limit available features, and reduce potential execution speed because it is built from generic components and is not hand crafted.

The real advantage of prototyping lies in the process of iteration. The analyst builds a prototype based on an understanding of the users' requirements. The prototype is shown to the users who operate it and make recommendations for change. The prototype is updated to reflect the suggestions and the users operate it again. This process continues until the users are satisfied.

Prototyping has its disadvantages. The most common may be that users may be so overwhelmed by the excitement of using the first prototype version of a system that a common reaction is "We'll take it as is!" The danger, of course, is that the user will fail to explore all possibilities that the new system could offer and limit the design to what is apparent in the first prototype.

7.6.5 Macros: Automating Your Work

Macros are similar to programs in that they are a task's sequence of steps recorded so that the task can be easily repeated. Macros are not compiled but are maintained in text form and interpreted each time they run. Macros require a host environment like Word or Excel for operation. Once a macro is recorded the code can be examined and edited if desired. Since macros are recorded in the **Visual Basic for Applications** (VBA) language an examination of that language follows. This section presents macro recording and editing in Excel and serves as an introduction to the creation and maintenance of program code.

Microsoft Office allows you to repeat tasks more efficiently and accurately by recording a task's steps for later use. The recording is known as a **macro** and is easily accomplished using the **Macro Recorder** provided by Excel and some other Office programs. More sophisticated automation goes beyond macro recording and permits the implementation of a dynamic user interface using **Visual Basic for Applications** (VBA). VBA is a complex and powerful topic. The subject of this section is automation using macros. The focus of this section is on macros and VBA.

7.6.5.1 Macro Recorder

The Macro Recorder is like a tape recorder that records what it senses. Here the recorder tracks the sequence of keystrokes, mouse clicks, and menu selections invoked to get a task completed. The macro is given a name and an associated short-cut key. Once complete the user presses the short-cut key and the macro is run. Saying the macro is run means that the sequence of keystrokes, etc. is replayed: the VBA program that the keystrokes were translated into is executed.

Recording a Macro We will illustrate recording a macro by using data in this table. The macro will sort these records by department.

	A	B	C	D
1	Expense	Amount	Department	Item
2	Personnel	$4,230	Marketing	Payroll
3	Supplies	$762	Production	Boxes
4	Supplies	$512	Sales	Order Forms
5	Utilities	$355	Marketing	Electricity
6	Personnel	$12,500	Production	Payroll
7	Supplies	$130	Marketing	Stationary
8	Utilities	$390	Marketing	Heat
9	Supplies	$3,000	Marketing	Desks
10	Utilities	$147	Sales	Electricity
11	Utilities	$1,200	Production	Electricity
12	Personnel	$5,012	Sales	Payroll
13	Utilities	$950	Production	Heat
14	Supplies	$268	Sales	Boxes

To begin recording a macro bring up the Macro Recorder by selecting Record Macro from the Code group of the **Developer Tab** as shown. Note: PowerPoint does not permit recording macros and Access macro programming (not recording) is invoked from the **Create Tab.**

Invoke the Macro Recorder

Once the Macro Recorder is selected the Record Macro dialog box appears. A default name (Macro1, Macro2 . . .) for the macro is suggested which you may either accept or alter. If you accept the default the name may be changed later. In this example we give the macro a suitable name: Sort_by_Department. Notice the use of underscore instead of a space in the macro name. Notice also that we typed "d" in the Shortcut key box. This allows us to run the macro later by pressing the control key and the d-key simultaneously.

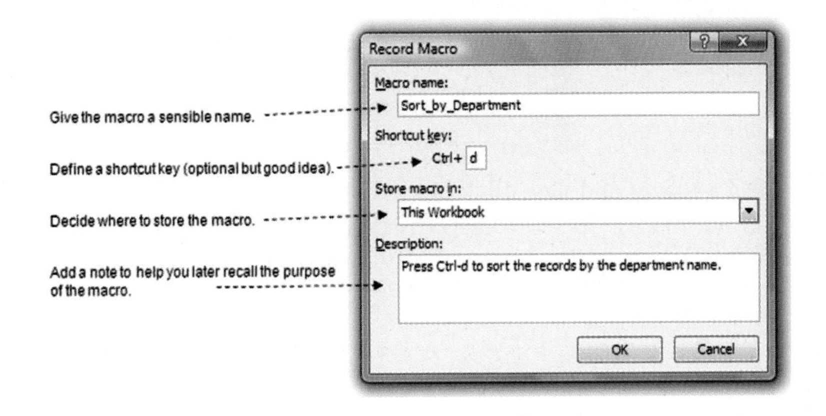

Record Macro Dialog Box

By clicking Ok the macro recoding begins. Perform the task you intend to record. Click anywhere in the table to select it. Click Sort from the **Home Tab** and make appropriate selections. Click Ok and the records are sorted.

When you are finished recording the macro click Stop Recording on the **Developer Tab** and the recording will be saved with the name given in the Record Macro dialog box. The records are sorted and look like this:

Records Sorted and Macro Recorded

	A	B	C	D
1	Expense	Amount	Department	Item
2	Personnel	$4,230	Marketing	Payroll
3	Utilities	$355	Marketing	Electricity
4	Supplies	$130	Marketing	Stationary
5	Utilities	$390	Marketing	Heat
6	Supplies	$3,000	Marketing	Desks
7	Supplies	$762	Production	Boxes
8	Personnel	$12,500	Production	Payroll
9	Utilities	$1,200	Production	Electricity
10	Utilities	$950	Production	Heat
11	Supplies	$512	Sales	Order Forms
12	Utilities	$147	Sales	Electricity
13	Personnel	$5,012	Sales	Payroll
14	Supplies	$268	Sales	Boxes

You could record another macro to sort the table by Item. Call that macro Sort_by_Item and associate the shortcut key CTRL-i to that macro. Now press CTRL-d and then CTRL-i and you will see the records are sorted in a different sequence as each shortcut key is pressed. Note: shortcut keys are case sensitive.

Editing a Macro If you make a mistake while recording a macro the best way to fix it is to start over. The macro is recorded in a language known as Visual Basic for Applications (VBA). VBA is explained later in this chapter, but if you want to take a peek at what VBA looks like, open a macro for editing by selecting Macros from the **Developer Tab.** The list of your macros appears.

Library of Recorded Macros

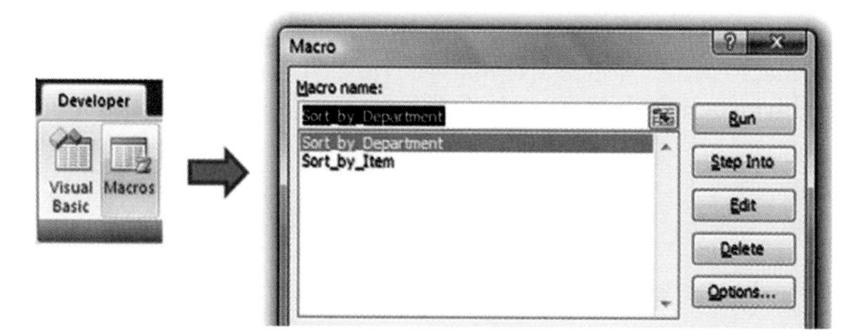

If you select a macro and then click Options you may change the shortcut key and description for that macro. To see what VBA code looks like select a macro and click Edit. The code that was recorded automatically for Sort_by_Department is shown here:

Macro VBA Code Automatically Recorded

```
Sub Sort_by_Department()
'
' Sort_by_Department Macro
' Press Ctrl-d to sort the records by the department name.
'
' Keyboard Shortcut: Ctrl+d
'
    Range("B6").Select
    ActiveWorkbook.Worksheets("Sheet1").Sort.SortFields.Clear
    ActiveWorkbook.Worksheets("Sheet1").Sort.SortFields.Add Key:=Range("C2:C14") _
        , SortOn:=xlSortOnValues, Order:=xlAscending, DataOption:=xlSortNormal
    With ActiveWorkbook.Worksheets("Sheet1").Sort
        .SetRange Range("A1:D14")
        .Header = xlYes
        .MatchCase = False
        .Orientation = xlTopToBottom
        .SortMethod = xlPinYin
        .Apply
    End With
End Sub
```

As you can see VBA is a bit complex. However, if you consider only the lines beginning with "Range" (the other lines are explanatory comments and are not steps performed by the macro) you see that a lot of processing power is packed into very few commands.

Also notice that Sort_by_Department begins and ends with lines that contain Sub. This is because a macro is formally a **subroutine** in the VBA programming language. In any computer programming language tasks are individually stored as named functions or subroutines and VBA is no exception.

7.6.5.2 Beyond Shortcut Keys

Shortcut keys are a handy way for the user to activate a macro but the specific keys to press are often forgotten. Also, there are a limited number of keys that may be used for shortcuts because there are a limited number of keys on the keyboard. An improvement would be to add interface elements that the user can click to activate your macros. You have two basic options.

Assign a Macro to the Quick Access Toolbar You can customize the Quick Access Toolbar by adding a button to it for your macro. This way the macro is conveniently available for you in a prominent position. Follow these steps:

1. Right-click on the Quick Access Toolbar.
2. Select Customize Quick Access Toolbar.
3. Select Macros in the Choose commands from drop down list.

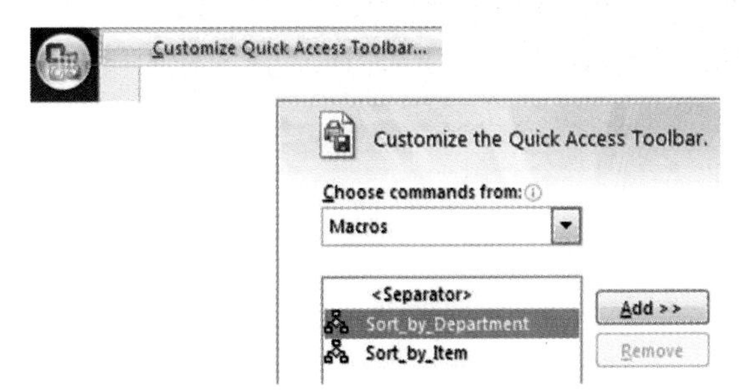

4. Select the macro you want and click Add (see above).
5. Select the macro just added and click Modify (see next page).
6. Select an icon for the macro.
7. Click Ok.

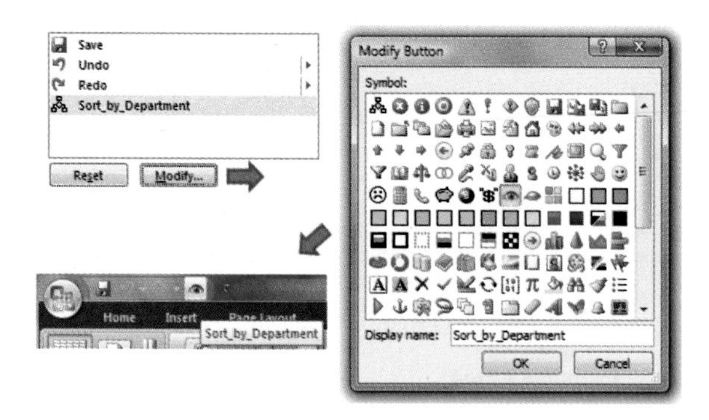

Assign a Macro to a Button on the Worksheet The other option is to add a button directly to the worksheet. This requires the use of the Form Controls Toolbox. Make the toolbox visible by selecting Insert from the **Developer Tab.** Note: Controls are a sophisticated addition to a spreadsheet and work closely with VBA. Here we will only explore the Command Button control.

Form Control Toolbox

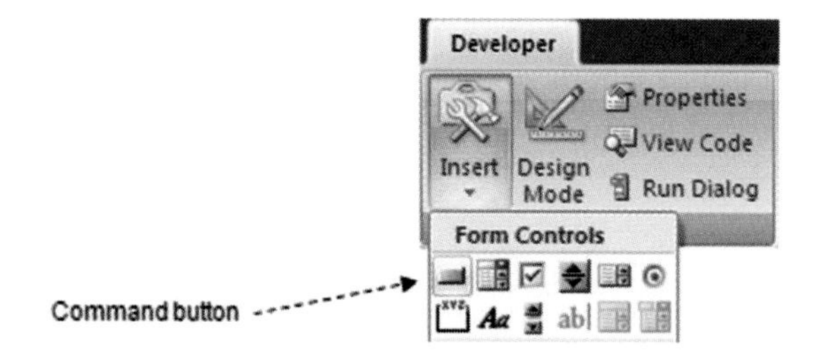

Click the Command Button icon and then click anywhere on the spreadsheet. Drag out the button to the size you want. Release the mouse and the Assign Macro dialog box appears. The result will look something like this:

Command Button Placed on a Spreadsheet

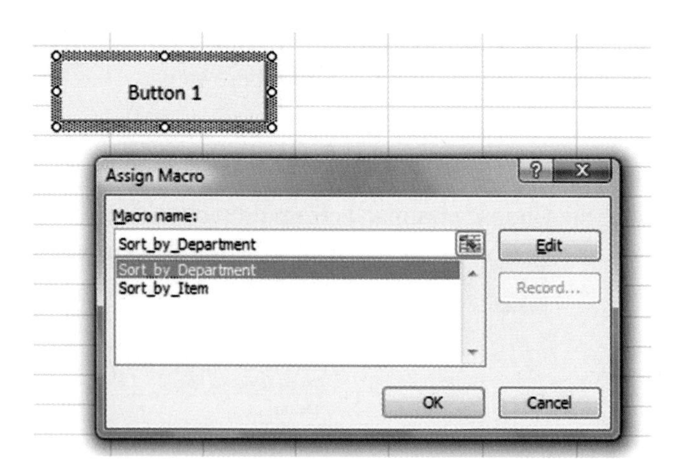

Select the macro you want to attach to the button and click Ok. To change the caption from the default ("Button 1") to "Sort by Department" follow these steps:

1. Right-click on the button.
2. Click Edit Text.
3. Type the new caption.

The button face immediately changes as shown here.

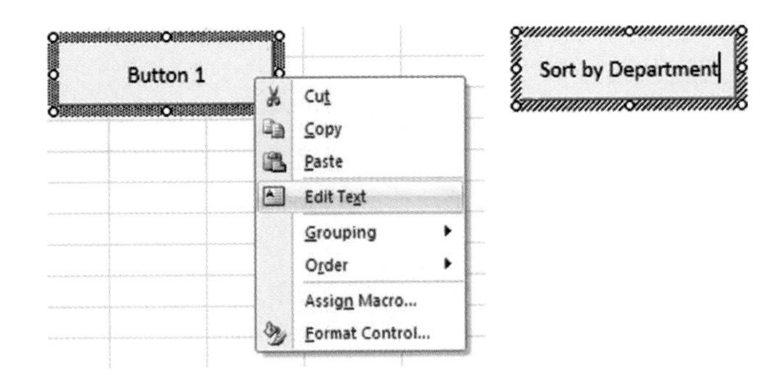

Altering a Command Button's Caption

A second button could be added to allow sorting by item (that was the second sort macro we created). After adding the second button the spreadsheet would look like this:

	A	B	C	D
1	Expense	Amount	Department	Item
2	Supplies	$762	Production	Boxes
3	Supplies	$268	Sales	Boxes
4	Supplies	$3,000	Marketing	Desks
5	Utilities	$355	Marketing	Electricity
6	Utilities	$1,200	Production	Electricity
7	Utilities	$147	Sales	Electricity
8	Utilities	$390	Marketing	Heat
9	Utilities	$950	Production	Heat
10	Supplies	$512	Sales	Order Forms
11	Personnel	$4,230	Marketing	Payroll
12	Personnel	$12,500	Production	Payroll
13	Personnel	$5,012	Sales	Payroll
14	Supplies	$130	Marketing	Stationary

Sort by Department

Sort by Item

Two Command Buttons Added

Other Controls Excel and other Office programs offer a collection of controls (radio buttons, check boxes, lists, etc.) in addition to the button demonstrated here.

7.6.5.3 Saving Your Work

Saving a document containing macros is a familiar process with a little twist. In the case of Excel, if you created a new workbook and added a macro you will see this message when you save your work:

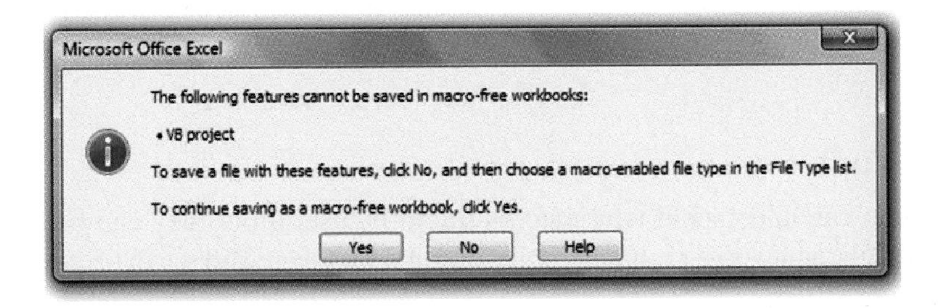

Saving a Workbook Containing Macros

Fixing the situation is easy. Click No and in the Save As dialog box that appears next direct Excel that the workbook is to be saved as a Macro-Enabled workbook this way:

Allowing Macros

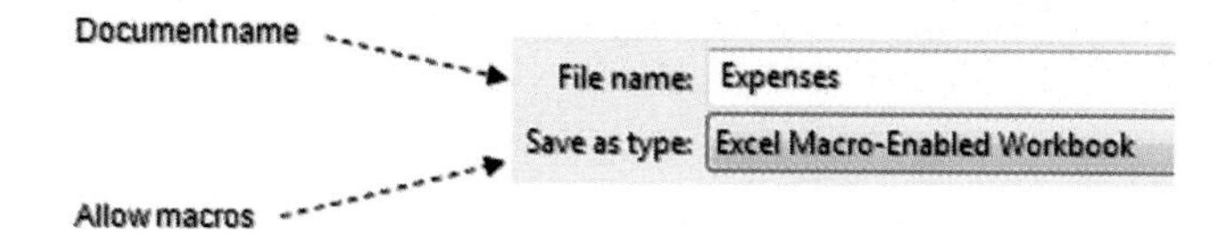

The reason you must do this is because Excel will not allow a macro to be stored in a document with the **XLSX** file extension. If you receive an XLSX document from another person or download it from a Web site you know that it is safe to open because it cannot include executable code (macros). Any code could be malicious, so this safeguard protects your computer and your data.

Workbooks with macros are stored in **XLSM** documents. Documents with embedded macro code can cause problems if the intention of the author is malicious. Macros and the VBA language are quite powerful and, if in the hands of the wrong person, dangerous. The security section of this chapter (later) discusses what you can do to protect your computer.

7.6.5.4 The Personal Workbook

So far the macros we created were for use in the Excel book that we were working in. At times it might be useful to have a macro that could be used in any of your workbooks. Suppose you have several workbooks that each has a table containing records of company expense data as we have been using. Suppose that each workbook is for sales from a different month and you would like the sort macros (built earlier in this chapter) available to all workbooks.

Excel automatically creates a workbook named PERSONAL.XLSM that is used to store any shared macros. If you want a macro available to all of your workbooks select Personal Macro Workbook when you store the macro.

Store a Macro in the Personal Macro Workbook

Word provides a document, NORMAL.DOTM, that performs for Word the same function as PERSONAL.XLSX for Excel.

Tip: Macros stored in PERSONAL.XLSM are available only to you. Macros stored in any other Excel workbook are available to others if you send them a copy of the XLSM document. Since you do not send others your PERSONAL.XLSM file macros stored there are not available to others.

7.6.5.5 Security

No doubt you can understand why macros might be useful but they can be dangerous, too. The VBA language is a complete programming language and it can be used to access your computer's files and change or delete data. It could even render Windows unusable. Although macros that you create serve your purposes, you must learn Excel's security provisions to protect against malicious macros created by and distributed by others.

When you open a workbook with macros, Excel will not allow you to run the macros. It informs you of the presence of macros with this message on the Information Bar:

Information Bar: Macros Are Disabled

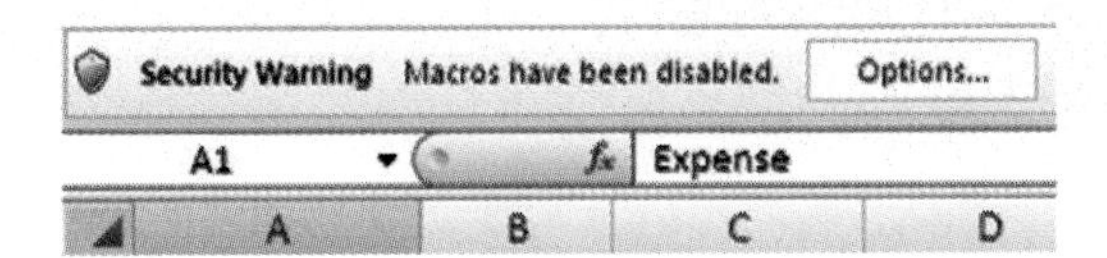

If you ignore the message and attempt to run a macro, Excel will not allow it.

Macros Do Not Run

To allow macros to run, click Options in the Information Bar and then enable macros in the Microsoft Office Security Options dialog box as shown.

Allow Macros to Run

Once macros are enabled you can click the buttons or use the shortcut keys that trigger your macros. The next time, however, that you open your workbook you will be surprised to learn that you must repeat the process of enabling macros. This will get tiring after a while, so we will explore more advanced security management options that avoid this speed-bump.

Trust Center The Trust Center is where you exercise greater control over the execution of macros in workbooks. To access the center, click Macro Security on the **Developer Tab** and then select Macro Settings. The default setting is selected (shown below). You could select Enable all macros and the annoying message would never appear again. This is not recommended!

Note: The Trust Center may also be accessed by clicking the Office button, then clicking Excel Options, and then clicking Trust Center.

Trust Center

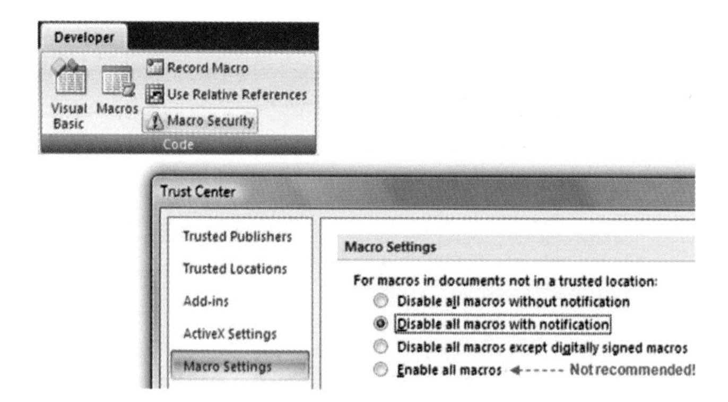

If you enable all macros you will never be informed of the presence of macros in a workbook and you could open a workbook with malicious code that runs as soon as it opens. You would never have the opportunity to prevent the code from running. Do not choose this option! Choose Trusted Locations instead.

A trusted location is a folder on your disk that you designate to hold workbooks with macros that you give permission to run. Normally, these are workbooks you created or those sent to you by people you trust. Any workbook in that folder may run macros without your explicit permission. All workbooks in other locations with macros will still require permission as described above. In the Trusted Locations page of the Trust Center click Add a new location.

Adding a Trusted Location

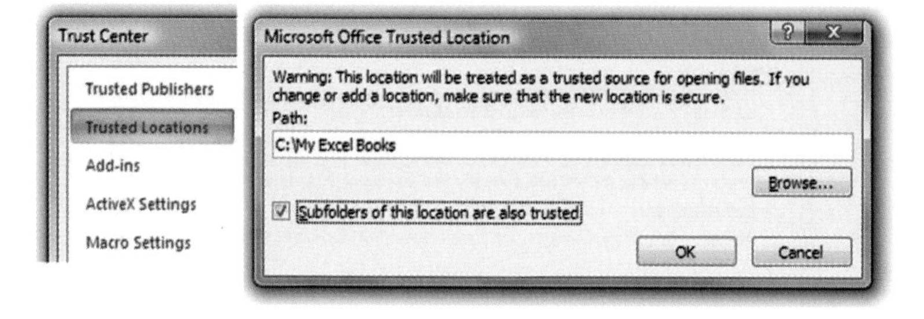

Now store any workbook that you create (or books created by people that you trust) in the trusted folder.

7.6.5.6 Macro Examples

In this section we present several macros that illustrate the power of using this automation technique. Since macros can be used in all Office programs we will demonstrate practical Excel and Word macros. Note: The macro recorder is not available in PowerPoint and all macros must be coded in VBA.

Creating a Worksheet Title A simple, but useful, macro inserts some standard text into a worksheet. You could use this technique to identify the worksheet as yours and also provide the date you created it. If you store the macro in PERSONAL.XLSM then you could use it to easily identify all worksheets that you produce.

For this example we want the text inserted beginning in the active cell rather than in a specific cell coded in the macro. For this reason be sure to select Use Relative References in the **Developer Tab** before recording the macro. We will call the macro Title and assign Ctrl-T as the shortcut key.

Now type the text (perhaps your name or your company name). Add other text as you wish and in another cell use the TODAY() function to obtain the current date to record when the worksheet was created. Since TODAY() always is updated as the date changes, you will need to fix the date so it never changes. Make active the cell with the date then press F2 followed by F9. Format all the cells as you wish and then stop recording.

To use the macro make any cell active and then press the shortcut key, Ctrl-T, or select Title from the macro list. The macro runs and inserts the title and date as shown. As you can see the, the TODAY() function was replaced by the date value itself.

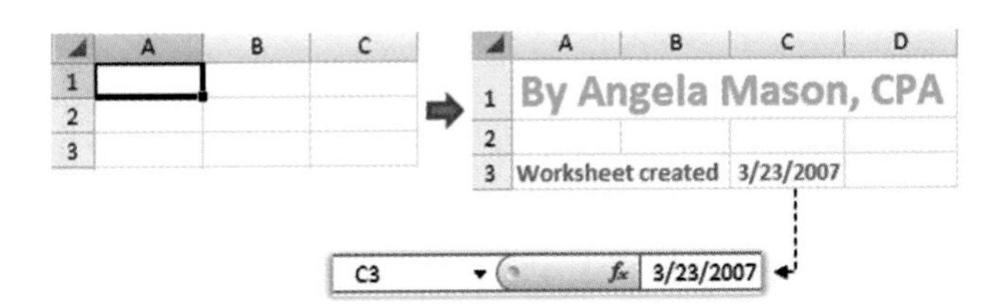

A Practical Macro

Mail Merge A macro could be used to prepare a letter for mailing to a list of customers. Assuming that you have already created a Word document and already linked to a set of records, a macro could come in quite handy. We start with a list of records in an Excel workbook:

	A	B	C	D	E	F
1	First Name	Last Name	Home Location	City	State	Zip
2	Fred	Smith	1902 Ash St	Santa Fe	NM	89002
3	Roberta	Goodall	2207 Utica Blvd	Utica	NY	14017
4	June	Waters	Green Ave.	Philadelphia	PA	19119
5	Albert	Zandar	Valley View Rd.	Worcester	MA	01610
6	Becky	Cromish	Juanita Rd.	Philadelphia	PA	19030

Records to Automate in Mail Merge

Next, navigate to the document that has been merged to these records and open it. Once the document is open the first record is merged in and the Preview Results icon on the **Mailings Tab** allows you to scroll through the merged letters.

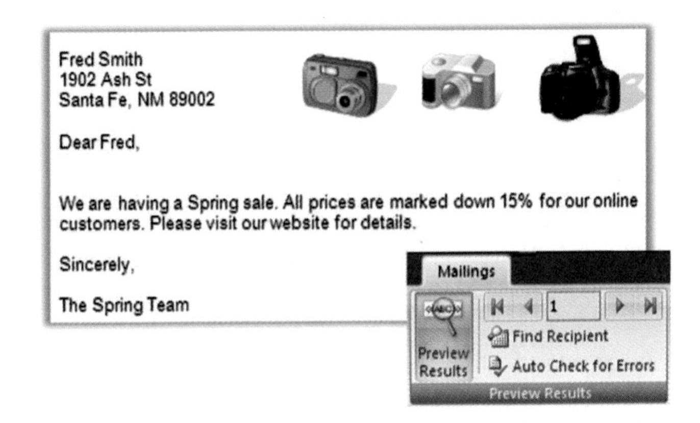

Merged Letters

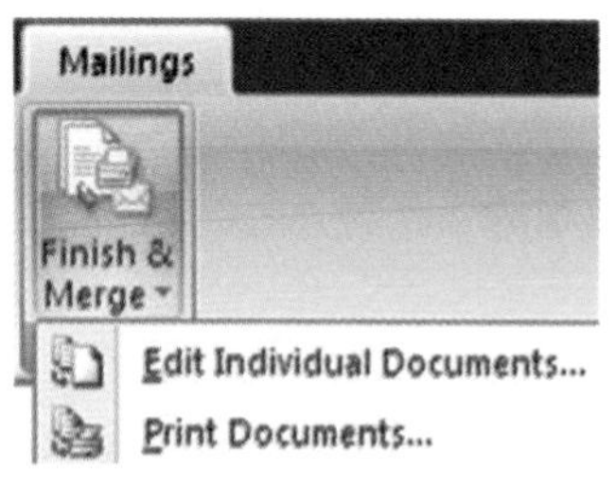

The final step would be to finish the merge by either printing all letters as is or editing individual letters. All of these steps could be automated by recoding a macro in Word and then running it each time letters were to be produced.

Start by opening a new Word document. Select Record Macro (from the **Developer Tab** as in Excel) and store the macro in NORMAL.DOCM (like PERSONAL.XLSM this applies to all Word documents). Also give the macro a name (here we called the macro Print_Letters).

Creating the Mail Merge Macro

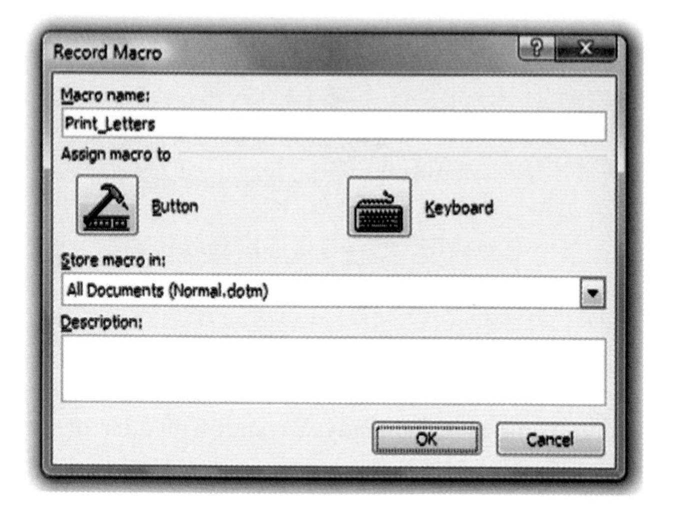

The next time you wish to print the letters:

1. Open Word
2. Select Macros from the Developer Tab.
3. Double-click Print_Letters.

Running the Mail Merge Macro

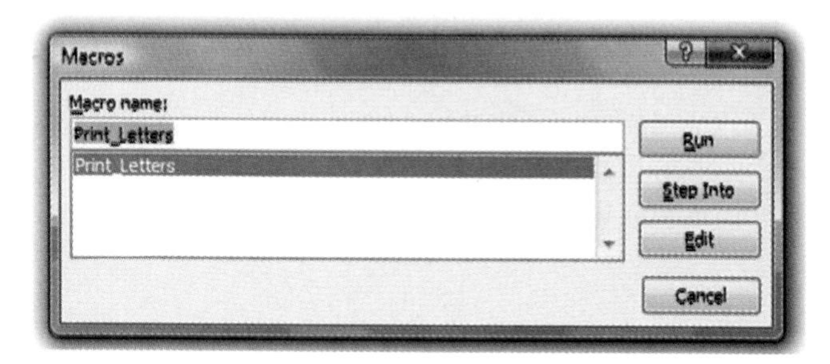

Import Data, Process and Analyze It Automation can be used to link together a series of steps that together perform a complex operation. In this example we will import an XML file containing data about sales and then present an analysis of the data. Presumably the data would change each day the business is open. Automation allows us to obtain a fresh look at the business daily. Here are the steps we would follow to perform this complex task. First, here is the data after it has been imported:

Imported XML Data (partial listing)

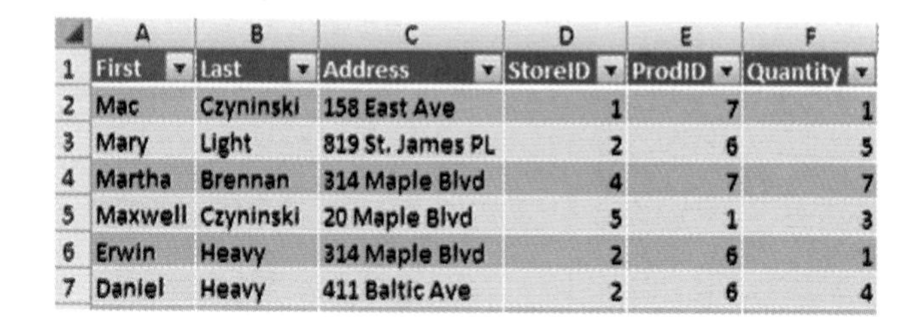

	A	B	C	D	E	F
1	First	Last	Address	StoreID	ProdID	Quantity
2	Mac	Czyninski	158 East Ave	1	7	1
3	Mary	Light	819 St. James PL	2	6	5
4	Martha	Brennan	314 Maple Blvd	4	7	7
5	Maxwell	Czyninski	20 Maple Blvd	5	1	3
6	Erwin	Heavy	314 Maple Blvd	2	6	1
7	Daniel	Heavy	411 Baltic Ave	2	6	4

Notice that the store of each purchase is coded numerically and not displayed by name. The same is true of the product purchased. We want our analysis to display names of stores and products rather than numbers so we plan to obtain names from two lookup tables stored in a different workbook.

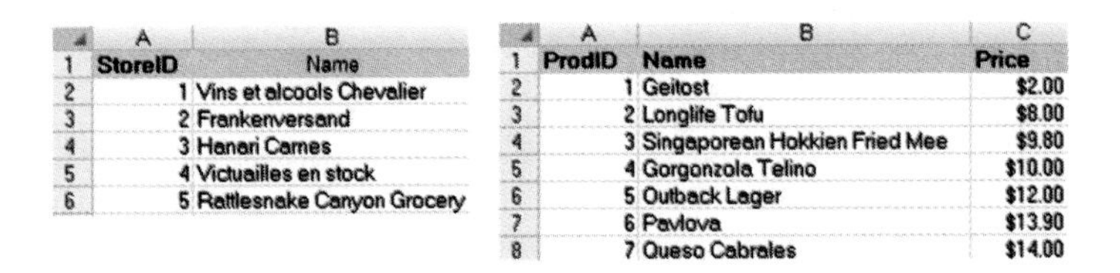

StoreID	Name
1	Vins et alcools Chevalier
2	Frankenversand
3	Hanari Carnes
4	Victuailles en stock
5	Rattlesnake Canyon Grocery

ProdID	Name	Price
1	Geitost	$2.00
2	Longlife Tofu	$8.00
3	Singaporean Hokkien Fried Mee	$9.80
4	Gorgonzola Telino	$10.00
5	Outback Lager	$12.00
6	Pavlova	$13.90
7	Queso Cabrales	$14.00

Lookup Tables in a Different Workbook

We would next insert new columns for Store, Product, Cost, and Extended Cost in the worksheet with the imported data and use VLOOKUP functions to achieve this result:

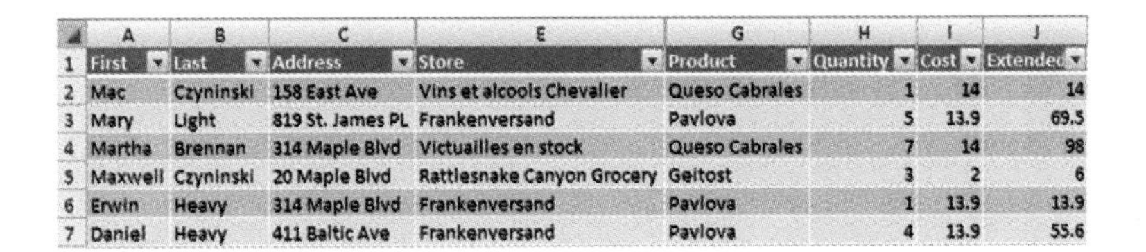

First	Last	Address	Store	Product	Quantity	Cost	Extended
Mac	Czyninski	158 East Ave	Vins et alcools Chevalier	Queso Cabrales	1	14	14
Mary	Light	819 St. James PL	Frankenversand	Pavlova	5	13.9	69.5
Martha	Brennan	314 Maple Blvd	Victuailles en stock	Queso Cabrales	7	14	98
Maxwell	Czyninski	20 Maple Blvd	Rattlesnake Canyon Grocery	Geitost	3	2	6
Erwin	Heavy	314 Maple Blvd	Frankenversand	Pavlova	1	13.9	13.9
Daniel	Heavy	411 Baltic Ave	Frankenversand	Pavlova	4	13.9	55.6

Records with VLOOKUPs

Once the data is loaded and new columns added a pivot table is used to display results.

Row Labels	Sum of Extended
Frankenversand	$ 1,205.20
Hanari Carnes	$ 899.50
Rattlesnake Canyon Grocery	$ 501.40
Victuailles en stock	$ 951.10
Vins et alcools Chevalier	$ 923.10
Grand Total	$ 4,480.30

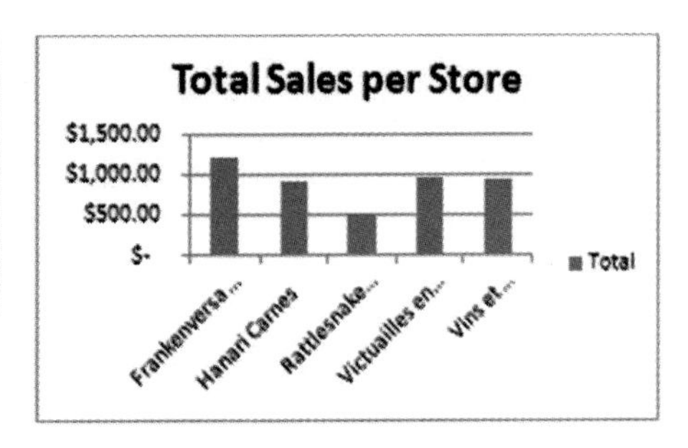

Pivot Table Displays Sales Results

Other charts could be prepared, too. Other views of the same data provide different inferences:

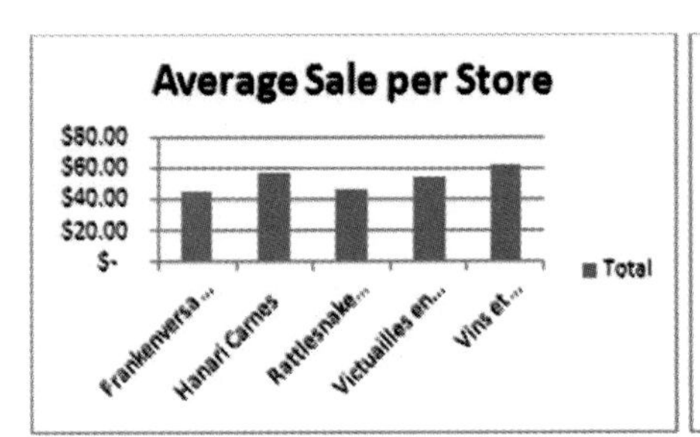

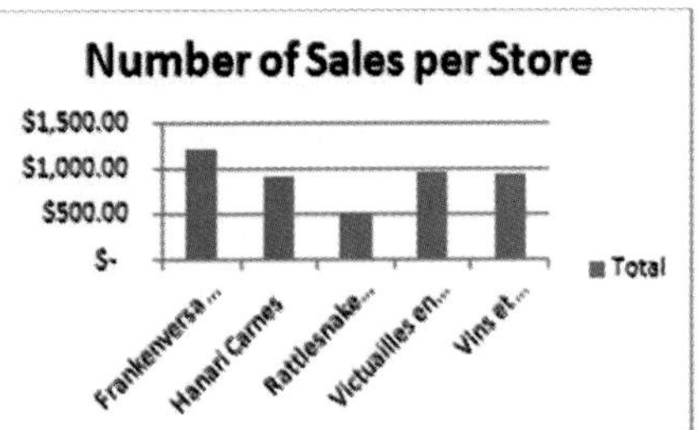

Other Information

Finally, we could take advantage of all of the computed data and obtain this result:

Comprehensive Result

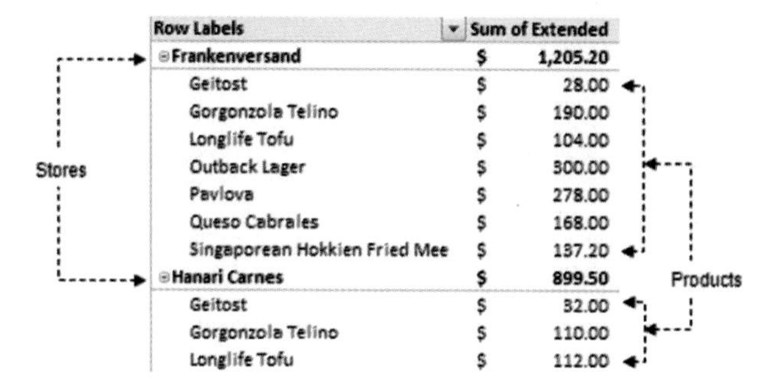

Row Labels	Sum of Extended
Frankenversand	$ 1,205.20
Geitost	$ 28.00
Gorgonzola Telino	$ 190.00
Longlife Tofu	$ 104.00
Outback Lager	$ 300.00
Pavlova	$ 278.00
Queso Cabrales	$ 168.00
Singaporean Hokkien Fried Mee	$ 137.20
Hanari Carnes	$ 899.50
Geitost	$ 32.00
Gorgonzola Telino	$ 110.00
Longlife Tofu	$ 112.00

All of the steps presented here could be automated in one macro. Imagine the director of sales getting daily access to data and analysis of the data this easily!

7.6.5.7 VBA: Visual Basic for Applications

Visual Basic for Applications is a complete programming language. As such it is a very large and complex topic. This section of the chapter introduces you to VBA and some general programming concepts. If you desire to learn more about VBA you will find many books on that topic alone. VBA is a version of **Visual Basic** and is more or less the same as **VBScript** (or Visual Basic Script) which is discussed later in this chapter. While VBA permits operations that are specific to Office 2007 programs, the general mechanism for controlling the operations of the program is identical.

VBA provides an editor that gives you easy access to all of your macros. The easiest way to open the editor is to select a macro to edit:

Open the list of macros and select Make Negative, a macro that multiplies the active cell's value by −1.

Select Macro to Edit

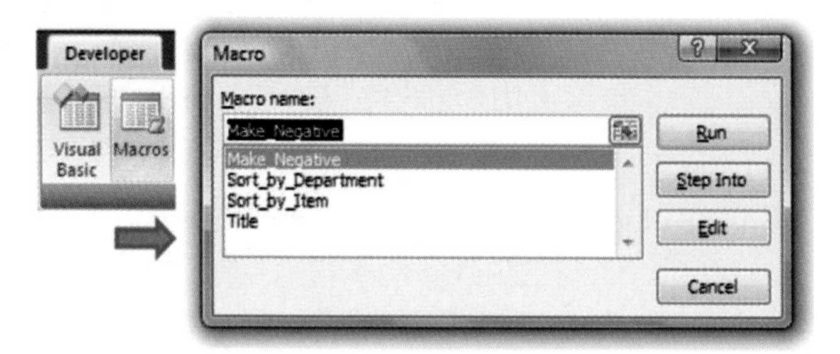

Here Make Negative is shown open in VBA editor. Notice the Sub declarations that mark the beginning and end of the macro. This is true for all macros. Lines beginning with an apostrophe are comments. The active code is just one line that works this way:

1. Get value found in active cell.
2. Multiply it by −1.
3. Store the result in the active cell.

Macro's VBA Code

```
Sub Make_Negative()
'
' Make_Negative
'
    ActiveCell.Value = ActiveCell.Value * -1

End Sub
```

When you select a macro to edit, the code is displayed in the VBA editor. The editor presents an organized view of the code objects that are found in your workbook. The components of the workbook are listed down the left-hand side. Included in the list are modules where macro code is normally (not always) stored.

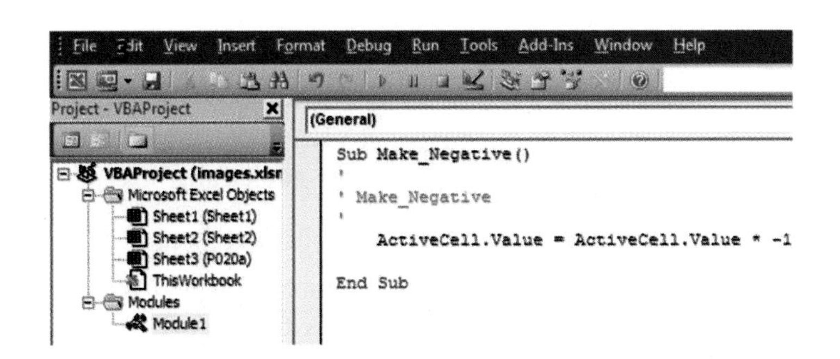

A Macro's VBA Code Shown in the VBA Editor

Some macros cannot be recorded by the macro recorder because there are no keystrokes that could do what the macro is intended for. In that case the macro would be coded by hand. To create a new macro (really a subroutine) open the VBA Editor and move to after the last line of any other macro (after End Sub) and type the new macro. Remember that all macros begin with the word Sub followed by the name of the macro.

All macros are stored in modules. As you examine the VBA Editor notice Module 1 at the bottom of the left-hand side list. A workbook can have any number of modules and it makes no difference what module a macro is in. If for some reason you want to create a new module, right click Modules and Insert a Module.

Here we will create a macro that calculates the square root of the cell one column to the left. We will call it Square_Root. Start by typing the macro's header right below the ending of the previous macro. As soon as the header is typed the editor displays this:

The editor added End Sub and now we complete the rest:

Beginning a New Macro in the VBA Editor

```
Sub Make_Negative()
'
' Make_Negative
'
    ActiveCell.Value = ActiveCell.Value * -1

End Sub
Sub Square_Root()


End Sub
```

The notation might seem odd but it is actually quite simple:

Completing the Square_Root Macro

```
Sub Square_Root()

    ActiveCell.FormulaR1C1 = "=RC[-1]^0.5"

End Sub
```

- **FormulaR1C1** — Make whatever comes next the formula for the active cell.
- **RC[-1]** — Get a value from the cell one column to the left.
- **^** — Raise the value just obtained to a power.
- **.5** — This is the power for a square root.

Sure it seems strange, but once you get used to it VBA code is quite straightforward. Here are a few more examples. Keep in mind that VBA is a big topic and you should consult a complete VBA book if you want to pursue this topic fully.

Select a Cell The power of macros is the power to set and update values, formats, formulas, and functions in cells. These operations require selecting a specific cell or range of cells. The use of Range (as shown next) illustrates how to make a cell the active cell. In this example A3 becomes the active cell. A range could be selected by replacing A3 with a range specification.

Since A3 is the active cell, ActiveCell.Value in the next line actually references the value in cell A3. As used here this line actually puts the value "Hello" into A3.

The next line sets the A3's format to bold. Selection refers to whatever cell or range of cells is selected. While only one cell can be active a whole range can be selected. Here, if True were replaced with False bold would be turned-off for that cell.

Offset from Active Cell

```
Sub Load_Cell()

    Range("A3").Select

    ActiveCell.Value = "Hello"

    Selection.Font.Bold = True

End Sub
```

Offset The Offset **property** of the active cell is used to point to a cell that is located relative to the active cell. In this example the offset points to the right one column. Here the Square_Root macro is rewritten and called SQR_toRight so that the square root is stored one cell to the right of the active cell. The square root is calculated from the number in the active cell.

Offset allows you to reference other columns and rows. Here are a few examples:

- **(0,1)** — One column to right and same row.
- **(1,2)** — One row down and two columns to the right.

- **(-1,0)** — One row up and same column.
- **(-2,-1)** — Two rows up and one column left.

In this example, the square root of the active cell's value is stored one cell to the right (0,1).

Offset from Active Cell

```
Sub SQR_toRight()

    ActiveCell.Offset(0, 1).Value = ActiveCell.Value ^ 0.5

End Sub
```

Change Font Any cell or range of cells can be selected as illustrated earlier. The selection **object** has a **property** font which itself has several properties. This example demonstrates how to reference the font's properties using the **with . . . end** with syntax. Note that each of the font's properties have a preceding period or "dot."

Formatting Text

```
Sub Change_Font()

    With Selection.Font
        .Name = "Verdana"
        .Size = 20
    End With

End Sub
```

The complete set of all objects, properties and their allowed values (known as the Document Object Model or **DOM**) is beyond the scope of this book. You should consult online and printed references if you are interested in this topic.

Loops Often, it is desired to repeat the same operation on a list of cells. This is known as **iteration** and in VBA loops are used to perform this operation. In this example a list of cells are formatted with the background color being set.

Repetition: Loops

```
Sub Set_Color()

    Do Until ActiveCell.Value = ""
        ActiveCell.Select
        Selection.Interior.ColorIndex = 35
        ActiveCell.Offset(1, 0).Select
    Loop

End Sub
```

The subroutine begins with the active cell. If the active cell has a non-null value the loop is entered and background color of the active cell is set. The next cell down the column is selected and control returns to the Do statement. If the new active cell is not empty the loop is entered again and the active cell is formatted. The process continues until an empty cell is found.

Using a Macro with a Loop

C3 · Apple

	A	B	C
1			
2			
3			Apple
4			Cherry
5			Pear
6			
7			Orange
8			Grape

C6

	A	B	C
1			
2			
3			Apple
4			Cherry
5			Pear
6			
7			Orange
8			Grape

Be careful to always give a condition that will terminate the loop. Otherwise the loop never stops. This unfortunate circumstance is known as an **infinite loop.**

Branching In programming, decisions are often determined by evaluating a data value and then taking a branch based on the outcome. This is analogous to using an IF function in Excel. In VBA, the If statement is used to test a condition and then execute code depending on the outcome of the condition. The general syntax of the If statement is shown here.

The If Statement

```
Sub Test_Value()

    If ActiveCell.Value = 5 Then
        ActiveCell.Offset(0, 1).Value = "Active Equals 5"
    Else
        ActiveCell.Offset(0, 1).Value = "Active Does Not Equal 5"
    End If

End Sub
```

When Test_Value is used in two cells this outcome results:

The If Statement in Use

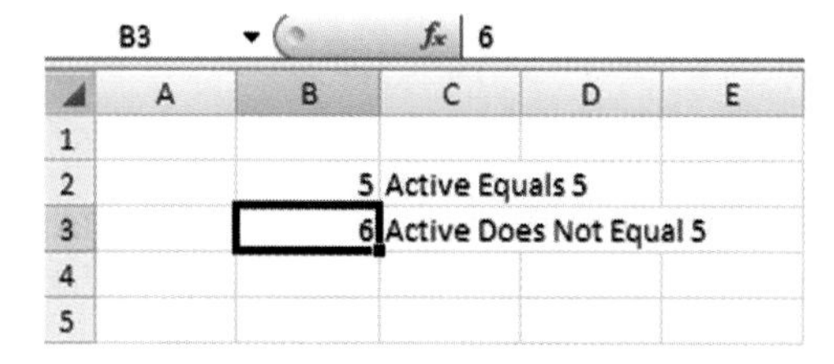

User Input and Output If you want to add a fancy touch to obtaining data from the user, consider employing the InputBox as shown here:

Using InputBox

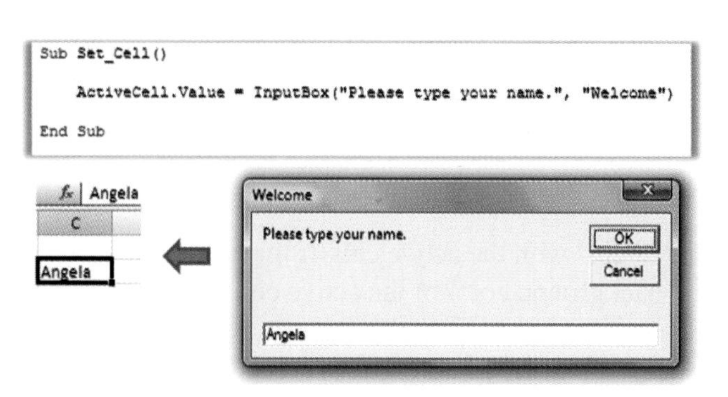

```
Sub Set_Cell()

    ActiveCell.Value = InputBox("Please type your name.", "Welcome")

End Sub
```

Notice that the box has two **parameters.** The first is the prompt displayed where the user types input and the second is the title displayed at the top of the box.

7.7 Programming

Logic is a step-by-step list of instructions written for a computer to follow as it processes data and computes results.

In this chapter we build on your understanding of the programming concepts learned earlier by developing an appreciation for how data is processed. You will learn how records are examined and selected (decision making), and how computations are performed. Underlying these concepts is logic.

Logic is the basis for the second part of the IPO model. To refresh your memory the IPO model is as follows:

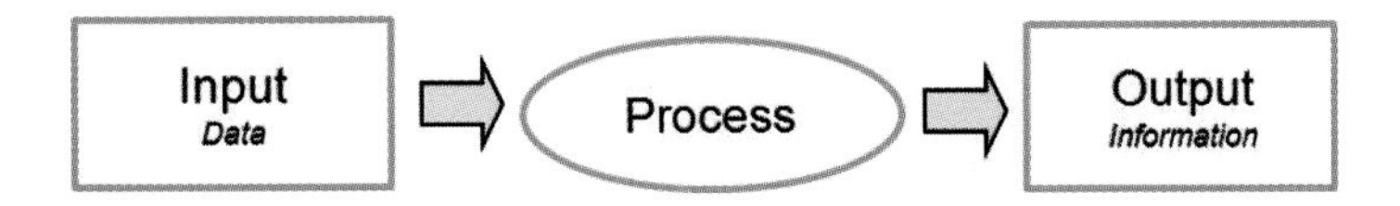

Input-Process-Output Model

7.7.1 Charts that Depict Logic

Processing data (a sequence of step-by-step instructions) follows a pattern. The pattern depends on the nature of the processing to be accomplished. Before learning the particulars of how to express processing logic as computer instructions it is important to understand the process to be automated.

A flowchart is used to illustrate a process. A basic flowchart identifies the starting and ending points of a process, the sequence of actions in the process, and the decision or branching points along the way. A solution to a problem may include many flowcharts.

Flowcharts use special shapes to represent different types of actions or steps in a process. Lines and arrows show the sequence of the steps and the relationships among them. While there are numerous shapes that are used, several are common and are described here:

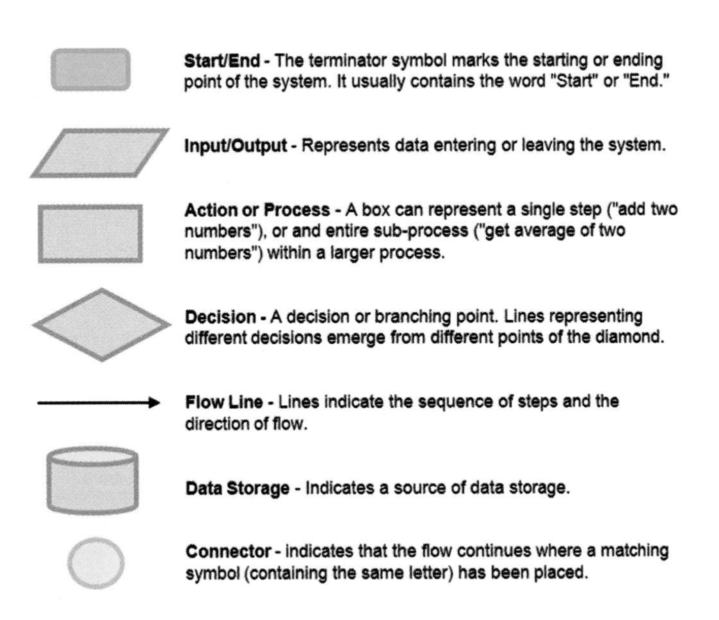

Flowchart Symbols

Here is an example flow chart that depicts the logic for calculating the average of two numbers:

Logic for Calculating the Average of Two Numbers

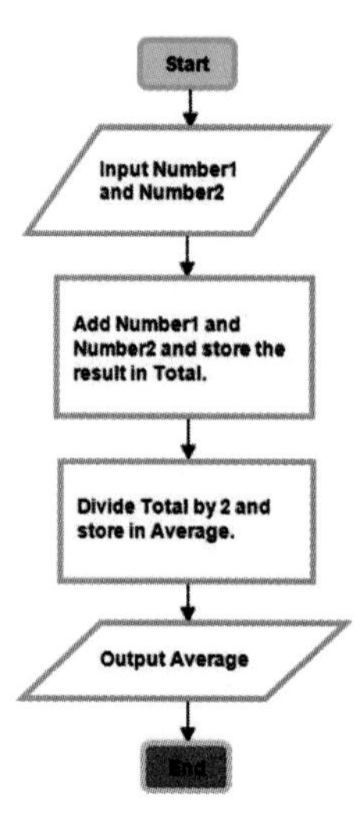

Another example shows how decisions are visually depicted. An ATM machine often must determine if an account has a sufficient balance to allow a requested withdrawal amount. If funds are sufficient then the ATM returns the amount requested otherwise it returns zero. This chart depicts this process:

ATM Logic: Determining if a Withdrawal Request Is Ok

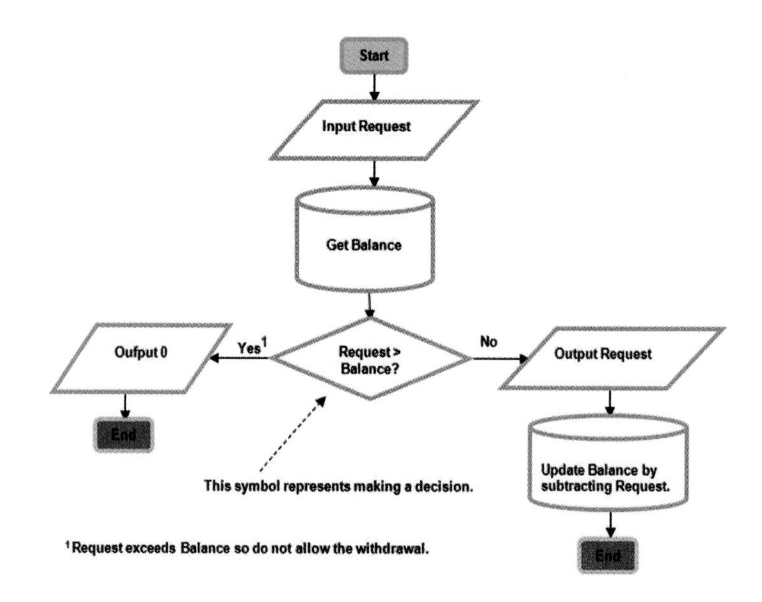

A chart can also show how a table of records is scanned (**iteration**) and only those records meeting a particular selection criterion are displayed. In this example all records of a table are scanned and only records of students from Louisiana ("LA") are displayed:

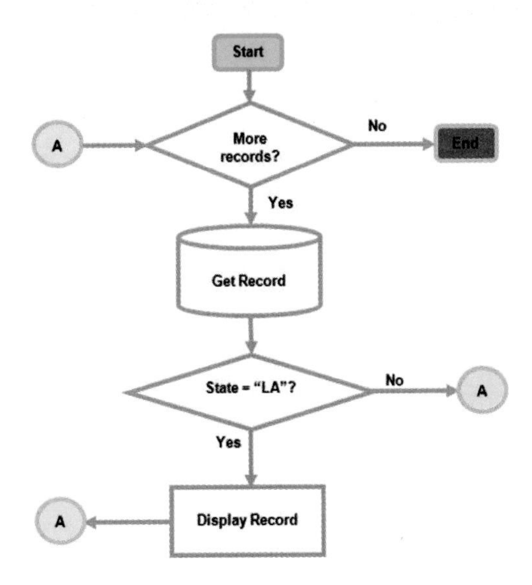

ATM Logic: Logic for Selecting Records from a Table

7.7.2 From Charts to Programming

Charts are used by humans as models of the steps that a computer will follow as data is processed. Of course the computer cannot understand the charts so they must be translated into a language the computer knows. There are many "computer languages" —in the next sections you will learn to translate logic from flow charts into an easy to use, common, and very powerful English-like computer language.

Note: some computer languages are case-sensitive and some are not. The language that is presented here is **Visual Basic Script** which is known as **VBScript** with extensions for processing sequential files and presenting output. The extensions are added for pedagogical purposes enabling VBScript exercises to run on a server and be automatically graded. TheVBS language is not case-sensitive.

7.7.3 Functions

Although the same flowchart can be used regardless of the computer language, it is the syntax of the language that dictates what the resulting code looks like.

Flowcharts are translated into a computer language and the **code** is contained in units called subroutines or functions. Each unit has a name, and the code within it performs the steps outlined in the flow chart. Consider the first flowchart above (the chart describing how to average two numbers). Assuming that we wish to contain that logic in a function named "compute_average" the code would be just like this:

```
function compute_average (number1, number2)
            total = number1 + number 2
            average = total / 2
            compute_average = average
end function
```

To ensure that you understand how this works the original flow chart is presented with the code you just examined:

The Logic of a Flowchart Is Implemented as a Function

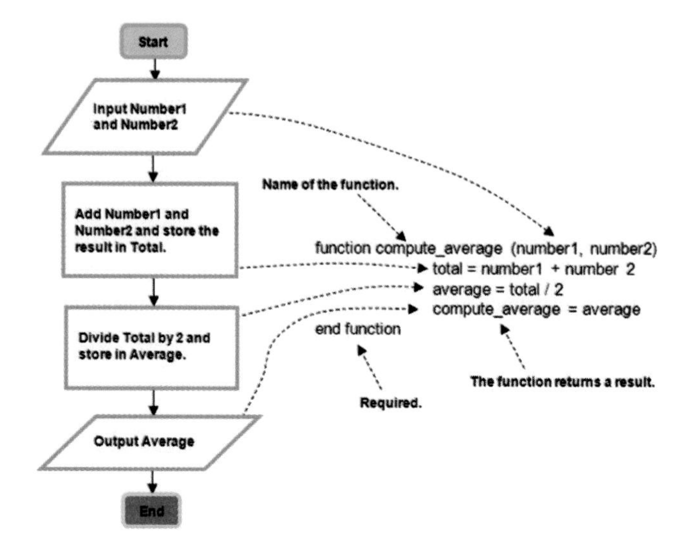

Parameters are also called arguments.

7.7.4 Input to a Function Is by Parameters

The list of data values to be input to a function is matched with parameters declared in the function's header. The comma delimited list of values is enclosed in parentheses after the name of the function. In the example above the function compute_average has two parameters in the input list. Note: The word "function" followed by the function's name is required.

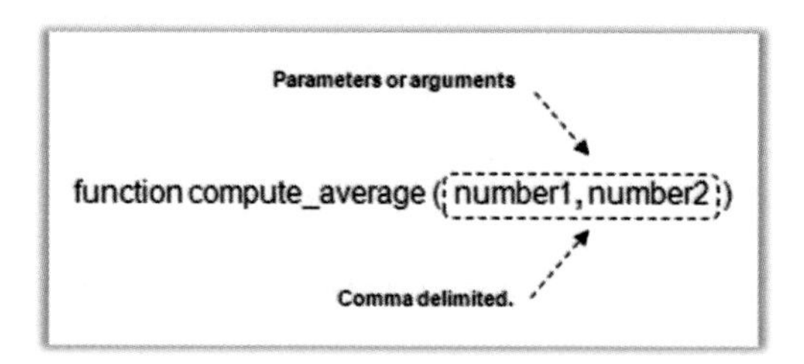

The names of the parameters in the function are defined by you. It is a good idea to use names that are meaningful. For example, a function that computes interest on an investment might be declared this way:

```
function interest_earned (investment_amount, interest_rate)
```

Note: function or parameter names may not have a space. Use the underscore instead of a space.

If the compute average function were used to compute the average of 20 and 16 it would be run this way:

```
function compute_average (20,16)
```

7.7.5 Computations: Operators and Data

Computations are easily performed using data values and operators. Operators are no doubt familiar to you. Here is a list:

Fundamental Computational Operators

Computational Operator	Usage
+	Addition
-	Subtraction
*	Multiplication
/	Division
^	Exponentiation
()	Parentheses

Data can be expressed in two ways:

- **Constant Values** — Constants are values that never change. Examples of constant data are 3.14, -8.9, "red". The first two examples are **numbers** and the last example is a **string.** Constants values are not stored separately in memory but are included in the source code of the program.
- **Variables** — Variables are names for storage locations that hold data values. The value in a storage location may change but the name of the location (the variable name) never changes.

Always surround a string data value (constant and variable) with quotes. Never use quotes anywhere else except in the DISPLAY statement shown later.

The parameters of a function are variables and receive values when the function is started. All other variables are assigned values while the function is running. Assuming we wish to average 20 and 16, the content of memory would change as shown here:

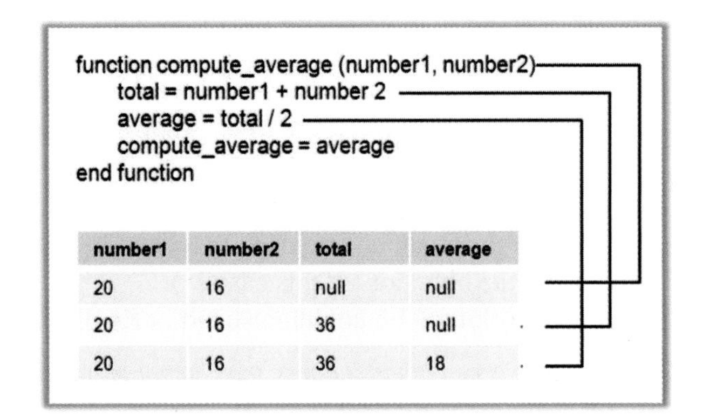

Variable Storage Changes Value

In the middle line of code 2 is a constant, and average and total are variables.

7.7.6 Output from a Function Uses the Function's Name

Once the work of the function is complete a value can be returned by the function to some other function or program that called the function. As shown in the example above the value is returned by assigning that value to the function name. Here is how it was done:

A Function Returns a Value

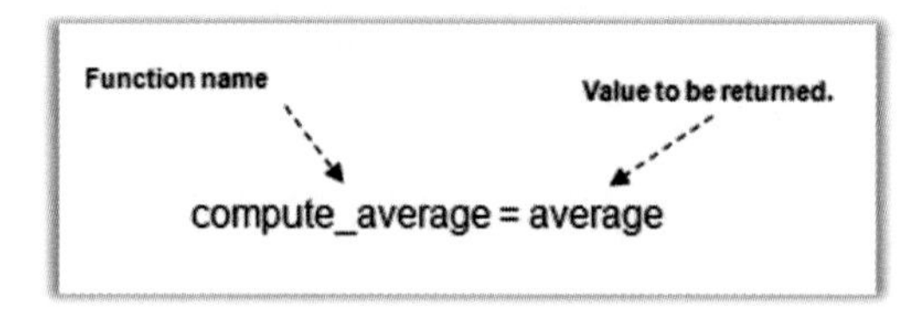

While VBScript operates this way it is not done this way in all languages. Use of the return statement is more standard in other than VBScript.

7.7.7 Branching

Decision making is known as branching. The decision to go one way or the other is based on evaluating a **condition** and taking action based on the evaluation. Conditions in code are displayed in flowcharts in a diamond. Consider this portion of an earlier **flowchart** in which an ATM machine will dispense cash if the request does not exceed the balance:

IF Statement Is used for Decision Making

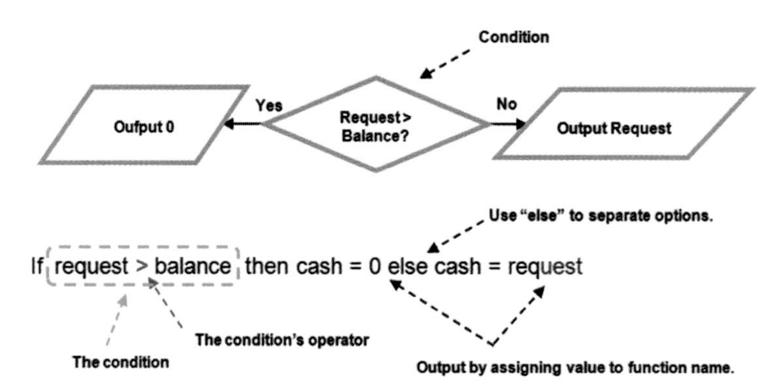

Conditions Require a Logical Operator Each condition asks a question in which there are two and only two possible answers. This is known as **binary logic** because only two outcomes exist. Two values are compared and the relationship between them is determined based on the operator that associates the two values.

The condition above asks: "Is the withdrawal request more than balance?" There can only be two outcomes: either the request is more than balance or it is not more than balance. If request is more than balance then the customer will not be able to withdraw because the account has insufficient funds so the ATM will return zero dollars.

Since there are only two possible outcomes the result of the condition is either **True** or **False.** Deciding whether the result is True or False depends on the values (in this case Request and Balance) and the operator (in this case >).

The example we are working with could be stated in English this way:

"If it is true that Request is more than Balance then do not allow the withdrawal (ATM = 0) but otherwise do allow the withdrawal (ATM = Request)."

The six operators summarized here:

The Six Fundamental Operators of Logic

Logical Operator	Meaning	Alternate
=	Equal	
<>	Not Equal	
>	Greater Than	
<	Less Than	
>=	Greater or Equal	At Least
<=	Less or Equal	At Most

Incorporating the IF statement into a function named ATM returns the correct amount of cash that will be dispensed. The function looks like this:

ATM Function

```
function ATM (request)
   If request > balance then cash = 0 else cash = request
   ATM = cash
end function
```

Here are a few examples of IF statements and the results that are produced:

```
min_age = 55
age = 61
If age >= min_age then discount = .2 else discount = 0
result: discount = .2
```

```
color="yellow"
If color = "yellow" then found_color=1 else found_color=0
result: found_color=1
```

7.7.8 Functions Calling Functions

Using functions is a great way to package a group of processing steps that are frequently reused. It can be useful to write functions that call other functions. Here is an example of a simple function that illustrates this concept. The function maximum will return the larger of two numbers that it receives:

```
function maximum (num_1, num_2)
      If num_1 > num_2 then maximum = num_1 else maximum = num_2
end function
```

Suppose that a couple is dining at a restaurant and has a coupon that gives the lower cost meal for free. The restaurant's computer could be given the following instructions when it computes the bill:

```
function dinner_cost (meal_1,meal_2, tip_percent)
     higher_cost_dinner = maximum(meal_1,meal_2)
     tip = higher_cost_dinner * tip_percent
     dinner_cost = higher_cost_dinner + tip
end function
```

As you see dinner_cost accepts three parameters. The two meal prices are immediately sent to the function maximum which returns to dinner_cost the price of the higher priced meal. The third parameter, tip_percent, is used to add on the computation of the tip. Assuming the two meals cost $25.00 and $20.00 and the tip percent is 15% the function would work together this way:

1. 25 and 20 are sent by dinner_cost to maximum.
2. Maximum determines 25 is larger and returns that value.

3. Dinner_cost receives the 25 and multiplies it by tip_percent giving tip.
4. Dinner_cost returns the total of the higher meal cost plus the tip.

Two Functions

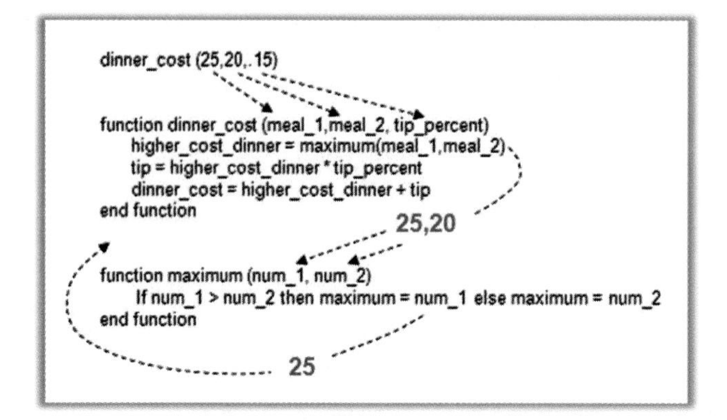

Suppose you want to compute the total cost for a purchase where the total includes the product price and shipping cost (based on the product's weight). Since shipping is computed for all products sold it is useful to store the logic for calculating shipping cost in a function that can be used and reused without rewriting the processing rules. We start by writing the function total_cost:

```
function total_cost (price, weight)
    total_cost = price + shipping(weight)
end function
```

Shipping is another function defined elsewhere.

You can see that total_cost returns the product price plus the shipping cost — just what was originally specified. The shipping cost is obtained by calling another function and passing it the product's weight. This function shipping computes shipping cost by comparing the weight in two conditions. In the following code, notice how an IF statement may have an alternative condition by using ELSEIF.

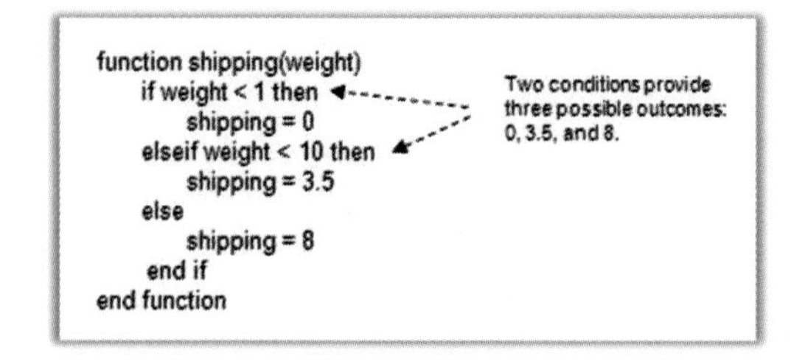

Any number of ELSEIF conditions may be added to an IF statement.

Not all languages use the same syntax for the multiple alternative decisions, however this structure is available in all languages.

7.7.9 Data Other than from Parameters (Stored Data)

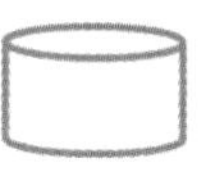

Sometimes a function requires data that is not given to it as parameters. This data typically comes from secondary (persistent) storage and is represented by the data storage symbol. External data (from storage) has names just as parameters and variables do. The difference is that you must use the names as given to you because those names identify specific locations in secondary memory.

The data storage symbol normally will have the word "Get" or "Update" shown inside it. These verbs indicate the particular use of data storage in the logic at that point. Gets do not translate into code but Updates do. Consider this flowchart presented earlier:

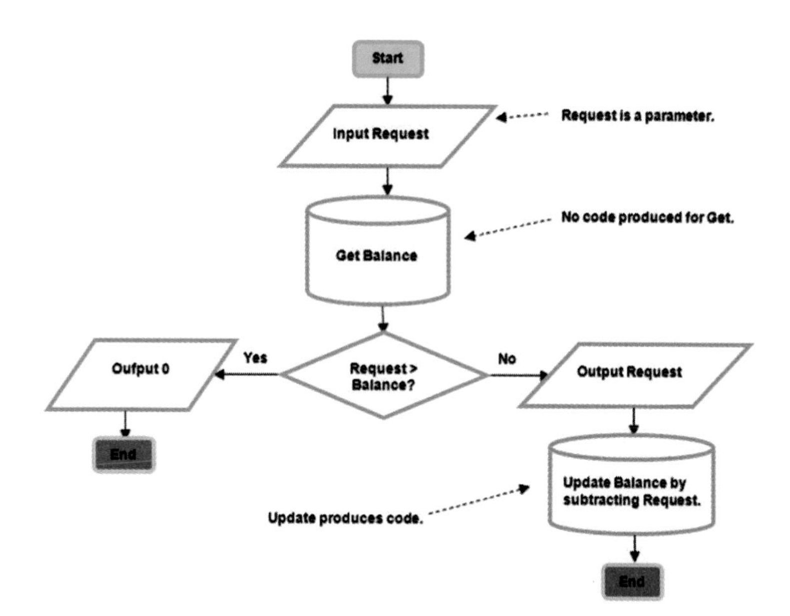

Data from Storage Retrieved and Updated

Here is the code produced for this chart:

```
function ATM (request)
    if request > balance then
        cash = 0
    else
        cash = request
        balance = balance – request
    end if
    ATM = cash
end function
```

7.7.10 Loops: Iteration

Processing data frequently involves repeating the same code as it is applied to a collection of records. One of the most common procedures is selecting records from a table and then performing an operation on the selected records (like displaying them, computing the sum of data from all selected records, finding the maximum value in a column, etc.).

For the next example assume a "Customers" table of records as shown below:

Customers Table with Three Records

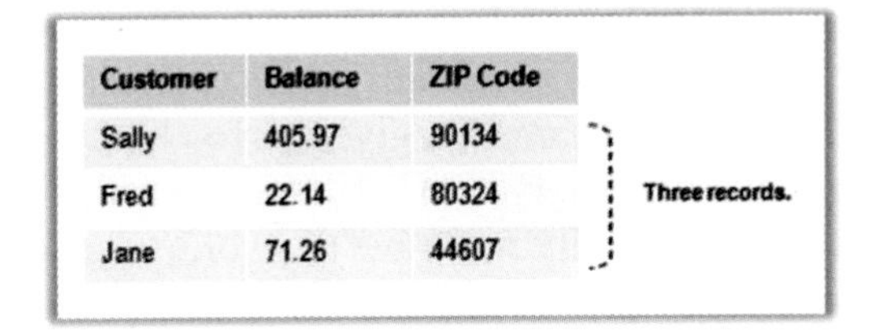

Customer	Balance	ZIP Code
Sally	405.97	90134
Fred	22.14	80324
Jane	71.26	44607

Since the table comes from permanent storage the names at the top of each column must be used. Since there are several values in each column we must indicate which row we are referencing so we use a **subscript.** To obtain the balance for the 2nd record (27.14) do it this way:

Using a Subscript

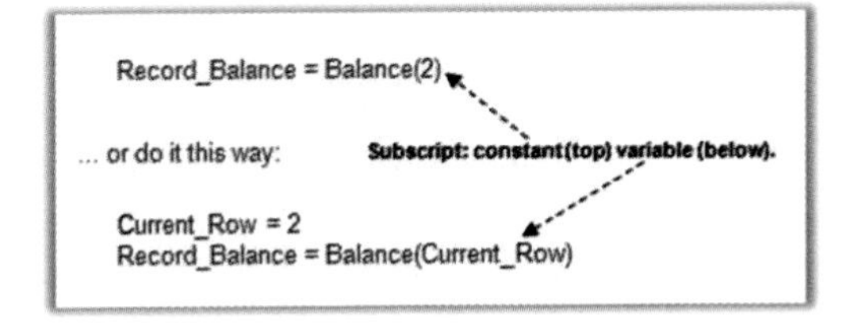

Record_Balance = Balance(2)
... or do it this way:
Subscript: constant(top) variable (below).
Current_Row = 2
Record_Balance = Balance(Current_Row)

Each Value in an Array Is Obtained Using a Subscript

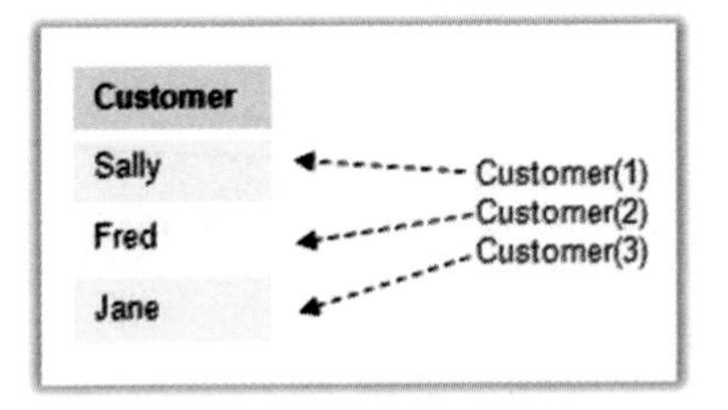

Each column of data in permanent storage is an array and has a name.

Using a constant subscript will not work if you want to use the same code to process more than one record. If you wish to examine several or all records in a table, a **variable subscript** is required as shown in the example that follows. Since we are working with a table the processing activity involves examining all records and selecting those that are relevant—therefore a variable subscript is required.

Repetition requires the use of a **loop** and the process is known as **iteration.** Here is the code that will iterate through all records of the Customers table shown above (the explanation follows):

Code to Iterate through All Records in a Table

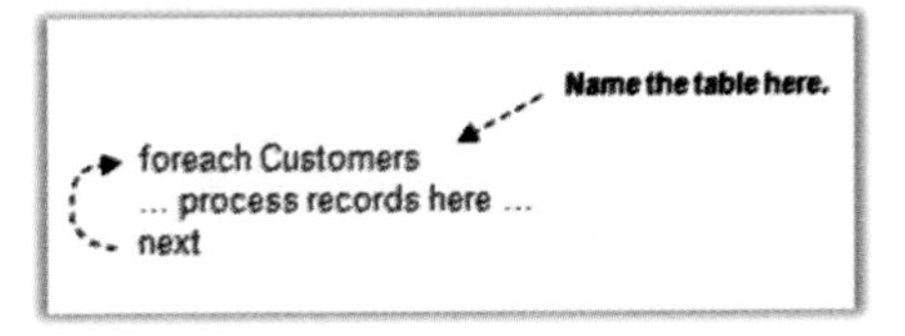

In this example, the code to be repeated is bounded by the **FOREACH** and **NEXT** statements. NEXT simply ends the repeated code ("the loop") but the "foreach" statement must be examined a little more fully.

FOREACH can be interpreted as "Repeat this code for each record in the Customers table." Since there are three records in the table the foreach . . . next loop will run three times. Each time the automatically created variable subscript, customers_row, will increase in value from 1 to 2 to 3. Here the total of all customer balances is computed.

A Loop Accesses all Items in an Array

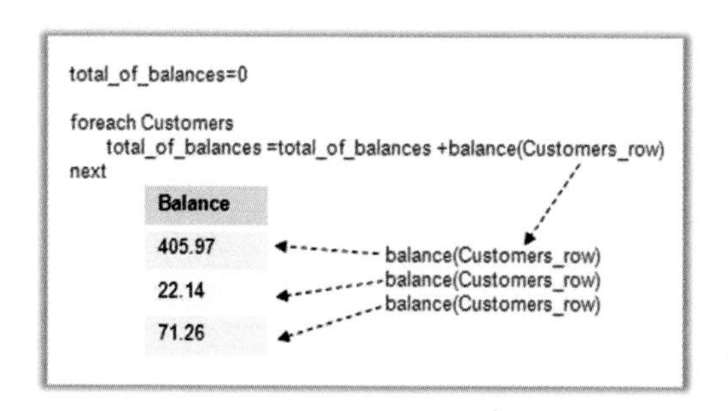

Suppose that we want to know how many customers owe at least $50.00. When the loop finishes, Big_Spenders will hold the value two because there are two customers who owe at least $50.00.

The variable subscript is automatically formed from the table name and the word row.

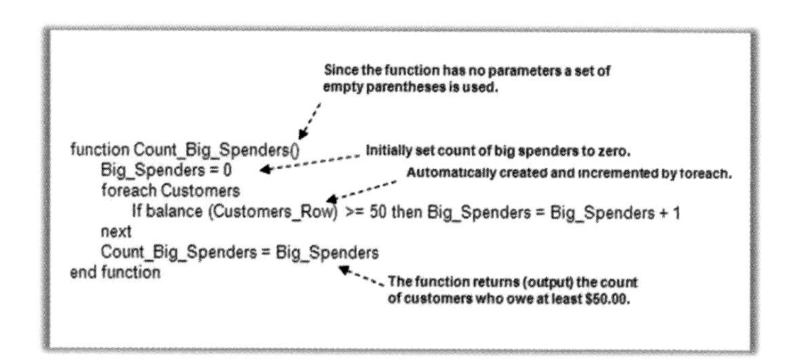

7.7.11 Creating a Table

In the previous section the Customers table was given to you. Suppose it were not? In that situation you could create a table as part of your code. This section describes how to do that by showing you how the Customers table (shown previously) would be created:

Creating a table begins with a TABLE statement and ends with /TABLE. The table statement provides a name for the table and the delimiter that separates column names and data values in records. Here is the TABLE statement for Customers:

Defining a Table

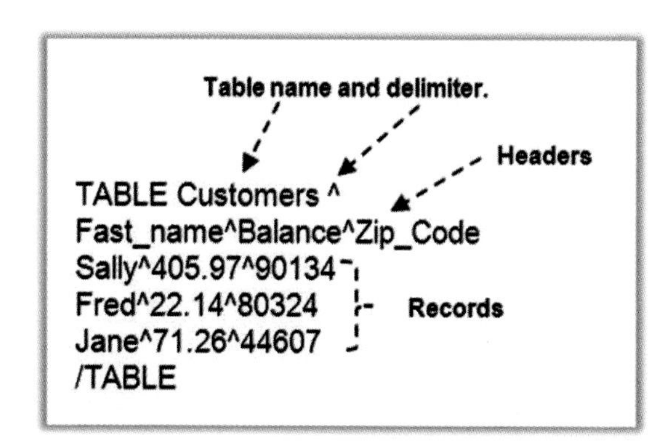

Never use the same name at the same time for a function, table, column, variable, or parameter. Each use of a name must be unique.

Include the completed table definition with your function as shown below. Presuming that the table was created as described this function and table definition will return the balance of a particular customer. The function accepts one parameter, name_to_search_for, which is the first name of the one customer we wish to find the balance of.

Combining Code with a Table

```
function get_balance(name_to_search_for)
foreach customers
    if name_to_search_for = First_name(customers_row) then
        get_balance = balance(customers_row)
    end if
next
end function

TABLE Customers ^
Fast_name^Balance^Zip_Code
Sally^405.97^90134
Fred^22.14^80324
Jane^71.26^44607
/TABLE
```

Searching for a string value requires a little thought. Strings are sequences of characters which may be upper or lower case. The string "apple" does not equal "APPLE" and neither equals "aPpLe" or "AppLE." To ensure that string values match use either case-conversion function. Here upper is used. A similar function lower is available, too. Upper("aPpLe") returns "APPLE." Case-sensitivity applies only to string data values, no where else.

String Case Conversion

```
if upper(name_to_search_for) = upper(Last_name(customers_row)) then
        get_balance = balance(customers_row)
end if
```

7.7.12 Display of Data or Results

The final activity in data processing is to display results. This is accomplished with the **DISPLAY** statement which causes data (words and numbers) to be displayed on the computer screen. These two statements together display a message and data on the same line:

Displaying Output

```
display "Your withdrawal was approved. Your balance is now: "
display Balance
```

If you want to move to the next line before continuing use display with new_line this way:

Separating Lines of Output

```
display "Withdrawal Amount: "
display Request
display new_line
display "New balance: "
display Balance
```

Numbers can be formatted several ways:

Formatting Numeric Output

```
display formatcurrency(Balance)

    Balance displays with $ and two digits after decimal point.

display formatnumber(Average,x)

    Average displays with x digits after decimal point. Make x: 0, 1, 2, 3...
```

7.8 Web Development

Developing Web applications normally involves using a programming language and a database management system. **HTML** and **XHTML** are used for building the user interface. Web applications are popular due to the omnipresence of the Web browser as a client, sometimes called a **thin client.** The ability to update and maintain Web applications on a server without distributing and installing software on potentially thousands of client computers is a key reason for their popularity.

Web applications follow the **client-server** model in which the server provides resources in response to requests from multiple clients. In the early days of networked client-server computing an executable program, providing the user interface was distributed to each client and was installed on each user's personal computer. Today, Web applications dynamically generate a series of Web documents (pages) in a standard format such as HTML/XHTML supported by common browsers. Client-side scripting in a standard language such as **JavaScript** is commonly included to add dynamic elements to the user interface. Generally, each individual Web page is delivered to the client as a static document, but the sequence of pages can provide an interactive experience, as user input is returned through Web form elements embedded in the page. During the session, the Web browser interprets and displays the pages, and acts as the universal client for any Web application.

A significant advantage of building Web applications to support standard browser features is that they should perform the same regardless of the operating system platform installed on any client. Rather than creating specific clients for Windows, Mac OS X, or Linux, the application can be written once, maintained on a server, and deployed almost anywhere.

Web applications usually follow a **three-tier** client-server **architecture** in which the user interface, application process logic, and data management are developed and maintained as independent modules, most often on separate platforms.

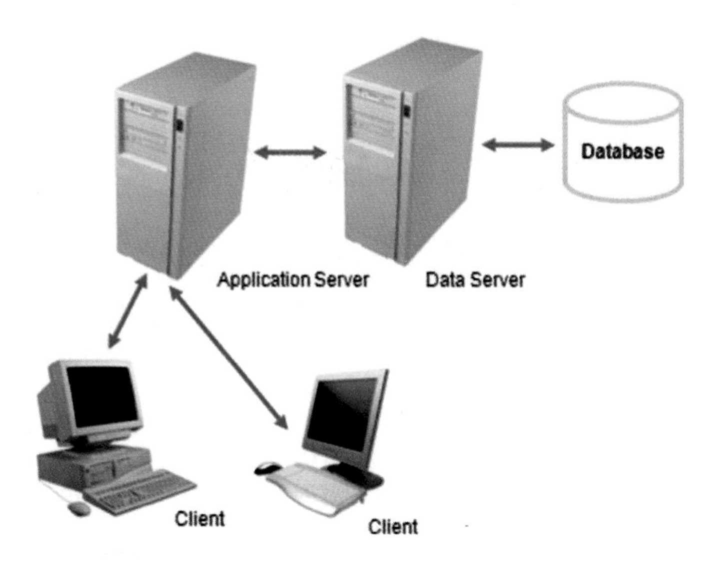

Web Application Three-Tier Client-Server Architecture

More information about the client-server architecture is found in the networking chapter. The focus on this chapter is computer programming and what follows is a discussion about basic Web application programming techniques. Application code on a server can be written in any language that the server can process. The language, however, must be able to coordinate with the application server's Web server software (**Apache** and **Internet Information Server** are the most commonly used). It is that software which manages the communication with clients and with the database server. Web server software receives client requests and activates application programs in response. It also delivers the client response that is prepared by the application program.

The Role of Web Server Software

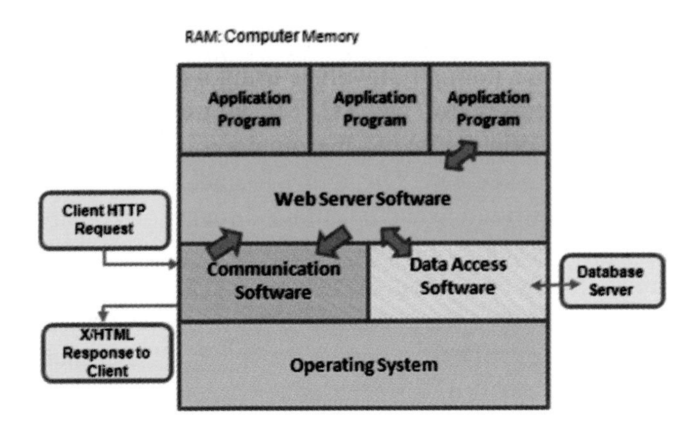

The **request-response** dialog is a standard feature of Web applications. The browser knows the standard communication protocols (HTTP and HTTPS) and also knows how to render the HTML or XHTML response that it receives from the server. The balance of this section illustrates how a server application program receives requests from a client, obtains necessary data, and formats a response.

Today, several programming languages are commonly used for development of Web application programs. **PHP** running on an **Apache** Web server and connected to the **MySQL** database manager is a well coupled combination of technologies. The three programs—PHP, Apache, and MySQL—are available without cost, and are packaged together as **LAMP** (for Linux servers) and **WAMP** (for Windows servers). Installing LAMP or WAMP requires administrator rights on a Linux or Windows server.

Microsoft's **.NET** environment is another collection of products and technologies that combines the features necessary to implement response-request applications. .NET is based on Microsoft's **.NET Framework** which is tightly coupled to the Windows operating system. The Visual Studio development platform offers several programming languages that can be used for Web development with **C#** and **Visual Basic** being the most popular. Database access is easily handled, too. Microsoft's Web server, **Internet Information Server** or **IIS** provides the linkage between components as it runs the **ASP .NET** Web application framework.

ASP, which stands for **Active Server Page,** is Microsoft's server-side script engine for dynamically generated Web pages. Most ASP pages are written in the same Visual Basic Script presented in an earlier section. The remainder of this section illustrates the implementation of request-response programs using ASP and VBScript. Instruction about connecting to a server DBMS (Database Management System) is also provided. At the conclusion of this section you will be able to build client-server programs and complete hands on exercises found at the end of the chapter.

Note: The server's response to the client is in the form of Web pages prepared in **HTML** and **XHTML.** For information about those topics refer to the chapter that discusses those languages in detail. **JavaScript** is discussed in the HTML and XHTML chapter, too. On the server the database is accessed using **SQL.** The SQL chapter presents the SQL language which can be used while developing Web applications.

Web Page User Input Web site visitors may be satisfied by clicking on hyperlinks and navigating to other URLs. That type of interaction is passive, in that the user is just a visitor and does not interact with a Web site other than to jump from page to page. The possibility of interaction, in which the user enters data and makes specific transactional requests, is valuable and accomplished by presenting the user with an HTML (or XHTML) Web page that includes a **form** for user input embedded within the page.

A Web page form is a rectangular area within a page that includes various controls that the user manipulates. These controls include **checkboxes, radio buttons, text areas, selection lists,** and **submit** and **refresh buttons.** Refer to the HTML chapter for details.

Web Page Forms A form is marked off by an opening form tag and a closing form tag. All interactive controls are placed between those tags. The opening form tag includes three important parameters:

- **Form Name** — Each form may be given a name that is unique within a Web page. Since a page could contain more than one form it is a good idea to name forms. Although it is not necessary, named forms are easier to connect to JavaScript code that could be included for execution in the Web browser.
- **Action** — The action is required. This is the specific Web address of the application program on a server that will receive the form and its content and process the request. The address includes the URL of the server and the path to the specific program that is requested. Since we are exploring ASP using VBScript programs the program names will have an extension of .ASP.
- **Method** — The method dictates how the form data will be packaged and transmitted to the server. There are several ways to do this but the most secure, and the only way recommended, is called **post.**

Here is a form that prompts a user for an ID and a password and provides a button that, when clicked, will submit the form to a server application program. Notice that an input box control is used for the ID and passwords. Also notice that each input control is given a name. That name is mandatory and must be unique for each control within a form and the name.

Login Web Form

```
<form name=logon_form action=http://myServer.com/logon.asp method=post>
ID: <input name=ID> <br>
Password: <input name=password type=password> <br>
<input type=submit value="Click to Logon">
</form>
```

Since a Web page is just text a simple editor like **Notepad** can be used. Make sure to use the extension **HTM.**

The Server Application Program An ASP program is really a Web page with processing logic included within. The page will have an extension of **ASP** and can also be prepared using Notepad. Any HTML (or XHTML) can be included in the page as if it were an HTM page. The portion of the page with processing logic is marked off by this pair of special tags:

An ASP Page

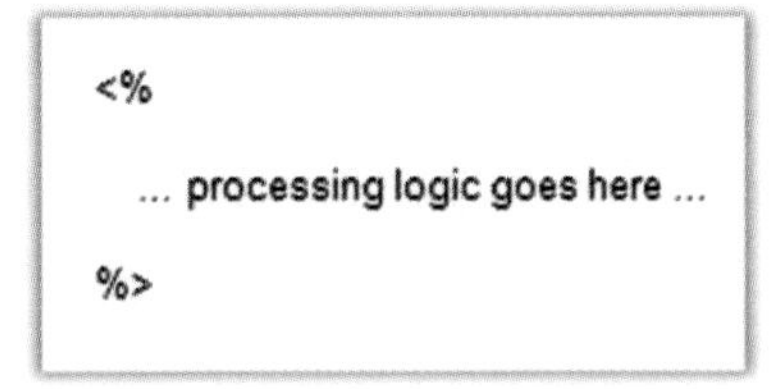
<%
... processing logic goes here ...
%>

Outside of the special tags any HTML is permitted. Inside the tags is Visual Basic Script code. In this logon request example, the code would accept the ID and password typed by the user and validate their correctness by accessing a database with user records.

Accepting User Input into an Application Program The response-request model requires that user input be received by a server application program for subsequent processing. The mechanism used in ASP is the **request object.** Specifically, this object has the **form property** that provides a list of all data values submitted by the user. The purpose of this property is to transfer the user entered data into program variables that can be processed. Note: All data transferred to a server application program is in string format. If the data is really numeric it must be data type converted in the application program.

The code to transfer form data to program variables is shown here. Keep in mind:

- Names used in the request.form property must exactly match form control names.
- Program variable names can be whatever the programmer wishes.

Transferring Form Data to Program Variables

```
<%
user_id = request.form("ID")
user_password = request.form("password")
%>
```

Accessing a Database It is easy to connect a server application program to a database manager provided the programmer:

- Knows the name and location of the database.
- Has authorization to access the database.
- Knows the code needed to open and use a connection to the database.

Connecting to a database requires building a connection string which:

- Identifies the specific DBMS (MySQL, Access, Oracle, SQL Server, etc.)
- Names the database.
- Provides authentication data (ID and password).

In this example we assume a SQL Server database named accounts. The IP address of the data server will be 401.251.8.67. The database ID and password will be as shown. Here the connection string is included in the example:

Connecting to a Database Manager

```
<%
user_id = request.form("ID")
user_password = request.form("password")
connString = "Provider=sqloledb; DATA SOURCE= 401.251.8.67;" &_
    "database='accounts';UID=x47;PWD=E902*32;"
%>
```

Remember, each DBMS requires a different connection string format. Here the string is spread over two lines due to space limitations. VBScript permits line continuation using the &_ character combination. Lines being concatenated may not have a blank line between them.

Once the string is built a connection is activated and may be used to execute SQL commands. The connection is activated as shown here. At the end of the program the connection should be closed to return memory and other resources to the operating system.

Activating a Connection

```
<%
user_id = request.form("ID")
user_password = request.form("password")
connString = "Provider=sqloledb; DATA SOURCE= 401.251.8.67;" &_
    "database='accounts';UID=x47;PWD=E902*32;"
Set aConnection= Server.CreateObject("ADODB.Connection")
aConnection.Open connString
    ... SQL operations go here...
aConnection.close
set  aConnection = nothing
%>
```

Processing SQL With the database connection open the next step is to search for a user record. The ID and password received from the Web page form will be validated using a database. First the SQL must be created as a string.

The variables user_id and user_password are holding values obtained from the user. User_id's value will be used to build an SQL statement to determine if the ID is valid. In the next illustrations only the SQL operations area of the example is shown. Assuming the database's table of user accounts is named customers, this is how a SELECT statement is built to obtain one customer record.

Building an SQL String

```
SQL = "select * from customers where id = " + user_id
```

If we assume the user ID received from the Web page was 613, this is the string that would be stored in the variable SQL as a result of the code shown above:

The SQL String

```
select * from customers where id = 613
```

Now that the string is built, it is executed. On receiving a response (called a **record set**) from the DBMS these possibilities could occur:

- ID is not valid (no record found).
- ID is valid but the password is incorrect (record found).
- ID and password are valid.

The following code executes the SQL string and handles the three possible outcomes. At the end of the SQL operations area the record set is closed. Response to the user is given using the response object's write property as shown.

Processing SQL

```
set customerRecord = aConnection.execute(SQL)

If customerRecord.eof then
    response.write "ID is invalid."
elseif customerRecord("password") <> user_password then
    response.write "Invalid password."
else
    response.write "Welcome!"
end if

customerRecord.close

set customerRecord = nothing
```

Formatting Output There is really no mystery to the appearance of output as rendered in the browser. Response.write sends the browser a text stream which includes ordinary HTML or XHTML for formatting instructions. If we wanted to emphasize the output already demonstrated it could be produced this way:

Formatting Output

```
If customerRecord.eof then
    response.write "<font color=orange>ID is invalid.</font>"
elseif customerRecord("password") <> user_password then
    response.write "<font color=red>Invalid password.</font>"
else
    response.write "<h1>Welcome!</h1>"
end if
```

Processing a Record Set A shopping Web site would allow visitors to view information about products as they shop. Records about products would likely be in a database. Here is how ASP can be used to respond to a request to view an alphabetized list of all products costing less than $50. Notice the use of **moveNext.** The logic of the loop that processes the record set, customerRecord, requires that the end of the record set be reached. Unless moveNext is used no progress is made through the record set and the end is never reached. This is known as an **infinite loop** and is an example of a **logic error.**

Iterating a Set of Records

```
SQL = "select * from products where price < 50 order by productName"
set customerRecord = aConnection.execute(SQL)
do until customerRecord.eof
    response.write customerRecord("ProductName") + "<br>"
    customerRecord.moveNext
loop
customerRecord.close
set customerRecord = nothing
```

Chapter ASP Exercises At the end of this chapter you will find ASP exercises. For each you will write an ASP application program in VBScript. Each program, known as a script, is typed into a text file with extension ASP. Include the <% and %> tags and type your code between them. The data needed for the connection string will be given to you. Start your program with a function named "main." Your code will look like this:

Completing Exercises

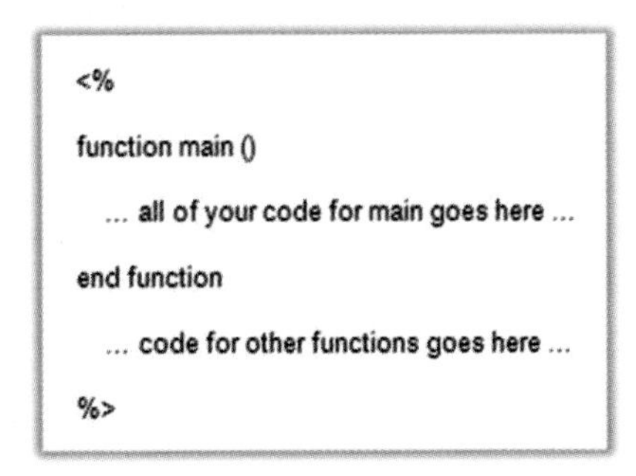

```
<%
function main ()
    ... all of your code for main goes here ...
end function
    ... code for other functions goes here ...
%>
```

If main is to receive data as parameters then change references in main's declaration accordingly.

7.9 Summary

Computer programming is about translating ideas into a reality that is experienced by a computer user. The reality can be visual (clicking a mouse button or viewing a web page), informational (reviewing a stock portfolio or viewing a clothing catalog), entertaining (viewing a movie or playing a game), transactional (reserving an airline ticket or taking a test). Programs provide e-mail, instant messaging, and Internet phone services. Everything that occurs when a computer is used involves software created by a computer programmer.

Hardware is the physical part of a computer system. It includes the electronic circuitry, input and output devices, data and program storage devices, and memory for program execution. It would be impossible to process data into information with a computer alone. Computer programs, from the operating system on up, give a series of instructions that command the hardware to act in specific ways.

Computer programming involves writing instructions for a computer to follow as it processes data. The instructions are usually written in a high-level language and later translated into the computer's native language: machine language. There are different programming paradigms and architectures, with object-oriented programming having become quite popular in the last decade. Rapid development and the reuse of code along with comprehensive system testing have become important objectives of program developers.

Several fundamentals are important to a programmer regardless of the programming language used. The structure of data and the basic operations of conditional testing and iteration are found in all languages. The programmer does have many languages to select from. Each has its own syntax and form and has features and potential that makes it especially suited for particular tasks. Sharing data and communication between programs is possible because of the standardized binary code, ASCII, Unicode, and the emergence of XML as a platform neutral data transport.

Developers are aided by various tools that are built into data management products. Tools for generating forms and reports make data entry and reporting easier and faster. Code generators can shorten the time for a programmer to complete a finished application. The macro processing environment in Office 2007 allows automation of common tasks, like mail merge, that combines data from Excel with letters prepared in Word. A macro recorder translates mouse clicks and menu selections into VBA program code that can be explored, edited, and refined later.

Programs follow a course of action known as an algorithm. The specific steps can be presented visually in a flow chart which can then be translated into program code. Various flowchart symbols indicate certain types of operations that follow known patterns like input of data, branching, iteration, and display of output. Operations exist in any programming situation, whether standalone or on the Web.

Web applications involve three partners: the client's interface, processing logic implemented in an application program, and a database. The three-tier client-server architecture model provides the framework for Web-based applications. Programs written to support Web applications require a connection to a database manager and a method for processing data in cooperation with a database.

EXERCISES

Exercise 7.1

What is the difference between application and system software?

Exercise 7.2

What is the difference between compilers and interpreters? Why would one be used instead of the other?

Exercise 7.3

What is unique about machine language?

Exercise 7.4

What is syntax? Give three examples of programming language syntax.

Exercise 7.5

What is binary code?

Exercise 7.6

What does a linkage editor produce and why is that significant?

Exercise 7.7

What is a bytecode interpreter? What does it do?

Exercise 7.8

What is the system development lifecycle? In what stages would programmers be actively involved?

Exercise 7.9

How do bottom-up and top-down design differ?

Exercise 7.10

Discuss the differences between unit and system testing. Why are both important in a testing program?

Exercise 7.11

What is a data structure and why are they important to programmers? Give two real world examples each of a queue and stack. Do not use examples presented in this book.

Exercise 7.12

What is different between constants and variables? Give an example of each.

Exercise 7.13

Give an example of a compound condition and draw a truth table that depicts the condition's possible outcomes.

Exercise 7.14

Contrast procedural and non-procedural programming languages. Give an example of each.

Exercise 7.15

Discuss the three categories of programming errors and give an example of each.

Exercise 7.16

What is a function?

Exercise 7.17

What is a logical operator?

Exercise 7.18

What is iteration and why is it an important programming tool?

Exercise 7.19

Describe the three-tier architecture used for Web development.

Exercise 7.20

Discuss the role of Web server software. What functions does it perform?

Exercise 7.21

What is an infinite loop? What does it mean to a programmer?

The Following Are Hands-on Exercises

Exercise 7.22

Record a macro in Excel named Set_Font that sets the font of the active cell to bold and underlined.

Exercise 7.23

Add a button to the worksheet and run Set_Font when the button is clicked. The button should have a "Set Font" on the face.

Exercise 7.24

In the module where Set_Font is stored add a new subroutine named Normal_Font that restores the font of the active cell to not bold and not underlined. Add a button that runs Normal_Font and has the name Normal_Font on the button face.

Exercise 7.25

Write a subroutine named Conditional_Color that changes the interior color of the active cell. Assume the active cell contains a numeric value. The two ColorIndex values to use are 10 and 27. If the value of the active cell is positive set the interior color to 10 otherwise set it to 27.

Exercise 7.26

Write a subroutine named Square_List that begins with the active cell and continues to the next row down until an empty cell is encountered. For each cell processed square the numeric value in it and store the result two columns to the right.

Exercise 7.27

Write a subroutine named Get_Input that uses the InputBox to obtain a number from the user and store the data value in the active cell. Next, the subroutine will divide the number in half and store the result one row below the active cell.

Exercise 7.28

Write a function named SQUARE_IT that correctly implements the steps shown in this flowchart:

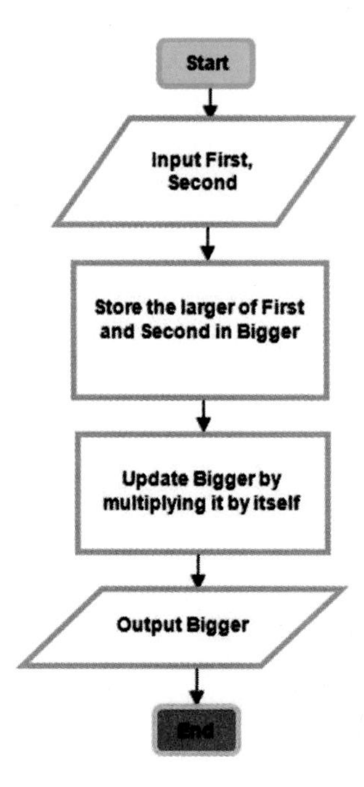

Exercise 7.29

Write a function named square_max which:

1. Accepts two numeric parameters (any names are fine).
2. Finds the maximum of the numbers.
3. Squares the maximum number.
4. Returns (outputs) the square.

Exercise 7.30

Assume a table named customers with two columns: name and debt.

Write a function named count_customers that accepts no arguments and returns the number of records in the table customers.

Exercise 7.31

Assume the same table named customers used in the previous exercise.

Write a function named get_debt that accepts one argument (the name of a customer) and returns that customer's debt.

Exercise 7.32

Perform these steps:

1. Consider this table:

Last Name	First Name	Address	Zip Code
Kline	John	47 Main Ave.	43902
Masters	Thomas	108 Main Ave.	
Water	Mary	108 Center Blvd.	47091
Houseman	Richard	401 Mills Ave.	43902
Jones	Sam	47 Main Ave.	
Delman	Wendy	401 Mills Ave.	

2. Use a TABLE statement to create an index for this table. The table will have two columns: Address and Row. Address is a data value shown above. Row is the row number that each record is found in. Use any delimiter you wish.
3. Name the table customer_index.
4. Write a function named get_record_num that accepts one argument (the address of a customer) and returns the customer's data record number.

Exercise 7.33

Use the connection information given you by the instructor and create a connection string.

The Following Are ASP Exercises. Refer to the ASP section for instruction about how to prepare your solutions.

Exercise 7.34

Assume this Web page:

```
<form name=transaction action=http://310.43.5.123/transact.asp method=post>
<input type=hidden name=custAccountNum value=89037>
How much do you wish to deposit? <input name=amountNum> <br><br>
<input type=submit value="Click when ready.">
</form>
```

Write an ASP page that will accept and display the two values submitted in the form. You do not connect to a database for this exercise. Include your code in function main().

Exercise 7.35

Assume this Web page:

```
<form name=transaction action=http://310.43.5.123/transact.asp method=post>
<input type=hidden name=custAccountNum value=89037>
Enter new balance: <input name=NewBalance>
<input type=submit value="Click when ready to update balance.">
</form>
```

Write an ASP page that includes a function main() so that it:

1. Accepts the HTML data from the Web page form.
2. Prepares the SQL string that would update the Balance column for the customer's account in the customer's table.
3. Returns the SQL string.

Assume the customer table has numeric columns called AccountNumber and Balance. You do not connect to a database for this exercise.

Updating a database record is similar to retrieving a record using a SELECT statement. The WHERE clause used while updating is identical to the SELECT's WHERE clause. Here is an example of the SQL that updates a student's record with a semester final grade. Notice how the connection is used; no record set is returned. Notice that the student's ID and grade are hard coded in the SQL string. For your answer use the data received from the client and build the SQL string. Do not connect to the database. The function main() will build the SQL string and return it.

```
SQL = "update students set grade = 97 where studentID = 403"

aConnection.execute(SQL)
```

Exercise 7.36

Assume this Web page:

```
<form name=transaction action=http://310.43.5.123/transact.asp method=post>

<input type=hidden name=productID value=16>

<input type=hidden name=productPrice value=17.47>

Select quantity you wish to purchase: <select input name=QTY>
    <option>1</option>
    <option>2</option>
    <option>3</option>
</select>

<input type=submit value="Click when ready.">

</form>
```

Write the ASP page that includes a function main() so that it:

1. Accepts the HTML form data for price and quantity.
2. Computes the product of price and quantity giving the extended cost.
3. Returns the extended cost.

You do not connect to a database for this exercise. Remember, data obtained by an ASP program is always in string format. Calculating the product requires numeric data. To convert numbers stored as strings to real numbers use VBScript's CDBL function this way:

```
testScore = CDBL(testScoreAsString)

testScoreBonus = testScore * bonusPercent
```

Exercise 7.37

Assume a database table named products with these column definitions:

Column	Data Type
productName	String
productCategory	String
productPrice	Currency
productWeight	Number

Write an ASP page that includes a function main() so that it:

1. Builds a record set of all product records where the productCategory is 43.
2. Calculates the total of all product Prices.
3. Returns the total.

The connection information will be given to you by your instructor.

DATA AND INFORMATION, DATABASE AND SQL

CHAPTER 8

Information systems (IS) support human **decision making.** An IS is typically assumed to include computer hardware and software but this is not always the case. Humans may record data for later analysis in non-computerized environments like a diary or a notebook. Regardless of the recording configuration, the foundation of any information system is the **data** that becomes relevant to humans when it is processed into **information.** Data itself is not particularly useful, but when it is processed and analyzed it may become information which is the basis for decision making.

Before we explore Information Handling more fully we should develop a clear understanding of basics. In the first chapter we learned about the Input-Process-Output model and the relationship between data and information. In this chapter we explore in depth what data is and how it can be perceived as information.

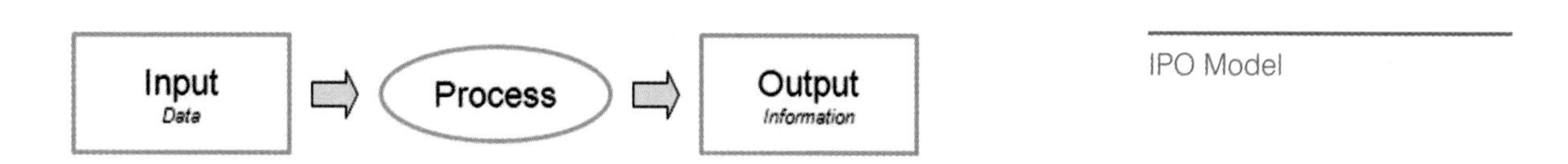

IPO Model

Data are facts that may or may not be relevant to decision making. Facts (numbers, characters, words, images) alone mean nothing until they are combined with other data and thus provide a context for understanding – they then become the basis for information. The process of providing a **context** for data is known as **data processing** and that is the fundamental activity of an information system. A computer-based information system is a set of components arranged to collect data, process it, and convert it into information. In effect, it is the integration of hardware and software technologies with humans.

Data processing often involves including data preserved in a storage device (disk, jump drive, CD, etc.) and the IPO model can be updated to reflect data storage this way:

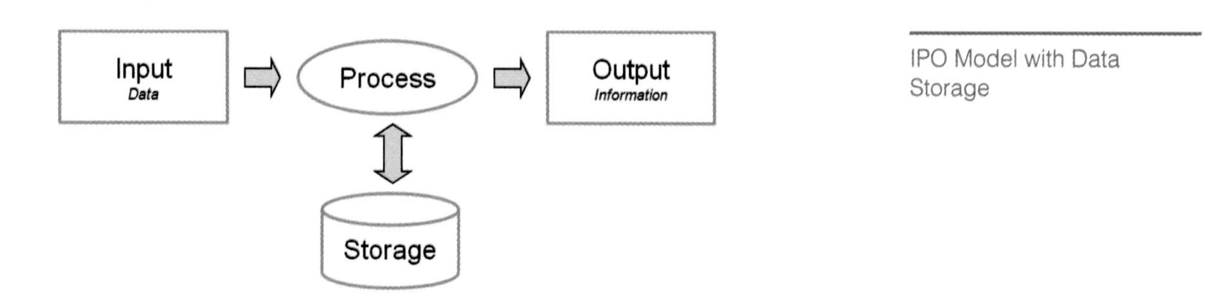

IPO Model with Data Storage

Technology is found everywhere in the home and workplace — in laptop and desktop computers, personal digital assistants (PDAs), and wireless telephones, but people remain the core consumer of information. The use of hardware and software greatly enhances our ability to derive useful information from the vast deluge of data that we experience and have access to. Technology can be used to collect, analyze, and package information so that it becomes a useful tool for individuals and business.

In an earlier chapter we learned about the **Input-Process-Output** model and the relationship between data and information. In this chapter we discuss in more depth what data is and how it can be perceived as information.

Here we first explore the relationship between data and information and develop the concept of **file processing** with data stored in records which provide a context for the data. We also introduce consideration of how records might be stored for efficient retrieval. We then move on to a discussion of **database management system** (DBMS) technology that is used to manage databases. The emphasis is on relational database management systems (RDBMS) with Microsoft Access used as a vehicle to present numerous examples. The last section of this chapter presents **SQL** (Structured Query Language) which is used to enter, manipulate, and retrieve data from a database. SQL is contrasted with **QBE** (Query by Example) used in Access. Examples of database design and creation using Microsoft Access are presented. Numerous hands-on exercises about file processing, Access, and SQL are found at the end of this chapter. First we introduce data and information.

8.1 Data and Information

There is a subtle but very important difference between data and information:

- Data are facts.
- Information is data (facts) grouped together and put into a context.

This difference is best illustrated by example:

Here is one piece of data – a fact: *18.43*

Here are some additional data: *8.21* *210.00* *59.81*

The addition of three more data values does not produce information. Looking at 18.43, 8.21, 210.00, and 59.81 tells us nothing. We presume that these are numbers but what do they represent? Do the numbers even belong together? Without some additional clues it is impossible to tell. Formatting the numbers like this adds something:

$18.43 *$8.21* *$210.00* *$59.81*

Still, however, we do not know what the currency represents. Labels might help:

Gas	*$18.43*
Lunch	*$8.21*
Rent	*$210.00*
Groceries	*$59.81*

Now the numbers are making more sense. We are building a **context** for the data. The context allows us to ascribe meaning to the data.

The transformation of data into information is subjective. No specific rule dictates when the transformation is achieved. In fact even with the labels added we can still not be certain that the four currency amounts belong together. We might argue that we still do not know what the context is. Did we buy gas or sell it? Are these expenses or revenue? Who was involved? When did it occur? Perhaps we still need more context before we can claim information. What exactly does data in a context look like?

Information is data in a context.

Adding a final value, 9/3/2007, and label, "Date of Expenses," completes the picture. Now arguably we have a context and therefore we have information! This collection of data and labels becomes a **record:**

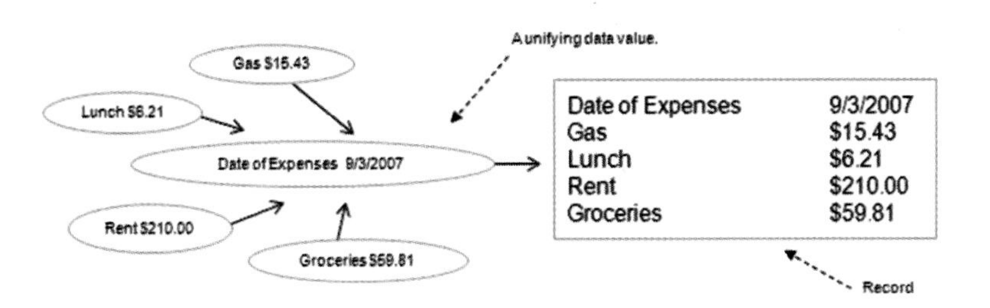

Information Is Data in a Context – a Record

8.2 Records, Tables, Files, and Decision Making

A record is data in a context and is considered the fundamental **unit of information.** What this means is that pieces of data that belong together provide a context for each other. As you see below the date of expenses and the four expense items (gas, lunch, rent, groceries) tell a story – they belong together – they are expenses for the same day – they form a record!

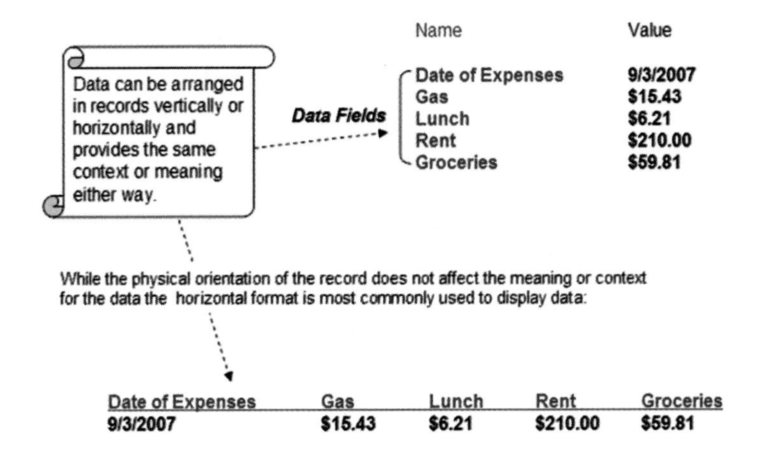

A Horizontal Record

A Record is the Basic Unit of Information.

Tables Records are usually grouped together in a **table** as shown next. It only makes sense to group together records that are about the same kind of data. It is important to realize that the first row, the row with the field names, is not a record. There are six records and not seven:

Header →	Customer	Item	Price	Quantity	Extended Cost	Shipping	Total
Records	Winston	Chair	$ 99.99	$ 2.00	$ 199.98	$ 32.00	$231.98
	Rudy	Desk	$219.00	$ 1.00	$ 219.00	$ 30.00	$249.00
	Samuels	Chair	$ 99.99	$ 6.00	$ 599.94	$ 60.00	$659.94
	Rudy	Rug	$107.00	$ 1.00	$ 107.00	$ 25.00	$132.00
	Jones	Clock	$ 25.67	$ 2.00	$ 51.34	$ 12.00	$ 63.34
	Winston	Desk	$301.00	$ 1.00	$ 301.00	$ 50.00	$351.00

A Table of Six Records

Sometimes a record is missing a piece or pieces of data. Missing values are said to be **null.** Null values do not represent blanks or zeros. A null value means that no data has ever been put in that location. The presence of null values can add to the complexity of processing data into information.

A Null Value

Last Name	First Name	Phone Number	Address	Zip Code
Green	Sally	675-1902	12 Main St.	29013
Samuels	Bertha	901-3098	16 Water Blvd.	
Ritter	Alfred	612-9012	192 Center Rd	89128

Null value.

A table is normally stored in a **file** on a computer's disk. The file is given a name so that the data it contains can be retrieved later:

Tables Are Persistently Stored in Files on Disks or Other Storage Devices

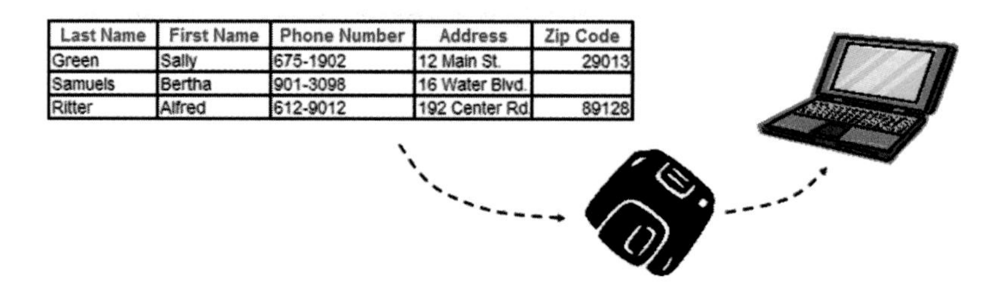

Last Name	First Name	Phone Number	Address	Zip Code
Green	Sally	675-1902	12 Main St.	29013
Samuels	Bertha	901-3098	16 Water Blvd.	
Ritter	Alfred	612-9012	192 Center Rd	89128

Decision Making We wish to fly from San Diego to Tampa. We will buy a ticket if the average ticket price of past prices for that route is higher than best current ticket price we can find, which happens to be $208.00. Do we buy a ticket?

This is summarized in the **logic flow chart** depicted next:

Decision Making Depicted in a Logic Flow Chart

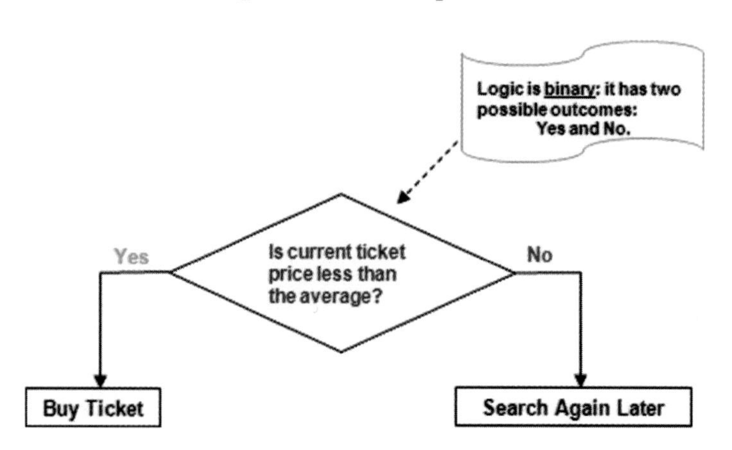
Logic is binary: it has two possible outcomes: Yes and No.
Is current ticket price less than the average?
Yes
No
Buy Ticket
Search Again Later

Using the table of flight information (below) we begin by selecting only the records for the relevant route (San Diego to Tampa) and then calculating the average ticket cost for the selected records. The process of selecting certain records from a table is called performing a **query** or applying a **filter.** Once the San Diego to Tampa records are selected the query result would look like this:

Relevant Records Selected with Filter Applied

Origin	Destination	Ticket Cost
San Diego	Boston	$ 59.00
Denver	Philadelphia	$ 198.00
San Diego	Tampa	$ 215.00
Portland	Boston	$ 112.00
San Diego	Tampa	$ 205.00
Denver	Chicago	$ 157.00
Tampa	San Diego	$ 200.00

Origin	Destination	Ticket Cost
San Diego	Tampa	$ 215.00
San Diego	Tampa	$ 205.00

Calculating the average ticket price completes the original objective. At this point instructions for processing the data are given and performed. The instructions are "add both selected ticket costs and divide by two." The result is an average price of $210.00 computed as ($215.00 + $205.00) / 2. Since the current selling price of tickets, $208.00, is lower than the average of past flights, $210.00, we believe that we have a good deal and decide to purchase the tickets now.

The method for applying the filter (locating specific records for retrieval) depends on how a table's records are organized in a file. The efficiency of different file organization methods varies depending on data retrieval requirements described later in this chapter.

8.2.1 Rules about Records

Data records placed into tables are governed by four important rules listed here:

Record Rules:
The order of the rows does not matter.
The order of the columns does not matter.
All records must have the same number of fields.
All data in a column (field) must be the same type.

Rules About Records

These first two rules are illustrated next. Examine both tables and ensure that the three records of the first table are replicated in the second. The row order and column order have been changed. Be sure that you can determine that the records are the same.

When we say that the order of rows and columns does not matter we mean that the **information content** of the records is unaltered by any storage arrangement.

A specific record order may make it easier for people to use the records but the information content is not different.

Last Name	First Name	Phone Number	Address	Zip Code
Green	Sally	675-1902	12 Main St.	29013
Samuels	Bertha	901-3098	16 Water Blvd.	
Ritter	Alfred	612-9012	192 Center Rd.	89128

First Name	Address	Phone Number	Zip Code	Last Name
Bertha	16 Water Blvd.	901-3098		Samuels
Alfred	192 Center Rd.	612-9012	89128	Ritter
Sally	12 Main St.	675-1902	29013	Green

Rules 1 and 2: The Same Records – Rows and Columns Scrambled – Same Information

The third rule requires that the structure of the table must be uniform from top to bottom. Each record must have the same number of data fields (columns) throughout the table with no exceptions. Examine below and notice how the irregularity of the records might make processing difficult or impossible.

How exactly would you (or a computer) interpret the data values shown here? What column headings would you use? The first column could be "First Name" followed by "Last Name" but then what? "Phone Number?" "Title?"

Rule 3: The Table Must Have a Consistent Structure

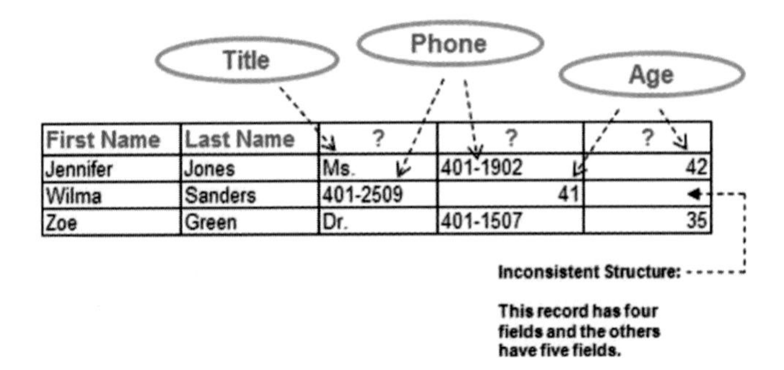

To conform to Rule 3 the table would be changed to this:

Rule 3 Satisfied

First Name	Last Name	Title	Phone	Age
Jennifer	Jones	Ms.	401-1902	42
Wilma	Sanders		401-2509	41
Zoe	Green	Dr.	401-1507	35

Null Value

The fourth rule builds upon Rule 3 by further ensuring the integrity of data stored in a table. The third rule requires that the structure of all records in a table must be the same. This means that the number of columns (data fields) in each record must be consistent. The fourth rule requires that all data in each column must be of the same type from top to bottom. Consider this figure and see if you understand the issues the illustration presents. Rule 3 is satisfied – all records have six columns (null values are ok), but Rule 4 is violated:

Rule 4: The Table Must Have Consistent Data

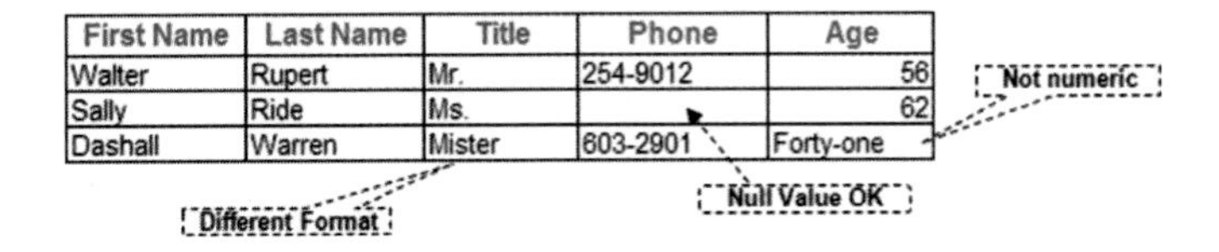

To conform to Rule 4 the table would be changed to this:

Rule 4 Satisfied

First Name	Last Name	Title	Phone	Age
Walter	Rupert	Mr.	254-9012	56
Sally	Ride	Ms.		62
Dashall	Warren	Mr.	603-2901	41

8.2.2 How Records Are Stored

Collections of records are stored together in a file which is typically stored on a disk. The particulars of how sections of the disk are allocated for files are quite advanced and beyond the scope of this book. Here, however, the simplest type of file storage, a **flat file,** is described. Flat files are easily created and edited using a simple text editor like Notepad.

As in any file, a record is a collection of data values (including null values if they exist). A record occupies one row in a file. Consider this table:

Last Name	First Name	Phone #	Address	Zip Code
Brown	Fred	618-2314	215 Main St.	34023
Smith	Betty	292-1902	47 Oak Ave.	
Trent	Michael		101 Center Blvd.	34029

If this table were to be stored as a flat file prepared using Notepad (or some similar program) we would have a row of column names followed by a row for each record. Notepad does not provide a grid for the storage and display of column names and data values. Instead each name or value must be separated from those adjacent by use of a **delimiter.**

The most common delimiter is a comma, and a flat file which uses a comma as a delimiter is known as a "**comma delimited file.**" The table above created as a comma delimited file looks like this:

```
Last Name,First Name,Phone #,Address,Zip Code
Brown,Fred,618-2314,215 Main St., 34023
Smith,Betty,292-1902,47 Oak Ave.,
Trent,Michael,,101 Center Blvd.,34029
```

Delimiters

Almost any character that is not typically found in data may be used as a delimiter. Here the same table is presented using ^ to delimit data values and column names.

```
Last Name^First Name^Phone #^Address^,Zip Code
Brown^Fred^618-2314^215 Main St.^ 34023
Smith^Betty^,292-1902^47 Oak Ave.^
Trent^Michael^^101 Center Blvd.^34029
```

Very Important: Whether or not null values are found, the same number of delimiters would be used in every record. Notice the **null values** in the previous table and look at the flat file implementations (with either delimiter) and be certain that you understand what was done to accommodate null values:

8.2.3 File Organization

Once records have been created and stored on a disk file they can be used for decision making, which involves retrieving relevant records and analyzing the content of those records.

There are two methods of organizing records in a file. When deciding how to organize your data consideration must be given to ease of use and efficiency of data retrieval. Each method presents particular benefits:

- Sequential Record Placement
- Random Record Placement

Sequential Record Placement Alphabetical listings are a good example of sequentially arranged records. Finding a particular friend's phone number is easier when the records are alphabetized by last name and then first name:

Sequentially Arranged Records – Alphabetical by Last Name

Last Name	First Name	Phone #	Address	Zip Code
Apple	Sally	891-1902	108 Main Ave.	
Brown	Fred	618-2314	215 Main St.	34023
Green	Jimmy	292-1902	47 Oak Ave.	
Randolf	Michael	672-1907	108 Center Blvd.	34029
Smith	Walter	292-1902	47 Oak Ave.	

When records are arranged sequentially each new record is sorted into the proper place as it is added to the table.

Suppose that a new record (below) for Wilma Jones on 204 East Lane is added to the table above. Since the records are arranged alphabetically you should be able to determine where the new record will be stored in the table. *Before adding a record, be sure to check that Record Rules 3 and 4 are not violated. Since the new record has the same number of columns (5) and the same type of data as the records above, it is ok to add it.*

A Record Is Added to a Sequential Table by Sorting it into Place

A record to be added to the table.

Jones	Wilma	902-1892	204 East Lane	39012

Last Name	First Name	Phone #	Address	Zip Code
Apple	Sally	891-1902	108 Main Ave.	
Brown	Fred	618-2314	215 Main St.	34023
Green	Jimmy	292-1902	47 Oak Ave.	39012
Jones	Wilma	902-1892	204 East Lane	39012
Randolf	Michael	672-1907	108 Center Blvd.	34029
Smith	Walter	292-1902	47 Oak Ave.	

Sorting records into proper place while adding them to a table takes time and effort but the sequential ordering of the records is often useful. In this example searching for a particular friend is easy because the names are in alphabetical order.

Adding records without sorting them into place is faster and takes less effort.

Random Record Placement If the physical order of records is not important then random record placement may be used. Generally this means that records are **appended** to the end of the file as they are created – they are not sorted into place. Records are appended in chronological order – the order they are created in.

So if your list of friends and their phone numbers were stored in the order that each was added to the list, the records might look as shown below. You will see that the information content is the same as in the table above but the order of the records is different (rule #1). The downside is that retrieval of specific records may be slower and more complicated. Here the new record for Wilma Jones is appended to the end of the table:

Randomly Arranged Records – Chronological Order

Last Name	First Name	Phone #	Address	Zip Code
Green	Jimmy	292-1902	47 Oak Ave.	
Apple	Sally	891-1902	108 Main Ave.	
Randolf	Michael	672-1907	108 Center Blvd.	34029
Brown	Fred	618-2314	215 Main St.	34023
Smith	Walter	292-1902	47 Oak Ave.	
Jones	Wilma	902-1892	204 East Lane	39012

Most recently added record is appended to end of table.

Random record arrangements often are used because of the extra effort required to sort records into sequential order each time a new record is added to a table.

Besides, what sequential order would you want the records sorted into? Suppose you wanted the records sorted alphabetically for retrieval by name and in some other order such as by phone number. If you want the records sorted by name and also phone number what do you do? Since records can only be physically stored in one order this requirement becomes a challenge.

The solution is to add the records to the table in the order that they are created (use random organization) and additionally use indexes (described later) for retrieval. Because random files alone do not easily lend themselves to record retrieval the addition of indexes allows specific records in random files to be quickly and easily located.

8.2.4 Retrieving Records

As noted earlier, processing data involves analyzing data found in specific records. Searching a table for records can be accomplished in different ways depending on how the records are organized.

There are two ways of retrieving records from a table:

- Top Down Search
- Index Search

Top Down Search Searching typically involves starting from the first record and scanning down through all records until a match is found or until all records are considered. This is known as a "top down search."

Suppose (below) that you want to find Walter Smith's phone number. You start at the top and consider the first record which belongs to Jimmy Green. Since Jimmy Green is not Walter Smith you go to the next record where you find Sally Apple and not Walter Smith. You continue this process until you reach the 5th row where you find Walter Smith. The 5th row (record) gives you Walter's phone number. It took five **comparisons** to find the record you wanted. We say the search stopped after five comparisons.

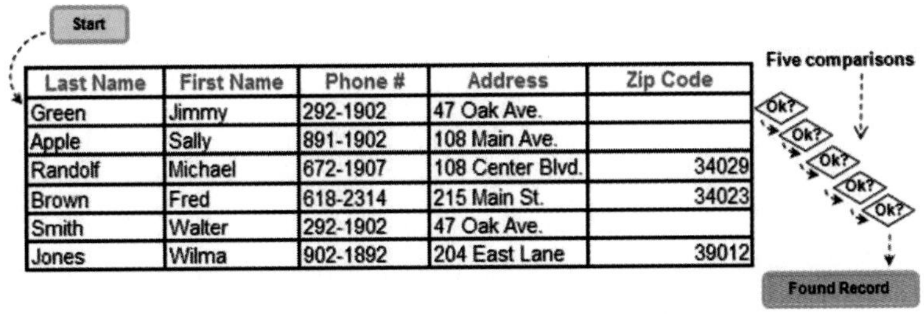

Start

Last Name	First Name	Phone #	Address	Zip Code
Green	Jimmy	292-1902	47 Oak Ave.	
Apple	Sally	891-1902	108 Main Ave.	
Randolf	Michael	672-1907	108 Center Blvd.	34029
Brown	Fred	618-2314	215 Main St.	34023
Smith	Walter	292-1902	47 Oak Ave.	
Jones	Wilma	902-1892	204 East Lane	39012

Five comparisons
Ok? Ok? Ok? Ok? Ok?
Found Record

Top Down Search for Walter Smith

When we search for records we must be mindful of how efficient the search is. Top down searches (while easy to understand) are not particularly efficient. Since a record could be in any row of the table then on the average one half of the records will be considered before the desired record is found. This is summarized as follows:

$$\mathbf{C}_{\text{(number of comparisons)}} = \mathbf{N}_{\text{(number of records)}} / \mathbf{2}$$

In this example we can stop the search as soon as Walter Smith's record is found. If, however, we wish to select a group of several records that match a certain criteria then we must perform an "**exhaustive search**" of the table. All six records must be considered because multiple records might match the search criteria (filter) so we must examine every record. This is different from a search for one specific record (previous figure) where we stop after the 5th comparison.

Suppose that we want to view the records of only those people living at "47 Oak Ave.". The search would operate as shown this way:

Exhaustive Search Applying a Filter for "47 Oak Ave."

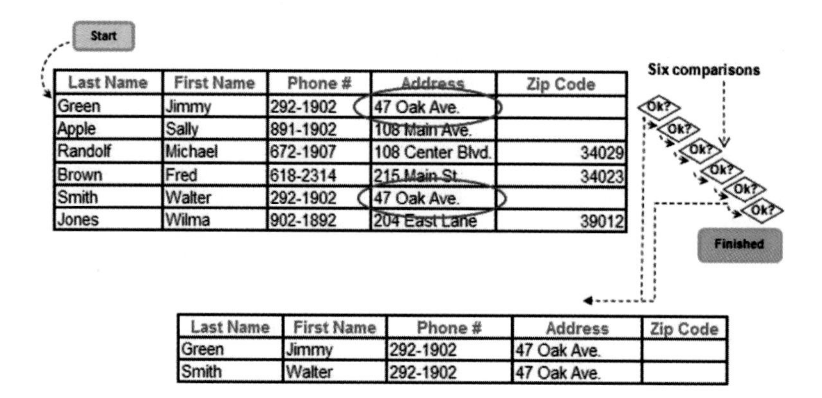

Index Search We will learn a lot more about indexes later but a short discussion is appropriate now. The benefits of using an index are more **flexibility** and **faster retrieval** of records. An index associates specific records with specific data values that someone might be searching for (like a person's last name, phone number, or street address).

The value of using an index is illustrated in the following figure which presents a random data table of six records and also shows two indexes used for accessing the six data records.

A Random Data Table with Two Indexes

Random Data Table:

Last Name	First Name	Phone #	Address	Zip Code
Green	Jimmy	292-1902	47 Oak Ave.	
Smith	Walter	292-1902	47 Oak Ave.	
Randolf	Michael	672-1907	108 Center Blvd.	34029
Brown	Fred	618-2314	215 Main St.	34023
Apple	Sally	891-1902	108 Main Ave	
Jones	Wilma	902-1892	204 East Lane	39012

Sequential Index

Last Name	First Name	Row
Apple	Sally	5
Brown	Fred	4
Green	Jimmy	1
Jones	Wilma	6
Randolf	Michael	3
Smith	Walter	2

Name Index: by Last and First Name

Phone #	Row
292-1902	1
292-1902	2
618-2314	4
672-1907	3
891-1902	5
902-1892	6

Phone Index: by Phone Number

The records in the data table are not arranged in any particular order (it is a random table) but both indexes are specifically ordered. Each index (sequentially arranged) is designed to allow us to easily locate specific data records using alternate (name or phone #) search values.

An index is actually an additional table with a record for each record in the data file. Therefore, each index table must have the same number of records as the data file it references so each index file shown above has six records. Each index record points to a specific associated data record.

The reason that indexes are used is because performing a top down (or exhaustive) search through a large data file can be quite time consuming. Since index records are smaller (usually fewer data fields per record) the index can usually be searched faster than the data file. Here a top down search for "Jimmy" is presented:

Start

Last Name	First Name	Row
Apple	Sally	5
Brown	Fred	4
Green	Jimmy	1 -----▶ Found in row 1 of random table
Jones	Wilma	6
Randolf	Michael	3
Smith	Walter	2

Top Down Index Search for "Jimmy"

When searching an index (or sequential file) the time that it takes to locate a specific record depends on the search strategy used. Search strategies are discussed in a later section.

Aside:
Searching for specific records is usually fastest in an indexed random table.

However:
Adding records to an indexed random table typically takes longest because as each data record is added one or more index records are created and sorted into proper sequence in the index. This is the slowest operation for adding records.
It is usually fastest to add records to a non-indexed random file (no index record and no sorting) and a bit slower to add records to a sequential data file (each new data record is sorted into place but there is no index).

8.2.5 Example: A Delimited Flat File with an Index

Recall this table of data records which you saw earlier:

Last Name	First Name	Phone #	Address	Zip Code
Brown	Fred	618-2314	215 Main St.	34023
Smith	Betty	292-1902	47 Oak Ave.	
Trent	Michael		101 Center Blvd.	34029

The above records arranged in a ^ delimited flat file are as follows with First Name index at right:

Flat Data File

Last Name^First Name^Phone #^Address^,Zip Code
Brown^Fred^618-2314^215 Main St.^ 34023
Smith^Betty^,292-1902^47 Oak Ave.^
Trent^Michael^^101 Center Blvd.^34029

Index

First Name^Row
Betty^2
Fred^1
Michael^3

Building an index for accessing the data records by first name is straight forward. Each index record will have a first name and the number of the data record (row number) that first name is found in. Index records are arranged (sorted) in order (you will learn why shortly). Since there are three data records there will be three index records like this:

When building an index *never* rearrange the order of the data records!

8.2.6 Search Strategies when Using an Index

Fastest record retrieval is most commonly obtained with an indexed random file. There are two search strategies for searching an index:

- Top Down Search of an Index
- Binary Search of an Index

Top Down Search of an Index This involves starting with the first index record and running down the list of index records until you find what you are looking for or that you determine the value you are searching for cannot be found. This type of index search was illustrated earlier as "Top Down Index Search for "Jimmy."

A binary search (next section) almost always does a better job than a top down search. It is always desirable to locate records with fewer comparisons resulting in faster retrieval. So it is worth learning about binary searches and indexes.

Binary Search of an Index In a binary search some index records are examined and some are ignored. This strategy successively divides the index records into two equal parts. This is known as **splitting** the index into:

1. Those records that might contain the target index value
2. Those records that do not contain the target index value

Index records must be sorted alphabetically or numerically for a binary search to work.

Initially all index records are considered as candidates because the target value might be anywhere among the full set of index records. As the search progresses, index records that could not possibly contain the target value are eliminated from consideration. In fact, with each comparison one half of the remaining index records are dropped from consideration. The search narrows in on the target quickly. This procedure continues until the target index record is found or is determined not to exist because there are no further index records to examine.

Assuming that we are searching for Walter Smith here is how a binary search would work using this Last and First Name Index:

The middle of the records that might contain the target index record is examined. In a Binary Search the middle record is always selected for comparison in each round. Since there is an even number of records (there are six data records) either record #3 or #4 can be selected as the middle record. The choice is arbitrary and does not matter. For this example, index record #3 is selected. Notice that the index records are sorted alphabetically.

Last and First Name Index

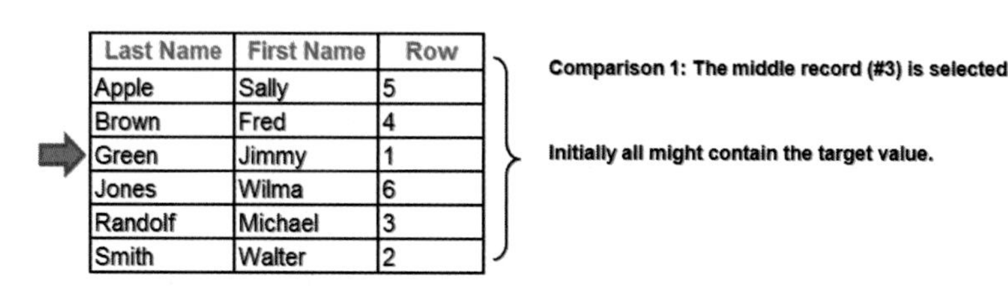

Last Name	First Name	Row
Apple	Sally	5
Brown	Fred	4
Green	Jimmy	1
Jones	Wilma	6
Randolf	Michael	3
Smith	Walter	2

Comparison 1: The middle record (#3) is selected.
Initially all might contain the target value.

Record #3 (the middle record) is for Jimmy Green. Since Walter Smith (the record we are searching for) is alphabetically after Jimmy Green (Smith is after Green) the first three records (Apple, Brown, Green) are eliminated from consideration and only the last three records (Jones, Randolph, Smith) are still considered. One half of the index records (the top three records) are ignored as the result of comparison one. This result is summarized below:

Last Name	First Name	Row
Apple	Sally	5
Brown	Fred	4
Green	Jimmy	1
Jones	Wilma	6
Randolf	Michael	3
Smith	Walter	2

Ignored: these do not contain the target record because Smith is alphabetically after Green.

Still considered: might contain the target value.

Now we move on to index comparison two. The middle record (#5) of the three records remaining in consideration (#4, #5, #6) is examined. It happens that index record #5 contains "Michael Randolf," so the search continues with one record still possibly in consideration:

Last Name	First Name	Row
Apple	Sally	5
Brown	Fred	4
Green	Jimmy	1
Jones	Wilma	6
Randolf	Michael	3
Smith	Walter	2

Comparison 2: The 5th record is selected.

Ignored: these do not contain the target record because Smith is alphabetically after Randolf.

Still considered: might contain the target value.

Index record #6 is examined and found to be for "Walter Smith." The desired record has been found in three comparisons! Data record #2 is where Walter Smith's data is found:

Last Name	First Name	Row
Apple	Sally	5
Brown	Fred	4
Green	Jimmy	1
Jones	Wilma	6
Randolf	Michael	3
Smith	Walter	2

Comparison 3: The 6th record is selected.

Found in row 2 of the data table.

Binary Search Speed So how fast is a binary search and is it really better than a Top Down Search? Performance differences can be dramatic. In a table of 1,000,000 records a linear (top down) search requires 500,000 comparisons vs. 20 comparisons for binary search! Adding another million records to the table would increase a linear search by 500,000 comparisons (now up to 1,000,000) but it would add only one more comparison to a binary search (now 21)!

If you are a bit familiar with mathematics then the following might interest you. *The mathematics of logarithms is beyond the scope of this book, so it is ok if you do not understand the mathematics shown here.*

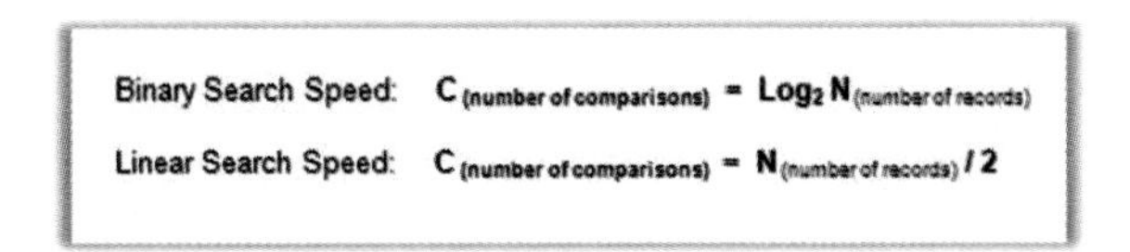

Binary Search Speed: $C_{(\text{number of comparisons})} = \text{Log}_2 N_{(\text{number of records})}$
Linear Search Speed: $C_{(\text{number of comparisons})} = N_{(\text{number of records})} / 2$

8.2.7 Linking Records in Different Tables

So far the tables you have seen are "stand alone" – that is they are not linked to other tables. An exception is the connection between a table and an index as illustrated here:

Binary Index Records

Last_Name^Row
Green^3
Jones^1
Sanders^2

Data Records

First_Name^Last_Name^Suffix^Phone^Prefix
Buster^Jones^Dr.^401-1902^
Wilma^Sanders^^401-2510^
Zoe^Green^^401-1507^Ms.

Physical pointers

Index records are linked to the data records by **physical pointers** (row numbers). This is the simplest type of linkage but not particularly recommended because physical pointers depend on the physical order of records and that violates the first rule about tables and records.

A better way to link records is with a logical connection. This affords more flexibility and reliability. With this method a column of data that is common to the linked tables must be present. In the following example the customer data records shown above are presented in table format. Additionally a table of customer purchases is also shown:

Customer Records

Logical Link (common to both tables)

First_Name	Last_Name	Suffix	Phone	Prefix
Buster	Jones	Dr.	401-1902	
Wilma	Sanders		401-2510	
Zoe	Green		401-1507	Ms.

Customer Purchase Records

Last_Name	Product	Price
Green	Coat	$ 109.53
Jones	Sweater	$ 43.77
Sanders	Pants	$ 31.45
Green	Sweater	$ 43.77
Jones	Shoes	$ 62.83
Green	Scarf	$ 17.50

The column common to both tables that will be used as the logical link is Last_Name. Logical links use data instead of row numbers to connect records. In this example each Customer Purchase record has a Last_Name value ("Green," "Jones," "Sanders") that links to a Customer record. *Note: the common column in both tables need not have same name but they must have same data type.*

If you look closely at the purchase records you notice that some last names occur more than once ("Green" and "Jones" but not "Sanders"). Each single purchase is linked to one customer. Some customers, however, made more than one purchase.

Data that provides a logical link to a record in another table is a foreign key.

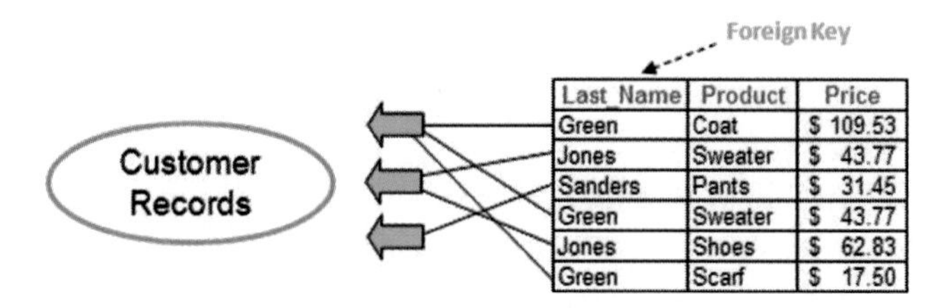

While foreign key values may be duplicated, the column they match in the other table must have unique data values. Looking back to the customer records you see three records each with a different last name. There is no duplication. These matching values are known as **primary keys.**

Customer Records

Primary Key — Foreign keys reference primary keys

First_Name	Last_Name	Suffix	Phone	Prefix
Buster	Jones	Dr.	401-1902	
Wilma	Sanders		401-2510	
Zoe	Green		401-1507	Ms.

Customer Purchase Records

Foreign Key

Last_Name	Product	Price
Green	Coat	$109.53
Jones	Sweater	$ 43.77
Sanders	Pants	$ 31.45
Green	Sweater	$ 43.77
Jones	Shoes	$ 62.83
Green	Scarf	$ 17.50

Primary key values are unique and foreign keys may be duplicated.

In this example several customers have multiple purchases. This is evident because some last names in the purchase table (foreign key) are duplicated and the last name (primary key) in the customers table is never duplicated. So we say "Each customer has several purchases." More commonly it is described as "One to Many" and is described and presented visually this way:

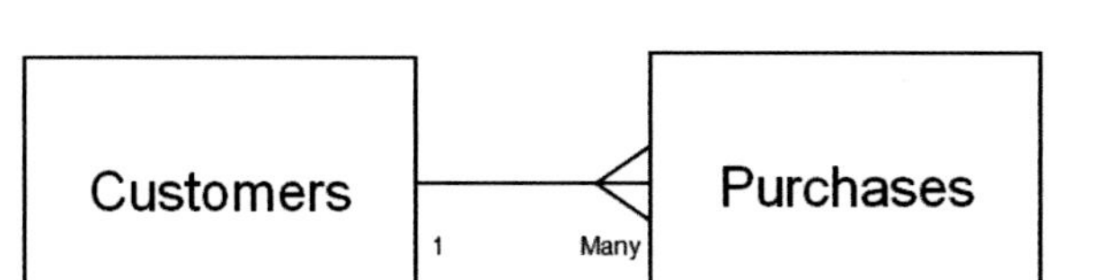

Referential Integrity: Each foreign key value must exactly match a primary key value. Foreign keys are always from the "many" side of the relationship.

Note: In large databases last name is not a good candidate for a primary key because often several customers have the same last name. Normally numeric IDs are used as primary keys.

8.3 Database

Information systems (**IS**) support human **decision making** and typically includes computer hardware and software. The foundation of any information system is the **data** that becomes relevant to humans when it is processed into **information.** Data alone is not particularly useful but when it is processed and analyzed it can become information.

A database management system (**DBMS**) is a computer program designed to manage a database. A database is a collection of data that is of interest to people. The concepts of database are rooted in our understanding of tables where data is arranged in records defined by rows and columns. The remainder of this chapter is about the manipulation of **relational** databases using a DBMS.

CustomerID	CompanyName	ContactName	ContactTitle
ALFKI	Alfreds Futterkiste	Maria Anders	Sales Representative
ANATR	Ana Trujillo Emparedados y	Ana Trujillo	Owner
ANTON	Antonio Moreno Taquería	Antonio Moreno	Owner
AROUT	Around the Horn	Thomas Hardy	Sales Representative
BERGS	Berglunds snabbköp	Christina Berglund	Order Administrator
BLAUS	Blauer See Delikatessen	Hanna Moos	Sales Representative
BLONP	Blondesddsl père et fils	Frédérique Citeaux	Marketing Manager

A Database Table Contains Records

Normally a database contains data about many interrelated subjects. An on-line retail store, for example, will have information about customers, products, and sales.

An Online Store's Data Entities

Each category or topic of data is called an **entity** and all entities are **related** (linked) to at least one other entity. Each entity is implemented as a **table.** The database for the online store would hold data about the store's data entities. A database's entities and **relationships** among them (depicted as boxes connected by lines) are shown in what is called an **Entity-Relationship (ER) diagram.** An ER diagram presents the database **schema:** a map of the database. ER diagrams are discussed later in this chapter and in the systems analysis chapter.

8.4 Database Management Systems

A database is data and a DBMS is a computer program used to manage and process data in a database. Both are software.

A **database** is a collection of records of information which are stored so that a computer program can access it to answer questions. A database management system (**DBMS**) is a program (software) designed to manage a database, and run operations on the data requested by various stakeholders. Typical examples of DBMS use include airline reservation systems, human resource management systems, financial and accounting systems, and customer support systems. In recent years, DBMSs have emerged as a fairly standard part of any company back office's information system.

A DBMS is a complex set of inter-related software programs that controls the organization, storage, and retrieval of data in a database. In a database, records are maintained in **tables** and the records are connected (related) to others in an organized way dictated by a map of the database known as a **schema.** The database structure (schema) is optimized to deal with large amounts of data stored on a permanent data storage device (most frequently a disk drive).

A database supports a query language which allows users to interactively interrogate the database, analyze its data, and update it. While there are numerous proprietary query languages in existence, the most commonly used and understood language is **Structured Query Language,** known as **SQL** for short.

Security is a major concern to **database administrators** (DBA). Apart from the use of passwords and other authorization techniques, few users are given access to an entire database and are limited to portions of a database defined in a **subschema.** As an example, a university database can contain all the data about an individual student, but staff in the registrar's office would only have access to academic data and staff in the bursar's office only to financial data. A student would presumably have access to view all personal data but would not be permitted to update it.

The database schema describes the objects that are represented in the database, and the relationships among them. There are a number of different ways for organizing a schema — these are known as **database models** (or data models). The model most commonly used today is the **relational model** (proposed by E.F. Codd of IBM in 1970 — "A Relational Model of Data for Large Shared Data Banks"), which represents all information in the form of multiple related tables each consisting of rows and columns (the definition is based on the mathematics of set theory). This model represents logical relationships by the use of values common to more than one table (**primary** and **foreign keys**). Older models such as the **hierarchical model** and the **network model** depend on a more explicit physical representation of relationships.

A **transaction processing system** (TPS) is a type of information system that typically relies on a DBMS to to collect, store, modify, and retrieve the transactions of an organization. A transaction is an event that generates or modifies data that is eventually stored in a database. There are two styles of transaction processing:

- **Batch Updating** — Transactions are collected and updated as a batch when it's convenient or economical to process them. The cost per transaction processed is assumed to be lower with batch processing but response time to the client is slower. Monthly statements from a financial institution are an example of batch processing.

- **Real-Time Updating** — This involves the immediate processing of data and instant confirmation of a transaction. The cost for real-time processing is higher because resources must always be available to handle peak demand. Because of advances in technology (such as the increase in the speed of data transmission and larger bandwidth) consumers have grown to expect real-time processing. ATMs and online reservation systems are examples.

The history of commercial relational database management systems (RDBMS) is long and involved with many dead ends. Today the market place is dominated by these offerings:

- IBM's **DB2** is considered to be one of the first database products to use SQL. The name was first used in 1982 as an IBM mainframe product. Today DB2 is available on other platforms including UNIX, Windows servers, and Linux.
- **MySQL** is a freely available **open source** product and runs on a variety of platforms including Linux and Windows. It is especially popular supporting Web-based applications. MySQL offers the advantage of providing an application programming interface (API) to many programming languages including: **C, C++, C#, Eiffel, Java, Perl, PHP, Python, Ruby,** and **Visual Basic.**
- Microsoft's **SQL Server** is a relational database management system based on the Sybase RDBMS. SQL Server is commonly used by businesses for small to medium-sized databases, but with the introduction of SQL 2005 greater adoption for larger enterprise databases has occurred.
- **Oracle** is one of the most popular DBMSs today. It runs on many platforms including UNIX, Apple Mac OS X, IBM, Linux, Windows, and Sun Solaris. It competes with DB2 for mid- and high-end applications. Oracle is one of the most mature RDBMSs in the market and also one of the most expensive.

More recent developments include **data warehousing** which incorporates a database that collects information from different sources. It provides data that is consolidated and integrated, subject-orientated, historical, and read-only:

- Consolidated and integrated: Data is organized with consistent naming conventions and measurements. It allows data from a data warehouse to be effectively used in a consistent manner.
- Subject-orientated: Most organizations own and process large volumes and categories of data and information. While much of the data may appear unrelated, cataloging schemes bind together data that is stored across an organization; a data warehouse organizes key business information from operational sources so that it's available for analysis.
- Historical: Data is from the past. It is accumulated and standardized so that it enables consolidation. It is not used for current transaction processing.
- Read-only: Data in a data warehouse is read-only. Since it represents a snapshot from a prior time it is never updated. The only operations which occur in a data warehouse are querying data.

Database Types There are numerous ways that data can be arranged in a physical structure. Performance and avoidance of duplicated data are important design objectives.

- **Relational** — A relational database is implemented as data tables with logical pointers (keys) that connect records in various tables. Databases of this type are more common that any others and business database applications are almost exclusively of this type. Relational databases provide great opportunity for efficiency and flexibility as described shortly.
- **Object-oriented** — In this type of database data is arranged in objects. Objects will also have programming logic capabilities. Use of this type of database is more specialized and is not common.
- **Multidimensional** — This type of database is a data aggregator which combines data from a multitude of data sources. It can also be known as a meta-database. Databases of this type are used by business analysts and managers who require a big picture view to support business decision making. Multidimensional databases would combine data about products, customers, competitors, government regulations, finance, etc., for **meta-analysis** and **decision support.**
- **Hierarchical** — This type of database was favored by IBM in the past and is tree structured. Records are arranged in a hierarchical fashion making some queries fast and some very slow. Hierarchical databases are rare now.
- **Network** — This is an older type of database structure that used physical pointers to connect records. It is generally not in use any longer. Records may have multiple pointers to other records.

Flexibility A DBMS provides a significant departure from the limits of a file processing system. In a file system the structure of records must be known by the programs that process them. This means that if a record's structure changes then all programs that access that file must also be changed. As you can imagine this quite possibly could lead to mistakes if some programs were not altered appropriately.

A relational database system (RDBMS) provides a solution to this problem by separating the data structure from the program (RDBMS) that processes the data. The linkage between the records and the RDBMS is through meta-data that describes the data structure. The RDBMS uses the meta-data which is stored in a separate file and guides record retrieval and update operations. The relationship between data structure and progressing program is described here:

Meta-Data Makes Database Processing Flexible

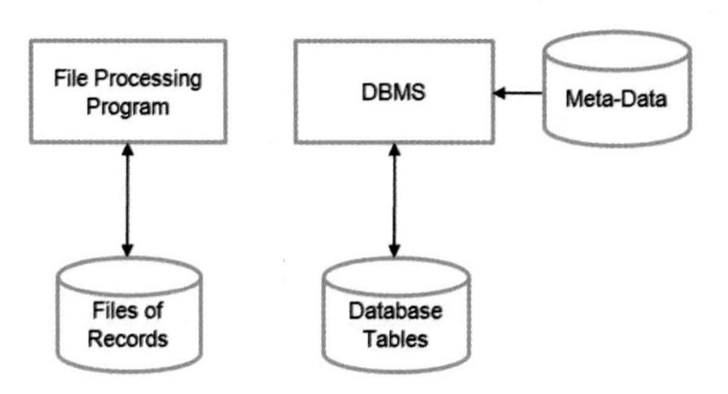

If the database tables are changed the meta-data is changed but no programs need be altered. Updating meta-data is automatic and is a byproduct of altering database table definitions.

Today the relational model is the basis for most databases in use. To better appreciate the simplicity of the relational model the next section discusses database design and it is followed with a presentation of the relational database language SQL.

8.5 Relational Database Theory

To better understand how a RDBMS operates and to enable you to take better advantage of its functionality, it is important to understand what databases are and how they are designed. A database is a collection of data about a topic or topics of interest. Each topic is called an **entity.** So what exactly is an entity? It is a table of records. As shown earlier.

8.5.1 Relational Databases

Today, almost all databases are of the type described here. They are called **relational databases.** The term relational is used because entities (tables) are related to one another. The collection of related tables comprises the database.

Each table contains data arranged in rows and columns and represents data about a complete topic (for example: all students, all customers, or all bank accounts, etc.).

Each row is a record (for example, one student, one customer, or one bank account). Each column is known as a column or field or attribute and contains data that is descriptive for each record (for example, grade point average, balance due, or account number). This illustration displays the relationship between these components:

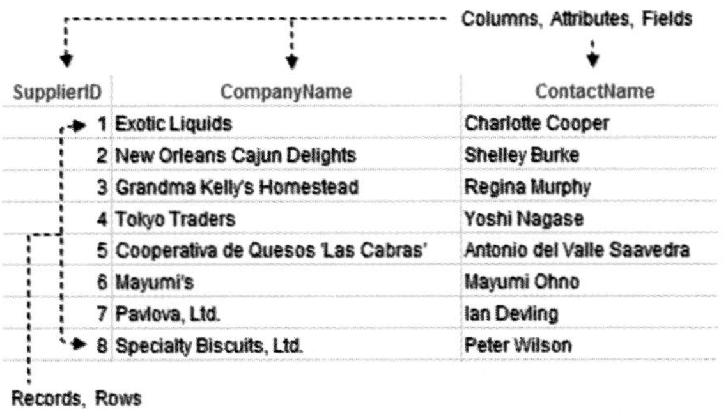

Columns, Attributes, Fields

SupplierID	CompanyName	ContactName
1	Exotic Liquids	Charlotte Cooper
2	New Orleans Cajun Delights	Shelley Burke
3	Grandma Kelly's Homestead	Regina Murphy
4	Tokyo Traders	Yoshi Nagase
5	Cooperativa de Quesos 'Las Cabras'	Antonio del Valle Saavedra
6	Mayumi's	Mayumi Ohno
7	Pavlova, Ltd.	Ian Devling
8	Specialty Biscuits, Ltd.	Peter Wilson

Records, Rows

A Relational Database Table: Records and Columns

The power of using a Relational Database Management System (**RDBMS**), like Access, is that data can be stored more efficiently and with less likelihood of corruption if it is divided among a group of related tables. As you will learn later, data redundancy is the cause of many problems and is to be avoided. Dividing data into correctly formed and properly related tables is the objective of database design.

Relational database management systems separate the physical structure of the data from the logical relationships among the data. Database design is considered next.

8.5.2 Designing a Database

The design of the database is known as the **schema.** A database base has both a **physical schema** and a **logical schema.**

Logical Schema The logical schema depicts the various tables that a database is to be built from. This schema does not give consideration to the physical implementation of the database. The emphasis here is on matching the layout to the database to matching the needs of users.

Database designs are often depicted graphically with boxes representing each entity. This figure shows several entities that might be in a database for a product sales company.

Database Entities

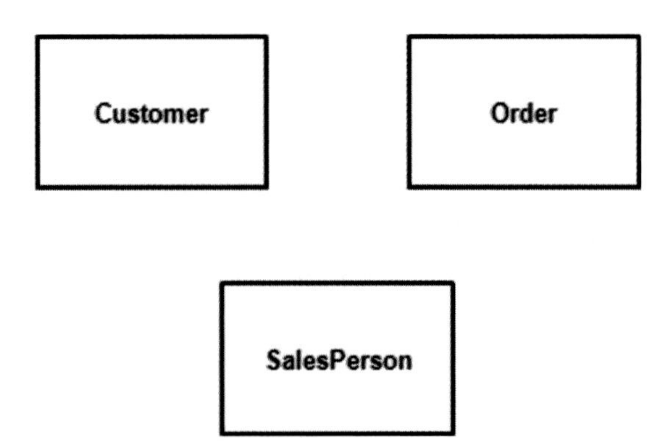

Each entity in a database should be related to the others for the database to make sense. It would make no sense to include in the business database an entity (a topic) about professors.

While not all entities are directly related to each other there must be a chain of **relationships** among all entities. In other words, it must be possible to trace a link from one entity to another until all entities are encountered. The figure is redrawn here depicting the chain of relationships showing that Customer and SalesPerson are indirectly linked through an Order.

Relationships among Database Entities

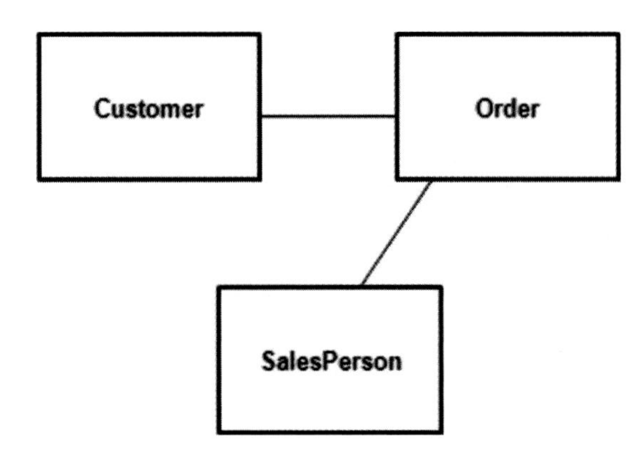

Cardinality The nature of the relationships can be examined further and quantified. This **quantification** is called **cardinality.** Consider the relationship between SalesPerson and Order. If we were to describe the relationship in English it would be like this:

- Each SalesPerson sells several Orders.
- Each Order has one SalesPerson.

Several is interpreted as "any number of" and is usually written as "Many."

This means that each SalesPerson record may be linked to any number of Orders because: Each SalesPerson sells several Orders. In other words, the number of Orders each SalesPerson is connected to will vary; in fact, a new SalesPerson may be linked to zero Orders. This situation is known as "many" and is stated this way: Each SalesPerson has many Orders.

This also means that each Order record must be linked to a single SalesPerson record because: Each Order has one SalesPerson. This situation is known as "one" and is stated this way: Each Order has one SalesPerson.

The relationship cardinality between SalesPerson and Order is described as:

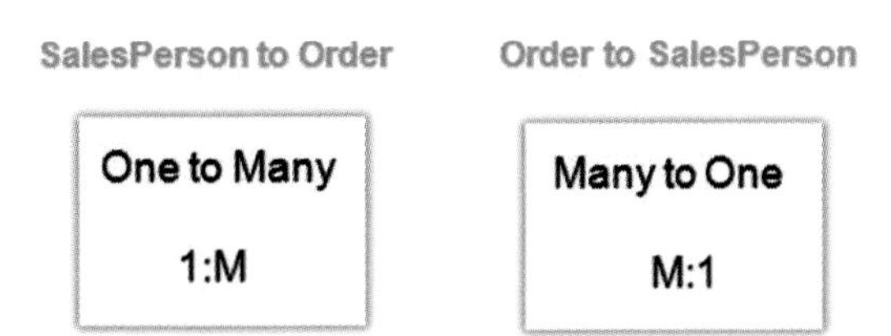

SalesPerson to Order Cardinality

Relationships are implemented by using **primary keys** and **foreign keys.** It is these keys that allow the DBMS to connect records. This operation is known as joining records and is somewhat analogous to using VLOOKUPs and HLOOKUPs in Excel.

Primary Key A primary key is a column in a database table that has a unique value for each record. The importance of the primary key cannot be overemphasized. It is used to help locate specific records just like a lookup does in Excel. Since each record has a unique primary key value there can be no confusion when retrieving specific records.

In the portion of the SalesPerson table shown here you can see that SalesPersonID is the primary key. Each SalesPerson has a unique number:

All Primary Key Values Are Unique

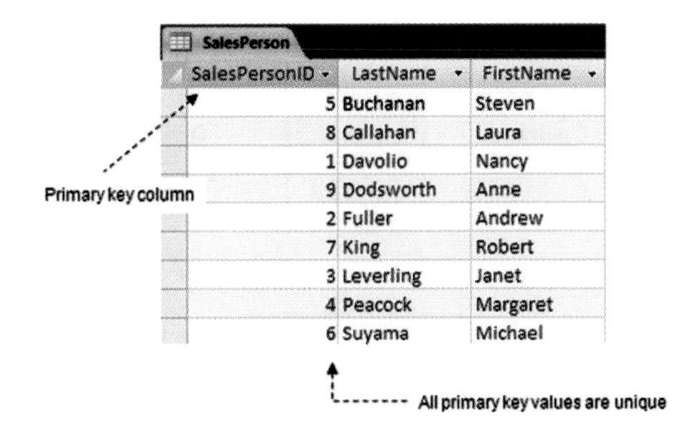

SalesPersonID	LastName	FirstName
5	Buchanan	Steven
8	Callahan	Laura
1	Davolio	Nancy
9	Dodsworth	Anne
2	Fuller	Andrew
7	King	Robert
3	Leverling	Janet
4	Peacock	Margaret
6	Suyama	Michael

While all tables (entities) should have a primary key it is essential that the "one" side of the relationship have a primary key. Without a primary key, relationships could not be determined.

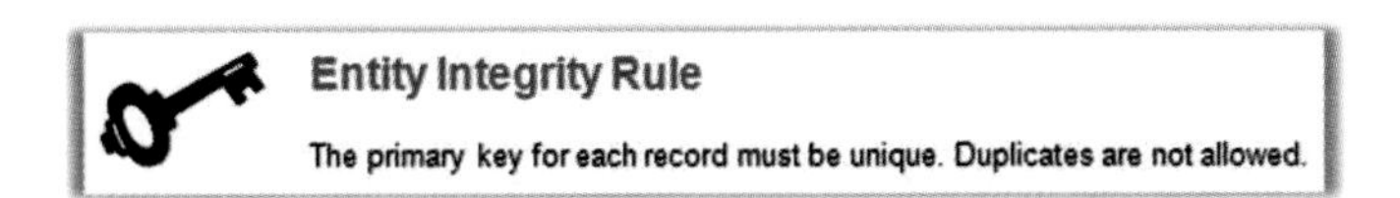

Foreign Key The *many side* of the relationship always has a foreign key which references the one side. This column provides the connection between each record on the *many side* and its parent on the *one side.*

The Order entity (table) looks as shown here. SalesPersonID is the foreign key. Notice that three SalesPersons (3, 4 and 5) made more than one sale (Order).

Order Is the Many Side of the Relationship

Order

OrderID	CustomerID	SalesPersonID	OrderDate
10248	VINET	5	11/29/2006
10249	TOMSP	6	11/30/2006
10250	HANAR	4	12/3/2006
10251	VICTE	3	12/3/2006
10252	SUPRD	4	12/4/2006
10253	HANAR	3	12/5/2006
10254	CHOPS	5	12/6/2006
10255	RICSU	9	12/7/2006

Foreign key column

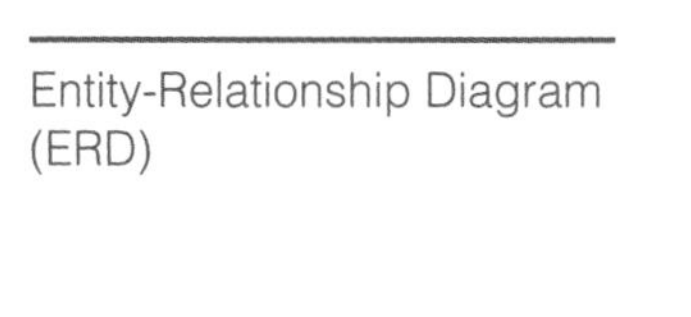

When tables are related one has a foreign key and the other does not. The foreign key is always found on the "many" side of the relationship. The primary key is found on the "one" side.

Tip: The foreign key column need not have the same name as the primary key column but they must be the same type of data (numbers, text, dates, etc.). Also, each foreign key value must exactly match a primary key value or be null.

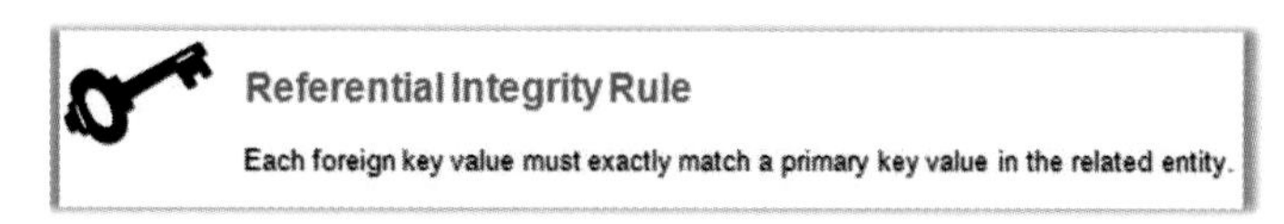
Referential Integrity Rule
Each foreign key value must exactly match a primary key value in the related entity.

Now that primary and foreign keys are understood the relationships shown earlier can be redrawn as an **Entity-Relationship Diagram** shown below.

Entity-Relationship Diagram (ERD)

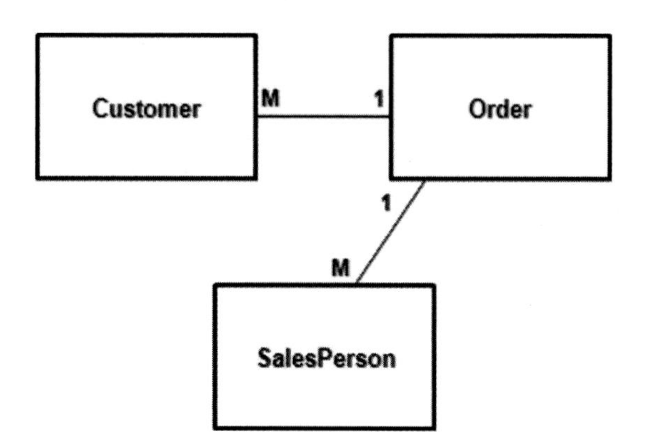
Customer
M
1
Order
1
M
SalesPerson

Why Relate Tables? The reason that relating tables is crucial is because if data about entities were not separated into tables all records would be combined in a single table. The result would be substantial duplication of data, and data duplication is quite unhealthy for a variety of reasons.

In the example we have been following, if records were not maintained in separate tables each Order record would require that a complete SalesPerson record (lastname and FirstName) be built in with other data about the order.

Redundant Data

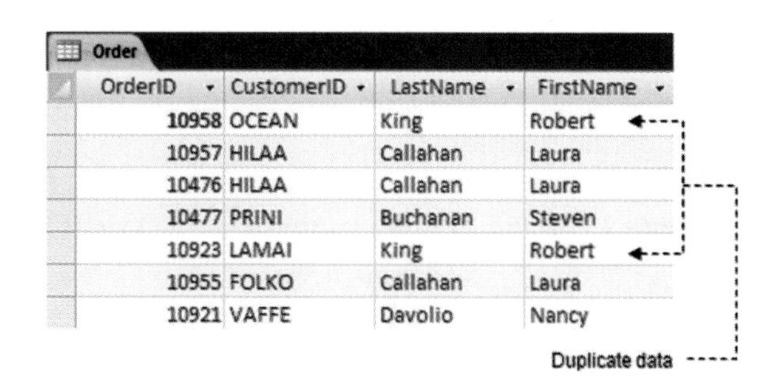

Order

OrderID	CustomerID	LastName	FirstName
10958	OCEAN	King	Robert
10957	HILAA	Callahan	Laura
10476	HILAA	Callahan	Laura
10477	PRINI	Buchanan	Steven
10923	LAMAI	King	Robert
10955	FOLKO	Callahan	Laura
10921	VAFFE	Davolio	Nancy

Duplicate data

8.5.3 Data Redundancy

Duplicated data promotes problems including causing slower DBMS performance and the potential for data integrity errors. Data redundancy is usually responsible for these problems:

- **Wasted space** — Duplicate data requires additional storage space. Storage is a resource and should not be unnecessarily wasted.
- **Slower processing** — When more data is available than is needed processing slows down as the additional data is considered.
- **Data inconsistency** — Duplicated data is subject to becoming inconsistent if updates are not applied to all instances of the same data.

A skilled database designer understands how to remove redundancy as tables are created. The process of removing redundancy is called **normalization.**

8.5.4 Normalization

Normalization is a large topic, and generally beyond the scope of this book, but a simple example might help. When you examine a table look for duplicated data as you see here:

A Table with Redundant Data

ProductName	UnitPrice	CompanyName	Address
Konbu	6	Mayumi's	92 Setsuko Chuo-ku
Tofu	23.25	Mayumi's	92 Setsuko Chuo-ku
Genen Shouyu	15.5	Mayumi's	92 Setsuko Chuo-ku
Pavlova	17.45	Pavlova, Ltd.	74 Rose St. Moonie Pond
Alice Mutton	39	Pavlova, Ltd.	74 Rose St. Moonie Pond
Carnarvon Tigers	62.5	Pavlova, Ltd.	74 Rose St. Moonie Pond
Vegie-spread	43.9	Pavlova, Ltd.	74 Rose St. Moonie Pond

Usually columns with significant duplication indicate that they belong in a different table. The solution to a table with duplication is almost always to break it into two tables. In this example, you can see that several products were supplied by the same company. Rather than duplicate the supplier name and address those columns (CompanyName, Address) should be separated out into a different table and the redundancy among records should be eliminated this way:

A Table Divided

ProductName	UnitPrice
Konbu	6
Tofu	23.25
Genen Shouyu	15.5
Pavlova	17.45
Alice Mutton	39
Carnarvon Tigers	62.5
Vegie-spread	43.9

CompanyName	Address
Mayumi's	92 Setsuko Chuo-ku
Pavlova, Ltd.	74 Rose St. Moonie Pond

Redundancy is gone but a new problem has developed, we no longer know what company supplied each product. The links between supplier and product have vanished. The new problem is easily fixed by adding primary and foreign keys this way:

Tables Linked by Adding Keys

Foreign key

ProductName	UnitPrice	SupplierID
Konbu	6	6
Tofu	23.25	6
Genen Shouyu	15.5	6
Pavlova	17.45	7
Alice Mutton	39	7
Carnarvon Tigers	62.5	7
Vegie-spread	43.9	7

Primary key

CompanyName	Address	SupplierID
Mayumi's	92 Setsuko Chu	6
Pavlova, Ltd.	74 Rose St. Mo	7

The relationship between tables in a database is known as **cardinality** and is depicted in an **Entity-Relationship Diagram** (ERD).

Assume these tables with related records as indicated:

Related Records

Customers

CustomerID	CompanyName	Country
GROSR	GROSELLA-Restaurante	Venezuela
HILAA	HILARION-Abastos	Venezuela
LILAS	LILA-Supermercado	Venezuela
LINOD	LINO-Delicateses	Venezuela

Orders

CustomerID	OrderDate	Freight
HILAA	7/16/1996	81.91
GROSR	7/30/1996	66.29
LILAS	8/16/1996	84.81
LILAS	12/12/1996	7.99
HILAA	12/26/1996	184.41
LINOD	1/6/1997	34.82

If you look at the diagram above you can see:

- Each customer may be linked to one or several orders.
- Each order is linked to just one customer.

Therefore:

- For each customer there are any number of orders (we call it "many" orders)
- For each order there is one customer (we say "one" customer)

The relationship from customer to order is said to be:

- "One to Many" or "1:M"
- "Each single customer is associated with any number of orders."

The relationship from orders to customers is said to be:

- "Many to One" or "M to 1"
- "Each of many orders is associated with one customer."

The Entity-Relationship Diagram (ERD) Depicts Table Relationships

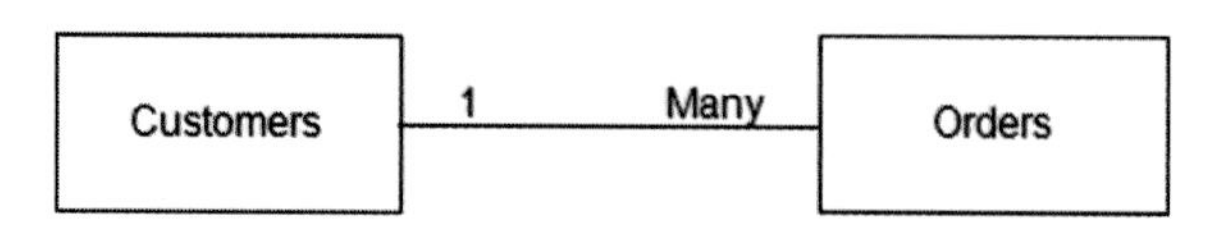

A box in an ERD represents a table of records and is known as an "entity."

In a relationship **many** really means "any number of." The diagram is read as "Each customer has any number of orders."

8.5.5 Many to Many Relationships

The relationship between each pair of entities is not always one to many. As the logical schema evolves some entities will be found to be in a many to many relationship. Consider this pair of entities:

Two Entities in Many to Many Relationship

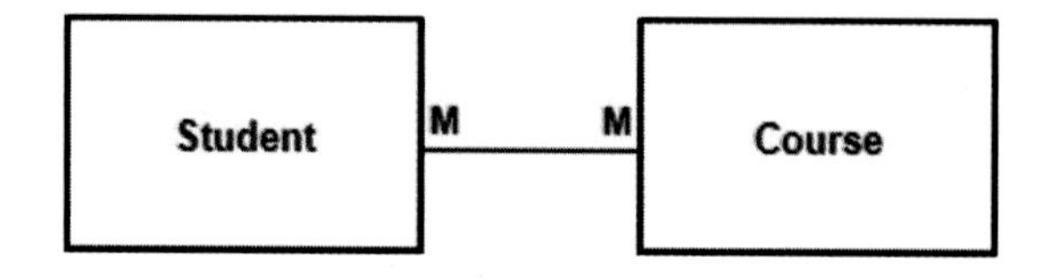

This situation is true at all colleges and universities. Data that associates three students with three courses they might be involved in is shown here:

Student	GPA	Major	Class	Times
Wally	2.98	Geography	Psych 100	MWF 8:15
Ruth	3.49	Math	Psych 101	MWF 8:16
Ruth	4.49	Math	Econ 207	TH 9:30
Mark	2.51	Art	Psych 101	MWF 8:16
Mark	3.51	Art	Econ 207	TH 9:30
Mark	4.51	Art	Paint 318	MW 2:45

Many to Many Data Shows Redundancy

It is not hard to spot the redundancy so it must be eliminated. If we divide up the table into two parts while removing redundancy we would get this:

Student	GPA	Major
Wally	2.98	Geography
Ruth	3.49	Math
Mark	4.51	Art

Class	Times
Psych 101	MWF 8:16
Econ 207	TH 9:30
Paint 318	MW 2:45

Redundancy Removed by Creating Two Tables

Now, however, we have lost the connections between records. We need to add foreign keys to link students with classes; but how many foreign keys do we allow per student? Or does the foreign key go in the class section record? The answer is that we do not worry about those questions because the resolution to a many to many relationship is to create a new table that sits between the others. This new table is called an **intersection** or **cross-reference** and is depicted and implemented as the enrollment table this way:

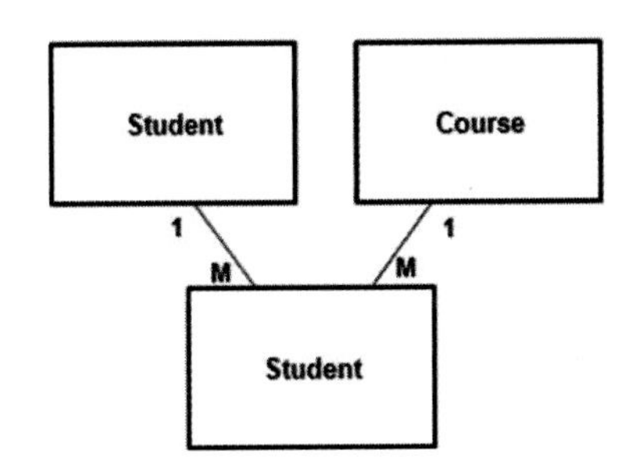

Student	Class
Wally	Psych 100
Ruth	Psych 101
Ruth	Econ 207
Mark	Psych 101
Mark	Econ 207
Mark	Paint 318

Many to Many Resolved with an Intersection Table

8.5.6 Physical Schema

Once the logical design is created and validated, consideration is given to providing the database's physical layout or schema. Here **tables** are defined and the specific **data types** found in each column are specified. **Constraints** that govern data values allowed in each column are given as well. All of these specifications are collected in the **data dictionary** and reflected in **meta-data** that the RDBMS uses to manage the database. Constraints include:

- **Data type** — These include integer, currency, string (character), date, time, and more.
- **Data values** — These are lists of specific, acceptable data values; for example: a list of all state abbreviations.
- **Data ranges** — Ranges of allowable values may be specified; for example a person's age must be at least zero.
- **Record uniqueness** — Each table should have a single data column with data values that uniquely define each record. This is known as the primary key and must be specified.
- **Relationships** — Table relationships defined by foreign and primary keys must be identified.

Once the physical schema is prepared and validated the database may be built. What follows is a description of how to implement a database and its tables in Access.

Creating a Database in Access Begin the creation of an empty Access database this way:

1. Click the Office button.
2. Click New.
3. Next enter a database name and location (path) for the database. Access provides a default database name that you may use if you wish, otherwise provide a name.
4. Click Create.

Creating a New Database

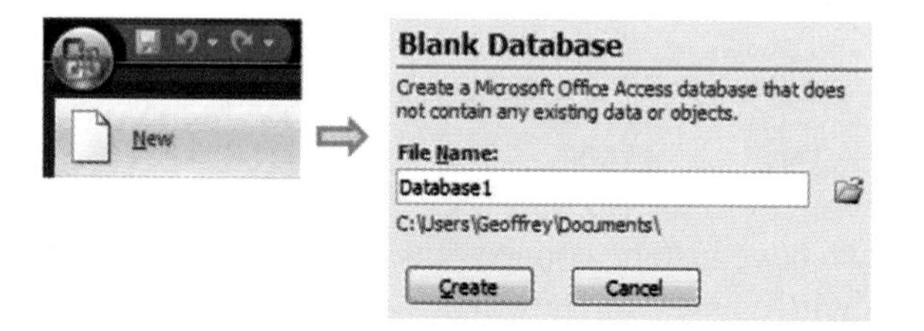

You now have a new but completely empty database. The next step is to build tables.

Aside: Remember that an Access database is a file with the extension ACCDB.

Adding a Table to a Database A new database contains no tables and it therefore holds no data. In this section we explore how to add tables to a database and in the following sections we discuss how to add and import records.

It makes little sense to begin randomly adding tables to a database. The smart thing to do first is to prepare a database design, a schema, and then build tables defined in the design. Refer to the earlier section about database theory for an understanding about tables and their relationships.

Adding a new table to a database requires naming the table and defining the table's columns. Once you are ready to build a table follow these steps:

1. Click Table in the Tables group of the **Create Tab.**
2. Access opens the new table in Datasheet view allowing you to type data into the new table. Do not add records now. Notice that Access gives the table a temporary name: Table1, Table2, etc.
3. Click Save on the Quick Access Toolbar.

Building a Table

When the window closes, Access asks you to give the table a descriptive name.

Naming a Table

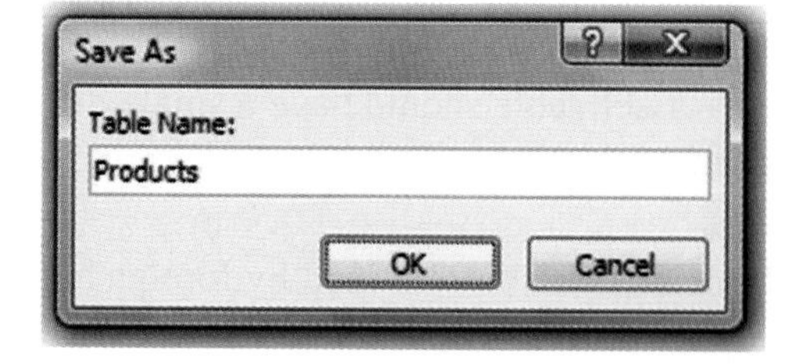

Now that the table has been created, you will want to define the names and type of data required by each column. Double-click the table's name and it opens in Datasheet View. Select Design View (click the View button on Home ribbon) and type the column names that will make up your table's columns. Also select the data type for each column.

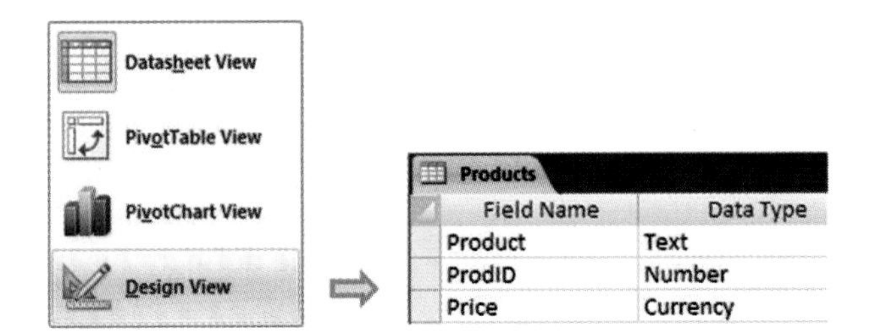

Table Design View

Defining the Type of Data for Each Data Field For text and number fields you should provide additional specifications. For **text fields** specify the maximum number of text characters for the field. The specification is entered in the lower left corner of the Design View screen after the Text data type is selected.

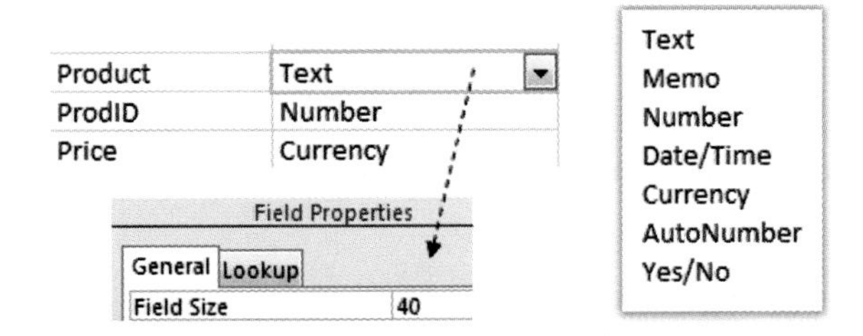

Table Specifying the Data Type and Size for a Table's Column

Other types of data include:

- **Memo** — Select this to store extra long text columns (longer than the 255 character maximum for allowed for text columns).
- **Number** — For numeric fields select the type of numeric data to be stored. This is also done in the lower left corner of Design View. The different numeric data types might seem a little confusing but they are really straight forward. Select an integer type if the number will never have decimal places. Select single, double, or decimal if the number does have decimal places.
- **Date/Time** — This type allows data stored as dates and/or time.
- **Currency** — If you want to store dollars and cents select the currency data type.
- **AutoNumber** — Use this for a primary key field if you want Access to assign unique numbers to the data automatically. It is for primary key fields only.
- **Yes/No** — This allows a column to hold just two values: Yes and No.

Defining a Primary Key Each database table should have one field selected as a primary key field. The primary key is used to guarantee the database's data integrity and to speed access to specific records. This field must have a data value that is unique among all records in a table. In this example we want to use ProdID as the primary key. To use it as the primary key follow these steps:

1. Open the table in Design View.
2. Right-click to the left of ProdID and select Primary Key.

Declaring the Primary Key

Field Name	Data Type
Product	Text
ProdID	Number
Price	Currency

Table Relationships You know from previous discussion that a database is usually a collection on related tables. Certainly you understand that a join is possible only because foreign and primary keys have been defined and linked. Once your tables are created and primary keys selected it is time to define relationships. In our current example we have added a second table to the database – the Orders table defined this way:

A Second Table

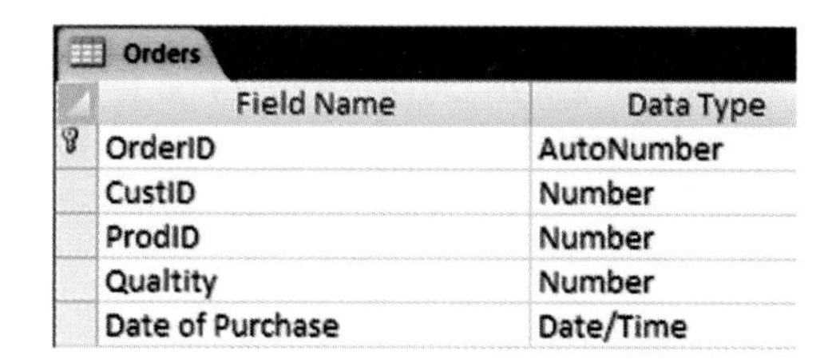

Field Name	Data Type
OrderID	AutoNumber
CustID	Number
ProdID	Number
Qualtity	Number
Date of Purchase	Date/Time

Select Relationships from the Database Tools Tab and then the Show Table dialog box appears. Double-click both table names and then click Close.

Editing Relationships

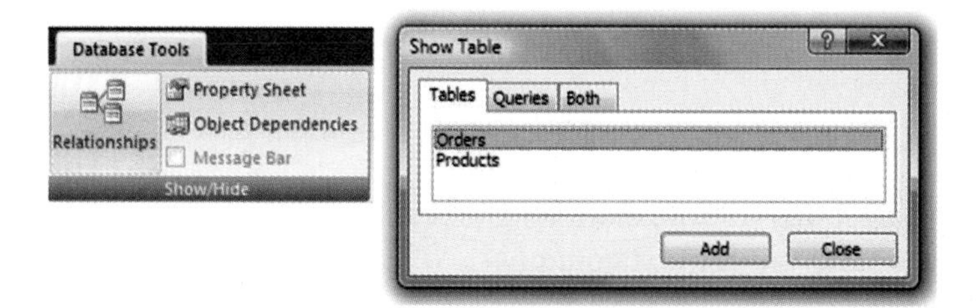

Once both tables are selected the Relationship Window appears with both tables presented.

Relationship Window

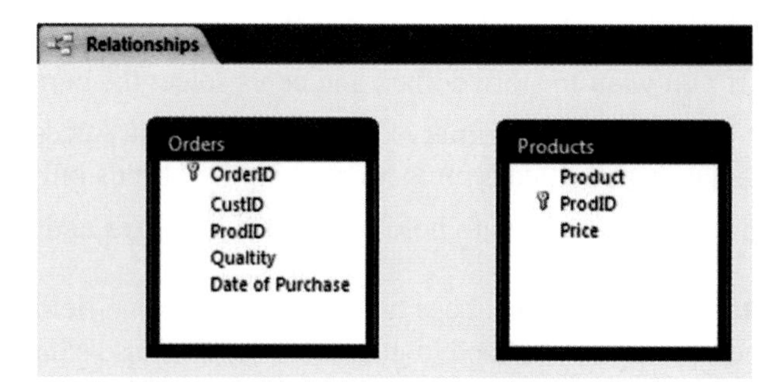

Now drag the foreign key (ProdID) from the Orders table to ProdID in the Products table and release the mouse. Access asks you about the relationship. Check Enforce Referential Integrity and click Create.

Note: Referential integrity ensures that foreign keys match primary keys. Both keys must be of the same data type for referential integrity to work.

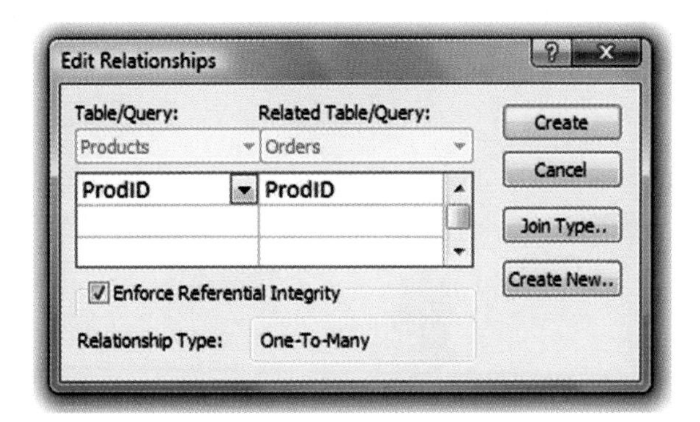

Define the Relationship

Finally the Relationship window displays the ERD with the relationship cardinality shown.

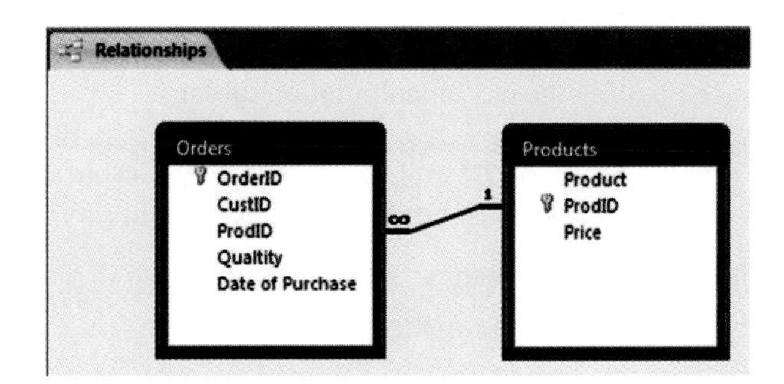

Relationship Complete

8.5.7 Database Application Architecture

Architecture is the structure and arrangements of the components of an application. It also includes the interface requirements of a program, and relationship between the program the database manager.

A single user database application can be implemented in Access. Here the user interface, program logic and database management responsibilities are bundled in Access as shown here:

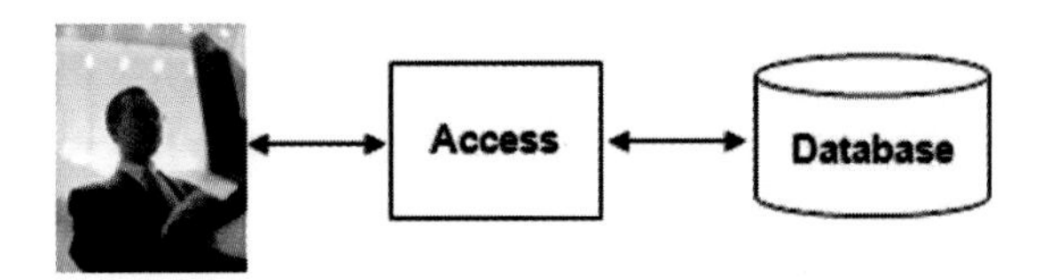

Single User Architecture

Client-server is an architecture which typically revolves around a network (although a network is not required) and separates the client (the consumer of data and other resources) from the server (which distributes those resources). Numerous clients are typically connected to the application server at the same time. Generally the database is maintained on a separate server for **security** and **performance** reasons. The interface is presented in the client computers often by a Web browser.

Client-Server Architecture

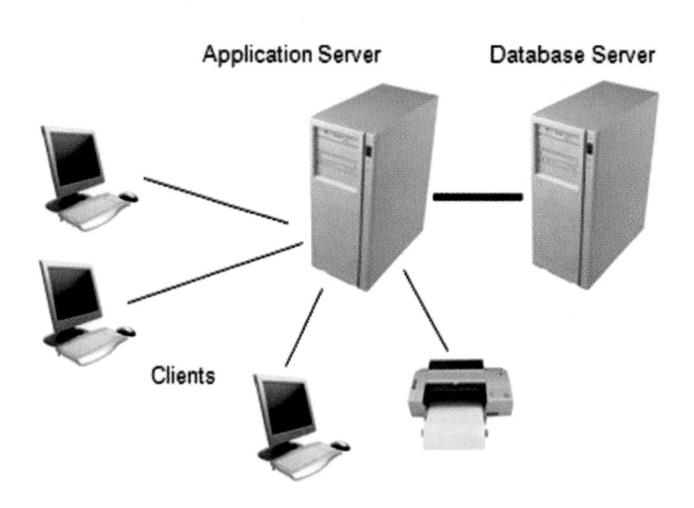

8.6 SQL: The Language of Data

The best way to appreciate data is to work with it; by that we mean to run queries that select, sort, and display records or portions of records. In this section you will learn about the language of data: **SQL** or **Structured Query Language.** This English-like language was designed to make possible the easy manipulation of data.

What Data Are We Working with? SQL understands data arranged in tables of records. Tables, as you will recall, must conform to the following four rules:

1. The order of the rows does not matter.
2. The order of the columns does not matter.
3. All records must have the same number of fields.
4. All data in a column (field) must be the same type.

Tables are normally stored in a database on a computer storage device such as a disk. For now we'll concern ourselves with retrieving existing data from a database's tables. Here we see a portion of a table which you should examine for yourself to be sure that it conforms to the four rules. Database tables must have a name and this table's name is "customers."

Records in the Customers Table

CustomerID	CompanyName	ContactName	ContactTitle	Address	City	postalcode	country
BERGS	Berglunds snabbköp	Christina Berglund	Order Administrator	Berguvsvägen 8	Luleå	40516	Sweden
COMMI	Comércio Mineiro	Pedro Afonso	Sales Associate	Av. dos Lusíadas, 23	Sao Paulo	20821	Brazil
ERNSH	Ernst Handel	Roland Mendel	Sales Manager	Kirchgasse 6	Graz	8010	Austria
FAMIA	Familia Arquibaldo	Aria Cruz	Marketing Assistant	Rua Orós, 92	Sao Paulo	20821	Brazil

Columns in a table are also known as attributes and fields.

Rows of a table are records.

Looking at this table you notice eight columns of data representing the table's eight **fields** or **attributes.**

Retrieving Records: SELECT The beauty of SQL is that it allows you to manipulate data using English-like statements. While the full range of SQL permits adding, updating, and deleting records, in this chapter we will focus only on queries (record retrieval) using the SELECT statement.

SELECT is used to specify which columns (**projection**) and which rows (**restriction**) of a table are to be displayed. We narrow down the range of columns and rows as we focus our search more closely. SELECT allows us to perform these operations:

- **Projection:** Select the columns to display.
- **Restriction:** Select the rows to display.

The general format of the SELECT statement is:

SELECT *which columns*
FROM *table*
WHERE *which rows*

Here a full table is shown with examples of fewer selected columns, rows or both:

SELECT Is Used to Project Columns and Restrict Rows

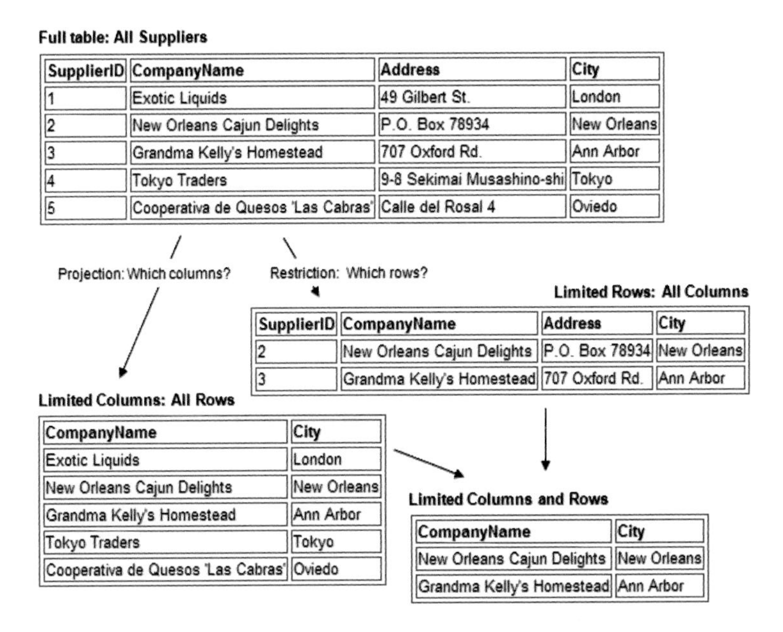

Full table: All Suppliers

SupplierID	CompanyName	Address	City
1	Exotic Liquids	49 Gilbert St.	London
2	New Orleans Cajun Delights	P.O. Box 78934	New Orleans
3	Grandma Kelly's Homestead	707 Oxford Rd.	Ann Arbor
4	Tokyo Traders	9-8 Sekimai Musashino-shi	Tokyo
5	Cooperativa de Quesos 'Las Cabras'	Calle del Rosal 4	Oviedo

Limited Rows: All Columns

SupplierID	CompanyName	Address	City
2	New Orleans Cajun Delights	P.O. Box 78934	New Orleans
3	Grandma Kelly's Homestead	707 Oxford Rd.	Ann Arbor

Limited Columns: All Rows

CompanyName	City
Exotic Liquids	London
New Orleans Cajun Delights	New Orleans
Grandma Kelly's Homestead	Ann Arbor
Tokyo Traders	Tokyo
Cooperativa de Quesos 'Las Cabras'	Oviedo

Limited Columns and Rows

CompanyName	City
New Orleans Cajun Delights	New Orleans
Grandma Kelly's Homestead	Ann Arbor

8.6.1 Projection: What Columns Will Be Displayed?

The columns displayed by a query are known as the query's **projection.** If we want to view all columns from the customer's table (shown earlier) we do it this way:

*SELECT * FROM customers*

Where * means "all columns" and is known as a **full projection.**

If, however, fewer than all columns are desired then replace the * with a comma-separated list of columns that you wish to view. A **partial projection** results.

To project each company's name, address, and city use the following SQL:

A Partial Projection

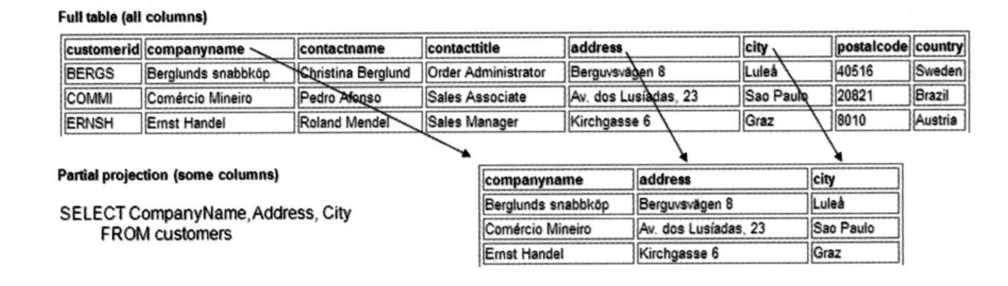

Full table (all columns)

customerid	companyname	contactname	contacttitle	address	city	postalcode	country
BERGS	Berglunds snabbköp	Christina Berglund	Order Administrator	Berguvsvägen 8	Luleå	40516	Sweden
COMMI	Comércio Mineiro	Pedro Afonso	Sales Associate	Av. dos Lusíadas, 23	Sao Paulo	20821	Brazil
ERNSH	Ernst Handel	Roland Mendel	Sales Manager	Kirchgasse 6	Graz	8010	Austria

Partial projection (some columns)

```
SELECT CompanyName, Address, City
    FROM customers
```

companyname	address	city
Berglunds snabbköp	Berguvsvägen 8	Luleå
Comércio Mineiro	Av. dos Lusíadas, 23	Sao Paulo
Ernst Handel	Kirchgasse 6	Graz

A restriction uses a WHERE clause to limit the rows that are displayed.

8.6.2 Restriction: What Rows Will Be Displayed?

So far our examples have returned all rows (records) of the table. If you wanted to limit the records to be displayed based on a selection criteria then you would be applying a **restriction** to the selection.

Here is an example:

If you wanted to view only the records of customers in Madrid, the following SQL SELECT statement would do it for you and the results of running the query follow:

A Restriction: Customers from Madrid

```
SELECT * FROM customers
    WHERE city = 'madrid'
```

A restriction is in the WHERE clause.

CustomerID	CompanyName	ContactName	ContactTitle	Address	City	postalcode	country
BOLID	Bólido Comidas preparadas	Martín Sommer	Owner	C/ Araquil, 67	Madrid	28023	Spain
FISSA	FISSA Fabrica Inter. Salchichas S.A.	Diego Roel	Accounting Manager	C/ Moralzarzal, 86	Madrid	28034	Spain
ROMEY	Romero y tomillo	Alejandra Camino	Accounting Manager	Gran Vía, 1	Madrid	28001	Spain

In SQL <u>always</u> surround character values with single-quote marks.

In this SELECT statement the value "madrid" is surrounded with single-quote marks because the data in the country column is character data.

8.6.3 Compound Queries: Multiple Restrictions

Multiple restrictions can be combined in a **compound query.** For example, if you wanted to view all records of Mexican customers in postal code 00533 then the following SQL is correct:

A Compound Restriction: Mexican Customers in Postal Code 05033

```
SELECT * FROM customers
    WHERE country = 'mexico' and PostalCode = 05033
```

CustomerID	CompanyName	ContactName	ContactTitle	Address	City	postalcode	country
PERIC	Pericles Comidas clásicas	Guillermo Fernández	Sales Representative	Calle Dr. Jorge Cash 321	México D.F.	05033	Mexico
TORTU	Tortuga Restaurante	Miguel Angel Paolino	Owner	Avda. Azteca 123	México D.F.	05033	Mexico

In this example the value 05033 is numeric so no quotes are used. In fact, the query could have been rewritten as shown next. Do you see the difference and do you know why it also works properly?

*SELECT * FROM customers*
    WHERE country = 'mexico' and PostalCode = 5033

In SQL <u>never</u> surround numeric values with quote marks.

Look closely at the restriction that depicted the result shown above and pay close attention especially to the word **and** in the WHERE clause. As **and** is used it means that both conditions on either side of **and** must be true for a record to be selected. In other words, a record must be for a Mexican customer **and** must also be from PostalCode 05033.

A compound restriction uses the operators **and** and **or** to connect conditions. **Truth tables** are used to summarize compound restrictions.

Truth Tables

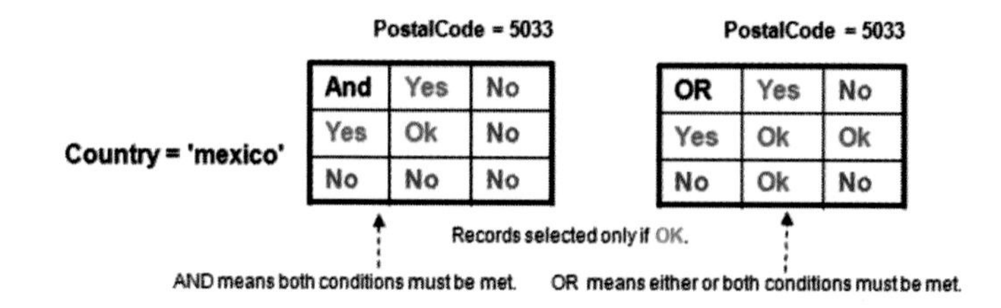

The figure below shows the results of the query with the and operator changed to **or.** Apparently there are some Mexican customers in a different PostalCode:

A Compound Restriction: Using the OR Operator

```
SELECT * FROM customers
   WHERE country = 'mexico' or PostalCode = 05033
```

OR requires that at least one or both be true:

- Country = 'mexico'
- PostalCode = 05033

CustomerID	CompanyName	ContactName	ContactTitle	Address	City	PostalCode	Country
ANTON	Antonio Moreno Taquería	Antonio Moreno	Owner	Mataderos 2312	México D.F.	05023	Mexico
CENTC	Centro comercial Moctezuma	Francisco Chang	Marketing Manager	Sierras de Granada 9993	México D.F.	05022	Mexico
PERIC	Pericles Comidas clásicas	Guillermo Fernández	Sales Representative	Calle Dr. Jorge Cash 321	México D.F.	05033	Mexico
TORTU	Tortuga Restaurante	Miguel Angel Paolino	Owner	Avda. Azteca 123	México D.F.	05033	Mexico

8.6.4 Combinations: Projections with Restrictions

Projections and restrictions can be (and usually are) combined. This SQL (results shown below) partially projects three columns for each German company in postal code 60528, apparently only one company satisfies the restriction.

Partial Projection with a Restriction

```
SELECT CompanyName, Contactname, Phone
   FROM customers
      WHERE country = 'germany' and PostalCode = 60528
```

CompanyName	Contactname	Phone
Lehmanns Marktstand	Renate Messner	069-0245984

8.6.5 Operators

A restriction permits records to be selected only if a **condition** is met. The condition is expressed after the key word WHERE and combines two values with an **operator** between them. In all examples shown so far the = operator, which means "equal," was used.

If you wanted to view a full projection of all non-Swedish companies use the <> operator which is the opposite of = and means **not equal.** The SQL that follows does this and the result is shown in the figure below. Notice that no Swedish company appears in the first records as shown.

A Restriction Using the <> Operator: Non-Swedish Customers

```
SELECT * FROM customers
   WHERE country <> 'sweden'
```

customerid	companyname	contactname	contacttitle	address	city	postalcode	country
COMMI	Comércio Mineiro	Pedro Afonso	Sales Associate	Av. dos Lusíadas, 23	Sao Paulo	20821	Brazil
ERNSH	Ernst Handel	Roland Mendel	Sales Manager	Kirchgasse 6	Graz	8010	Austria
FAMIA	Familia Arquibaldo	Aria Cruz	Marketing Assistant	Rua Orós, 92	Sao Paulo	20821	Brazil

Each condition must include an operator. Operators allow comparison of a column to a value. Here are the operators that you should know:

Common Operators

=	equal
<>	not equal
>	greater than
<	less than
>=	greater than or equal to (aka: "at least" or "not less than")
<=	less than or equal to (aka: "at most" or "not more than")

The **less than** operator is used to restrict selected records to those with values lower than a specific value. The database has a products table with the necessary columns; the SQL and the result are displayed below.

A Restriction Using the < Operator

```
SELECT ProductName, UnitPrice
   FROM products
      WHERE UnitPrice < 20
```

ProductName	UnitPrice
Chai	18
Chang	19
Aniseed Syrup	10
Konbu	6
Genen Shouyu	15.5
Pavlova	17.45

The restriction shown above could have been rewritten as:

```
WHERE 20 > UnitPrice
```

Rewritten this way, the clause reads "20 **greater than** UnitPrice." Make certain that you understand why both WHERE clauses are equivalent.

8.6.6 Other Operators

Several other operators extend the potential for selecting specific records. The following operators are described in this section: BETWEEN, IN, NOT, LIKE.

BETWEEN: Restricting a Range of Values The **BETWEEN** operator is used to select records based on a range of values. In this example customers with postal codes in the range from 30000 to 43000 are displayed. The SQL and the results follow:

A Range Restriction Using the BETWEEN Operator: Postal Code Range

```
SELECT * FROM customers
   WHERE PostalCode BETWEEN 30000 and 43000
```

customerid	companyname	contactname	contacttitle	address	city	postalcode	country
BERGS	Berglunds snabbköp	Christina Berglund	Order Administrator	Berguvsvägen 8	Luleå	40516	Sweden
FOLKO	Folk och fä HB	Maria Larsson	Owner	Åkergatan 24	Bräcke	40516	Sweden
GODOS	Godos Cocina Tipica	José Pedro Freyre	Sales Manager	C/ Romero, 33	Sevilla	41101	Spain
LAMAI	La maison d'Asie	Annette Roulet	Sales Manager	1 rue Alsace-Lorraine	Toulouse	31000	France
REGGC	Reggiani Caseifici	Maurizio Moroni	Sales Associate	Strada Provinciale 124	Reggio Emilia	42100	Italy

IN: Restricting to a List of Values The **IN** operator is used to select records with any of a group of data values. As you can see by examining the following SQL the IN operator is a convenient way to select from a list of values. Here customers from Germany and Mexico are selected:

The IN Operator Is Used to Check a List of Values

```
SELECT CompanyName, ContactName, Country, Phone
   FROM customers
      WHERE Country IN ('germany','mexico')
```

You might have realized that the use of IN (above) is equivalent to multiple values selected by a compound condition. This SQL produces the same result as the SQL above:

A Compound Condition May Be Used as the Equivalent to Use of the IN Operator

```
SELECT CompanyName, ContactName, Country, Phone
   FROM customers
      WHERE Country = 'germany' or Country = 'mexico'
```

NOT: Negating a Restriction (turning it around) The **NOT** operator "turns the logic around." In this example companies NOT in Germany or Mexico are selected.

A Restriction Using the NOT Operator: Other than German and Mexican Companies Displayed

```
SELECT CompanyName, ContactName, Country, Phone
   FROM customers
   WHERE Country NOT IN ('germany','mexico')
```

CompanyName	ContactName	Country	Phone
Around the Horn	Thomas Hardy	UK	(171) 555-7788
Berglunds snabbköp	Christina Berglund	Sweden	0921-12 34 65
Blondesddsl père et fils	Frédérique Citeaux	France	88.60.15.31
Bólido Comidas preparadas	Martín Sommer	Spain	(91) 555 22 82
Bon app'	Laurence Lebihan	France	91.24.45.40

Consider several SQL examples presented earlier in this chapter. In each case the use of NOT would produce the exact opposite result from what was discussed before. Here are several examples:

Using the NOT Operator

```
SELECT * FROM customers
   WHERE PostalCode NOT BETWEEN 30000 and 43000

SELECT ProductName, UnitPrice
   FROM products
      WHERE NOT UnitPrice < 20
```

And the last example would produce the same result if this WHERE clause was used instead:

```
WHERE UnitPrice >= 20
```

LIKE: Restricting to Similar Values: You can use the LIKE operator to select records with **similar** data values. In the next figure records with a city name beginning with B are selected. The percent sign is called a "**wildcard.**" The SQL is:

A Restriction Using the LIKE Operator with a Wildcard: Cities Beginning with B

```
SELECT CompanyName, ContactName, City, Phone
   FROM customers
      WHERE City LIKE 'B%'  <-------------- Similar: Cities that begin with 'B'.
```

CompanyName	ContactName	City	Phone
Galería del gastrónomo	Eduardo Saavedra	Barcelona	(93) 203 4560
LILA-Supermercado	Carlos González	Barquisimeto	(9) 331-6954
Magazzini Alimentari Riuniti	Giovanni Rovelli	Bergamo	035-640230

If the WHERE clause above were changed to this City LIKE '%B%' then all cities with a "B" anywhere in the name would be displayed. Here is a partial listing of the result:

A Restriction Using the LIKE Operator with a Wildcard: Cities Containing a B

CompanyName	ContactName	City	Phone
Alfreds Futterkiste	Maria Anders	Berlin	030-0074321
Blondesddsl père et fils	Frédérique Citeaux	Strasbourg	88.60.15.31
Cactus Comidas para llevar	Patricio Simpson	Buenos Aires	(1) 135-5555
Chop-suey Chinese	Yang Wang	Bern	0452-076545
Folk och fä HB	Maria Larsson	Bräcke	0695-34 67 21
Furia Bacalhau e Frutos do Mar	Lino Rodriguez	Lisboa	(1) 354-2534

SQL's % wildcard is replaced in Access (Microsoft's desktop database program) by * as a wildcard.

8.6.7 Computing Results

Sometimes your work requires data that does not yet exist so it must be calculated. SQL permits this and the next examples demonstrate how. Another table in our database, order details, has columns including the UnitPrice of an item and the Quantity of that item purchased. If you wanted to know the extended cost (UnitPrice times Quantity) of each item sold then calculate it this way:

Computing a New Column's Value

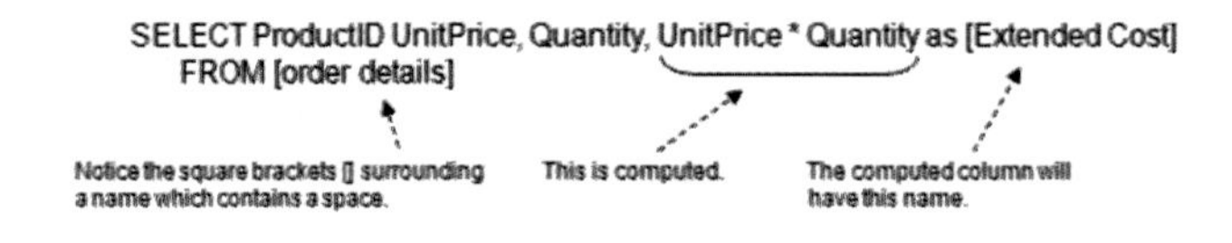

ProductID	UnitPrice	Quantity	Extended Cost
11	14	12	168
42	9.8	10	98
72	34.8	5	174
14	18.6	9	167.4
51	42.4	40	1696
41	7.7	10	77
51	42.4	35	1484

Note: Column names, table names, and the names of calculated columns with a space as part of the name must be surrounded in square brackets [].

8.6.8 Aggregate Functions

Another way to compute results is to use an aggregate function. There are several aggregate functions that work like this:

Aggregate Function: MAX

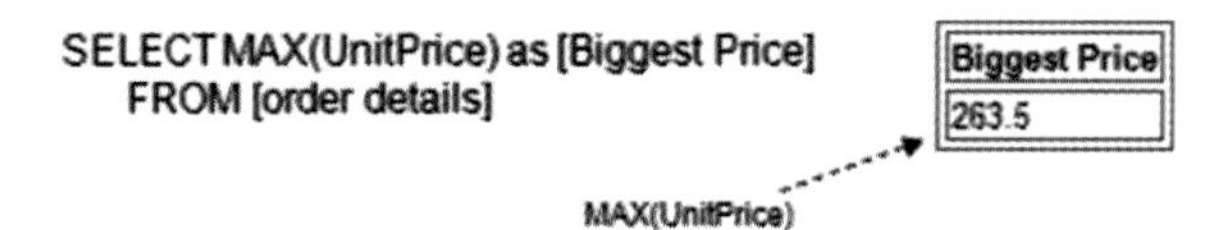

Other aggregate functions that are used similarly are: **MIN, AVG,** and **SUM.** Here are two examples:

Aggregate Functions

```
SELECT AVG(UnitPrice) as Average
    FROM [order details]
```

```
SELECT SUM(UnitPrice * Quantity) as [Total Cost]
    FROM [order details]
```

Another aggregate function, **COUNT,** works slightly differently – it gives the number of records returned by a query. Apparently there are 2,155 records in the order details table. Take a look:

Counting Records

```
SELECT count(*) as [Record Count]
    FROM [order details]
```

Record Count
2155

To learn the number of distinct countries that customers are from, use the COUNT operator with the DISTINCT qualifier this way:

Counting DISTINCT Values

```
SELECT count (DISTINCT country) as [Number of Customers]
    FROM customers
```

Number of Customers
21

To project the list of distinct countries that customers are from use DISTINCT this way:

SELECT DISTINCT country FROM customers

TIP: If you are projecting multiple columns only use the word DISTINCT once before the first projected column's name.

8.6.9 Sorting Records: ORDERED BY

Sometimes it is easier to understand the records returned by a query if the records are viewed in a particular order. For example, suppose that we want a list of all employees. Here is the SQL that lists three columns from the database's employee table. The SQL used to sort the same records alphabetically by LastName is also shown here:

Sorting Records Using ORDERED BY

```
SELECT Lastname, FirstName, HireDate
    FROM employees
```

Lastname	FirstName	HireDate
Fuller	Andrew	8/14/1992
Leverling	Janet	4/1/1992
Peacock	Margaret	5/3/1993
Suyama	Michael	10/17/1993
Callahan	Laura	3/5/1994
Dodsworth	Anne	11/15/1994

```
SELECT Lastname, FirstName, HireDate
    FROM employees
    ORDER BY LastName
```

This performs the sort. → ORDER BY LastName

Lastname	FirstName	HireDate
Callahan	Laura	3/5/1994
Dodsworth	Anne	11/15/1994
Fuller	Andrew	8/14/1992
Leverling	Janet	4/1/1992
Peacock	Margaret	5/3/1993
Suyama	Michael	10/17/1993

There are times when you want the records sorted in reverse order. Suppose you wanted the highest numbers displayed first or suppose that you wanted the most recent dates displayed first. You would still use order by but additionally you would use the key word **desc.** This example shows how to display most recent dates first:

Sorting in Descending Order

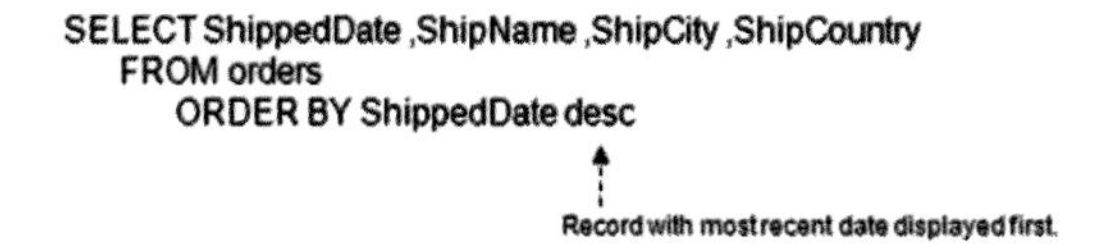

SELECT ShippedDate ,ShipName ,ShipCity ,ShipCountry
FROM orders
ORDER BY ShippedDate desc
Record with most recent date displayed first.

This next example shows that the output from a restriction can also be sorted. Here the restriction uses a different type of data: dates. Notice how the restriction is set up in the following SQL. The results are presented next:

Combining a Restriction and ORDERED BY

```
SELECT Lastname, FirstName, HireDate
    FROM employees
        WHERE HireDate BETWEEN '1/1/1993' and '12/31/1993'
            ORDER BY Lastname, FirstName
```

Single quotes required for dates.

Lastname	FirstName	HireDate
Buchanan	Steven	10/17/1993
Peacock	Margaret	5/3/1993
Suyama	Michael	10/17/1993

8.6.10 What If More than One Table Is Needed?

Sometimes the answer to a question requires records from more than one table. For example, suppose that we want to list all orders placed by a customer in Venezuela. Since the orders table does not identify the country of the customer we must **join** the two tables (orders and customers) together and restrict records to customers in Venezuela.

Linked Tables

Orders
OrderID
CustomerID ------------ link ------------► CustomerID
EmployeeID
OrderDate
RequiredDate
ShippedDate
ShipVia
Freight
ShipName
ShipAddress
ShipCity
ShipRegion
ShipPostalCode
ShipCountry *(this is the shipping destination – not the customer country)*

Customers
CustomerID
CompanyName
ContactName
ContactTitle
Address City
Region
PostalCode
Country = 'Venezuela'
Phone
Fax

Joining tables often involves tables with identical column names. To avoid ambiguity prefix each column name with the name of a table followed by a period. This is known as dot notation.

Joining Tables For tables to be joined they must share a common data column. The figure below shows portions of both tables. From what is shown you can see that CustomerID is common to both tables. Order does not hold the country of the order (the Customer table does) so the order records must be joined with customers records which do have the country.

Joining Tables Requires a Common Column

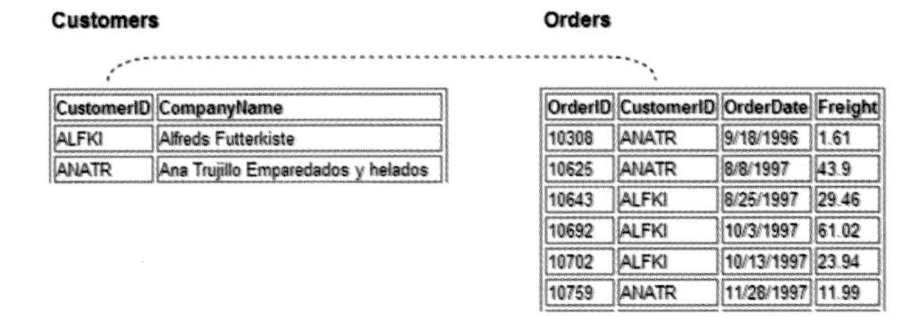

Customers

CustomerID	CompanyName
ALFKI	Alfreds Futterkiste
ANATR	Ana Trujillo Emparedados y helados

Orders

OrderID	CustomerID	OrderDate	Freight
10308	ANATR	9/18/1996	1.61
10625	ANATR	8/8/1997	43.9
10643	ALFKI	8/25/1997	29.46
10692	ALFKI	10/3/1997	61.02
10702	ALFKI	10/13/1997	23.94
10759	ANATR	11/28/1997	11.99

Writing the query to perform the join is actually straight forward. The SQL follows and the result is shown after. Notice that CustomerIDs match on each row – this is a consequence of the join. The left CustomerID is from the Orders table and the other is from the Customers table. Note: only a few columns from each table are shown below due to space limitations.

Join Using Dot Notation

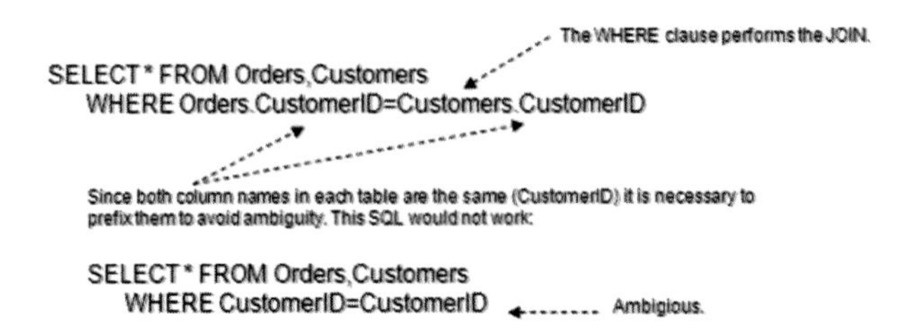

The WHERE clause performs the JOIN.
SELECT * FROM Orders,Customers
WHERE Orders.CustomerID=Customers.CustomerID
Since both column names in each table are the same (CustomerID) it is necessary to prefix them to avoid ambiguity. This SQL would not work:
SELECT * FROM Orders,Customers
WHERE CustomerID=CustomerID
Ambigious.

The result of a join is a new table with columns from both of the joined tables:

Joining Tables Requires a Common Column with Matching Values

From Orders : From Customers

CustomerID	OrderDate	Freight	CustomerID	CompanyName	Country
VINET	7/4/1996	32.38	VINET	Vins et alcools Chevalier	France
TOMSP	7/5/1996	11.61	TOMSP	Toms Spezialitäten	Germany
HANAR	7/8/1996	65.83	HANAR	Hanari Carnes	Brazil
VICTE	7/8/1996	41.34	VICTE	Victuailles en stock	France
SUPRD	7/9/1996	51.3	SUPRD	Suprêmes délices	Belgium

Match

Joining Tables Using a Restriction Since we may want only orders placed by companies in Venezuela the query is modified here. As you study the result below you will see that one customer, LILA-Supermercado, is repeated several times. This is because that one customer placed several orders. Since we joined the tables using the common column CustomerID we see that at least three orders were linked to the same customer.

Joining Tables with a Restriction

```
SELECT * FROM Orders,Customers
    WHERE Orders.CustomerID=Customers.CustomerID
        and Country = 'Venezuela'
```

CustomerID	OrderDate	Freight	CustomerID	CompanyName	Country
HILAA	7/16/1996	81.91	HILAA	HILARION-Abastos	Venezuela
GROSR	7/30/1996	66.29	GROSR	GROSELLA-Restaurante	Venezuela
LILAS	8/16/1996	84.81	LILAS	LILA-Supermercado	Venezuela
LILAS	9/3/1996	0.12	LILAS	LILA-Supermercado	Venezuela
LILAS	10/16/1996	12.75	LILAS	LILA-Supermercado	Venezuela

Three orders for one customer.

We could use a diagram to depict the **relationship** between the two tables:

Records Are Related

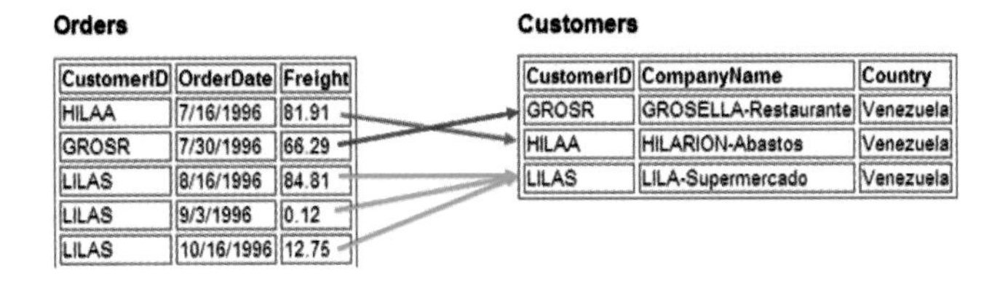

Orders

CustomerID	OrderDate	Freight
HILAA	7/16/1996	81.91
GROSR	7/30/1996	66.29
LILAS	8/16/1996	84.81
LILAS	9/3/1996	0.12
LILAS	10/16/1996	12.75

Customers

CustomerID	CompanyName	Country
GROSR	GROSELLA-Restaurante	Venezuela
HILAA	HILARION-Abastos	Venezuela
LILAS	LILA-Supermercado	Venezuela

If you look at the diagram above you can see:

- Each customer may be linked to one or several orders.
- Each order is linked to just one customer.

Any pair of tables that are related have common columns of data. These columns are used to join the tables in a WHERE clause. Unrelated tables may not be directly

If we were interested in learning which products were included in each order we would want to join the orders and products tables. The orders and products tables are not directly related but it is possible to join them by also including the [order details] table using a compound restriction. Here is the ERD showing the table relationships and the SQL showing how the join is done:

Joining Three Tables

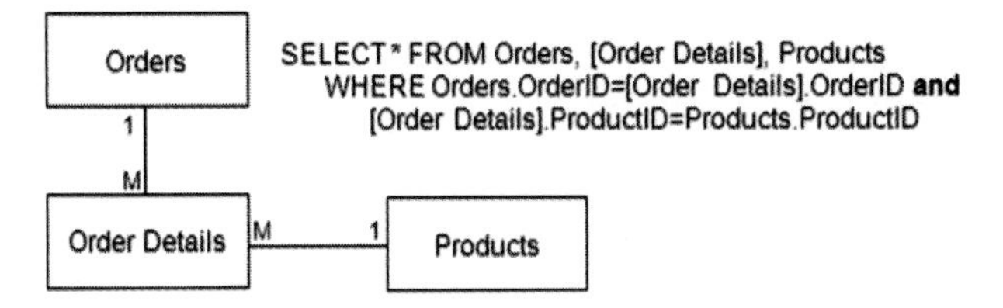
Orders
1
M
Order Details
M
1
Products
SELECT * FROM Orders, [Order Details], Products
WHERE Orders.OrderID=[Order Details].OrderID and
[Order Details].ProductID=Products.ProductID

If tables to be joined are not directly related, all intermediate tables must also be included in a join.

Primary and Foreign Keys When tables are joined, both tables must share a common column. We will now investigate this in more depth. As you noticed recently the data values in the common column, CustomerID, were duplicated in the orders table (the many side) and they were unique in the customers table (the one side). The common columns are known as **key** columns.

For table joins:

- The many side may have duplicated key values. The "many" side's common column is the **foreign key.**
- The one side has unique key values. The "one" side's common column is the **primary key.**

In the SQL that performed the join the primary and foreign keys are identified as shown next:

Duplicated Foreign Keys Reference Unique Primary Keys

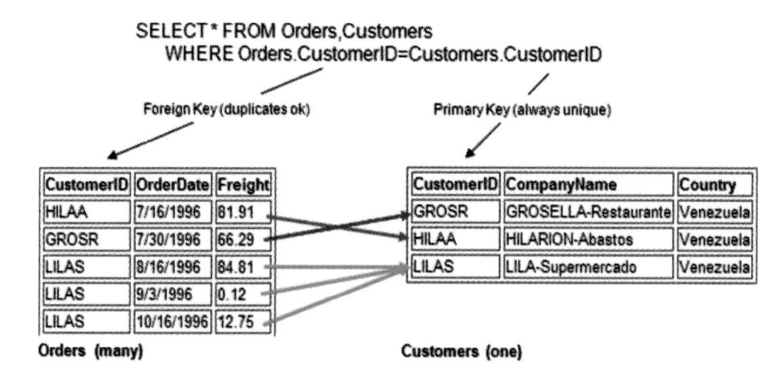

8.7. Queries in Access

Microsoft Access, part of Office 2007, offers an alternative to SQL for performing queries and database updates. Access provides **Query by Example** (**QBE**) which is a graphical method for defining a database query. Any query defined in QBE has a direct SQL equivalent. Access, in fact, translates QBE setups to SQL for processing and Access allows the user to view the SQL equivalent for any QBE.

8.7.1 Asking a Question: Creating a Query by Example

In a query the list of columns to be displayed is known as the Projection of the query.

Asking a question about the data within a database is called asking a **query.** For this example we build a query that displays several columns from the Products table.

To build the query follow these steps:

1. Click Query Design in the Create Tab.
2. Double-click Products.
3. Click Close.

These steps are summarized visually next:

Beginning a Query

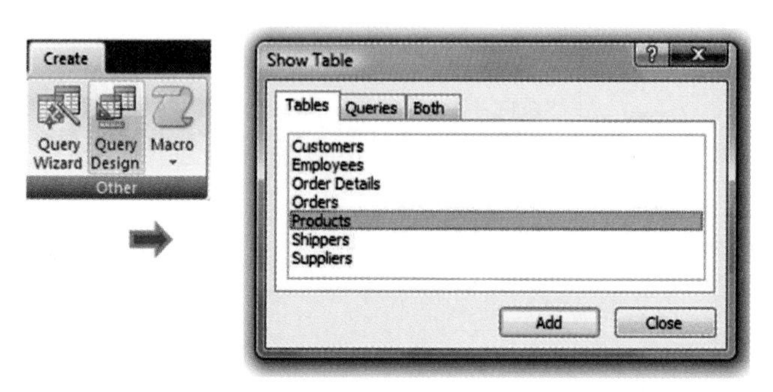

After clicking Close you are ready to select the columns of the Products table to be included in your query.

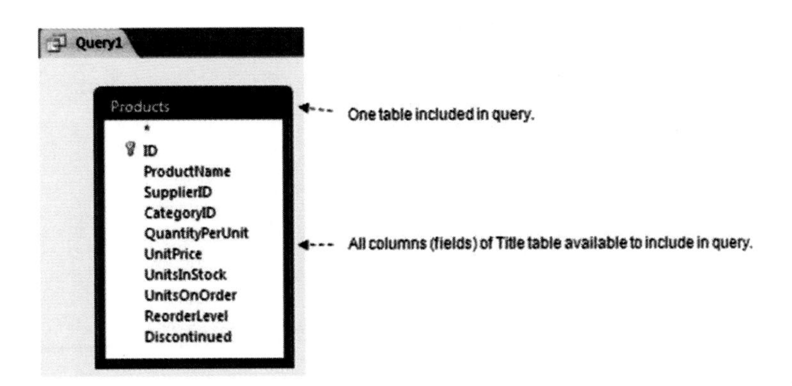

Ready to Select Columns

Next we form the specifics of the query. Notice that all columns of the Titles table appear in the box displayed in the top left of the window. The Product table's fields are all available in this query.

The next step is to select the **fields** (**columns** or **attribute**s) to be **projected** in the query. Assume that for this query, we wish to know the ProductName, UnitPrice and UnitsInStock for all products. Double click on the three field names in the box shown.

The selected fields will appear from left to right in the order that you select them as you can see below. When the query is run three columns of results display the values of the selected columns for each record in the Products table.

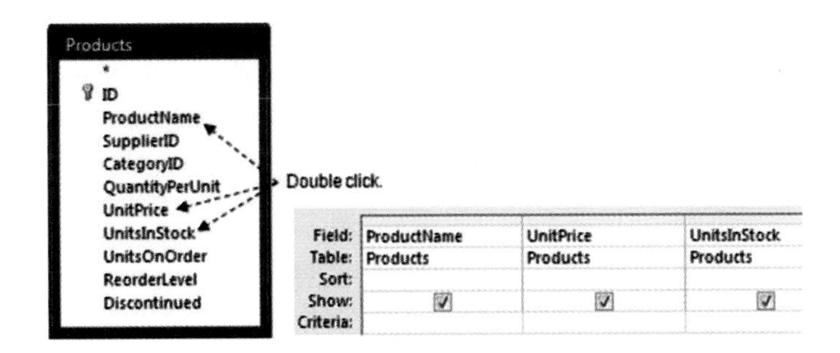

Three Columns Selected for the Query Appear from Left to Right

Run the query by clicking Run in the Query menu or click **!** on the **Design Tab.** Here are the results:

Design
View Run
Results

Query1

ProductName	UnitPrice	UnitsInStock
Chai	18	39
Chang	19	17
Aniseed Syrup	10	13
Chef Anton's Cajun Seasoning	22	53
Chef Anton's Gumbo Mix	21.35	0
Grandma's Boysenberry Spread	25	120
Uncle Bob's Organic Dried Pears	30	15
Northwoods Cranberry Sauce	40	6

The Query Result

In a query the rules limiting the set of rows to be displayed is known as the Restriction of the query.

Restricting Query Results to Certain Rows Sometimes it is desirable to limit the records selected and displayed by the query. In the prior example all rows in the Products table were selected. Suppose that we only want to view records of Products costing at least 20 per UnitPrice. The solution is to return to design mode and then place a **restriction** on the records selected as shown here.

Return to Design Mode and Add a Restriction

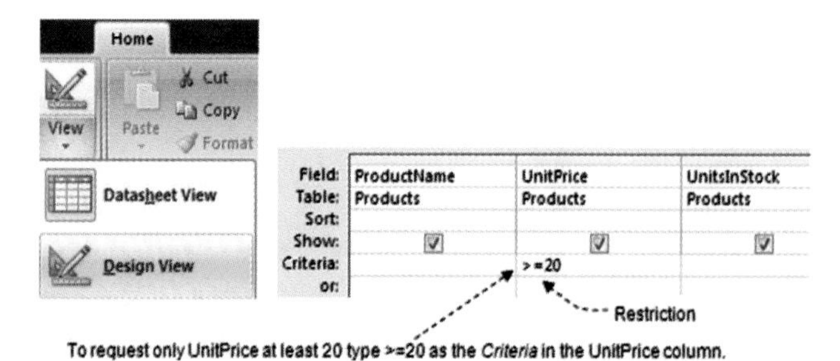

To request only UnitPrice at least 20 type >=20 as the *Criteria* in the UnitPrice column.

Now run the query again and only selected records will appear.

Display Restricted to Products with UnitPrice at least 20

Query1

ProductName	UnitPrice	UnitsInStock
Chef Anton's Cajun Seasoning	22	53
Chef Anton's Gumbo Mix	21.35	0
Grandma's Boysenberry Spread	25	120
Uncle Bob's Organic Dried Pears	30	15
Northwoods Cranberry Sauce	40	6
Mishi Kobe Niku	97	29
Ikura	31	31

8.7.2 Complex Queries

Sometimes one table does not hold all of the data required to satisfy your query. Sometimes you want to limit records using more sophisticated restrictions than demonstrated so far. Sometimes you want to update records as they are processed. This section discusses all of these activities.

Joining Tables When the records of more than one table are necessary to answer a query the tables must be **joined.** This operation is easily handled by a relational DBMS like Access when the primary and foreign keys are identified and the relationships among entities are known. As we discuss joining tables we will use an Access database with three tables related this way:

The Biblio Database

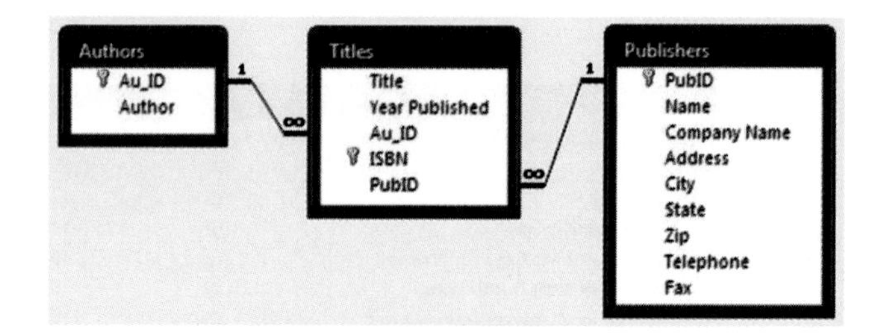

Suppose that we wanted to know the book title and publisher name of all books published after 2000. Since the desired data is found in the combination of two tables (Titles and Publishers) we must perform a query that **joins** these tables.

Each Title record has a **foreign key** that references a Publisher record. So we will **join** the tables using the Title's foreign key PubID.

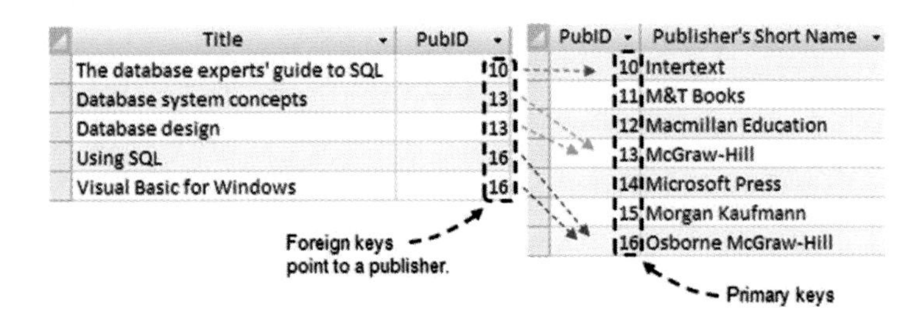

Title	PubID
The database experts' guide to SQL	10
Database system concepts	13
Database design	13
Using SQL	16
Visual Basic for Windows	16

PubID	Publisher's Short Name
10	Intertext
11	M&T Books
12	Macmillan Education
13	McGraw-Hill
14	Microsoft Press
15	Morgan Kaufmann
16	Osborne McGraw-Hill

Tables Are Joined by Linking Keys

To perform the query get started in the usual way. Select both the Titles and Publisher tables this time. Once both tables are selected, Access draws a connecting line to show the relationship between the entities as it completes the ERD. The Entity-Relationship-Diagram that Access creates for the query is shown here:

Entity-Relationship Diagram Depicts Relationships between Tables

This diagram shows that there are many Titles for each Publisher. The infinity symbol next to the Titles box represents many. The one next to the Publishers box means that every one Publisher has printed some number of Titles (many Titles) but that each title has only one publisher.

Here a few actual records from each table are shown. You should be able to see that one publisher (#14) has published three books. Each of the three books has the same foreign key value: 14. That value matches the primary key value (14) of the publisher of all three volumes.

When tables are related one has a foreign key and the other does not. The foreign key is always found on the "many" side of the relationship.

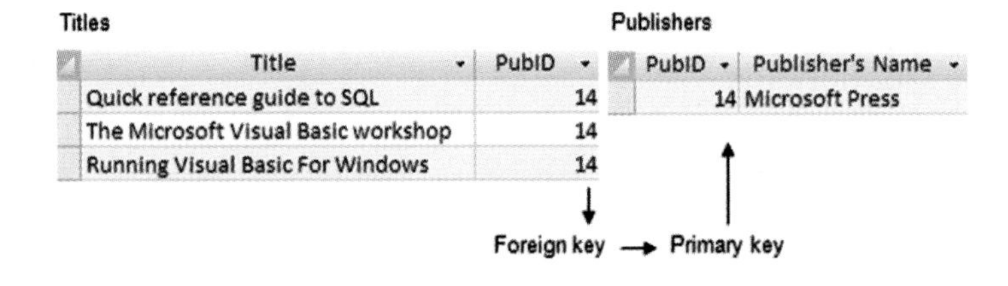

Titles

Title	PubID
Quick reference guide to SQL	14
The Microsoft Visual Basic workshop	14
Running Visual Basic For Windows	14

Publishers

PubID	Publisher's Name
14	Microsoft Press

Three Titles Have the Same Foreign Key Value

Now select the book title and publisher names and year published. Set the criteria for all books published no earlier than 2001.

Field:	Title	Name	Year Published
Table:	Titles	Publishers	Titles
Sort:			
Show:	☑	☑	☑
Criteria:			>=2001

Join Query Setup

Next click the Query Run button to perform the query and the results will be displayed as demonstrated before.

Join Result

Title	Publisher's Name	Year Publish
Data structures, files and databases	Macmillan Education	2004
A visual introduction to SQL	Wiley	2006
Database : structured techniques for	Wiley	2005
Database processing : fundamentals,	SRA	2005
Database analysis and design	SRA	2001
Principles of database systems	Computer Science Press	2000
Fundamentals of database systems	Benjamin/Cummings	2006

The connection between Titles and Publishers is automatic because of the foreign key definition built into the database by the database's designer. How conveniently a complex query can be done in so few keystrokes!

8.7.3 Advanced Queries

Access allows you to be more sophisticated about how you specify selection criteria in queries. The following examples illustrate several of the options available to you.

Prevent Showing Duplicate Records in a Query. When you run a query it is possible that two rows of the result might be exactly the same. The query below produces a row for each book published.

A Query May Produce Duplicate Records

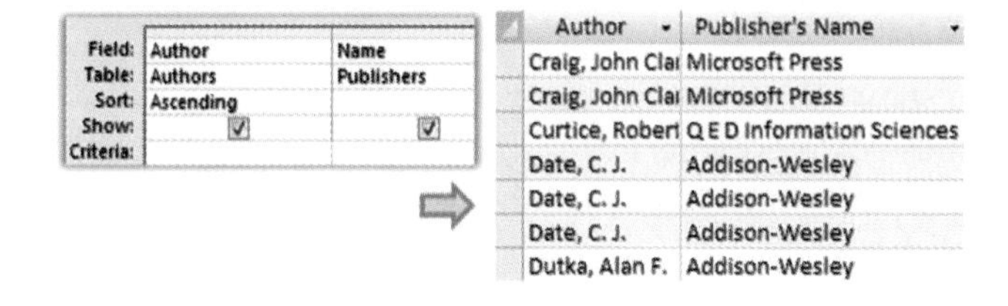

Notice that C.J. Date apparently authored three books with Addison-Wesley. To eliminate duplicate rows open the Property Sheet and then select Yes for Unique Records. Now rerun the query and the duplicates disappear! NOTE: To obtain the Property Sheet box first right-click in the top half of the Query Designer anywhere not covered by the Entity-relationship Diagram (ERD). Next select Properties and finally left-click at the same location.

Eliminating Duplicate Records

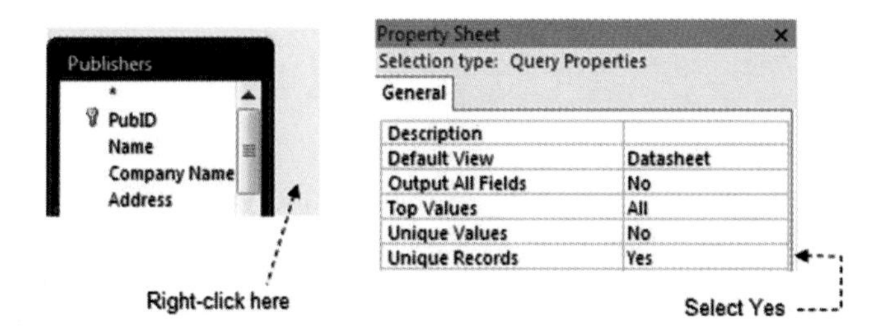

Selecting Records with a Field that Contains a Specific Word You might, however, want to select records that contain a certain value within a column's data. In this example all books that have "database" as part of their title are retrieved. The next figure shows how the query is set up and the results of running the query.

Notice that the **Like** operator is used. Also note that the value you are searching for is surrounded by asterisks which are known as a **wildcards.** The asterisks can be replaced by any characters found in the data thus allowing "database" to be at the beginning of the field, the middle or the end. The query returns only records where the title contains "database."

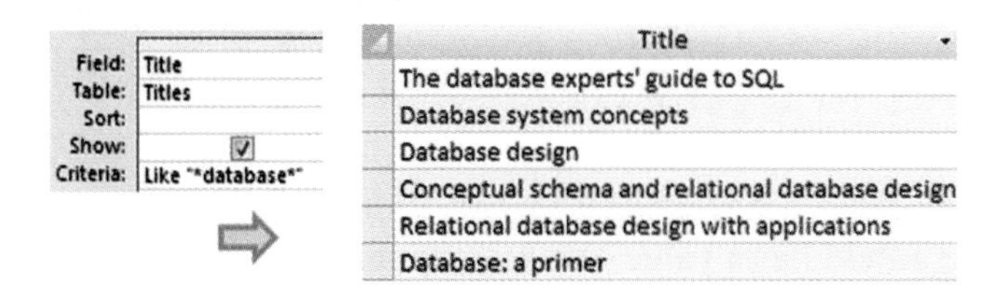

Selecting Records Where a Column Contains Specific Text

If Like had been used this way only books with titles beginning with "database" would be retrieved:

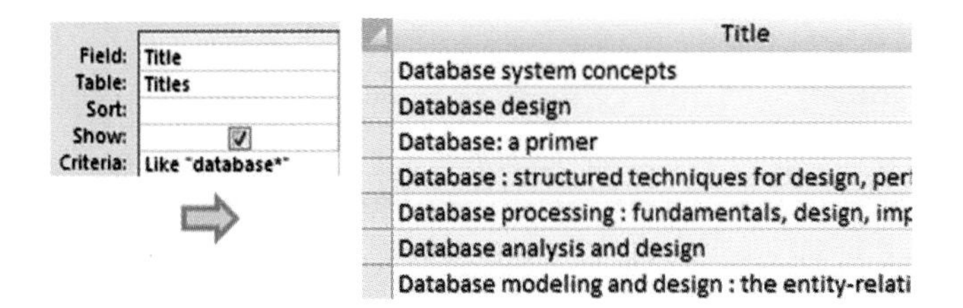

Use the Wildcard a Little Differently

Selecting Records Where a Field May Contain One of Several Values Sometimes you may wish to select records where a certain field has one of several possible values. There are two ways to do this. In the example shown next, publisher names found in two states are displayed. Both selection methods are illustrated:

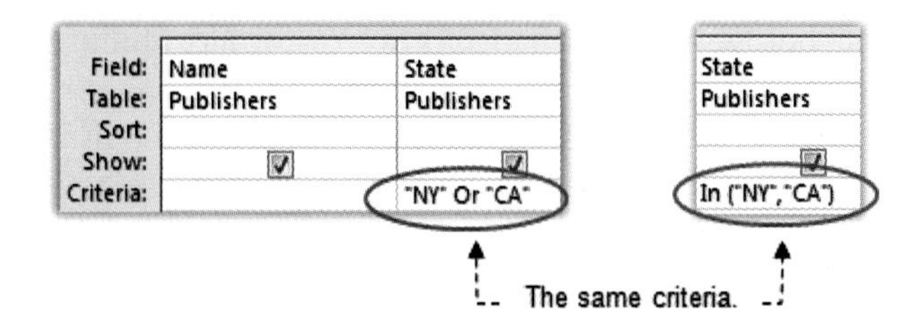

Selecting a Field with One of Two Values

Tip: the state code values are surrounded in quotes because they were declared in the database table design as text fields. Had they been numbers then the quotes would be incorrect.

Selecting Records with a Field that Contains Other than a Specific Value You may wish to select records where a field specifically does not contain a certain value. Use the Not operator as shown here:

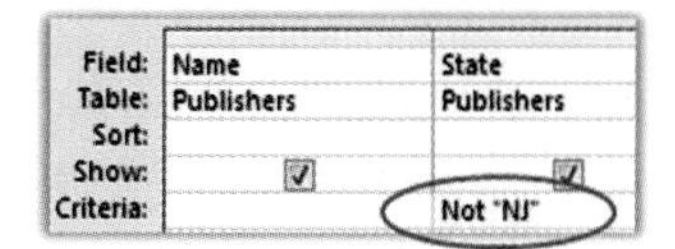

Selecting a Field Containing Other than a Specific Value

Selecting Records Where a Field Has a Null Value Now and then you might want to select records where a specific field has no value. A non value is called a **null.** The use of the Null operator is illustrated here.

Selecting a Field with Null Values

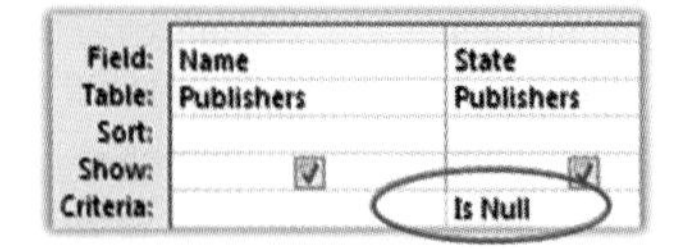

Selecting Records Where a Field's Value Is Within a Range You may wish to select all records where a field has a value in a specific range. In the example shown next all Titles with a publishing year between 2002 and 2007 are displayed. Two methods for setting up this query are shown.

Ways to Select a Field with a Range of Values

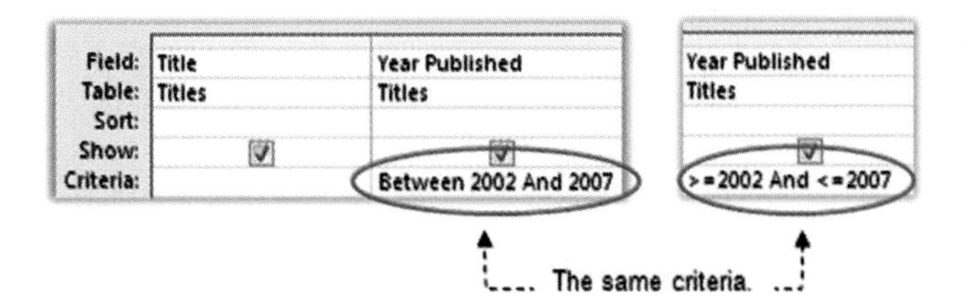

8.7.4 Updating Records

At times it is necessary to update data. The easiest way to update records is to open a table and type the replacement date where the data is to be changed. That works nicely where individual data values are to be changed but there are situations when updating many records simultaneously is desired.

We want to send a thank you letter to all authors who published in 2007. To help us we added a new column to the Author table named SendLetter. Each record had SendLetter initially set to "N" but we want to change it to "Y" for any author who published in 2007. Updating records is accomplished using a query.

We will join Titles and Authors selecting only Titles published in 2007. Next we update the SendLetter column in the Authors table to "Y" for any selected records. Set up the query as you would expect: include both tables and select the two relevant columns (Year Published and SendLetter). Next click Update in the **Design Tab** which causes the Query Designer to add a row for update values. Run the query and the records for authors who published in 2007 are updated.

Updating Records

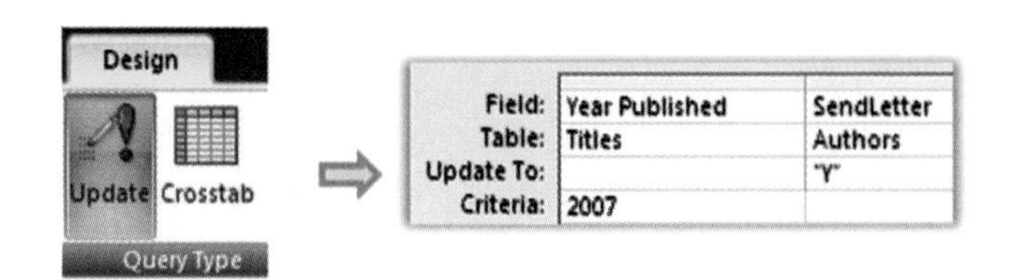

8.7.5 Deleting Records

Individual records are deleted by opening a table first. Next, right click at the left side of the record to be deleted and then click Delete record from the popup menu.

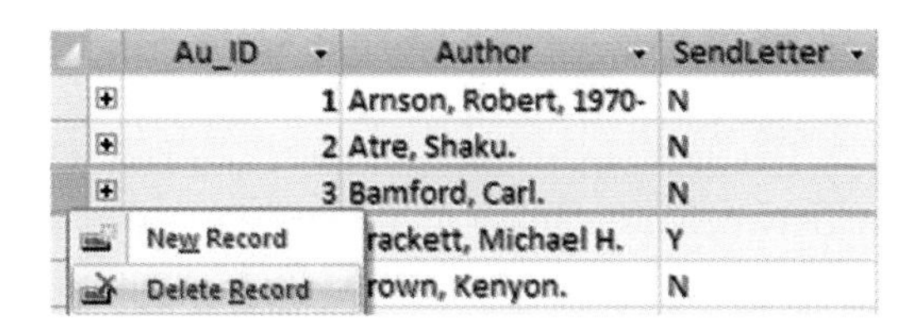

Deleting One Record

Deleting a group of records that match selection criteria requires a query. Set it up as you normally would and then select Delete from the **Design Tab.** Delete appears, select Where in the list that appears to the right of Delete. Run the query and the records are deleted after you confirm your intent to delete records. Note: Deleted records cannot be recovered. There is no Ctrl-Z to undo record deletions. There is no Recycle Bin to restore deleted records from.

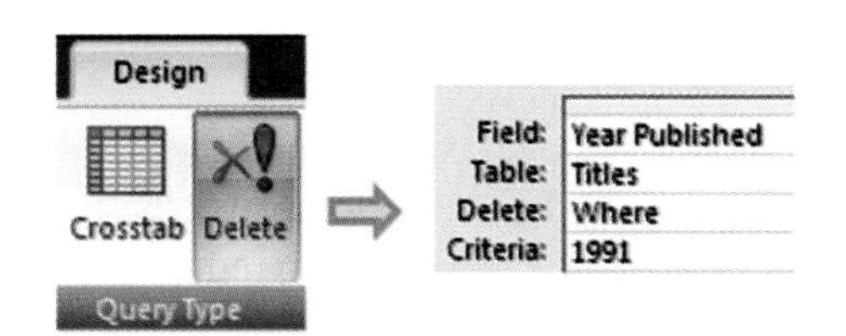

Deleting a Group of Records

8.7.6 QBE and SQL

Database queries are created in either of two ways:

- **QBE** — Query by Example
- **SQL** — Structured Query Language

You are now familiar with both. QBE is the standard query format that Access provides and you have already experienced using it. SQL is more powerful in that any query that can be formulated in QBE has an equivalent in SQL. The reverse is not true. Here you see a query in QBE and the same query written in SQL.

Field:	ProductName	UnitPrice	UnitsInStock
Table:	Products	Products	Products
Sort:			
Show:	☑	☑	☑
Criteria:		>=20	

```
SELECT Products.ProductName, Products.UnitPrice, Products.UnitsInStock
FROM Products
WHERE (((Products.UnitPrice)>=20));
```

QBE and SQL Form the Same Query

As you look at the QBE and SQL versions of the same query see if you can detect how the SQL was derived from the QBE. Every QBE query that you design can be viewed in SQL by selecting SQL View from the View menu. If you are interested in learning more now about SQL allow Access to help you, define queries in QBE and take a look at the equivalent SQL.

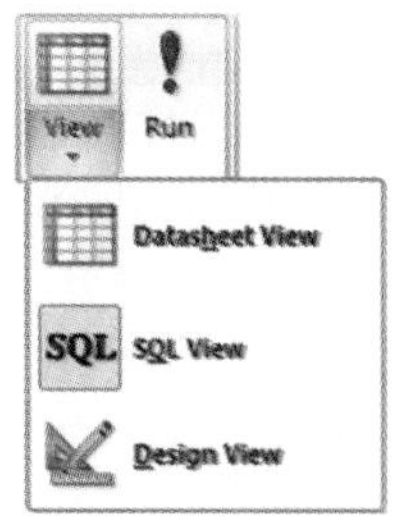

8.8 Summary

This chapter progressed from a discussion of the fundamental building block of an information system, data, through database and data modeling to the language of database,

SQL. The relationship between data and information is described in the **Input-Process-Output** model. An understanding of the important difference between data and information was developed — the difference between facts and that which supports decision making. The difference between a database and a DBMS was presented with relational database techniques emphasized. Upon conclusion of this chapter, and the associated exercises that follow, a deep understanding of this vital component of information systems will be achieved.

Records arranged in tables are the fundamental building block of an information system. The tables may be implemented as flat files or as part of a database. In flat files, connections between records are generally physical which places limitations on flexibility and efficiency of use. Database systems, and in particular relational database systems, rely on meta-data as the bridge between the application and the tables. Designing a database correctly has a profound impact on the database's value. Two stages of design, logical and physical, were discussed. The logical design identifies the entities of the database and relationships among them. This design is depicted in an Entity-Relationship-Diagram or ERD. The physical design involves the detailed description of the tables, their data fields and data value constraints and their primary and foreign keys.

The purpose of a database is to store data, to ensure the data's integrity, and to provide the data in the form of information to users who require it. Query languages are used for this purpose. The standard language for interaction with a relational database is SQL which was described in this chapter. Also presented was the Access implementation of QBE which is a graphical alternative to SQL.

EXERCISES

Exercise 8.1

Rearrange the content of this table so that the rows and columns are organized differently. Be sure that the information content of your result is not different from the original.

Address	First Name	Phone #	Last Name	Zip Code
12 Main	Mark	901-2192	Mason	17210
6 Mills	Hestor	703-2324	Rugby	21043
4 Water	Jennifer	901-4508	Bruce	84908

Exercise 8.2

Create a flat file with horizontal records for these receipts. Add records in the order of receipts from left to right. Include a header row for the four data columns. Make sure that the four rules about tables are not violated. Use ^ as a delimiter. Do not include colons in the headers.

Receipt:

Date: 1/27/2007
Amount: $47.63
Item: Sweater
Tax: $0.00

Receipt:

Date: Feb. 3, 2007
Amount: $65.00
Item: Shoes
Tax: $0.00

Receipt:

Date: 1/31/2007
Amount: Ten Dollars
Item: Book
Tax: $0.55

Exercise 8.3

Fix the following table so that the fourth rule about tables is not violated.

Name	Salary	Hire Date	# Degrees After
Randy	$ 44,902.00	24-Jan-07	2
Wendy	$ 37,902.00	1/15/2005	none
George	$ 39,082.00	11/2/2006	1

Exercise 8.4

Fix this data so that Rule 4 is not violated.

First Name	Last Name	Suffix	Phone	Title	Age
Happy	Jester		309-2341	Ms.	29
Seth	Anderson		9022901		twenty-six
Bo	Randers	Sr.	902-9273	Mr.	31

Exercise 8.5

Assume this random table:

Last Name	First Name	Phone #	Address	Zip Code
Kline	John	384-2345	47 Main Ave.	43902
Masters	Thomas	602-1903	108 Main Ave.	
Water	Mary	602-3892	108 Center Blvd.	47091
Houseman	Richard	618-2314	401 Mills Ave.	43902
Jones	Sam	384-9023	47 Main Ave.	
Delman	Wendy	602-3432	401 Mills Ave.	

Redraw the table after this record is added:

Smith	Lester	384-3892	401 Mills Ave.	47091

Exercise 8.6

Assume the table that results from Exercise 8.5 and create an index for binary search by address.

Tip: when you sort addresses, 108 Center Blvd. and 108 Main Ave. will appear earlier in the list than 47 Main Ave. This is because "address" is not numeric data even though it looks numeric. If address were numeric data then 47 would appear in the index first because 47 is before 108, however, since it is character data 108 Center Blvd. is first.

Exercise 8.7

Assume the table that results from Exercise 8.5 and create a binary index for record retrieval by zip code (numeric data). This is a situation where the target values (zip codes) are duplicated. Tip: null values sort into place before non-null values. Where two zip codes are the same, the one recorded originally first (of the two) remains before the other.

Exercise 8.8

Assume a random table with a record for each US state. Each record has two data fields: the abbreviation of the state's name and the state's population. When performing a top-down search, how many comparisons would you expect to be needed to find the population of Illinois? Tip: Illinois is the 13th state alphabetically but the correct answer is not 13.

Exercise 8.9

Create two alphabetical flat file indexes for the table shown here. One index will be for Origin and the other for Destination. Each index record has a city followed by a record number. The fields are delimited by a ^. Where two index rows have the same city of origin the lowest data row number is first.

Origin	Destination	Ticket Cost
Washington	Boston	$290.45
Denver	San Francisco	$198.00
Portland	Grants Pass	$168.23
Washington	Nashville	$112.00
Phoenix	Selma	$208.32
Denver	Los Angeles	$157.00
Selma	Washington	$198.00

Exercise 8.10

Assume the following data table. If you were to use a top down search how many comparisons on the average would be needed to locate a specific record?

ProductName	UnitPrice
Cranberries	$16.03
Ikura	$31.00
Tacos	$38.00
Alice Mutton	$23.43
Tofu	$31.23
Fabioli	$13.54
Perth Pasties	$32.80
Gnocchi	$38.00
Gouda	$17.08
Semmelknodel	$33.25
Gudbrandsdalsost	$36.00
Mozzarella	$33.80

Exercise 8.11

Create a binary index as a flat file for the table in Exercise 8.10 based on Product Name. The index will have two columns: ProductName and Row. Use ^ as a delimiter.

Exercise 8.12

Fix the data table and index so that none of the record rules are violated. Also ensure that index records correctly reference the proper rows in the data table. Arrange the index records to allow a binary search of the index based on age. Do not change the order of the data records.

Data Records

First Name	Last Name	Prefix	Phone	Age
Jessica	Halter	Ms.	492-8902	20
George	Rus	534-5142	eleven	
Mark	Krauss	Mr.	201-9023	12

Index Records

Record #	Age
6	11
three	12
1	twenty

Exercise 8.13

Download BIBLIO.ACCDB (ask instructor where if you do not know). Create a query that displays the name and city of all publishers in New York State (state code = NY). The result is as shown here:

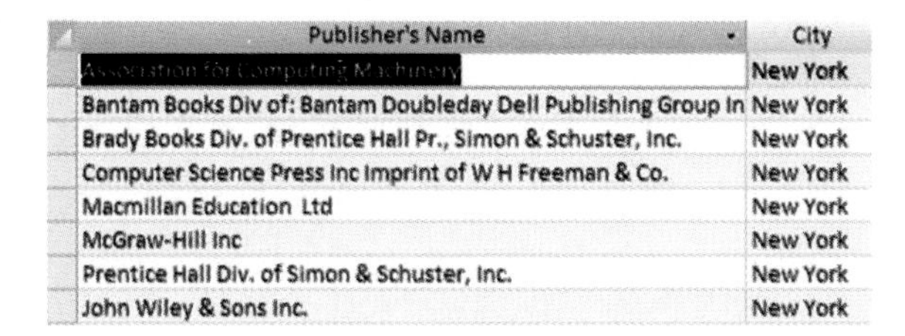

Publisher's Name	City
Association for Computing Machinery	New York
Bantam Books Div of: Bantam Doubleday Dell Publishing Group In	New York
Brady Books Div. of Prentice Hall Pr., Simon & Schuster, Inc.	New York
Computer Science Press Inc Imprint of W H Freeman & Co.	New York
Macmillan Education Ltd	New York
McGraw-Hill Inc	New York
Prentice Hall Div. of Simon & Schuster, Inc.	New York
John Wiley & Sons Inc.	New York

Exercise 8.14

Create a query that displays the title and publisher name of all books published in New York State. The partial result of the query is shown here:

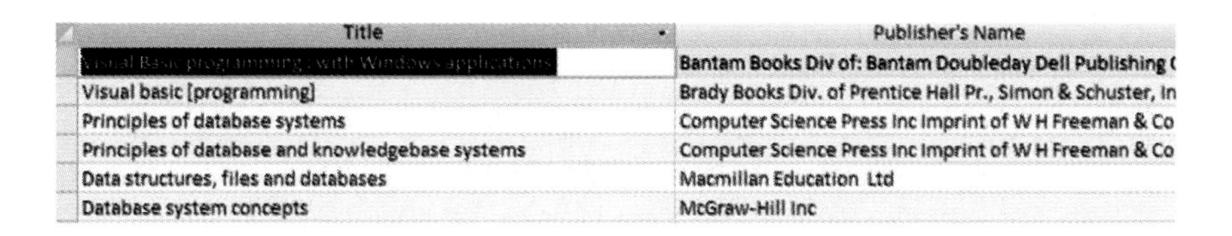

Title	Publisher's Name
Visual Basic programming : with Windows applications	Bantam Books Div of: Bantam Doubleday Dell Publishing (
Visual basic [programming]	Brady Books Div. of Prentice Hall Pr., Simon & Schuster, In
Principles of database systems	Computer Science Press Inc Imprint of W H Freeman & Co
Principles of database and knowledgebase systems	Computer Science Press Inc Imprint of W H Freeman & Co
Data structures, files and databases	Macmillan Education Ltd
Database system concepts	McGraw-Hill Inc

Exercise 8.15

Create a query that displays the title and author names of all books published in New York State. The partial result is shown here:

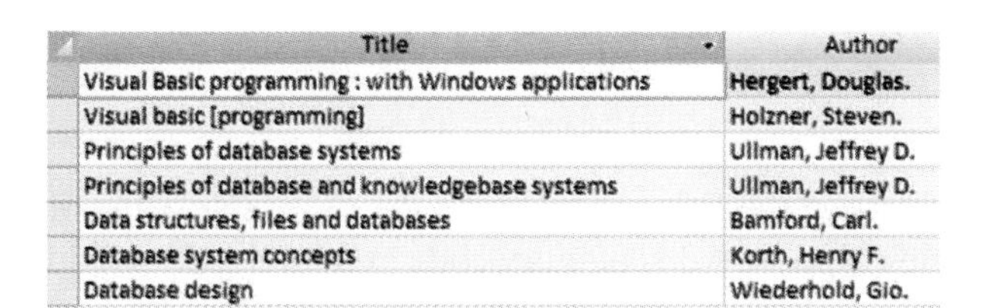

Title	Author
Visual Basic programming : with Windows applications	Hergert, Douglas.
Visual basic [programming]	Holzner, Steven.
Principles of database systems	Ullman, Jeffrey D.
Principles of database and knowledgebase systems	Ullman, Jeffrey D.
Data structures, files and databases	Bamford, Carl.
Database system concepts	Korth, Henry F.
Database design	Wiederhold, Gio.

Exercise 8.16

Export the result of Exercise 8.15 to Excel format. Right-click the query and select Export then select Excel. The partial result of the export is shown here as displayed in Excel.

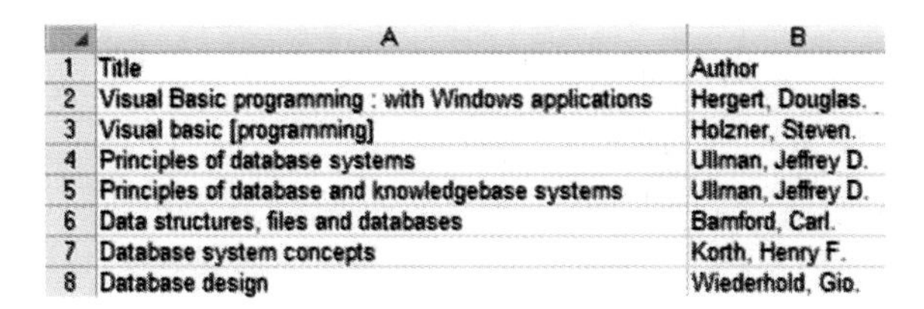

	A	B
1	Title	Author
2	Visual Basic programming : with Windows applications	Hergert, Douglas.
3	Visual basic [programming]	Holzner, Steven.
4	Principles of database systems	Ullman, Jeffrey D.
5	Principles of database and knowledgebase systems	Ullman, Jeffrey D.
6	Data structures, files and databases	Bamford, Carl.
7	Database system concepts	Korth, Henry F.
8	Database design	Wiederhold, Gio.

Exercise 8.17

Create a query that displays the names of authors who wrote books published in New York. Here is the correct answer (partial result); see if you can do this.

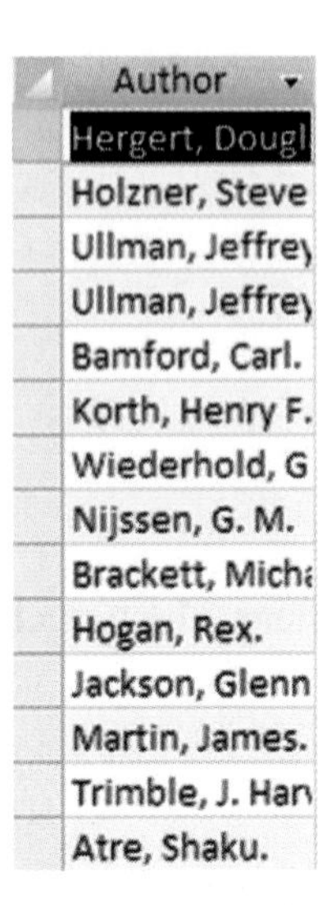

Author
Hergert, Dougl
Holzner, Steve
Ullman, Jeffrey
Ullman, Jeffrey
Bamford, Carl.
Korth, Henry F.
Wiederhold, G
Nijssen, G. M.
Brackett, Micha
Hogan, Rex.
Jackson, Glenn
Martin, James.
Trimble, J. Harı
Atre, Shaku.

Exercise 8.18

Modify the query in 8.17 so that duplicate names are eliminated.

Exercise 8.19

Create a database with two tables. Link the tables referentially after you select a primary key for each table. Add several records to each table and make sure that Access is properly enforcing referential integrity. Finally run several queries that involve joining the tables. Make certain that the records in each table are properly linked.

Exercise 8.20

Add a new table, Book Category, to BIBLIO.ACCDB that links to the title table. Make the new table a list of book categories with two fields: category code and category description. Add category code as a foreign key field in the book table. Edit the database relationships to add referential integrity to this new relationship. The new table will look like this:

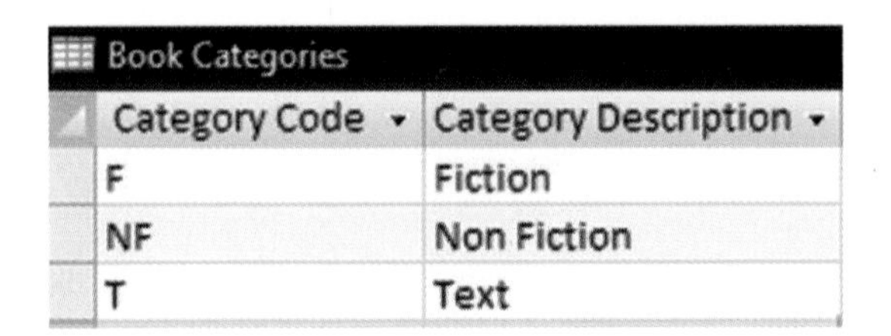

Book Categories

Category Code	Category Description
F	Fiction
NF	Non Fiction
T	Text

Exercise 8.21

Assume a database about professional baseball. The database would include data about teams, players, cities, and statistics for each at bat. Complete the diagram below by filing in the entity names and drawing the correct relationship cardinality:

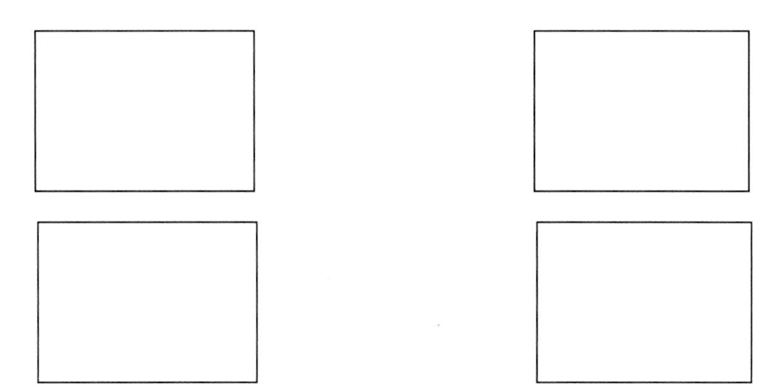

Exercise 8.22

Assume an insurance database about automobiles and licensed drivers. The database would include data about vehicles, owners, drivers, and accident instances. Complete the diagram below by filing in the entity names and drawing the correct relationship cardinality:

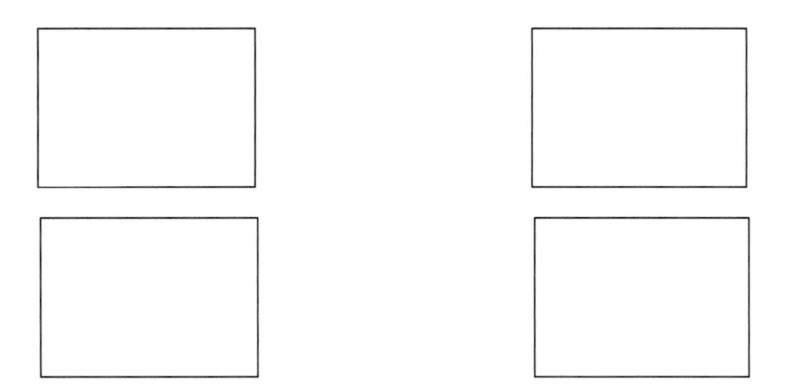

Exercise 8.23

Use BIBLIO.ACCDB and perform a query that returns ONLY these three fields in this order:

- Author from the author's table.
- Publisher's name (not company name) from the publisher's table.
- Publisher's state from the publisher's table.

Show authors with a last name beginning with H or C. You must use the like operator for this. Specify H before you specify C. Only include publishers which have no state code. Make sure that you do not sort the records.
Tips:

- Select the titles table first.
- Although you are selecting columns from two tables all three tables must be included in the query.
- This is a compound query — be sure that you get the logic right. Make certain that the "no state code" restriction applies to both the "begins with H" and to the "begins with "C" restrictions.

When you set up the query correctly the result will have one row as shown here:

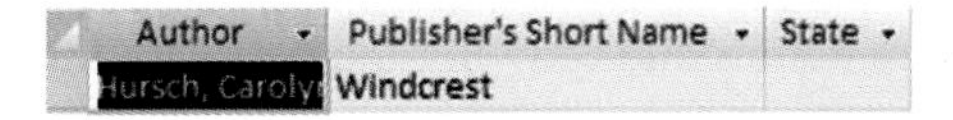

Author	Publisher's Short Name	State
Hursch, Caroly	Windcrest	

When the result is correct submit the SQL. Do not submit the records returned by the query.

Exercise 8.24

Use SCHOOL.ACCDB and perform a query that returns these three fields in this order from the Class table for classes taught by a professor with a PhD only:

- Catalog Number
- Title
- Time

Make sure that you do not sort the records. Tips:

- Select the professor table first.
- For this assignment you are joining both tables. You must add a selection criterium to the degree column of the professor table.

Export the query result as COURSES BY PHD.TXT file and submit it. Use comma as a delimiter. Include column headers. The first several records of the query result look like this:

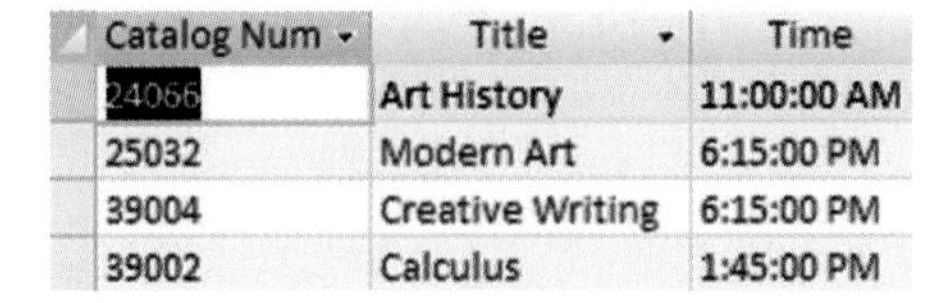

Catalog Num	Title	Time
24066	Art History	11:00:00 AM
25032	Modern Art	6:15:00 PM
39004	Creative Writing	6:15:00 PM
39002	Calculus	1:45:00 PM

The following are SQL exercises. The instructor will tell you how to access the SQL Lab to complete these exercises.

Exercise 8.25

Write a query that performs a full projection of all customer records. Use the customers table.

Exercise 8.26

Using the supplier's table write a query that performs a full projection of all French suppliers. Sort the records alphabetically by city.

Exercise 8.27

Write the SQL that will perform a partial projection of the products table that displays the name, price, and stock level for all products. A portion of the result looks like this:

ProductName	UnitPrice	UnitsInStock
Chai	18	39
Chang	19	17
Aniseed Syrup	10	13

Exercise 8.28

Change the query of Exercise 8.27 so only products with insufficient inventory are displayed. Also display two additional columns as shown below. Insufficient inventory is defined as when units on hand plus units on order sum to less than the reorder level:

$$UnitsInStock + UnitsOnOrder < ReorderLevel.$$

To make this work you will need to do a restriction which checks inventory on hand plus inventory ordered against the reorder level. The query will return these records and look exactly as this:

ProductName	UnitPrice	UnitsInStock	UnitsOnOrder	ReorderLevel
Nord-Ost Matjeshering	25.89	10	0	15
Outback Lager	15	15	10	30

Exercise 8.29

Write the SQL which selects records in Region 1 from the territories table. Project only the columns shown here in the partial listing:

TerritoryID	TerritoryDescription
01581	Westboro
01730	Bedford
01833	Georgetow
02116	Boston
02139	Cambridge
02184	Braintree
02903	Providence

Exercise 8.30

Write the SQL to display (in this order) the first name, last name, title, and hire date of all employees who are sales representatives. Sort the records so that the most recently hired sales representative is first in the list exactly as shown here. Tip: The most recent date is the highest value. So sort the records in descending order.

FirstName	LastName	Title	HireDate
Anne	Dodsworth	Sales Representative	11/15/1994
Robert	King	Sales Representative	1/2/1994
Michael	Suyama	Sales Representative	10/17/1993
Margaret	Peacock	Sales Representative	5/3/1993
Nancy	Davolio	Sales Representative	5/1/1992
Janet	Leverling	Sales Representative	4/1/1992

Exercise 8.31

Write the SQL that will return the number of records from the products table where the unit price is at least 55. Only display the count and name the returned column exactly as shown below.

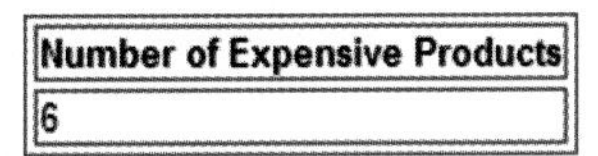

Number of Expensive Products
6

Exercise 8.32

How many orders were shipped on time? Lateness is defined as the order being shipped after the required date.

Exercise 8.33

Write the SQL to learn how many different cities customers come from. The result will look exactly like this:

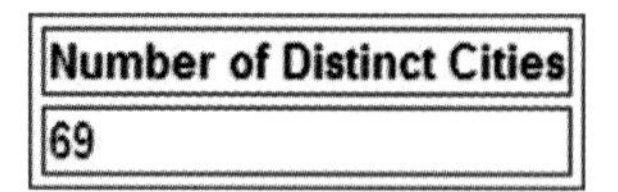

Number of Distinct Cities
69

Exercise 8.34

Write the SQL to project the ProductName supplied by any company based in Spain. Use the products and suppliers tables, they share a common column: SupplierID. The result will return exactly these two records:

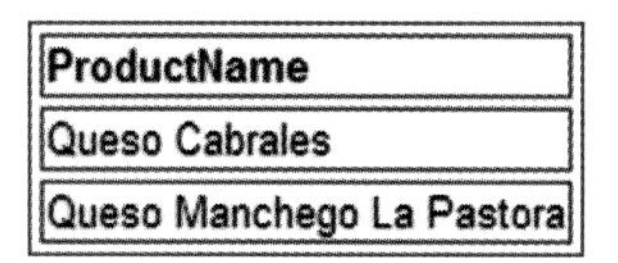

ProductName
Queso Cabrales
Queso Manchego La Pastora

Exercise 8.35

Write the SQL to display an alphabetical list (by LastName) of all employees who sold an order shipped to Portugal. Join the orders and employees tables using a common column: EmployeeID. This is the result of the query:

FirstName	LastName
Steven	Buchanan
Laura	Callahan
Nancy	Davolio
Anne	Dodsworth
Robert	King
Janet	Leverling
Margaret	Peacock

Exercise 8.36

Write the SQL that joins these tables in this order: customers to orders, orders to order details, order details to products. Project all columns. Here is the relevant ERD:

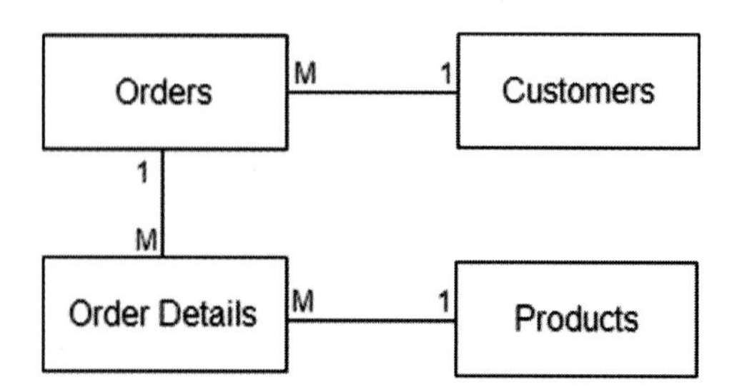

HTML, XHTML, AND XML

CHAPTER 9

HTML is an abbreviation for a particular form of **hypertext** that is used to create Web pages. A Web browser renders the Webpage according to the hypertext so that its appearance on the screen is attractive and easy to use. The letters, HTML, stand for **Hypertext Markup Language.**

Hypertext is used to prepare documents that are displayed in Web browsers and are linked to one another. The beauty of linking documents is that as the viewer reads (or views) a document, any topic of interest (that is linked to the current document) may be jumped to. Viewers **navigate** among Web sites by following hyperlinks. The viewer then reads the new document and may jump from that to other documents.

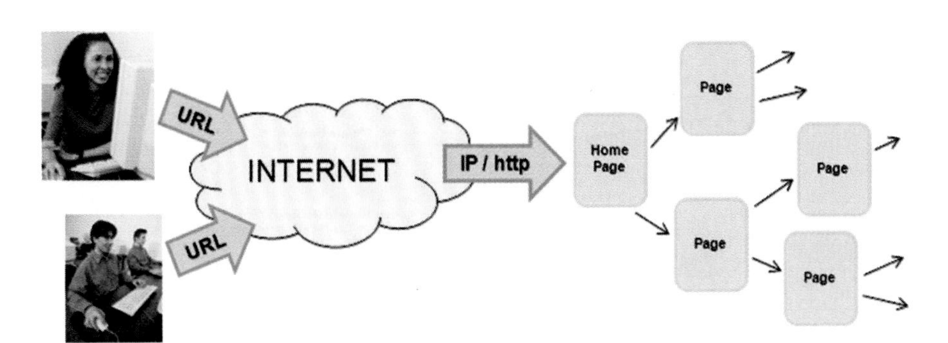

Hypertext – Linked Documents

Markup is about the formatting commands that the browser follows when rendering an HTML document for view. Markup is not particularly a computer oriented term as it existed in the printing industry for several centuries. In the context of a Web browser (Internet Explorer, FireFox, Opera, Safari, etc.) the display **rendering** can be thought of as multimedia since the HTML document may contain words, sound, images, video, and other active components.

HTML	Make this text <b>bold</b>.
Browser	Make this text **bold**.

Markup – Formatting Documents

HTML was introduced prior to the public availability of the Internet in the mid 1990s. It was the markup language understood by early Web browsers like **Netscape** and **Mozilla.** Since no industry-wide HTML standard existed, browser developers began to invent new formatting commands which resulted in a lack of consistency among browsers.

The industry recognized the advantages of standardization and recreated the entire HTML language in a standard published in 2001 and known as **XHTML** or "**Extensible HTML.**" The standard published by the **WC3** (World Wide Web Consortium) was since updated in 2004. XHTML is less forgiving than HTML. The Web page author or designer must pay closer attention to the language **syntax** when using XHTML. HTML has somewhat loose syntactic rules. While this encouraged its adoption by those unfamiliar with Web publishing, over time the insatiable demand for greater sophistication in Web sites required standardization.

Since HTML and XHTML are almost functionally identical and the formatting commands have mostly the same names, it is useful to learn the languages in sequence. The HTML portion of this chapter provides the basics of hypertext and its use. The XHTML section further explains and demonstrates how to use the functionally called for in the XHTML standard. A key feature of XHTML as explained in this chapter is the use of **CSS** (cascading style sheets).

Hypertext Markup Language (HTML) was designed to display data and to focus on how data is presented. Extensible Markup Language (XML) was designed to describe data and to focus on what the data is about. Both languages are used to provide communication between producers and consumers of information. XML is a **markup language** for documents containing **structured information.** XML is a way of describing data and an XML file can contain the data, too, as in a database of structured records. Its primary purpose is to facilitate the sharing of data across different systems, particularly systems connected by the Internet.

XML Structures Data

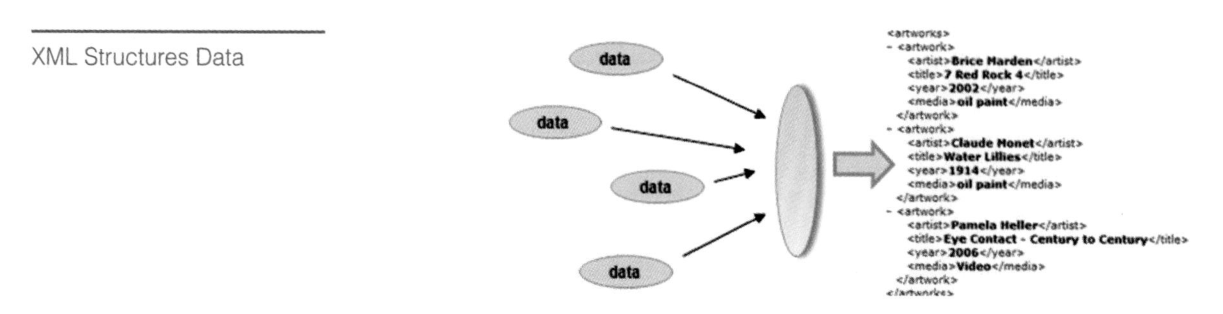

Both XML and HTML contain markup symbols, known as **tags,** to describe the contents of a page or file. HTML, however, describes the content of a Web page (mainly text and graphic images) only in terms of how it is to be displayed and interacted with. For example, the letter "p" placed within HTML tags starts a new paragraph. XML describes the content in terms of what data is being described. For example, the word "phonenumber" placed within markup tags could indicate that the data that followed was a phone number. This means that an XML file can be processed purely as data by a program.

9.1 HTML: Hypertext Markup Language

HTML is a common (possibly the most common) markup language used for the creation of Web pages. It provides the rules to describe the structure of a document so that it can be displayed in a Web browser. The structure might contain words, images, video, color, sound, and links to other documents and so on.

HTML suffers from lack of **standardization.** Web browsers commonly make assumptions about HTML's intent and proceed with rendering the Web page while ignoring errors in the HTML **syntax.** Over time, the trend in official standards has been to create increasingly strict language syntax; however, browsers still continue to render pages that are far from valid HTML.

This section discusses the basics of hypertext and HTML. Following are the instructions about text formatting and including images and hyperlinks follow. These descriptions apply to both HTML and XHTML.

9.1.1 Hypertext

For a document to be prepared as a hypertext document use a text editor like Notepad, or a special HTML editor. It is first necessary to understand a few concepts:

A Web page's file extension must be HTM or HTML.

- **Page** — data or information that may be of interest to a viewer is organized in pages. Each page may contain complete information about a topic or provide links to other pages that provide additional information. Pages may contain almost any kind of data, for example: text, pictures, video and sound, and are called **hypermedia.** Pages are also known as **documents.**
- **Jump point** — the point within a document that a viewer uses to **navigate** to another document is called a jump point or **hyperlink.** Normally a hyperlink is displayed in color and underlined. When the mouse is moved over it the cursor usually changes from a pointer to a hand with a pointing finger.
- **Universal Resource Locator** — each document (page) that is the target of a link must be located for the jump to happen. The page's address, the **URL (Uniform Resource Locator),** for a target page is embedded in an HTML document. A URL is the unique address for a file that is accessible on the Internet, so the protocol is not limited to HTTP, but may also be HTTPS, FTP, etc.

  Webpage URLs are of the form: **http://**............ where "http" stands for hypertext transfer protocol. **HTTP** is the set of rules that control how Web pages are delivered through the Internet. A Web page named "mypage.htm" might have this URL: http://someserver.com/mypage.htm.
- **Tag** — a code within the HTML document that tells the browser what to do with the text that follows. Tags are used to create page headers, menus and titles, emphasize text, include images, and create hyperlinks, and so on. Tags begin with a less than sign, <, and end with a greater than sign, >. Between < and > are the name of the tag and sometimes other **attributes** that tell the tag how to behave.

9.1.2 HTML Basics

Creating hypertext documents in HTML takes a little getting used to. Mostly you type what you want and then surround the text with tags to format its appearance.

A **tag** is a code that instructs the browser to do something special with the content that follows. Typically, you give the name of the tag followed by optional attributes that provide additional control over how the browser uses the tag. The general format of a tag is:

General Tag Format

```
<TAG_NAME PARAMETERS...>
```

Several tags mark important sections of an HTML document:

- **html** — This element tells a browser that this is an HTML document.
- **head** — The head element can contain information about the document which is not displayed. The following tags can be in the head section: <base>, <link>, <meta>, <script>, <style>, and <title>.
- **body** — The body element defines the documents' body. It contains all the contents of the document (like text, images, colors, graphics, etc.).

These tags divide the document this way:

Tags Mark Major Portions of a Page

```
<html>
<head>
<title>My Website</title>
</head>
<body>
The content of the document...
</body>
</html>
```

Deprecated tags: Older HTML tags and attributes that have been superseded by other more functional or flexible alternatives (whether as HTML or as CSS) are declared as deprecated in HTML4 by the W3C - the consortium that sets HTML standards. Browsers will continue to support deprecated tags and attributes, but eventually these tags are likely to become obsolete and so future support cannot be guaranteed.

Since a tag tells the browser how to treat content it is also necessary to inform the browser when to stop the special treatment. For example, the <b> tag instructs the browser to display all text that follows it in bold letters. When you want to return to normal text, use the **closing** bold tag </b> as in this example:

Closing Tags

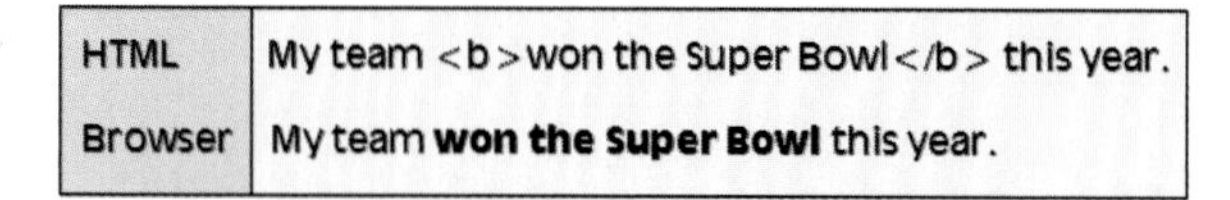

HTML	My team <b>won the Super Bowl</b> this year.
Browser	My team **won the Super Bowl** this year.

Many tags have closing tags; some do not. A few examples of tags:

Common HTML Tags

HTML	Browser
<b> ... </b>	**Bold**
<i> ... </i>	*Italic*
<u> ... </u>	Underline
<center> ... </center>	Center
 	New Line
<hr>	Horizontal Line
<font color=...> ... </font>	Color text
<h1> ... </h1>	Header
<a href=...> ... </a>	Hyperlink
<img src=...>	Image

9.1.2 How to Create and Display a Web Page

Once you get the idea about tags and what they are used for you should try to create your own Web page. Follow these steps:

HTML is not case sensitive but XHTML is. To prepare for mastering XHTML it would be a good idea to use lower case tag names while learning HTML.

1) Start a text editor program like Notepad.
2) Type your HTML in the edit window.
3) **CRITICAL:** Save your work with the htm file extension and select All Files in Save As type box.
4) Keep Notepad open.
5) Display your work in the browser this way:
   a) Start your browser.
   b) Select Open from the File menu.
   c) Use the Browse option from the dialog box that appears to locate your work.

   To change your web page:

1) Return to Notepad and edit the HTML code.
2) Save the document (File > Save menu in Notepad).
3) Return to the browser and click Refresh on the toolbar (or select View menu then click Refresh).

Notepad is not a WYSIWYG ("what you see is what you get") editor; you will not immediately know what you have accomplished. For that reason it is necessary to display your work in a browser.

9.1.4 Formatting Text

HTML allows you to format your text in various ways. In most cases you surround the text that you want to format with a pair of tags. The three simplest formats are:

- **Bold:** Text that is surrounded by the <b> and </b> tags appears in **bold** letters.
- **Underline:** Use the <u> and </u> tags to underline words.
- **Italic:** Put text in *italics* with <i> and </i> tags.

You can also **nest** format tags. For example, <b><i> ... some text here ... </i></b> creates bold italic text. Here are some examples of tags and nesting:

```
<b>bold text</b>
<u>underlined <i>italic</i> text</u>
<i>italic text</i>
<i><u>nested </u>tags</i>
```

Formatting Text

You were probably surprised to learn that if the four previous examples were in a Web page's HTML as shown the browser would display the result in one single line this way:

bold textunderlined *italic* text*italic text**nested tags*

The Browser Ignores Carriage Return

This happens because browsers ignore the carriage return ("line feed") that you are familiar with from typing with a word processor. Since the line feed is ignored by the browser the Web page author must add one after each line.

Line Feed If you wish to force a line feed use <br>. This tag works alone; there is no closing </br> tag. If the example above were rewritten using the <br> tag the results would be different as shown on the right:

Using a Line Feed

HTML	Browser
<b>bold text</b> 	**bold text**
<u>underlined <i>italic</i> text</u> 	underlined *italic* text
<i>italic text</i> 	*italic text*
<i><u>nested </u>tags</i>	*nested tags*

Centering on a Page Any page content, including text, may be centered in the browser window using the <center> and </center> tags. Surround the content to be centered with those tags this way:

Centered Text

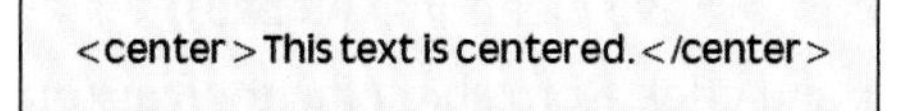

<center> is an example of a deprecated tag. It is recommend instead to use the <div> tag with the align attribute set to "center.". The <div> tags surrounds a section of a webpage's HTML code. The <div> tag is used for centering a portion of a webpage as shown here:

Centered Text

```
<div align=center>This text is centered.</div>
```

Subscripts and Superscripts A pair of tags allows smaller text above the surrounding text (a superscript) or below the baseline (a subscript). Here are examples that show the tags and the outcomes:

Subscripts and Superscripts

HTML	Browser
8² = 64	$8^2 = 64$
H₂O	H_2O

Headers HTML allows for six levels of headers. *Text typed otherwise is sized according to the browser defaults or is controlled by other tags.* Normally you use larger text for **headers** or **section separators.** Header tags automatically bold what is displayed. Surround the text with <h1> and </h1> for the largest header and<h6> and </h6> for the smallest as shown here:

Header Tags Offer Six Predetermined Text Sizes

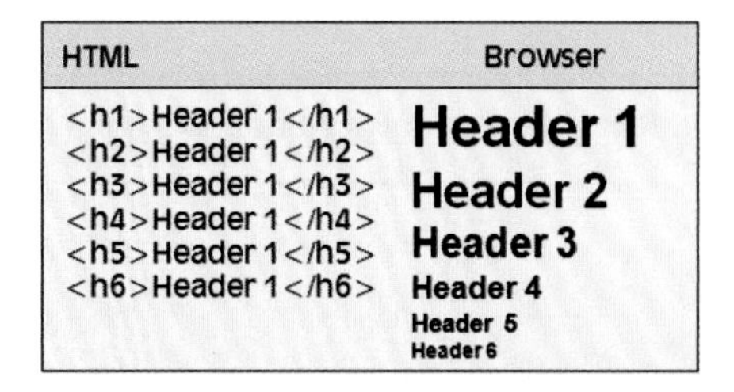

HTML	Browser
<h1>Header 1</h1>	Header 1
<h2>Header 1</h2>	Header 2
<h3>Header 1</h3>	Header 3
<h4>Header 1</h4>	Header 4
<h5>Header 1</h5>	Header 5
<h6>Header 1</h6>	Header 6

It is reasonable to nest other tags inside a header tag. Here is an example:

HTML	<h1>Corporate <u>Profits</u><h1>
Browser	**Corporate <u>Profits</u>**

Nesting inside a Header Tag

Font Style, Color, and Size HTML provides a font tag which allows general control over the appearance of text. The font tag requires a minimum of one **attribute** but several may be used. A closing font tag is required. Each attribute requires a value and is used in this form: **attribute-value.** Attribute-value pairs are separated by a space. The three attributes of the font tag are:

- **face** — the name of a font style.
- **size** — the size of the text.
- **color** — the text's color.

Here is an example:

HTML	Default font. <font face="Tango">Tango font.</font>
Browser	Default font. Tango font.

Changing a Font

If multiple parameters are used the order does not matter but separate each parameter by a space. If the parameter's value has a space in it then the value itself must be surrounded by quotes. For example:

HTML	Default font. <font size=+2 face="Marigold"> This is different.</font>
Browser	Default font. This is different.

Setting Multiple Attributes

The **size** parameter can be used in two ways: **absolute** and **relative.** Absolute use selects a specific font size (size=3). There are seven sizes for text numbered from 1 to 7, where 1 is the smallest text in a document and 7 is the largest. Relative use makes the font size larger or smaller than the current font (size=+2 or size=-3). The relative sizes should range from +1 to +6 and -1 to -6.

Any changes made by the font tag are in effect until a closing font tag is encountered.

Tip: Do not nest tags in a title.

Page Titles Use the title tag to put a **title** on the top of the window. This tag requires a closing tag.

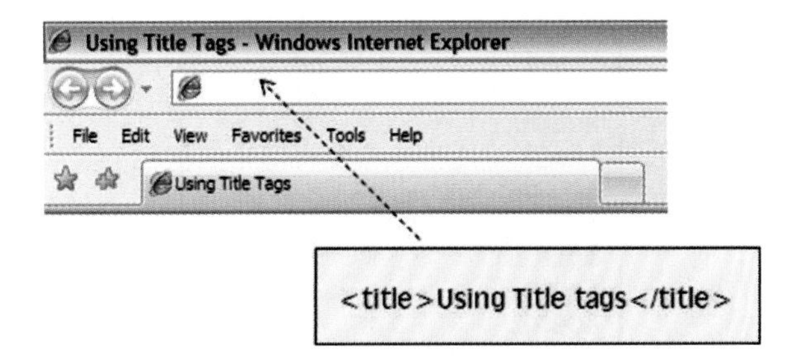

Using a Title Tag

Horizontal Rule Separate sections of a page with a horizontal rule (a line) by using the <hr> tag. Use the **size** parameter to make the line thicker (the default is 1 so <hr> and <hr size=1> are the same). The higher the number, the thicker the line.

To fill-in the line use the keyword NOSHADE like this: <hr noshade size=10 >. This horizontal rule is presented as flat instead of three dimensional. Use the color parameter to change the rule's color (example: color="magenta").

The Horizontal Rule

<hr>

<hr size=20>

<hr size=20 NOSHADE>

<hr size=20 color=magenta NOSHADE>

Displaying Lists of Things Web sites often display items in a list. There are two styles of lists: **ordered** and **unordered.** In an ordered list the items are numbered and in an unordered list they are shown with a "bullet."

- **Ordered List** — Begin with the ordered list tag, <ol>, and end with the closing ordered list tag, </ol>. In between the tags include the individual items to be listed; start each item with a list item tag, <li>. The list item tag has no closing tag.
- **Unordered List** — Creating an unordered list is just as simple; change the ordered list tags to unordered list tags, <ul> and </ul> and the numbering before each list item becomes a large bullet.

Ordered and Unordered Lists

HTML	<ol> <li>Apples <li>Pears <li>Cherries </ol>	<ul> <li>Apples <li>Pears <li>Cherries </ul>
Browser	1. Apples 2. Pears 3. Cherries	• Apples • Pears • Cherries

Tip: Any item in a list may be additionally formated using any other format tags (<u>, <b>, <i>, <font . . .> etc.). For example:

<li><font color=orange>Orange</font> is my <u>favorite</u> fruit!</li>

An ordered list need not start numbering at one. Adjust the starting value this way:

<ol start = "4">

Special Characters Not all characters that might be desired in a Web page are found on the keyboard. The copyright symbol ©, for example, is one such character. Rendering special symbols in the browser requires a sequence of characters in HTML that the browser will interpret in the correct fashion. This table lists several special characters and the HTML code that renders them:

Special Characters

HTML	Browser
£	£
©	©
®	®
™	™
<	<
>	>
&	&
¢	¢

9.1.5 Display an Image

Including an image in a Web page is straight forward. Use the IMG tag with the following syntax:

```
<img src=IMAGE_NAME>
```

Quotes around the name are required if the image name or address contains a space.

There is no closing image tag. Replace IMAGE_NAME with the name or URL (http://.....) of the GIF, JPG, PNG, or other image to be included. If the image is in the same folder as your HTML document just use the file name. If the image is anywhere else (other than the folder that contains your HTML page) then use the image's full URL. Example:

Including an Image

Location of Image
Same folder as web page
<img src="birthday party.jpg"[1]>
Elsewhere
<img src="http://webimages.com/birthday party.jpg">

[1]Quotes around the URL are required if the address contains a space.

It is common in a website to locate images in a separate folder, such as the "images" folder. In this case, assuming that images is a sub folder to the document's folder the URL would reference the images folder **relatively** this way:

Using a Relative URL

```
<img src="images/birthday party.jpg">
```

9.1.6 Hyperlinks

A hyperlink connects a page to another document or resource. The viewer clicks on underlined words to navigate to the target.

Link to Another Page The hyperlink is constructed from the <a ..> and </a> tags this way:

Hyperlink

```
<a href=URL1,2>Underlined text that the viewer clicks.</a>
```

[1]URL is:

- *The name of a page in the same folder as the page with href=mypage.htm, or*
- *The full path (href=http://.../mypage.htm) to a page elsewhere.*

[2]Quotes around the URL are required if the address contains a space.

Here is an example of an ordered list of hyperlinks (HTML followed by result):

A URL is the location of a document or resource somewhere on the Internet. URLs are specified for:
- **Documents as: http://someserver.com/somepage.htm**
- **Images as: http://otherserver/myimage.gif**

Ordered List of Hyperlinks

HTML	<ol> <li><a href=http://Microsoft.com>Microsoft</a> <li><a href=yahoo.com>Yahoo</a> </ol>
Browser	1. Microsoft 2. Yahoo

Incorporating an Image in a Hyperlink Replacing underlined words with an image is as simple as removing the words and replacing them with an <img...> tag. The link to Google with an image is done this way (assuming google.gif is in the same folder):

Image Used in Hyperlink

The image referenced in the <img...> tag is outlined in the same color as all hyperlinks, and when clicked on the hyperlink will be activated. This is how to remove the outline around the image; use the **border** attribute like this:

Hiding a Border

```
<a href="http://www.google.com/">
      <img src="google.gif" border=0></a>
```

Link to E-mail The same tag is used to link to an email address. If you want your Web page to allow a link to an e-mail program and have it address the e-mail to a specific recipient do it this way:

Linking to E-Mail

```
<a href=mailto:information@ajax.biz>information</a>
```

9.1.7 Other Features

HTML is a rich environment with many features and options. While a comprehensive list is too involved to present in this chapter, several additional features are described in this section.

More Control Using Tables HTML allows more precision in the control over the appearance of portions of a Web page with the use of a table. A table is essentially a grid of rows and columns. Each table **cell** may contain text, images, or even another table. The table is formed from three basic tags each of which must have a closing tag:

- <table> starts and ends a table.
- <tr> starts and ends a table's row.
- <td> starts and ends a cell within a row.

Here is an example that shows how a table is created using HTML. As you can see, a table is a nested structure of the three tags listed above:

Tables Help Organize a Page

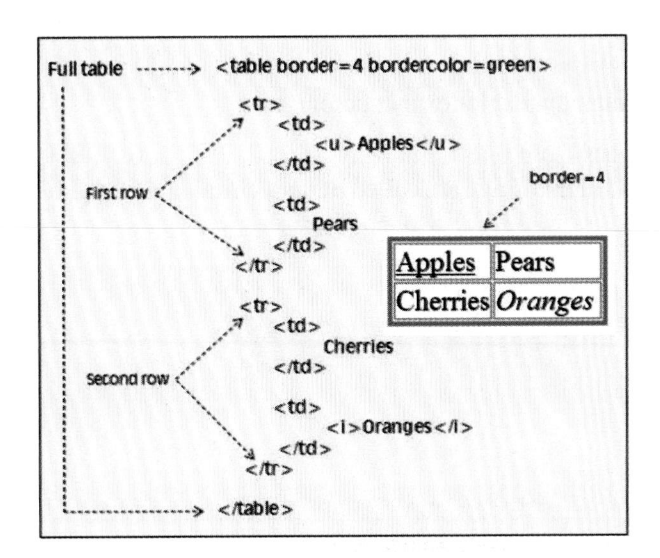

The border parameter controls the thickness of the table's border. The default value is 1. A value of 0 eliminates the border and larger numbers make thicker borders. The color of the border is controlled by the **bordercolor** attribute and is used as: bordercolor=color where color is the name of a color or a RGB color (introduced later in this chapter).

The background color of a table is controlled by the **bgcolor** attribute and it is used as bgcolor=color.

Page Background Color If you wish the page to have a uniform **background color** the <body> tag is used to accomplish that effect. The **bgcolor** parameter controls the background color this way:

Setting the Page's Background Color

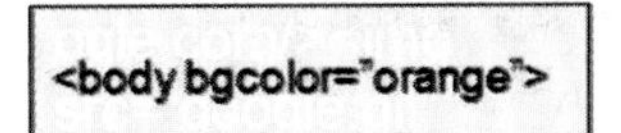

Most colors that can be imagined can be used. Silver, blue, yellow, orange, gold, black, pink, white, green, and so on are available. For more specific control over color sections use **RGB** colors.

RGB (Red-Green-Blue) Colors Each computer color is comprised of **red, green,** and **blue** (RGB) components. All colors are formed by combining these three **primary colors.** The amount of each color in the mix determines the outcome. RGB colors are specified by # followed by six characters in a sequence of three codes; first red, then green, then blue. Each color code is two characters long.

RGB Color Examples

#DEB887
#5F9EA0
#7FFF00
#D2691E
#FF7F50
#6495ED
#FFF8DC
#DC143C
#00FFFF

The code defines how much of each color is desired in the blend. Look at the chart above to get an idea of how RGB colors are constructed. Specifically, each primary color is given two digits and the range for each color is:

RGB colors must include an amount for red, green, and blue even if the amount of a color is zero (none). The order of colors always must be red, green, then blue. RGB colors always begin with #, and they always have six characters after the #.

- 00 (none of that color) to
- FF (the maximum available for that color)

Each digit ranges from 0 to F this way: 0, 1, 2, 3, 4, 5, 6, 7, 8, 9, A, B, C, D, E, F. Numbers expressed in this range are called **hexadecimal** numbers. Points in the two digit range include:

- 00 (0%)
- 3F (25%)
- 7F (50%)
- BF (75%)
- FF (100%)

Setting the Background RGB Color

Page Foreground Color The foreground color of a page is the color text is rendered in. Normally this is black because the page color is normally white. If you make the page background color too dark the text will not show. For that reason setting the foreground color could be useful. This example shows how to set both colors in the body tag:

Setting the Page's Background and Foreground Color

```
<body bgcolor="blue" color="white">
```

Page Background Image It is also possible to display an image as the background of a Web page. If you do this, changing the background color will have no effect. The background image will tile (repeat itself vertically and horizontally). Here is how to set the background image:

Setting the Page's Background Image

```
<body background="whitemountains.jpg">
```

Sound in a Web Page There are several ways to incorporate sound in a Web page. The **bgsound** tag plays the background sound in a page. When the viewer visits a page, the sound will automatically play. The syntax is as follows:

Adding Sound to a Web page

```
<bgsound src=SOUND_FILE loop=X>
```

Replace SOUND_FILE with the name of a sound file. The file should have an extension of **.wav** or **.mid.** Replace X with the number of times the sound will play or -1 for the sound to play continuously. You may also add the volume attribute as shown. Volume values range from 0 (mute) to 100.

```
<bgsound src=SOUND_FILE loop=1 volume=500>
```

Adjusting the Volume

Positioning Objects More Precisely Using the Style Attribute HTML tables were presented as a means for exercising some control over where items appear in a Web page. Since the height and width of the cells is automatically controlled by the web browser it is impossible to obtain precise positioning using tables. Use of an object's **style** attribute allows precision.

```
<img src='telephone.jpg'
    style="position:absolute; top:50; left:200">
```

The Style Property

In this example an image is positioned 50 pixels from the page top and 200 pixels from the left margin:

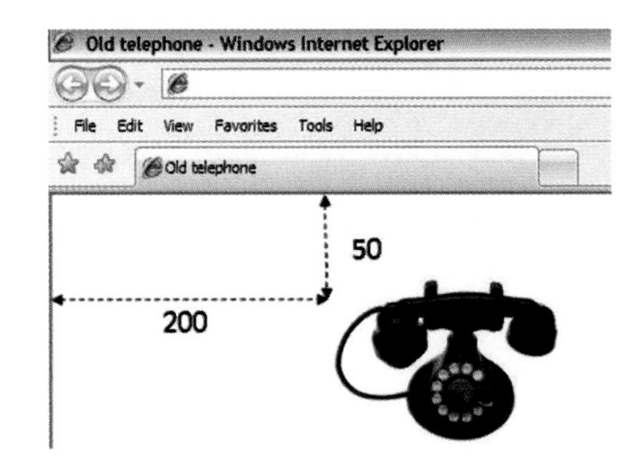

Precise Positioning

The style attribute provides many additional options. Style is a feature of XHTML and is discussed later in this chapter.

9.1.8 Forms

A form is a rectangular section of a Web page that contains **controls** that the viewer is able to interact with. Common controls include:

- Input box
- Radio button
- Checkbox
- Selection list
- Textarea
- Submit button

Normally the viewer enters data into input boxes and text areas or makes selections from radio buttons, checkboxes, and selection lists. Once the form is complete the viewer clicks the submit button and the form is delivered to a server where a program processes it. Web server processing is beyond the scope of this book and is not discussed here.

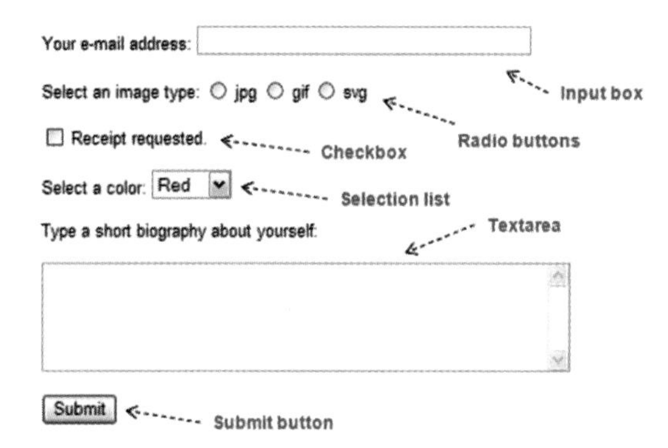

HTML Form Showing Controls

The controls are placed on a Web page this way:

Input Box The input box display size and maximum size may be specified, too.

```
<input>
<input size=40>
<input size=40 maxlength=100>
```

Radio Button Group Radio buttons present a choice to the viewer so they are grouped by using the same name.

```
<input type=radio name=imageType value=J>
<input type=radio name=imageType value=G>
<input type=radio name=imageType value=S>
```

Checkbox A checkbox is like an on/off switch because it records one of two values.

```
<input type=checkbox>
```

Selection List The selection list uses two types of tags. Option tags are nested within select tags. The size attribute determines how many options are displayed when the list is not expanded. The list expands when selected with the mouse.

```
<select size=1>
<option>Red</option>
<option>Green</option>
<option>Blue</option>
<option>Pink</option>
</select>
```

A variation of the selection list allows options to be arranged in groups this way:

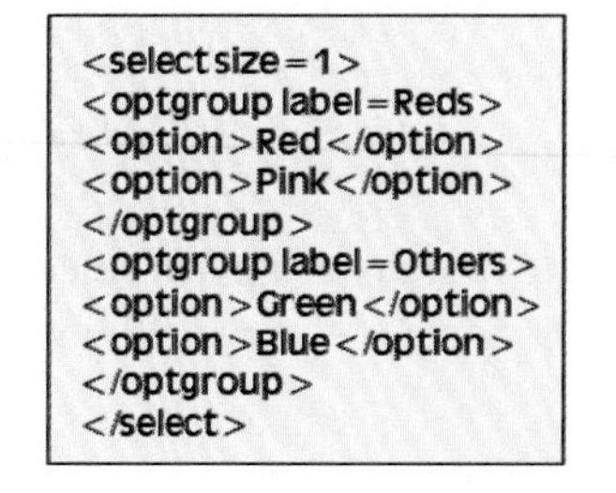

```
<select size=1>
<optgroup label=Reds>
<option>Red</option>
<option>Pink</option>
</optgroup>
<optgroup label=Others>
<option>Green</option>
<option>Blue</option>
</optgroup>
</select>
```

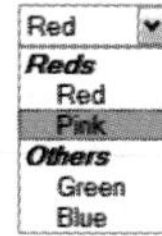

Textarea The size of the textarea may be specified using the rows and cols attributes. It also requires a closing tag.

```
<textarea rows=10cols=50></textarea>
```

Submit Button The submit button will display "Submit Query" on its face unless the value attribute is used.

```
<input type=submit value=Submit>
```

9.2 XHTML: Extensible Hypertext Markup Language

The Extensible Hypertext Markup Language, or XHTML, is a language that has at least the same expressive possibilities as HTML, but has a stricter syntax. XHTML is an application of **XML (Extensible Markup Language)**. XHTML is a successor to HTML and many people consider XHTML to be the "current version" of HTML. It is not, but it is a separate, parallel implementation of a markup language that Web browsers understand. The **W3C** (World Wide Web Consortium) continues to recommend the use of both XHTML and HTML for Web publishing.

The World Wide Web Consortium (http://www.w3.org/) is an international consortium that develops Web standards. W3C's mission is: "To lead the World Wide Web to its full potential by developing protocols and guidelines that ensure long-term growth for the Web."

The need for greater standardization of HTML was recognized because Web content is now delivered to many devices, like mobile equipment, in addition to traditional computers. In these small devices extra resources are not available to support the parsing complexity of the syntactically looser HTML. At present, most Web browsers recognize HTML and XHTML, but other devices recognize XHTML only. The drive for standardization may someday remove HTML support from browsers.

The changes from HTML to XHTML 1.0 are minor. The most obvious charges are:

- Document must be **well formed** meaning all elements must conform to the rules and requirements of XHTML.
- All tag names must be in **lowercase.**
- All attribute values must be **enclosed by quotes** (either 'single' or "double" quotes may be used).
- Tags must be **properly nested.**
- Each document must have a **root element** which is normally a pair of <html> tags.
- The document must begin with a DOCTYPE declaration.

Any tag that does not have a closing tag must be self-closed. For example: <br> is replaced by <br />. Since all tags must be lower case <BR /> is not valid. Surrounding attribute values means that <img src="myFamily.jpg" /> requires quotes as shown even though the image file name contains no spaces.

Apart from the changes noted above the most significant feature of XHTML is the use of the **style** attribute for controlling the appearance of most Web page content. Styles may be recorded in a separate page, known as a cascading style sheet or **CSS** and used throughout a Web site.

Keep in mind that XHTML is not forgiving. The use of syntax must be correct. If one portion of a tag is incorrect the tag is ignored; no error message appears. In HTML only the incorrect portion of a tag is ignored.

9.2.1 Document Types and Structure

All XHTML documents must be well formed and that begins with a DOCTYPE declaration. The html, head, and body elements all must be present, and the title must be present inside the head element. The structure of a document and the relationship among the elements of a document (the **objects**) follows what is known as the **Document Object Model** (DOM).

The DOCTYPE declaration names the document type definition (DTD) in use for the document. A DTD defines the actual elements, attributes, and element relationships that are valid in documents. The DOCTYPE declaration also allows validation software to identify the HTML DTD being followed and verify that the document is syntactically correct.

The basic document structure is:

XHTML Document Structure

```
<!DOCTYPE ...>
<html>
<head>
<title>... title required here ... </title>
</title>
</head>
<body>
  ... page content here ...
</body>
</html>
```

The DOCTYPE declaration is not a part of the XHTML document itself. It is not an XHTML element, and it should not have a closing tag. The DOCTYPE declaration must always be at the beginning of an XHTML document because it informs the browser how to treat the remainder of the document. The DOCTYPE declaration defines the document type. There are three kinds of DocTypes:

- **Transitional doctype** — This is the HTML 4.01 Transitional DTD, which includes deprecated presentation attributes and elements that W3C expects to phase out as support for style sheets matures. Authors should use the Strict DTD when possible, but may use the Transitional DTD when support for presentation attribute and elements is required.
- **Strict doctype** — Strict is an XML version of HTML. It is a trimmed down version of HTML4.01 that emphasizes structure over presentation. Deprecated elements and attributes including most presentational attributes, and frames are not allowed. Strict documents easily adapt to style sheets and different browsing situations.
- **Frameset doctype** — This is the HTML 4.01 Frameset DTD, which should be used for documents with frames. This DTD is identical to the HTML 4.01 Transitional DTD except that the FRAMESET element replaces the BODY element. Frames are dropped in the strict doctype definition so this doctype is not commonly used.

For now use this declaration:

DOCTYPE Loose Declaration

```
<!DOCTYPE HTML PUBLIC "-//W3C/DTD HTML 4.01 Transitional//EN"
 "http://www.w3.org/TR/html4/loose.dtd">
```

The DOCTYPE declaration should be on one line. Space limitations prevent displaying it that way here.

Once browser support for HTML is completely replaced by XHTML use this declaration instead and alter the <html> tag as shown. The page's content is placed between the <body> tags as shown above.

```
<!DOCTYPE html PUBLIC "-//W3C//DTD XHTML 1.0 Strict//EN"
  "http://www.w3.org/TR/xhtml1/DTD/xhtml1-strict.dtd">

<html xmlns="http://www.w3.org/1999/xhtml">
```

DOCTYPE Strict Declaration

Note: The <html> tag declares **XML** as the **namespace** for the XHTML language. A namespace is a language **vocabulary** and the XML vocabulary is the basis for XHTML. XML is described later in this chapter.

9.2.2 Styles

The style attribute of a tag is used to format the content defined by that tag. The easiest way to demonstrate the use of this attribute is by example. The <p> tag or paragraph tag is used to format a section of text. The style attribute can be used with this tag to specify many formats including the font and text color this way:

```
<p style="font-family: arial; color:blue">
  This is blue text in Arial font.</p>
```

Use Style for Formatting

Contrast this with conventional HTML where the same result could have been achieved like this:

```
<font face=Arial color=blue>
  This is blue text in Arial font.</font>
```

Conventional Formatting

So far this is not much of a change; it seems the <p> tag replaced the <font> tag. While not obvious now, there is much more of a difference than is apparent. You might recall that the font tag supports three attributes: font, color, and size. The style attribute provides many more than three ways to format text. Style gives considerably more control over Web page content then conventional HTML.

Be aware that in the style attribute each property is separated from a value with a colon. Each property-value pair is separated from others by a semi-colon. The complete list of property-value pairs is surrounded by quotes since this is XHTML.

We will next examine lists to help understand how the style attributes work. The concepts presented here apply to virtually all tags.

Using the style attribute, lists may be customized better than before. The symbol or number at the front of each item in an unordered or ordered list may be specified using the **list-style-type** attribute this way:

```
<ul style="list-style-type: TYPE"> or

<ol style="list-style-type: TYPE">
```

Formatting a List

Replace TYPE with the name of a type appropriate to the list using this guide:

List Format Options

Unordered List		Ordered List	
Type	Result	Type	Result
disc	Filled circle	decimal	1,2,3,4
circle	Unfilled circle	lower-alpha	a, b, c, d
square	Filled square	upper-alpha	A, B, C, D
lower-roman	I, ii, iii, iv		
upper-roman	I, II, III, IV		

Here is an example. Notice the required use of the closing </li> tag:

Changing the Style of a List

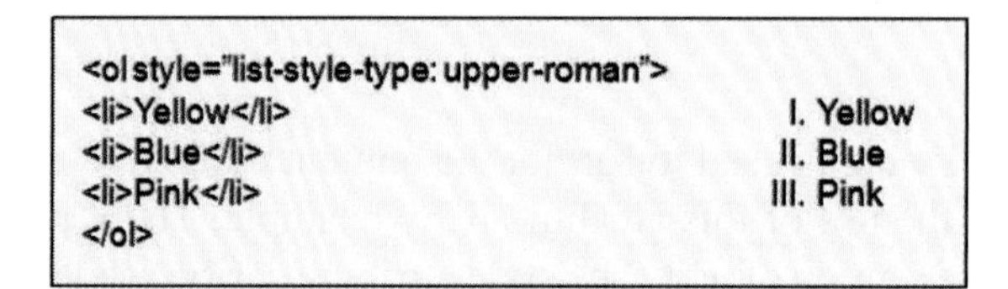

```
<ol style="list-style-type: upper-roman">
<li>Yellow</li>
<li>Blue</li>
<li>Pink</li>
</ol>
```

I. Yellow
II. Blue
III. Pink

Later in this chapter you will find a comprehensive list of many of the style attributes and values that are available for use in a Web page.

9.2.3 Style Rules

Rather than coding the style "in-line" in the tag for each page element it is possible to define how all instances of a tag will appear. For example, to specify in one place that all <h1> tags appear with green text the <style> tag is used to create a style rule this way:

```
<style>
h1 {color: green}
</style>
```

A rule may have any number of values set. In this example all <h1> tags will appear in the browser as green letters in Arial font on a red background.

```
<style>
h1 {color: green; background-color: red; font-family: arial}
</style>
```

If it is desired that all <h1> tags as well as <h2> and <h3> tags share the same formatting then one style rule can accommodate the three tags this way:

```
<style>
h1, h2, h3 {color: green; background-color: red; font-family: arial}
</style>
```

If the style tags delimit several rules then type additional rules like this:

```
<style>
h1, h2, h3 {color: green; background-color: red; font-family: arial};
ul {list-style-type: square}
hr {background-color: yellow; height: 20px}
</style>
```

Style rules are contained in the <head> section which also contains the title. Here is an example:

Style Rules Placed in the Head Section

```
<!DOCTYPE...>
<html xlmns="http:/www.w3.org/1999/xhtml">
<head>
<title>Corporate Earnings</title>
<style>
h4, h5 {color: blue; font-family: arial};
ul {list-style-type: square}
</style>
</head>
<body>
  ... page content here ...
</body>
</html>
```

9.2.4 Classes

As shown above, a style rule provides uniform formatting to all instances of a particular tag. If it were desired to create a format style that could be applied to any tag a **class** is used. The class is given a name and specification in the style tag this way. Notice that the class name follows a period:

```
<style>
.favoriteColor {color: red}
</style>
```

Remember that the class name is surrounded by quotes because it is an attribute value. The class is used in a page element this way:

```
<p class="favoriteColor">This is my favorite color.</p>
```

A style attribute value in a tag always takes precedence over a style rule. If the style rules were this:

```
<style>
p { color: green; background-color: black}
.favoriteColor {color: red}
</style>
```

Either of these tags would produce red letters.

```
<p class="favoriteColor">This is my favorite color.</p>
<p style="color: red">This is my favorite color.</p>
```

Style rules are usually coded in a Web page as shown here, but it is not uncommon for a Web site designer to want the style rules replicated in all pages of the website. Rather than copy and paste the rules from one page to another, style sheets are preferred.

9.2.5 Style Sheets

A **cascading style sheet** is a plain text file with style rules stored in it. The rules are exactly those that could be typed surrounded by style tags as described earlier. In a style sheet the <style> tag is not used and the file extension must be **CSS.** Just as Notepad is used for creating (X)HTML documents it may be used for CSS documents, too. The rules from the previous section would be typed in a CSS file this way:

```
p{ color: green; background-color: black}
.favoriteColor{color: red}
```

Each XHTML page that is to include the style rules in a CSS would link the CSS file like this:

```
<link rel="stylesheet" type="text/css" href="mystyle.css"/>
```

The <link ...> tag is in the <head> section of the document. The relationship between a Web page, a style sheet, and the browser is depicted in this illustration:

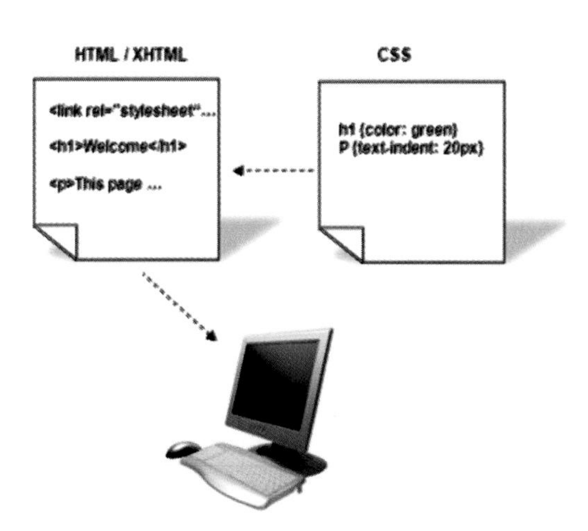

A Web Page Links to a Style Sheet

9.2.6 The Style Attribute

The XHTML examples shown so far illustrate very few of the attribute-value pairs that are available. In this section style attributes available for different tags are listed. Each example also gives a demonstration value for the attribute. The number of attributes is too numerous to permit offering detailed explanations for each. It is not possible to list all attributes – this is a partial list. The best way to learn what each attribute does is by experimentation.

Style is an attribute of most tags. The value of the attribute is always surrounded by quotes and can be used to control multiple formatting features (color, font size, cursor, etc.) at once. Formatting using the style attribute is local to each tag that uses this attribute. The technique follows the pattern of **attribute-value pairs.** For example: setting the text color of a paragraph to red is done this way:

The Style Attribute

```
<p style="color:red">
```

If more than one formatting is defined both are included as the value of the style attribute and are separated by semi-colons. In this example a horizontal rule is drawn in blue with a height (thickness) of 10 pixels. Remember that the <hr> has no closing tag so it must be explicitly closed as shown here:

Using Multiple Formatting Values

```
<hrstyle="color:blue; height: 10px" />
```

The body tag can be used to control the formatting of the entire Web page. Refer back to the section on document types and you will remember that <body> ... </body> tags surround the page's content. Formatting specified in the opening body tag applies to the entire page. Remember that the body tag is not self-closing because there is a separate closing body tag at the end of the document. Here is an example:

Styling the Whole Page

```
<body style="font-size: 15px; letter-spacing; 7px">
```

When tags using the style attribute are **nested,** the inner most style takes precedence over other directives. For example, if a paragraph is formatted with 7px letters and the body tag is styled as above then the 7px will apply to the paragraph while the rest of the page is in 15px. Nesting is illustrated here:

Nested Tags Using the Style Attribute

```
<body style="font-size: 15px; letter-spacing; 7px">
<p style="font-size: 7px"> ... </p>
</body>
```

General Formatting for Text These attributes are used in many tags including: <body>, <li>, <ol>, <p>, <table>, <td>, <tr>, <ul>.

font-family: Verdana, Arial	
font-size: 13px	
text- align: left	*Also use: right, center, justify.*
text-indent: 15px	*Indent first line.*
line-height: 150%	*Set spacing between lines. Use 200% for double spacing.*
color: green	*Set text color.*
font-weight: bold	*Also use: normal and lighter.*
font-style: italic	*Also use: normal.*
text-decoration: line-through	Also use: underline, and overline.
letter-spacing: 5px	*Pixels between letters.*
word-spacing: 10px	*Pixels between words.*

Setting the Cursor

cursor: wait	*Also use: help, pointer, crosshair, and hand.*

Formatting Specific Tags

<a href...>

a:hover {color: lime}	*Color of URL as mouse hovers over it.*
a:link {color: blue}	*Color of a URL not visited.*
a:visited {color: green}	*Color of a URL that has been visited.*

<body>

background-color: green	*Background color of whole page.*
background-image: url(IMAGE)	*IMAGE displayed on background of page.*
background-repeat: no-repeat	*No image tiling.*
color: white	*Foreground (text) color of page.*
font-family: Verdana, Arial	*Font for page.*

<hr>

background-color: green	*Line color.*
color: green	*Line color*
height: 3px	*Line thickness.*
width: 300px	*Use of a percent (as 25%) is permitted.*

<img ...>

float: left	*Wrap text around an image. Also use right.*
height: 55px	*Automatically changes width proportionately.*
margin: 5px	*Distance from image to edge of page.*
width: 20px	*Automatically changes height proportionately.*
visibility: hidden	*Also use: visible. Manipulate using action code.*

<ol>

list-style-type: upper-roman	*Also use: lower-alpha, upper-alpha, lower-roman*

<p>	
border-color: purple	*Color around a paragraph. Border-width must be > 0.*
border-style: solid	*Also use: dotted, dashed, double, groove, ridge, inset, outset.*
border-width: 2px	*Changes thickness of border.*
margin: 8px	*Space outside a paragraph.*
text-indent: 10px	*Indent first line of paragraph.*
<table>	
background-color: yellow	*For whole table.*
background-image: url(IMAGE)	*For whole table.*
border: 6px	*Border thickness. 0 = no border.*
border-color: green	*Color of border around table.*
border-style: solid	*Also use: dotted, dashed, double, groove, ridge, none.*
height: 200px	*Height in pixels.*
padding: 7px	*Padding inside all cells.*
width: 600px	*Width in pixels.*
width: 50%	*Width as % of page.*
<td>	
background-color: yellow	*For one cell.*
border-style: solid	*Also use: dotted, dashed, double, groove, ridge, none.*
padding: 7px	*Padding inside one cell.*
width: 50px	*Width in pixels.*
<tr>	
background-color: yellow	*For whole row.*
<ul>	
list-style-type: square	*Also use: disc and circle.*
Positioning	
position: absolute	*Also use relative.*
top: 100px	Pixels from top of page (absolute) or down from prior element (relative).
left: 57px	Pixels from left of page (absolute) or right from prior element (relative).

9.2.7 Events and Action

The **document object model,** which defines the structure of a Web page, allows the page author to control the attributes of page elements while the page is displayed in a Web browser. This is a very large topic in its own right and would be impossible to cover other than lightly here. This section highlights a few features of XHTML that add life to a Web page. This section is just a taste of what is available. If this section is interesting then a further investigation of this topic is suggested.

Events Objects can recognize when certain events occur. For example, an image can sense when it is clicked or double clicked by a mouse. Trapping an event is done by including appropriate attributes that can then trigger actions. Commonly used event attributes are: onclick, ondblclick, onmouseover, onmouseout, onload, and onkeypress. Here an <img> tag is shown ready to trap single mouse clicks.

```
<img src="birthday party.jpg" onclick="... action here ..." />
```

Actions Actions are triggered when an object senses the occurrence of an event. An action is one or more commands given to the browser when an event happens. The easiest way to code an action to responsd to an event is as script code that is associated with an event attribute. In this example an image will become hidden (invisible) when it is clicked.

```
<img src=" birthday party.jpg " style="visibility: visible"
   onclick="style.visibility='hidden'" />
```

The Object's ID Usually it is not sufficient to trigger actions that apply only to the object that sensed the event. Events like button clicks are often used to trigger links to other pages, submissions of forms with data, etc. To provide linkage to other objects the document object model provides a special attribute that allows any object to be addressed by any other. The **ID** attribute takes on a value that is unique for each object on a page. An object's ID is defined this way as shown for a <p> tag:

```
<p ID="objecteID" style="attribute: value; attribute: value ...">
  ...
</p>
```

JavaScript is Case-sensitive

Put it Together with JavaScript When an object in a page is used to control another object often the language JavaScript is used. JavaScript is a scripting language that most Web browsers understand. The language code is surrounded by <**script**> tags and is divided into **functions.** Here is a short example that develops these concepts. We start with an image that will sense a click. When the click happens the function changeText() is invoked.

```
<img src="clickme.gif" onclick="changeText()" />
```

Next a paragraph is added. The function changeText() will alter the text displayed in the paragraph. Notice the use of ID which will allow changeText() to access the paragraph.

```
<p ID="myParagraph">Click the button to change this text.</p>
```

Once both tags are created the page appears this way in a browser.

Click Me

Click the button to change this text.

Finally the function is added; changeText prompts the viewer to type something and then what is typed becomes the text of the <p> tag. Here is the JavaScript code:

```
<script>
function changeText(){
        newText=prompt('Please type something.','');
        myParagraph.innerText=newText;
}
</script>
```

When the image is clicked, changeText() prompts for and displays new text as shown:

JavaScript Is Used to Perform Actions Triggered by Events

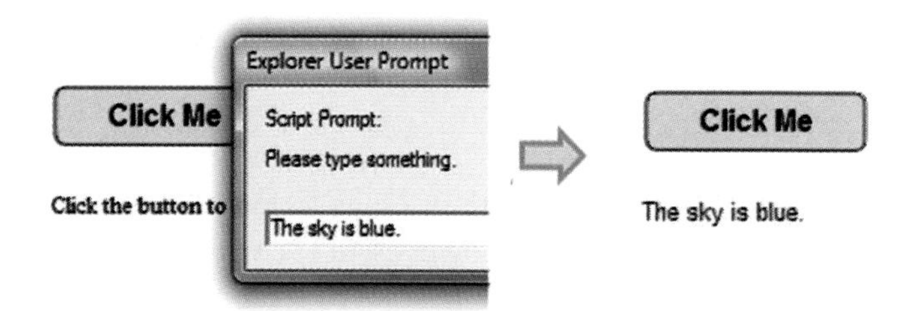

9.3 Office 2007 and Web Pages

Office 2007 can produce Web page output for display from Word, PowerPoint, and Excel. Your active document may be saved as an htm (Web page) document this way. Click the Office button and then click Save As. In the dialog box select Web Page as file type and type a file name. You may add a page title if you wish.

Presenting Office 2007 Output as a Web Page

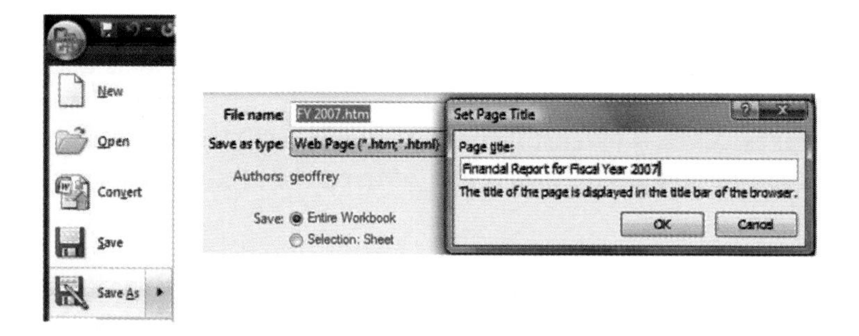

The **Save As** dialog box offers a **Change Title . . .** button which displays the **Set Page Title** dialog box as shown.

Web page code produced by Office 2007 is complex and could be hard for you to customize. Take a look at the title and opening paragraph of this chapter as produced in (X)HTML by Word 2007. By the way, the listing shown begins on line 474 of the HTM document generated by Word – imagine what the rest of the document looks like!

X/HTML Produced by Word 2007

```
<p class=MsoNormal><b style='mso-bidi-font-weight:normal'><span
style='font-size:26.0pt;font-family:"Arial","sans-serif"'>HTML and XHTML</span></b></p>

<p class=MsoNormal><span style='font-size:11.0pt;font-family:"Arial","sans-serif"'> </o:p>

<p class=MsoNormal><span style='font-size:11.0pt;font-family:"Arial","sans-serif"'>HTML
is an abbreviation for a particular form of <b style='mso-bidi-font-weight:
normal'>hypertext </b>that is used to create Web pages. A Web browser formats
the hypertext so that its appearance on the screen is attractive and easy to
use. The letters, HTML, stand for: <b style='mso-bidi-font-weight:normal'>Hypertext
Markup Language</b>. <o:p></o:p></span></p>
```

Other (X)HTML Editors The Internet abounds with offers for free downloads of (X)HTML editors. There are editors for CSS documents as well. Some editors can add JavaScript code and <script> tags to a Web page. If you want to get beyond the potential of Notepad you might want to check out the Internet or invest in an advanced tool such as Dreamweaver.

9.4 XML: Extensible Markup Language

The Extensible Markup Language (XML) is a general-purpose markup language that can be used to hold **structured data** and, as a **meta language,** it can be a basis for other languages. Like HTML and XHTML the document elements are defined by tags. Similarly, the XML document is also a text file.

9.4.1 Markup Tags

Is XML just like HTML? Yes and no. Both use tags to instruct a browser or other program about the content of the document. However, in HTML, both the tag semantics and the tag set are fixed. An <h1> is always a first level heading and the tag <phonenumber> is meaningless.

XML specifies neither tags nor their meaning. In fact XML is really a meta language for describing languages because it provides a facility to define tags and the structural relationships between them. Since there is no predefined tag set, there cannot be any preconceived semantics. All of the meaning of an XML document's data will either be defined by the programs that process them or by cascading style sheets (CSS).

XML tags never contain spaces. XML tags are always in lower case.

9.4.2 Meta Language

A **meta language** is defined as a language used to make statements about other languages. In that sense XML is a meta language because it is used as the definiton of other language syntaxes. XML is **extensible** because, unlike HTML, the markup symbols are unlimited and self-defining. This means that XML can be used as the basis for many data sharing languages.

XML Is not a Programming Language Neither XML or HTML or XHTML are programming languages. All are markup languages which are descriptive; they do not include processing logic. XML can be used to hold (and describe) data processed in an application by a programming language but it is just a vessel for the data and not the rules that process the data.

9.4.3 What XML Documents Look Like

XML documents are simple text files. They have no special formatting and standard text editors like Notepad may be used to edit XML documents. This section points out the basic structure of an XML document. The first line of a document is the document's **XML declaration** which informs the processor (Web browser or other program) that this is an XML document based on version 1.0 of XML:

```
<?xml version="1.0"?>
```

The remainder of the document holds data structured as records for transport from a source to a recipient (browser, etc.). In this example data about three works of art are marked up this way:

```
<artworks>
  <artwork>
   <artist>Brice Marden</artist>
   <title>7 Red Rock 4</title>
   <year>2002</year>
   <media>oil paint</media>
  </artwork>
  <artwork>
   <artist>Claude Monet</artist>
   <title>Water Lillies</title>
   <year>1914</year>
   <media>oil paint</media>
  </artwork>
  <artwork>
   <artist>Pamela Heller</artist>
   <title>Eye Contact - Century to Century</title>
   <year>2006</year>
   <media>Video</media>
  </artwork>
</artworks>
```

Notice that the full document has a pair of **root tags** (<artworks> and </artworks>) and that other tags were created to be descriptive of the data they surround. <artwork> is container that holds four separate other tags: <artist>, <title>, <year>, and <media>. The data represented by the XML above is of records that could be represented this way:

XML Data in Tabular Form

artist	title	year	media
Brice Marden	7 Red Rock 4	2002	oil paint
Claude Monet	Water Lillies	1914	oil paint
Pamela Heller	Eye Contact - Century to Century	2006	Video

As you examine the table above try to relate specific records and data values to the content of the XML that precedes it. Where XML departs from HTML is that the tags (<artist>, <title>, etc.) have meaning and convey the purpose of the content. (The artist Brice Marden produced 7 Red Rock 4 in 2002, etc.). XML does not inform the browser about how the data is to be displayed.

9.4.4 XML Document Presentation

If the data were being sent to a non-display device, like a cell phone or other electronic device, display considerations would be unimportant. If the data above were sent to Internet Explorer the browser would render it this way by default:

XML Data Rendered in Browser

```
  <?xml version="1.0" ?>
- <artworks>
  - <artwork>
      <artist>Brice Marden</artist>
      <title>7 Red Rock 4</title>
      <year>2002</year>
      <media>oil paint</media>
    </artwork>
  - <artwork>
      <artist>Claude Monet</artist>
      <title>Water Lillies</title>
      <year>1914</year>
      <media>oil paint</media>
    </artwork>
  - <artwork>
      <artist>Pamela Heller</artist>
      <title>Eye Contact - Century to Century</title>
      <year>2006</year>
      <media>Video</media>
    </artwork>
  </artworks>
```

A complex element is known as a container and it defines a data structure.

Although the native display shown above is quite similar to the original XML document itself, display in the browser window does have an advantage. Look closely at the browser display and you will notice dashes to the left of some tags. The presence of a dash means that the specific tag is a complex object that holds or contains other containers or data elements. For example, the portion of the display shown here is of a container called "artwork" and it holds four data elements. In this case artwork defines a record.

A Container Holds a Data Structure

```
- <artwork>
    <artist>Brice Marden</artist>      ]
    <title>7 Red Rock 4</title>        ]<------ A Data Structure (one record of four data fields).
    <year>2002</year>                  ]
    <media>oil paint</media>           ]
  </artwork>
```

The dash has other significance, too. If you click it the elements between that tag and the associated closing tag hide. The closing tag hides, too. When clicked, the dash changes to a plus sign indicating a data structure that may be expanded. If all dashes in front of artwork are clicked, as shown here, only the data structure tags are visible. Notice that artwork is itself a container holding three artwork structures.

Data Structures May Be Hidden

```
  <?xml version="1.0" ?>
- <artworks>
  + <artwork>
  + <artwork>
  + <artwork>
  </artworks>
```

```
  <?xml version="1.0" ?>
+ <artworks>
```

Controlling Presentation While the browser faithfully displayed all data elements in the document, a technique presented earlier in the study of **XHTML** can be used to dress up the presentation of XML data. We return to **Cascading Style Sheets** (CSS).

A **CSS** is a plain text file that lists style properties. It is saved with an extension CSS. The general format of a CSS file is a collection of specifications that follow this structure:

```
selector{property: value}
```

Selector identifies the XML element (tag) which a style rule applies to. Property is the name of the CSS property and value is the value applied to that property for that selector. See the HTML and XHTML sections of this chapter for a list of CSS properties and values. If a selector is defined as having multiple CSS formatting styles then separate each with a semi-colon as shown here. Also notice that three elements (tags) share the same formatting.

```
artist {
            display: block;
            font-weight: bold;
            margin-top: 5pt;
            margin-bottom: 5pt;
            font-family: Arial;
            font-size: 20;
            background-color: #8FBC8F;
            padding: 2px;
            cursor: pointer
}

title, media, year {
            margin-left: 5pt;
            font-size: 15;
            background-color: #F5F5DC;
            padding: 2px;
            font-weight: bold;
}
```

Assuming that the above style sheet was saved as art.css then this declaration is added to the XML document to link it to the CSS. Note: art.css is assumed in the same folder as the XML document:

```
<?xml-stylesheet type="text/css" href="art.css"?>
```

Including a Style Sheet

The resulting browser display is shown here:

Brice Marden

7 Red Rock 4 | 2002 | oil paint

Claude Monet

Water Lillies | 1914 | oil paint

Pamela Heller

Eye Contact - Century to Century | 2006 | Video

XML Data Displayed with Cascading Style Sheet

9.4.5 XML Document Data Validation: DTD and Schema

To ensure that data in an XML document is valid a **Data Type Definition** (DTD) or a **schema** is used. A document description is a formal statement in plain text of the rules governing how content (data) can (or must) appear in an XML document that follows these particular rules. Data validation is especially important when computer programs are sharing data over a network. Since it is critical for the sender and receiver to share an understanding of the structure of the data being transported between them, a document description used at both ends of the transmission can be valuable.

A Document Definition Ensures Common Understanding of Data Structure

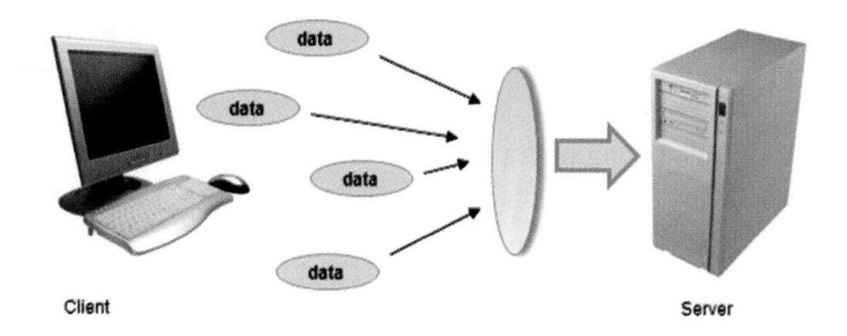

As seen earlier the browser was able to infer records based on the hierarchical structure of the XML tags. The browser was not able to determine what type of data (numbers, text, etc.) each field was. The two methods available for validating the structure of an XML document as it is passed between systems are DTD and schema. Deciding on whether to use a DTD or a schema is somewhat subjective. These guidelines might help:

- **DTD** — In general, DTDs work better for text intensive data structures.
- **Schema** — a schema works better for varied data collections that include data other than text.

9 4.5.1 Data Type Definition

A Data Type Definition (**DTD**) is a set of **rules** that defines the **elements** of an XML document and the elements' **attributes.** Any XML documents that use the same DTD use the same rules. The rules are called the grammar of a language and, since XML is an extensible language used to define other languages, the DTD is the definition (the grammar) of a new language.

A data type definition is stored in a plain text file with an extension DTD. It is linked to an XML document by using the **DOCTYPE** declaration. Linking a DTD to an XML document causes the XML document's recipient to validate all data contained within the document according to the rules defined in the DTD. Assuming a DTD named "art.dtd" it would be linked to an XML document by typing the DOCTYPE declaration in the XML document this way:

```
<!DOCTYPE artworks SYSTEM "art.dtd">
```

A data type definition is stored in a plain text file with extension DTD.

To show you exactly where the link specification is placed, the first several lines of the XML document are shown here:

```
<?xml version="1.0"?>
<?xml-stylesheet type="text/css" href="art.css"?>
<!DOCTYPE artworks SYSTEM "art.dtd">
<artworks>
    ...
</artworks>
```

In this DOCTYPE example, artworks is the **internal name** of the DTD used and SYSTEM "art.dtd" informs the processor to fetch an **external document** "art.dtd" to be used as the definition for the DTD "artworks." The internal name of the DTD must be the same as the name of the root element. Note: art.dtd is assumed in the same folder as the XML document. The content of art.dtd is:

External DTD

```
<?xml version="1.0"?>
<!ELEMENT artworks (artwork+)>
<!ELEMENT artwork (artist, title, year, media)>
<!ELEMENT artist (#PCDATA)>
<!ELEMENT title (#PCDATA)>
<!ELEMENT year (#PCDATA)>
<!ELEMENT media (#PCDATA)>
```

It should be fairly easy to understand the DTD. The first line informs that this is an XML document. The remaining lines define the **elements** of the hierarchical **data structure.** If necessary, refer to an earlier section to recall the original XML document. The root element <artworks> is listed first. Since multiple <artwork> instances occur within <artworks> . . . </artworks> the element name "artwork" is listed with a plus sign after it. The parentheses surrounding artwork + indicate the content of the **container** artworks.

Since each <artwork> (also a container) has an artist, title, year, and media, those elements are referenced by artwork and contained, comma delimited, within parentheses too. The last four elements do not reference other elements (as artworks and artwork do) so **#PCDATA** (parsed character data) is used to indicate an element that is a specific data value.

Clearly if two communicating processors share this DTD then there can be no ambiguity about the structure of the data within the document. The DTD need not be maintained in a separate file but can be contained within the XML document itself this way:

Internal DTD

```
<?xml version="1.0"?>
<?xml-stylesheet type="text/css" href="art.css"?>
<!DOCTYPE artworks [
<!ELEMENT artwork (artist, title, year, media)>
<!ELEMENT artist (#PCDATA)>
<!ELEMENT title (#PCDATA)>
<!ELEMENT year (#PCDATA)>
<!ELEMENT media (#PCDATA)>
]>
  <artworks>
    ...
  <artwork>
```

The relationship between an XML document and CSS and DTD documents is shown here:

The Relationship Between XML, DTD, and CSS Documents

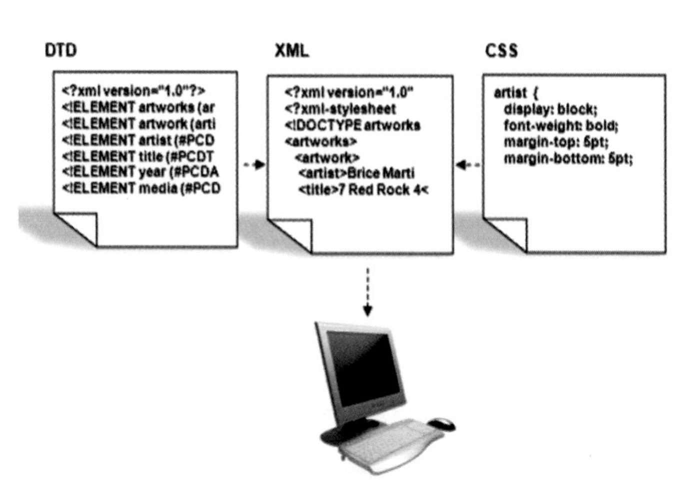

An XML schema is stored in a plain text file with extension XSD.

9.4.5.2 Schema

Similar to a DTD an XML schema defines rules for the structure and content of an XML document. The overall structure of the document is specified and all the components of the XML document are identified, too. The purpose of using a schema is to ensure that the data contained within an XML document is of the correct type and in the correct form. The schema is in effect a **template** that specifies the form the XML document must take. When a program processes an XML document the data it contains is validated against the schema.

Schemas are an improvement over DTDs because they offer more control over the type of data contained within the document. PCDATA (from a DTD) may be any type of data but in a schema specific data types are defined. Here several of the many data types are identified and described:

XML Schema Data Types

XML Data Type	Definition
string	Character or text data.
decimal	Numeric data.
integer	Numeric data.
date	A date value.
time	A time value.
positiveInteger	Integer greater than zero.
anyURI	A Uniform Resource Identifier – address of a resource like a DTD or CSS. Normally a file name or URL.
boolean	A logical value that may be true / false or 1 / 0

The schema is referenced at the beginning of the XML document. Since an XML document's schema follows a standard set of data definitions (see partial list above) that set is identified early in the document. The list of definitions defined in the schema is known as a **namespace** (ns) and is stored in a text file with an extension **XSD.** Assuming a schema in "art.xsd" the schema is referenced by the XML document this way:

A Namespace Defined in an External Schema

```
<?xml version="1.0"?>
<artworks xmlns:xsi="http://www.w3.org/2001/XMLSchema-instance"
                    xsi:noNamespaceSchemaLocation="art.xsd"> 1
  <artwork>
    ...
  <artwork>
</artworks>
```

[1]The namespace declaration is shown on two lines here due to space limitations. In an XML document type the declaration on a single line.

The XSD document, schema file, which is also an XML document, will have this format:

Structure of XSD Document

```
<?xml version="1.0"?>
<xsd:schema xmlns:xsd="http://www.w3.org/2001/XMLSchema">
        ... schema elements here ...
</xsd:schema>
```

Notice that both documents reference http://www.w3.org/2001/XMLSchema. This is because both documents use the same vocabulary — the **XML namespace** which is defined and maintained by the W3C. That namespace is the basis for all languages derived from XML, and it provides tag names that permit defining a schema.

Schema Elements The main body of the XSD (the schema file) is the enumeration of elements that define a XML document's basic structure. The schema also defines a hierarchy of elements if several are grouped together. There are two categories of elements:

- **Simple definitions** — elements that may not contain any other elements.
- **Complex definitions** — elements that may contain other elements.

The complete XSD for the artworks example is listed here. On examination of the schema it is apparent that artwork is a complex definition and artist, title, year, and media are simple definitions:

Complete XSD

```
<?xml version="1.0">
<xsd:schema xmlns:xsd="http://www.w3.org/2001/XMLSchema">
  <xsd:element name="artwork">
    <xsd:complexType>
      <xsd:sequence>
        <xsd:element name="artist" type="xsd:string"/>
        <xsd:element name="title" type="xsd:string"/>
        <xsd:element name="year" type="xsd:integer"/>
        <xsd:element name="media" type="xsd:string"/>
      </xsd:sequence>
    </xsd:complexType>
  </xsd:element>
</xsd:schema>
```

Notice that all XML tags have a closing tag or are self-closed like this:

Self-Closing an XML Tag

```
<xsd:element name="artist" type="xsd:string"/>
```

The schema is reasonably straightforward but several items should be pointed out:

- **Tags** — All schema tags begin with xsd:
- **xsd:element** — Each element, simple or complex, begins with this tag and has a name.
- **xsd:complex Type** — Complex elements require this tag. Complex elements are likely to be records.
- **xsd:sequence** — This marks the beginning and end of the list of elements that form the complex element's structure. This tag is optional. If it is included then the data elements must be found in the XML document in the specified order.
- **xsd:string** — A data type definition included in the XML schema namespace. Here it is used to define a data type; it is not used as a tag.
- **xsd:integer** — A data type definition included in the XML schema namespace. Here it is used to define a data type; it is not used as a tag.

The schema (XSD) shown above could be prepared a little differently. If the elements title and year were to be used in other complex structures the schema would be written as shown here. Notice that the sequence elements title and year use the "ref=" syntax to refer to an xsd:element defined elsewhere.

Referencing XSD Elements

```
<?xml version="1.0">
<xsd:schema xmlns:xsd="http://www.w3.org/2001/XMLSchema">
  <xsd:element name="artwork">
    <xsd:complexType mixed="true">
      <xsd:sequence>
        <xsd:element name="artist" type="xsd:string"/>
        <xsd:element ref="title"/>
        <xsd:element ref="year"/>
        <xsd:element name="media" type="xsd:string"/>
      </xsd:sequence>
    </xsd:complexType>
  </xsd:element>
  <xsd:element name="title" type="xsd:string"/>
  <xsd:element name="year" type="xsd:integer"/>
</xsd:schema>
```

A Bit More about Schema Elements XML is an extensive language but there are several other schema elements that are easily understood and worth mentioning. **Attributes** often provide data values that are not found as part of the data elements. Attributes and simple elements can be used somewhat interchangeably with the same information content being transferred. HTML can illustrate the concept of attributes this way:

Attributes in HTML Tag

```
<img src="myPicture.gif">
```

Here src is an attribute and "myPicture.gif" is the value of the attribute.

This is best explained by example. Here an XML structure is presented with an accompanying schema.

XML Structured Data

```
<person sex="female">
  <firstname>Julia</firstname>
  <lastname>Eastburn</lastname>
</person>
```

In the schema that follows notice that the element "person" has an attribute named "sex" which is defined as of type "gender." The **simpleType** definition "gender" has a **restriction** which is limited to two **enumerated values** "male" and "female." This schema rejects data in which an element "person" has a sex value other than "male" or "female." Such bounds placed on acceptable data values are known as **constraints.**

XML Schema with Data Value Constraint

```
<xsd:element name="person">
  <xsd:complexType>
    <xsd:attribute name="sex" type="gender"/>
    <xsd:sequence>
      <xsd:element name="firstname" type="xsd:string"/>
      <xsd:element name="lastname" type="xsd:string"/>
    </xsd:sequence>
  </xsd:complexType>
</xsd:element>

<xsd:element name="gender">
  <xsd:simpleType>
    <xsd:restriction base="xsd:string">
      <xsd:enumeration value="male"/>
      <xsd:enumeration value="female"/>
    </xsd:restriction>
  </xsd:simpleType>
</xsd:element>
```

XML restrictions can be used to limit data values to an enumerated list of acceptable values as you have seen. This table includes other constraints:

XML Schema Constraints

Constraint	Definition
enumeration	Defines a list of acceptable values.
fractionDigits	Specifies the maximum number of decimal places allowed.
length	Specifies the exact number of characters allowed.
maxExclusive	Specifies the upper bounds for numeric values (the value must be less than).
maxInclusive	Specifies the upper bounds for numeric values (the value must be less than or equal to this value).
maxLength	Specifies the maximum number of characters.
minExclusive	Specifies the lower bounds for numeric values (the value must be greater than this value).
minInclusive	Specifies the lower bounds for numeric values (the value must be greater than or equal to this value).
minLength	Specifies the minimum number of characters.
totalDigits	Specifies the exact number of digits allowed.

This final example shows how to limit a whole number data value to a specific range of values:

XML Schema Constraint

```
<xsd:simpleType name="examScore">
  <xsd:restriction base="xsd:integer">
    <xsd:minInclusive value="0"/>
    <xsd:maxInclusive value="100"/>
  </xsd:restriction>
</xsd:simpleType>
```

The relationship between an XML document and CSS and XSD documents is shown here:

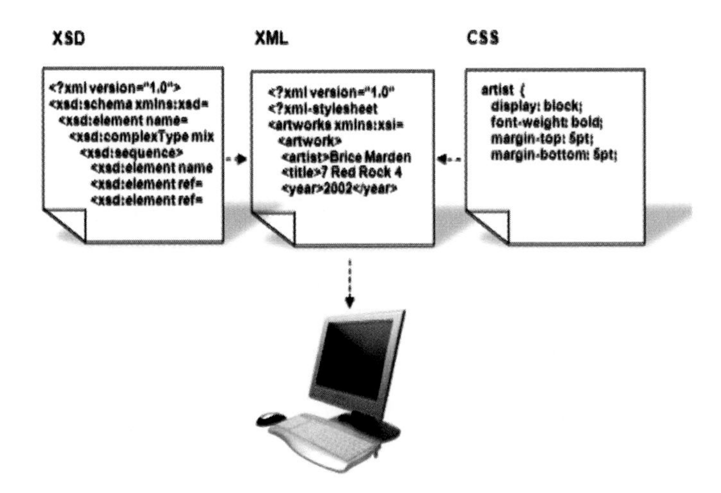

The Relationship Between XML, DTD, and XSD Documents

9.4.6 Using XML in Access and Excel

Microsoft Office programs are conversant in XML. Both Excel and Access can be used to import, process, and export XML based data. It is therefore possible to communicate data between those programs if a data format common to both is used. XML is perfect for the task.

In this section we discuss XML operations in Excel and Access. Since a schema file (XSD) is required when you export data in XML format we will discuss editing that file, too.

9.4.6.1 XML in Excel

First we will take a look at Excel. To work with XML you need access to the **Developer** ribbon. If you have not activated that ribbon do so now this way:

1. Click the Office button.
2. Select Excel options.
3. Select the top option: Personalize.
4. In the section Top Options for Working with Excel check Show Developer Tab.
5. Click Ok.

Extra Developer Ribbon

Excel can **read** (input) and **write** (output) XML files. As you might imagine Excel would prefer to have a schema (or DTD) to guide it as XML files are read or written. It turns out that Excel can figure out the schema when it needs to without the benefit of an external DTD or XSD.

Reading XML Data Assuming you have an XML file ready Excel can read it easily but you have to make a choice about how the records are imported. The simplest way is to read the records into a worksheet table. We will try that first.

Start by click the Office button and then click Open. From the standard Open dialog box select only XML files.

Opening an XML File

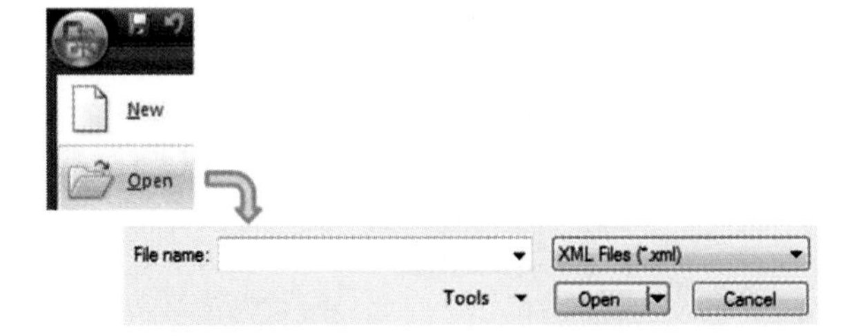

Navigate to your file and double click it to open it. The Open XML dialog box appears. Select the first option and open the file as an XML table. Click Ok and the records load into your worksheet. You may see a message informing you that a schema was not found and that Excel will create it; this is normal. Click Ok to move on and data is arranged in a table and filter mode is set as shown here.

XML DATA Imported into Excel

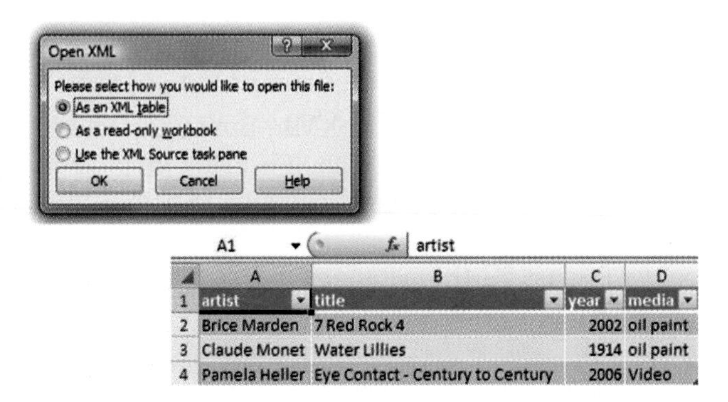

	A	B	C	D
1	artist	title	year	media
2	Brice Marden	7 Red Rock 4	2002	oil paint
3	Claude Monet	Water Lillies	1914	oil paint
4	Pamela Heller	Eye Contact - Century to Century	2006	Video

You may now manipulate the table using any of the Excel operations that you are familiar with. The big drawback is that you have no ability to alter and save the records. We need to examine the other option for reading XML data.

When an XML file is selected, choose to use the XML Source Task pane. The table is not loaded, and instead the XML Source task pane appears with the XML file's schema displayed in hierarchical form. Note that the data types are not displayed. Remember that Excel infers the schema as it reads the XML file.

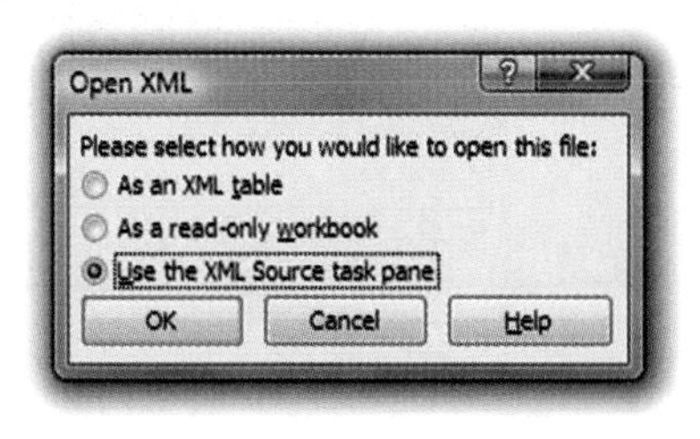

Schema Displayed in the XML Source Task Pane

None of file's data is displayed anywhere on the worksheet. You have control over the selection and placement of specific data elements anywhere you like. The process of placing data elements on the spreadsheet is known as mapping.

Mapping The easiest thing to do is to map the entire record. Simply drag the record structure name (artwork) to the location where you want the records to appear.

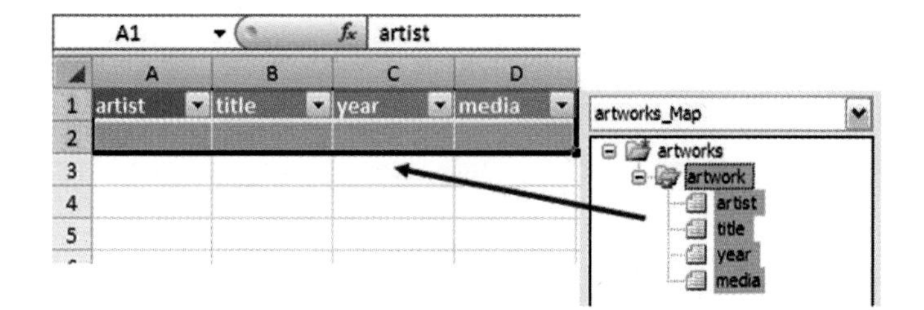

Mapping a Record

The records have still not appeared. That is accomplished by clicking **Refresh Data** on the **Developer** ribbon. What has happened is that you created a link (a map) between the external file and specific locations in your worksheet. You are free to edit the data as you wish. Even add new records to the end of the table. Manipulate the records using the tools that Excel offers and, if you wish, save the updated date to the same or a different XML file.

Refreshing the Mapped Data Set

A1 artist

	A	B	C	D
1	artist	title	year	media
2	Brice Marden	7 Red Rock 4	2002	oil paint
3	Claude Monet	Water Lillies	1914	oil paint
4	Pamela Heller	Eye Contact - Century to Century	2006	Video

Writing XML Data If you just want to save the changed records click Export on the Developer ribbon and in the Save dialog box that appears navigate to the location where the file will be saved. Either reuse an existing file (updating the file's records) or type a new file name.

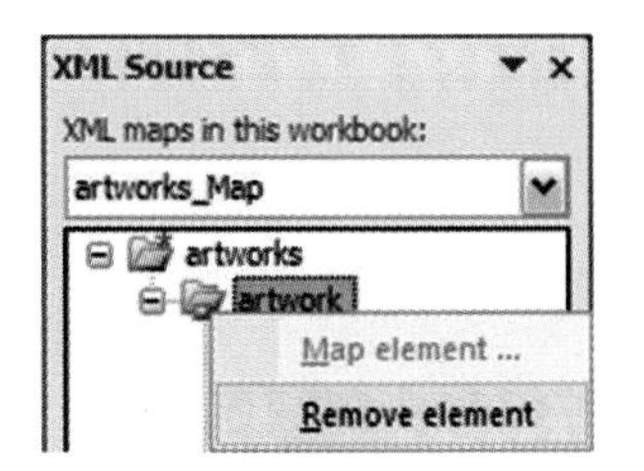

Mapping Some of the Schema Elements
You do not need work with the whole record. Excel allows you to map individual columns as you wish. If a map is currently active it must be removed. This means that you must cut the linkage between specific worksheet cells and the XML file. In the XML Schema task pane, right click on the mapped element (artwork) and remove the map.

Now map the three elements artist, title, and year by dragging each individually as shown here.

Partial Mapping

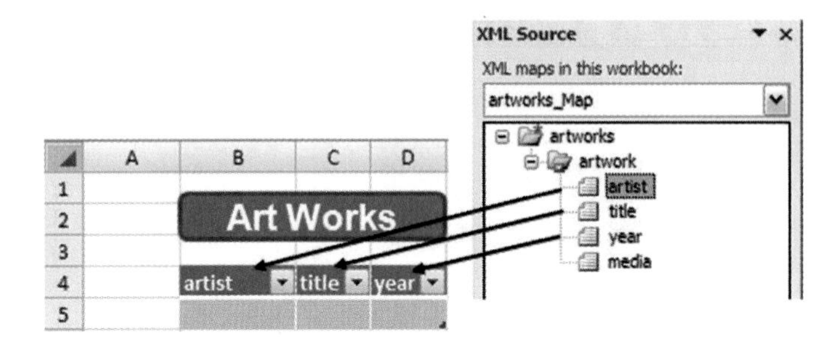

Click Refresh and three columns of the records appear. You may manipulate the date and export as previously described. You could also add a record by typing it below the last record in the table and then exporting to the same file just imported. That would have the effect of updating the file.

Records Displayed

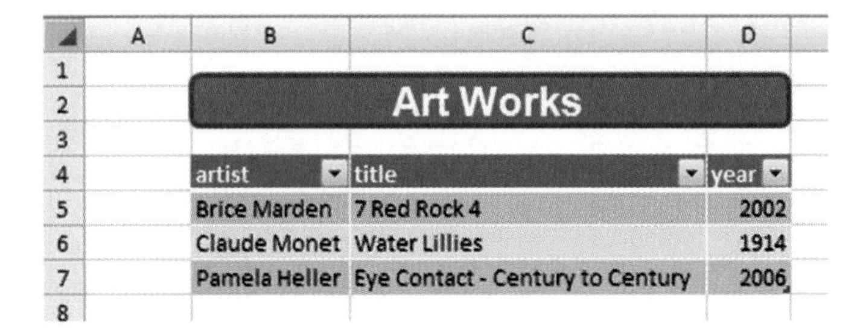

What Happens to the Schema Maps? Each time you import an XML document Excel creates a schema by interpreting the data it is reading. When you move on to the next XML file and a new schema is created the previous schema is added to a library and maintained in the workbook. The library also remembers the XML file associated with each schema. If you want to switch to a different XML file view the schema list (click down-arrow) and select the map (and file) you want to work with. Any active mappings are removed. The new schema appears in the **XML Source** window.

A Practical Example This example shows how you could store your data in XML format and use it for analysis over time. Suppose you were a teacher with a roster of your students and their grades were delivered in XML format from an electronic grade book. Suppose also that you had available your school's grading scale in XML format. You could import both files and use the second as a source for converting numeric grades to letter grades.

Import the student table first and then import the grading scale table. Each time you import a new file the active map is removed allowing you to continue. After both tables are imported it is easy to use a VLOOKUP to retrieve the letter grade for the number grade read from the file. After typing the function shown in C3, Excel automatically copied it into C4:C11 because Excel knew that a table was active. The references in the VLOOKUP look messy but they are not. Just click in the cells or table ranges for each portion of the function and it will be automatically built.

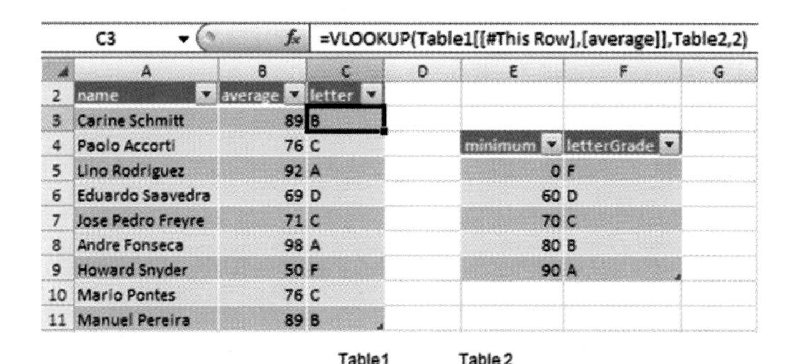

name	average	letter
Carine Schmitt	89	B
Paolo Accorti	76	C
Lino Rodriguez	92	A
Eduardo Saavedra	69	D
Jose Pedro Freyre	71	C
Andre Fonseca	98	A
Howard Snyder	50	F
Mario Pontes	76	C
Manuel Pereira	89	B

minimum	letterGrade
0	F
60	D
70	C
80	B
90	A

Two XML Tables and a VLOOKUP

What About the XSD File? The examples that we just worked through demonstrate that an external schema file is not necessary for Excel's use as XML data is read and written. Excel internally develops a schema from the data it has read. As shown above, you may manipulate the mappings and export XML using the mapped columns.

Recall that when Excel read the file it informed us there was no schema so it created one by inferring it from the XML data. If, however, you open an XML file which does have an associated XSD (both must have the same file name) Excel uses that schema and does not create one.

Sometimes it is desirable to have more control over how data is read, validated, and written. For that reason, learning to craft a schema to the specifics of your data management requirements is worth mastering.

9.4.6.2 XML in Access

Reading XML Data Access makes it easy, too. Remember that as a **DBMS** (database management system) Access is required to follow stricter data management rules than Excel does. Consequently the notion of mapping is not carried over to Access. When you import a table the entire table is loaded. You may use the sophisticated query tools in Access to modify the view of the data.

To load an XML file select **XML File** in the **Import** group on the **External Data Tab.** Navigate to the file and accept the default in the Import XML dialog box.

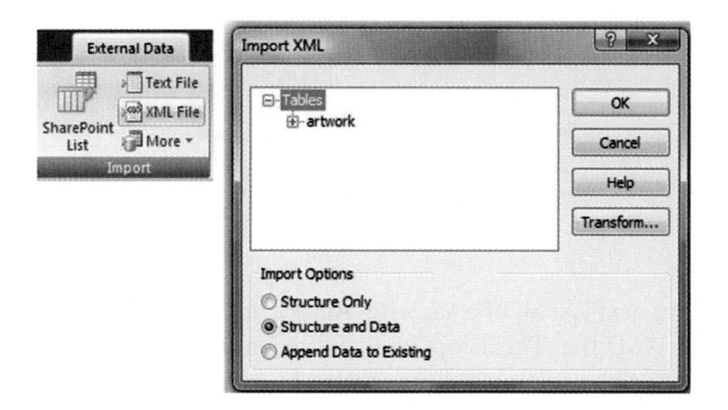

Importing XML to Access

Click Ok and the file will load and a new database table will be created with the same name as the record structure defined in the XML.

Two XML Tables in an Access Database

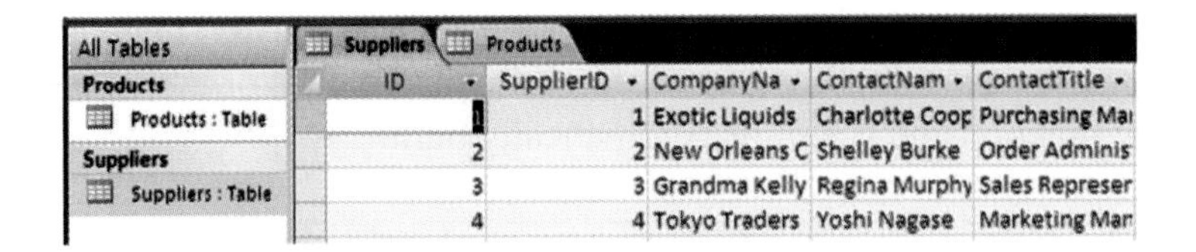

ID	SupplierID	CompanyNa	ContactNam	ContactTitle
1	1	Exotic Liquids	Charlotte Coop	Purchasing Mai
2	2	New Orleans C	Shelley Burke	Order Adminis
3	3	Grandma Kelly	Regina Murphy	Sales Represer
4	4	Tokyo Traders	Yoshi Nagase	Marketing Mar

To perform analysis using both tables you may need to help Access link the tables by editing the table relationships.

Edit Relationships

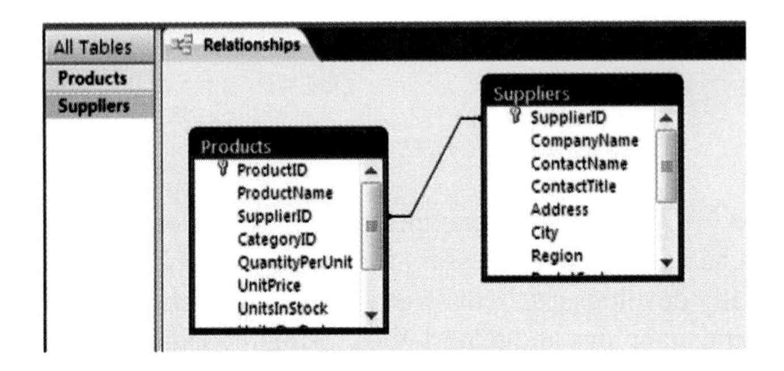

Once the relationships are established the query power of Access opens up.

A Multi-Table Query

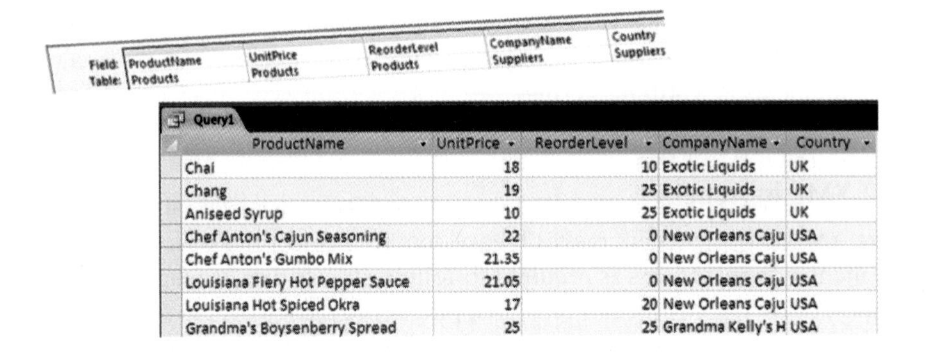

ProductName	UnitPrice	ReorderLevel	CompanyName	Country
Chai	18	10	Exotic Liquids	UK
Chang	19	25	Exotic Liquids	UK
Aniseed Syrup	10	25	Exotic Liquids	UK
Chef Anton's Cajun Seasoning	22	0	New Orleans Caju	USA
Chef Anton's Gumbo Mix	21.35	0	New Orleans Caju	USA
Louisiana Fiery Hot Pepper Sauce	21.05	0	New Orleans Caju	USA
Louisiana Hot Spiced Okra	17	20	New Orleans Caju	USA
Grandma's Boysenberry Spread	25	25	Grandma Kelly's H	USA

Writing XML Data Any table or the result of any query can be written to an XML file. In the **Export** group click **More** and select **XML File.**

Exporting XML from Access

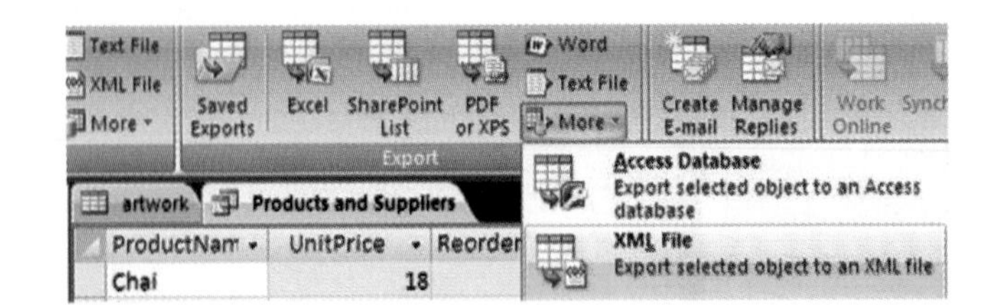

What happens next is a bit of a surprise. Access, unlike Excel, also writes a copy of the schema to an XSD file. This is optional, but recommended. It is also a way to learn more about schemas by examining those created by Access.

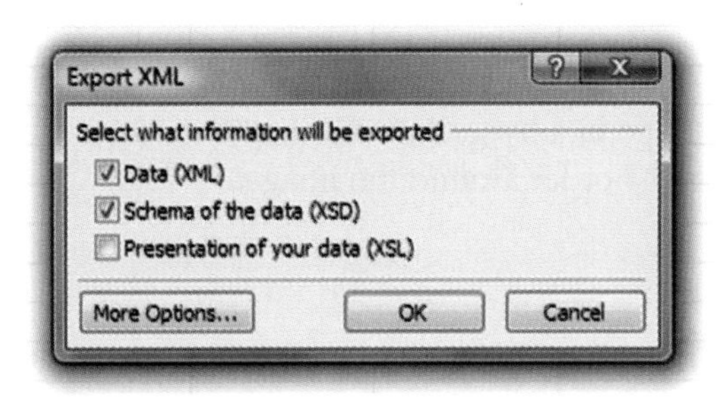

Access Creates an XSD, Too

9.4.7 Other XML Editors

A search of the Internet will result in numerous offers for free downloads of XML editors. There are editors for CSS, DTD, and XSD documents as well. If you want to get beyond the potential of Notepad you might want to check out the Internet.

9.5 Summary

HTML (Hypertext Markup Language) is the set of markup codes inserted in a text file intended for display in a web browser. The markup informs the browser how to display a Web page's words and images for the viewer. Each individual markup code is referred to as a tag. Some tags come in pairs that indicate when some display effect is to begin and when it is to end and some do not.

HTML is a formal Recommendation by the World Wide Web Consortium (W3C) and is generally adhered to by the major browsers. The current version of HTML is supported somewhat differently among different Web browsers so in the interest of standardization and adding advanced features Extensible Hypertext Markup Language or XHTML was developed.

XML is a tool for structuring data in a document so that the data may be passed among and shared by programs. The structure of the data can be evident upon examination of the XML document but it can be more precisely defined using a Data Type Definition (DTD) or an XML schema (XSD). A cascading style sheet (CSS) can be used to format the data for presentation in a browser. An important advantaged offered by this approach is the potential for sharing data among applications on computers running different operating systems and using different programming languages for processing shared data.

EXERCISES

Exercise 9.1

Using HTML only write the complete HTML code that would produce this page. The first row is a header size three. Use no <br> tags.

Welcome to My Webpage

The font for the remainder of this page is `Courier New`.

Exercise 9.2

Using HTML only write the code that uses an image in a hyperlink. Assume the image is "clickme.gif" and that URL is "http://www.nbc.com." There should be no border around the image.

Exercise 9.3

Using HTML only create a Web page with a table. The table should have two rows and two cells per row. The border should = 1. Do not use any <br> tags. Header 2 is displayed with header tags. Preformatted text uses the <pre>...</pre> tags. Remember that a table is created using <table>, <tr>, and <td> tags.
The contents of the cells are shown here:

Header 2	An Ordered List: 1. Item 1 2. Item 2
An Unordered List: • First Item • 2nd item • Third item	`This is preformatted text`

Exercise 9.4

Prepare your resume as a Web page using HTML only. It should contain the following:

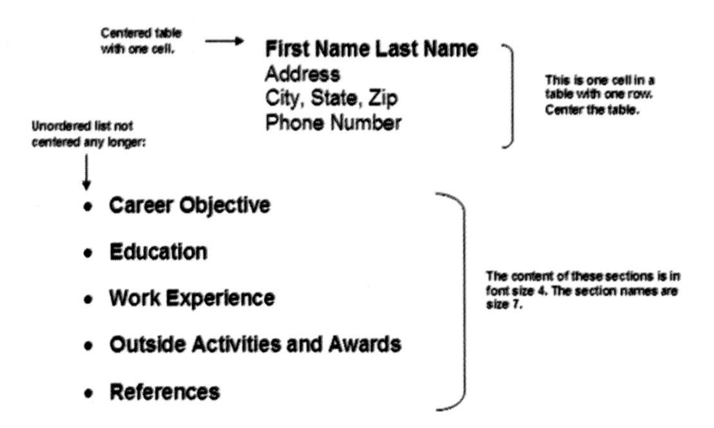

All items shown above are font size 7. What looks bold is bold. For the five categories on the left (Career Objective, etc.) type inside each section whatever applies to you. What you type inside the five categories is to be size 4 and not bold. The font you select is up to you.

The only way to position the top four lines in the center of the page is to use a table with one row and one cell. Put the four lines in the cell. Center the table.

Exercise 9.5

Using XHTML, type the body tag that will create a page with the background color red (75%), blue (50%), and no green. Also use the body tag to get the page font to "Verdana." Remember to use a style attribute in the body tag. Tip: For the color use an RGB color and remember it begins with a pound sign (#).

Exercise 9.6

Using XHTML create the unordered list exactly as shown here. Use only one style attribute, Do not set the font.

- **Shoes**
- **Clothes**
- **Jewelry**

Exercise 9.7

Using XHTML, type an image tag that displays the image "clickme.gif" and changes the cursor to a hand when the mouse passes over the image. Onmouseover is not used here.

Exercise 9.8

Write a tag that begins a paragraph with this style in this order: a dashed, pink border 15 pixels in thickness.

Exercise 9.9

Prepare a cascading style sheet document that performs the following style specifications in this order:

- All headers size 3 are to be green, underlined text, in arial font.
- All tables will have a size 5 dotted red border.

Exercise 9.10

Write the X/HTML that would produce this ordered list:

I. $2^2 = 4$
II. $2^3 = 8$
III. $2^4 = 16$
IV. $2^5 = 32$
V. $2^6 = 64$
VI. $2^7 = 128$
VII. $2^8 = 256$

Exercise 9.11

Create an XML document that contains this data. Use the text editor Notepad and save the file with the proper extension. Tip: Each row is a sales record, use <salesrecord> as the tag to mark each record.

	A	B	C	D	E
1	Month	Sales Rep	Region	Flavor	Cases Sold
2	July	Baker	North	Vanilla	361
3	February	Denton	East	Chocolate	23
4	August	Williams	North	Strawberry	282

Exercise 9.12

Create an XSD for this data. UnitPrice should be treated as decimal data. UnitsInStock must always be positive. Make appropriate decisions for the all data fields. Only include the portion of the XSD beginning and ending with the xsd:sequence tags.

ProductName	UnitPrice	UnitsInStock
Chai	$ 18.00	39
Chang	$ 19.00	17
Aniseed Syrup	$ 10.00	13
Chef Anton's Cajun Seasoning	$ 22.00	53
Chef Anton's Gumbo Mix	$ 21.35	0
Grandma's Boysenberry Spread	$ 25.00	120
Uncle Bob's Organic Dried Pears	$ 30.00	15
Northwoods Cranberry Sauce	$ 40.00	6
Mishi Kobe Niku	$ 97.00	29

Exercise 9.13

Use Excel to create a table of records that reflects this data. Be sure to include column headers in the first row. Begin the table in A1 of Sheet 1 of the workbook.

```
<?xml version="1.0"?>
<states>
  <state>
  <name>New Hampshire</name>
  <song>Old New Hampshire</song>
  <flower>Purple lilac</flower>
  <bird>Purple Finch</bird>
  </state>
  <state>
  <name>New Mexico</name>
  <song>O, Fair New Mexico</song>
  <flower>Yucca flower </flower>
  <bird>Roadrunner</bird>
  </state>
  <state>
  <name>Hawaii</name>
  <song>Hawaii Ponoi</song>
  <flower>Pua Aloalo</flower>
  <bird>Nene</bird>
  </state>
</states>
```

Exercise 9.14

Prepare a simpleType xsd:string component named userID. The data will be string data from four to ten characters in length. Only include the portion of the XSD beginning and ending with the xsd:simpleType tags.

Exercise 9.15

Create a DTD for this data:

```
- <gradingScale>
  - <gradeLevel>
      <minimum>0</minimum>
      <letterGrade>F</letterGrade>
    </gradeLevel>
  - <gradeLevel>
      <minimum>60</minimum>
      <letterGrade>D</letterGrade>
    </gradeLevel>
  - <gradeLevel>
      <minimum>70</minimum>
      <letterGrade>C</letterGrade>
    </gradeLevel>
  - <gradeLevel>
      <minimum>80</minimum>
      <letterGrade>B</letterGrade>
    </gradeLevel>
  - <gradeLevel>
      <minimum>90</minimum>
      <letterGrade>A</letterGrade>
    </gradeLevel>
  </gradingScale>
```

Exercise 9.16

Write the XML tag that links an external schema "car.xsd" to the root element automobiles in an XML document.

Exercise 9.17

Write the DTD that defines this XML data. Name the document "automobiles.dtd".

```
<automobiles>
  <automobile>
    <make>Honda</make>
    <year>2007</year>
    <color>Red</color>
  </automobile>
  <automobile>
    <make>VW</make>
    <year>2008</year>
    <color>Green</color>
  </automobile>
</automobiles>
```

Exercise 9.18

Type this data into an Excel worksheet. Import the worksheet to Access. Export the records from Access as XML and select XML and XSD as the information to be exported.

Last_Name	Product	Price
Green	Coat	$109.53
Jones	Sweater	$43.77
Sanders	Pants	$31.45
Green	Sweater	$43.77
Jones	Shoes	$62.83
Green	Scarf	$17.50

Exercise 9.19

Write the complete XML schema for an element automobile where each record contains make (string), color (string), and year (integer) as shown here. Only include the portion of the XSD beginning and ending with the xsd:element tags.

make	color	year
Honda	Red	2007
VW	Green	2008

Exercise 9.20

Extend Exercise 9.19 by adding a constraint limiting the year to no earlier than 2000. Only include the portion of the XSD beginning and ending with the xsd:restriction tags.

E-Commerce

Chapter 10

E-commerce, or electronic commerce, is business focused on using the Internet and other electronic technologies as a channel through which to communicate and negotiate with customers. The channel is often used to distribute products as well. Because of the directness of communication between vendor and customer **disintermediation,** the removal of **supply chain** intermediaries results. Customers may examine more product options and benefit from the experience of other customers by reading their product reviews online. Vendors may spend less on marketing and selling and perhaps on distribution as well. It seems like everyone wins. The U.S. Census Bureau defines e-commerce as the value of goods and services sold online which includes the use of the Internet and proprietary networks that run systems such as **Electronic Funds Transfer** (EFT) and **Electronic Data Interchange** (EDI).

E-commerce primarily consists of selling, marketing, distributing, buying, and servicing of products or services over Internet. The infrastructure for this arrangement includes local Internet service providers (ISP), international communication carriers, and the millions of Internet servers as well.

E-commerce is a large-scale **business application** that processes substantial volumes of commercial transactions. To the businesses and other organizations that engage in e-commerce it involves coordinating the use of services that those organizations count on to do business: online marketing, online transaction processing, supply chain management, Electronic Funds Transfer, Electronic Data Interchange (EDI), automated inventory management systems, and automated data collection systems.

In this chapter we discuss what e-commerce is about today and what current trends are driving the future.

10.1 Commerce

Commerce is the exchange of goods and services, usually for money. When you buy something at a clothing store you are participating in commerce. When you sell your possessions on eBay, you are participating in commerce. When you think about commerce these roles are recognized:

- **Buyers** — These are people with money who purchase a good or service.
- **Sellers** — Those who offer goods and services to buyers.
- **Producers** — The people who create the products and services that sellers offer to buyers.

Commerce is a fairly simple concept. All of commerce at its simplest level involves buyers, sellers, and producers.

10.1.1 The Elements of Commerce

Practicing commerce requires that the elements of commercial transactions be considered. Here are the elements of commerce encountered in the sale of some product by a retailer to a customer:

- **Product or Service** — If you would like to sell something to a customer, at the most fundamental is what you are selling. A product can be physical like a lamp or hat, or it can be a service like selling tickets or hotel reservations.
- **Place** — You must have a place from which to sell, and perhaps inventory, your products. The place can be physical(a warehouse), or ephemeral (a Web site) that presents a catalog of services and is driven by a database and hosted by a server.
- **Marketing** — Figure out a way to get people to come to your place. Locating your place at a busy corner is a way to gain exposure. Sending out an e-mail order catalog and being listed in a **search engine** are others.
- **Order Processing** — You must accept and record orders. At a grocery store this is handled by the checkout line. In a Web site a **shopping cart** application processes orders.
- **Money** — You need to accept money. If you operate a booth at a farmer's market you can accept cash, check, or credit cards, but a Web site probably would mandate **electronic funds transfer** for monetary interchange.
- **Fulfillment** — You have to deliver a product or service. Customers leave a video rental store with a DVD, but students registering for a course only receive an e-mail confirming the transaction.
- **Returns** — You need a way to handle returns. This could involve receiving, checking, and restocking a physical product into inventory or changing a **database** record from sold to unsold status.
- **Customer Service** — A store selling dishwashers has a staff or people to repair and service broken equipment. An on-line reservation broker could allow customers to re-book their own hotel and airline reservations when their travel plans change. Rebooking causes records to change in a database, repairing dishwashers requires inventory of spare parts, repair vans, and technicians.

As you can see for the previous discussion, in an e-commerce sales channel all of the elements would be present, too:

- **Product** — Either physical and shipped from warehouse or digital and electronically mediated like airline and hotel reservations and music for sale by downloading.
- **Place** — Web site.
- **Marketing** — E-mail, search engine placement, affiliate groups. Also important are database driven cross-selling programs; programs which identify opportunities to sell additional products to existing customers.
- **Order Processing** — Shopping cart application.
- **Money** — A merchant account handling credit card payments. There are other possibilities, too.
- **Fulfillment** — Drop shipping from a warehouse or electronically using the Web and using DBMS, Web server, and browser software.
- **Returns** — Accept physical returns or update database records.
- **Customer Service** — Some information request responses can be automated; many are handled with e-mail correspondence. Also useful are on-line forms, knowledge bases and FAQs. A Web interface can be used to automatically provide order processing status information for customers' peace of mind.

10.1.2 Disintermediation and the Supply Chain

Disintermediation, in Economics, is the removal of mediators in sell-purchase relationships. It is thought that if consumers have direct access to more information they will make better choices and products purchased directly should cost less. Examples of mediators may be found in all aspects of life: bank teller, salesperson, librarian, distributor, wholesaler, broker, financial advisor, doctor, travel agent, agent, and lawyer. In business dealings, intermediaries are found in the **supply chain.**

Supply chain management is the control and administration of materials, information, and financial resources as they move through a process of activities from supplier to manufacturer to wholesaler to retailer to consumer. Supply chain management involves coordinating and integrating these flows among companies and customers. The goal of a supply chain management system is to reduce inventory and associated costs.

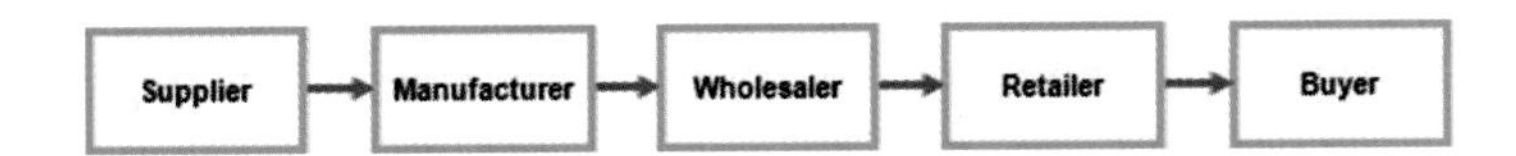

The Supply Chain

Each stage in the chain causes expense; removing barriers to the flow of materials, information, and product reduces cost. The online, real-time environment provided by the Internet enables numerous opportunities to successfully manage the supply chain.

Cutting Out the Middleman Reducing transaction intermediaries has long been an objective of any person or organization wishing to cut expenses. Instead of going through traditional distribution channels companies may now deal directly with their customers via the Internet. Disintermediation is also connected to the idea of **just in time** manufacturing, as the elimination of the need for inventory storage removes one function of an intermediary.

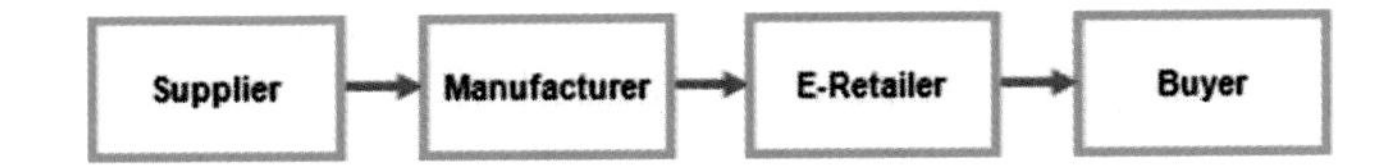

Supply Chain Disintermediation

The supply chain is shortened even more if **digital products,** like airline reservations, movie tickets, etc., can be transported electronically. With no need for warehousing other than in a database, and no physical construction or manufacturing of products, disintermediation has a dramatic impact:

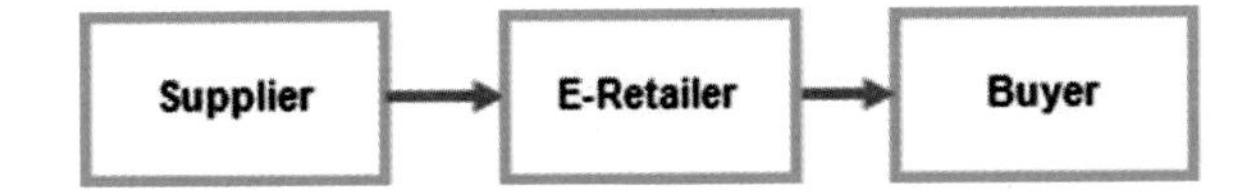

Supply Chain Disintermediation

The business to consumer (**B2C**) supply chain, for example, is typically comprised of five stakeholders:

- Supplier
- Manufacturer
- Wholesaler
- Retailer
- Buyer

It is not unreasonable to conclude that the Internet could reduce the relevant stakeholders to three as retailers sell directly to customers:

- Supplier
- Retailer
- Buyer

Disintermediation initiated by consumers (searching as far back the supply chain as possible) is possible because of high market transparency made possible by access to information. Buyers may become aware of supply prices directly from the manufacturer and bypass wholesalers and retailers in order to buy directly from the manufacturer and pay less.

One important factor is a reduction in the cost of servicing customers directly. A prime example of disintermediation is **Dell, Inc.,** which sells its products directly to the consumer — bypassing traditional retail chains. A well known example of disintermediation in the non-Internet world is **Wal-Mart,** which attempts to reduce prices by eliminating layers of intermediaries between the supplier and the buyer. In Wal-Mart's case, and that of similar big box stores, an online presence offers products to consumers who purchase online and pick up at the retailers location. This **bricks and clicks** arrangement exposes many products to many customers (via online – the **virtual store**) and minimizes shipping expense (one large delivery to one physical location).

10.2 E-commerce

The meaning of the term electronic commerce has changed over the last 30 years. Originally, the term meant the facilitation of commercial transactions electronically, usually using technology like **Electronic Funds Transfer** (EFT) and **Electronic Data Interchange** (EDI). Both were introduced in the late 1970s, for example, to send commercial documents like purchase orders or invoices electronically.

Breaking e-commerce into two parts we find the "E" is about electronic systems and "commerce" is about business. E-commerce is defined as a set of activities that support business operations on a network. The development and proliferation of **Automated Teller Machines** (ATM) and **telephone banking** in the 1980s were also forms of e-commerce. In the dot.com era of the 1990s, e-commerce became commonly defined more as Web commerce — the purchase of goods and services over the Internet.

When the Internet first became generally known to the public in the mid-1990s, many forecasters predicted that e-commerce might soon overtake traditional business models and become the dominant method of buyer-seller dealing and negotiation. Advances did not happen that fast due to several reasons including:

- Insufficient availability of Internet access.
- Lack of broad bandwidth.
- Lack of secure communication protocols.
- Lack of public trust.

Today these problems are mostly considered solved due to the use of **HTTPS** (Secure Hypertext Transfer Protocol which encrypts transactional data), proliferation of **broadband** Internet access, and positive public experience with electronic mediated shopping.

E-commerce is about buyers and sellers of products and services performing transactions over the Web. E-commerce encompasses many commercial activities including support for these relationships:

- **Business to Business** (B2B) — commercial relations between business enterprises.
- **Business to Consumer** (B2C) — commercial relations between business enterprises and retail consumers.

Although many early B2C enterprises floundered during the dot com collapse of 2000 and 2001, many established brick-and-mortar retailers remained active online. Some recognized the potential of the Internet as a channel to augment their traditional delivery system. Wal-Mart, as noted earlier, is one such example of many. Other e-commerce relationships presented later include:

- **Customer to Customer** (C2C)
- **Business to Government** (B2G)
- **Government to Citizen** (G2C)

10.2.1 Electronic Funds Transfer

Electronic Funds Transfer (**EFT**) provides for payments and collection of receipts using electronic networks and equipment. Electronic banking is a common example of EFT. To consumers it means direct deposit of paychecks into savings or checking accounts, 24-hour access to cash, online or telephone bill paying, and other transactional activities. EFT is also important to business. It encompasses a system of transferring money from one bank account directly to another without paper money changing hands and thus helps speed fulfillment of business to business transactions.

The Federal Reserve Board provides the framework that establishes the rights, liabilities, and responsibilities of EFT participants. Known as Regulation E, it regulates **ATM** transactions, **point-of-sale** (POS) transfers in stores, **telephone bill-payment** services, and preauthorized transfers to an account such as **direct deposit** and **social security payments.** EFT is highly regulated.

10.2.2 Electronic Data Interchange

Electronic Data Interchange (**EDI**) is the computer-to-computer interchange of **structured information.** Standardized digital messages in specific formats form the basis of common transactions such as:

- Insurance claims.
- Purchase orders.
- Inventory management.
- Payments.
- Deposits.
- Cash management.
- Receipt confirmation.

It provides user authentication, standardized formatting of transactional data, validation of content, transaction acknowledgment, data encryption, and other services. EDI is an electronic replacement for paper-based transactions and provides the potential of low-cost and reliable communication of structured information. It is capable of facilitating closer integration between an organization and its partners.

The first known application of standardization in transaction content occurred in the 1948 Berlin Airlift with the development of a standard cargo manifest. Electronic transmission of standardized data began during the 1960s in the railroad and trucking transportation industries. Since EDI standards cover the format of data and are independent of specific computer and networking technologies, EDI transactions can be transmitted using the Internet and private networks as long as sender and receiver agree on transaction format.

There are several advantages of using EDI which provide distinct benefits to the user:

- Time-saving.
- Elimination of distributing hard copies of information throughout an organization.
- Data accuracy because all parties receive the same data.
- Ability to track the origin of data.
- Lower communication and handling costs.
- Faster transaction turn-around time.
- Elimination of the unnecessary re-capture and distribution of data.

Another advantage is the closeness of business relationships that develop between organizations that adopt EDI. The commitment to use EDI requires semi-permanent alterations to corporate information systems enabling transaction automation. Such projects reflect a desire of the participants to be partners and are not to be taken casually. The strategic potential inherent in these relationships is significant.

There are not many documented disadvantages of using EDI but those most frequently cited are:

- Installation and customization expense.
- Staff training requirements.

EDI provides relatively fast delivery of electronic documents from sender to receiver. A reasonably sophisticated information technology infrastructure is needed including data processing, data management and security, and networking capabilities. Faster transfer of data with fewer errors streamlines business process.

10.2.3 Automated Teller Machines

The automated teller machine (**ATM**) allows a bank's customer to conduct banking transactions from almost anywhere in the world. The first ATMs were different; since bank database systems were not connected to other banks by computer networks, banks were exclusive about who they gave ATM privileges to: their own customers only. Today the ATM is a banking terminal that accepts deposits, dispenses cash, and transmits a completed transaction notice to the home bank. The magnetic stripe on the ATM card holds the user's account number, PIN, and other identification information.

Once it became apparent that customers demanded the convenience of anywhere-anytime access many banks inaugurated the service. Today, banks not members of an ATM network are rare and considered to be at a competitive disadvantage. Not only do they miss the opportunity to service a larger customer base, but they also miss out on interest revenue known as **float** that is earned as funds in transit pass through their systems.

10.2.4 Telephone and Online Banking

Telephone banking is the use of the telephone system by a customer to check bank balances, pay bills, move money between accounts and other investments, and so on. The Internet provides a platform for the same activities and is known as **online banking.** This environment allows customers to do their banking outside of bank hours and from anywhere where Internet access is available. Because online banking is based on computer automation it is possible for the customer to import data to personal finance programs such as **Microsoft Money** or **Quicken.**

Several developments can be traced to online banking:

- Account aggregation allows customers to monitor all of their accounts in one place.
- Expanding customer willingness to perform technology dependant transactions.
- A growing number of banks operate exclusively online. These banks have low costs compared to traditional banks and can offer high interest rates.

10.3 Types of E-commerce

E-commerce does not follow a particular business model but involves the use of computer and network technology to provide a platform for the automation of commercial and other transactions. The partners in a transaction can involve business, customers, the government, citizens, and regulatory agencies. In this section several types of e-commerce relationships are explored.

E-commerce relationships can be divided into several categories each of which is described in this section:

- Business to Business (B2B)
- Business to Consumer (B2C)
- Customer to Customer (C2C)
- Business to Government (B2G)
- Government to Citizen (G2C)

Before delving into those relationships it is worth mentioning some of the applications that support e-commerce and upon which it depends:

- **Customer relationship management** — CRM systems are used by companies to manage the sales, marketing, service, and other relationships with clients. These systems can be used to produce automatic **personalized marketing** based on customer information stored in the system.
- **Enterprise resource planning** — ERP systems integrate the data and data processing activities of a government, business, or other organization into a single system.
- **Inventory management** — These systems are used to replenish inventory **just in time** to fulfill customer demand while minimizing the cost of carrying in inventory.
- **Document management** — The dream of a paperless office is not new. These systems are used to track and store electronic documents or images of paper documents. Some systems are integrated into other applications; so that users may retrieve existing documents (viewing e-tickets online is an example).
- **Shopping cart** — This server-based application presents a vendor's products to customers who place selections in a shopping cart before completing the order check-out.

- **Payment systems** — A main requirement in e-commerce: the ability to accept a form of electronic payment and payment systems fulfill this requirement.

Apart from formal systems to support e-commerce there are other systems that support communication and have been used as discussion vehicles between sellers and consumers:

- Email.
- FAQ lists.
- Chat rooms enabling consumers to discuss a product or prospective purchase with a live sales representative.
- Discussion forums including posting customer evaluation of products.
- Agents that track a customer's movement through a vendor's Web site and provide the sales staff with tips about a customer's areas of interest.

10.3.1 Business to Business

Business to business electronic commerce (**B2B**) refers to inter-company transactions, including wholesale trade and business purchases of resources, manufactured parts, services, and capital resources. It also includes many types of financial transactions between companies, such as reinsurance, acquisition of commercial credit, and security trading. The basic objective it to shorten the supply chain and achieve greater economies of scale and lower transaction costs.

B2B relationships today cover almost the entire spectrum of inter-business commerce. Use of EDI and EFT are fundamental to B2B operations. Online markets have been established for just about everything including computers and electronics, energy, advertising, health care services, industrial machinery, agriculture, telecommunications, apparel, chemicals, aircraft and automotive parts, financial instruments, food and beverages, intellectual property, metals, office supplies, paper, printing services, shipping, laboratory supplies, plastics, and travel services.

10.3.2 Business to Consumer

Business to consumer e-commerce (**B2C**) is a form of electronic commerce in which products or services are sold from a business to a consumer. Companies that provide products or services directly to customers are called direct sellers. There are two types of direct sellers:

- **E-tailers** — Upon receiving an order, the e-tailer ships products directly to the consumer for delivery. A well-known example is **Amazon.com.**
- **Manufacturers** — Some manufacturers sell directly to consumers via the Internet. The objective is removal of intermediaries and the establishment of direct customer relationships. **Dell.com** is an example.

The B2C commerce must provide customers with safe and secure, and easy-to-use and convenient procedures when paying for merchandise. In early B2C days some potential customers were uncomfortable making payment to an unknown merchant shielded by a Web site. Customers were put off by being unable to ask questions of a sales staff. Due to use of FAQs and other means of dialog that reluctance has largely melted as evidenced by the growth of online buying.

Common examples of B2C commerce include:

- Online banking and electronic funds transfer.
- Travel reservations and ticketing.
- Music download and purchase.
- Pharmaceutical purchase.

It has been suggested that several important advantages are derived from B2C including:

- Shopping can be faster and more convenient.
- Offerings and prices can change instantaneously.
- Customer service and call centers can be integrated with a Web site.
- Broadband electronic communications enhance the buying experience.

10.3.3 Customer to Customer

Consumer-to-consumer electronic commerce (**C2C**) is an Internet supported form of commerce that has existed for thousands of years. We know of it in the form of barter, swap meets, flea markets, yard sales. Most of the successful C2C examples using the Internet take advantage of some type of intermediary which helps customers find other customers and provides a mechanism for payment processing. In some cases product delivery is provided also. The best known example of this is the auction site **eBay.**

The C2C model is best described as commerce conducted between two consumers. In this example, commerce is conducted between a consumer who is auctioning and consumers who are bidding for it. The consumer who is auctioning decides the price of the product. The consumers who are bidding analyze the product and decide how much they value it.

10.3.4 Business to Government and Citizen to Government

Since the government is involved in these models government profit is not a motive. Business and individuals make use of government sponsored Web sites to obtain information and perform useful transactions. Businesses sell products and services to governments as they do to other businesses. Electronic mediation is as useful here in supply chain management as it is in B2B relationships. The state of Ohio, for example, created the Electronic Commerce Center which provides the infrastructure and needed services that allow state agencies to engage in EDI with their vendors.

Citizens transact with governments in several ways. The most notable are:

- Automobile license renewal.
- Tax payment.
- Worker compensation claim filing.

10.3.5 E-commerce Expectations

The following list summarizes some expectations that lure business toward an e-commerce strategy:

- **Lower transaction costs** — A well designed and constructed Web site can lower order-taking costs and customer service costs by automating processes.

- **Larger purchases per transaction** — Much the same as with physical retail shopping, customers often purchase more than they expected to when visiting a an online store.
- **Business cycle integration**— A Web site well integrated into the business cycle can offer customers more information than previously available. Customers track orders, pay bills, and micro-manage investments.
- **People shop in different ways** — Customers have long been familiar with mail order firms and with viewing home shopping shows on television. Web sites build on buying from home behavior and add more options:
    - The ability to build an order over several days.
    - Configure custom orders — like a personalized computer system.
    - Compare prices between multiple vendors easily.
    - Search large catalogs easily.
- **Larger catalogs** — A Web site can offer a catalog larger than what would reasonably be distributed by the post office. The catalog can be searched easily, too.
- **Enhanced customer interaction** — Using automation it is possible to interact with a customer frequently at little cost. Information provided by the customer can be used to customize the customer's view of a Web site.
- **New business models** — With the cost of catalog distribution and order taking falling almost to zero it may be possible to offer products for lower price.

E-commerce is not likely to replace all brick and mortar merchandising. Customers like to try out products before they buy and to receive products immediately when they decide to purchase. With the exception of software products, try before you buy is impossible in an electronic environment. Several operations, however, lend themselves particularly well to e-commerce:

- Online Banking
- Online Auction
- Online Reservation Systems

10.4 Who Participates

Online intermediaries are companies that facilitate transactions between buyers and sellers. They often receive a fee for assisting with the transaction. There are four main types of e-commerce intermediaries which are discussed here.

10.4.1 Brokers

Brokers match buyers and sellers and generally receive a fee. Some brokers offer referral services and provide buyers with information about sellers or their product offerings. These services are somewhat like telephone directories with search facilities. **Craigslist** and dating services are well known examples of brokers. Most brokers tend to be passive and post listings of products and services in response to requests from sellers.

Some brokers allow sellers to pay fees to be listed, or to provide additional information about their products. Other brokers are known as **catalog aggregators** and provide buyers with a catalog of catalogs which contain information from numerous sellers about products, services, and prices. Some of the aggregators take orders on behalf of sellers and charge the seller a fee for this service. Aggregators standardize information coming from vendors enabling customers to make comparisons of similar products and services.

10.4.2 Auctioneers

Auctioneers take a more active role than brokers. They assist in the transaction by setting up the market place for customers to find sellers and their products and they provide the place for the auction to occur – the Web site. They also usually handle payment options. The Federal Trade Commission describes an online auction as "a 'virtual' flea market with new and used merchandise from around the world." The FTC cautions that auctions can be risky and that among consumer fraud complaints it receives every year, those associated with online auction activity always rank near the top. The most common complaints involve late shipments, no shipments, or shipments of products that were not as advertised. Also common are complaints about missed or incorrect payments. Well known auctioneers include **eBay** and **Yahoo Auctions.**

Several common sense tips are offered for those wishing to participate in an auction as buyers:

- Understand the auction's procedures. Auction sites each have their own rules.
- Know about the seller before bidding. Read feedback forums with comments from other buyers about the seller.
- Know who pays for shipping and insurance and determine in advance if a product requires special handling. Since some products may be broken in transit, know in advance what the return policies and procedures are for damaged products.
- Pay by credit card if possible. Federal law permits a credit card holder to dispute charges if the goods were never delivered or if they were misrepresented.

10.4.3 Exchanges

Exchanges are similar to brokers in that buyers and sellers are brought together. Unlike auctions, exchange transactions are usually double-sided in that both parties are buyers and sellers. The exchange provides an arena for bartering to take place. Barter may involve trading goods for other goods or for credit toward future exchange.

Exchanges provide several important services which include:

- Standardized trading rules so that buyers and sellers understand the procedures. Stock markets are prime examples of an exchange.
- Price transparency, meaning that buyers and sellers know the cost of transactions as they occur. It is assumed that access to more information allows participants to make better decisions.
- Centralized clearing which reduces transaction costs and provides transaction verification and documentation.

10.4.4 Dealers and Resellers

Unlike the brokers, auctioneers, and exchanges, dealers and resellers take ownership of products provided by suppliers and resell them to buyers. Some dealers simply purchase goods and resell them at a fixed price. Others, like **Priceline.com,** allow customers to bid for a product (like airline tickets or hotel reservations). The bid is accepted or not depending on the dealers reserve or minimum price.

Since dealers hold product inventory, storage and shipping can be a concern. For this reason many of the notable dealer and resellers handle products that can be delivered electronically and require no physical storage. Prime examples include **Travelocity** and **Orbitz** (travel products) and **Apple** (music downloads).

10.4.5 How Big Is E-commerce?

The United States Census Department tracks business activity and provides statistics. Here we will take a look at two interesting trends in retailing. Online retail activity data from 1999-2006 shows a reasonably consistent upward trend.

Extent of Retail E-commerce

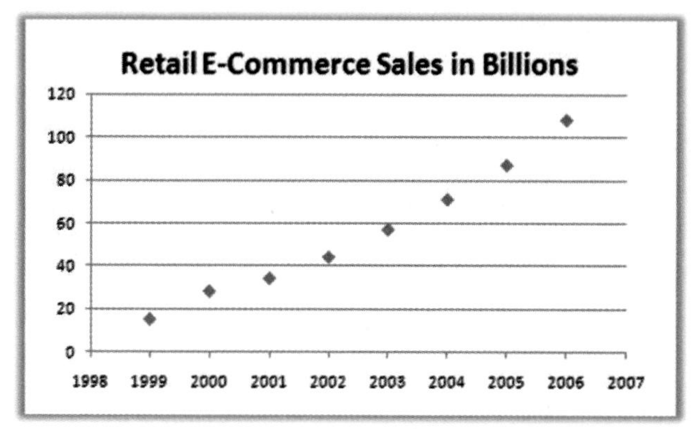

Data Source: U.S. Census Department

When e-commerce's percent of total retail sales is plotted we also notice an upward trend. Percent of retail sales is projected to pass 3 percent in 2007.

Retail E-commerce as Percent of Total Retail

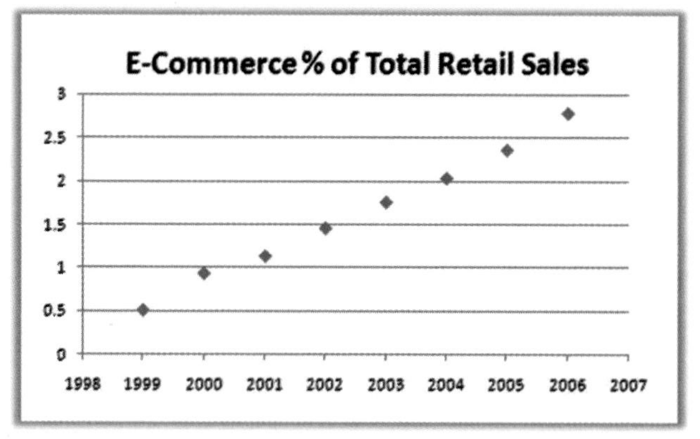

Data Source: U.S. Census Department

The extent of e-commerce's replacement of brick and mortar operations seems a long way off, but the seemingly steady increase in real dollars and percent of total retailing should not be ignored.

10.5 Web Traffic

Since e-commerce today mostly resides on the Web it is important that Web traffic be monitored by businesses that participate. Web traffic is the amount of data sent and received by visitors to a Web site and is determined by the number of visitors and the number of pages they visit. Businesses monitor their Web site's traffic to learn which parts of their Web site or specific pages are popular. They also want to determine if there are any trends, such as one specific page or product category being viewed mostly by consumers in a particular country or within a specific demographic group.

Terms used to describe the recording and interpreting of Web site statistics include Web metrics, Web analytics, Web stats, and site stats. Statistics reveal numerous aspects of traffic including the number of new and returning visitors to a site, and how visitors navigate through the site's content. Essentially the information informs about the content of a site and how visitors use it. Traffic statistics are a measure of Web site performance.

10.5.1 Measuring Traffic

There are numerous ways to monitor Web traffic. The data that is obtained may be used to help structure sites, focus on security problems, or indicate speed bumps (lack of information or poor organization) that get in the customers' way. Several methods for measuring Web traffic are discussed here.

- **Traffic statistics** — Statistics that are found in the Web server's log file contain an automatically generated list of all the pages served. A **hit** is generated when any file is served. The log also records the IP address (visitor's computer address) giving the possibility of learning the geographic location of the visitor.
- **Tracking applications** — External applications can record traffic by inserting an almost invisible image (1 by 1 pixels) in a section of HTML code in every page of the Web site. Using this technique, outside agencies record page hits and provide reports of page activity to client businesses.
- **Toolbars** — Another technique used for collecting traffic makes use of toolbars that users install for free in their Web browser. One such example is from **Alexa Internet** (owned by Amazon.com) that reports the user's page requests to a central host. There the data is aggregated and estimates about traffic volume and **reach** are generated. Reach is expressed as the percentage of all Internet users who visit a given site. Alexa publishes traffic and reach estimates daily. According to Alexa (and numerous other tracking organizations) **Yahoo** is presently the world's most visited Web site (or **portal**). The last section of this chapter presents reach statistics for a number of e-commerce businesses.
- **Packet sniffing** — A less common technique is known as packet sniffing. With this method random samples of traffic data are examined and used to extrapolate information about Web traffic as a whole.

Several categories of data are often collected and analyzed when monitoring web traffic:

- **Visitor count** — The number of visitors and return visitors.
- **Page count** — The average number of page views per visitor – (a high number might suggest that visitors go deep inside the site or it could indicate difficulty while locating desired information).
- **Popular pages** — Most requested pages – the most popular pages.
- **Visit time** — Average visit duration.
- **Time per page** — Average page duration – how long a particular page is viewed.
- **Busy times** — What time of day and in what seasons are the Web site most active. This information might provide clues about when to offer promotions.
- **Referrers** — What page did the visitor arrive at the site from? Referrers can be tracked and may reveal valuable information about the paths that visitors follow to a Web site.

10.5.2 Increasing Web Traffic

Increasing traffic to a Web site is mostly desirable and several techniques may be employed for that purpose:

- Indexing a site in search engines.
- Purchase advertising, including bulk (spam) e-mail, pop-up ads, and search engine advertisements.
- Purchasing non-Internet based advertising.
- Links from referrer sites.

10.5.3 Excessive Traffic

Too much Web traffic can slow down a Web site or even prevent any access to it. These outcomes are caused by more page requests going to a Web server than it can handle. This situation is generally caused by these reasons:

- **Denial-of-Service Attacks** — DoS attacks force Web sites to close (temporarily) after a malicious attack floods a site with more requests than it can cope with. A DoS attack is an attempt to make a server resource unavailable to its intended users. Viruses (which are self-replicating) have been used to generate large-scale distributed denial-of-service attacks.
- **Unanticipated popularity** — A sudden spike of publicity (due to a news item, a rapidly propagating rumor or email, or a link from a popular site) may accidentally cause a Web site to overload. The popularity may be temporary, in which case the owner waits until the popularity passes and business resumes as usual. If the level of visitation remains high and response time suffers then the problem can be solved by adding bandwidth in the form of additional server capacity or increase in communication capacity.

10.6 Success Factors in E-commerce

In most cases, a company engaging in e-commerce depends on more than quality products for its success. Other factors include good customer service, a well-organized business, and a well-designed Web site supported by robust network infrastructure. Those and other factors include:

- **Market research** — Competent market research and analysis by a good team that produces a sound business model. E-commerce is not exempt from good business planning.
- **Interface** — Provide an easy, user-friendly, and secure way for customers to complete transactions.
- **Documentation** — Provide a clear understanding of the products or services offered. Answer all questions in the Web site without the need for a customer to speak with a sales agent.
- **Security** — Provide a reliable and secure processing environment. Backup servers and other protection including firewalls and anti-virus software should be used. Routine database backup should be performed and **disaster recovery** procedures should be established and tested.
- **Inviting** — Operate near, but not on, the cutting edge of technology. Maintain technological freshness, but do not forget that the fundamentals of good business practices are indifferent to technology.

- **Value** — Provide value to customers — this is no different from non-electronic commerce. Merchants can achieve this by offering a product or product-line that attracts potential customers at a competitive price.
- **Incentive** — Providing an incentive for customers to buy and to return and buy more. Sales promotions for repeat purchases and special offers and discounts may help achieve some of this objective. E-mail should be used to remind customers about the incentives between visits.

10.7 Challenges and Impediments to Success

The two main challenges faced by e-commerce businesses are **building traffic** and maintaining **customer loyalty.** Because of the wide availability of online information, customers are thought to be price sensitive and easily lured away by lower price competitors. As in non-e-commerce acquiring and holding on to new customers can be difficult. Here are several reasons why:

- **Unfulfilled expectations** — Failure to understand customer expectations, and motivations. It is critical to know why customers buy what they do.
- **Unsatisfactory Web experience** — Poor Web site implementation due to over-use of glitz at the expense of substance and easy navigation. Underestimation of hardware, software, and communication requirements needed to support the business strategy.
- **Navigation** — Poorly designed or bug-infested Web sites that customers find hard to navigate or trust.
- **Motivation** — Inability to predict competitive reaction. What will competitors do? Will they introduce competitive brands or build more competitive Web sites?
- **Awkward process** — Underestimation of time requirement to complete a transaction. Customers are turned-off by slowness and out dated informnation in a website
- **Security** — Concerns about security. People sometimes will not use credit cards over the Internet due to concerns about theft and credit card fraud. This is a generic concern. A good website design may alleviate security concerns for visitors to that website. The https protocol provides secure ttranactions over the Web.
- **Suitability** — Unsuitable products that are either not wanted or cannot be profitable sold with an e-commerce business model. Product suitability is discussed next.

10.8 Product Suitability

Certain products and services are more suitable for online sales and some are more suitable for offline sales. Clearly **digital products,** including music, movies, software, photography, travel reservations and tickets, and financial transactions are good candidates for e-commerce sales. Digital products have a close to zero shipping cost.

Marketers can also sell certain non-digital products and services successfully as well. Generally, such products should have a high **value-to-weight ratio** meaning that shipping cost is a small portion of the product's value.

Products that have a low value-to-weight ratio are unsuitable for e-commerce. So are products that have a limited shelf-life or might spoil, products that require trial fittings (clothing), and products where color integrity is important (fine art).

10.9 Transactions

Transactions are at the center of commerce. For a seller to participate some tools and services are required to make it happen:

- **Merchant account** — An account that lets payments be electronically collected.
- **Order taking software** — Shopping cart programs that record customer orders and submit orders for processing.
- **Communication software** — Software to process the transactions and to communicate with banks and other parties.
- **Secure server** — A server that houses the Web site, provides data management and storage, and processes transactions securely.

10.9.1 Merchant Accounts

A Merchant Account allows you to accept and process credit card payments. There are many charges associated with accepting credit cards including:

- **Transaction charge** — A base charge per transaction.
- **Monthly minimum charge** — A flat rate that is charged if the minimum is not met.
- **Statement fee** — A monthly fee charged regardless of the amount of charges in a month.
- **Application and setup fees** — Fees when getting started.

An online merchant not processing payments electronically may miss out on a lot of business.

There are alternatives to merchant accounts like **PayPal** and **Propay** that let merchants set up accounts to accept payment from customers without having to have a merchant account. There are still charges and limitations, but these may fit your needs and are worth investigating.

10.9.2 PayPal

PayPal is business that allows payments and electronic money transfers to be made through the Internet. It serves as an electronic payment channel that is used by many business and individual customers. It is now a wholly owned subsidiary of **eBay.**

PayPal is a secure service which carries funds that are being transferred from one PayPal account to another. Buyers and sellers create accounts at PayPal. For a buyer to make a payment that user's account must have sufficient funds to cover the purchase or the buyer must have sufficient credit established elsewhere. Funds are transferred to the seller's account at PayPal. The seller does not receive the funds immediately but must make a withdrawal from their PayPal account to receive payment.

Some are critical of the PayPal arrangement because lack of immediate access to funds received and some claim that PayPal charges numerous hidden fees. While these concerns might be legitimate, PayPal's success is notable as reported on eBay's Web site:

- PayPal had 114 million total payment accounts at the end of Q2-06, a 44 percent increase from the 79 million reported at the end of Q2-05.
- The dollar volume of payments initiated through PayPal was $9 billion in Q2-06, a 37 percent increase from the $6 billion reported in Q2-05.

10.9.3 Google Checkout

Google Checkout is a newer online payment processing service designed to simplify paying for online purchases. Users create a Google account in which they store credit card and shipping information which enables them to purchase at participating stores. Google's approach is connected to their main revenue source, advertising. Google allows online merchants to sell through the advertising they place on Google.

Checkout and PayPal are similar services but not likely in direct competition since Checkout relies on credit card payments and PayPal allows transfers between accounts. Google's announcement of Checkout in mid-2006 did elicit concern about PayPal causing a 7 percent drop in eBay's stock price. EBay preemptively signed a deal with Yahoo who will use PayPal to let its customers pay for Yahoo services. EBay has also banned eBay users from making payments using Google Checkout.

This is a newer, and therefore less established, service than PayPal, but considering Google's overall success to date it is reasonable to presume that Google Checkout might become a major player in the future.

10.9.4 Secure Electronic Transaction

Secure Electronic Transaction (**SET**) is a standard **protocol** for securing credit card transactions over open networks like the Internet. It was developed by MasterCard, Visa, Microsoft, Netscape, and IBM beginning in the mid-1990s and is being advocated as an emerging standard for delivery of secure electronic transactions. It has been adopted by most banks. SET is an **open standard** meaning that its definition is available to all merchants, financial institutions, and software and network vendors.

SET provides for the privacy and authenticity of electronic transactions. It relies on cryptography, encoding and decoding messages, to maintain secrecy. A user is given an **electronic wallet** and a transaction is conducted and authenticated using a combination of **digital certificates** and **digital signatures.**

A digital certificate can be considered an electronic identity that establishes a consumer's credentials when doing transactions on the Web. A certification authority like **VeriSign** issues certificates which contain the holder's name, a unique ID number, the expiration date, the key used for encrypting transactions and digital signatures, as well as the digital signature of the certificate issuing authority (so a recipient can verify that the certificate is authentic).

Authentication is achieved through the use of a **digital signature.** Using a special algorithm, SET can sign a transaction by encoding a specific sequence of numbers into the transaction message by using the sender's key. The recipient authenticates the sender, and therefore the data contained in the digital certificate, by comparing the encoded numbers with a sequence of numbers that it is expecting.

SET appears to be becoming the de facto standard of payment method on the Internet between the merchants, banks, and credit-card companies.

10.9.5 Electronic Checks

Electronic checks are actually printed checks that the customer authorizes the merchant to print. The customer provides checking account and bank routing information and the merchant prints a check on blank check stock and deposits it at the bank as with any other check.

10.9.6 Digital Cash

Digital cash is the focus of a system that allows a person to pay for goods or services by transmitting a number from one computer to another. Similar to the serial numbers on real dollar bills, all digital cash numbers are unique; each is issued by a bank and represents a specified sum of real money. Digital cash is **anonymous** and **reusable,** just like real cash. When a digital cash amount is sent from a buyer to a vendor, there is no way to obtain information about the buyer. This is a key difference between digital cash and credit card systems.

10.9.7 Smart Cards

A smart card is the size of a credit card but has electronic circuitry inside that can process data and participate in transactions. Inside of a smart card a microprocessor is usually found. The microprocessor on the smart card is there for security; it cannot be accessed without authentication as a magnetic strip on a credit can be. Smart cards are more commonly used in Europe than in the United States. Some cards combine RFID technology which connects the card to a reader without requiring physical contact with it.

10.9.8 Micropayments

Micropayment systems accumulate individual, very small payments in a larger batch for processing. The system overhead and cost per transaction can overwhelm the value of a sale by a merchant. By batching payments together the processing cost can be spread over a number of transactions. Common use of micropayment systems is found on highway toll operations, public transportation systems, and student dining room service.

10.9.9 SSL

The Secure Sockets Layer protocol was developed by Netscape to protect the content of documents transmitted on the Internet. It uses encryption and requires a public and private key for encoding and decoding messages. SSL establishes a secure connection between client and server. The browser alone cannot secure the transaction, therefore a SSL certificate on the server, issued by a trusted authority, is needed to decode client messages containing transaction and financial data. https in the address bar and a padlock on the status bar of the browser window indicate that information will be sent encrypted over the Internet.

10.10 Fraud and Other Concerns

The U.S. Department of Justice defines Internet fraud as "any type of scheme that uses one or more components of the Internet to present fraudulent solicitations to prospective victims, to conduct fraudulent transactions, or to transmit the proceeds of fraud to financial institutions or to others." Numerous examples of Internet fraud abound, several common types are described here.

10.10.1 Stolen Credit Cards

Most Internet fraud is done through the use of stolen credit card information which may be obtained in many ways**. Identity theft** can occur by credit card or other information being copied from retailers, either online or offline. There have been many cases of hackers intrusively obtaining large quantities of credit card information from companies' databases. Refer to the security chapter for more information.

Despite the public claims of merchants and credit card issuers, using credit cards for online purchases can be insecure especially when merchants manually complete transactions. For this reason, even so called secure transactions are not fully secure, since the information is decrypted to standard text in order to process it. This is one of the points where credit card information is typically stolen.

Reporting Credit Card Fraud If you lose or have your credit card stolen, you should immediately report it to your card issuer. Once you report the incident, you are no longer responsible for unauthorized charges made on your card.

Credit card fraud can be reported to the **Federal Trade Commission** (FTC) and to local and regional authorities. It is the standing policy of the FTC not to investigate reports where the value of fraud does not exceed $2,000. Local law enforcement may or may not further investigate a credit card fraud, depending on the amount, type of fraud, and where the fraud originated from.

10.10.2 Phishing

Phishing is the act of attempting to fraudulently acquire information by distribution of e-mail messages asking prospective victims to verify their account or confirm billing information. The messages appear to be real because the graphics, layouts, and fonts of actual Web sites are used.

Phishing has been widely used to target customers of large institutions like Citibank, Bank of America, eBay, and PayPal. Since these businesses each have a large customer base, widely distributed **spam email** is likely to be delivered to actual customers. These customers might be deceived into believing the e-mail was legitimate and in turn answer questions such as "What is your social security number?", "What is your account ID and password?", and so on.

Microsoft's Internet Explorer has a built-in Phishing Filter. The Internet and WWW chapter has details on how IE and phishing filter works.

10.10.3 Click Fraud

Advertisers often pay a fee based on some other Web site's referrals (clicks) to the merchant's Web site. Click fraud occurs when Web sites which are paid for providing links to advertisers force clicks to ads on their own Web sites via **Spyware.** The advertiser then pays a commission on the cost-per-click that was artificially increased.

10.10.4 Pharming

Pharming is the exploitation of vulnerability in domain name servers (machines responsible for resolving Internet names into their real numeric IP addresses) that allows traffic to a Web site to be redirected to another Web site. If the Web site receiving the traffic is a fraudulent copy of a legitimate Web site, it can be used to phish or steal a computer user's ID number or account number and passwords.

The term pharming is a combination of farming and phishing. The term phishing refers to obtaining access credentials such as user names and passwords.

10.10.5 Auction and Retail Schemes

According to the Federal Trade Commission, fraudulent schemes on online auction sites are the most frequently reported form of Internet fraud. These schemes often purport to offer high-value items (art, classic cars, expensive watches, collectibles, etc.). The successful bidder of an auction will pay for the advertised items and may find that the vendor delivers nothing or delivers an item of far less value than what was promised.

10.10.6 Market Manipulation

Attempts to manipulate the securities market for personal gain require rapid dissemination of information about a target company. The Internet is ideal for this type of fraud. The two most common types on Internet driven stock manipulation are:

- **Pump and Dump** — Schemes which are an attempt to spread fraudulent information in an effort to cause dramatic price increases in thinly traded stocks. Perpetrators then sell off their holdings and collect profits before the stock price falls back to its usual level.
- **Short Selling** — Schemes that take a similar approach by causing the price of a stock to fall. Short sellers have contracts to sell stock at a predefined future price. If the price falls, the short seller will purchase the stock at the lower price and immediately sell it at the higher contract price.

10.10.7 Spam

Spam floods the Internet with numerous copies of the same message. It is an attempt to force the message on people who would probably not otherwise wish to receive it. Much spam is commercial advertising, but some is for get-rich-quick schemes, and sale of inferior products. Spam costs the sender very little to send.

10.11 Deciding Whether to Begin E-commerce

Many businesses have entered the e-commerce market. Not all survive. It is important to remember that e-commerce is about electronic systems that support business operations on a network. There is no substitute for a solid business plan – after all this is about business that happens to use technology as a communication and delivery vehicle. It is crucial to understand the potential that technology offers but its limitations must be known as well. Several points are worth noting:

- **New opportunities** — Business opportunities that e-commerce presents often challenge traditional approaches to business.
- **A new way to do business** — E-commerce is still relatively young, and although growing rapidly, has not yet settled into repeatable patterns. The dot com burst of the early 2000s eliminated numerous early online entrepreneurs.
- **Technology changes fast** — Technology lifecycles are often of less than a year in duration. Comprehensive capacity and cost planning can help make a commercial Web site successful.
- **Not yet mainstream** — Although growth continues to be positive, e-commerce is not yet considered mainstream by most businesses. Many consumers, afraid of fraud or technology, prefer conventional business interaction.

Deciding whether or not to participate in e-commerce involves the traditional planning and implementation of steps that all business ventures are defined by.

10.11.1 What to Consider

E-commerce does not always meet the needs of a business so how does it decide whether or not to engage in that practice? If the market for a company's products is tiny, or if the products are otherwise unsuitable for e-commerce, then building a commercial Web site would not make sense. The revenue from a small market may not support the expense of a Web site and products with a low value-to-weight ratio may require delivery expense that leaves no room for profit. Other products like perishables present obvious disadvantages. E-commerce is hard and easy; here are both perspectives:

E-commerce challenges:

- Obtaining traffic for the Web site.
- Getting traffic to return a second time.
- Differentiating from the competition.
- Motivating purchases. Browsing the website is easy but not all hits end up in generating revenue for the site.
- Integrating an e-commerce Web site with existing business processes.

The easier part:

- Creating the Web site.
- Taking the orders.
- Accepting payment.

If a company concludes that their products offer acceptable market potential on the Web then some things to consider are:

- **Suppliers** — The same concern that any normal store or mail order company has. Without good suppliers you cannot offer products.
- **Price Point** — Price comparisons on the Web are extremely easy for the consumer.
- **Customer Relations** — E-commerce offers a variety of different ways to relate to your customer. E-mail, FAQs, knowledge bases, forums, chat rooms, etc. Integrating these features into a Web site helps differentiate from the competition.
- **The Back End** — Order fulfillment, return processing, and customer service will make or break any retail establishment. They define the relationship with the customer.
- **Other Tools** — Customers need motivation to visit a Web site and make purchases. Several ways to stimulate visits include:
  - Affiliate programs – discussed later.
  - Special discounts to preferred customers.
  - Repeat buyer programs.
  - Seasonal or periodic sales.

The company considering entry into e-commerce should contemplate these questions:

- What similar products or services does this target market buy now? All new or newly offered products and services take market share away from something else. How will competitors react? Will consumers be interested in new products?

- How will the new product or service offerings add value for the customer? Successful competition in a well attended market requires differentiation by product characteristics or transaction procedures and support. Will a new offering stand apart as better made, provide more or better benefits and features, and be sold at a competitively acceptable price?
- Which audience segments will be most receptive to those products? Who are the best prospects and what might they want? Product line extensions will likely be sold to an existing audience. A new market or new a product likely requires new customer relationships.

Assuming that the evaluation of these considerations is positive, construction and marketing of the Web site remains ahead.

10.11.2 Implementation

Before constructing an e-commerce Web site these questions should be considered and answered:

- **Are you going to design your site yourself? If so, you will need:**
  - Experience or training in Web design.
  - A server or access to a commercial server.
  - Web design software.
  - Likely a scanner or digital camera — for product photos.
  - FTP software for uploading files to your Web site.
- **Are you going to sell products from your site? If so, you will need:**
  - A merchant account — or some way to accept payments.
  - Shopping cart software — or some way for shoppers to enter and keep up with their orders.
  - Secure servers if you're accepting credit card payment or other personal payment information.
  - Fulfillment software to keep track of inventory and orders.
- **Are you offering a large number of products? If so, you'll need:**
  - A database.
  - Knowledge about how to incorporate a database into a Web site.
- **Does your product or service require sound, video, or animations? If so you need:**
  - Video or audio capture equipment.
  - Software for editing video or audio clips.
  - A broadband Internet connection.

Implementing an E-commerce Site Let's say that you would like to create an e-commerce site. There are three general ways to implement the site. The three general ways, listed in order of decreasing flexibility and increasing simplicity, are:

- **Enterprise computing** — Enterprise computing means that you purchase hardware and software and hire a staff of developers to create your e-commerce Web site. These are indicators suggesting this approach:
  - Immensely high traffic.

    - A large catalog of products — especially if the catalog is changing constantly.
    - Other business processes already in place to be integrated to the e-commerce offering.
- **Virtual Hosting** — The vendor maintains the equipment and software and sells them in standardized application packages. Part of the package includes security, and almost always a merchant account is available. Database access is normally a part of the package. You provide the Web designers and developers to create and maintain the site.
- **Simplified E-commerce** — This approach is used by most small businesses and individuals getting into e-commerce. The vendor provides a template system for creating an online store. Forms are filled out and the vendor's software then generates all of the Web pages for the store. Good examples of this sort of offering include **FreeMerchant, Yahoo Stores,** and **MyCart.**

Shopping Cart Software Assuming a business has a merchant account — or alternative method of processing payments — now visitors must be given a way to shop. A good shopping cart allows customers to:

- Preview and select products.
- Preview the checkout stage.
- Delete items if they change their mind.
- Enter payment and shipping information.

Numerous shopping cart applications are offered, so it makes little sense to build one in-house unless the nature of the products or customers are especially unique.

Tools to look for in a good shopping cart program include:

- The potential for making ordering and checkout pages look similar to the rest of the Web site.
- SSL capabilities.
- Interactivity with online authorization services.
- Management tools to manage the online store.
- Merchandising features that help cross-sell products.
- Inventory tracking functions.
- Order review and confirmation tools including e-mail order notifications.
- Sales tax and shipping cost calculators.
- Frequent-shopper and special discount functions.
- Import/export with standard data managers like Access and Excel.
- Web-based administration tools allowing changes to be administered remotely from a Web browser.

10.12 Compromise Solutions

Bricks and clicks is a business strategy or business model in e-commerce in which a company attempts to integrate both online and physical presences. It is also known as **click and mortar** or **bricks and clicks.** This **hybrid model** seems sensible because the Internet by itself can perform only some of the numerous activities required to run a successful business. Success will always involve the ability to produce or acquire and deliver high-quality products and distribute these products, communicate with customers, handle returns and repairs, and possibly perform maintenance and service.

Despite the initial advantage of strictly online businesses (easy to start and expand rapidly because of their low capital requirements and virtual nature) they are also easy to replicate. E-commerce is replete with copycats who swamp markets with similar offerings and mostly compete on price alone. Often the organization with the deepest pockets and not necessarily the best products or service survives.

By contrast, many market segments have a handful of traditional manufacturers, distributors, and retailers that have built competitive barriers through brand building and investments in physical infrastructure. E-commerce only operations may not be able to compete against such established merchants.

The bricks and clicks strategy has most frequently been used by traditional retailers who have deep supply chains. It may be easier for a traditional retailer to establish an online presence than it is for a start-up company to employ a successful e-commerce only strategy, or especially for an online retailer to establish a traditional brick and mortar presence.

Brick and click firms might have the advantage in business practice because they are able to use their competencies and assets, which include:

- **Core Competency** — Successful firms tend to have core competencies that they perform better than their competitors. When a brick and mortar firm goes online it is able to use this core competency.
- **Branding** — Existing firms often have invested large sums in years of brand advertising. This equity can be leveraged on-line.
- **Stability** — Existing firms may appear more stable because they have been in business for many years and enjoy greater public awareness. People trust them more than pure e-commerce firms.
- **Existing Customer Base** — Because existing firms already have customers, they can more easily obtain economies of scale in marketing and distribution.

Affiliate programs A big part of today's e-commerce is the affiliate programs. If you are an online merchant, how can you get people to your site to buy your products? One popular option that serves both of these functions is an affiliate program. There are arrangements in which an online merchant Web site pays affiliate Web sites a commission to send them traffic. Affiliate Web sites post links to the merchant site and are paid according to a particular agreement. This agreement is usually based on the number of people the affiliate sends to the merchant's site or the number of people they send who buy something. An affiliate program can provide a cheap and effective marketing strategy.

10.13 Success Stories

Not all e-commerce entries are successful. The dot com burst of 2000-2001 claimed numerous casualties. While understanding the causes of failure can be most informative this section describes some well known examples of successful online enterprises. Each description is accompanied with late 2006 reach statistics provided by **Alexa Internet.**

eBay EBay manages an online auction and shopping Web site, where people buy and sell goods and services worldwide. EBay generates revenue from a number of fees. There are fees to list a product and fees when the product sells. The eBay fee system is quite complex. EBay's success has allowed it to purchase **PayPal** outright and it owns 25 percent of **Craigslist.** Reach is 2.9 percent which means that each day 2.9 percent of all Internet users visit eBay's Web site.

Amazon Amazon.com was one of the first companies to successfully sell goods over the Internet and it was one of the few companies to ride the dot-com bubble and survive the burst. Launched in 1995, it initially was an online bookstore but it later diversified into other product lines, adding computer software, video games, DVDs, music CDs, electronics, like mp3 players, apparel, furniture, food, and more. Amazon operates in many countries. Reach is 2.68 percent.

Craigslist Craigslist is a centralized network featuring free classified advertisements of jobs, housing, personal ads, and listings for sale, for barter, wanted, services, and more. It was founded in 1995 in San Francisco, and as of mid-2006 is established in about 300 cities in various parts of the world. According to Alexa it serves over 4 billion page views per month and reach is just under 1 percent of Internet user traffic.

Google Google is one of the world's most popular **search engines.** It began as a research project by two PhD students and has evolved into a highly successful business. No longer only a search engine, Google provides e-mail (Gmail), mapping applications (Google Earth), instant messaging (Google talk – now merged with Gmail), and other applications. Google has embarked on the development of online office applications that, if successful, may complete with Microsoft's popular Office Suite. Google's main source of revenue is advertising. Its success has given it deep cash reserves and allows it to branch out in numerous directions. Its most recent major acquisition is **YouTube** which it purchased for 1.6 billion dollars. It is not surprising that such a popular Web site would enjoy reach of 25 percent!

Yahoo! Yahoo! is a Web **portal** offering a wide range of products and services which include: A popular search engine, Yahoo! Mail (a Web-based e-mail service, Yahoo! Messenger (an instant messaging client), online discussion groups (Yahoo! Groups), online gaming chat, various news feeds, online shopping, online auction facilities, and a lot more. At 27 percent it has the highest reach of any Web site. Over 4 billion pages are served daily.

Although still a very dominant player in e-commerce, Yahoo! is seen as recently losing some of its edge. For example, it came close to purchasing YouTube but was edged out by Google. Advertising sales are also down especially from large marketers.

MySpace and Facebook MySpace is a social networking Web site that allows people to maintain communities of friends who share photos, journals, and interests. A relatively new Web site, it became an overnight phenomenon. Created in 2003 it was purchased in July 2005 for $580 million by News Corporation (the parent company of Fox Broadcasting). Daily reach is 3.6 percent of all Internet traffic.

Facebook is another social networking Web site. Originally focused on college students it has branched out and offers communities for many other special interest groups. The site is free to users and generates revenue from advertising. Facebook was created in 2004 at Harvard University and within three weeks of its inauguration over 50 percent of all Harvard undergraduates had signed up! By the end of 2004 there were over 1 million registered users. It is a highly popular Web site with reach of 5 percent.

Dell Dell computer is a major manufacture of computers and peripheral equipment. Through its **direct business model,** it designs, manufactures, and customizes products and services to customer requirements, and offers an extensive selection of software and peripherals. With over $57 billion in 2006 sales the business model seems to work:

Dell's five tenets of the model from the annual corporate report are:

- **Efficient Path to the Customer** — The most efficient path to the customer is through a direct relationship, with no intermediaries to add confusion and cost.
- **Single Point of Accountability** — One entry point for customers to access all resources that relate to a sale: sales support, technical support, and customer support.
- **Build-to-Order** — Every customer gets exactly what they want.
- **Low-Cost Leader** — Dell is highly efficient in supply chain management.
- **Standard Based Technology** — Dell technology conforms to industry standards. Customers benefit from industry research and development and obtain flexibility and choice.

10.14 Summary

E-commerce is commercial activity carried out using a technology infrastructure. It is business first which uses technology as a vehicle for performing business activities. As in all commerce a supply chain carries raw materials eventually to consumers. Shortcuts through the supply chain are advantageous, perhaps lowering prices and transaction costs. Disintermediation of the supply chain, the creation of shortcuts, can be facilitated by electronic based commerce systems.

Commerce is the exchange of goods and services for money or other goods and services. For e-commerce to be successfully applied money must be transferred from buyers to sellers. Electronic Data Interchange standards provide a platform which together with Electronic Funds Transfer protocols allows secure money exchanges to happen rapidly, reliably, and at low cost.

Commerce has different partners and participants. Business, consumers, and governments are engaged. Businesses are driven by profit. Consumers are driven by obtaining low cost, high quality service, and ease of experience. Governments are driven by reducing budgets. Each class of stakeholder can benefit from e-commerce.

Commercial success is measured in profit and profit depends on having customers. A Web site operator monitors Web site traffic in terms of new visitors, repeat visitors, geographic location if possible, and considers seasonality of time of day, week, and year. Tools for increasing traffic are available but nothing is better than a good product at a good price, presented well with good quality service delivered by the Web site operator who pays attention to the business.

Successful Web sites require forethought. Sensible design with the goal of easy customer navigation and order fulfillment are important. A good shopping cart application running on a secure server is mandatory. A merchant account or some other method of exchanging money is clearly required. Security is always important for the merchant and the customer and various protections should be considered and implemented.

The decision to attempt an e-commerce operation should be thought out and considered with regard to the nature of the product or the offering, the competition, ease of obtaining products to sell, and many other factors. Existing brick and mortar businesses have certain advantages having an already established market presence and distribution channel that allows local drop-off.

There have been some astonishing successes in e-commerce. There are many more failures that go unreported. e-commerce is not an end in itself; it is a vehicle that if well used can lead to spectacular outcomes.

EXERCISES

Exercise 10.1

Discuss online sale of music from the perspective of supply chain disintermediation.

Exercise 10.2

Describe the differences between processing credit cards for payment and using a service like PayPal. In your answer consider the merchant and consumer perspective.

Exercise 10.3

Imagine that you are a Web site operator and notice that traffic is less this quarter than it was in the same quarter one year ago. What would you consider doing to stimulate more traffic? Prepare a plan.

Exercise 10.4

If you were to build a commercial Web site, what security measures would you take?

Exercise 10.5

What is the role of the Web browser and of certain protocols in providing security for the consumer?

Exercise 10.6

Some products work better in e-commerce than others. The weight-to-value ratio is a measure that is used to evaluate the suitability of products. Identify four products and their suitability for e-commerce sale this way:

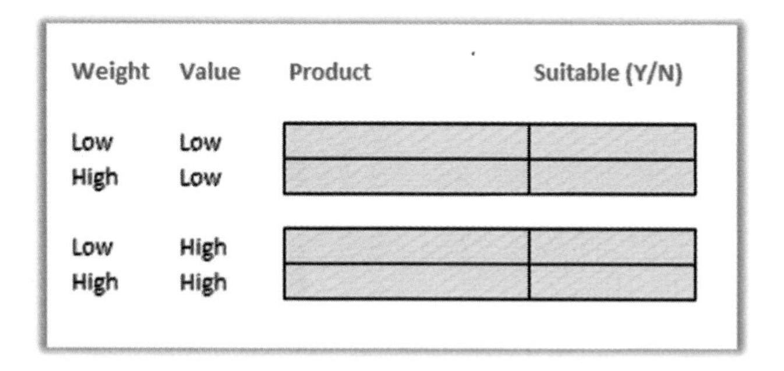

Weight	Value	Product	Suitable (Y/N)
Low	Low		
High	Low		
Low	High		
High	High		

Exercise 10.7

Considering the future of e-commerce, what do you think are the limits or challenges that it faces over the next several years?

Exercise 10.8

Identify a business segment not currently participating in e-commerce that you think is likely to get involved soon. Why do you think it has not participated yet?

Exercise 10.9

What should the role of government be in regulating e-commerce?

Exercise 10.10

You are entrepreneurial. What is your idea for the next big e-commerce success?

SECURITY, ETHICS, AND PRIVACY

CHAPTER 11

Privacy and security have always been important. Greater attention is focused on these concerns now more than ever because of increasing opportunities for intrusion into networked computer systems. Individuals, businesses, governments, and other institutions must be aware.

Information privacy, sometimes known as **Internet privacy,** is about protection of data when transmitted, stored, and received over the structure of the Internet. It includes the ability to exercise control over what information is protected and who can access that information. Internet privacy is within the broader subject of computer privacy.

Many computer and network users speak about the importance of maintaining secure systems and networks that guard the privacy of their data. It is interesting, however, that numerous stories abound, revealing how lax or uninformed many individuals and organizations are about security.

Organizations that acquire and store personal or private data must consider these questions because each has significant consequence. When data is gathered:

- What purpose is it to be used for?
- How will it be verified?
- How will it be secured?
- When will it be destroyed?

Access to information, consumer and business products, credit and financial services, vacation opportunities, medical information, and many other types of data and services is more available than ever before. Due to the Internet, we can order music, books, and gifts online, we can book travel arrangements, and manage our bank accounts twenty-four hours a day. Surely we are grateful that the Internet provides the vehicle for this access, but it also opens the door to unwanted **intrusion.**

While the Internet creates opportunities for a more enjoyable and convenient life, it also provides an opening to personal and corporate information. News about the newest computer virus, the actions of hackers and discovery of stolen databases have become routine.

It is increasingly difficult to imagine a business that does not collect or hold personal information — Social Security numbers, names and addresses, credit card numbers, or bank and other account numbers — about customers, students, employees, or patients. If this information is inappropriately accessed, it could put these individuals at risk for **identity theft.** Importantly, not every information compromise results in identity theft, and the type of information compromised does affect the degree of potential damage.

Fortunately, securing a computer and network is mostly a well understood matter of identifying potential threats, developing plans and procedures for guarding against risks, and implementing and monitoring protection. Unfortunately, while well understood, these steps are too often forgotten. The use of strong passwords, installation of firewalls, regularly updating anti-virus software, encryption of wireless networks, and other actions can help considerably with protecting a computer, a network, and stored data.

People and organizations with a casual interest in information privacy are at risk. People with an interest in unauthorized entry or damage to computer systems abound. The availability of the Internet provides relatively easy pathways into unprotected systems. Computer system **vulnerabilities,** system holes, weaknesses allowing an attacker to violate the confidentiality, integrity, access control, or audit mechanisms of the system are more common than expected. Attackers are known as:

- **Hacker** — A computer programmer specializing in the discovery of exploits in systems, or in obtaining unauthorized access to systems through skills, tactics, and detailed knowledge of vulnerabilities.
- **Cracker** — A person who engages in circumvention of computer security systems through illicit actions to obtain and use passwords or other means to breech system security.
- **Script Kiddie** — A negative term for computer intruders with little or no skill who simply follows directions without fully understanding the meaning of the steps they are performing. By being lucky these people can cause damage to systems. Groups of these intruders are known as Cybergangs and often are just having fun at the expense of others.
- **Intruder** — Hackers, crackers, and others performing illicit intrusion or damage to computer systems or data.

Several terms have come into common usage when we consider security, ethics, and privacy:

- **Cyber Security** — Cyber security involves protecting computer systems, networks, and information by preventing, detecting, and responding to attacks.
- **Cyber Terrorism** — The use of target computers, networks, and data to cause physical, real-world harm or severe disruption.
- **Information Warfare** — The use of information technology to obtain a competitive advantage over a competitor.
- **Corporate Espionage** — The practice of obtaining information about a business organization that is considered secret or confidential without the permission of the holder of the information. Information obtained this way is often used to gain unfair competitive advantage.

This chapter introduces the risks to privacy attendant with poor security. Corporate and individual concerns are discussed. The causes and effects of a lowered guard are presented and followed with a discussion of opportunities for tightening up. Various Internet-based schemes are cited, too. A three tier security model is also presented. The chapter concludes with a discussion of ethics and responsibilities. The chapter begins with a brief discussion about recent events.

11.1 Recent Events

Security breaches are quite common. That should not be a surprise since the media frequently alerts us to these events. Some are large and some are small. Some are accidental and some the result of deliberate action. It is important to be aware of the difference between **data loss** and **malicious data loss.** The difference is important and often ignored as the public becomes aware of recent attention-grabbing stories like those described here. While millions of Americans' personal data records have been lost or stolen there is little evidence of an increase in identity theft or financial fraud. In other words, data loss is not uncommon but harm due to data loss may be less common than many think.

While the public focuses on large-scale data loss, personal identity theft is predominantly due to lost wallets, stolen credit cards and checkbooks, and not to violated computers and communication networks. Relatives, friends, and co-workers are the thieves in the majority of cases.

The events described in this section are publicly known because the personal data of many people was lost or stolen in each occasion. How many unpublished events are we unaware of? What about the non-public intrusion into personal computers and home networks? We will discuss that later, but for now some public stories.

Transportation Security Administration The Transportation Security Administration lost a computer hard drive containing Social Security numbers, bank data and payroll information for about 50,000 employees. Authorities realized the hard drive was missing from a controlled area at TSA headquarters. The TSA Administrator sent a letter to employees apologizing for the lost data and promising to pay for one year of credit monitoring services. Of course, once data is compromised, monitoring will not re-secure the data it will merely identify attempts to use it inappropriately.

The external (portable) hard drive contained information and while its loss of personal data was significant it did not come close to what happened at the Department of Veterans Affairs.

Department of Veterans Affairs The Department of Veterans Affairs reported that 1.8 million personal and business records of veterans and doctors had been stolen. The information was on a hard drive in a computer that was taken from a hospital in Birmingham Alabama. Unfortunately, that was not the DOV's first experience with data loss as you will shortly read.

T.J. Maxx and Marshall's As many as 40 million T.J. Maxx and Marshall's customer credit and debit cards may have been compromised due to a security breech at CardSystems Solutions, a card payment processor. The exploited database contained customer records with data about retail transactions, and driver's license and checking account numbers. The intrusion is thought to have gone on for over four years through the use of point-of-sale terminals which are connected to the Internet.

University of California at Los Angeles The University of California at Los Angeles (UCLA) announced that hackers gained access to a university database and exposed private information about approximately 800,000 current and former faculty, students, and staff. It is believed that the initial intrusion occurred in October 2005 and was likely ongoing. The university reported that the hackers were particularly interested in names and social security numbers. This break-in is the largest yet reported by an academic institution. Other institutions with similar exposures include Ohio University, the City University of New York, the University of Southern California, Tufts University, the University of Colorado, and the University of Mississippi.

Department of Veterans Affairs An earlier data loss experience of the DOV involved the records of over 26 million veterans. The information was stolen from the home of a Veterans Affairs employee when the employee's computer was stolen. The laptop and removable hard disk contained veterans' names, social security numbers, birth dates, and more. Fortunately it turned out that the theft was a routine residential burglary and no evidence was found that the thieves knew the significance of the data they acquired. One wonders how an employee, in violation of Department policy, was permitted to bring home a database with confidential data.

H&R Block H&R Block Inc. mistakenly distributed free copies of its tax return software that included the Social Security numbers of recipients' on the mailing label. The Social Security numbers were embedded within a string of 47 numbers and letters printed on the mailing label. Because the numbers were not separated out and identified as Social Security numbers it would not necessarily be easy for anyone other than the recipient to recognize the privacy breech. Therefore thieves were less likely to have exploited it. The company first became aware of the problem when a recipient called to point it out. No evidence of identity fraud has been connected to this incident.

People's Bank: Connecticut Nearly 90,000 customers of Bridgeport, Connecticut-based People's Bank learned that information from their accounts was compromised when a computer tape with that data was lost. The tape was lost by UPS en route to the credit-reporting bureau TransUnion. It contained personal data that included names, Social Security numbers, addresses, and checking account numbers. As in the other examples, no known associated fraud has yet been uncovered.

Metropolitan State College: Denver Metropolitan State College in Denver lost personal data on more than 93,000 students due to the theft of one of the college's laptop computers. A college employee had been using the data, including Social Security numbers and student names, to write a grant proposal at home, where the computer was stolen. Ironically, the same employee was also using the unprotected data to write a master's degree thesis. No fraudulent use of the lost data is known of. What policies, if any, were violated here?

University of Mississippi Web pages on the University of Mississippi's Web site were found to list the names and Social Security Numbers of about 700 university students. The files were "published" as a backup file on an Internet server by a staff member in the dean ofstudents office. Like most similar situations, it was in clear violation of policy. Since the documents had been on the Internet for so long, the data had been indexed by the major search engines. Anyone searching the Internet by the name of one of the affected students would have been given a link to the page with that student's Social Security Number.

Providence Health Systems: Oregon Providence Health Systems of Oregon agreed to repay the state of Oregon for costs of more than $95,000 as part of a deal resolving an investigation into the largest data breach reported in Oregon until then. Medical records of over 365,000 patients, stored non-encrypted, were in a car stolen from an employee of Providence Health Systems. The data was not recovered.

Georgetown University Hospital A consultant was able to download the Social Security numbers, names, and dates of birth for thousands of Georgetown University Hospital patients by accidentally discovering the unsecured data on the Web site of Web-based pharmacy, InstantDx. The consultant accessed the data by using a password he discovered hard-coded into Medisoft (online pharmacy management software used by InstantDx), which that company claims is used by 70,000 medical providers.

11.2 Corporate Concerns

Corporations, like individuals, are concerned about privacy and security. While individuals are mostly alerted to the harm that might be caused by malicious loss of data, corporations are concerned about that and more. In this section risks to corporations are discussed. Concerns of individuals are discussed in the following sections. Some risks are common to both and some to mostly corporations (denial of service for example). The section that then follows presents opportunities for prevention. You will notice that many of the actions to be taken (installation of firewalls for example) may apply both to individuals and corporations.

11.2.1 Denial of Service

A denial of service attack is described as an aggressive attempt to prevent legitimate users of a service from using that service or the server it is installed on. Common examples of this risk include attempts to:

- Overload a network with packets slowing and perhaps crippling legitimate network traffic.
- Disrupt communication connections between two machines.
- Prevent public's access to a service or server.
- Prevent a specific individual from accessing a service.

Two of the more common techniques used for denying service are:

- **Bandwidth Consumption** — The intruder attempts to consume all bandwidth available to the server (or service) by generating a large number of packets which are directed to the target.
- **Consumption of Other Resources** — An intruder attempts to overload the processing power of a server. This is done by consuming memory and other resources that are needed for the system to operate. This attack can be achieved by the installation of a fast replicating virus.

11.2.2 Unsecured E-mail

Corporations spend significant expense to maintain safe e-mail systems. Of particular concern is the desire to maintain control over the proprietary content of internal communication between employees. Software and hardware is used to prevent employees from unknowingly downloading viruses and spyware and then infecting corporate networks. For that reason corporations often desire that all internal communication use the corporate internal network. Employees may have a different point of view since many use e-mail accounts on third party services for e-mail.

Corporate networks often have multiple layers of defense against hackers and require employees to use special software for access to e-mail systems. Often multiple passwords, or passwords that are frequently changed, are required. A growing number of employees believe that these layers of security are excessive and get in the way of productivity. Some sophisticated users, in search of convenience, forward their internal e-mail to Web-based systems (like **Yahoo Mail** or **Google Gmail**) that are accessed with standard Web-browsers which allow passwords to be stored (in cookies) and therefore provide immediate access to e-mail. Messages sent and received using Web-based systems bypass the corporate e-mail system and are not subject to the **filters** and other security provisions that are in place. Not only does this open the possibility of unintentionally downloading and installing **malware** (software designed to infiltrate or damage a computer system) which might then propagate through a corporate network, the possibility of legal liability exists as well.

Some federal laws require that corporate e-mail be archived and made available during litigation. Not only is web-based e-mail not archived corporately, but once transmitted on a public network, there is no way of controlling who reads what. Hospitals, for example, are strictly governed with regard to the confidentiality of patients' medical records but doctors have been found to use Web-based e-mail systems to enable them to work at home.

One easy solution is to prevent employees from forwarding internal e-mail to Web-based systems. The problem is that it is not a permanent solution because once an employee uses an external system for a correspondence, forwarding e-mail is no longer an issue. Many companies try to audit employee e-mail as reported by the security firm **Proofpoint** which said that more than 60 percent of businesses regularly audit their staff's outbound e-mail, with 38 percent employing a "corporate snoop" to read e-mails. The problem is that over-policing of e-mail tends to create mistrust and to de-motivate the workforce.

11.2.3 Online Fraud Risk

Online fraud rates for merchants are higher than fraud rates of brick-and-mortar stores. Fraud rates for "Card-present" transactions (where a customer personally presents a credit card) are usually about 1 percent of sales but online fraud rates exceed 1.4 percent (costing over $3 billion in 2006) according to the electronic payment and security management provider **CyberSource.** In spite of the security code found on the back of most credit cards, online fraud continues to outpace fraud for in-store purchases.

Many merchants are using fraud management tools to battle the perpetrators. A significant automated tool growing in popularity is the technique of **Geolocation** which is used to evaluate the risk of an online transaction based on geographic data derived from IP addresses. Other tools used to potentially differentiate legitimate and fraudulent purchasers include **order velocity monitoring** that assess purchases based on metrics such as total dollar amount and frequency and positive lists that report buyers known to be good customers. Despite the increase in automated tool usage, however, more merchants than ever before are reviewing some orders manually, CyberSource reports.

The risk with online purchases is to business and not generally to individuals for two reasons:

- **Business responsibility** — Businesses must repay credit card companies for illegal purchases when reported by consumers. Consumers are not charged when credit cards are stolen and used to make purchases.
- **Falling sales** — Consumers will stay away from specific merchants that have received bad press about fraudulent incidents. The general willingness to participate in E-commerce may also suffer. In fact, according the **Gartner,** the technology research firm, about 15 million U.S. Internet users will not participate in online commerce.

Increasingly it is **smaller merchants** that are suffering. This is because of their inability to afford fraud detection and management solutions and because the relative high cost of fraud can significantly damage a smaller business. In fact, among smaller business, Gartner reports that fraud rates may exceed 3 percent of business. Further, the lack of sophisticated monitoring systems denies smaller business the opportunity to identify fraudulent transactions rapidly. In addition, the cost of security as a percentage of sales is greater for small business, thus adding to the challenge.

A recently emerging fraud technique involves **gift cards** issued by stores. Criminals visit stores and write down the numbers on gift cards that are displayed, often at checkout counters. They wait a few days assuming that it is likely that someone has activated the card and then they use the card number to make purchases at the retailer's Web site (where physical possession of the card is not required). Covering the gift card number until the card is activated is an obvious protection, but other techniques (not mentioned here to prevent fraudulent use) are increasing.

11.2.4 Business Considerations

Identity theft and other fraud affects consumers and businesses in many ways. Not only may businesses suffer direct financial loss due to crime but inadequate security and poor business practices may open a company up to fines, liability suits, and, as already mentioned, loss of customers.

No one can totally prevent identity theft due to the involvement of humans, but there are steps that a company can take to minimize risk factors for themselves and consumers. Safe **information handling** practices are the key to keeping identifying information out of the hands of criminals. These are some of the questions that should be asked and answered:

- **Information acquisition** — Does the business have a good reason for requesting the information that it wishes to gather? Is it acquiring it in a safe manner so that it cannot be overheard or seen by others?
- **Storage** — What computer security measures are placed around the systems storing personal data? Is data access restricted and not open to common access within the organization?
- **Data access** — Is personal identifying information (customer account numbers, social security numbers) available only to those employees with a need to know?
- **Database** — Is the corporate database access audited and password controlled?
- **Data disposal** — How is data disposed of when no longer needed? Are paper documents and digital databases containing personal information rendered unreadable prior to disposal? Paper should be physically shredded and magnetically recorded data rendered unreadable using software **scrubbers.**
- **Personnel** — Are regular background checks conducted on all employees with access to confidential and identifying information? The list of such employees is extensive and includes customer service representatives, sales staff, mail room staff, cleaning crews, temp workers, and computer service technicians.

11.2.5 Port Scanning and Back Door Access

Port scanning software sends out requests to connect to target computers on each port sequentially and makes a note of which ports respond. Ports that seem open may be subject to more in-depth probing. Note: A communication port, discussed in the networking chapter, is an electronic opening that allows the computer to send and receive data from external sources.

A port scan is a method used by hackers to determine what ports are open or in use on a system or network. If the port scan is being done with malicious intent, the intruder would generally prefer to go undetected. Once unprotected ports are detected an intruder may gain access to the computer system. Sometimes network security applications can be configured to alert administrators if they detect connection requests across a broad range of ports from a single host.

Not all port scanning is for malicious reasons. Large organizations often employ this method to detect vulnerabilities in their servers.

11.3 Individual Risks

Those individuals concerned about information privacy often cite a number of risks — events that can and often do compromise privacy — which may be encountered through Internet use. Unfortunately, ensuring security can be perceived as complex, causing people to shy away from understanding the issues. This section covers not only legitimate privacy risks, but also risks perceived as overemphasized. The risks discussed here are relevant to both individuals and organizations of all sizes.

11.3.1 Cookies

Cookies are perhaps one of the most widely recognized privacy risks. Although **HTML** (Hypertext Markup Language) pages most commonly use cookies for legitimate purposes, cases of abuse do occur.

An **HTTP** (Hypertext Transfer Protocol) cookie consists of a piece of data stored in a text file on a user's computer. The purpose of storing data is to allow the state of the user's interaction with a Web site to be maintained for future visits by the user. The data in the cookie might represent the user's preferences for menu colors and preferred categories of products offered by the Web site – that seems harmless enough. Cookies are also used, however, to store user identification like names, mailing addresses, account numbers, and passwords. While it is convenient for frequent purchasers (as cookies are used to automatically complete data in an on-line purchase form) the presence of sensitive data stored in a cookie is a security risk. Systems often do not generally make the user explicitly aware of when a cookie is in use.

The originally cookies were developed with the intention that only the Web site that originally created them would retrieve them. However, in actuality, programmers can bypass this intended restriction. **Spyware** programs can harvest personal data by reading cookies and sending the data to a server.

Many users choose to disable cookies in their Web browsers. This eliminates the potential privacy risks, but may limit the functionality of many Web sites. All significant Web browsers have this disabling ability built-in, with no external program required.

As an alternative, users may frequently delete any stored cookies. Internet Explorer, for example, provides this functionality by selecting Internet Options from the Tools menu and then selecting Delete from the General tab as shown here.

Using Internet Explorer to Delete Cookies

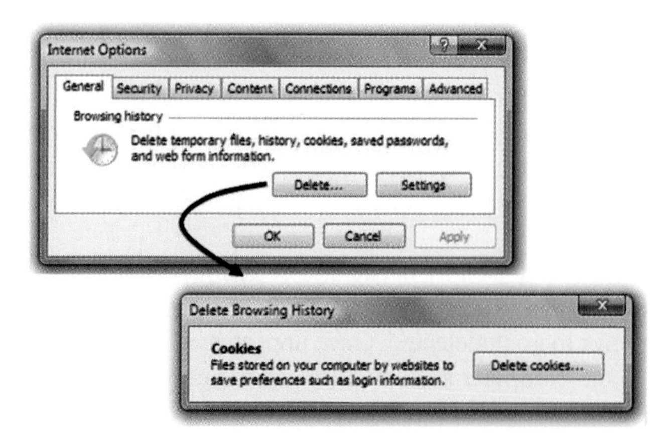

For more information about Internet Explorer's protection and security settings refer to chapter about the Internet and WWW.

Some browsers like Mozilla Firefox, for example, have an option to have the system clear cookies automatically whenever the user closes the browser. This is accessed in Firefox by Options on the Tools menu as illustrated here:

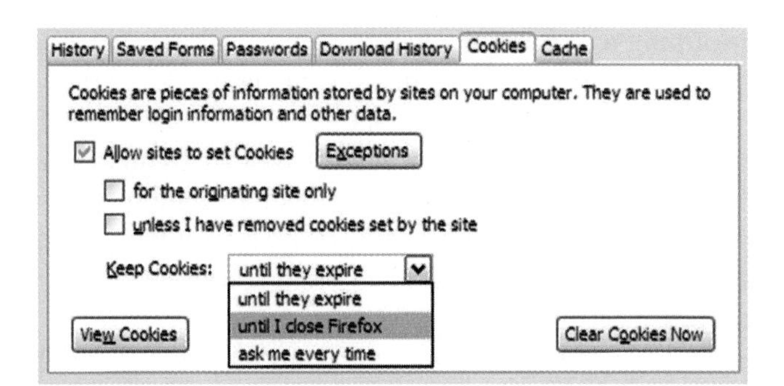

Firefox Allows Cookie Management Options

11.3.2 Virus

A computer virus is a **self-replicating** computer program intended to alter how a computer operates, without the permission or knowledge of the user. While some virus authors create these programs for fun, many viruses cause substantial (and at times unrecoverable) damage to data and perhaps hardware. Though the term virus is generally used to identify a range of **malware,** a virus must **replicate** and execute itself. The later criterion is often met by a virus which substitutes itself for existing executable files with a virus-infected copy.

While viruses can be intentionally destructive—destroying data, for example—some viruses are benign or merely annoying. Some viruses are designed to damage the computer by altering programs, erasing files, or even reformatting the hard disk. Others are not designed to do any damage, but just to replicate and make their presence known by presenting funny messages, images, and audio messages. However, even benign viruses can create problems because they consume computer memory and other machine resources used by legitimate programs. Erratic behavior can result and cause system crashes. In addition, many viruses are bug-ridden, and these bugs may lead to system crashes and data corruption.

Virus distribution can be subdivided into a number of types:

- An **e-mail virus** is a virus attached to an e-mail message for transportation between computers. These may copy themselves by mailing copies to all people in the victim's address book.
- A **macro virus,** written in a scripting language like those found in Microsoft Office programs such as Word and Excel, is spread by infecting documents and spreadsheets.

Virus Distribution

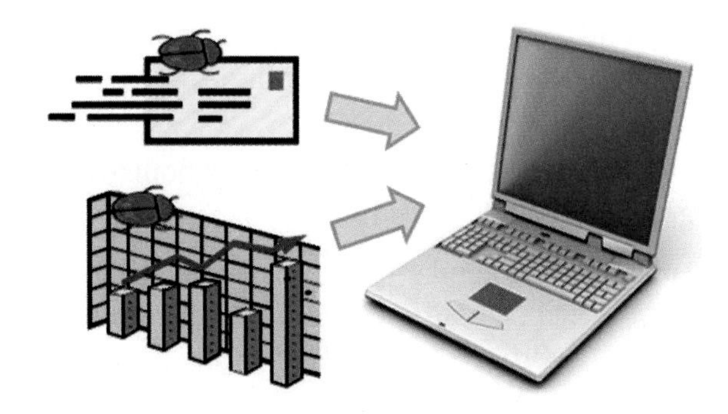

Computer viruses first emerged in the 1980s and were distributed by increased use of bulletin board systems and software sharing. Since the mid-1990s, macro viruses have become more prevalent.

To replicate itself a virus must access computer memory and execute program code. To facilitate that, many viruses attach to legitimate executable program files. Often when a user starts an infected program, the virus' code may be executed first thus blocking the program from performing as it normally would.

Windows is the most popular operating system target for virus writers but some viruses exist on other platforms. Any operating system (OS) can theoretically run viruses. Some operating systems are less secure than others. Unix-based OS's are more secure because they allow users to isolate programs by running them within their protected space in their own directories (this is known as a sandbox) and thus being prevented from infecting a whole system. There are relatively few known viruses targeting Mac OS X (a Unix-based operating system).

Several other classifications of viruses are commonly known and include:

- **Boot sector virus** — A boot sector virus substitutes its own code for the master boot record (MBR) of a computer. The MBR controls the boot sequence and runs every time the computer starts up making it extremely dangerous. A boot sector virus if usually very difficult to remove while Windows is running because it is resident in memory at all times.
- **Resident virus** — A virus that resides in computer memory once it runs. Boot sector viruses are a notable example.
- **Logic bomb** — Program code intentionally inserted into a software system that will set off a malicious function at a pre-defined time or when specified conditions (like withdrawal of a certain amount of money from a bank account) are met. Viruses of this type that attack on a certain date or time are known as **time bombs.**
- **Overwrite virus** — A virus that overwrites a file with its own code, helping spread the virus to other files and computers. The content of an infected file is effectively destroyed.
- **File virus** — A file virus infects executable files. These are non-memory resident viruses that search for infectable files themselves. When such a virus runs, it searches for files of specific name, type or extension on a hard drive and infects them.
- **Polymorphic virus** — This type of virus changes form so that once it infects files or programs it becomes hard to detect. The intent is to disguise the virus' **signature** so that anti-virus software will not recognize it.
- **Encrypted virus** — This is a virus encrypted to avoid detection. Each virus has a signature (a known pattern) but if encrypted the pattern may not be recognized by anti-virus software. Polymorphic viruses are usually encrypted.
- **Stealth viruses** — A stealth virus hides itself to avoid detection. In a sense this is a variation of a polymorphic virus because the objective is hiding from detection. While the virus itself may not be noticed a good antivirus program should be able to find a stealth virus by looking for evidence or intrusion in memory as well as in areas that viruses usually attack.
- **Multipartite virus** — A virus that attempts to attack both the boot sector and the executable, or program, files at the same time.

Worms and Trojan horses are similar to viruses in that they are destructive to computer systems and data, but there are differences. These are discussed individually next.

11.3.3 Worm

A worm is programmed software that uses computer networks for transportation between computers and takes advantage of security flaws in operating systems to create copies of itself. Once installed, the worm may cause the same types of damage associated with a virus. A worm will scan a network for other computers having a security flaw and attempts to enter the unguarded computer through open ports. It replicates itself to the target machine and then begins scanning for new targets. While a worm is self-replicating like a virus a key difference is that the worm takes responsibility for penetration of target systems. It does not need to attach itself to an existing program for transport. Worms can also harm a network by consuming bandwidth and by preventing legitimate network traffic.

Several common types of worms include:

- **E-mail worms** — These worms are spread via e-mail messages, but once implanted take responsibility for their own replication and distribution.
- **Instant messaging worms** — IM worms use the network connections of instant messaging applications for distribution often traveling to all computers on the user's contact list.
- **File-sharing networks worms** — These copy themselves into a shared folder on a storage device (usually a hard disk). Once implanted the worm can copy itself to all computers which access the shared folder.
- **Internet worms** — These generally use a computer's TCP/IP communication ports directly instead of searching for IM or e-mail applications. TCP/IP ports are easily identified by worms. Once safely through the port, the worm has access to the machine (not only an application) and can be particularly dangerous.

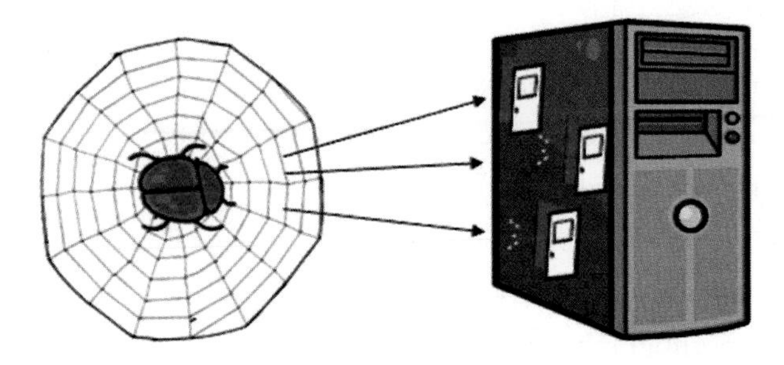

Worms Penetrate Ports

11.3.4 Trojan Horse

Trojan horses are imposters. They are files that claim to be something that they are not. A Trojan horse appears to do something desirable (like a screen saver) but what it does in fact is something entirely different, and usually malicious, such as erase files, damage data, or reformat a hard disk.

Trojan horses can not replicate so they are not a viruses in the strict sense. A Trojan horse must be invited onto a computer to spread. Entry is often obtained when a user opens an e-mail attachment or downloads and runs a file from the Internet. The classical Greek myth of the Trojan horse derives the name of this malware class.

There are two common types of Trojan horses:

- **Corrupted software** that is otherwise useful and has been altered by the insertion of malicious code that executes while the program runs.

- **Standalone programs** that pretend to be something else like an image file, a screen saver, or other utility in order to trick the user into running the program.

Because Trojan horse programs cannot operate without user intervention, each new victim must run the program if it is to perform damage. This means that the user must become part of the security systems by being sure about what programs are run. The user is advised to avoid opening unexpected attachments on e-mails. The infected program can also arrive in an Instant Message or can be downloaded from a Web site.

Trojan Horses Are Not What They Appear to Be

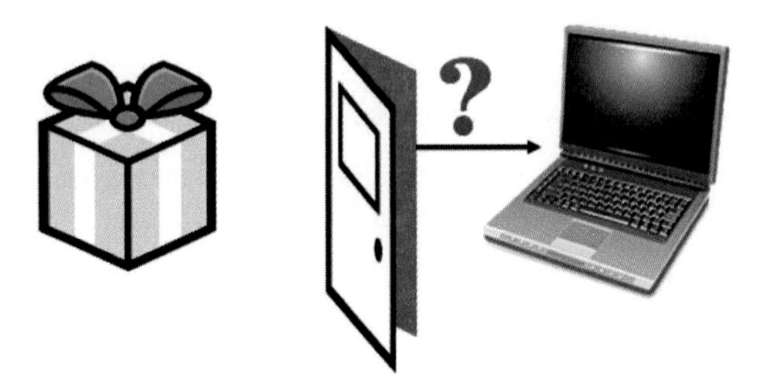

A computer's open ports are primary doorways for a Trojan horse's entry. These ports are used for Window's file sharing, instant messengers, and other communication activities. These services and programs may open a network port giving Trojans a means for interacting with the computer from anywhere on the Internet. A firewall may be used to limit access to open ports.

The damage that may be caused by a Trojan horse includes:

- Erasing data.
- Corrupting data.
- Download of unwanted and undesirable files.
- Allowing remote access to the victim's computer.
- Launching denial of service attacks.
- Logging keystrokes.
- Installing a backdoor on a computer system.
- Distribution of pornography.

11.3.5 Spyware

Spyware refers broadly to malicious software (malware) designed to partially control a computer's operation without the knowledge and consent of the user. Historically the term usually suggested software that invisibly monitors the user; it typically now refers to a program that alters computer operation for the benefit of a third party. The AARP's Public Policy Institute believes that spyware is rapidly becoming the tool of choice for thieves using the Internet to commit identity theft.

Spyware collects different types of information about a user and then sends that information over the Internet to a host. Somewhat benign programs track the Web sites a user visits and send this information to a marketing firm's server where a marketing profile about the user may be created and maintained. Malicious programs may try to record what a user is typing in an attempt to harvest log-on IDs and passwords or credit card numbers. Some programs, known as **adware,** launch popup advertising windows.

Spyware Reads Cookies

Spyware differs from viruses and worms in that it does not usually self-replicate. Like a Trojan horse the program must be run (installed) by the user. Often spyware is not installed alone but is installed as part of a larger program that does provide the user with some desired functionality. Spyware rarely harms a user's computer or data.

The installation of spyware often involves Microsoft's Internet Explorer. It is the most popular Web browser and has had a number of security issues. Availability and access make it the largest target. Since the browser is deeply integrated with the operating system the combination is a very inviting target platform.

11.3.6 Keystroke Logging

Keystroke logging is a technique embedded in some programs enabling the recording and reporting of the user's keystrokes. Usually the recorded keystrokes are uploaded to a server. User personal information is the most commonly targeted data. Logging programs may be installed by the user as a Trojan horse or unknowingly to the user as a worm.

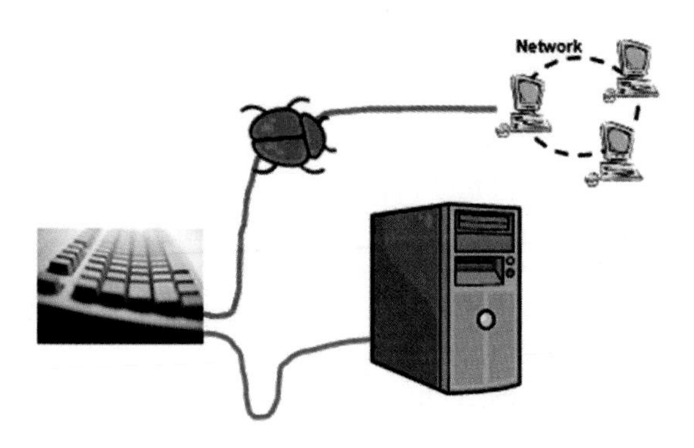

Keystroke Logging

Virtually any data may be recorded. This list of potential use of one such program is from the marketing Web site of **Blazingtools Software** that sells this type of software:

- Visual surveillance (screenshots).
- Captures the passwords behind the asterisks.
- Captures button clicks.
- Logs Web sites visited.
- Captures IM and Yahoo chats.
- Keyword Detection and Notification.
- Records contents of password protected Web pages.
- Monitors Windows Clipboard.

11.3.7 Phishing

Phishing is an attempt to trick a person into giving away their private account information by confirming it at the phisher's Web site. The confirmation request is frequently disguised as an official e-mail from a business that attempts to lure the recipient to reveal sensitive information. The e-mail might inform that the user's credit card account will expire unless verified. The phisher's e-mail message will usually include a legitimate logo of a known business.

Recent phishing attempts have largely targeted the customers of banks and institutions that deal with finance. Spoofed e-mails are sent to a randomly chosen group of prospective victims with the phisher's hope that a portion will be received by actual customers of the target company (the company whose logo is used). Most recipients will not be customers but a subset may be and they might fall for the bait and respond. E-mails supposedly from the IRS (Internal Revenue Service) have also been used to acquire data of U.S. taxpayers.

Phishing is not a risk easily averted by use of software. User vigilance and care are required to avoid revealing sensitive private data. Software can help, however. **Vista** and **Internet Explorer** introduce Microsoft's **Phishing Filter.** This optional feature connects with an online database of known phishing Web sites and alerts you to communication attempts from those sites. It remains your responsibility to decide how to respond.

Vista and Internet Explorer Provide a Phishing Filter

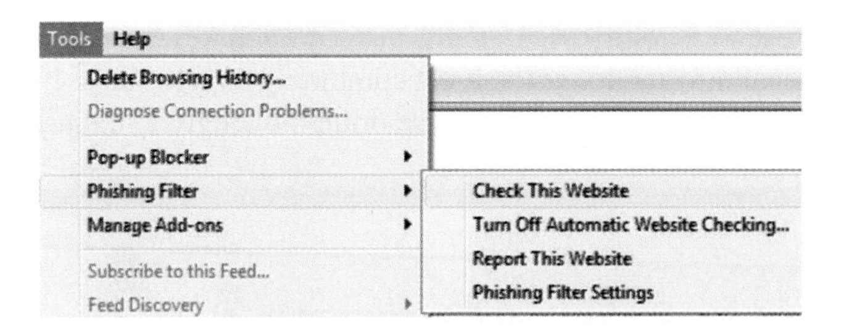

Developers of phishing and other malicious activities thrive on lack of communication and limited sharing of information. Using an online service that is updated several times an hour, the new Phishing Filter in Internet Explorer 7 consolidates the latest industry information about fraudulent Web sites and shares it with Internet Explorer 7 customers to warn and help protect them.

The Phishing Filter combines client-side scans for suspicious Web site characteristics with an opt-in online service. It helps protect users from phishing scams in three ways:

1. It compares the addresses of Web sites a user attempts to visit with a list of reported legitimate sites that is stored on the user's computer.
2. It analyzes sites that users want to visit by checking those sites for characteristics common to phishing sites.
3. It sends the Web site address that a user attempts to visit to an online service run by Microsoft to be checked immediately against a frequently updated list of reported phishing sites.

Internet Explorer 7 uses the Security Status Bar to signal users (in yellow) if a Web site is suspicious.

How Does the Phishing Filter Work? The Phishing Filter is off by default; meaning that it does not transmit any suspect data to Microsoft and will only check visited Web sites against locally stored data until the user decides to turn the Filter on. The locally stored data is a list of Safe Sites that is downloaded and installed with Internet Explorer 7 when it is installed.

When you visit a Web site, IE7 first checks the local Safe Sites list. If the URL is there or it appears in the local cache (because you visited it already), things will go no further. If, on the other hand, the site is not in those lists then the users must opt in to use the Phishing Filter. If it is enabled IE will then transmit details of the URL being visited for checking.

Internet Explorer 7 uses a notification area called the Security Status Bar. If a Web site is suspected as a phishing site the Address Bar turns yellow and the Security Status Bar warning will appear.

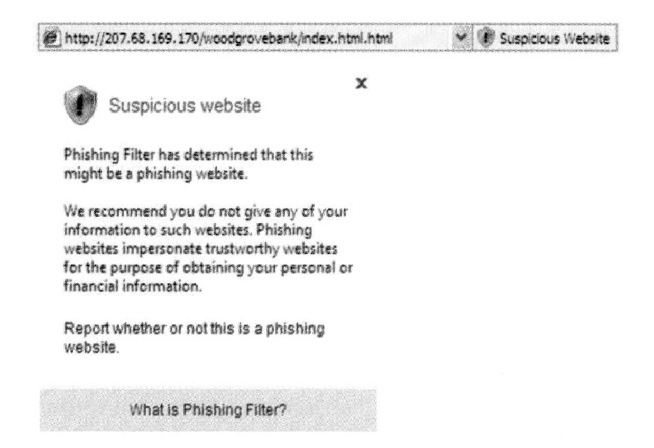

Suspected Phishing Site

If the Web destination has been confirmed as a known phishing site, Internet Explorer 7 signifies the threat level in red and automatically navigates the user away from that site.

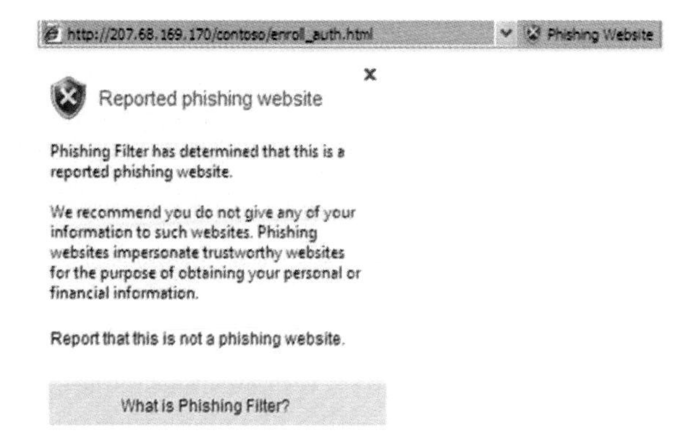

Known Phishing Site

Internet Explorer permits you to report a suspected or confirmed phishing site. Microsoft maintains a list of confirmed phishing sites that you will be alerted to as you surf in the future.

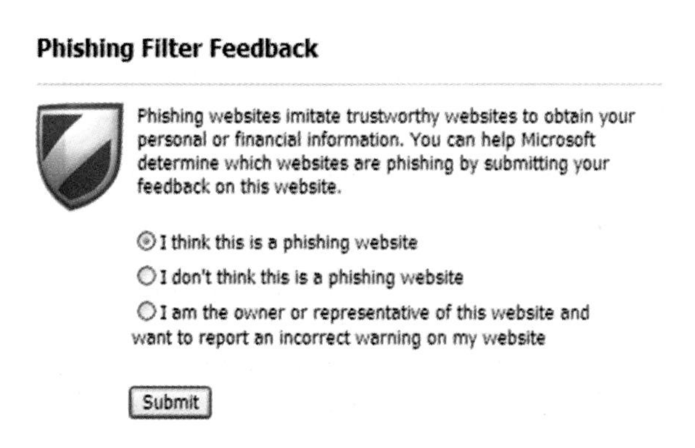

Report Phishing Site

If you do not wished to be warned about phishing sites the Phishing Filter can be turned off at any time via Internet Explorer's Advanced settings tab.

Phishing Control

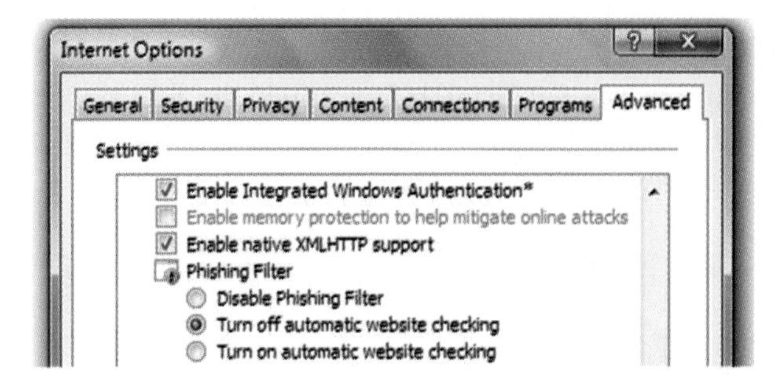

11.3.8 Web Bug

Web bugs are tools used to monitor the activity of customers at a Web site. A Web bug is an object (often a 1×1 pixel image, or a transparent **GIF** image or an image of the same color of the Web page background) that is embedded in an e-mail and is usually invisible to the user. It allows checking that a user has viewed the e-mail.

Web bugs are often used by e-mail marketers to verify that e-mail addresses are valid and that the content of e-mail is viewed by the recipient. When the user reads an e-mail that contains images the images are requested from the server. This is because an e-mail programs requests all components of an e-mail message as the display is rendered. Since images are components, the server delivers the image and records the location (IP address and e-mail address) of the computer that requested the image. When the server receives the image's URL request, the operator of the server now knows that the recipient's e-mail address is valid.

Tracking via Web bugs may be prevented by using e-mail clients that do not download images whose URLs include e-mail addresses. Examples of such e-mail programs which filter such URLs include: Google's Gmail and Yahoo's e-mail.

11.3.9 Spam

Spamming is an abuse of e-mail or other electronic-based messaging systems to send unsolicited and often undesired bulk messages. While e-mail is the most common type of spam, the term applies to abuses in other media like chat rooms and instant messaging.

Spamming is economically attractive to advertisers since they have no operating costs other than the management of their mailing lists. Also, it has often proven difficult to hold spammers accountable for their activities. The barrier to entry is low, spammers are numerous, and the volume of spam e-mail is substantial. The risks fall mostly in the areas of lost productivity (reading unwanted e-mail) and fraud. Spamming is viewed by the public as unwanted as junk mail and telephone solicitation and is the subject of legislation in some areas.

The most common types of spam are:

- **E-mail spam** involves sending unsolicited messages to many recipients. Unlike legitimate commercial marketing e-mail, spam is sent without the permission of the recipients, and frequently uses tricks (like misspelled words in the subject) to bypass e-mail filtering. Most spammers deliberately conceal the origin of their messages. Techniques include:
    - **Spoofing** e-mail return addresses. This involves using invalid return addresses. In a broader sense a spoofing attack is a situation in which one person or program

successfully masquerades as another by falsifying data and thereby gaining an illegitimate advantage over unsuspecting users.

- Use of **spambots** (often delivered and installed as worms) to send low volumes of e-mail from many users' computers. This way large volume spam is distributed without being stopped by high volume filters.
- **Messaging Spam** makes use of IM systems, such as Instant Messenger or Yahoo Messenger. These systems may provide a user directory which includes demographic information. The advertiser harvests the directory's data and sends unsolicited messages to members selected from the directory.

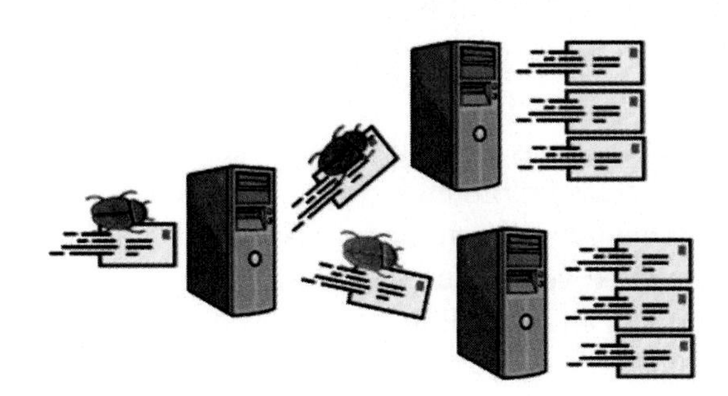

Distributing Spam Using Spambots

11.3.10 Identity Theft

Identity theft occurs when someone uses someone else's personal information without their permission in an attempt to commit fraud or other crimes. Identity theft usually involves illegal acquisition of personal data — especially Social Security numbers, bank account or credit card numbers, telephone calling card numbers, and any other valuable personal data. **Identity fraud** is a crime and involves using illegally obtained personal data for fraudulent activities.

According to the U.S. Department of Justice, much identity theft today occurs non-electronically as criminals can easily obtain personal data in public places. This can be done by watching from nearby as telephone numbers or credit or debit card numbers are typed into a cell phone. Criminals may also listen to cell phone conversations in a public space in which credit-card numbers are given for hotel or rental car reservations. Some engage in **dumpster diving** through trash in search of credit card or bank statements, cancelled checks, or other documents that display a person's name, address, and more.

The Internet also provides an arena for criminals to obtain identifying data. Many people respond to **phishing** spam that promises benefit but requests identifying data. Spyware, too, can obtain and report personal data.

If you lose or have your credit card stolen, you should immediately report it to your card issuer. Once you report the incident, you are no longer responsible for unauthorized charges made on your card.

11.3.11 Password Hacking

Password hacking is one of the easiest and most common ways intruders obtain unauthorized entry into a computer system. Use of strong passwords that are difficult to **crack** (or guess) is highly recommended but users often neglect this. Therefore, passwords are one of the weakest links in information chain. Passwords rely on secrecy but once a password is compromised, its original owner is not the only person who can access the system with it.

There are numerous ways to learn the password of others including:

- **Password guessing** — As the name implies some passwords are not too difficult to guess. Quite often people use their name, birth date, or a child's name as a password. Nothing obvious, or easily guessed, should ever be used as a password.
- **Dumpster diving** – As odd as this sounds, some people earn a living going through what is discarded by others (mostly businesses). Passwords (or other sensitive information) that are written or printed are subject to this type of theft. Like fishing, the act involves casting a net and seeing what turns up. The point is that putting secret information on paper that is then deposited in the trash is foolish because there are people who may search in surprising ways.
- **Shoulder surfing** — The use of direct observation techniques, such as looking over someone's shoulder, to get information.
- **Brute force attack** — This is a technique of exhaustively working through all possible combinations of letters, numbers, and special characters in order to guess a password. While it theoretically would be possible for a person to conduct this type of detection it would be very time consuming. Computer programs, however, can rapidly **iterate** through all possibilities until the correct match is found. For a computer to perform this type of attack it must be able to break in to the program that validates passwords.
- **Dictionary attack** — Trying to determine a password by searching a large number of possibilities. It is similar to a brute force attack, where all possibilities are searched through exhaustively, except that a dictionary attack only tries possibilities which are most likely to succeed, typically derived from a list of words in a dictionary. Generally, dictionary attacks succeed because many people have a tendency to choose passwords which are easy to remember, and typically choose words taken from their native language.
- **Packet sniffing** — A packet sniffer (sometimes known as a **network analyzer**) is computer software or computer hardware that can intercept and log traffic passing over a network. As data streams travel back and forth over the network, the sniffer captures each packet and eventually decodes and analyzes its content. This procedure is commonly used to analyze network problems, detect network intrusion attempts, monitor network usage, and gather and report network statistics. However, if packets are being collected and examined the content could fall into the wrong hands and reveal passwords, account numbers, log on IDs, and other confidential data.

11.3.12 Zombie

A zombie is a computer attached to the Internet that has been compromised by a security cracker, a computer virus, or a Trojan horse. A compromised machine is often one of many computers linked in a **botnet,** and is used to perform malicious tasks of one sort or another under **remote control.** Most owners of zombie computers are unaware that their system is being used in this way. Zombies have been used extensively to send e-mail spam.

11.3.13 Rootkits

A rootkit is a set of software tools intended to conceal running processes, files or system data from the operating system. Rootkits have been used increasingly by malware to help intruders maintain access to systems while avoiding detection.

A rootkit can take full control of a system. A rootkit's only purpose is to hide files, network connections, memory addresses, or registry entries from programs used to detect special privilege accesses to computer resources. While a rootkit may be incorporated with programs having legitimate purposes, it is important to note that a rootkit may be used maliciously.

11.3.14 Online Auction Fraud

Internet auction sites give buyers a virtual flea market with new and used merchandise from all over the world. These sites give sellers a global storefront from which to market their goods. While many (or most) transactions are concluded honestly, the online auction business can be risky business for buyers and sellers.

Most complaints generally are about sellers and deal with late shipments, no shipments, or shipments of products that are not the same quality as advertised, bogus online payment, or escrow services. Complaints also single out fraudulent dealers who lure bidders from legitimate auction sites with seemingly better deals. Among the thousands of consumer fraud complaints the FTC (Federal Trade Commission) receives every year, those dealing with online auction fraud consistently rank near the top of the list.

11.3.15 Scams

An age old scam that has adapted well to the Internet is advance fee fraud. It is a confidence trick in which the target is persuaded to advance sums of money in the hope of realizing a much larger gain. Among the best known variations on this type of scam is the Nigerian Letter also known as 419 fraud. The number 419 refers to Nigerian Criminal Code article 419 which prohibits obtaining property by false pretences.

The 419 scam originated as the oil-based economy of Nigeria deteriorated in the 1990s and scammers first used this scam as a means of manipulating business visitors interested in questionable deals in Nigerian business. Prospective "investors" are contacted,with an offer similar to: "A rich person needs to discreetly move money abroad, would it be possible to use your account?". Promises of a large return open otherwise cautious people to theft.

The global spread of email and easy access to email-harvesting programs has allowd the cost of sending scam letters through the Internet to fall dramatically.

11.4 Protection

At the front line of security are network hardware devices known as firewalls. Other programs and devices are available, too. Users of these technologies bear responsibility for properly configuring and managing these tools. In this section several categories of protection are presented and discussed.

11.4.1 Firewall

A firewall is used to limit access to a computer's open **ports.** Firewalls are hardware or software functioning in a networked environment engineered to prevent forbidden communication. Firewalls are especially helpful in preventing worms from illicit entry.

Essentially a firewall is a filter between a computer and the network that allows passage only to packets with permitted IP addresses. Firewalls can be implemented as software or hardware. Software firewalls are more flexible but hardware firewalls operate faster.

The most common type of filtering is **IP address filtering.** Here the firewall administrator maintains a list of acceptable IP addresses of origin and destination:

- Origin IP addresses are the numeric addresses of those servers and clients the administrator is allowing the local computer to receive messages (packets) from. Since worms do not advertise, their point of origin they will likely be blocked by a well managed firewall.
- Destination IP addresses are the addresses of those computers the administrator does not wish communication to be sent to. Spyware programs would likely be stopped from uploading harvested data since the administrator will not have included the destination IP addresses in the firewall's database.

IP address filtering is actually one of several techniques used in firewalls for guarding communication. IP filtering is the technique most commonly used for protecting personal computers. Here are some other methods:

- **Domain name** filtering replaces the IP address with readable names, called domain names. The concept of origin and destination address is retained but English-like names are used instead of numeric IP addresses.
- **Port blockage** is a filtering technique (mostly used on servers) that involves shutting down specific communication ports. A server makes its services available through the Internet by using one numbered port for each service (e-mail, HTTP, etc.) that is provided by the server. Although ports are normally dedicated to specific purposes, a worm, or other such aggressor, can enter a machine through any port it becomes aware of. Worms are designed to probe for entry opportunities by testing the full range of port numbers, so shutting unused ports is an excellent idea.
- **Content filtering** involves the firewall searching through packets on arrival or departure and blocking movement of any packet containing words or phrases on a list maintained by the administrator.

Vista's Firewall

11.4.2 Anti-Virus Software

Anti-virus software are computer programs that attempt to identify, stop, and eliminate (erase or quarantine) computer viruses and other malicious software (malware). Anti-virus software typically uses two different techniques to accomplish this:

- In the **dictionary approach,** the program examines files to look for known viruses by matching definitions (known as **signatures**) in a virus dictionary.
- Identifying **suspicious behavior** from any computer program which might indicate infection.

Commercial anti-virus software usually uses both of these approaches but the emphasis is on the virus dictionary approach.

In the dictionary approach, as a file is examined the anti-virus software refers to a database of known viruses that have been identified by the authors of the anti-virus software. If a piece of program code in the file matches any virus signature (the code's pattern) identified in the dictionary the anti-virus software can take one of the following actions:

- **Repair** the file by removing the virus.
- **Quarantine** the file (make the file inaccessible so its virus can no longer operate or spread).
- **Delete** the infected file.

To maintain protection the virus dictionary requires frequent updates (generally nightly) by downloading an updated virus signature database from the vendor's Web site. Dictionary based anti-virus software examines files when they are created, opened, closed, or sent or received as e-mail attachments.

The suspicious behavior approach monitors the behavior of all programs. If a program tries to write data to an executable program or sets the execution priority of a program unusually high, the anti-virus software can flag that abnormal behavior, and alert a user or take one of the actions listed above. Since this approach is not dependant on a maintained dictionary, protection is provided against new viruses with uncharted signatures. The downside of this approach is the requirement for user interaction and the sounding of a large number of false positives perhaps making users less likely to follow the warnings.

11.4.3 Anti-Spyware Programs

Anti spyware programs are designed to remove or block spyware. Programs such as **Spybot,** Search & Destroy, and Lavasoft's **Ad-Aware** are popular and are found in versions available for free.

Anti-spyware programs can identify and remove spyware in two ways:

- **Real-time protection** preventing the downloading and installation of spyware.
- **Detection and removal** of spyware as the hardware (memory and secondary storage) is scanned.

Detection and removal is simpler, and such programs scan the hardware by inspecting the contents of the **Windows Registry,** the **operating system files,** and **installed programs.** Files and registry entries which match a list of known spyware components are quarantined or erased.

Real-time protection from spyware works as real-time anti-virus protection does: the software scans incoming network packets, and blocks the activity of components believed to represent spyware.

Anti-spyware tools require a frequent updating of the database of threats. Anti-spyware experts and developers routinely discover and evaluate new threats and make their signatures available for download. Anti-spyware software without a regular source of updates is of limited value.

11.4.4 Digital Signatures

Digital signatures, like written signatures, are used to provide authentication of the associated input, usually called a message. A message may be anything from electronic mail to a contract. Digital signatures are used to simulate the security properties of a signature in digital, rather than written, form providing two essential safeguards:

- **Author identification** — The digital signature identifies the author.
- **Content integrity** — The presence of the signature indicates that the content is unchanged since signed by the author.

The recipient decodes and verifies the signature, and therefore the author, using a combination of private and **public keys.** Digital signatures are provided by a third-party certifying authority like **VeriSign, Network Solutions, OpenFortress,** and **CoSign.**

Many software systems make use of digital signatures without the end users being aware. A practical example that would involve your intervention is the use of digital signatures for protecting an Excel or Word document. **Office 2007** allows you to attach a digital signature to a document authenticating that you are really the author of the document. Once your signature is attached, the document is converted to read-only so that it may not be altered and all recipients can be assured that you are the author. This is especially important for two reasons:

- **Content unchanged** — The content of the document is authentic – it is just as you prepared it. Assuming the recipient trusts you they will trust the content.
- **Macro safe** — Some Office documents contain small programs known as macros. Some macros may be malicious. Assuming the recipient trusts that you do not write malicious macros the document may be opened without concern. Documents with macro code can be allocated to a trusted location as described later in this chapter.

Office provides two types of digital signatures:

- **Signature line** — A signature line looks like a typical signature placeholder that might appear in a print document, but it works differently. When a signature line is inserted into an Office document, the document author can specify information about the intended signer, as well as instructions for the signer. The presence of the signature line causes a dialog with the recipient who must digitally sign as recipient. After a document is digitally signed, it will become read-only to prevent modifications to its content.
- **Invisible signature** — Unlike a signature line, an invisible digital signature is not visible within the contents of the document itself, but recipients of the document can determine that the document has been digitally signed.

Digital Signature in Office 2007 Document

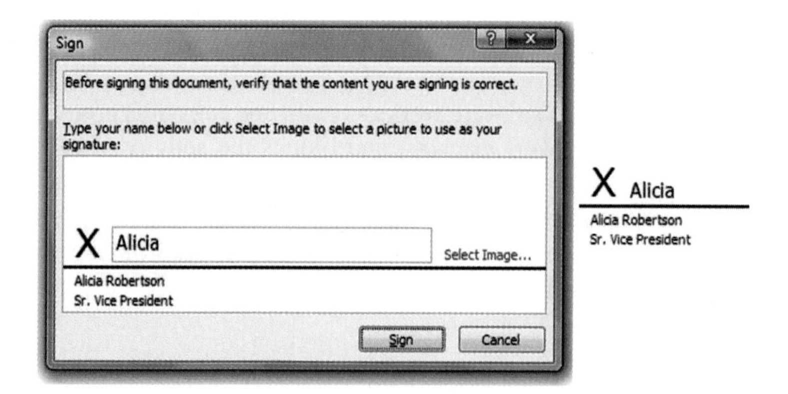

Use of digital signatures in Office 2007 documents is explained fully later in this chapter.

11.4.5 Proxy Server

A proxy server allows clients to make indirect network connections to network services. Once a connection to the proxy server is established the client may request resources available on other servers. The requested resource is obtained by the proxy server by connecting to the specified server or by locating it from a cache. Because a proxy server acts as a link between clients and servers it can also serve as a firewall.

TOR Tor ("The Onion Router") is free software which implements **onion routing** — a system allowing users to communicate anonymously on the Internet. Originally sponsored by the US Naval Research Laboratory, Tor is supported by the Electronic Frontier Foundation (EFF). TOR is like a series of proxy servers.

Anonymous Web browsing operates by preventing a client's IP address from being available to the Web sites that one is visiting. It is potentially of value to any Internet user who wants to ensure that their sessions are private. It can be used to avoid traffic monitoring by organizations or businesses which want to find out which Web sites members or employees visit.

Onion routing communications is based on a distributed network of trusted servers called onion routers. Each server passes Web packets to the next and at each server the physical location of the prior server (the IP address) is erased from the packet thus eliminating the trail indicating the packet's path.

Aside from personal anonymity, a further advantage of this approach (separating the logical and physical location of a web service) is that denial of service attacks can be prevented. An anonymous server would be a difficult target for a worm or virus to locate.

11.4.6 Sandbox

A sandbox is a software tool available for safely running programs. It is typically used to execute untested program code during the development process. It may also be used to test suspicious programs. The sandbox usually provides a tightly-controlled environment for the program to run in including protected disk and memory resources. The sandbox normally denies the program access to the network and limits use of the operating system's file system to those files stored in the test area's allowed space.

Another use of a sandbox is to install new software for testing before putting the software into general use.

11.4.7 Backup and Recovery

Backup involves copying data and programs so that these copies may be restored in the event of a system loss or data corruption. Backups are primarily used for two purposes:,

- **Disaster recovery** — restoring operation to a computer following a disaster.
- **Data recovery** — restoring files after accidental corruption or deletion.

Backing up data (and programs) is very important and should not be taken lightly. Several considerations are relevant:

- Scheduled backups improve data recovery reliability.
- Making multiple copies of a backup can increase the likelihood of data recovery.
- Storage of backup copies should be physically removed from the original source providing protection in the event of a physical disaster like a fire.

- Data compression is important where there is more data than media space but uncompressed data are mostly easier to recover.

Deciding what to backup is important and not necessarily obvious. Backing up too much data redundantly may cause the data storage facility to fill too quickly. However, if sufficient data is not backed, critical information may not be restorable. The key is to backup only those files that have changed. These considerations are the work of the data administrator.

The best path to recovering from a disaster is to have a documented recovery plan that is well tested. The plan (even for personal computers) should cover restoration of the data, hardware, and software critical for operations to restart.

11.4.8 Strong Passwords

The first line of defense in preventing unauthorized access to data is by use of strong passwords. Passwords that are easily guessed (birthdates, names, favorite foods, etc.) should never be used. It is best to form a password with a mix of numbers and letters and special characters. Passwords should be changed frequently and they should never be written down or displayed in a placed where they might be viewed. If it is necessary to record passwords to help you remember them it is suggested to use an encrypted PDA.

11.4.9 Browser Security

Due to its ubiquitousness, Microsoft's Internet Explorer is a convenient target for vandals. While the release of IE 7 has improved security, users should still be alert to the potential for intrusion and especially should be aware of suggestions that could help tighten down the browser. Some ideas pertain to all browsers.

- **Password storage** — do not let the browser store passwords.
- **Different passwords** — do not use the same passwords for different online environments.
- **Spam offerings** — do not buy anything offered by a spammer.
- **Firewall** — This should be obvious. Install one if you do not have one. Always keep it active.
- **Too good to be true** — do not accept offers that are too good to be true.
- **Children** — do not allow children (who download games and other programs) to use the same computer used to pay bills and perform other transactions.

Browser security is very important and fairly easy to control. Refer to the Internet and WWW chapter for suggestions.

11.4.10 Software Installation

Installing new software causes changes to the Window's Registry and to the content of your computer's storage devices. Change can be dangerous and can cause unexpected consequences. Therefore, before installing new software:

- **Backup** — Make backup copies of all data (spreadsheets, databases, documents, etc.).
- **Restore point** — Make certain to establish a Vista or operating system restore point.

- **Registry backup** — Software installations update the operating system's registry. Backup the registry before installing software.
- **Location** — Decide in advance where on the hard disk you plan to install the software.
- **Customization** — Many programs offer installation alternatives. Think through the options and do not accept them blindly.

11.4.11 Encryption

Encryption is the process of obscuring information to make it unreadable without special knowledge. It is sometimes referred to as scrambling. An algorithm is used for performing encryption and decryption (returning the information to its original state). A key is used for encoding and decoding the information.

Computer encryption is based on the mathematics of **cryptography,** which has been used throughout history. The existence of coded messages has been verified as far back as the Roman Empire. But most forms of cryptography in use these days rely on computers, simply because a human-based code is too easy for a computer to crack.

Most computer encryption systems belong in one of two categories:

- **Symmetric-key** — Each computer has a **key** (a secret code) that is used for encoding and decoding messages. The same key is used by both computers. This method is not particularly secure because keys are distributed and the encoding algorithms are not especially complex.
- **Public-key** — This method uses a combination of a **private key** and a **public key.** The private key is known only to one computer, while the public key is given to any computer that wants to communicate securely with it. To decode an encrypted message, a computer must use the public key, provided by the originating computer, and its own private key. Public-key encryption is commonly used in computer networks. A popular public-key encryption utility is called **Pretty Good Privacy** (PGP). Public key cryptography is also known as **asymmetric cryptography** because of the dual and different keys used.

In cryptography, **plaintext** is information used as input to an encryption algorithm; the output is termed **ciphertext.**

Public Key Infrastructure The public key infrastructure is an arrangement that binds public keys with respective user identities by means of a trusted **certificate authority** (CA) — a trusted third party which issues digital certificates for use by other parties. Digital certificates contain public key and private key pairs. The CA certifies and attests that the public key contained in the certificate belongs to the organization or server identified in the certificate. A CA's obligation in such schemes is to verify an applicant's credentials and delivering certificates to legitimate users.

Wireless Encryption The content of communication between your computer and a wireless router should be hidden by using encryption. This technique encodes data so that the information content remains intact but outsiders are prevented from interpreting intercepted data. The prevalent use of **Wi-Fi** for home and small business use provides a wide open door as many users do not encrypt their network. The major concerns that encryption addresses are:

- **External access** — Anyone with a wireless equipped computer in proximity to an unencrypted network can potentially use that network for personal access to the Internet. This is common in urban areas where users at times piggy-back on their neighbors' networks thus avoiding Internet connection fees.

- **Data loss** — Once access is obtained to an unencrypted network that is not password protected (most are not) it is not much of a stretch to examine data communicated by the network.

11.4.12 Transport Layer Security

Transport Layer Security (**TLS**) and its predecessor, Secure Sockets Layer (**SSL**), are protocols which provide secure communications on the Internet for such things as Web browsing, e-mail, and other data transfers. Secure HTTP (**S-HTTP**) is a commonly used implementation of public-key encryption that relies on SSL. SSL was originally developed by **Netscape** and is now part of TLS.

TLS allows applications to communicate across a network in a way designed to prevent eavesdropping and message tampering. TLS provides authentication and communications privacy over the Internet. Typically, only the server is authenticated.

When using a browser, you can tell when you are using a secure protocol in a couple of different ways. You will notice that the http in the address line is replaced with **https** and you should see a small padlock to the right of the URL.

HTTPs

11.4.13 System Hygiene

Keep the computer system running efficiently and maintain current operating software. As a computer is used the hard drive becomes increasingly cluttered. Three useful programs can help remove clutter, fix file errors, and generally improve performance. These programs should be run reasonably frequently. Windows and most operating systems provide these or similar programs:

- **Checkdisk** scans the file directories and searches for errors within files. Those errors that can be corrected are fixed and those that cannot are avoided by the operating system in the future.
- **Disk Defragmenter** scans the entire disk drive and looks for segments of unused disk area. The segments are consolidated resulting in larger areas of contiguous space for the storage of larger files. Regular use of this program helps keep a computer running more efficiently and may prevent unexpected loss of data. It also helps the computer find files and documents faster.
- **Disk Cleanup** allows the selection for deletion of unused or little used files. Removal of unused files opens up disk space for other purposes. This program finds infrequently used files in areas of a disk that are normally ignored.

Maintain current versions of operating software by downloading and installing **service packs** provided and recommended by the software's vendor. These updates are typically created to provide additional security protection, to close security loopholes, and to add additional functionality to the software. Use the **automatic update** feature of the operating system to keep current.

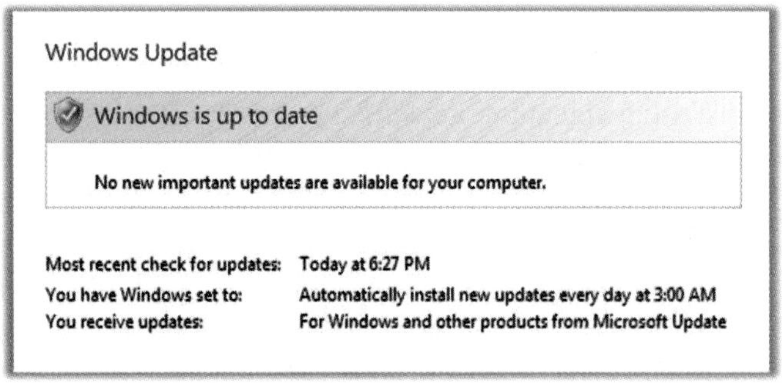

Windows Update

Windows is up to date

No new important updates are available for your computer.

Most recent check for updates: Today at 6:27 PM
You have Windows set to: Automatically install new updates every day at 3:00 AM
You receive updates: For Windows and other products from Microsoft Update

Windows Update

11.4.14 Other Security Measures

Protection of a computer system is very important and many provisions make it secure. Here are a few more directions to consider:

- **Uninterruptible power supply** — A UPS provides emergency backup power in the event of an electrical outage. The UPS contains batteries that are maintained fully charged when in normal use. The emergency charge available to a computer is usually sufficient to allow the computer to be shut down properly and that is important. When a computer stops abruptly two types of damage may occur:
  - **Physical damage** — Components may suffer. For example, a sudden loss of power could damage any components with moving parts like a disk drive or a printer.
  - **Data damage** — When data is updated it is eventually stored on a disk or other storage device. The operating system and database management software accumulate data updates and send several to the storage device at one time. A sudden system crash could prevent some updates already thought to be complete from actually occurring.
- **Physical security** — How about locking computers, communication equipment, and other devices behind a closed door? Preventing direct access to equipment is a major line of defense. It is not a substitute for firewalls, anti-virus software, etc., but it is a smart augmentation to any security program.
- **Strong authentication schemes** — As mentioned elsewhere in this chapter users often select poor passwords. Some suggestions for enforcement of stronger passwords include:
  - Have at least 8 letters, digits, and characters.
  - Have at least 3 letters.
  - Have at least 1 digit.
  - Do not use your username.
  - Do not use your username backwards.
  - Do not use your username with letters rearranged.
  - Have no more than two pairs of repeating characters.
  - Must be changed at least every 30 days.
  - Do not use an old password (going back one year).
  - Do not use a dictionary word from any language.
- **Biometrics** — Methods for uniquely recognizing humans based upon one or more intrinsic physical or behavioral traits. Biometric techniques can be used to authenticate access by individuals. These include physiological and behavioral:

- **Physiological** — Related to the shape of the body: fingerprints, face recognition, hand geometry, facial pattern recognition, and iris recognition.
- **Behavioral** — Written signature, keystroke dynamics (timing information that describes exactly when each key was depressed), and voice patterns.
- **Honeypot** — A trap set to detect or deflect unauthorized use of information systems. Usually a computer appears to be part of a network but it is actually isolated, protected, and monitored and set up to entrap intruders. The server is set up so that it seems to contain information or a resource that would be of value to attackers. The IP address of intruders is recorded and added to a database of unauthorized user addresses that will be rejected by the organization's other servers if access is attempted.
- **Policies** — Various organizational policies and procedures can be established to stipulate the proper use of corporate computer, network, software, and data resources. Many companies have rules that govern personal use of Web browsers and e-mail services, for example. Rules are only as good as their enforcement, and that of course is a concern of management. An important consideration is data access which defines what files and file folders (directories) are available to each employee and what access (read/write) is permitted.

11.5 Vista

Use the security provisions of your computer's operating system. The newest version of Windows, Vista, provides several important security advances over the prior version Windows/XP. Several important security features provided by Vista are explained in this section.

Enhancing security was a top objective of Microsoft while developing Office 2007 and Windows Vista. In Office, security measures centered on preventing malicious code in an Office document from executing and performing damage to data or a computer system. Other security measures include use of digital signatures to ensure that document content has not been altered without authorization or corrupted. As before, documents may be password protected and digitally signed.

11.5.1 Trust Center

The Trust Center is where you exercise greater control over the execution of macros in documents. To access the center, click Macro Security on the **Developer Tab** and then select Macro Settings.

Accessing the Trust Center

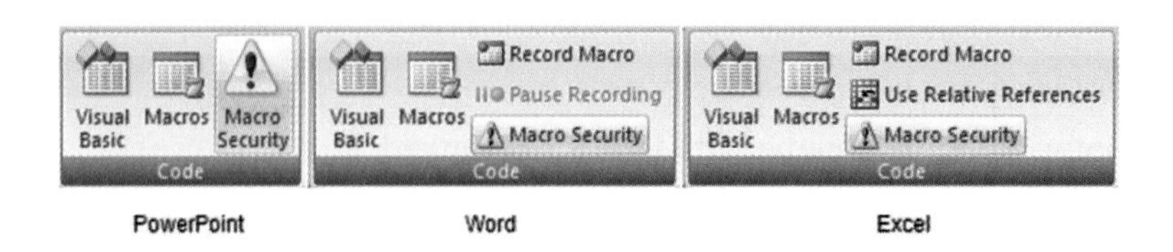

The default setting is selected (shown on the next page). You could select Enable all macros and the annoying message would never appear again. This is not recommended!

Note: the Trust Center may also be accessed by clicking the Office button and then clicking Excel (or Word or PowerPoint) Options and then click Trust Center.

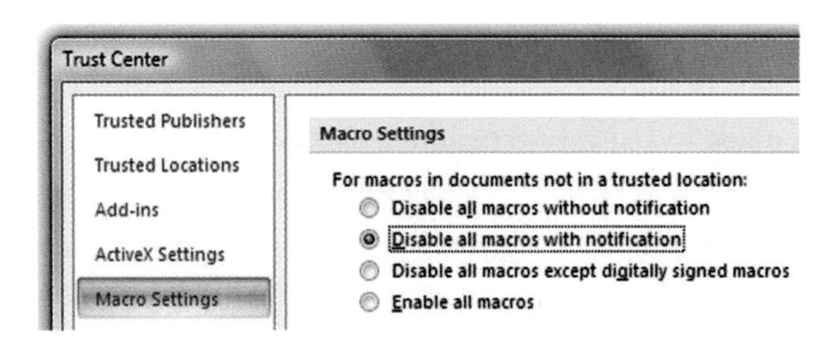

Trust Center

If you enable all macros you will never be informed of the presence of macros in a workbook, or other document, and you could open a workbook with malicious code that runs as soon as it opens. You would never have the opportunity to prevent the code from running. Do not choose this option! Choose Trusted Locations instead.

A trusted location is a folder on your disk that you designate to hold documents with macros that you give permission to run. Normally, these are documents you created or those sent to you by people you trust. Any workbook in that folder may run macros without your explicit permission. All documents in other locations with macros will still require permission as described above. In the Trusted Locations page of the Trust Center click Add a new location.

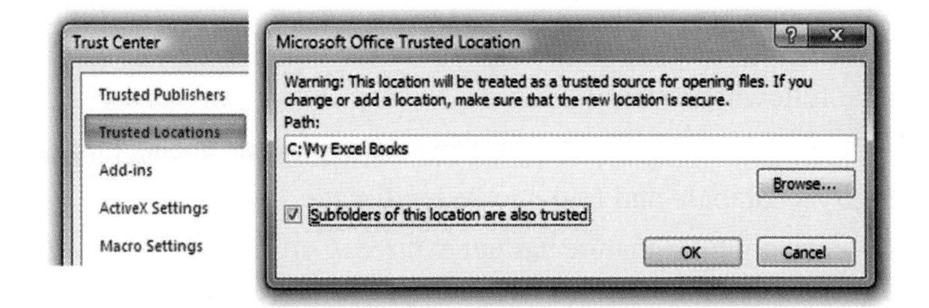

Adding a Trusted Location

Now store any document that you create (or documents created by people that you trust) in the trusted folder.

11.5.2 Document Passwords

To allow only authorized reviewers to view or modify your content, you can help secure your entire document with a password. Passwords can be set to prevent a document opening for reading or to prevent a document from being re-saved without authorization. To add either or both protections:

1. Click the Office Button.
2. Click Save As.
3. Click Tools.
4. Click General Options.

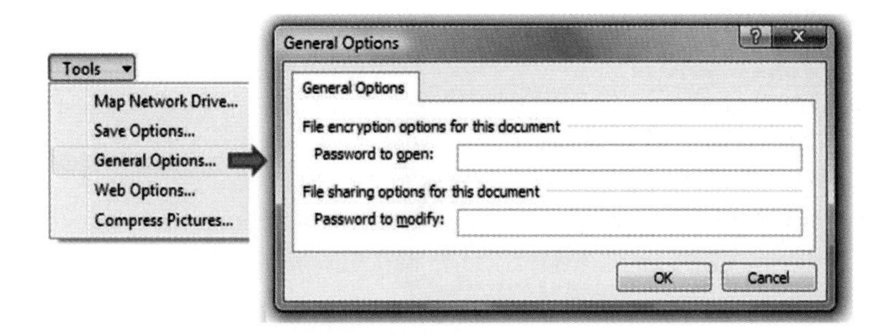

Setting Passwords

In the General Options dialog box there are two password options. You may use either or both as described here:

- **Password to open** — Use this to require a password before a document is opened.
- **Password to modify** — Use this to require a password before the document is re-saved.
- **Both passwords** — You can assign both passwords — one to access the file and one to provide specific reviewers with permission to modify its content. Make sure each password is different from the other.

11.5.3 Digital Signatures

A digital signature is used to authenticate or verify that people and products are who and what they claim to be. For example, confirming the source and integrity of a software publisher's code by verifying the digital signature used to sign the code. Digital signatures help to establish the following assurances:

- **Authenticity** — The digital signature helps to assure that the signer is who they claim to be.
- **Integrity** — The digital signature helps to assure that the content has not been changed or tampered with since it was digitally signed.

Office 2007 allows you to digitally sign Office 2007 documents. To make these assurances, the content must be digitally signed by the content author, using a signature that satisfies the following criteria:

- **Valid** — The digital signature is valid. The certificate is checked against a certificate authority's database and found to be legitimate.
- **Current** — The digital signature has not expired. Certificates that ensure digital signatures are issued by a certification authority, and can expire or be revoked.
- **Trusted** — The signing author is trusted by you or your organization.
- **Certified** — The certificate associated with the digital signature is issued by a reputable certificate authority (CA). Certification may be purchased from a CA or Office will create one for you.

Signing a Document Signing a document is not particularly difficult, but you must decide what type of signature you wish to use:

- **Signature line** — This option adds a visible signature line to your document. Move the cursor to where the signature will be inserted and click Signature Line from the Ribbon's **Insert Tab.** Complete the fields in the dialog box that appears and click Ok. A signature line appears in the document.

Inserting a Signature Line

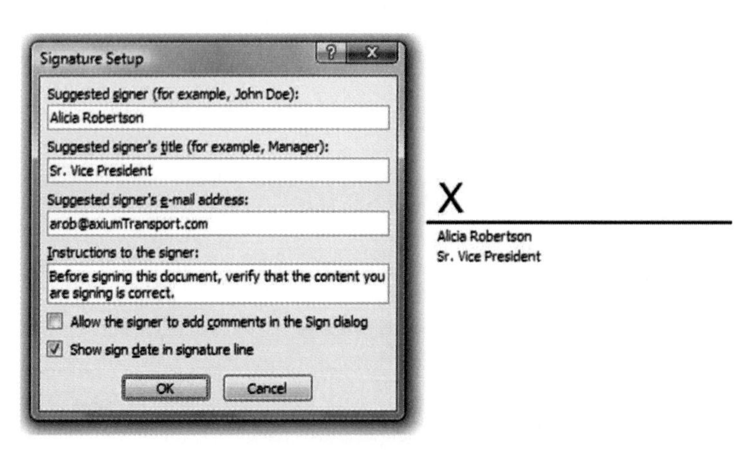

Next you will want to sign the document. Double click the signature. If you do not have a digital signature on file then you must follow these steps to create one:

Creating Your Digital Signature

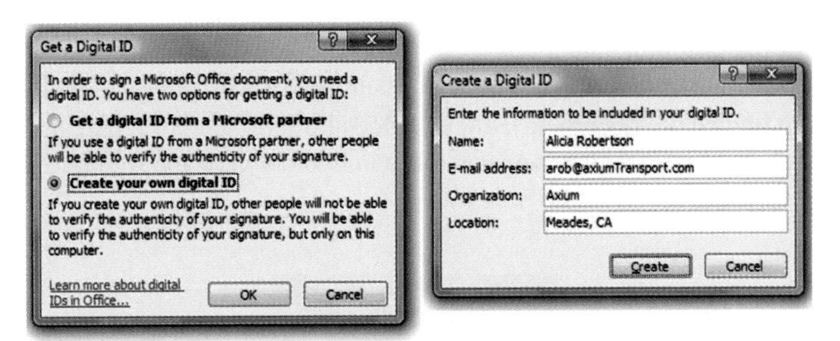

Once you have a digital signature you sign the document. In the dialog box that appears the author types his or her name as shown in the illustration. Had the author possessed a scanned copy of her signature that image could be used in place of the typed name.

Signing the Document

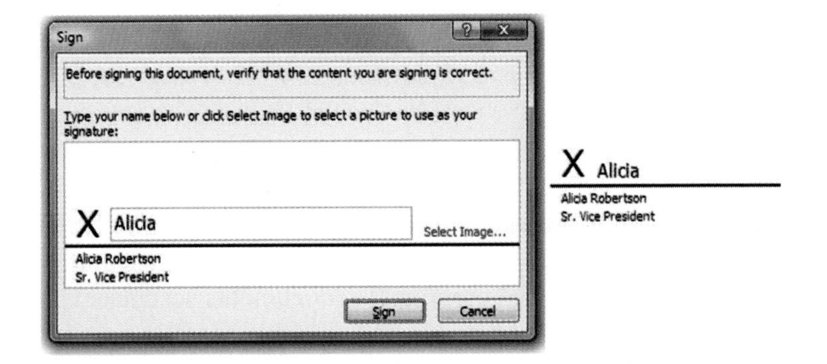

Once the document is signed this message reminds you that if you change the document in any way you must sign it again if you wish the document to remain certified.

Signing Reminder

- **Invisible signature** — If you wish your signature to be invisible instead, add the signature this way. Click the **Office** button then select Prepare and Add a Digital Signature. A dialog box appears in which you type the purpose for signing the document and click Sign.

An Invisible Signature

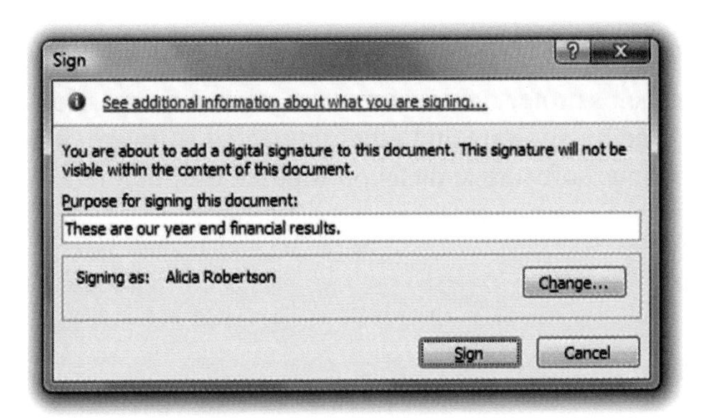

Opening a Signed Document When you open a signed document you will find it in read-only mode. That means that you may view, but not change, the content. Excel notifies you of the read-only status on the Window caption. Word displays a message at the bottom left of the program's window.

If you want to learn who signed the document, or if you want to remove the sign (allowing you to update the document), click Office and then select Prepare and View Signatures. The Signatures task pane appears allowing you to view the signature content and remove the signature if you wish.

Signature Task Pane

Signatures on signature lines may be examined by double clicking the signature. Removal is as already explained.

Office 2007 is a very significant overhaul of Microsoft's Office productivity programs. The most obvious change is the interface, but new security features limit execution of active code (macros and VBA programs) to documents designated by specific file extensions. For additional protection documents may be stored in a designated trusted location. Digital signatures and embedded comments are tools enabling you to collaborate with a reasonable level of security as you share data and work with colleagues.

11.5.4 Firewall

Vista's firewall is an improvement over XP's firewall first presented in Windows XP Service Pack 2. As an example of the enhanced control it offers Vista will allow blocking programs (such as instant messaging) from contacting or responding to other computers.

11.5.5 Windows Service Hardening

Vista restricts critical Windows services from doing abnormal activities in the file system, registry, or network that could be used to allow malware to install itself or attack other computers.

11.5.6 Windows Defender

Windows Defender helps protect your computer against pop-ups, slow performance, and security threats caused by spyware and other unwanted software. It detects many types of potentially suspicious software and can prompt the user before allowing applications to make potentially malicious changes.

Windows Defender

11.6 Three-Level Security Model

Security is indeed a complex topic. Many risks and protections were described in this chapter's pages. Here a three-level security model is presented which summarizes what has been discussed.

1. Protect a computer system from outside intrusion. Install and maintain these:
    a. Firewall
    b. Anti-virus software
    c. Anti-Spyware software
2. Back up data:
    a. Use a different storage device.
    b. Store backups in a remote location.
    c. Prepare (and test) a recovery plan.
3. Keep the system healthy:
    a. Defragment the disk frequently.
    b. Check and scan the disk for errors.
    c. Cleanup the disk by removing un-needed files.
    d. Maintain the operating system by downloading and installing service packs.
    e. Be vigilant and do not accept and install programs that are not documented or whose origin is not identified.

The schematic that follows graphically depicts the protections and actions that are suggested by the Three-Level Security Model.

Security Model

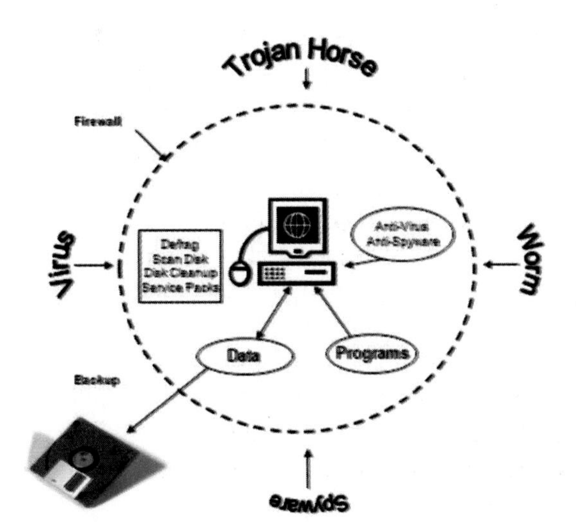

11.7 Ethics and Privacy

A discussion of computing ethics examines ethical rules and principles within an organizational context. Computing professionals and others with access to data and computer systems will be called on to make decisions regarding professional and social conduct. The importance of computer ethics increased through the 1990s especially fueled by the growth of the Internet. Privacy issues as well as concerns regarding computing technologies such as spyware have called into question ethical behavior in the use of technology.

Information ethics is the field that investigates the ethical issues arising from the development and application of information technologies. It provides a framework for considering moral issues concerning informational privacy, problems arising from the system life-cycle (creation, distribution, and processing) of information, and issues concerning ownership and copyright. Information ethics broadly examines issues related to ownership, access, privacy, security, and the community of stakeholders.

Information technology affects fundamental rights involving copyright protection, intellectual freedom, accountability, and security. Also, professional codes offer a basis for making decisions and applying ethical solutions to situations involving information control, privacy and distribution.

The topic is quite broad but includes several important considerations.

11.7.1 Code of Ethics

A code of ethics is a set of rules and conventions that are commonly agreed to within a business, academic, or governmental organization. Also included are industry and legal regulations. A prominent expectation of any ethics code includes protecting the privacy of customers and proprietary corporate data that an employee or other stakeholder has access to.

Why Have a Code of Ethics? Although it is generally agreed that ethical behavior is valuable, people often ask why have a code of ethics anyway? The answers are many, but a common set of ideas might include the following:

- To define accepted and acceptable behaviors.
- To promote high standards of practice.
- To provide a benchmark for members to use for self evaluation.
- To establish a framework for professional behavior and responsibilities.
- As a vehicle for occupational identity.

IT Code of Conduct Information systems professionals are in a unique position because of their great access to personal and corporate data. The rapidly accelerating advance in the demand for more and more varied data only enhances the focus on the behavior and responsibilities of those involved in this field.

A code of ethics serves to guide the employees or members of an organization. Specific behavioral policies and procedures are derived from a code. As an example, these are the section titles from the first part of the **Association for Computing Machinery** (ACM) Code of Ethics. The ACM code is a four-point standard governing ethical behavior among computing professionals. It covers the core set of computer ethics from professional responsibility to the consequences of technology in society:

- Contribute to society and to human well-being.
- Avoid harm to others.

- Be honest and trustworthy.
- Be fair and take action not to discriminate.
- Honor property rights including copyrights and patent.
- Give proper credit for intellectual property.
- Respect the privacy of others.
- Honor confidentiality.

11.7.2 Intellectual Property

With the widespread proliferation of the Internet people have access faster to more data and other content than ever before. The global reach of the Internet crosses national boundaries causing multiple ethical and legal traditions to meet and sometimes conflict. This mix affects questions of ownership of intellectual property.

While laws and custom in the United States is quite developed and quite specific, in other countries the situation is more lax. From the perspective of the United States this can be said about several important concerns:

- **Copyright** — Today's technology presents serious challenges to copyright compliance. It is easy to copy, manipulate, or re-publish digital images and because of the nature of digital information, any copies will be perfect duplicates of the original. When installing a program a copy is made to the hard drive, when launching a copy is made into memory, when visiting a Web page a copy is sent over the network. All these activities are allowed in the US under the US Copyright Act and do not violate US copyright law. What is not allowed is to make copies of program source code.
- **Patent** — A software patent is a patent on any activity or performance of a computer guided by means of a computer program. Patents and copyright differ substantially. Any software written is automatically covered by copyright. This allows the owner to prevent anyone from directly copying the source. Patents cover the underlying methodologies embodied in a given piece of software, or the function that the software is intended to serve, independent of the particular language or code that the software is written in. While the copyright protects the code a patent protects the process. Patented software may not be reverse engineered and re-implemented by anyone else in the same or different programming language.
- **Trade secret** — A trade secret is a formula practice used by a business to obtain an advantage over competitors or customers. It is confidential information and not a product in its own right. Unlike a patent it does not expire. A further distinction is that to acquire a patent, full information about the method or product is supplied to the US Patent Bureau and will then be publically available to all. After expiration of the patent, competitors can copy the method or product legally. Trade secrets are not disclosed to the world at large. Instead, owners of trade secrets seek to keep their special knowledge out of the hands of competitors.
- **License** — A software license does not imply ownership of the software by the licensee, instead it grants the licensee rights to use the licensed software in compliance with the specific terms of the license. Software remains the holder of the copyright and possibly the patent.
- **Free Software License** — A software license which grants recipients rights to modify and redistribute the software which would otherwise be prohibited by copyright law. **Open source** software is licensed and distributed this way.

- **Fair Use** — Fair use is established in United States copyright law and allows limited use of copyrighted material without requiring permission from the rights holders. Under the fair use rule of copyright law, an author may make limited use of another author's work without asking permission. Fair use is based on the belief that the public is entitled to freely use portions of copyrighted materials for purposes of commentary and criticism. The foundation for fair use law is the US tradition of free speech. In the world of software, fair use does not extend to copying programs for use without compensation to the author. It would be permissible, however, to reproduce screen shots of a computer program's interface as an illustration in an instructional manual.
- **Open Source** — Open source is a development and distribution method for software that harnesses the power of collaboration, distributed peer review, and transparency of design. According to the **Open Source Initiative** (OSI), a non-profit corporation formed to educate about and advocate for the benefits of open source the objective of open source development is better quality, higher reliability, more flexibility, lower cost, and especially an end to vendor domination in market segments. Open source software remains the property of the copyright holder but is issued with a **free software license.** Ownership is maintained to ensure that no user could claim ownership and then deny the free software license to others.

Important and well known open source projects include **Linux, MySQL, PHP, Perl, Blender, Java,** and **Python.** The OSI defines an open source software license to include:

- **Free redistribution** — The open source license may not restrict any party from selling or giving away the software.
- **Source code** — The program must include source code, and must allow distribution in source code as well as compiled form.
- **Derived works** — The open source license must allow modifications and derived works, and must allow them to be distributed under the same terms as the license of the original software.
- **Technology-neutral** — No provision of the license may be predicated on any individual technology or style of interface.

Copy Protection Copy protection, which is also known as copy prevention, is any technical measure designed to prevent unauthorized duplication of information. Copyright, patent, and licensing laws do offer legal protection but are not enforceable if infringements are not detected. To ensure better protection, software vendors add built-in protection to their products.

Copy protection is often debated, and is thought to sometimes infringe on some user property rights: for example, the legal right to make a backup copy of a computer program they have purchased, to install and use computer software on multiple computers, or to upload their music into their digital audio player for easier access and listening. Regardless of the debate, the need for protection is a given to most vendors.

As an example, publishers of music and movies in digital form have turned to encryption to make copying more difficult. The **Content Scramble System** (CSS) is a copy protection scheme used on almost all DVDs. It uses a key built into DVD players that matches a key encoded in legitimate copies of commercial digital content. Unauthorized copies will not play because the key is not writeable to DVD-R or DVD-RW discs and the copy will not have the key that matches the key expected by the player.

The trend in software copy protection is different. Since software is installed mostly on computers with Internet access, the network can be used to obtain a **registration key** from a server which permits **product activation.** Keys are issued to match a product's serial number and once a serial number is registered a second registration key will not be issued for that same number. If a person gives a copy of a purchased program to a friend the registration key will not be duplicated. The software chapter has more information about software installation.

11.7.3 United States Laws

Privacy has different meanings for different people. It is about the desire and the ability of an individual or group to keep their lives and personal data and affairs out of public view, or to control the flow of information about themselves. Personal privacy can be at odds with public right to know. Federal legislation has attempted to address this issue in notable ways, several of which are describe here:

- **Identity Theft Protection Act of 2005** — The bill sets national standards to safeguard individual personal information, to notify consumers of data breaches, to require businesses to improve their safeguards for sensitive consumer information, to give consumers the right to freeze their credit reports to thwart identity theft, and to limit the solicitation of social security numbers by commercial entities.
- **Information Protection and Security Act of 2005** — This act addresses the security and privacy risks of radio frequency technology in government-issued RFIDs. The act makes it a misdemeanor for any person or entity to willfully read a person's ID remotely using radio waves without the knowledge of that person.
- **Junk Fax Prevention Act of 2005** — This act is the junk fax equivalent of the telephone do not call act. It gives citizens the right to prevent marketers from sending junk faxes to recipients' fax machine. What it also does is allow junk faxes to be sent until a person requests they not be sent.
- **Family Educational Privacy Act of 2003** — Known as FERPA, this is a Federal law that protects the privacy of student education records. The law applies to all schools that receive funds under an applicable program of the U.S. Department of Education.
- **Notification of Risk of Personal Data Act of 2003** — This legislation requires businesses or government agencies to notify individuals if a database has been broken into and personal data has been compromised, including Social Security numbers, driver's licenses, and credit cards. The objective is to reduce the threat of identity theft.
- **CAN-SPAM Act of 2003** — This act controls the distribution of commercial e-mail. It permits e-mail marketers to send unsolicited commercial e-mail as long as it contains an opt-out mechanism, a valid subject line, the legitimate physical address of the mailer, and a label if the content is adult. If a recipient opts out, a sender has ten days to cease sending the spam.
- **Sarbanes-Oxley Act of 2002** — The financial reporting processes of most organizations are driven by IT systems and this act places specific requirements on those who are responsible for the security, accuracy, and reliability of the systems that manage and report financial data.
- **USA Patriot Act of 2002** — The act increased the ability of law enforcement agencies to search telephone and e-mail communications and medical, financial, and other records. It also updated the Computer Fraud and Abuse Act of 1986.
- **The Children's Online Privacy Protection Act of 2000** — This act applies to the online collection of personal information by persons from children under thirteen

years of age. It details what a Web site operator must include in a privacy policy, when and how to seek verifiable consent from a parent or guardian, and what responsibilities an operator has to protect children's privacy and safety online.

- **Digital Millennium Copyright Act** — The DCMA of 1998 criminalizes production and distribution of technology that is used to circumvent measures that control access to copyrighted works.
- **Health Insurance Portability and Accountability Act of 1996** — HIPAA established standards for the privacy and security of health information. It also established standards for electronic data interchange (EDI) of health information.
- **Computer Matching and Privacy Act of 1988** — Describes the manner in which computer matching involving Federal agencies may be performed. The act provided detailed procedures to control data matching but it also approved sharing of data among federal government agencies. Information collected for one purpose may be used for different purposes by a different federal agency. Though integrity and fairness seem assured by the act, privacy is not.
- **Electronic Communications Privacy Act of 1986** — Extends government restrictions on wire taps from telephone calls to include transmissions of electronic data by computer. The act prohibits unlawful access and certain disclosures of communication contents. The law sets out the provisions for access, use, disclosure, interception, and privacy protections of electronic communications.
- **Computer Fraud and Abuse Act of 1986** — This act was intended to reduce hacking of computer systems. It has been amended several times. It criminalized several activities including knowingly accessing a computer with the intent to defraud and obtain anything of value.

11.7.4 International Agreements

The international community is involved too. Their interest especially lies with intellectual property protection. The World Intellectual Property Organization (WIPO) is an agency of the United Nations. Its purpose is "to encourage creative activity, promote the protection of intellectual property throughout the world". Much of the important work is done through committees, including the Standing Committee on Patents (SCP), the Standing Committee on Copyright and Related Rights (SCCR), and the Advisory Committee on Enforcement (ACE).

A most notable aspect of the WIPO's work is the 1996 Copyright Treaty. Specifically the treaty's preamble declares its purpose is to "introduce new international rules and clarify the interpretation of certain existing rules in order to provide adequate solutions to the questions raised by new economic, social, cultural and technological developments."

Going Overboard? It may be tempting to clamp down hard in the interest of security, but consider this:

- **Cell phone usage** — Your cell phone helps you keep in touch with families and friends, but it also makes it easier for governments to track your location.
- **Web searchers** — Your personal Web searches about sensitive information might seem secret, or are they? While you might assume they are known only to you and search engines like Yahoo, MSN, or Google these companies are creating a database of personal information which might be potentially available to any party wielding a subpoena.

- **Watch list** — When next trying to board a plane you might be turned away after being mistakenly placed on a government watch list based on incorrect data.
- **Data mining** — Governmental authorities are not always content to exploit personal data when someone is suspected of a crime. Instead, increasingly government agencies analyze the details of private lives, looking for potential threats.
- **Secret searches** — Can the government monitor your Web browsing without a warrant? Under the Patriot Act, the FBI can secretly conduct a physical search or wiretap on American citizens to obtain evidence of crime without proving probable cause, as the U.S. Constitution Fourth Amendment explicitly requires. Whether this can be extended to Web searches has not been resolved yet by federal courts.

11.8 Summary

Security and privacy is important to corporate and individual computer system owners. It is also important to consumers. Numerous recent events demonstrate how easy it is for personal data to be compromised. Security is the responsibility of a computer owner and network administrator. Software vendors provide tools to this end but unless the tools are installed, properly configured, and maintained, privacy will be an accident and not an expected outcome. Some security measures that guard privacy are not software dependant and reply instead on the good judgment and actions of users when handling programs and data. The most important protection against unwanted instruction and malicious data loss is you.

Corporations and individuals face similar and different risks. Business could suffer from business interruption or even shutdown if adequate protection is not provided. Loss due to on-line fraud and business reputation are real threats and should be guarded against. Individuals face loss of personal data as well as damage to personal computer systems and software. Collectively known as malware, bothersome and dangerous intruding cookies, viruses, Trojan horses, spyware, and others can easily infest an unprotected system.

Protection comes in the form of software and hardware. Operating a firewall to limit a system's interchange with other networked computers is a first line of defense. Anti-virus and anti-spyware programs either identify attacking software during its attempted installation or as it begins running – both types of protection should be used. Protection of individual documents, spreadsheets, and databases is smart. Digital signatures and passwords should be considered when authoring and distributing documents. System passwords should be strong and not casually created. Encryption and secure connections should be used especially in a wireless environment and when conducting financial transactions. You are the most important component of any security system. It is your commitment to a secure environment that is a necessary condition for all the rest to work.

Windows Vista was designed with enhanced security as the top objective. Numerous features were built in to that end. In cooperation with Office 2007, documents with macro programs can be isolated to a trusted location; documents can be protected with passwords and digital signatures. New defensive features that are part of Vista include a built-in firewall, Windows Defender, and hardened protection around system services. Internet Explorer version 7 also offers stronger protection: a better popup blocker, isolation of active content, better protection when downloading and installing software and well-defined security zones. Erasing browsing history and cookies is easier than before and should be used too – especially when working on a shared computer.

A security model is recommended that suggests protecting a computer system from outside intrusion, regularly backing up data, and regular system maintenance that includes defragmenting, error checking, and cleaning unused data from the disk. The operating system should be maintained up to date with patches and service packs.

In concert with the recommended vigilance and protection, questions of ethics strongly influence how we operate. People with access to data about individuals have responsibilities to guard and not reveal what is personal or organizational. Software is intellectual property and is protected by copyright and patent laws – each offering different level and type of protection. Software developed under the open source model follows a different track and has become quite popular. In spite of legal protection, software vendors build copy prevention into their product's installation routines.

United States federal legislation has addressed many privacy and security concerns including: protection for personal, student, and financial data, protection of children, and prevention of junk e-mail,faxes, and other intrusions. Federal law also grants the government more right to collect more data and share it more comprehensively among federal agencies. Questions about the trade-off between the quest for security while maintaining privacy are on the table as public awareness grows of cell phone use and Web-surfing monitoring, data mining that reveals personal data, and even secret searches authorized by acts of Congress.

EXERCISES

Exercise 11.1

Discuss two common techniques for denying users to a service provided by a corporation.

Exercise 11.2

Discuss the technique for maintaining the state of the user's interaction with a Web site to be maintained for future visits by the user.

Exercise 11.3

Discuss three virus types.

Exercise 11.4

What type of malware takes responsibility for its transportation? What are the common types of this malware?

Exercise 11.5

One type of malware is known as an imposter. Identify it and discuss at least three types of damage it might cause.

Exercise 11.6

One type of malicious activity involves asking people to give away their private information. What is this technique known as? Briefly describe how it is accomplished.

Exercise 11.7

E-mail filters may identify and stop large e-mail volume from being sent from the same point of origin. To get around this protection a particular type of worm may be used. What is this worm known as and what does it do?

Exercise 11.8

What is identity theft? What does it involve?

Exercise 11.9

What type of protection limits access to computer's communication ports? Discuss the two types of address filtering it provides.

Exercise 11.10

Anti-virus software may take three actions when an infected file is identified. Identify and discuss these actions.

Exercise 11.11

What are digital signatures and why are they used?

Exercise 11.12

Why is backup important? Describe what backups are used for.

Exercise 11.13

What is data encryption? Why is it important?

Exercise 11.14

Discuss three actions that you should take before installing new software.

Exercise 11.15

System hygiene involves keeping your computer running efficiently. What are service packs and why are they important?

Exercise 11.16

With so much of life now online some investment schemes involve fraudulent offerings. What does this involve and what should a smart investor be alert to?

Exercise 11.17

Discuss how and where RFID technology can be used in your school. How is it currently used in kitchen appliances, hospitals, and the sports industry?

Exercise 11.18

Find biometric devices used in two different locations such as at an airport and in your office. Discuss any privacy concerns you may have in using these biometric devices.

Exercise 11.19

Research a well known security event such as the Morris worm, Code Red, or Moonlight Maze. Discuss what happened, who was responsible and what the outcome was.

Exercise 11.20

What challenges does the WIPO face in enforcing provisions of the 1996 Copyright Treaty? What role can the United States play in this and other international intellectual property protection agreements?

Decision Support Systems

Chapter 12

Decision support systems, or **DSS** as they are commonly known, support decision-making activities. They are information and knowledge based systems that include:

- **Data Mining** — Analysis of data from different perspectives and its summarization into useful information.
- **Artificial Intelligence** — Computer programs that can engage in human-like reasoning.
- **Management Information Systems** — Systems that collect data about business activity and report trends to management.
- **Metadata** — Data about data; used to facilitate the understanding and use of data.
- **Data Warehouse** — Repository of an organization's data.
- **Data Integration** — Providing a unified view of data from different sources.
- **On Line Analytical Processing** — Query processing system that provides a multidimensional view of data.

A DSS is a computerized system for helping make decisions. The realization of decision support systems, however, is very broad since a DSS can take many different forms. A DSS can range from data analysis in an Excel worksheet to an integrated meta-analysis system. All decision support systems help decision makers gather intelligence, generate alternatives, and make choices.

While there is no standard definition of what a DSS is or what components it is composed of, there is general agreement that a DSS:

- Provides support for **unstructured,** or **semi-structured** decisions.
- Problems supported have **incomplete** or **uncertain** knowledge.
- Includes tools for testing various **scenarios.**

There are common themes as you will see in these descriptions of DSS:

- A **computer-based** system that aids the process of decision making (Finlay).
- **Interactive** computer-based systems that help decision makers utilize data and **models** to solve unstructured problems (Sprague and Carlson).
- An interactive, flexible, and **adaptable** computer-based information system; especially developed for supporting the solution of a non-structured management problems. It utilizes data, provides an easy-to-use interface, and allows for the decision maker's own insights (Turban).
- A model-based set of procedures for processing data and **judgments** to assist a manager in decision making (Little).
- A DSS couples the intellectual resources of individuals with the capabilities of the computer to improve the **quality of decisions** (Keen and Scott Morton).

- Extendible systems capable of supporting **ad hoc** data analysis and decision modeling, oriented toward **future planning,** and used at irregular, unplanned intervals (Moore and Chang).

The analysis emphasis for any DSS is usually specific to the type of processing it provides. Several foundations have been identified in the DSS literature and include:

- **Model-driven** — Emphasis on analysis of data using statistical, financial, optimization, or simulation models. This approach is **programmed** in that the process follows established rules or algorithms.
- **Communication-driven** — Support for groups collaborating on shared decision-making tasks.
- **Data-driven** — Emphasis on analysis of large volumes of data including internal company data and perhaps external data. Data mining falls within this category. This approach tends to be **non-programmed** in that the relationships among data elements and categories are not known in advance.
- **Document-driven** — This type of DSS retrieves and analyzes information found in documents. Data is unstructured and in a variety of formats.
- **Knowledge-driven** — Problem-solving expertise stored as facts, rules, and procedures is used to analyze data.

DSS is extensively used in business and management. Executive **dashboards** and other performance analysis software allow faster decision-making, identification of negative trends, and better allocation of business resources.

DSSs tend to support making **one-time decisions.** Data and knowledge relevant to the decision is accumulated and presented to the decision maker. Decisions of a more routine nature tend more to be supported by management information systems.

Executive Information Systems There is no specific differentiation between DSS and Executive information Systems (EIS) which has become thought of as:

- Supporting unstructured decision making.
- Used by executive level of management.
- Used as a strategic analysis tool.
- Wide use of summary data from many sources.

The discussion in this chapter does not draw a distinction between DSS and EIS; both are considered to fall under the broad DSS umbrella. A DSS can be used to support strategic thinking at one end of the spectrum and at the other a DSS can be used to assist in semi-routine decision making such as in granting loan approvals.

12.1 Decision Making

A decision is a choice between alternatives. Decision making is based on assumptions about the likelihood and desirability of the alternatives. The estimated value of the alternatives' outcomes is a significant factor in selecting a choice. Decision making is a reasoning process.

Decision making is especially important for management and leadership. It is easy and tempting when faced with a new problem or decision to react with a decision that seemed to work before. It's easy to get stuck in a circle of solving the same problem over and over again. A DSS can help by applying processes and techniques to improve decision making and the quality of decisions.

Decision making requires creativity in identifying and developing options. Several well-established techniques include:

- **Brainstorming** — Creates new ideas, solves problems, motivates, and develops teams. Brainstorming needs to be a structured activity. It enables people to suggest ideas at random but follows a process that allows the group to prioritize ideas, rank options, and suggest actions.

- **SWOT** — The Strengths, Weaknesses, Opportunities, and Threats analysis provides a framework for reviewing strategy, position, and direction of a company or business proposition. It is primarily a strategic planning tool. SWOT is explained fully in the systems analysis chapter.
- **PEST** — A Political, Economic, Social, and Technological analysis is a business measurement tool that can be used to review a strategy or position, direction of a company.
- **SLEPT** — Social, Legal, Economic, Political, and Technological analysis is a tool used to analyze a business environment. It is similar to SWOT and PEST but emphasizes other factors as identified in its title.
- **Cause and Effect** — Also known as a **Fishbone** diagram is a graphic approach to identifying the causes of outcomes. It identifies possible causes for an effect or problem, sorts ideas into useful categories, and can be used to structure a brainstorming session.

To address the large number of considerations involved in many decisions, computer-based decision support systems have been developed to assist decision makers in considering the implications of various courses of thinking. The structure they impose can help reduce the risk of human errors.

Decision Making in Groups Decision making in groups requires communication and negotiation. **Group decision support systems** (GDSS) were developed to encourage and support collaboration and integrated thinking for complex decision making. Participants use networks to enable collaboration.

Group decision support systems can be classified in terms of support offered for different configurations of when and where team members participate.

- Same time AND same place.
- Same time BUT different place.
- Different time AND different place.
- Different time BUT same place.

When people meet at the same time discussion is said to be **synchronous** otherwise it is **asynchronous.**

The benefits of electronic enabled group meeting support systems include:

- Opportunity for equal participation.
- Enables greater participation bringing more knowledge and analytical skills to the task.
- Electronic recordkeeping supports organizational memory between meetings.
- Provides group access to knowledge and databases.

Group decision making facilitates the process of group interactions and depends upon rules for concluding a group decision. The process supports time and place considerations, data and knowledge sharing, and stored group memory. Deciding involves negotiation and the rules for deciding fall into these categories:

- **Unanimity** — Everyone agrees on a given course of action. Care must be taken to avoid the bandwagon effect of **group think** in which everyone jumps on board without careful consideration to their objections.
- **Majority** — Agreement among at least 50 percent of group members. Unlike a unanimous decision, with majority rule there remain defeated members and rejected ideas. Execution of the group's decision requires support of all members, so care must be taken with majority rule decisions.

- **Consensus** — Here a majority approves a given course of action and the minority agrees to go along with it. If the minority opposes the course of action it is modified to remove objectionable features.

12.2 Components of a DSS

Since there is no formal definition of a DSS the components vary among systems. The commonly identified components include:

- **Database management system** — The DBMS stores organizational information. Data is commonly obtained from transactional systems and may be aggregated. Relational database management systems are typically used.
- **Knowledgebase** — A collection of internal and external databases and data warehouses. It includes rules that define data associations; the rules are defined by **metadata.** The knowledgebase also includes an **inference engine** to aid in determining new rules and data associations.
- **Model-base management system** — The MBMS handles models that represent the relationships among facts and events. The models usually provide simulations of real events and may be statistical, mathematical, financial, or economic.
- **User interface** — The component that allows a user to interact with the system.
- **Analytical and presentation tools** — Tools to help an organization understand the issues it faces more clearly. The primary focus is to help identify as many issues as possible and to structure these issues into useful categories. These are user controlled with access provided by the user interface. The tools might include:
  - Statistical analysis tools
  - Data mining tools
  - Geographical information tools
  - Operations research tools including queuing models and linear programming tools

A general model of a DSS is presented here:

DSS Model

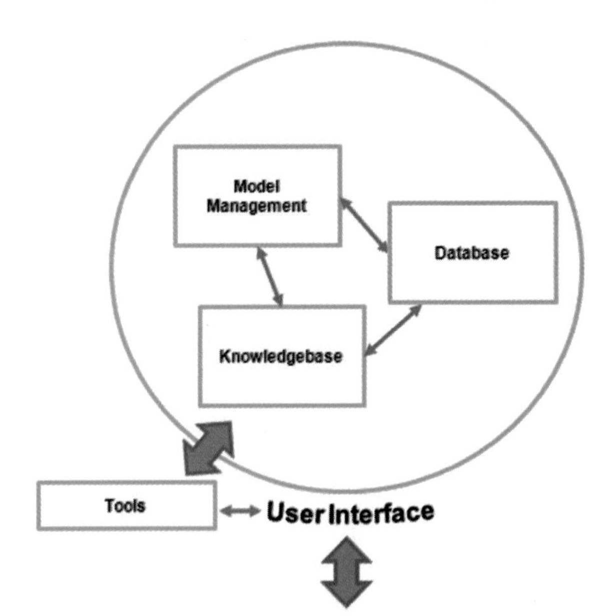

Stakeholders are important too. The categories of stakeholders are:

- **Decision maker** — The person or persons with the ultimate responsibility for arriving at a decision.
- **Domain experts** — People with knowledge of the **problem domain,** sometimes known as the problem space.
- **System experts** — People skilled at operating the DSS.
- **Data collectors** — People responsible for locating and gathering data from heterogeneous sources. The data is organized and standardized and defined by **metadata.**

12.2.1 The Role of Metadata

Metadata is data about data. It may describe an individual data item or a collection of data items. Metadata is used to manage data, assist with its use and facilitate **data integration.** Metadata varies with the context of use. Metadata is stored in a **data dictionary** which provides the information contained in metadata to the programs that comprise a DSS.

Metadata assists people in the use of data. Some examples of metadata help illustrate its significance:

- In a museum collection, where the content is the art works on display as well as those stored for future display, metadata would include the work's title, the artist, year complete, and media (paint, clay, etc.) and the work's location.
- In a library, where the data is the content of the shelved titles, metadata about each book would include a description of the content, the author, the publication date, and the work's location.
- In a data warehouse, where the data is the content of the stored data, metadata would identify the name of the database, a description of the content, the physical storage arrangement (relational database, flat file, spreadsheet, etc.), the storage location (disk drive, magnetic tape), the owner's name, and access permission rules. For each individual data item, the metadata would include the name of the field, the data type and its length.

Metadata is a guide to mapping data as it is transformed from the operational environment to the data warehouse environment. The data dictionary helps the DSS locate the contents of the data warehouse as illustrated here:

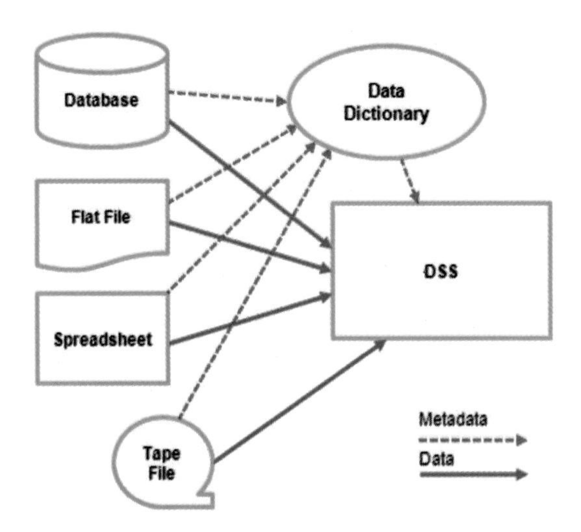

Metadata Informs the DSS about Data Sources

12.2.2 Data Warehouses

Data warehousing is a process of centralized data management and retrieval. Data warehousing is a recent term although the concept itself has been around for years. Fundamentally, a data warehouse is a central repository of all organizational data. Organizational data usually is prepared by transactional business systems, accounting systems, financial systems, human resource systems, and more. Usually the data stored in the warehouse is a copy of the original, thus eliminating the possibility of damaging critical business data. As data is copied into the warehouse it may also be reformatted into a homogenous structure enabling easier analysis. The data may also be **aggregated** because a DSS is not often concerned with detailed transactions.

Centralization of data is a key to maximizing user DSS access and analysis. A data warehouse is not an operational business system, but is usually a large database that is updated periodically from a range of sources. They are sometimes used to bring data together from a range of incompatible or isolated internal systems.

12.2.3 On-line Analytical Processing

On-line Analytical Processing (**OLAP**) is software that enables analysts, managers, and executives to gain insight into data through access to a wide variety of possible views of information that has been transformed from raw data. OLAP is designed for manipulating **multidimensional data** from a variety of sources that has been stored in a data warehouse. The software can create various views and representations of the data. OLAP software provides fast, interactive and, consistent access to shared data. OLAP provides the capability for complex calculations, **trend analysis,** and sophisticated **data modeling.**

OLAP can achieve several tasks. Some uses of OLAP include:

- Budget forecasting
- Financial reporting
- Knowledge discovery
- Performance management

The analysis techniques performed by OLAP include:

- **Trend analysis** — Analysis of data over sequential time periods.
- **Slicing** — Creating data subsets for on-screen viewing and closer inspection.
- **Consolidation** — The aggregation of data. For example, sales offices can be rolled-up to districts and districts rolled-up to regions.
- **Drill-down** — The display of detailed data from which consolidated data was derived.
- **Rotation** — Reorientation of the analysis view enabling examination of data from different perspective. It is often performed along the time axis in order to analyze trends and find patterns.

Multidimensional Data Structures A multi-dimensional structure is arranged so that every data item is located and accessed based on the intersection of the dimension members which define that item. The physical structure of the data may be two dimensional (as in a table) but the analysis may require comparison between data elements in the table.

Use of a pivot table explains this concept as it can automatically sort, count, and total data stored in tabular format. It allows deeper analysis than conventional sort and subtotal operations. Data analyzed using Excel's pivot table is illustrated using this table (partially displayed).

Source Data

	A	B	C	D	E
1	Month	Sales Rep	Region	Flavor	Cases Sold
2	January	Baker	North	Vanilla	49
3	July	Baker	North	Vanilla	361
4	April	Baker	North	Chocolate	70
5	April	Baker	North	Strawberry	69
6	September	Baker	North	Strawberry	102
7	March	Baker	South	Vanilla	61
8	December	Baker	South	Vanilla	35
9	December	Baker	South	Chocolate	19
10	June	Baker	South	Strawberry	80
11	June	Baker	East	Vanilla	130
12	February	Baker	East	Chocolate	25

The table of source data presents sales of ice cream by month for different sales people. The number of cases sold per flavor and in each region is available for analysis. While the data is stored in the two-dimensional tabular format as shown, depending upon the interest of the decision maker it is possible to analyze sales by sales person, region, flavor, and even month.

The concept of a pivot table is that the data element to be analyzed (cases sold – **dependant variable**) is the pivot between two other variables (known as **independent variables**). Here a pivot table shows the total amount of cases sold by each sales person in the first four months of the year.

Pivot Table

Sum of Cases Sold	Month			
Sales Rep	January	February	March	April
Baker	330	366	621	835
Denton	360	658	793	1164
Williams	225	436	528	712
Grand Total	915	1460	1942	2711

The analysis can be enhanced to differentiate among the different ice cream flavors this way:

Drilling-Down in a Pivot Table

Sum of Cases Sold		Month			
Sales Rep	Flavor	January	February	March	April
⊟Baker	Chocolate	144	103	202	284
	Strawberry	49	83	146	193
	Vanilla	137	180	273	358
Baker Total		330	366	621	835
⊟Denton	Chocolate	80	213	280	386
	Strawberry	125	146	147	262
	Vanilla	155	299	366	516
Denton Total		360	658	793	1164
⊟Williams	Chocolate	73	134	202	278
	Strawberry	83	77	96	121
	Vanilla	69	225	230	313
Williams Total		225	436	528	712
Grand Total		915	1460	1942	2711

Sometimes a different view format is useful. The pivot table above can be redrawn as a chart offering the potential for additional insight. The same data (cases sold by flavor and sales person) is presented as a chart. It is easy to notice that most sales occur in the warm months and that Denton and Baker are more successful sales people than Williams is.

A Chart Present a Different View

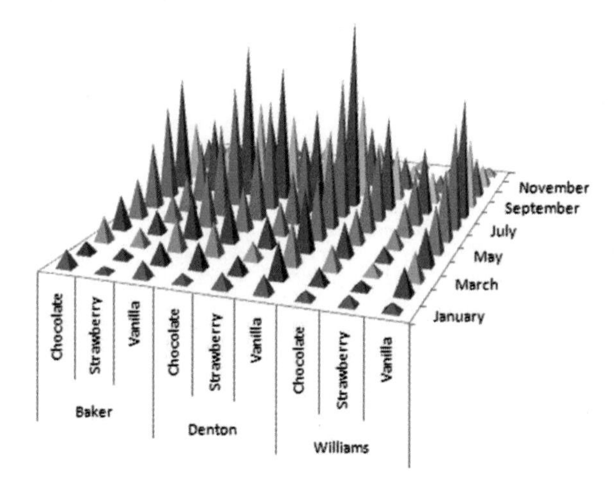

Each column added to the table represents an additional dimension. For example, if a column for the year of sale were added it would be possible to perform a year-to-year analysis. Business often finds it quite useful to compare the same month, or quarter, from the prior year to the current one. **Longitudinal studies** provide important insight and are commonly employed in business.

12.3 Characteristics and Capabilities of DSS

Since there is no exact definition of DSS there is no agreement on the standard characteristics and capabilities of DSS. A list of the ideal capabilities and characteristics of DSS might include:

- Support for semi-structured and unstructured problems.
- Support for individuals and groups including group communication and collaboration.
- Support different data types.
- Access to homogenized data structures.
- DSS should be adaptable and flexible.
- DSS should be interactive and provide ease of use.
- Fast query response.
- Provide various analysis techniques.
- Allow different presentation styles.

12.3.1 Management Information Systems

Management Information Systems **(MIS)** provide an operational view of business activities. MIS reports derive data from transactional systems and present summarized aggregations of operational data. MIS output is used by managers to direct **current operations** but is not used for strategic decision making.

Characteristics of MIS include:

- Reporting systems built on existing **transaction** processing systems.
- Used to support **structured** decision making.
- Used to support **tactical** level management.

MIS is linked to management by objectives in that the MIS is used to monitor key performance indicators. These are metrics used to quantify objectives that reflect performance of an organization and assess the present state of the business. The outcome of this analysis may be to prescribe a course of corrective action. MIS helps an organization to measure progress toward their organizational goals. The analysis is not open-ended, as it is with strategic thinking, but is focused on assessing performance toward measurable objectives.

The output of MIS includes:

- **Scheduled reports** — Most MIS reports are transactional in nature and regularly produced as a byproduct of business activity. Examples include a monthly financial statement, a daily employee attendance report, and weekly bank report of a bank's deposits.
- **On-demand reports** — A manager wants focus on a topic of interest. Usually this is the first step in taking a deeper look at an operational situation.
- **Exception reports** — A report that is produced when something unusual happens. For example, when employee turnover exceeds a certain pre-defined threshold. MIS reports may show trends but often they just report ordinary business activity.

12.3.2 MIS Reporting Using Excel

Tools for MIS reporting include database queries using SQL (refer to the SQL chapter for more information) and use of Excel to analyze operational data in a spreadsheet. Numerous other tools exist, too, but the point is that MIS analysis is transactional in nature. Here Excel's use as an MIS tool is demonstrated.

If a manager were interested in focusing on the performance of one sales person a filter could be used to hide data about all other salesperson performance. Since Williams was identified earlier as the lower performing sales person the manager might wish to view William's records only:

Month	Sales Re	Regio	Flavo	Cases So
June	Williams	North	Vanilla	204
December	Williams	North	Vanilla	35
November	Williams	North	Chocolate	38
May	Williams	North	Strawberry	64
March	Williams	South	Vanilla	46
September	Williams	South	Vanilla	154
August	Williams	South	Chocolate	202
February	Williams	South	Strawberry	17
December	Williams	South	Strawberry	15
June	Williams	East	Vanilla	126

Filtering Limits Records to Those of Interest

If the manager wanted to know how well Williams' sales were in each region for each flavor the data would be sorted by region and flavor this way:

Month	Sales Rep	Region	Flavor	Cases Sold
May	Williams	East	Chocolate	68
November	Williams	East	Chocolate	34
February	Williams	East	Strawberry	23
July	Williams	East	Vanilla	161
February	Williams	North	Chocolate	59
May	Williams	North	Strawberry	64
June	Williams	North	Strawberry	90

Sorting Records Allows Additional Analysis

Now that the data has been sorted the manager could produce summary results:

Summary Results

Month	Sales Rep	Region	Flavor	Cases Sold
May	Williams	East	Chocolate	68
November	Williams	East	Chocolate	34
			Chocolate Total	102
February	Williams	East	Strawberry	23
			Strawberry Total	23
July	Williams	East	Vanilla	161
			Vanilla Total	161
February	Williams	North	Chocolate	59
			Chocolate Total	59
May	Williams	North	Strawberry	64
June	Williams	North	Strawberry	90
			Strawberry Total	154

12.3.3 DSS and MIS are Different

A hallmark of a DSS is the possibility of **integrating data** from different sources. The manager we have been following might have the insight that ice cream sales could be affected by outdoor temperature and would wish to associate temperature recordings data with sales data. Temperature data can be obtained easily from numerous sources by searching on the Web. Here temperature data for the Eastern region was located in a Web site.

External Data Located in a Web Site

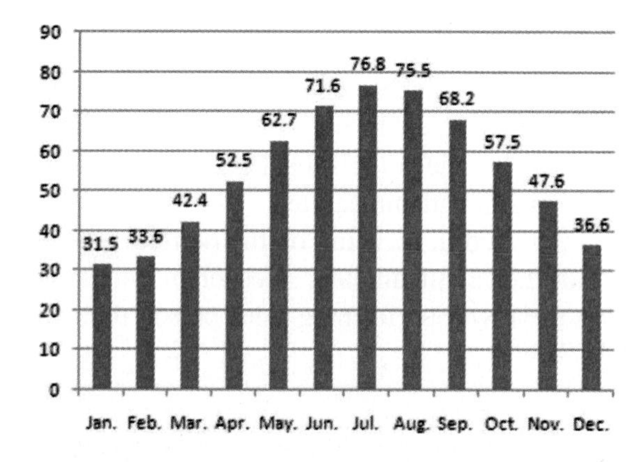

The manager uses Excel's import feature to accept the Web site's data and add it as a table in the workbook. As all four regions' data is imported a new table of average temperature per month and region is built that looks like this:

Imported Data in a New Spreadsheet Table

Month	East	North	South	West
January	31.5	29.3	41.0	34.7
February	33.6	31.2	43.7	37.0
March	42.4	39.4	55.1	46.6
April	52.5	48.8	68.3	57.8
May	62.7	58.3	81.5	69.0
June	71.6	66.6	93.1	78.8
July	76.8	71.4	99.8	84.5
August	75.5	70.2	98.2	83.1
Septembe	68.2	63.4	88.7	75.0
October	57.5	53.5	74.8	63.3
November	47.6	44.3	61.9	52.4
December	36.6	34.0	47.6	40.3

Excel could now be used to combine data from the sales performance and temperature tables to aid the manager in determining if temperature affects sale of ice cream. Of course it seems obvious that temperature would at least partially determine ice cream sales, but what seems obvious is not always correct. A DSS helps the decision maker sift through large volumes of data, applying statistical inference techniques, to learn the truth embedded in the data.

While an MIS is used for routine analysis, a DSS is used to perform **what-if analysis** as described in the next section.

12.3.4 Solving Problems Using Excel

Sometimes the solution to a problem is not so straight forward. Often various input values must be considered until the best solution is found. Excel offers several tools that help you accomplish that type of **What-If** analysis.

What-If Analysis Suppose that you were thinking about purchasing a house but you did not know the various mortgage interest rates and house prices that you can afford. A What-If analysis can help. First we introduce the PMT function which is used to calculate the payment for a loan based on constant payments and a constant interest rate. If the house we want to purchase costs $150,000 and the interest rate is 7% and we expect to pay monthly for 30 years the PMT function would be used this way:

Computing a Mortgage Payment

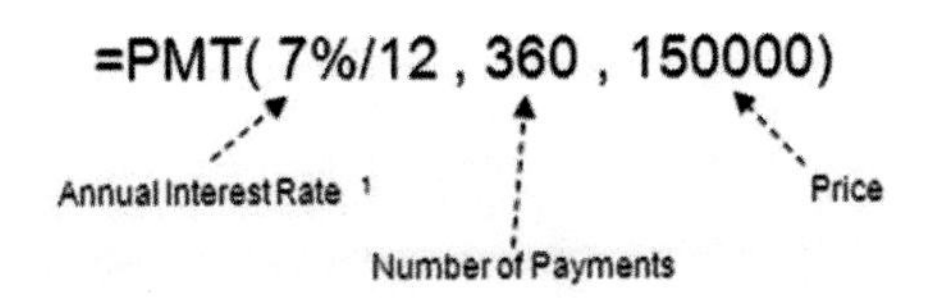

[1] Divide interest rate by 12 because payments are monthly.

It turns out that this combination of price and interest rate results in a monthly payment of $997.95. That is good if we are sure of the price and interest rate that we will end up spending, but what if we are not sure and would like to see various potential combinations of both. To test various combinations we must use a data table which allows us to compare two input values (in this case price and interest rate) over any range we wish.

First set up the PMT calculation as shown in cell B5 below. Any numbers in B1, B2, and B3 are okay; the data table will be used to establish the ranges to be analyzed. The purpose of setting this part up first is to establish the PMT function so that it can be used in the data table.

Data Table Step 1: Setup the Calculation

B5 =PMT(B3/12,B2,B1)

	A	B
1	Price	$ 150,000.00
2	Number of Payments	360
3	Interest Rate	7%
4		
5	Monthly Payment	$ (997.95)

Next add values to test along the row to the right of the PMT function in B5 and in the column below. Doing this sets up the combinations of values to be tested. Here house prices are listed vertically and interest rates are shown horizontally.

Data Table Step 2: Establish the Values to Test

B5 =PMT(B3/12,B2,B1)

	A	B	C	D	E	F	G
1	Price	$ 150,000.00					
2	Number of Payments	360					
3	Interest Rate	7%					
4							
5	Monthly Payment	$ (997.95)	5%	6%	7%	8%	9%
6		$ 75,000.00					
7		$ 100,000.00					
8		$ 125,000.00					
9		$ 150,000.00					
10		$ 175,000.00					
11		$ 200,000.00					

With the active cell containing the PMT function select the whole table and then select **What-If Analysis** from the **Data Tools** group of the **Data Ribbon.** From the drop-down list click Data Table and the Data Table dialog box appears. Since the row of table headers is the interest rates type B3 for the row input cell and B1 for the column input cell since the column values are home prices.

Data Table Step 3: Linking the Columns and Rows to the Calculation

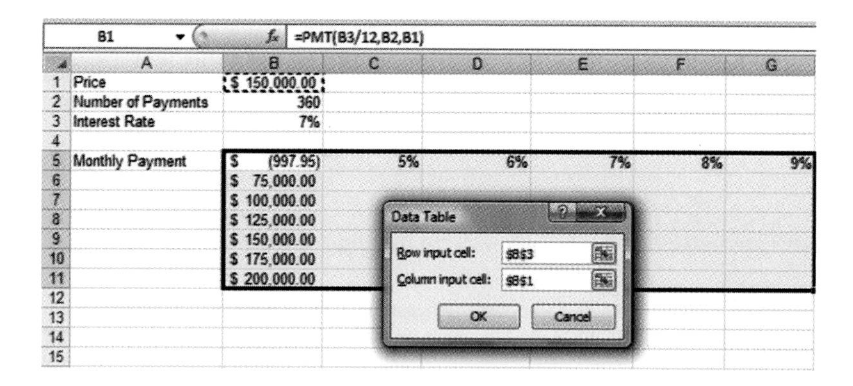

After clicking Ok the data table is complete. Here the monthly cost of various combinations of interest rate and home price are displayed:

The Data Table Is Complete

$ (997.95)	5%	6%	7%	8%	9%
$ 75,000.00	$ (402.62)	$ (449.66)	$ (498.98)	$ (550.32)	$ (603.47)
$ 100,000.00	$ (536.82)	$ (599.55)	$ (665.30)	$ (733.76)	$ (804.62)
$ 125,000.00	$ (671.03)	$ (749.44)	$ (831.63)	$ (917.21)	$ (1,005.78)
$ 150,000.00	$ (805.23)	$ (899.33)	$ (997.95)	$ (1,100.65)	$ (1,206.93)
$ 175,000.00	$ (939.44)	$ (1,049.21)	$ (1,164.28)	$ (1,284.09)	$ (1,408.09)
$ 200,000.00	$ (1,073.64)	$ (1,199.10)	$ (1,330.60)	$ (1,467.53)	$ (1,609.25)

Goal Seeking Goal seeking is the ability to calculate backward to obtain a valid input. In the last example we calculated numerous possible monthly payments based on combinations of interest rates and house prices. Examining the table above we could determine the combinations that are within our budget. How about if we wanted to try this a different way? Presumably we know what out budget is, so why not have Excel tell us what interest rate or house price we can afford. Goal seeking provides exactly that type of possibility. Goal seeking is found by selecting **What-If Analysis** from the **Data Tools** group of the **Data Ribbon.**

Goal seeking allows us to set the target (perhaps the mortgage payment we can afford) and ask how high a price we can afford. For example, we know that our monthly budget allows $900.00 for house expense. We cannot go as high as the $997.95 for the $150,000.00 home that we want at the 7% we know we can get. What is the maximum house price we can afford? Return to the cell with the PMT function and click What-If Analysis and select Goal Seek. The Goal Seek dialog box appears, complete it this way:

- **Set cell** — This is the cell with the target value that we want to reach. In this case we want the target to be the payment which is in B5.
- **To value** — This is the target value. In our case, $900.00.
- **By changing cell** — This is the value we have a question about – how high a house price we can afford. The number of payments and interest rate will not vary.

Setting up for Goal Seeking

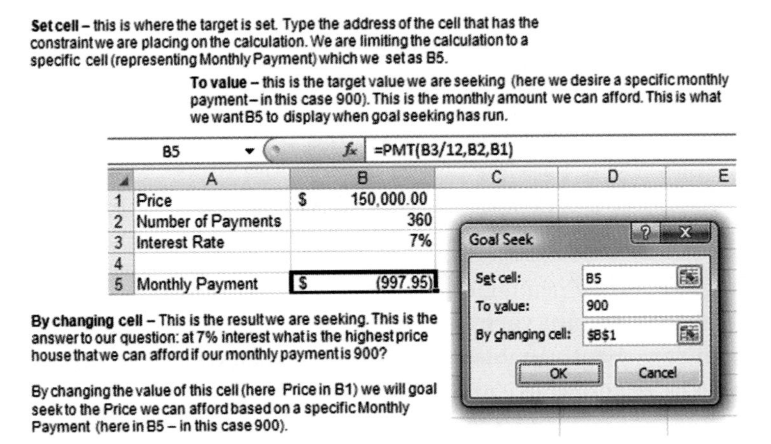

Click go and the result appears. We can afford a house costing $135,276.81.

Goal Reached

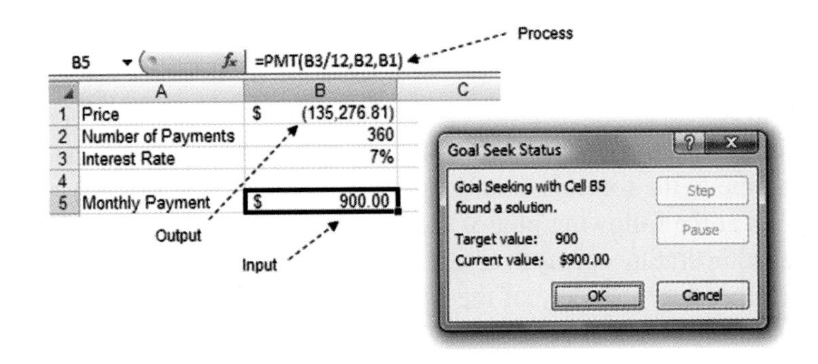

Here is a handy example. A student wishes to know what grade is needed on the final exam to bring a course average up to 80 percent. Assuming that 75 percent of course requirements are graded already and resulted in an average so far of 76.5, what final exam score is needed to reach the desired 80 percent?

The equation for determining the grade is typed in B5. By setting the goal for B5 to 80 based on changes in B3 the answer is that a last exam score must be 90.5.

Goal Reached

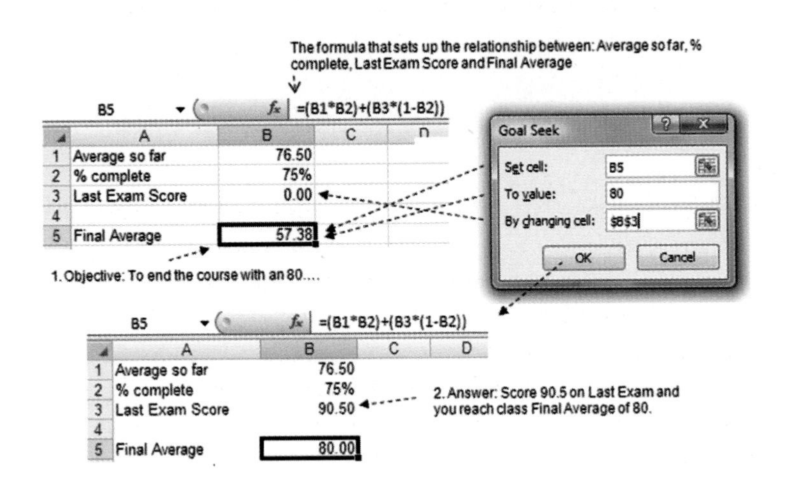

Forecasting Often data analysis involves attempting to predict **future** values based on the relationship among values that have been already observed. This is known as **forecasting** and is best explained by example. The figure below presents a chart depicting average temperature and heating cost data for the first six months of the year. Given this data is it possible to predict heating cost for July if a specific average temperature for July is assumed?

Average Temperature and Heating Cost for Half a Year

	A	B	C
1		Avg. Temp.	Heating Cost
2	January	21	$ 350.00
3	February	24	$ 290.00
4	March	31	$ 250.00
5	April	42	$ 220.00
6	May	55	$ 100.00
7	June	68	$ 60.00

The assumption is that heating cost depends on the average temperature. Therefore heating cost is the **dependant variable** and the average temperature is the **independent variable.** The independent variables are assumed to determine the value of the dependant variables. The relationship can be described this way:

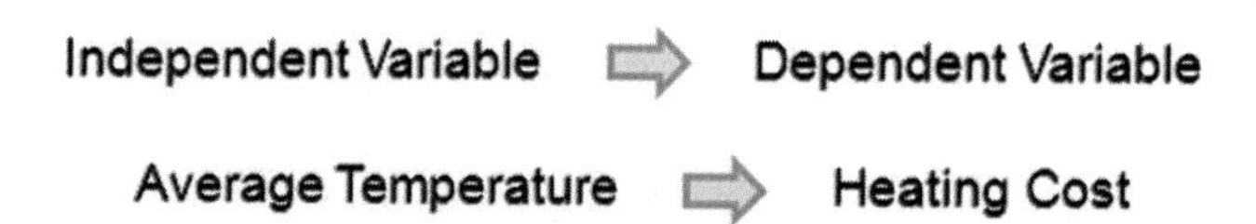

What could we expect the heating cost for July to be if we **assume** an average July temperature of 72 degrees? Note: forecasting always makes assumptions about the future. The outcome of the forecast is only as good as the assumptions.

Take a look at the following plot of the data from the figure above. As you can see rising average temperature seems to result in lower heating cost. We would expect July with higher temperature than any of the first six months of the year to have the lowest heating cost. Since this makes sense let us allow Excel to predict July's heating cost.

Plot of Average Temperature vs. Heating Cost

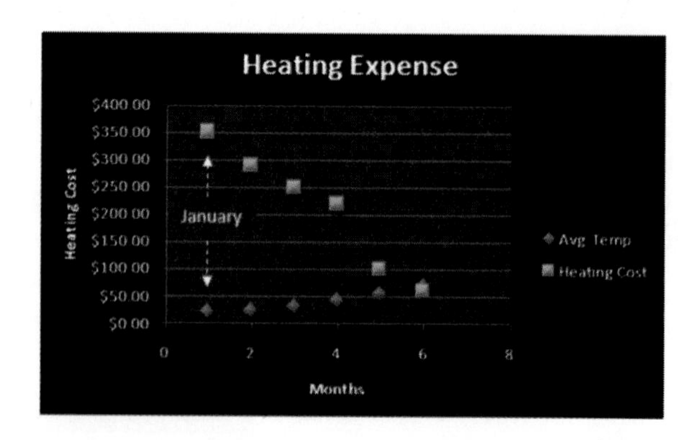

Here we use the FORECAST function which requires three arguments:

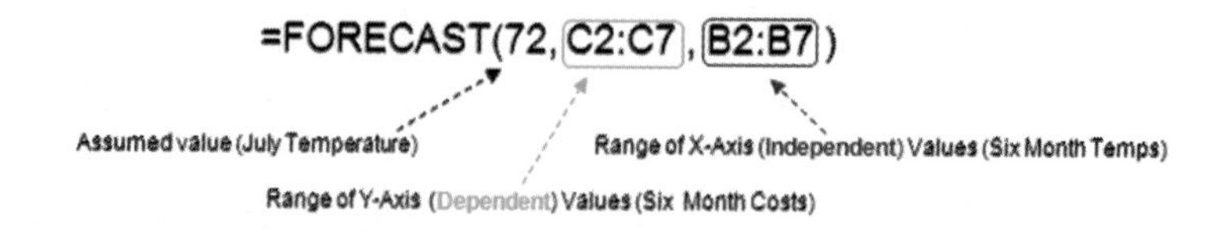

And the answer is? Based on an assumed July average temperature of 72 degrees the heating cost will be $23.15.

12.4 Examples of DSS

A DSS can theoretically be built to address many different knowledge domains. Here are several examples of DSS in use that illustrate the variety of application:

- **Clinical DSS** — Used for medical diagnosis.
- **Bank DSS** — Used for credit verification during a loan application process.
- **Engineering DSS** — Used to assess whether a firm can be profitable on projects that it is considering bidding on.
- **Railroad DSS** — Used to schedule maintenance based on rail condition and extent of rolling stock use.
- **Agricultural DSS** — Used to plan crop rotation based on climate and financial market forecast.
- **Airline DSS** — Use to determine optimal route and aircraft scheduling. Also used to help decide what markets to enter and leave.
- **Political DSS** — Used to influence political campaigns by accessing demographics and voting patterns.
- **Production DSS** — Used to schedule input and application of resources to manufacturing. Quality production at lowest cost possible is usually the goal.
- **Strategic Planning DSS** — Used to guide and manage the planning process. Used for **one-time** decision making. Also known as **EIS:** Executive Information Systems.

Examples of DSS for personal use include:

- **Diet** — Numerous Web sites offer tools for determine a proper diet based on personal data and income.
- **Relocation** — Web sites and other tools help a person assess job opportunity, equivalent salaries, cost of living, mortgage rates, crime rates, and school quality in different cities.
- **Purchase Decision** — Web sites allow consumers to compare products and prices. Customer reviews of products, products availability and prices from different merchants are available for comparison and analysis.

In addition to the applications identified above a DSS can be used in any field where organization of data and analysis is necessary.

12.5 Role of Artificial Intelligence

DSSs which perform selected **cognitive** decision-making functions, and are based on artificial intelligence or intelligent agent technologies are called **Intelligent Decision Support Systems** or IDSS. The term Artificial Intelligence or **AI** is used to mean the science and engineering of making intelligent machines. Some examples of its use include:

- **Banks** — Use of artificial intelligence systems to organize operations, invest in stocks, and manage properties.
- **Medicine** — A medical clinic can use artificial intelligence systems to organize bed schedules, make a staff rotation, and to provide medical information to staff as needed.

- **Technology** — Windows Vista uses AI to allocate and manage memory. Vista's **Superfetch** learns the computer user's usage patterns and preloads programs in anticipation of expected demand.

12.5.1 Conventional AI

Conventional AI is mostly classified as machine learning in which algorithms and techniques are employed that allow computers to **learn.** There are two types of learning: inductive and deductive:

- **Inductive machine learning** — Uses methods to extract rules and patterns out of massive data sets. Since the cause and effect relationships among observed data are not specifically known to exist, inductive learning is considered **tentative.**
- **Deductive machine learning** — Conclusions are reached from previously known facts. Since the outcome is necessitated by the inputs, deductive learning is considered to be **predictive.**

Conventional AI is applied in several ways:

- **Expert systems** — Process large amounts of known information and provide conclusions based on what is known.
- **Case based reasoning** — This application of AI searches a knowledgebase for previously solved problems that match a current question.
- **Bayesian networks** — Uses probability to predict outcomes based on the existence of known data. A model provides an estimate of the significance of known data which provides probabilistic weights for calculating an outcome.
- **Behavior based AI** — Is used to model human behavior and incorporates software agents that assists users and act on their behalf in performing non-repetitive computer-related tasks.

Computational Intelligence Development of knowledge presumes an iterative development learning process. Computational intelligence (CI) is closely related to machine learning. CI is not statistically or model driven but combines learning, adaptation, and evolution to create programs that are somewhat intuitive or even intelligent. CI methods include:

- **Neural networks** — Systems mimic human brain functionalities.
- **Fuzzy systems** — Systems that address reasoning in conditions of uncertainty, true or false, 0 or 1. Widely used in machine control where systems monitor and diagnose machine performance.
- **Evolutionary computation** — A machine learning technique used to evolve programs that perform specific tasks. EC is biological in nature and has been recently applied in evolvable hardware, which refers to hardware that can change its architecture and behavior dynamically and autonomously by interacting with its environment. Refer to the future of computing chapter for more information.

Decision Tree A decision tree is a tool that uses a graph to model decisions and their possible consequences. It is used to identify the strategy most likely to reach a goal successfully. The model appears as a sequence of decisions as represented by **nodes.**

The machine learning technique for inducing a decision tree from data is called **decision tree learning.** A decision tree derived this way is a predictive model; it is a mapping from observations about an item to conclusions about outcomes.

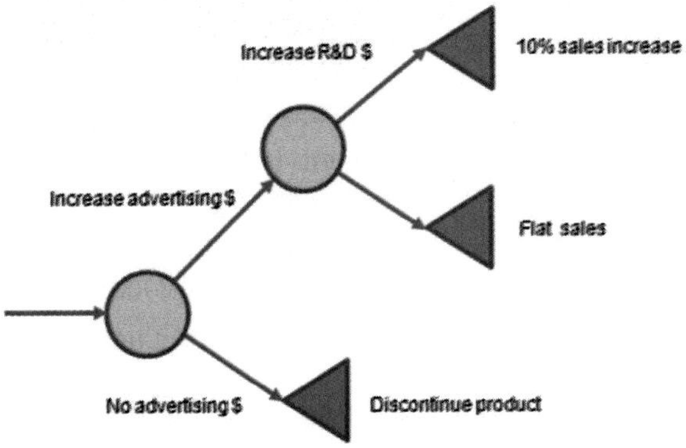

Increase R&D $
10% sales increase
Increase advertising $
Flat sales
No advertising $
Discontinue product

Decision Tree

12.5.2 Expert Systems

An expert or **knowledge-based** system blends subject-specific knowledge with the knowledge and analytical skills of human experts. Most commonly an expert system is a program which analyzes data by following a set of rules about a specific **problem domain.** These systems seem to apply reasoning while reaching conclusions.

Types of Problems Solved by Expert Systems Use of expert systems is especially valuable in organizations where the experience that judgments are based on cannot be easily taught to others. Expert systems used in this circumstance are designed to capture the knowledge and experience of experts and disseminate it to others within the organization.

Expert systems are used where it is not possible to code a programmed route to a problem's solution. This is because there is no one set of circumstances or symptoms that define a problem. With multiple entry points the outcomes cannot be predicted. Expert systems are not predictive.

Use of expert systems is found in many disciplines including these:

- Medical diagnosis
- War gaming
- Legal planning

As an outcome of AI research expert systems have demonstrated the possibility of practical application. Because of the requirement for narrow domain knowledge coupled with the knowledge of subject matter experts, generalized expert system solutions are hard to find.

Expert Systems and Problem-Solving Systems The difference between expert systems and traditional problem-solving systems is the way knowledge and expertise is coded. The traditional procedural approach finds knowledge coded in both a program's procedural code and its data structures. In an expert system it is the data structures only which hold knowledge.

- **Problem solving program** — In a tax computing program, data structures hold data about the taxpayer and the tax tables. The program is coded to apply the expertise of a tax expert who is knowledgeable with tax law. Programs of this nature are used by millions of Americans annually while preparing tax returns.
- **Expert system** — Data is found in the data structures. The expert's knowledge, the relationship between data elements – the rule set—is coded in the data structure here, too. This arrangement permits the expert system to be generic and therefore independent of the problem domain, which in this case is taxes.

There are two primary components to an expert system:

- **Knowledgebase** — A problem-dependent set of data structures called the knowledge or rule base. A knowledgebase is a special data storage architecture designed and optimized for knowledge management. It provides the collection, organization, and retrieval of knowledge. A knowledgebase follows a data model or an **ontology** that represents a set of concepts within a domain and the relationships between those concepts. Increasingly XML is used for hosting knowledgebase data structures.
- **Inference engine** — A problem independent program used to derive solutions from a knowledgebase. The engine follows rules implied in data structures to process data and format conclusions. It is a program that infers new facts from known facts using inference rules. An inference engine adds to the knowledgebase as it processes data.

12.6 Data Mining

Data discovery is the process of analyzing data from different perspectives and summarizing it into useful information. Data mining, which is also known as **Knowledge-Discovery** is the process of searching large volumes of data and automatically detecting patterns within it. Analytical tools such as classification, rule association, and data clustering are used. Data mining identifies trends that would usually be overlooked with simple data analysis. Sophisticated algorithms identify key attributes of business processes and outcomes.

Data mining is a relatively new term but not a new technology. For a long time, databases have been sifted by programs searching for data associations that might yield competitive opportunities. Data to scan is abundant. With market checkout highly automated, widespread use of ATM and debit card machines and increasing online and electronic commerce it is easy to find data. Faster processors, larger and faster disks, and greater pools of primary memory increasingly enable the application of this technology.

Data mining is used by many classes of organizations including businesses, the FBI, other organizations, and financial analysts.

Data, Information, and Knowledge

The basis for data mining is the hierarchy of data, information, and knowledge.

- **Data** — Facts that can be machine processed. This includes:
  - Operational or transactional data (sales, cost, inventory, payroll, and accounting, etc.).
  - Nonoperational data (industry sales, forecasts, economic, etc.).
  - Metadata about database models or data dictionary definitions.
- **Information** — Patterns, associations, and relationships among data provides information. Transactional data yields information about what has happened and when.
- **Knowledge** — Information examined over time or across different subject domains can be converted into knowledge. Analysis of the patterns and associations among different pools of data may yield relationships that would have otherwise been undetected.

12.6.1 What Can Data Mining Do?

Data mining is heavily used by retail, financial, and marketing companies with a consumer focus. Companies mine to determine relationships among factors such as price, product positioning, competitive offerings, economic factors and customer demographics. Data mining suggests models that enable companies to predict the impact of their actions on sales, customer satisfaction, and corporate profits.

Point-of-sale purchase records can be used to send target promotions to specific customers based on an individual's purchase history. Comments on warranty cards provide valuable opportunities to classify customers as candidates for particular promotions. Video rental companies use rental history as a basis for offering customer recommendations for subsequent rentals. Electronic companies use data mining to offer customers accessories to already purchased products.

Other uses for data mining are:

- **Market basket analysis** — Understand what products or services are often purchased together.
- **Market segmentation** — Identify the characteristics common to customers who buy the same products.
- **Customer turnover** — Predict which customers are likely to purchase the product of a competitor.
- **Interactive marketing** — Predict what a Web site customer is most likely interested in seeing.
- **Purchase patterns** — Understand when customers purchase certain products.
- **Fraud detection** — Identify which transactions are most likely to be fraudulent.

12.6.2 How Data Mining Works

Data mining provides the link between transactional and analytical systems. Software analyzes relationships and patterns in recorded transaction data using statistical, machine learning, and neural network techniques. The process of data mining includes these general steps:

- Obtain data, re-format it if necessary, and store in a data warehouse system.
- Provide access to business analysts.
- Analyze the data by application software.
- Present outcomes in a useful format, often a graph or table.

12.6.3 Required Technology

Data mining technology is available today for all common architectures: mainframe, client/server, and stand alone PC. There are two critical technological drivers:

- **Database Size** — The more data being stored and processed, the more powerful the system required. This requirement impacts on disk drive capacity and speed. Use of **RAID** technology can be valuable in data mining applications. More information about RAID is found in the hardware chapter.
- **Query complexity** — The more complex the queries and the greater the number of queries being processed simultaneously, the greater the amount of faster primary memory required. Processor speed and parallel architectures have a significant impact on query processing, too.

12.6.4 Issues

Data mining is coming into common use, but not without challenges or even controversy. Several concerns that are raised frequently include:

- **Technical** — The question of data structure is often considered. Most transactional data is stored in tables in relational databases. In a multidimensional structure, data in cubes is arranged with subsets created according to category. Multidimensional structures are optimized to facilitate multidimensional data mining but relational structures appear to perform better in client-server environments that move large data volumes through networks.
- **Management** — Data analysis can only be as good as the data that is being analyzed. Key to obtaining value from data mining is integrating data from disparate sources so that data does not conflict and is not redundant. Customer names obtained from different systems could be slightly different and require homogeneity if mining is to prove valuable.
- **Cost** — The more powerful the data mining queries, the greater the utility of the information being learned from the data, and the greater the pressure to increase the amount of data being collected and maintained. This in turn increases the pressure for faster, more powerful data mining queries which causes the cycle to repeat.
- **Privacy** — The issue of individual privacy has grown in importance with the emergence of data mining as a widely used tool of business and governments. Data mining makes it possible to analyze data recorded from numerous types of transactions and obtain a significant amount of information about individuals' buying habits, travel patterns, and even political and religious preferences.

12.7 Tools

Tools to provide automated decision support can be complete stand-alone application packages or can be customer crafted from several major components.

12.7.1 Data Management

A DSS aids people by allowing the analysis of data with the aim of supporting decision making. Data must be available for analysis and may be stored in various structures.

- **Spreadsheet** — Volumes of data are stored in business spreadsheets. Although not a sophisticated data structure, the examples earlier in this chapter validate the use of spreadsheet resident data for support of decision making.
- **Relational database** — A relational database is defined as a collection of records structured in tables with logical (data driven) connections among them. SQL is used to perform queries. Certain data structures cannot be stored relationally requiring use of other data models.
- **Multidimensional database** — Multidimensional databases which are sometimes known as **data aggregators** combine data from multitude data sources. Data may be stored in non-relational structures including networks, hierarchies, and arrays which are difficult to model in relational table structure. Multidimensional databases form the basis for knowledgebases. Metadata is important when multidimensional databases are used because data sources and definitions vary.

12.7.2 Model Management

Model-based DSSs depend upon the manipulation of a **model** or **queries** that define assumptions about the **problem domain** under consideration. Models incorporate data and parameters provided by decision-makers to aid in analyzing a situation.

Queries representing models are a function of OLAP systems and are actually a hybrid technology because they provide modeling, data retrieval, and data summarization.

12.7.3 User Interface

The user interface is the means by which people interact with a DSS. It can be as simple as Excel's interface or as sophisticated as a custom-built application using **SAP** as the foundation. The key functionality provided by the interface is:

- **Input** — Allowing the users to manipulate a system
- **Output** — Allowing the system to display the effects of the users' manipulation.

12.7.4 Digital Dashboard

A digital dashboard or **executive dashboard** is a visual information display tool that is based on the metaphor of a car's dashboard and its instruments. Business data is displayed in gauges, charts, and graphs making use of color and other visual effects. Data is drawn from corporate operational or informational databases and displayed in an accessible format. The dashboard's summary displays are often clickable leading to the underlying detail data. The display is usually in a portal-like environment with a customizable interface.

Digital Dashboard

Widgits A widget is a **graphic display interface** element that a computer user interacts with, such as a window, graphic display, or a text box. Widgets are used to build digital dashboards. Widgets are usually found on the desktop and operate in Windows from the System Tray. Widgets can be networked, access corporate databases, and provide a graphical display. The basic building blocks for graphical user interfaces are part of the operating system and found in system or API libraries. Widgets are described as virtual to distinguish them from the physical counterparts whom they represent.

Gadgets Windows Vista introduces a set of tools called gadgets that appear floating in front of open windows. Gadgets are useful programs or information sources. A business can distribute data for display using customized gadgets. Gadgets that are installed with Vista include these and other categories:

- Security
- System Performance Monitors
- Games
- Utilities
- Mail and Contacts

Vista's Gadgets

- Calendars
- News Feeds
- Music
- Lifestyle
- Information

Gadgets may be relocated and also removed. To add a gadget click the + at the top of Vista's Sidebar and select a gadget from the Gadget Gallery. To widen the selection click Get more gadgets online in the Gallery's lower right.

Gadget Gallery

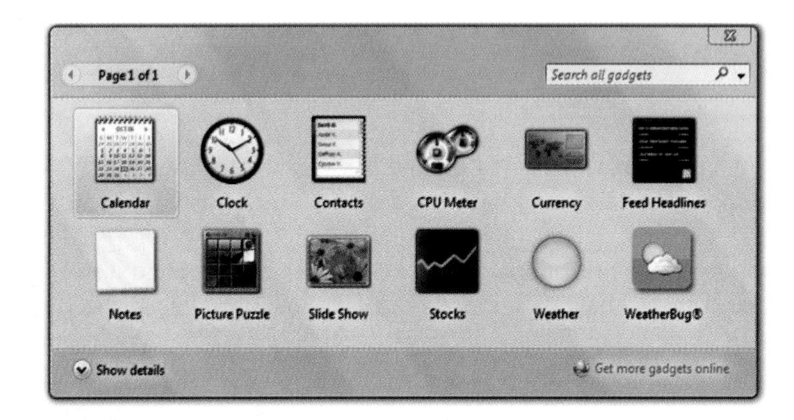

12.7.5 Web Based

A Web-based DSS delivers decision support information or decision support tools to a manager or business analyst using a **thin-client.** The server that is hosting the DSS application is linked to users in a **client-server** architecture. Since multiple simultaneous access is assumed the server's processing power (CPU and RAM) and persistent storage capacity (disk) must be considered. For performance reasons it is common for a Web-based, data-intensive application like a DSS to follow an architecture that separates the application from the data manager as shown here:

DSS/Client-Server Architecture

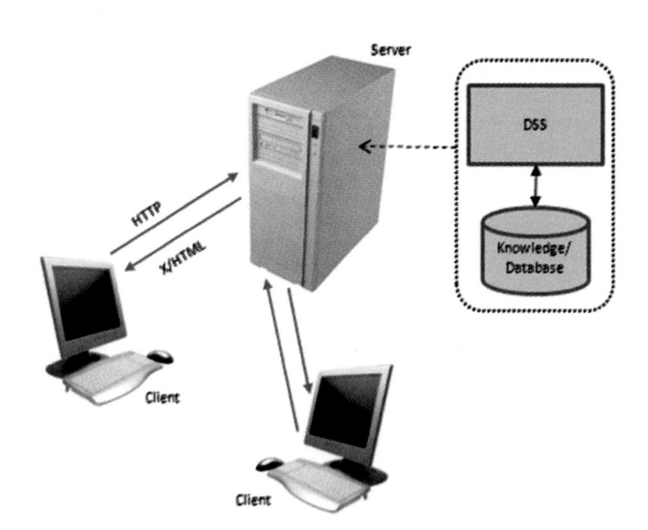

Client-server architectures are desirable because there is no incremental client expense since a Web browser is the application's local host. Data updating is easy since the Internet and standard protocols are used.

12.8 Summary

Decision support systems are built to assist humans with decision making. Decision making is the selection of a direction from among a collection of possibilities, each with an associated expected outcome. A strategic planning process that includes idea surfacing and evaluation of choices and their potential value is followed. Group decision making has a political dimension absent from singular decision making and is provided for in a collaborative DSS.

Decision support systems provide multi-dimensional data for analysis. Data is often obtained from divergent sources with unique format and organization. As data is collected and homogenized the role of metadata becomes important. The development of data warehouses has been parallel to the proliferation of OLAP.

Management information systems dominated the earlier use of computers and software for processing transactional data. MIS reporting on business transactions was suited to controlling and managing operations but it did not provide strategic insight into a company's potential. A DSS is different in that allows questions to be asked and reports on what-if possibilities instead of what-is.

The dream of Artificial Intelligence researchers has been to develop machines that mimic human reasoning. Limited success has been achieved. Most notably, expert systems, in spite of narrow problem domains, have demonstrated the practicality of AI concepts.

Data mining is a long-established technique that more recently has come under public awareness. Massive databases are scanned by software searching for patterns that reveal relationships among data. Opportunities to cross-sell, to adjust to changing demographics, and to prevent fraud are benefits from data mining.

The scope of the DSS is a matter of business decision. Technologies ranging from individual spreadsheet templates to complete DSS applications are available. Any DSS depends on a data store and analysis tools. The user interface unifies the components as the user manipulates the system and results are displayed. Web-based DSS applications are becoming common because of lower client expense and easy updating.

EXERCISES

Exercise 12.1

What is a DSS? Must a DSS be computerized to be useful?

Exercise 12.2

What is data mining? What organizations employ it and for what purposes? Give three examples of what it can be used for.

Exercise 12.3

How do semi-structured and unstructured decisions differ?

Exercise 12.4

What is an expert system? What makes it an expert and what is it an expert in?

Exercise 12.5

What is decision making? Research a technique that supports decision making and describe how the technique is employed.

Exercise 12.6

What are the components of a DSS? Describe what each is and how they interact to support decision making.

Exercise 12.7

DSSs can be classified based on the type of processing they provide. What is the difference between data- and document-based systems? Which would more likely be associated with model-driven systems? Why?

Exercise 12.8

Select three characteristics of a DSS and describe their significance.

Exercise 12.9

Data mining has several associated issues. Select two and describe concerns and prospective remedies.

Exercise 12.10

How does group decision making differ from individual decision making? Describe the key difference and the challenge that is presented to groups.

Exercise 12.11

What is the difference between a DBMS and a knowledgebase?

Exercise 12.12

What is an EIS? Does it differ from a DSS? How and why?

Exercise 12.13

What is an inference engine? How is it different from a search engine?

Exercise 12.14

How do a DSS and MIS differ? Are they compatible in any way? How?

Exercise 12.15

What is the difference between forecasting and goal seeking?

Exercise 12.16

What is metadata? Where does it originate from?

Exercise 12.17

Discuss data, information and knowledge as a hierarchy of increasing value.

Exercise 12.18

What is a multidimensional data structure? Why is a pivot table helpful in analyzing data stored in these structures?

Exercise 12.19

What is a decision tree?

Exercise 12.20

What is a digital dashboard? Identify and describe three commercial products that present visual displays from data maintained in relational or spreadsheet form.

Exercise 12.21

Is a multidimensional database relational? Could it be or is it structured differently? Why?

Exercise 12.22

What is machine learning? What are the differences between the two types of machine learning? Given an example how each might be used.

Exercise 12.23

What is a data warehouse and how might it support decision making? How does a data warehouse fit in with a DSS?

Solve the following exercises using Excel.

Exercise 12.24

Based on the price data for a stock as shown here what will the stock price be on December 17, 2008? In J5 use a function to forecast the stock price for 11/17/2008.

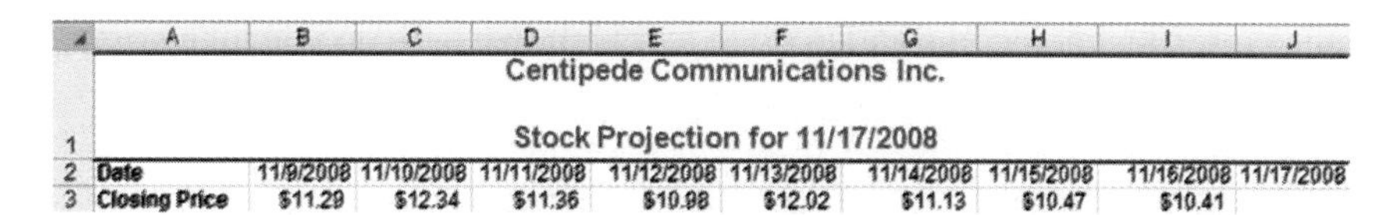

	A	B	C	D	E	F	G	H	I	J
1	Centipede Communications Inc. Stock Projection for 11/17/2008									
2	Date	11/9/2008	11/10/2008	11/11/2008	11/12/2008	11/13/2008	11/14/2008	11/15/2008	11/16/2008	11/17/2008
3	Closing Price	$11.29	$12.34	$11.36	$10.98	$12.02	$11.13	$10.47	$10.41	

Exercise 12.25

The data here associates an exam score with the number of practice exercises each of several students completed. If a student decides to complete three practice exercises what is their exam score likely to be? Forecast your answer in B12.

	A	B
1	Number Practice Exercises Completed	Exam Score
2	4	90
3	1	67
4	3	83
5	3	79
6	2	95
7	0	54
8	1	78
9	1	87
10	2	81
11	2	76
12	3	

Exercise 12.26

Set up a spreadsheet as shown here. In B6 type a formula that computes total profit. Profit per individual unit is price to customer minus cost per unit. Use Goal Seek to determine the number of units that must be sold to reach a profit objective of $1150.00? Round up your answer to the next integer.

	A	B
1	Material cost per unit	$ 2.00
2	Labor cost per unit	$ 3.00
3	Unit price to customer	$ 8.00
4	Units sold	
5		
6	Total Profit	$ -

Exercise 12.27

Set up a spreadsheet for determining a car sales person's paycheck as shown here. In B6 type a formula that computes pay for the month. Pay is calculated as base salary plus commission per car sold plus a bonus for each car sold above twenty. Use Goal Seek to determine how many cars must be sold to earn $7,500 for one month. Round up your answer to the next integer.

	A	B
1	Base salary	$ 1,000.00
2	Commission per car	$ 300.00
3	Bonus per car over 20 sold per month	$ 500.00
4	Cars sold this month	
5		
6	Paycheck for month	$ 1,000.00

Exercise 12.28

Assume that income tax is computed as the sum of:

- Income times the tax rate.
- The portion of income over $70,000 times the tax rate increased by a factor of 1.5.

Write a formula in B3 that computes income tax. Take home income in B4 is the difference between income before taxes and income taxes. At what income and tax rate levels shown here do you take home more than $60,000? Complete your work in Excel using a data table.

	A	B	C	D	E
1	Income before taxes	$ 71,000.00			
2	Tax rate	15%		Income tax rates	
3	Income tax	$10,950.00			
4	Take home income	$ 60,050.00	25%	30%	33%
5		$ 70,000.00			
6		$ 75,000.00			
7	Income before taxes	$ 80,000.00			
8		$ 85,000.00			
9		$ 90,000.00			

The Impact of Computing on Society

Chapter 13

Advances in technology always present society with new challenges. New jobs have been created to harness computing technology, existing jobs have changed, and some jobs have disappeared. This technology, in particular, presents health and security risks that were not anticipated in its early days. In this chapter we explore the positive and negative impacts of computing technology.

Computers have made an impact on most of the population. It would be a difficult challenge for anyone to demonstrate that computers have not touched their lives. Computers are embedded into much of what we touch and use. They enable the communication technologies we have learned to depend on. Computers make possible the special effects filmed in Hollywood. Computers are essential in business, help find cures for disease, plan space flights, predict the weather and the economy, and design new vehicles and clothes.

Computers make life easier and their impact is profound. The impact on each of us personally touches many aspects of our lives:

- **We Are Online** — Estimates generally agree that about 70 percent or 210,000,000 Americans use the Internet. Usage rates in some European countries are higher. World usage is estimated at about 1.1 billion people representing close to 17 percent of world population. We chat, e-mail, network with groups, buy and sell things, and speak our mind.
- **Careers Are Affected** — Medical use of computing technology is wide spread and well known. Publishing and the communication industry operate faster than ever. Artists use video and other electronic technologies in their work. Business depends on computer use for monitoring activities and customer relationships. Everyone who works in those and virtually any other field has been impacted by computers.
- **New Careers Emerge** — Jobs have changed and new ones created. The people who design networks and database and provide the communication infrastructure we depend on are performing work that was not known several decades before. Computer graphics is a relatively new profession. Computers have enabled rapid and extensive financial analysis opening new jobs in the financial services industry.
- **Health Issues Surface** — The advantage offered by using computers must be weighed against the unintended consequences of their use. Physical injury due to repetitive actions affects many people. Some people fear using technology improperly and become stressed. Exposure to excessive information can also cause stress.
- **The Work Environment Changes** — Some jobs have disappeared due to automation and some now require less knowledge than before. This situation, known as de-skilling, can cause salaries to fall for specific jobs. Traditional hierarchical organization structures change as technology speeds communication through the organization. Increasingly people work at home and eliminate transportation expense at the cost of isolation from the business community.

- **Social Concerns** — Some people exhibit addictive behavior with computer use. Excessive use and personal isolation seem related. Online-off shore gambling which is not regulated and the wide availability of pornography online are societal concerns. The overload of unfiltered information that we all face can offer us too much to think about and sap our energy.
- **Privacy and Personal Rights** — Online databases accumulate data about us and share it with other computers using the Internet. The volume of data collected would astound most people. With such volumes of data travelling worldwide the opportunity to pry into personal information is greater than ever.
- **Business Issues** — The business community benefits greatly from computer automation and communication technologies but it does face issues. Security incursions and the possibility of fraudulent transactions demand the need for constant vigilance. Equipment can break down or be destroyed in a disaster, so replacement and recovery plans are essential.

13.1 Online Community

When a group of people interacts electronically we build an online community. The Internet and the Web are the enabling technologies permitting much of the World's population to gather in a very large online community. Interacting electronically implies communicating and that is perhaps where computers have made their largest collective impact. Being online is about communicating with and in some cases retrieving information from businesses, friends, governments, and schools.

Major portions of the World's population are online. Estimates of use have been found to be quite consistent including this from March 2007:

World Internet Use

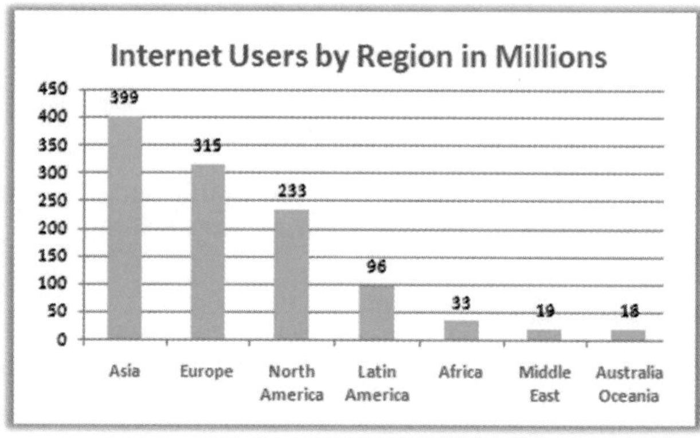

Data Source: Internet World Stats – March 2007

Clearly there are many people using the Internet. Asia, Europe, and North America are the clear leaders. When considering usage penetration among the people of the different regions a slightly different picture emerges:

Internet Penetration by Region

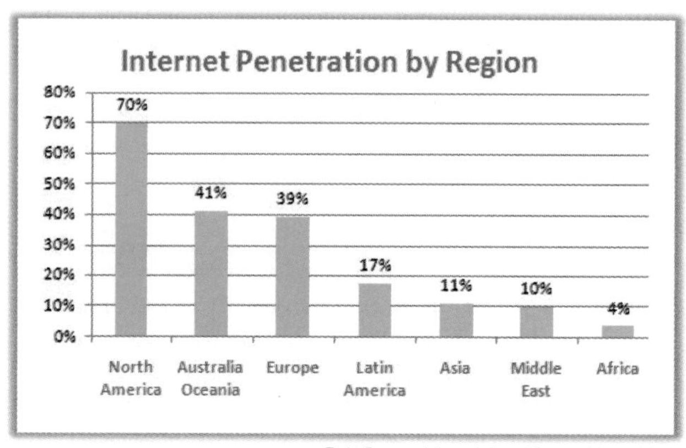

Data Source: Internet World Stats – March 2007

Now North America emerges as the online leader followed by Australia/Oceania and Europe. Usage lags in the Third World but data collected over the last several years indicates acceleration in the number of new users there.

13.1.1 Communicating

The primary personal use of computers is to aid in communication with other people and retrieve information. available online. It provides the foundation for personal online interaction, business transaction, and entertainment.

- **E-mail** — E-mail was the first widely used communication service and although it pre-dated the Internet it remains immensely popular today. E-mail is used to communicate with friends, colleagues, and businesses. It is hard to imagine a world without e-mail.
- **Instant messaging** — Various programs allow instant communication among individuals and groups. Programs and networks that operate in real-time deliver text, voice, and video anywhere in the world. Instant messaging is consistent with the anytime-anywhere culture that social scientists say has evolved.
- **Social networking** — Social networking Web sites are a more recent development in personal communication. Social networking Web sites like MySpace and Facebook allow people to maintain communities of friends who share photos, journals, and interests. While social networking sites can increase a person's circle of friends, they also can increase exposure to people with less than friendly intentions.

13.1.2 E-Commerce

E-Commerce is the use of the Internet and other electronic technologies through which business communicates and negotiates with customers. Because of the directness of communication **disintermediation,** the removal of supply chain intermediaries results. Vendors spend less on marketing and selling and perhaps on distribution as well. E-commerce depends on the use of communication protocols such as **Electronic Funds Transfer** (EFT) and **Electronic Data Interchange** (EDI) to enable transaction automation.

The Supply Chain

Each stage in the chain had associated expense, so removing barriers to the flow of materials, information, and products reduces cost. The online, real-time environment provided by the Internet enables numerous opportunities to successfully manage the supply chain. Instead of going through traditional distribution channels companies may now deal directly with their customers via the Internet.

Cutting out the middleman has long been an objective of any person or organization wishing to cut expenses.

E-Commerce Model

E-commerce is big and growing. Examination of online retail activity tracked by the United States Census Department shows an upward trend.

Extent of Retail E-Commerce

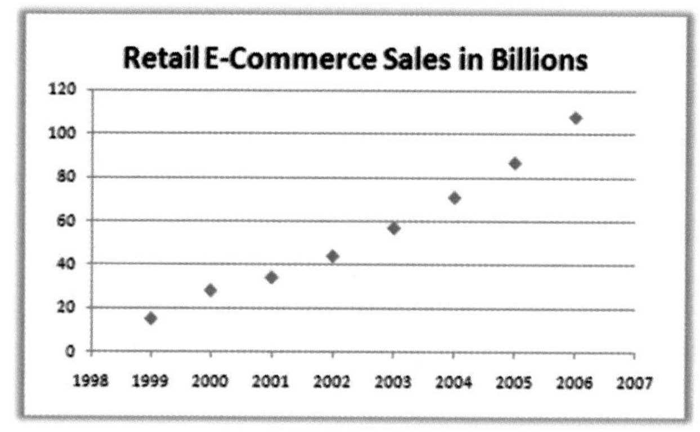

E-commerce as a percent of total retail sales also has shown an upward trend. Percent of retail sales is projected to pass 3 percent in 2007.

Retail E-Commerce as Percent of Total Retail

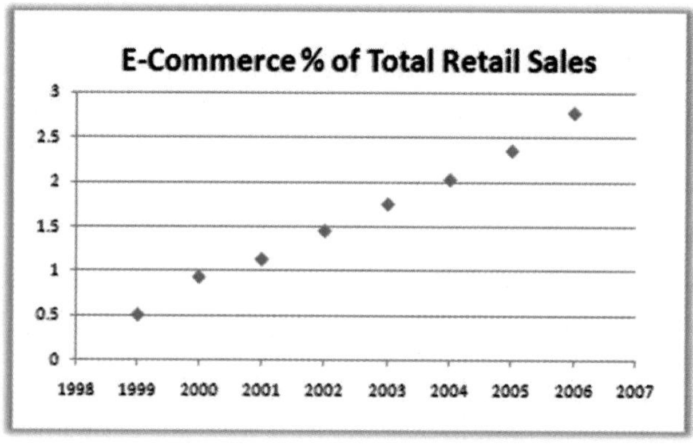

The idea of e-commerce replacing brick and mortar operations seems a long way off, but the seemingly steady increase in dollars spent on-line and percent of total retailing allocated to e-commerce should not be ignored.

Living in Cashless Society Cash usage in the United States has halved since the late 1990s, from 60 percent of all payments to 31 percent. The same is true with check usage, halving from 30 percent of all payments to just 15 percent. The reason for the big drop is the fast rise of debit and credit card payments, rising from 10 percent to 51 percent of payments. This suggests the possibility of a cashless society being made possible by substituting cash with cards. The rise of e-commerce on the Internet most definitely is a factor.

Card use may itself fall due to several emerging technologies. In Europe and Australia text messaging is used to trigger EFT transactions – no cash and no card are used. Radio Frequency Identification (RFID) technology can be built into a card allowing the holder to wave it past a reader and not hand it over to a salesperson. Tests are underway implanting the same technology under human skin potentially eliminating the need to carry cash, card, or electronic device. Biometric measures including face, iris, finger, and palm scans have not yet proliferated but the enabling technology exists and banks are interested.

The major inhibitor to online transactions is the fact that many consumers feel threatened by identity theft and online fraud. Cardless technologies could ameliorate these fears and stimulate additional e-commerce activity.

13.3 Computer Affecting Many Professions

Computer use has had a profound impact on numerous professions. From diagnostic tools in medicine to new media and techniques for artists, computers as just about everywhere.

Medicine The use of computers in medicine is widespread. It is impossible to inventory more than a few examples:

- **Health informatics** — Deals with the resources and methods required to acquire, store, retrieve, and use information in health and medicine.
- **Anesthesiology** — Computers monitor respirators, pumps, and vaporizers in the operating room during surgery.
- **Medical records** — Patient medical records are maintained in databases allowing more accurate record keeping and distribution of records to all of a patient's doctors.
- **Diagnostics** — MRI and other scanning equipment is computer controlled. Computer programs perform preliminary inspections of patient x-rays.

Business and Finance Successes in business depends on provides quality goods at a competitive price to customers. Computer use has penetrated all aspects of business including:

- **Manufacturing** — Computers are used to control production and manage inventory. Robots are used on assembly lines.
- **Finance** — Financial information systems enable companies to manage financial resources with more precision than ever.
- **Sales** — Automation of sales transactions has become commonplace fuelled by EFT and EDI. E-commerce depends on transaction automation.
- **Planning** — Decision support systems provide volumes of data for analysts to examine and model when developing business plans.

Science and Engineering Computers were born from science and engineering and use is wide spread:

- **Research** — Computers control experiments in laboratories and enable telescopes to track stars too dim for the human eye to see.
- **Aviation** — Aircraft developers use computer simulation to test new designs before building test models. Use of wind tunnels is not as prevalent now since computer models perform the same tests faster and with less expense.
- **Chemistry** — Software is used to model chemical reactions without mixing elements and molecules in test tubes.

Social Sciences The social sciences involve research, social policy planning, and delivering services. Computers have impacted all areas:

- **Social policy** — Massive databases allow social scientists to model the expected outcome of proposed social service programs.

- **Research** — Data mining is used by sociologists to identify demographic and behavioral trends among populations.
- **Program delivery** — Computer technology is used to manage the operations of social agencies.

Sports and Physical Education Computers are found in sports and physical education uses that range from management performance to analysis of athletes.

- **Records** — Competitive sports produces volumes of data. Sportscasters rely on databases for athletic performance information to inform their audience with.
- **Sport management** — Professional sports is a business – it has similar opportunities for monitoring and control as all business does.
- **Numerical analyses** — In exercise science, statistical applications and techniques are used to numerically analyze exercise and sport data.

Government and Law As would be expected governments use computer technology to perform law enforcement activities. Governments also enact laws to protect citizens using computers.

- **Intelligence** — Government systems intercept electronic communication searching for evidence of financial fraud and terrorist activities.
- **Intellectual property** — Copyright and patent law protects the rights of software developers.
- **Law enforcement** — Electronic devices monitor the physical location of persons under house arrest.
- **Identify theft** — Federal and state law provide safeguard for the protection of personal information.

Publishing and Communication The communication industry's job is to deliver information to those who desire it. No other industry, except perhaps financial services, is better suited to the use of computer automation.

- **Custom publishing** — Publishers use computer technology to seamlessly combine the work of several authors into a book with consistent organization and style.
- **24-hour news cycle** — News gathering and dissemination depend heavily on computer and communication technologies. Interviews across the globe and dazzling graphics are two examples. News gets updated on Web instantly, and is available to its users all the time.
- **WWW** — There is no rich communication channel more dependent on Internet technologies than the Web.

Travel The travel industry has changed dramatically due to computing.

- **Vacation planning** — Tourists use the Web to take virtual tours of possible vacation destinations.
- **Reservations** — The primary role of the travel agent in handling ticket reservation has long been supplanted by Web-based reservation systems.
- **Cross-selling** — Online systems that offer travel accommodations provide additional offers to customers including theater and recreation opportunities, travel insurance, and even clothing.

Art and Fine Arts Artists use computers as media and as a tool.

- **Videography** — Computers are used to edit video recordings.
- **Display** — Video and computer generated displays are becoming important as a tool in the art world.
- **Virtual galleries** — With gallery space always hard to come by, the Web offers the possibility of presenting to an audience that might otherwise not be available.
- **Graphic design** — Drafting has been replaced by computer aided design (CAD).
- **Theater** — Stage sets are computer controlled.

Education

- Online classes.
- Access to class material on tools like WebCT, BlackBoard, and eCollege.
- Online peer reviewed articles available on library sites.
- Groupware and collaboration tools.

13.4 The Computer Profession

The explosion of computing technology has spawned a whole new career area called **Information Systems** or **IS.** Businesses employ many people as programmers, system analysts, and as other related professionals. They work in a corporation's IS department. These jobs did not exist before the computer revolution.

The U.S. Bureau of Labor Statistics regularly forecasts job demand for all categories of work. Their more recent forecasts show continued, exceptional expected growth for most of the jobs described in this section.

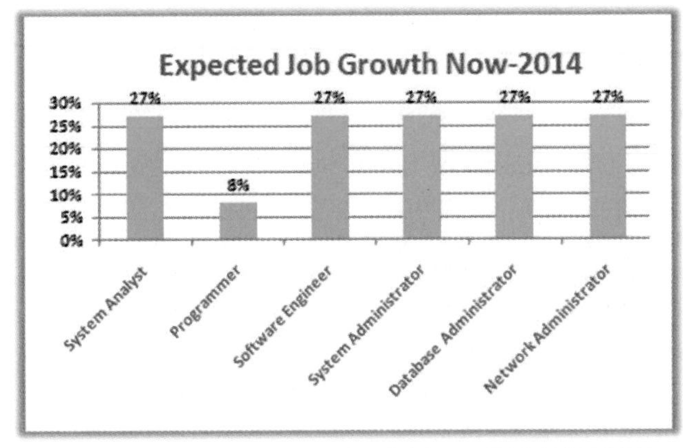

Data Source: U.S. Bureau of Labor Statistics

Job Growth Forecast

System Analyst Computer systems analysts solve computer problems and design the application of computer technology to meet the needs of an organization. They help to maximum benefit from investment in equipment, personnel, and business process design. Systems analysts may plan and develop new computer systems or devise ways to modify existing systems to meet new requirements. They are aware of the potential of technology but must also understand the business of the organization they are working for. Analysts tend to work in domains that use specific types of systems including: accounting, financial, scientific, or engineering systems. The type of system varies with the type of organization the analyst works for. System analysts are not technical developers, they do not write computer programs, design networks, or develop databases.

According to the United Stated Bureau of Labor Statistics the careers with the largest expected percentage increase in the number of jobs are that of computer scientist and systems analyst. The Bureau is predicting remarkable job growth rate of over 27 percent in the current forecast period which ends in 2014. The Systems Analysis chapter presents a full description this pivotal job.

Software Engineer Software engineers translate the recommendations of the system analyst into designs that are implemented by a development staff. They establish testing criteria to certify that programs were written correctly and that completed systems perform as required. While software engineers usually possess strong programming skills, they are more concerned with designing algorithms, analyzing and solving programming problems, and testing outcomes than with actually writing code.

Job growth is expected to equal that of system analysts.

Programmer The computer programmer writes computer programs in what are called programming languages such as **Java, C#,** and **Visual Basic.** This person must have the ability to take a design specification prepared by a system analyst or software engineer and implement the concepts as computer programs. This is an abstract process requiring the programmer to visualize in advance what the computer's monitor will display when the new program is run. Translating a concept to a finished product that others can appreciate and use requires a special creative talent.

Computer programmers often are grouped into two broad types—applications programmers and systems programmers.

- **Applications programmers** — These programmers write programs to handle a specific job, such as a program to track inventory within an organization. They also may revise existing packaged software or customize generic applications which are frequently purchased from vendors.
- **Systems programmers** — They write programs to maintain and control computer systems software, such as operating systems, networked systems, and database systems.

According to the U.S. Bureau of Labor Statistics, job growth is forecast to be at a slower rate than for most other computer related work. The Bureau expects this to happen because of the consolidation and centralization of business systems, developments in packaged software reducing the demand for customized solutions, advances in programming languages and tools which streamline the task of programming, and the growing ability of users to design, write, and implement more of their own programs.

System Administrator Systems administrators are the information systems employees responsible for the efficient use of computers and networks by organizations. Their job is to ensure that an organization's processing environment is designed with compatible equipment, including computers, the network, and software that work reliably. They also monitor and adjust the performance of networks and continually survey the current processing center to determine future network needs. They troubleshoot problems reported by users and network monitoring systems and recommend fixes and enhancements.

Employment of systems administrators is expected to increase as fast as system analysts and software engineers as firms continue to invest heavily in securing computer networks.

Computer Operator Someone has to keep the computers running, and that is the job of the computer operator. The operator is responsible for scheduling processing jobs, mounting tapes and disks on drives, and making sure the printer is loaded with paper. This work is normally performed in what is known as a **data center.**

Webmaster A webmaster is the person responsible for designing, developing, and maintaining a Web site. The webmaster of a Web site may also be called an administrator. Webmasters are typically generalists with HTML expertise who manage all aspects of Web operations. Depending on the size of operations the webmaster may also be a computer programmer able to code and deploy database-driven, interactive Web applications. The Computer Programming chapter has more information about Web application development. Information about HTML and XHTML may be found in another chapter.

Database Designer and Administrator (DBA) This person has a lot of responsibility and is paid quite well to perform these duties. The DBA has jurisdiction over the organization's data storage and works with database management systems, and determines ways to organize and store data. This responsibility includes data modeling (designing the database), selecting the database management system (DBMS) software, ensuring data accuracy and integrity, providing security for the data and making sure that the data are backed up and stored elsewhere in the event that an emergency requires restoration of data. The DBA responds to the system analyst or software engineer's requirements by building databases designed to meet specific performance criteria. The DBA must consider the hardware and operating system platforms on which the database runs and the network protocols that permit moving data among servers and clients.

As with the system analyst job growth for database administrators is expected to be exceptionally high.

Network Administrator (NA) While the DBA is responsible for the integrity of the data, the network administrator is responsible for making sure that the data gets delivered to the right people at the right time. The selection, purchase, installation, and maintenance of network servers, communication gateways, modems, and terminals belong to the NA. Like the DBA this person is well paid. Clearly a company cannot operate without data being available to workers when it is needed.

Network administrators design, install, and support an organization's local-area network (LAN) and wide-area network (WAN) architectures. They may also provide onsite administrative and training support for users of networking and communication tools. They maintain network hardware and software, analyze problems, and monitor the network to ensure its availability to system users. Administrators also plan, coordinate, and implement network security measures. Here, too, job growth is expected to be exceptionally high.

IS Director This person runs an organization's IS department. Sometimes the title is Vice President of Information Systems and sometimes it is Information Systems Manager. The IS director is responsible for the IS department's budget, hiring and firing of staff, staff development and retention, computer operations, and negotiating with other senior managers for project selection, financing and priority. This is the highest position in the IS department unless the organization has a CIO.

Chief Information Officer (CIO) Some large businesses have added the job of CIO to the ranks of top corporate management. The CIO, if a company has one, would sit as a senior officer on the strategic decision-making committees of the company. This person would be on par with the Chief Financial Officer (CFO) and report to the Chief Executive Officer (CEO). The IS Director would report to the CIO. The CIO is the top IS position in an organization. The emergence of the CIO position reflects the recognition in business and management that the delivery of timely, integrated, accurate, and useful information is of strategic value to many organizations.

13.5 Health Issues

There are several health concerns that result from computing:

- **Repetitive stress (or strain) injuries (RSIs)** — Repetitive action, often to fingers, wrists, and arms, can create discomfort or even permanent disability. You have heard of the common example: **Carpal Tunnel Syndrome** (pain and weakness in lower arms and hands).
- **Computer vision syndrome (CVS)** — A frequent computer user's eyes may become irritated, vision may blur, and they may experience headaches and even exhaustion. Taking a regular rest can be a good idea.
- **Low level electromagnetic fields** — Computers, like many electronic devices, emit magnetic fields. There is a possible, but as yet unproved, link with miscarriages and maybe even cancer. There are reduced levels of emission with most new products. In fact, federal and state laws govern the allowed levels of emission. Modern computer monitors present much less of an emission risk than the CRT systems of ten years ago.
- **Psychological stress** — A first-time computer user may be anxious about making mistakes and the consequences. Lack of sufficient training can lead a user to experience loss of data and communication messages and produce anxiety. Changes in the workplace can be stressful. Use of computer automation technology may require people to work differently. Workers may feel that systems require them to work faster, perform more accurately, and even instill a fear of competition against their co-workers.
- **Information overload** — Information overload is a term used in conjunction with various forms of computer-mediated communication (CMC) such as e-mail. It refers to having too much information to make a decision or remain informed about a topic. This condition results from a rapid rate of growth in the amount of information available, while days remain 24 hours long. Information and e-mail filters are becoming popular as screening devices. If not dealt with, Information overload can cause a person to freeze when asked to make a decision. The similar term **information pollution** has begun to appear in the literature.

  Filters can be an effective tool in stemming the flow of excessive information. E-mail programs like Outlook provide filtering tools. RSS aggregators, including Internet Explorer's aggregation tool, permit filtering news feeds. Learning better Web-search strategies is also helpful.
- **Isolation** — Computers are certainly changing the dynamics of human interaction and relationships. It has been generally assumed among social scientists that computer use breeds isolation but research suggests otherwise. Significant correlations between computer-mediated-communication (CMC) and loneliness have not been detected. A study at Penn State University found that those who send e-mail more frequently are more social, and even less socially isolated, because the computer is now being used as an additional means of communicating socially with others.

- **Cyberbullies** — The term refers to bullying and harassment by use of electronic devices though means of e-mail, instant messaging, text messages, blogs, mobile phones, pagers, and Web sites. The intention of cyberbullies is to cause emotional distress. Cyberbullying ranges from sending continuous e-mails to someone who has said they want no further contact with the sender to publishing personal contact information for victims at Web sites. Cyberbullying may include threats, sexual remarks, and racist, homophobic, or pejorative labels.
- **Environment** — Even the environment has been affected by computing technology. Semiconductor manufacturing pollutes air, soil, and groundwater. PCs and peripherals consume several billion dollars of power annually and power production can produce air pollution. Disposal of discarded computer equipment is a serious problem, especially because more than ten million systems are discarded each year. Some equipment is recycled, but advances in technology often obsolete equipment thus relegating older computer equipment to junkyards.

13.6 Work and Workspace Design

Aside from the new career paths that were described earlier, an IS career offers other advantages as well. Most IS professionals assume responsibility for challenging assignments, using technology that continues to change. Thus, IS professionals rarely get stale. In fact, it is quite common for an organization to provide continuing education programs just so that its staff can remain current.

Although new career opportunities abound, the proliferation of computing within organizations is not without a downside. Several issues and concerns are discussed next.

13.6.1 De-skilling

Computer software, like word processors for example, makes tasks easier to perform. A secretary, in the past, was expected to be an expert at spelling and at grammar. Not so any longer, because the software takes care of that. But what does it mean? The skill level required for a portion of a secretary's work is lower today than in the past. What are the consequences? If lower skills are expected then more people are qualified for the job. With more people qualified, the salary can be lower. De-skilling can mean lower wages or even no job. There are other examples. Consider a bank teller. Today a teller works with a computer that performs arithmetic and does other record keeping, so again the skills required in the past are not needed.

13.6.2 Job Losses

Some jobs are lost altogether. Robots have replaced assembly line workers. Bank tellers have been replaced by ATMs (automatic teller machines). Telephone switchboard operators have been replaced by automatic electronic switches. This is not a new phenomenon. In the days before automobiles the blacksmith was in great demand as horses provided the basic means of transportation. Technology creates change, some good, and some that displaces or is hurtful to others.

13.6.3 Communication and Organizational Structure

The automation of information flow has changed the way that people communicate within organizations, and the consequence has been job loss, this time for middle managers. A flatter web-like structure is replacing the traditional hierarchical structure, where information flowed up and down the levels. Middle managers, of the traditional structure, were the gatekeepers, through which information passed. They also held power functioning as the filters of information. E-mail and other communication tools make parts of these jobs unnecessary. We are witnessing business reengineering focusing on new methods and processes that drift towards leaner organizations with more direct and faster communication.

Flattening the Organization

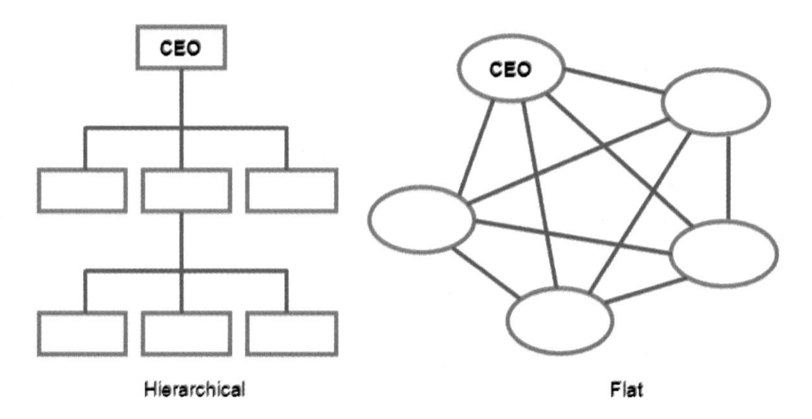

13.6.4 Geography

Communication technology allows organizations to spread out geographically. An expert in some aspect of the organization's production process need not be stationed at each plant or factory. Instead that person can use video conferencing technology, inexpensively through the Internet, to communicate face to face with plant engineers around the world. Companies are finding that they can reduce the travel expenses of bringing experts to where they are needed by using communication technology instead.

13.6.5 Telecommuting

A variation on the geography theme is telecommuting which is a work arrangement in which employees enjoy some flexibility in working location and hours. Commuting to a central work place is provided by telecommunication links. Some companies allow employees to work all or some of their hours at home. This saves office space for the company and saves commuting time and expense for the employee. Telecommuting allows employees to have flexible hours that can often help when the need to care for young children or elderly parents is involved. The handicapped and people living in remote areas may also become employable due to telecommunicating. Society benefits, too, as less fuel is consumed for transportation and less pollution is produced.

There is a downside. People are social and telecommuting breeds business isolation making job advancement more difficult to achieve. Informal communication (discussion at the water cooler or coffee machine) is largely lost. Corporations also face the increased risk of data loss and compromise to data integrity resulting from the loss of direct corporate control over the telecommuter's physical work environment.

13.6.6 Ergonomics

Ergonomics, sometimes known as **human factors,** is the scientific application of information about humans to the design of objects, systems ,and environments that humans use and interact with. This field has made contributions to the design of computing equipment making our use of computers and peripheral technology more comfortable and less likely to induce strain or injury. Ergonomics also focuses on promoting good user posture which may enhance user productivity, limit fatigue, and reduce the possibility of injury.

- **Keyboards** — Ergonomic keyboards are designed to reduce stress from the repetitive action of typing. Many designs use a wrist-rest as shown here. Other designs break the keyboard into sections to conform to normal rotation of the hands.

A Keyboard Prevents Wrist Strain
© WaD, 2007, Shutterstock

- **Mouse** — The repetitive movement of dragging a mouse over the mouse pad can cause wrist strain and discomfort. To address this concern the trackball mouse was introduced. It reduces hand movement and space requirements. A large ball called the **marble** is used for cursor motion. The sculpted form keeps the hand and arm relaxed and fits into the palm of the hand.

A Trackball Mouse
© Aga & Rafi, 2007, Shutterstock

- **Keyboard drawers** — A keyboard drawer can be used when desk space is cramped. This type of drawer is mounted just below the desk surface and contains the keyboard so no desk surface is needed. The drawer is opened when the computer is used and otherwise it is closed. Some drawers also provide placement for a mouse pad.
- **Document holders** — Document holders keep printed materials needed during computer tasks close to the user and the monitor. Proper placement of the holder may reduce or eliminate risk factors such as fatigue, eye strain, awkward head and neck postures, and headaches.
- **Anti-glare screens** — Sometimes the surface of a computer monitor produces reflections that could make viewing the screen difficult. An anti-glare screen covers the monitor and reduces glare while allowing the monitor's display to be viewed. Some anti-glare screens provide privacy by limiting the field of view to the user facing the computer directly and prevent nosy neighbors, especially in public places, from viewing screen content.

- **Docking station** — A docking station supports a laptop computer by providing hardware that remains on a desk and that is not needed when the computer is used away from home or office. Docking stations are often used to accessorize a laptop so that it is more like a desktop computer.
- **Notebook stand** — A notebook stand provides a secure, easy way to take advantage of limited desk space. The computer is raised above the desk which may protect the laptop from overheating by improving air circulation. A notebook stand can also be used to position a laptop at a more comfortable height for both viewing and entry of information.

Assistive Technology Ergonomics plays an important role in the conceptualization and design of technology solutions for people with impairments.

- **Public access** — The Americans with Disabilities Act of 1990 provides protections against discrimination to Americans with disabilities. One of the provisions of the Act is to ensure that disabled persons have access to public accommodations. The communication, banking, transportation, and other systems are considered public; assess for the disabled is mandated by law. Here an ATM keyboard presents Braille characters on key tops enabling use of the machine by a vision-impaired person.

ATM with Braille Symbols
© Denis Debono, 2007, Shutterstock

- **Braille keyboard** – Braille keyboards have Braille symbols on top of each key. The typist's feel of the keys ensure pressing the proper keys. The output will be conventional ASCII characters processed as if from any keyboard.
- **Braille terminal** — With a pure Braille terminal, input is performed by two sets of three keys plus a space bar. The collection of keys pressed creates Braille symbols and not the standard ASCII characters others are familiar with. Output is generated by a row of electromechanical character cells. Each cell has pins that rise above or fall flush with a plane that the user touches. The pattern of the raised pins exactly duplicates standard Braille symbols.
- **Magnifiers** — People with limited sight can benefit by using screen magnifiers like the one built into Windows. It is found in the Accessory folder's Ease of Use folder.

Web Page Displayed at 5X Magnification

- **Screen reader software** — This software aides those with hearing impartment by reading documents, Web pages, or other content and transforming the typed words into synthesized speech. This technology is also known as **text to speech.** Two popular screen readers are:
  - **JAWS** — Reads screen content and speaks what has been read.
  - **EYES** — Reads screen content and provides speech and Braille output.
- **Speech recognition** — Windows provides a way to command the computer using spoken commands instead of mouse clicks and keyboard strokes. Software that hears and understands human speech is sophisticated technology. The product, **Dragon Naturally Speaking,** is considered the best commercially available speech recognition program.

13.7 Social Concerns

Use of computers is not without societal concerns. Initiatives range from protecting children from undesirable material and predators, to banning certain materials are discussed frequently by the public. Several concerns are discussed here.

13.7.1 Child Protection

Probably the most discussed social concern is the protection of children. Numerous stories are known of children lured by inappropriate material. Attempts by predators to pose as children in online chat rooms and then attempt to contact children are known too.

- **Blocking Web sites** — Parents who wish to limit their child's access to Web sites can use a filter like a firewall to prevent navigation to other than permitted web addresses.
- **Sting Operations** — Law enforcement officers have been known to pose as children in chat rooms and attempt to lure predators to a meeting. Once arrival at the agreed location an arrest is made. Certainly parents would rather prevent access to the chat room and not rely on the presence of law enforcement office to protect their children.

Legislation The federal and state governments have enacted child protection laws. Most notable is perhaps the federal Children's Online Privacy Protection Act of 2000. This act requires a Web site that collects information from or about children (under 13) to publish a privacy policy which parents should read before allowing access to the Web site. Protection is really only as good as the vigilance of parents and their determination to teach their children to act responsibly.

13.7.2 Computer Addiction

Some people do spend a lot of time using computers. Webster's Concise Dictionary defines addiction as "A habit so strong that one cannot give it up." Can people really become addicted to computers? There are people who feel the compulsion to spend so much of their time computing that it causes problems with their health, finances, relationships, and career. These are the same kinds of problems caused by other addictions which we are more familiar with.

It remains a question of what they are addicted to. Are they addicted to the computers themselves, the programs they are running, or the real-life aspects embodied by those programs? These and many other questions surrounding excessive use of computers remain open. With today's commonplace use of computers, it has become difficult to distinguish users who are merely highly engaged in their computer use from those who could be considered truly addicted.

13.7.3 Pornography and Indecent Content

Pornography has been available online since before the Web became publically known. Its sale is considered to have been the first substantial successful use of the e-commerce paradigm. It remains a potent commercial force today and is expected to continue profitably for many years to come.

Some psychologists believe that online pornography is stronger, and more addictive, than ordinary pornography addiction because of its wide availability, explicitness, and the privacy that online viewing offers. In order to satisfy their addiction, addicts are said to regularly spend extended periods of time searching the Internet for new pornographic material.

13.7.4 Dangerous Information Available Online

Dangerous means different things to different people. Here are several examples of what some people have classified as dangerous material available online.

- **Banned books online** — Some cultures ban specific books and other writings from their membership. Much banned material can be found online in spite of group prohibitions.
- **Child online safety** — Pornography is readily available and, unless parents intervene, children can access it as easily as adults can. There is little debate about the harmful potential of pornography to children.
- **Build a bomb** — Plans to build an atomic bomb are easy to find online. Whether the plans are workable is unknown.
- **Political discussion** — Some repressive societies block Web sites that provide forums for political opinion. The content of political forums is likely most dangerous to the governments that block the sites and not to the site readers.
- **Personal data** — The media has reported numerous events where personal data, including social security numbers, has been posted on public Web sites. Although the data is itself not dangerous, its improper use leads to identity theft.

13.7.5 Risks of Nanotechnology

Nanotechnology is the science and engineering of building electronic circuits and devices from single atoms and molecules. The technology offers great promise in many fields including in healthcare, telecommunications, information technology, and pharmaceuticals. Nanotechnology research is leading to the potential for molecular manufacturing in which very small, powerful, and sophisticated processors, memories, weapons, and surveillance devices could be fabricated.

Some objection to the development of nano-devices centers on the possibility of tracking and monitoring devices being implanted unknowingly in humans while eating or drinking. Medicines are obvious possible carriers, too. Even airborne distribution would be possible. Health concerns are also raised.

13.7.6 Security and Privacy

Security is a very broad and important topic. E-mail messages are intercepted and hackers steal private information. There is good reason to be concerned. Not only are there vast data banks holding numerous varieties of personal data, but the Internet provides an extremely inexpensive and available communication link for the transfer of data. Credit bureaus (TRW, Equifax, etc.), hospitals and doctors, employment agencies, educational institutions, and governmental agencies store and supply data. The list seems endless. Most private industries are free to use information about you despite many laws to protect your freedom and privacy. There is a huge information marketplace that many companies and other organizations participate in. Information is bought and sold by almost all organizations.

Numerous stories abound about large-scale security breaches. In 2006, 26 million records (including social; security numbers) were stolen from the Department of veterans Affairs. T.J. Maxx, Marshall's, H & R Block and many more companies, schools and other organizations have reported security breaks. With data in digital form the potential for theft and misuse has escalated greatly.

The Security, Ethics, and Privacy chapter discusses federal legislation aimed at promoting personal and business privacy and protection.

13.7.7 Green Computing

Green computing is the study and practice of using computing resources efficiently and with a worldly perspective. Green computing principles take into account these factors:

- **Economic viability** — Does the system perform cost effectively?
- **Social responsibility** — Is the system used for social good, or at least not to harm society or groups of people?
- **Environmental impact** — Is there unnecessary harm to the environment?

Traditional business practices focus mainly on the economic viability of a computing solution. Social responsibility is about holding a group, organization, or company accountable for the effect of its computing systems on the people around it. A company acting responsibly would not allow its customers' personal credit data to be lost or revealed inappropriately. Environmental responsibility involves:

- **Buying green** — Having a green perspective when purchasing electronic equipment includes these considerations about electronic devices:
  - Contain fewer toxic constituents.
  - Use recycled materials in the new product.
  - Energy efficient.
  - Use minimal packaging.
- **Saving energy** — Computing equipment runs on electricity which is generated in a process that consumes energy resources and produces pollution. Turning off equipment not in use saves power. For example, turning off monitor at night and printer when not in use.
- **Saving trees** — It has been the dream of business for many years to go paperless. While business may view this as cost saving it would also reduce consumption of trees and therefore preserve the Earth's oxygen supply.
- **Proper disposal** — Computer equipment, and especially batteries, should be properly disposed of when no longer used. Batteries contain chemicals that are environmentally harmful. The hardware chapter provides tips about proper disposal of equipment.

- **Donation programs** — Donating used (but still operating) electronics for reuse extends the lives of valuable products and keeps them out of the waste stream for a longer period of time. Donating used electronics allows schools, nonprofit organizations, and lower-income families to obtain equipment that they otherwise could not afford.
- **Recycling programs** — Recyclers recover millions of pounds of materials from discarded electronics each year. Recycling electronics helps reduce pollution that would be generated while manufacturing a new product and from the need to extract valuable and limited natural resources. It also reduces the energy used in new product manufacturing.

13.8 Business Concerns

Businesses have concerns, too. The chapter on security and ethics has more information, but some issues to consider are described here.

13.8.1 Fraud

Online fraud rates for merchants are higher than fraud rates of brick-and-mortar stores. Fraud rates for transactions where a customer personally presents a credit card are usually about 1 percent of sales but online fraud rates exceed 1.4 percnt (costing over $3 billion in 2006) according to the electronic payment and security management provider **CyberSource.** In spite of the security code found on the back of most credit cards online fraud continues to outpace fraud for in-store purchases.

Merchants are using fraud management tools to battle the perpetrators. Growing in popularity is the technique of **IP Geolocation** which is used to evaluate the risk of an online transaction based on geographic data. **Order velocity monitoring** assesses purchases based on metrics such as total dollar amount and frequency of purchases on accounts associated with good buyers. Despite the increase in automated tool usage an increasing number of merchants are reviewing some orders manually.

13.8.2 Computer Crime

Computer crime is theft of computer resources or use of computer systems while committing a crime. It could range from illegal or unauthorized use of a computer to theft of data to destruction or alteration of data or programs. Who commits computer crime? Often it is an ideal employee, in a position of trust: an insider who is greedy or disgruntled and typically has no prior criminal record. Frequently the perpetrator sees the crime as a game. Much computer crime is not reported because it can be hard to trace and because an organization might be embarrassed to reveal that its security has been breached.

Types of Computer Crimes There are primarily four general types of computer crimes:

- **Computer as the target** — Crimes in which the computer is the target include such offenses as theft of intellectual property, theft of marketing information, and gain from use of computerized files (medical information, personal history, or financial status). Unlawful access to criminal justice and other government records is another crime that targets the computer directly.

- **Computer as the instrument of the crime** — This involves converting legitimate computer processes for illegitimate purposes. Crimes in this category include fraudulent use of financial processing systems to divert money from legitimate accounts. Use of computers to launch denial of service attacks on other computers is another example.
- **Computer is incidental to other crimes** — In this category the computer is not essential for the crime to occur, but it is related to the criminal act. This means that the crime could occur without the technology; however, computerization helps the crime to occur faster, permits processing of greater amounts of information, and makes the crime more difficult to identify and trace. Such crimes include money laundering and unlawful banking transactions. In an extreme case, a patient's medication information and dosage could be maliciously altered in a hospital computer database.
- **Crimes associated with the prevalence of computers** — The simple presence of many computers generates new versions of fairly traditional crimes. Software piracy, copyright violation of computer programs, black market computer equipment and programs, and theft of technological equipment are examples.

Property Rights Who owns software? The programmer or employer? Does a computer user purchase software and then own it? The answers are not as straightforward as you might think.

Generally, software remains the property of the author. A staff programmer who works for a company usually agrees to give ownership to the employer. But the end-user rarely obtains ownership. When you purchase software, you are really purchasing permission to use the software, but you do not own it. Since you are not the owner, you may not give copies of it to anyone. To do so is **stealing,** a violation of federal copyright law.

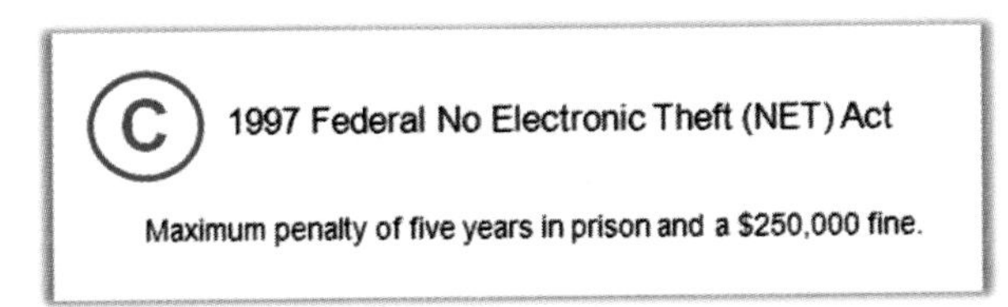

Copyright Violation Carries Substantial Penalties

Some software authors protect their right by use of copyright or patent. How much protection either affords is not really clear. Just like in any fast moving industry the best protection is gained by constant product improvement. The Security, Ethics, and Privacy chapter has more information about licensing and intellectual property rights.

13.8.3 Data and Equipment Protection

All computer users will want to protect data and equipment. For equipment there are several obvious and common sense suggestions: do not eat, drink, or smoke near a computer; keep the computer and peripherals clean; protect against extreme temperatures; and use a surge protector.

Protecting data is actually a more complex activity. Several suggestions are highlighted here:

- Make sure that un-needed material (disks & paper) are properly discarded.
- Separate job functions (programmers should not have access to live customer databases).
- Make daily backup copies of data and programs.
- Allow audit checks of data and data management and security systems.

Users should also read the Responsible Use of Computing policy of their organizations.

13.8.4 Disasters and Recovery

Security is a system of safeguards designed to protect a computer-based information system from accidental or deliberate damage or access. Often, an organization creates and enforces policies and procedures to protect the assets of the organization. Part of the approach is to prevent problems before they occur. Sometimes unfortunate events do happen, and many businesses would not be able to continue operations if their computer access was interrupted for even a few days.

But what could cause a shutdown? It would be worthwhile to take a moment and consider the vulnerabilities that an organization can be exposed to. They range from natural disasters to deliberate fraud or intrusion:

- Fire
- Flood
- Hacker
- Virus or other malware
- Disgruntled employee
- Eavesdropper

So, what should an organization do about this? A **disaster recovery plan** should be created and periodically tested. Perform dry runs to make sure that the organization knows how to deal with disaster. Check to make sure that backup copies of data and programs were properly made and stored in a safe place. Make sure that critical employees are notified of what has happened. Make sure that an alternative data processing site is available. This is not a trivial task, but many unfortunate companies forget to build and test their plan.

13.9 Summary

Computing has indeed had a very large impact on society. Whole new career paths have been created and the current job outlook is excellent. The widespread use of computing and networks does, however, make available data that might be considered private. Concerns about privacy should not be ignored.

About 70 percent of North Americans use the Internet. World usage is estimated at about 17 percent and growing fast. The potential for world-wide real time communication is a transforming force that changes how people engage in commerce, social activity, and personal relationships. Politics is changing, too, as candidates use the Web to raise funds, schedule campaign events, and recruit supporters.

Jobs are changing because of the introduction of computing technology in numerous fields. Libraries are highly automated making the work of a research librarian faster paced and more data intensive. Doctors use computers to aid in diagnosis and patient treatment. The communication industry works in a 24 hour news cycle thanks largely to computer and communication technology. Computers help police officers identify criminals and databases are used by customs officers to screen people at international points of entry.

The relatively new field of information systems emerged and developed alongside the growth of business use of computing systems. Supporting IS work are several new jobs (systems analysis, software engineering, and database and network administration) that are forecast to experience continued substantial growth well into the next decade. Recognition of the importance to business of the flow of useful and timely information has elevated the top information system professional to the executive ranks.

Computer use has had negative repercussions. Physical injury and stress have affected many people. Stress, in particular, is caused by information overload, fear of making mistakes or even prospective embarrassment due to using equipment or software improperly. Economically, jobs have disappeared due to computing and the skill level required for other jobs has diminished.

Some changes are evident in the organization of business. Business structures have become flatter and leaner as information flows electronically, faster and more directly through a business. Communication technology permits wider use of telecommuting which reduces personal and business expense but has the unintended consequence of isolation and may retard career advancement.

Society and business have concern raised due to the widening use of computer and communication technology. The addictive use of computers which may breed isolation affects personal relationships and careers. Security intrusions are a constant and real fear to persons and business alike. Fraud and computer crime trouble business and the danger of a computer related disaster is always present and recovery should be planned for.

The introduction and penetration of computing into business and into our lives has a double-edge. The benefits are frequently discussed but the negatives are always present and deserve attention.

EXERCISES

Exercise 13.1

How IT is affecting your major or job?

Exercise 13.2

Do you think IT literacy is as important as reading and writing skills?

Exercise 13.3

What is information literacy? Do you think computer literacy leads to information literacy?

Exercise 13.4

Do you think people who are not computer literate are disadvantaged?

Exercise 13.5

How do computer literary and information literacy differ? What can be done in universities and colleges to change computer literary to information literacy?

Exercise 13.6

Describe three jobs that have been affected by computing. Include at least one job that has been affected by deskilling.

Exercise 13.7

Identify and describe three specific applications of computing technology in the travel industry. In your answer name specific organizations that employ the applications you describe.

Exercise 13.8

What is an online community? How is membership and behavior governed?

Exercise 13.9

What is the role of the system analyst? Why do you think the U.S. Government consistently predicts a bright future (high job demand at good salaries) for this profession?

Exercise 13.10

Why do people use personal computers? Describe the three most significant reasons you use a computer. How much time each week do you spend on each of the three activities? What has the impact been on other aspects of your life?

Exercise 13.11

Identify and describe three specific applications of computing technology in the social sciences. In your answer name specific organizations that employ the applications you describe.

Exercise 13.12

How has computing changed the structure of business?

Exercise 13.13

Write a job description for a database administrator. Include objectives and responsibilities. Also identify required pre-requisite work experience.

Exercise 13.14

Select two health issues associated with computing. Discuss their implications and what is done to prevent and treat the associated problems.

Exercise 13.15

Could nano devices be implanted in humans unknowingly? Who might attempt that and why?

Exercise 13.16

What is ergonomics? Since it is not specifically a computing term why has it become important in computing?

Exercise 13.17

Computer addiction is a controversial topic. Some say it is not possible to be addicted to a computer but that addiction is possible to programs and the real-life environments they model. What do you think and why?

Exercise 13.18

What is a disaster recovery plan? If you were a small business operator of an on-line retail web site what would be included in your disaster recovery plan?

Exercise 13.19

Discuss green computing. What do you believe is the green initiative that could have the greatest ecological potential? What business interest might cause opposition to green computing?

Exercise 13.20

What is e-commerce? How has it changed the way commercial activity is conducted? In your answer describe the impact on individuals and business. Consider business from the perspectives of customer and merchant.

Exercise 13.21

What is computer crime and what characteristics do computer criminals possess?

Exercise 13.22

Is political discussion on-line dangerous? Consider it from the perspective of those who do think it dangerous and those who do not. What is your opinion?

Exercise 13.23

Why has the position of CIO been created? Search on-line for the names of CIOs of three prominent public organizations. Write a job description for a CIO. Tip: Corporate websites often list top executives.

Exercise 13.24

Do you believe that cash will one day become a relic of the past? How soon might that happen? What technologies might enable this development? What impediments might keep cash in human future for a long time?

FUTURE OF COMPUTING

CHAPTER 14

Predicting the future is tempting but risky. The title of this chapter suggests a look around the corner and that is what we will do. Rather than take a starry-eyed science fiction-like tour of the distant future we will examine research that is emerging now and discuss the potential impact of this technology's implementation.

The central expectation of researchers and technology developers is that computing circuits will shrink in size to atomic level. With on-off circuits, the basic building blocks of computing, miniaturized to this extreme it is not hard to imagine immensely powerful processors tightly integrated with gigantic clusters of memory. Smaller than can be seen by the human eye, we will find networked computers that can be airborne, and can permeate just about everything. It has not happened yet but that is the direction that computing seems to be going.

Imagine the potential of a blanket of connectivity in which intelligence is embedded in the objects of our daily lives. It might sound like science fiction, but already in development are designs that could lead to a world where household objects are fabricated by computer, smart dust monitors the climate, and embedded circuits monitor our bodies.

This scenario is described as **pervasive computing** and presumes an explosive level of connectivity. Managing networks of this scale may be too difficult for humans, and network management may be delegated to intelligent software programs called **agents.** Humans will interact with computers by speech and gesture. Computers and networks will be adaptive, intelligent, and self-organizing.

These advances will open a new era of **ubiquitous computing,** in which inexpensive servers bring Internet access to household appliances, clothing, and office equipment. People will take for granted that microwave ovens download cooking instructions from the Web. Clock-radios will reset themselves after a power outage. Smart refrigerators could monitor tagged products, learn your food preferences and shopping schedule, and eventually order all your groceries for you. Washing machines could monitor fabrics and colors—hot and cold water could be automatically selected as you toss tagged clothing into a washer; mixing colors and whites would be noticed by the machine and it would stop the wash. Tagged pill bottles in a medicine cabinet could allow doctors to monitor patient compliance with prescriptions remotely, and reminders would automatically be sent to patients if necessary.

Bridging the theoretical possibilities of today with the technological capability of tomorrow is not easy. The assumption is that computing will become ubiquitous. Atomic sized processors and memory will be collecting and communicating data from appliances, vehicles, the oceans, the atmosphere, books, our pets, and us. It is not clear how data flowing from trillions of networked, wireless, low-cost computational devices will be carried through the Internet. Can the data traffic be handled by XHTML and XML? Might new Internet protocols have to be devised? Atomic computing seems likely to happen. The infrastructure will be altered to support the demand. So what will it mean when so much data is collected and shared?

How ready are we for pervasive computing that surrounds us and helps us, but knows a lot about us? Some people are concerned that ubiquitous networks will present the possibility of new and enlarging violations of personal privacy. In addressing privacy matters a big challenge will be to find ways to allow citizens to opt in or out of the system as it becomes more pervasive. How that will happen is not now obvious, but it is important in order to prevent a public rejection.

14.1 The Server Farm

Software is becoming webified: Computer programs from word-processing and e-mail to corporate receivables and payables are going online. **Google** offers Gmail and features of office software. **Microsoft** is planning to offer its Office products online. It is making a shift from a traditional software model, with low capital costs and substantial margins, to the **software-as-services** model.

The transition to software-as-services is a business challenge: Instead of collecting big one-time payments for software, software services companies receive subscription revenue that trickles in over a longer period of time. The biggest challenge lies in building and maintaining the kind of infrastructure needed to distribute software, news, games, entertainment, information, and other content, and to provide storage on the Internet. To handle this change, the large companies are building their own data centers known as **server farms.**

Microsoft is constructing a 1.4-million-square-foot server and storage campus. **Yahoo** has a 50 acre site ready for development. Google has a 30 acre site under development. Google's facility will contain some, although not all, of the estimated half to one million servers that the company expects to operate in the near term as it services about 2.7 billion expected searches daily.

New microprocessors can process more data than current machines but at the cost of generating significantly more heat. That means greater air conditioning expense and more electricity consumption for power. In fact, Microsoft and Yahoo are locating their server farms close to hydroelectric power generation in Washington State. It is not unusual for a business that operates a server farm to spend a dollar on cooling for every dollar spent to power computers.

The End of the Computer Terminal As data and programs become centralized in server farms, the number and size of computers as we know them may shrink. Computers are going to be absorbed by their surroundings and embedded in carpets, magazines, radios, socks, and even in us. As networked computing disappears into the environment, it will become as ubiquitous as the electricity flowing through society. Some call this blanket a **digital skin,** which will transmit signals over the Internet almost as if it were alive. Billions, even trillions, of sensors will monitor streets, schools, factories, forests, oceans, the atmosphere, and people.

The Flash Drive Personal computing is likely to change, too. A simple tool, the flash drive, will allow us to carry our data and documents and process it wherever we find an

Internet appliance. Today **flash drives** using **flash memory** store five or more GB of data. 50, 100 and even 500 GB capacity is not far off. Internet appliances will offer banks of flash drive ports. With no flash drive plugged in, the device is simply a public Internet appliance allowing Internet browsing, checking e-mail, and sending messages. With a flash drive plugged in the appliance runs your preferred operating system and processes your data using your favorite programs obtained from server farms.

Security will be provided as the entire flash drive's content is **encrypted.** Internet server farms will provide storage space for compressed backup copies of encrypted data in case of flash drive malfunction or theft.

14.2 Hardware Advances

Moore's Law suggests that the number of electronic devices put on a microprocessor doubles every eighteen months. It has been predicted that Moore's Law will soon reach its end because of the physical limitations in miniaturization of **silicon** microprocessors and memories. The fabrication process used to pack transistors onto a chip is called deep-ultraviolet lithography (DUVL). It is a technique that focuses light through lenses to carve circuit patterns on silicon wafers. It has approached the transistor density limit that it is capable of. Extreme-ultraviolet lithography (EUVL) is a newer but temporary measure to extend the use of silicon-based technologies for several to ten or so years. EUVL uses mirrors instead of lenses to focus the light, which allows light with shorter wavelengths to accurately focus on the silicon wafer. With shorter wavelengths light can carve smaller gaps between transistors and therefore increase chip density.

EUVL, like DUVL, is well understood to have physical limits and two of the more interesting emerging technologies that might replace silicon-based computing are DNA computers and quantum computers.

- **DNA Computers** — There are several advantages to using DNA instead of silicon:
  - The large supply of DNA makes it a cheap resource.
  - DNA biochips can be made cleanly without use of toxic materials as used with silicon chip production.
  - DNA computers would be many times smaller than silicon-based computers while at the same time increasing speed and storage capacity.

  It is believed that one pound of DNA has the capacity to store more information than all the electronic computers ever built. The computing power of a pea-sized DNA computer should be more powerful than the world's most powerful supercomputer.

  Unlike current conventional silicon-based computers, DNA computers could perform calculations simultaneously. Conventional computers are linear, performing one task at a time. In conventional personal computers multitasking is an illusion performed by operating systems as computers process only one program at a time. Rapidly allocating time-slices to individual programs fosters the illusion. It is **parallel computing** that will allow DNA to solve complex mathematical problems like economic and weather forecasting in seconds — problems that might take conventional computers several hours to complete.

- **Quantum Computers** – Today's conventional computers work by manipulating bits that exist in one of two states: 0 or 1. Quantum computers are not limited to two states; they encode information as quantum bits, or **qubits.** A qubit can be a 1 or a 0, or it can exist as 1 and 0 simultaneously or somewhere in between. Qubits represent atoms working together to serve as processor and computer memory. Since a quantum computer can contain multiple states simultaneously it can process in parallel and has the potential to be millions of times more powerful than today's most powerful supercomputers.

Printing To a computer and a printer the instruction to describe what colors to print is a set of numbers and characters that are obscure and technical. People ascribe words not numbers or commands to mean colors. Words like, "that basket in the photo is reddish orange," "that egg is light blue," "that car is brilliant yellow." The computer uses other commands to represent human adjustments to color shades like "a tad lighter", or "a bit darker", or "a whole lot brighter". People think in words but computers use command values to drive devices like printers.

Companies like **Xerox** are working on software technology that will employ **speech recognition** software to accept human speech and translate it into print commands. The command, "Make the moon a brighter white," might be translated to CIELAB[88, -3, 64]. As with many newly emerging **computer interfaces,** there are problems to be worked out. For example, the command "Make the green brighter" might mean "Make the green crisper," or "Make the green sharper" to another person. "Make the blue deeper" might cause the sky, a dress, and the ocean in an image to all become deeper or darker. The software does not yet have the intelligence to differentiate at that level.

3D Printing Researchers are devising ways to ship data through networks to manufacture products remotely. Printers called **personal fabricators** will be used to make things like toys, dishes, and wine glasses. 3D printers are now making semiconductor and transistor models. Three-dimensional objects can be printed on machines like **Z Corporation**'s ZPrinter using designs from **CAD** (computer aided design) files. The printer uses special ink and prints one layer of an object at a time. After the layers are printed a chemical process heats the layers and they melt as if in a mold – a 3D object the CAD diagrams define emerges. These printers exist today. 3D printing is a category of **rapid prototyping** technology and is used to model new products. Eventually it is expected to be used in the home to produce 3D objects as needed.

14.3 Computers and the Environment

The most extensive environmental observations will come from satellite-based remote sensors in space. Scientists at NASA envision robust flows of environmental data coming from grids of networked satellites orbiting the Earth. A number of satellites are already monitoring the global environment now specifically collecting data about clouds, temperature, vegetation, and radiation. One of the most common applications for satellite images involves linking them to Geographic Information Systems (**GIS**), a combination used to study global land use patterns; map population migrations; track oil spills, forest fires, and deforestation; and monitor the health of oceans.

Satellite sensors will comprise only part of a broader distributed network – the infrastructure must be changed to support the explosion of data expected to be generated and transported. Billions of low-cost devices embedded throughout the environment will add to the data-management challenge. Researchers are also working on ways to transfer intelligence to the sensors themselves. This approach is based on a technology called **intelligent multitasking.** Embedded intelligence would eliminate the need for a centralized data processing facility. Each sensor would carry a microcomputer and communications abilities, providing for **collaborative signal processing** and **data sharing** and the ability to make **group decisions.** Sensors in an industrial setting could be designed to respond to toxic releases and spills, perhaps by shutting down a factory process. If the release extended beyond factory perimeters, local sensors would communicate with networked municipal sensors, in turn, initiating a series of protective actions directly within the community.

Eventually, remote sensing data will be accessible to the ordinary citizen on the street. Someone with a handheld wireless device will likely someday be able to access satellite data from the Internet, overlay it with GIS coordinates, and obtain on-the-spot weather information for any location on Earth. Homes in the future may link to weather data from online sources and monitor and control their own internal environments accordingly. The key to all these applications is they will take humans out of the loop—the sensor networks will be intelligent, proactive, and able to respond to environmental changes without human intervention at lightning speed.

The promise of real-time data flowing over self-managing networks could offer a major boost in the future to environmental protection. How do chemical pollutants move through oceans and the atmosphere? Can we link local ecological changes to changes in the global environment? Scientists investigating environmental questions now rely on computer models and incomplete databases of observed data. The deployment of small, networked, self-powered sensors that communicate with each other could set up **dynamic databases** that reduce the uncertainty in these ecological analyses. With better information will come better decision making, and with that, perhaps environmental policies that are more responsive to ecological needs.

Smart Dust Much of the research driving small, inexpensive sensors is found in the area of micro-electromechanical systems or MEMS. MEMS technology is used now to build silicon-based devices, some of them smaller than blood cells. Researchers are developing a sensor called **smart dust** designed to be so small that it floats in the air. The idea is to use them in great quantity, connected by networks, communicating with each other using wireless signals. The environmental possibilities are numerous: sprinkled out of airplanes monitoring the atmosphere or hovering inside factory smokestacks monitoring pollution, or used in farms measuring pesticide levels and soil chemistry. Smart dust is powered by batteries which contain toxic metals like lead and cadmium. This raises environmental concerns because dust travelling through the atmosphere might leave toxic deposits when the batteries fail.

Geographic Information System GIS is a system for collecting, storing, managing, and analyzing data and associated attributes which are referenced to locations on the Earth. Geographic information system technology can be used for sales tracking and determining new marketing opportunities tied to geographic regions. A company could find potential new customers demographically similar to existing customers in established markets.

With a geographic information system information is linked to location data about people, forests, buildings, bodies of water, and streets. GIS can integrate and relate any data with a spatial component, regardless of the source of the data. The location of mobile service workers, located in real-time by GPS devices, can be mapped in relation to customer homes, located by an address obtained from a customer database. GIS maps this data, giving dispatchers a visual tool to plan the best routes for mobile staff or to send the closest worker to a customer.

In business, geographic information systems are used for these and other reasons:

- **Store Location** — Selection of store location blending geographic, economic, and marketing data.
- **Market Analysis** — Analysis of demographic-geographic mix to help select new markets.

- **Agribusiness** — Used to determining the correct amount of fertilizers or pesticides needed at each point of a cultivated field.

Government use of GIS includes:

- **Local** — Placement of firehouses and police stations.
- **State** — Redistricting political boundaries.
- **Regional** — Determination of areas affected by pollution from neighboring regions.
- **Military** — Use of GIS for applications including cartography, intelligence, battle field management, terrain analysis, remote sensing, military installation management and monitoring of possible terrorist activity.

Recently there has been an explosion of mapping applications on the Web such as **Google Maps, MapQuest, Yahoo! Maps,** and **Rand McNally.** These Web sites give the public access to huge amounts of geographic data with an emphasis on street maps and aerial photography. Google Maps exposes an API (application program interface) that enables developers to create custom applications with street maps and aerial imagery.

While GIS has application in many areas including public health, transportation and logistics, real estate, national defense, crime mapping, natural resource planning, landscape architecture, and regional and community planning it is also becoming a **location-based service** (LBS). LBS data allows GPS enabled mobile devices to display their location in relation to fixed objects (nearest fire hydrant, restaurant, or gas station) and mobile objects (fire truck, children, or friends) to relay their position back to a central server for display or other processing.

14.4 Evolvable Hardware

Evolvable hardware (EH) is hardware that can change its architecture and behavior dynamically by autonomously interacting with its environment. EH brings together reconfigurable hardware with the fields of artificial intelligence, system fault tolerance, and autonomous systems.

Why Evolve Circuits? An existing circuit may need to adapt, alter its configuration, to compensate for faults or perhaps changes to the operational environment. For instance, space probes may encounter sudden high radiation environments, which alter a circuit's performance; the circuit must autonomously adapt to restore as much of the circuit's original behavior as possible.

Evolvable hardware falls into two categories:

- **Original Design** — Uses evolutionary development techniques to design a system that meets a specific predefined specification.
- **Adaptive Systems** — Reconfigure an existing design to counteract faults or a changed operational environment.

Adaptable Circuit **Hewlett-Packard** is researching the possibility of adaptable circuits that can be modified in products after a product has been sold and has been in use. Chips of this technology could be installed in printer cartridges and adapted as directed by an operating system to conform to the particular requirements of a printer the cartridge is used in. The impact to a cartridge manufacture like H-P would be the development of lower cost cartridges that could be used in a greater variety of printers.

14.5 Quantum Computing

Building a quantum computer is still very, very hard to do. Quantum computers could one day replace silicon chips, just as transistors replaced the vacuum tube in second generation computers. For now, the technology required to develop such a quantum computer is mostly beyond our reach. Research in quantum computing is generally still very theoretical.

The most advanced quantum computers have not gone beyond manipulating more than 16 qubits, meaning that they are far from practical application. However, the potential remains that quantum computers one day could quickly and easily perform calculations that are incredibly time-consuming on conventional computers.

If functional quantum computers can be built, they may be valuable in several ways:

- **Encryption** — Quantum computers could factor very large numbers, and therefore would be extremely useful for decoding and encoding secret information. If one were to be built today, all information on the Internet would be safe. Our current methods of encryption are simple compared to the complicated processing methods possible in quantum computers.
- **Database Search** — Quantum computers could also be used to search large databases in a fraction of the time that it would take a conventional computer.
- **Molecular Modeling** — Part of the promise of quantum computers is their ability to model how molecules react in contact with others. Quantum computing can calculate the interaction of different molecules that cannot be modeled using conventional computers. Applied this way, the traditional laboratory experiments of live animal and human testing would be eliminated.
- **Optimization Problems** — Most real-life business problems (logistics, production, and engineering) require that all possible solutions must exhaustively be tried when solving the problem. These problems involve allocating limited resources to minimize cost and defects or maximize production or profit. Conventional algorithms cannot solve these problems well so the approach often taken is to devise methods for gaining answers which are good enough for the given application. These approaches are called **heuristics** and include **genetic algorithms.** Quantum computers can be used to calculate approximate complete solutions to large exhaustive problems more quickly than the best-known methods running today on any supercomputer.
- **Other Applications** — Quantum computers could be used to study quantum mechanics, or even to design other quantum computers.

But quantum computing is still in its early stages of development, and many computer scientists believe the technology needed to create a practical quantum computer is years away. It is believed that quantum computers must have at least several dozen **qubits** to be able to solve real-world problems. The sixteen qubit accomplishment of today is not yet even close.

It has been shown in theory that a quantum computer will be able to perform any task that a classical computer can. However, this does not necessarily mean that a quantum computer will outperform a classical computer for all types of task. If we use classical algorithms on a quantum computer, the calculation would be performed in a fashion similar to a classical computer. In order for a quantum computer to show its true performance it needs to use new algorithms which can exploit **quantum parallelism.** This means that conventional programming techniques must be changed to optimize the use of quantum processors.

Classical computers can do the same computations as quantum computers, only needing more time and more memory. The catch is that they need exponentially more time and memory to match the power of a quantum computer. It is not expected that silicon-based technology has sufficient stretch to meet this demand.

14.6 Nanocomputing

Over the last few decades computer power has grown at an astonishing rate, doubling every couple of years. This increase is essentially due to the continued miniaturization of a computer's most elementary electronic component, the **transistor.** As transistors become smaller more can be integrated into a single microchip, and so computational power increases. This miniaturization process is now reaching a limit. There is a quantum threshold below which transistors will not function. Present state-of-the-art components possess features only a few hundreds of nanometers across (a billionth of a meter), if these chips were to be miniaturized further to the scale of tens of nanometers then their operation would be disrupted. The emergence of quantum activity, such as electrons traveling through the barriers between wires, would disturb operations. If the science of computation is to progress further an alternative to silicon-based transistor technology must be found. It will be necessary to develop components that will function through quantum effects rather than in despite of them.

14.6.1 Nano-Medicine

Nanocomputers are small enough that several hundred of them could fit inside the space of a human cell. Medical nano-monitors, known as **nanites,** could patrol your body, and provided with a database of your DNA information, could repel foreign invaders by forming an artificial immune system. The common cold would no longer exist; neither would threats of any biological or viral infection. Biological warfare would then cease to be a danger.

Nanites, which are composed of smart materials, could replace plastic surgeons and people would be able to remake their bodies as desired and even often. There would be no surgery, no bruises, the results would be overnight, and there would be no recovery needed. Nanites could replace the oxygen in your blood in case of fire or chemical spill, and allow people to walk away from normally fatal accidents. Nanites are expected to interact directly with muscles enabling movement otherwise impossible because of signals blocked by damaged and diseased nerves.

Aging is the real number one killer of humans. With new emerging genetic therapies it is hoped that the aging process can be reversed. With medical nanites, it is expected that we cannot only extend our lives but stop the aging process completely.

14.7 Optical Computing

An optical computer uses light instead of electricity to manipulate, store, and transmit data. Light photons, pulses of light energy, have fundamentally different physical properties than electrons, and researchers have attempted to make use of these properties to produce computers with performance and capabilities greater than those of electronic computers. Researchers are testing new conducting polymers to make transistor-like switches smaller and 1,000 times faster than silicon-based transistors. Optical computer technology is in the very early stages: functional optical computers have been built in the laboratory, but none have progressed past beyond the prototype stage.

Most research projects are aimed at replacing current computer components with optical equivalents, resulting in optical digital hybrid-computer systems for processing data. This approach appears to offer the best short-term prospects for commercial optical computing since optical components could be integrated into traditional computers. Development of complete optical computers is further off.

The fundamental building block of modern electronic computers is the transistor. To replace electronic components with optical ones, an equivalent **optical transistor** is required. In these devices the intensity of incoming light affects the intensity of the light transmitted through the material and the output to the next circuit. This is similar to the manner in which input voltages affect an electronic transistor's output voltage.

Optics can reduce power consumption. In a communication system optical circuits will typically use more power over short distances than electronic components would. Over longer distances and at greater data rates the power loss in conventional electrical lines is sufficiently large that optical communications will save power and provide cleaner data transport.

14.8 Bots

Eventually, future e-markets could become so complex, with so many participants and competing market variables, that human involvement could be a hindrance. Researchers and software companies have set hopes on so-called **software agents,** which learn about their user interests and act independently on the user's behalf. Autonomous e-markets of the future may find billions of software agents, representing the interests of users, processing data and disseminating information to humans and to other agents. Agents will **evolve** from facilitators to decision makers, as their degree of autonomy and responsibility increases with time. It is generally believed that ultimately transactions among software agents will become an essential portion of the world economy.

To computer scientists, particularly specialists in artificial intelligence, agents are nothing new. Researchers have been trying to build prototype agents for several decades. A number of primitive versions are in commercial use today sorting and filtering e-mail and responding to Web site inquiries. These agents, while somewhat useful, rely on the initiative and technical ability of the user. More advanced commercial agents called **bots** (from robots) is now being designed to reside on the Web and perform tasks that compare prices for online retail items or disable viruses online before they infect your computer. Researchers expect that agents will become robust and adaptive, learn from experience and will respond to unexpected situations with an array of different methods. An ideal agent would sense the current state of its environment and act independently toward its goal. Agents are software implementations and could presumably be embedded in microscopic computers that patrol the environment or human bodies.

14.9 Summary

It is a bit more than a decade since the widespread introduction of the graphical user interfaces which revolutionized computer use by opening the door for people unable or afraid to use older and more arcane computer command syntax. Then as now, however, common computer use remains in the realm of word-processing, messaging, data analysis, and imaging.

It is in this time period that the Internet, and the Web which it enabled, blossomed and prompted the wide interest in computing that we now observe. The near-term evolution of networked computing seems clear as applications and data are moved online to server farms and as computers shrink and become more mobile.

The quest for increased computer power and communication potential is pushing the physical limits of what it is possible to fabricate using conventional silicon-based technology. DNA, quantum and optical computer architectures are developing as alternatives. Each offers the potential for extreme miniaturization and high performance. None is yet ready for commercial application.

The potential of high speed, microscopic, networked processors and memories excites many people. Airborne atmospheric sensors, sharing data world-wide, would enable environmental protection on a scale not presently imagined. Intelligent monitors in the human body could alert doctors and a person's immune system when action is needed. Human bodies could possibly be automatically repaired and paralysis could possibly be overcome.

As hardware shrinks, and becomes more pervasive, evolving circuits could extend the usefulness of machines by allowing adaptation to changing environmental conditions. Software bots, embedded in these machines, and fuelled by the processing speed and data access of networked nano-machines, will serve as agents representing the interests of human users.

To many, these emerging technologies are science fiction and maybe they are right. It is worth remembering for a moment at least that the technologies of today were the science fictions of the past.

EXERCISES

Exercise 14.1

What does ubiquitous computing mean?

Exercise 14.2

What technology enables tagging products? How could it be used to harm personal privacy?

Exercise 14.3

How might the personal computer be replaced by a flash drive connected to an Internet appliance? What concern about privacy might this architecture raise?

Exercise 14.4

What is Moore's Law and why might it no longer predict the future of technological expansion? What must be done to overcome the limit that Moore's Law is facing?

Exercise 14.5

Why is the physical location of a server farm important? Discuss this from three perspectives.

Exercise 14.6

What is evolvable hardware? What impact might it have on the development and marketing of new technologies?

Exercise 14.7

What is smart dust? The technology is identified with environmental monitoring but could it be used in other applications? Suggest three non-environmental uses for smart dust.

Exercise 14.8

What is a DNA computer? What would it look like and what types of problems might it solve? How practical is this emerging technology?

Exercise 14.9

What is a software agent? Creatively invent three applications of software agents that would be useful to you.

Exercise 14.10

How might quantum computing contribute to enhanced encryption?

Exercise 14.11

What is a geographic information system? What data does it process? Invent and describe three applications in which GIS would be central.

Exercise 14.12

How might 3D printing be used? Invent and describe three applications for the home and three for business.

Exercise 14.13

What is a nanite? What can they do? What are they fabricated from?

Exercise 14.14

What is intelligent multitasking? What use might that technology enable?

Exercise 14.15

What is optical computing? When considering emerging computer technology, why does optical computing have the greatest short-term potential?

Exercise 14.16

Why might software as services present a challenge to the software industry? In addition to Microsoft, identify two software companies which might be adversely affected. Suggest strategies they could employ to protect themselves.

Exercise 14.17

Imagine that you are a venture capitalist with several million dollars to invest. You believe in the promise of emerging technology. Select five technologies to invest in and justify your choices. What portion of your investment would be allocated to each technology that you selected?

GLOSSARY

10base T A twisted-pair cable used for Ethernet.

A

Action An action is the response to an event that a program is directed to perform.

Ajax Asynchronous JavaScript and XML, is a Web development technique designed to make Web pages appear to operate more like programs found on the user's computer

Anti-Spyware Anti spyware programs are designed to remove or block spyware.

Anti-Virus Software Anti-virus software is computer programs that attempt to identify, stop and eliminate (erase or quarantine) computer viruses and other malicious software (malware).

Application Service Provider A business that provides computer-based services to customers over a network.

Array A list of data elements (or objects) that are of the same data type (number, string, date, etc.) and occupy a predetermined quantity of contiguous memory.

Artificial Intelligence Computer programs that can engage in human-like reasoning.

ASCII The ASCII code set represents each letter (upper and lower case), digit, punctuation and special character as a specific sequence of bits in an eight bit per byte system,

ASP ASP, which stands for Active Server Page, is Microsoft's server-side script engine for dynamically generated Web pages.

Assembly Language Shorthand for machine language.

Atanasoff-Berry Computer The Atanasoff-Berry Computer (ABC) was the first electronic digital computing device.

Avatar An avatar is an electronic image that represents something or someone and is manipulated by a computer user.

AVI Audio Video Interleave, known by its acronym AVI, is a multimedia video format with minimal compression and excellent quality.

B

Babbage Charles Babbage is considered to be the father of the computer.

Backup Involves copying data and programs so that these copies may be restored in the event of a system loss or data corruption.

Bandwidth Bandwidth is the measure of a channel's capacity.

BASIC Early programming language: It was originally designed in 1963 at Dartmouth College to enable shared access to the school's limited computer resource,

Binary All programs ultimately must be represented in the computer's memory (RAM) as a sequence of binary digits (1 and 0). Digital computers are binary machines, so only two states are possible: on and off. O

Binary Search In a binary search some index records are examined and some are ignored. This strategy successively divides the index records into two equal parts: Those records that might contain the target index value and those records that do not contain the target index value.

BIOS The Basic Input/Output System (BIOS) is a small program run by a computer when first powered on. Its primary function is to stabilize the machine and devices on the motherboard so that the operating system can be loaded and take control of the computer.

Bit A logical data value may be 0 or 1. Sometimes a bit is said to take on the values True or False.

Bluetooth A specific radio frequency wireless connection limited to very short distances.

Bots Software agents which learn about their user interests and act independently on the user's behalf.

Bps Bits Per Second. The number of bits transmitted per second.

Braille Keyboard Braille keyboards have Braille symbols on top of each key. The typist's feel of the keys ensure pressing the proper keys.

Branching In programming decisions are often determined by evaluating a data value and then taking a branch based on the outcome.

Browser A web browser is an application that enables the user to retrieve, display and interact with web pages provided by a server.

B-tree A data structure well-suited for implementation of binary database indexes,

Bus A bus is a subsystem of the motherboard that transfers data or power between computer components inside a computer or between a computer and external components which are typically controlled by device driver software.

Bus Topology The bus topology involves a single cable (bus) that all computers and other devices are connected to but it is not connected in a loop as in the ring topology.

Byte A unit of data storage consisting of 8 bits. It represents a single character, digit or punctuation.

Bytecode Interpreter A compromise between compiling and interpretation is a partial translation that yields what is known as bytecode. The translation is not into machine code that is native to any particular processor, but instead an efficient platform independent representation of the program is produced .

C

C Programming language: allows the programmer excellent communication with the operating system and with hardware devices.

C# An object-oriented programming language developed by Microsoft as part of their .NET initiative.

C++ Programming language: an object oriented derivative of C.

Cache Memory It is used as a buffer to reduce the time of data transfer between the processor and devices like the monitor and storage devices.

Cardinality The quantification of the relationship among database tables in known as cardinality.

CASE Computer Aided Software Engineering, usually abbreviated CASE, is the use of programs to assist in the analysis of requirements and the design, development and maintenance of software.

Centralized Processing One computer system handles all of the data processing responsibilities for the organization.

Chat Room A chat room or chartroom is a term used primarily by mass media to describe any form of synchronous conferencing.

Checkdisk Checkdisk is a program that scans the file directories and searches for errors within files.

CIO The Chief Information Officer is the top IS position in an organization.

Class A blueprint, base, or prototype from which objects are created.

Client-Server Client-server is an architecture which typically revolves around a network (although a network is not required) and separates the client (the consumer of data and other resources) from the server (which distributes those resources).

Coaxial Cable This type of cable delivers high-speed transmission, which is relatively free from outside noise.

Cobol Its name is an acronym, for COmmon Business Oriented Language, and is primarily of use in business and administrative applications.

Codec It is a device or program capable of performing encoding and decoding on a digital data stream or signal.

Communication Channel A communication channel is an electronic or optical highway that carries a communication signal between computers or other electronic devices.

Compatibility Mode Compatibility mode allows content created in Office 2007 to be converted or downgraded to a form that can be used by previous versions of Office.

Compiler Translates Source Code to Binary Machine Code

Computer A machine that can be programmed to accept data and process it into useful information.

Computer Based Information System When an Information System involves a computer it is a computer based information system (CBIS).

Computer Crime Computer crime is theft of computer resources. It could range from illegal or unauthorized use of a computer to theft of data to destruction or alteration of data or programs.

Computer Literacy Computer literacy is the broad understanding of the technology and its applications.

Computer Program A computer program is a series of commands that instructs the computer how to process data.

Condition A question with two (and only two) possible outcomes is known as a condition. All binary questions are conditions and all result in two possible outcomes: True (or Yes or 1) or False (or No or 0).

Context for Data The process of providing a context for data is known as data processing and that is the fundamental activity of an information system.

Control Panel The Control Panel is the doorway to control of hundreds of the computer's individual components.

Cookie An HTTP (Hypertext Transfer Protocol) cookie consists of a piece of data stored in a text file on a user's computer.

Copy Protection Any technical measure designed to prevent unauthorized duplication of information.

CPU The central processing unit (CPU), also called the processor, is the critical component in a digital computer that processes data by executing instructions that are contained in computer programs.

CSS A cascading style sheet (CSS) is a plain text file with style rules stored in it. Style rules are the formatting directives followed by the browser while rendering the document for display.

Cursor As the mouse moves around a pointer, known as the cursor, moves on the computer screen reflecting the physical movements of the mouse.

D

Data Data are facts and can be thought of as raw material.

Data Compression Compression techniques are used to reduce the number of bytes required to store certain kinds of data. Compression is also used to permit faster transmission of data between computers.

Data Integration The use of different software tools to share data from multiple sources among users and applications.

Data Mining Analysis of data from different perspectives and its summarization into useful information.

Data Model Data modeling is the process of designing structures for organizing data. The data structures are created in a database which is controlled by a DBMS.

Data Redundancy Data redundancy causes several significant problems and should be avoided: extra storage space is required, Processing takes longer, data integrity errors may occur.

Data Structure An arrangement of storing data in a computer's memory (primary and secondary) so that it can be used reliably and efficiently.

Data Validation Ensuring that data is of the correct type (date, number, character) as it is entered or edited. Validation also involves checking data values against acceptable lists or ranges.

Data Values Data can be expressed in two ways: constant values and variables that hold values.

Data Warehouse Repository of an organization's data.

Database A database is a collection of data that is of interest to people in support of decision making and record management activities. A DBMS is required to manipulate the data.

Database Administrator The DBA has jurisdiction over the organization's data storage and works with database management systems, and determines ways to organize and store data.

DBMS A database management system (DBMS) is a computer application designed to manage a database.

Decentralized Processing Each part of an organization does its own data processing. Each unit is totally independent of the others. Programs and data are not shared.

Decision Support System A Decision Support System (DSS) is used to support higher level decision-making. Often a DSS will integrate organizational data with models that are used to predict organizational outcomes.

Decision Tree A tool that uses a graph to model decisions and their possible consequences.

Defragment a Disk Defragmenting a disk involves scanning the entire disk drive and consolidating unused disk area into larger areas of contiguous space for the storage of larger files.

Delimiter A character that is used to separate column headers and data values in a text file.

Denial of Service A denial of service attack is described as an aggressive attempt to prevent legitimate users of a service from using that service or the server it is installed on.

De-skilling Reduction in skills required for a particular job.

DFD A data flow diagram (DFD) is a graphical representation of the movement of data through an information system.

Digital Dashboard A visual information display tool that is based on the metaphor of a car's dashboard and its instruments.

Digital Signature Digital signatures, like written signatures, are used to provide authentication of the associated input, usually called a message.

Disaster Recovery A disaster recovery plan should be created and periodically tested. Perform dry runs to make sure that the organization knows how to deal with disaster.

Disaster Recovery Plan A plan for regaining access to data, computer systems, and software to resume operations after a disaster.

Disintermediation The removal of supply chain intermediaries/

Distributed Processing Computers are linked together in a network. Data processing responsibilities for the organization are handled by local parts of the organization where data originates and is most frequently accessed.

DNA Computer Biological computing device.

DOCTYPE Declaration The DOCTYPE declaration informs the browser of what type of document the browser is about to render and therefore how to treat the document.

Domain Name Service Domain Name Service (DNS) performs the translation of URLs into numeric IP addresses.

DSL Digital Subscriber Line (DSL) is a family of technologies that provide digital data transmission over the wires of a local telephone network.

DTD To ensure that data in an XML document is valid a Data Type Definition (DTD) or a schema is used.

E

E-commerce E-commerce or electronic commerce is business focused on using the Internet and other electronic technologies as a channel through with to communicate and negotiate with customers.

Electronic Data Interchange EDI is the computer-to-computer interchange of structured information.

Electronic Data Processing Electronic Data Processing (EDP) systems were the first data processing applications. Here computer hardware and software were employed to automate repetitive tasks.

Electronic Funds Transfer EFT provides for payments and collection of receipts using electronic networks and equipment.

Encapsulation The process of shielding an object's implementation details from the programmer.

Encryption Encryption involves disguising data before it is transmitted over a network. Data is decrypted at the receiving end. Encrypted data is harder for an intruder to intercept and comprehend.

ENIAC ENIAC, the abbreviation for Electronic Numerical Integrator and Computer, is usually considered to be the first modern, general purpose computer.

ERD An Entity Relationship Diagram (ERD) represents the objects of a database and the relationships that connect them.

Ergonomics Sometimes known as human factors, is the scientific application of information about humans to the design of objects, systems ,and environments that humans use and interact with.

ERP Enterprise Resource Planning systems (ERPs) integrate the data and data processing activities of a government, business or other organization into a single system.

Ethernet IEEE 802.3. The Ethernet standard defines a network with no centralized server. Individual nodes control what is transmitted without external governance.

Event An event is a recognizable action that occurs in computer software or hardware that a program can be directed to respond to. The most common event is a mouse click.

Evolvable Circuits A circuit that may adapt, alter its configuration, to compensate for faults or perhaps changes to the operational environment.

Executive Information System Executive Information System (EIS) is really an extension of a DSS. Here, external data (economic, industry specific, governmental) is integrated with organizational data. Decisions made with support of an EIS often are one time only decisions.

Expert Systems An expert or knowledge-based system blends subject-specific knowledge with the knowledge and analytical skills of human experts.

Extranet Used by a group of organizations to provide communication among their members.

F

Favorite Center The Favorite Center in Internet Explorer provides a consolidated place form which to access favorite websites, RSS feeds, and browsing history.

Feedback Output from an information system used as input in a subsequent round of processing.

Fiber Optics The transmission medium is light waves. Since the signal is being carried by light data travels at the speed of light which is extremely fast.

Fiber Optics The transmission medium is the glass or plastic cable itself that is transparent and carries light waves.

File Association The linkage between a file and the program required to process the document is known as the file association. Associations are implemented using file extensions.

File Extension The file extension (the part of a filename after the period or dot) describes the type of file.

File Organization When deciding how to organize your data consideration must be given to ease of use and efficiency of data retrieval.

File Path A file path describes the location of a file on a storage device.

File System This is the portion of the operating system that manages files (documents) on storage devices. Typical operations include copy, delete, rename, move, open, etc.

Firefox Mozilla Firefox is a graphical Web browser developed by the Mozilla Corporation and has a large community of external contributors.

Firewall A firewall is used to limit access to a computer's open ports. Firewalls are hardware or software functioning in a networked environment engineered to prevent forbidden communication.

FireWire FireWire is used for fast data transfer with peripheral devices.

Flash Memory Flash memory is solid state (an integrated circuit) and not rotational like a disk

Flowchart A flowchart is graphical representation used to illustrate the logical steps to be performed by a process.

Folder A folder holds icons for a group of related objects.

Font The style of characters printed or displayed on a monitor. Font is also known as typeface.

Forecasting Forecasting is a statistical technique used to predict future values based on the relationship among values that have been already observed.

Foreign Key A foreign key is the column in a database table that references another table's records by pointing toward a matching primary key value in the other table.

Formatting Formatting involves changing the appearance of data.

Formula A formula describes the steps followed to perform a computation.

Fortran The first third generation programming language.

Free Software License A software license which grants recipients rights to modify and redistribute the software which would otherwise be prohibited by copyright law. Open source software is licensed and distributed this way.

FTP Short for File Transfer Protocol, FTP is the protocol for exchanging files over the Internet.

Full Duplex A full duplex line permits data to flow in both directions at the same time.

Function A function is a portion of program code that performs a predefined activity. In Excel, a function is used to perform calculations that Excel knows how to do like sum, standard deviation, average and lookups.

G

Gateway An entrance from one network to another to another network.

Geographic Information System GIS is a system for collecting, storing, managing, and analyzing data and associated attributes which are referenced to locations on the Earth.

GIF Suitable for sharp-edged line art (such as logos). This takes advantage of the format's lossless compression which preserves very sharp edges (in contrast to JPEG). GIFs are used for small animations and low resolution film clips.

Gigabits per Second One billion bits per second.

Gigabyte A unit of data storage consisting of about 1000 megabytes or a billion bytes.

Gigahertz One billion hertz.

Goal Seeking Goal Seeking is a technique available in Excel to determine what input values are required in obtaining a per-determined outcome.

Graphical User Interface The Graphical User Interface (GUI) is a collection of icons, menus, buttons and other graphical representations of objects that the user manipulates with hardware like a mouse or touch screen.

H

Hacker A computer programmer specializing in the discovery of exploits in systems, or in obtaining unauthorized access to systems through skills, tactics, and detailed knowledge of vulnerabilities.

Half Duplex Data flows in both directions on a line but not at the same time.

Hardware The physical part of the computer. All computing, communication and peripheral equipment is hardware.

Hertz A unit of frequency describing the number of electrical cycles that occur in a second. The speed of a computer's processor is measured in hertz. The larger the number, generally the faster the microprocessor

History List This is the history of all Web sites you visited. It is maintained by the Web browser.

Hollerith Herman Hollerith designed a system for the U.S. Census Bureau that sorted and analyzed data stored on paper cards with holes representing data values.

HTML HTML is an abbreviation for a particular form of hypertext that is used to create web pages. The letters stand for Hypertext Markup Language.

HTTP Hypertext Transfer Protocol (HTTP) is a method used to transfer or convey information on the Internet. Its original purpose was to provide a way to publish and retrieve HTML pages.

HTTPS HTTPS is a scheme used for normal HTTP connections, but which signals the browser to use an added encryption layer for transmitted data.

Hub A device for connecting multiple lines together, making them act as a single segment.

Hyperlink A hyperlink (often referred to as simply a link), is a reference or navigation element in a document to another section of the same document, another document, or a specified section of another document, that automatically brings the referred information to the user's browser when the navigation element is selected (clicked).

Hypermedia Web pages are said to be hypermedia pages meaning that they could contain more than one type of data (text, images, sound, etc.).

Hypertext A hypertext document contains links to other documents. The links or jump points are known as hyperlinks and often appear as underlined words in a web page.

I

Icon Icons are graphical representations of objects: programs, documents, data files and folders (a collection of the other objects).

Identity Theft Identity theft occurs when someone uses someone else's personal information without their permission in an attempt to commit fraud or other crimes.

Index An index associates specific records with specific data values that someone might be searching for (like a person's last name, phone number or street address).

Inference Engine Used to determine new rules and data associations in a knowledgebase.

Information Handling There are four facets to Information Handling: data gathering, manipulation, analysis and presentation of results.

Information Overload This condition results from a rapid rate of growth in the amount of information available, while days remain 24 hours long.

Information Privacy The protection of data when transmitted, stored, and received over the structure of the Internet.

Information Security The process of preventing and detecting unauthorized use of your computer.

Information System An Information System (IS) is a set of components arranged to collect data, process it, and convert it into information.

Infrared Light rather than radio waves carries the signal.

Inheritance The process of defining new objects as descendents of existing objects.

Instant Messaging Instant messaging (IM) is a form of real-time communication between two or more people based on typed text.

Integrated Circuit An electronic circuit that combines numerous transistors and other electronic components and their connections in a single package thus eliminating the problems of distance between components.

Internet The Internet is a worldwide network of computers connected by high-speed telephone and other communication links. It is also known as a network of networks.

Internet Protocol Internet Protocol (IP) is the protocol responsible for handling the routing of the packets.

Internet Service Provider ISPs provide basic end-user access to the Internet.

Interpreter Interprets program code as the program is running.

Intranet Intranets are used by organizations to facilitate internal communication but present barriers to external access (inbound and outbound).

IP Address Every machine on the Internet has a unique identifying number, called an IP Address.

IPO Model The relationship between data and information is often summarized in the Input–Process–Output (IPO) model. In essence, an information system processes raw material into something that is useful to people following the steps of accepting input, processing it and creating output.

ISDN Integrated Services Digital Network (ISDN) is a circuit-switched telephone network system, designed to allow digital transmission of voice and data over ordinary telephone copper wires.

Iteration Often times it is desired to repeat the same operation on a list of cells or records. This is known as iteration and in a computer program loops are used to perform this operation.

J

Jacquard The Jacquard Loom, invented by Joseph Jacquard in 1801, used the holes punched in wooden cards to control the weaving of patterns in textiles. This loom was the first machine to use data stored as holes in punch cards to control a sequence of operations.

Java Java is a programming language different from other languages, It is compiled to bytecode for distribution allowing it to operate on different computer systems running different operating systems.

JavaScript Program code contained in a Web page and run on the client computer. Use of this language permits interactive control within a Web browser.

Join Joining tables is the operation that combines data from related database tables by matching primary and foreign key values.

JPEG The format most used for storing and transmitting photographs on the Web. It is preferred to formats such as GIF, which has a limit of 256 distinct colors that is considered insufficient for color photographs.

Justification Text justification is about the positioning of text in relation to the page's margin.

K

Keystroke Logging A technique embedded in some programs enabling the recording and reporting of the user's keystrokes.

Kilobits per Second One thousand bits per second.

Kilobyte A unit of data storage consisting of about one thousand bytes.

Kilohertz One thousand hertz.

Knowledgebase A collection of internal and external databases and data warehouses. It includes rules that define data associations; the rules are defined by metadata.

L

Landscape Mode When text is printed across the longer dimension (11) and from top to bottom (8.5) the orientation is known as landscape mode. Landscape mode is particularly useful if a document contains a table or otherwise requires wide display.

License A software license does not imply ownership of the software by the licensee, instead it grants the licensee rights to use the licensed software in compliance with the specific terms of the license.

Linked List A linear list of data elements (or objects) that is dynamically sized as a program is running depending on the immediate storage requirements of the program.

Linux A Unix-like computer operating system that is one of the most significant examples of open source development and free software.

Local Area Network Local area networks, LANs for short, are generally in a single geographical area.

Logic Logic is the step-by-step instructions for processing data. Logic follows a specific pattern.

Logical Operator A condition (or question) compares two values and determines if the comparison is true or false. The comparison is accomplished by way of using a logical operator.

Loops Often times it is desired to repeat the same operation on a list of cells or records. This is known as iteration and in a computer program loops are used to perform this operation.

Lovelace Ada Lovelace is often considered the first computer programmer.

M

Machine Language Machine language is the native language of the processor. It is completely expressed in binary meaning it is limited to a vocabulary of 0 and 1.

Macro Macros are used in Office 2007 programs as a way of recording a sequence of keystrokes that you likely wish to repeat.

Macro Recorder The Macro Recorder is like a tape recorder that records what it senses. It tracks the sequence of keystrokes, mouse clicks and menu selections in Excel or Word invoked to get a task completed.

Mail / Merge Mail / Merge involves merging an external mailing list with a document so that customized letters may be prepared for each person in the list.

Mainframe Mainframes are computers used mainly by large organizations like government agencies, large companies, universities, the military, and research laboratories for mission critical requirements.

Malware Malware, short for malicious software, refers to software applications designed to damage or disrupt a user's system.

Management Information System A Management Information System (MIS) is a step above EDP in complexity and value to the organization. MISs prepare management control reports on a regularly scheduled basis.

Mapping Linkage between the logical location of files in folders and the physical locations on a storage device.

Markup Markup is about the formatting commands that the browser follows when rendering an HTML document for view. for: Hypertext Markup Language.

Megabits per Second One million bits per second.

Megabyte A unit of data storage consisting of about one million bytes.

Megahertz One million hertz.

Merchant Account Allows a vendor to accept and process credit card payments.

Meta Language A meta language is a language used to make statements about other languages. XML is a meta language because it is used as the definition of other language syntaxes.

Metadata Data about data; used to facilitate the understanding and use of data.

Meta-Search Engine A search engine that sends user requests to several other search engines, and perhaps databases, and returns the results from each engine in one consolidated Web page.

Method An object's behavior.

Metropolitan Area Network A MAN usually networks together LANs in a region such as a city or college or corporate office campus.

Microprocessor The microprocessor (an integrated circuit that serves as a central processing unit or CPU in a computer system) made possible the development of the microcomputer, small, low-cost computers that could be owned by individuals and small businesses.

Microwave The use of radio to carry a communication signal.

Modem A modem is a device that modulates a carrier's signal to encode a computer's digital data, and later demodulates the signal to decode the data at the receiving end. The purpose is to produce a signal that can be transmitted easily and decoded to reproduce the original digital data.

Monitor A monitor, or video, is the device that displays data on its screen - it display signals generated by a computer as images on a screen.

Moore's Law Suggests that the number of electronic devices put on a microprocessor doubles every eighteen months.

Motherboard This is where the core components of a computer reside. A computer is typically constructed with the processor (CPU), main memory (RAM), and other basic components on the motherboard.

Mouse The mouse is a point and click interface for entering commands which works well in graphical environments.

MP3 An encoding format that uses a compression algorithm designed to greatly reduce the amount of data required to represent audio recording, yet still sound like a faithful reproduction of the original uncompressed audio.

MPEG A family of digital video compression standards.

Multidimensional Data Structure A multi-dimensional structure is arranged so that every data item is located and accessed based on the intersection of the dimension members which define that item.

Multidimensional Database Sometimes known as data aggregators combine data from multitude data sources.

Multimedia Media that uses multiple forms of information content (text, audio, graphics, animation, and video, interactivity) to inform or entertain the (user) audience.

Multiplex A multiplex configuration involves several computers sharing the same channel.

Multitasking Running several programs simultaneously is multitasking. This enables a computer's resources to be used more efficiently.

N

Nanites Medical nano-monitors of the future could patrol human bodies, and provided with a database of DNA information, could repel foreign invaders by forming an artificial immune system.

Nanocomputing Computers small enough that several hundred of them could fit inside the space of a human cell.

Network Adapter Card A network card, network adapter or NIC (network interface controller) is a piece of computer hardware designed to allow computers to communicate over a computer network.

Network Administrator Responsible for making sure that the data gets delivered to the right people at the right time.

Network Card A network card, network adapter or NIC (network interface controller) is a piece of computer hardware designed to allow computers to communicate over a computer network.

Network Neutrality Network neutrality is a broadband network free of restrictions on the kinds of equipment attached and the modes of communication allowed. No users would receive preferential access.

Non-Procedural Languages Tell a computer what (not how) to do.

Normalization The process of removing duplicated data from database tables.

Null Value In a record a missing data value is said to be a null value.

O

Object Most items stored in a computer are objects. Files, images, documents, databases and programs are objects. In PowerPoint the individual components found in each slide are known as objects.

Object A template for all instances that have identical behaviors and properties which are known as methods and properties.

Object Oriented Programming The concept of object-oriented programming or OOP is that a computer program is a collection of individual units (objects) that maintain their own data and behaviors.

Office Button The Office 2007 button, located on the top-left of the window, replaces the File menu and provides access to functionality common across all Office programs.

OLAP On Line Analytical Processing — Query processing system that provides a multidimensional view of data.

Open Source A development and distribution method for software that harnesses the power of collaboration, distributed peer review, and transparency of design.

Open Source Software This is software whose program source code is available under a copyright license that permits users to review, alter, and enhance the software, and redistribute it as modified.

Operating System A program to control hardware, present a user interface, manage files, and run other programs. It is the is the master program controlling all resources within a computer.

Optical Computer Uses light instead of electricity to manipulate, store, and transmit data.

P

Packet A packet is an electronic envelope that contains data and is transported from server to server until it reaches its destination.

Packet Sniffing Random samples of traffic data are examined and used to extrapolate information about Web traffic as a whole.

Packet-Switching Routing packets among servers and other devices while travelling through the Internet.

Paste Paste is an operation that places content in the Clipboard into a selected location in a document or the file system.

Paste Special This operation is available in Excel and allows additional control over the placement of Clipboard content in target destinations.

Path A file path describes the location of a file on a storage device.

PDF The Portable Document Format (PDF) was created by Adobe Systems, Inc and uses the PostScript printer description language making it highly portable across computer platforms.

Peer-to-Peer Direct connection between computers that avoids use of servers.

Phishing Phishing is an attempt to trick a person into giving away their private account information by confirming it at the phisher's website.

PHP PHP is a scripting language that generally runs on a web server host. PHP programs generally produce web page output in response to client requests of a server.

Pivot Table A pivot table is used to compare the data values in multiple columns of a table. A pivot table can perform the work of sorting and subtotallting faster and perhaps more accurately.

Pixel An image is made up of numerous dots, called pixels.

PNG PNG was created to improve and replace the GIF format. It generally can achieve greater compression than GIF, and give a wider range of transparency options and wider range of color depths than GIF.

POP3 Post Office Protocol version 3 (POP3) is an Internet protocol to retrieve e-mail from a remote server over a TCP/IP connection.

Pop-Up Blocker A pop-up blocker is software in a web browser designed to prevent undesirable windows from being launched.

Port A communication port is a doorway between an external device and a computer system.

Port Scanning A method used by hackers to determine what ports are open or in use on a system or network.

Portrait Mode Pages are normally vertical in that the height is greater than the width. This format is known as portrait mode.

PPM PPM (pages per minute) indicates how many pages a printer is able to produce each minute.

Primary Key A primary key is a column in a database table that has a unique value for each record. Primary keys are never duplicated.

Primary Memory A computer's RAM is considered main memory (or primary storage): the working area used for loading, displaying and manipulating programs and data.

Procedural Languages Tell a computer how to behave.

Processor The central processing unit (CPU), also called the processor, is the critical component in a digital computer that processes data by interpreting and executing instructions that are contained in computer programs.

Program A computer program is a series of commands that instructs the computer how to process data.

Programmer The computer programmer writes computer programs in what are called programming languages such as Java, C#, and Visual Basic.

Programming Computer programming (sometimes known as coding) is the process of writing, testing, and maintaining the code of computer programs.

Projection Specification of the database table columns to be returned by a query is know as the projection.

Property The characteristics of an object

Protected Mode A feature of Vista that prevents code in web pages from manipulating files or programs on the client computer.

Protocol Protocol refers to an established procedure of conduct. Computers and software follow protocols when their activities must be coordinated.

Prototype A prototype is a model of what is being built.

Q

QBE Query by Example (QBE) is the query design mode offered in Access 2007. It provides a graphical interface as an alternative to writing queries in SQL.

Quantum Computer Processes data encoded as quantum bits, or qubits.

Query This operation retrieves selected data from database tables. It is similar to, but more powerful than, a spreadsheet filter.

Queue A list (that might be implemented as an array or linked list) in which data added to the list first is processed first.

R

Radio Frequency RF is also known as wireless technology. It is gaining popularity as more and more families and small businesses are wiring homes and offices.

RAM Random Access Memory. This memory holds programs as they execute and temporarily holds data as it is processed.

Record A record is data in a context and is considered the fundamental unit of information.

Relational Database A database with data arranged in related tables is known as a relational database. Access 2007 is a relational database management system and performs operations on relational databases.

Relative Addressing This is the default mode of cell addressing in Excel. When functions or formulas with cells referenced this way are copied the cell references are altered by Excel.

Resolution The number of individual pixels contained on a display and it is expressed as the ratio of pixels on the horizontal axis to the number on the vertical axis.

Restriction Specification of database table rows to be returned by a query is known as the restriction.

RFID Radio-frequency identification (RFID) is an automatic identification method which relies on embedded RFID tags or transponders for storing and remotely retrieving data.

RGB Color Each computer color is comprised of red, green and blue (RGB) components. All colors are formed by combining these three primary colors.

Ring Topology The ring topology involves a single cable that connects each workstation in a circle.

ROM Read-Only Memory. It cannot easily be written to and its main uses are the distribution of firmware (software that is very closely related to hardware).

Router A router is a computer networking device that buffers and forwards data packets across an internetwork toward their destinations.

RSS RSS (Really Simple Syndication) is a way of sharing information over the Internet.

RSS Aggregator Software that uses a Web feed to retrieve syndicated Web content such as blogs, podcasts, and RSS feeds.

S

Safari Safari is a Web browser developed by Apple Inc., and is available as part of Mac OS X.

Sandbox A sandbox is a software tool available for safely running programs.

Satellite Satellites are used to overcome the distance limitations imposed by the line of sight restriction of other wireless communication media.

Scanner A scanner is a device that analyzes an image (most commonly a photograph) or document (printed text or handwriting) and converts it to a digital image.

Schema Data is stored in a database in records that are defined as a collection of fields. This data structure is called the database schema or data model.

Screen Saver Originally used to prevent screen burn-in today they are mostly used for entertainment, cosmetics and most importantly security.

Search Engine An Internet search engine is a program that runs on a server and helps users find web pages of interest. It provides hyperlinks allowing navigation to the selected pages.

Secondary Memory Secondary storage is persistent. This means that it holds data and programs even when there is no power in the computer. The most common kind of secondary storage is a hard disk.

Secure Electronic Transaction SET is a standard protocol for securing credit card transactions over open networks like the Internet.

Select This is the key word that all SQL data retrieval operations begin with.

Server Those machines that provide services (like Web servers or FTP servers) to other machines are servers.

Server Farm Large data centers with numerous servers.

Service Pack A service pack is an update to a program provided by the vendor. Service packs are used to fix program bugs, add enhancements and close security loopholes.

Shareware Shareware is a method for marketing commercial software, in which a trial version is distributed in advance and without payment. Frequently shareware is downloaded from a website providing a convenient try before you buy environment.

Shopping Cart Software Allows customers to: preview and select products, preview the checkout stage, delete items if they change their mind, enter payment and shipping information.

Shortcut A shortcut is a link to a folder, file or program, represented by an icon.

Simplex Communication in one direction only.

Smart Card The size of a credit card but has electronic circuitry inside that can process data and participate in transactions.

Smart Dust Small, inexpensive sensors that float in the air. Use to monitor polution and weather.

SMTP Simple Mail Transfer Protocol (SMTP) is the most commonly used standard for e-mail transmissions across the Internet.

Social Networking Social networking websites are a more recent development in personal communication and e-commerce. This development allows people to maintain communities of friends who share photos, journals and interests.

Software Software is data and computer programs. It is not physical and cannot be directly seen.

Software Architecture Software architecture is the structure and arrangements of the components of an application.

Sort Sorting records involves rearranging the visible order of records. Sorting records is always required before computing subtotals.

Sort-Merge Key To compute aggregations among records it is necessary for each record to possess a unique data value. This is especially important when tables are merged. This key is known as a sort-merge key.

Source Data Automation The use of special equipment to collect data at the source and send it directly to the computer for processing.

Spam Spamming is an abuse of e-mail or other electronic based messaging systems to send unsolicited and often undesired bulk messages.

Speech Recognition Speech recognition is the prospect of a computer understanding spoken words and translating them into commands directed to the computer or words typed into a document or e-mail message

Spreadsheet Spreadsheet programs permit the manipulation of data arranged in a grid of rows and columns which define cells.

Spyware Spyware refers broadly to malicious software (malware) designed to partially control a computer's operation without the knowledge and consent of the user.

SQL SQL or Structured Query Language is an English like, a non-procedural language designed to make possible the easy manipulation of data managed in a relational database.

SSL The Secure Sockets Layer protocol was developed by Netscape to protect the content of documents transmitted on the Internet.

Stack A list (that might be implemented as an array or linked list) in which data added to the list last is processed first.

Stakeholder All people concerned with the development of a new information system are considered to be its stakeholders. .

Star Topology The star topology involves a collection of terminals or workstations (computers) connected to a single central computer.

Storage Processing data often requires including data that was stored earlier during collection or production. Storage is provided by hard disk, jump drive, CD and DVD, tape, and other storage devices.

Streaming Streaming media is multimedia that is continuously received by the client while it is being delivered by the provider.

Structured Programming A task-oriented design technique. There are two approaches: Top-Down Design and Bottom-Up Design.

Super Computer A supercomputer is a machine that processes data exceptionally fast. Supercomputers are used for calculation-intensive tasks.

Supply Chain Materials, information, and financial resources as they move through a process of activities from supplier to manufacturer to wholesaler to retailer to consumer.

SVC Scalable Vector Graphics (SVG) is an XML markup language for describing two-dimensional vector graphics that can be animated and interactive.

Switch A networking device that directs packets to a specific hardware device attached to a network.

SWOT A strategic planning tool used to evaluate a business and the environment it operates within.

System Analyst The systems analyst studies the information related needs of an organization to determine how people, business processes and computer technology can be best arranged to help accomplish the objectives of the business.

Systems Analysis Systems analysis is the process of learning about and understanding the needs that organizations have for computer automation. These needs are then translated into information system designs and ultimately into hardware selections and computer programs.

Systems Development Life Cycle The traditional Systems Development Life Cycle (SDLC) model has been used successfully for many years. The conceptual and implementation phases of the SDLC contain a sequence of stages that are described as the Waterfall Model.

T

T1 Digital signal 1 (also known as T1 or DS-1) is a long distance telephone-carrier line that carries multiple signals at the same time.

Tabbed Browsing Tabbed browsing involves opening multiple web pages in the same browser window.

Table Records are usually grouped together in a table.

Tag A tag is a code that instructs the browser to do something special with the web page content that follows.

TCP/IP A set of two of the most important Internet communication protocols.

Telecommuting Some companies allow employees to work all or some of their hours at home. This saves office space for the company and saves commuting time and expense for the employee. Telecommuting allows employees to have flexible hours that can often help when the need to care for young children is involved.

Terabyte A unit of data storage consisting of about 1000 gigabytes.

Text Justification Text justification is about the positioning of text in relation to the page's margin.

Token Ring IEEE 802.5. The most common local area network alternative to Ethernet implements a strict, orderly access method.

Top Down Search Searching that involves starting from the first record and scanning down through all records until a match is found or until all records are considered.

Touch Screen A touch screen is an overlay that covers the computer's monitor and can receive movements of a user's finger in a fashion similar to the touchpad.

Transitions The application of timing and visual formatting when moving from one PowerPoint slide to the next is known as transitions.

Transmission Control Protocol Transmission Control Protocol (TCP) is the protocol responsible for reliable end-to-end delivery of packets.

Trojan Horse Trojan horses are imposters. A Trojan horse appears to do something desirable (like install a screen saver) but what it does in fact is something entirely different, and usually malicious, such as erase files, damage data or reformat a hard disk.

Trust Center The Trust Center is used in Office 2007 applications to permit greater control over the execution of macros in documents.

Truth Table A truth table can be used to summarize the possible outcomes as a logical condition is evaluated.

U

Ubiquitous Computing A network arrangement where inexpensive servers bring Internet access to household appliances, clothing, and office equipment.

Unicode Unicode is an industry standard designed to allow text and symbols from all of the major writing systems of the world to be consistently represented and manipulated by computers.

Uninterruptible Power Supply A UPS provides emergency backup power in the event of an electrical outage.

Universal Resource Locator A URL is an Internet address.

Unix An operating system perhaps ahead of its time, Unix was designed as portable, multi-tasking, and multi-user.

USB The Universal Serial Bus (USB) allows peripheral devices to be connected without the need to plug expansion cards into the computer's external bus.

V

VBA Visual Basic for Applications is a complete programming language. It is the language that macros are recorded in.

Virtual Machine Software that essentially mimics a computer so that several copies of an operating system, for example Windows and Linux, can run on one physical machine at the same time.

Virtual Memory Virtual memory is a memory management technique, used by multitasking computer operating systems like Windows. This technique allows the computer to pretend it has more real primary than it actually does.

Virtual Reality Virtual Reality (VR) is a technology which allows a user to interact with a computer-simulated environment.

Virus A computer virus is a self-replicating computer program intended to alter how a computer operates, without the permission or knowledge of the user.

Vista The newest version of Windows, Vista, provides offers several important security advances over the prior version Windows/XP.

Visual Basic Visual Basic is one of the most used languages today, especially in business. Visual Basic is available in several forms and is heavily supported by Microsoft.

Voice Over Internet Protocol Internet telephony, commonly known as Voice over Internet Protocol (VoIP), is the routing of voice conversations over the Internet or through any other IP-based network.

W

Waterfall Model A model to manage the system development lifecycle.

WAV Standard digital audio file format for storing sound data; allows audio recordings to be captured and stored; often used to save CD-quality audio.

Web The Web, or World Wide Web, is an information service of the Internet.

Web Bug Tool used to monitor the activity of customers at a Web site.

Web Service A web service is a software system designed to support interoperable machine to machine interaction over a network.

Web Site A collection of Web pages, images, videos, and other digital content and hosted on a particular domain on the World Wide Web.

Wide Area Network Wide area networks (WAN) provide connections for computing devices that are geographically diverse.

Wi-Fi A variation on the delivery mechanism between the modem and the computer is to use a wireless system to transmit the modem's signal to the computer which has a receiver.

Windows Defender Windows Defender is an anti-spyware program.

Windows Registry A database which stores settings and options for the operation of the computer including information about the hardware, software, and users.

Wire Pair The oldest and most common form of medium is ordinary telephone wire known as wire pair or twisted pair.

Wireless Access Point A wireless access point (WAP or AP) is a device that connects wireless communication devices together to form a wireless network.

Word Processor Word processors use a graphical interface that allows the author to view and directly edit an accurate representation of the end result as the document is being created.

Worm A worm is programmed software that uses computer networks for transportation between computers and takes advantage of security flaws in operating systems to create copies of itself. Once installed, the worm may cause the same types of damage associated with a virus.

X

XHTML XHTML or Extensible HTML, is a standardization and recreated the entire HTML language.

XML The Extensible Markup Language (XML) is a general-purpose markup language used to describe almost any kind of data structure. It is not a programming language but is used primarily to allow data sharing across different systems,

XSD Similar to a DTD, an XML schema defines rules for the structure and content of an XML document. A schema is prepared in a text file with an extension XSD.

INDEX